Catholicism in Rhode Island

✠ ✠ ✠

Catholicism in Rhode Island
and the
Diocese of Providence
1921–1948

✠ ✠ ✠

by

Robert W. Hayman

VOLUME THREE

Diocese of Providence
2020

Visit our website at **www.StillwaterPress.com** for more information.

First Stillwater River Publications Edition

Library of Congress Control Number: 2019120795

ISBN: 978-1-950339-70-9

1 2 3 4 5 6 7 8 9 10
Nihil Obstat: Rev. Jonathan DeFelice, O.S.B.
    Censor Librorum
Book designed by James F. Brisson
Published by Stillwater River Publications, Pawtucket, RI, USA.

Publisher's Cataloging-In-Publication Data
(Prepared by The Donohue Group, Inc.)

Names: Hayman, Robert W., author. | Catholic Church. Diocese of Providence (R.I.),
 sponsoring body.
Title: Catholicism in Rhode Island and the Diocese of Providence. Volume 3, 1921–1948 /
 by Robert W. Hayman.
Description: First Stillwater River Publications edition. | Pawtucket, RI, USA : Stillwater
 River Publications, 2020. | Series: [Catholicism in Providence] | "Diocese of Provi-
 dence." | Includes index.
Identifiers: ISBN 9781950339709
Subjects: LCSH: Catholic Church. Diocese of Providence (R.I.)--History--20th century. |
 Providence (R.I.)--Church history--20th century.
Classification: LCC BX1415.R5 H383 2020 | DDC 282.7452--dc23

The views and opinions expressed in this book are solely those of the author
and do not necessarily reflect the views and opinions of the publisher.

This Volume is dedicated to all the Priests, Religious and Laity with whom I have served during my years of Priesthood.

CONTENTS

ACKNOWLEDGEMENTS

This volume took many years to write. During the process of writing I received help from many individuals without whose assistance the writing of this volume would have taken even longer. They are too many to acknowledge them all but my gratitude to them is great. However, I do need to acknowledge explicitly the assistance I received from a few. Sr. Juliette Laporte, s.s.a. translated numerous documents from French to English. Her work helped to verify my understanding of many documents. Bishop Louis E. Gelineau and Fathers Lionel Blain and Edward St. Godard read and commented on the sections on the Sentinellist Movement. Fr. Jonathan DeFelice, O.S.B. read the entire manuscript in his function as *Censor Liborum* and gave me the benefit of his insights. Finally, I owe a great debt of gratitude to Elaine Kehoe for her copyediting work and to Clifford Garber, who did the layout work on the book. Their corrections and suggestions have greatly improved the text. I take full responsibility for any mistakes of interpretation or understanding found in this volume.

Catholicism in Rhode Island

✠ ✠ ✠

Bishop William A. Hickey

CHAPTER I

Bishop William A. Hickey and Catholic Education

The New Bishop

The third Bishop of Providence, William Augustine Hickey, was born in St. John's Parish, Worcester, Massachusetts, on May 13, 1869. He was the son of William and Margaret (Troy) Hickey. His father, a sergeant of the Worcester police department, had enlisted in the Union Army as a six-month volunteer at the beginning of the Civil War and served with the rank of captain. When the elder William Hickey was discharged, he enlisted in the Union Navy and served in that branch until the end of the war. Shortly after the war ended and the Grand Army of the Republic was formed by the Civil War veterans, William Hickey joined that organization and was one of its best-known members in the Worcester district. The bishop's mother, Margaret Hickey, had worked energetically in the cause of the Irish Land League. An early biographical notice of Bishop Hickey noted that Mrs. Hickey was "a lady of splendid talents . . . a woman of the most charming personality whose memory was held in the highest esteem by all who knew her."[1]

Since there were no Catholic Schools in Worcester at that time, young William began his education at the Ash Street and Washington Street primary schools and quickly showed the academic talent that was to mark his entire career as a student. During his early years he served as an altar boy at St. John's Church and in Notre Dame Convent. He finished grammar school at the age of fourteen and, in 1882, entered the Worcester Classical High School graduating in 1887. He then enrolled at Jesuit-run Holy Cross College in Worcester where he gained first honors in almost all his classes prior to his graduation with an A.B. degree in 1890.[2]

After he declared his desire to study for the priesthood, the Bishop of Springfield, Patrick T. Reilly, sent him to study at the major seminary of St.

<hr/>

[1]   *Providence Visitor*, February 7, 1919; *Providence Journal*, October 5, 1933.
[2]   Ibid.

Sulpice in Paris. At the end of three years, Bishop Reilly called him home and assigned him to St. John's Seminary, Brighton, for a single term prior to his ordination to the priesthood in Holy Cross Cathedral, Boston, on December 23, 1893.[3]

In early 1894, Bishop Reilly assigned his new priest to St. Patrick's Parish, a mixed Irish and French Canadian parish in Whitinsville, Massachusetts. While at Whitinsville, Fr. Hickey began an intensive study of French, which became a lifelong hobby for him. Because of his mastery of French, Msgr. Denis O'Connell, when rector of the North American College in Rome, asked him to translate into English the *Life of Christ* by Abbe E. Le Camus, D.D., director of a College in Castelnaudary, France. Le Camus' work had been published in two volumes in Paris in 1883 and was one of the more popular devotional works of the time. Fr. Hickey's translation was published by the Cathedral Library Association in New York.[4]

Between 1897 and 1903, Fr. Hickey served as an assistant in parishes in Brookfield, Blackstone, Holyoke, and Clinton, Massachusetts. The Brookfield, Blackstone and Clinton parishes had, like St. Patrick's, a mixture of Irish and French Canadians while Precious Blood Parish in Holyoke was exclusively a French-Canadian parish. Fr. Hickey's years in Holyoke were among the happiest of his priesthood.[5]

In 1903, Bishop Thomas D. Beaven, who had succeeded Bishop Reilly in Springfield, appointed Fr. Hickey pastor of St. Aloysius Parish in Gilbertville, Massachusetts. Shortly before he arrived in Gilbertville, the Sisters of St. Anne, a French-speaking order had closed the school and withdrawn from the parish because they lacked sufficient personnel for all their schools. One of Fr. Hickey's first concerns was to reopen the school, which he did with the cooperation of the Sisters Faithful Companions of Jesus, who came from Fitchburg to take charge of it. Fr. Hickey then set out to encourage the parents in the parish to send their children to the school. Before long he found it necessary to build an addition to the school to accommodate two new classrooms. At St. Aloysius, Fr. Hickey's talent for languages proved a great asset. Because of the ethnic diversity of his parish, he was called upon to preach each Sunday in four languages, English, French, Polish and Lithuanian.[6]

After thirteen years in Gilbertville, Bishop Beaven, in 1917, transferred Fr. Hickey to St. John's, Clinton, one of the largest parishes in central Massachusetts, where he had previously served as an assistant. The new pastor soon took over the direction of the school, which was under the charge of the Sisters of the Presentation of the Blessed Virgin Mary. Under his care, it quickly became one of the finest in the Springfield diocese. In

[3]   Ibid.
[4]   *Providence Journal*, April 6, 1919; Thomas F. Cullen, *The Catholic Church in Rhode Island* (North Providence: The Franciscan Missionaries of Mary, 1936), p. 186.
[5]   J. Albert Foisy, *The Sentinellist Agitation in New England* (*Providence Visitor* Press, 1930), p. 60.
[6]   *Providence Visitor*, February 7, 1919; *Providence Journal*, April 6, 1919.

order to better provide for the students and faculty, Fr. Hickey launched a drive for the building of a new twelve-room school. His new parishioners cooperated in the endeavor with great generosity.[7]

At Clinton, Fr. Hickey quickly won the esteem of his fellow citizens, who unanimously elected him to the town's finance committee in February 1916. His good business sense and sound judgment soon came to be appreciated by the taxpayers of the town. With the United States declaration of war in 1917, 284 members of St. John's Parish left the parish for military duty. Fr. Hickey carefully kept a list of all of them with their home addresses and their units. He himself was called on to serve as a "four-minute speaker." In this capacity he made many speeches in which he urged his audiences to support the war effort by buying bonds.[8]

When, in October 1918, Bishop Matthew Harkins submitted his request for the appointment of another auxiliary following the death of Bishop Dennis M. Lowney on August 13, 1918, he once more put the name of his Vicar General, Msgr. Peter E. Blessing, as his first choice. As the second on the list, he placed the name of Msgr. Thomas S. Duggan, Vicar General of the Diocese of Hartford, and that of Fr. Hickey third. In placing Msgr. Blessing first on the list, Bishop Harkins was again arguing that, for pastoral reasons, the diocese needed to have an Italian-speaking bishop able to minister to the newly arrived Italian population of the diocese more than a French-speaking bishop. Cardinal De Lai and the Sacred Congregation of the Council, however, for a second time recommended to Pope Benedict XV that a priest with a knowledge of French was more important. In nominating Fr. Hickey over Monsignors Blessing and Duggan, the Congregation also recommended that Pope Benedict appoint Fr. Hickey as coadjutor bishop with the right of succession. The *Providence Sunday Journal* for February 2, 1919 carried the news of Fr. Hickey's choice as coadjutor. Bishop Beaven, rather than the ailing Bishop Harkins, ordained Fr. Hickey bishop of the titular see of Claudiopolis on April 10, 1919 in the cathedral in Providence. Following Bishop Hickey's ordination, Bishop Harkins, aware that he was failing mentally as well as physically, wrote to the apostolic delegate for permission to turn over the administration of the diocese to Bishop Hickey. After receiving the required permission, Bishop Harkins announced Bishop Hickey's appointment as Administrator of the diocese in a letter to the priests that was published in the local papers on May 22, 1919, the day that Bishop Harkins celebrated his fiftieth anniversary as a priest.[9]

---

[7] Ibid.
[8] Ibid.
[9] Robert W. Hayman, *Catholicism in Rhode Island and the Diocese of Providence, 1886–1921* (Diocese of Providence, 1992), 61–65.

The National and Local Context

The Rising Threat to Catholic Education

Among the issues that caused Bishop Hickey concern during his first years as bishop was the attempt by some Americans to destroy the system of Catholic grammar schools that had grown to such a great extent following the Third Plenary Council of Baltimore in 1884. When in 1917 large numbers of young men were drafted into the army, many Americans were appalled to discover that many of those drafted could not read or write the English language. To remedy this and other educational deficiencies revealed by the draft, the American Council on Education along with other groups proposed a study of American education with a view of suggesting remedies to the problem of illiteracy. In October 1918, the heads of the National Education Association, with the help of some Congressmen, drafted what later came to be called the Smith-Towner bill when submitted to Congress. The bill called for the establishment of a Federal Department of Education with a cabinet-level official at its head. It also proposed the appropriation of tax monies to be distributed by the proposed Secretary of Education to the states, which were intended to be used for ending illiteracy and for the "Americanization" of people from foreign countries. As a condition for receiving the money appropriated by Congress, the states would be required to enact and enforce adequate compulsory school attendance laws and to make English the basic language of instruction in all public, private and parochial schools. It further provided that no part of the appropriation could be used in any way for a religious or privately endowed, owned or conducted school or college. Congress adjourned in March 1919 before taking any action on the proposed bill.[10]

Bishop Hickey was one of the first, if not the first, of the American bishops to criticize the final evolution of the proposals in the educational reform measures embodied in the Smith-Towner bill. In a speech to the La Salle Alumni Association on Sunday, January 23, 1921, Bishop Hickey characterized the pending Smith-Towner bill as "unjust, unfair, undemocratic, un-American, and impolitic." A week later in a lecture in Cathedral Hall on Sunday, January 30, he charged that passage of the bill would revolutionize the American system of education by taking control of education out of the hands of parents and placing it in the hands of one man, the proposed Secretary of Education. The *Visitor* printed the bishop's remarks in the form of a brochure and, on the following Friday, the *Providence Visitor* printed the text of his address in its February 4 issue. When on March 14, 1921, Rev. George B. Thomas, pastor of the Trinity Union Methodist Church in Providence preached a sermon on the Smith-Towner bill in

---

[10]   *Providence Visitor*, March 21, 1919; February 4, 1921.

which the *Providence Journal* reported that he praised the bill as representing the highest ideals of Americanism, Bishop Hickey delivered a rebuttal to the *Journal*, which was printed the following Friday. In his comments on Rev. Thomas' sermon, the editor of the *Visitor* charged that Rev. Thomas was actuated by bigotry when he claimed that the opponents of the measure were un-American.[11]

Bishop Hickey's anxiety about the freedom of Catholic and other parents to choose the manner in which their children were educated increased in November 1922. In that month, the voters in the state of Oregon passed, by a slim majority, a law requiring children between the ages of eight and sixteen, who had not completed the eighth grade, to attend the public schools. Similar legislation was introduced in the states of Michigan and Washington. The Archbishop of Oregon City, the religious of his diocese and other interested parties successfully challenged the Oregon law in the federal courts and the attempts in Michigan and Washington to secure similar legislation also failed. However, Bishop Hickey was one of those who took the threat posed by the attempts to outlaw Catholic elementary education seriously. These attempts prompted him to speak out on the danger he perceived by urging the people of his diocese to defend their rights as parents and to join with him in supporting and extending the Catholic schools in the diocese.

The Peck Education Act

The patriotism stirred by America's entry into the First World War stirred calls for national unity, which found expression in calls for the naturalization or Americanization of foreign-born residents. In 1919, the Rhode Island legislature enacted an Americanization Act, which made night classes in English compulsory for persons aged sixteen through twenty-one who did not meet state standards of literacy in that language. In the early 1920s, many states passed English-only laws in revising legislation, which concerned the public schools. In its January 1920 session, the Rhode Island legislature created a Special Commission on Public Schools Finance and Administration to examine the challenges that confronted Rhode Island. The General Assembly renewed the Commission's mandate in 1922 in order that it might complete its work. The Commission's report, containing a draft of all proposed legislation, was presented in the House of Representatives on February 28, 1922, with the proposed changes in existing legislation printed in italic type.

At the beginning of March, the author of the report, Dr. Charles Carroll,

---

[11] *Providence Visitor*, January 28, February 4; March 18, 1921; May 11, 1923; *Providence Journal*, January 24, 31; March 14, 18, 1921. On Sunday, March 20, 1921, the *Journal* printed Rev. Thomas's reply to Bishop Hickey's letter.

then State Director of Vocational Education and the author of a recently
published study, *Public Education in Rhode Island*, carried a typewritten copy of
the Commission's report to Bishop Hickey since the printed report was not
then available. Carroll acted at the behest of the Commission. The Commission asked the bishop to examine the proposed legislation and make
such comments and criticisms as seemed advisable. On April 9, Gov. Emery
San Souci called on Bishop Hickey and the two discussed various pieces of
pending legislation, among them the bills pertaining to education.[12]

In the General Assembly itself, much of the legislators' time was taken
up early in the session with the question of electing a replacement for
Judge John Doran whose death, in June 1921, had created a vacancy on
the Superior Court bench. The first name proposed for the seat was that of
a Woonsocket lawyer and politician, Elphege J. Daignault, who was soon
joined as a candidate by Antonio A. Capotosto, a state assistant attorney
general, and Hugh B. Baker, a district court judge from Newport. As the
three candidates represented different factions within the Republican Party,
the choice of one candidate over another courted the risk of alienating the
other factions. After a great deal of political maneuvering the Republican
leaders of the Assembly decided a second district court seat was needed. In
the end, the Republican caucus chose Mr. Capotosto and Judge Baker over
Mr. Daignault and the Franco Americans who championed his cause.[13]

With the question of the judgeships decided, the General Assembly was
able to turn its attention to other matters. On March 15, Rep. Frederick
S. Peck had submitted a bill in the House that incorporated the Commission's proposed reforms. In the mind of the Commission, the key provision
of the proposed legislation was the appropriation of substantial state funds
to be distributed to the various cities and towns of the state in order to enable them to bring the base pay of public schoolteachers to $650 a year.
By more closely equalizing the pay of schoolteachers in Rhode Island, the
Commission hoped to see the overall quality of the education offered in
the state rise. In order to provide for a more uniform quality of education
in the state, the bill proposed to remove the task of supervising the state's
public and private elementary schools from the jurisdiction of the local
school committees and give it over to the State Board of Education on the
same basis of as the high schools. The proposed act also repeated an earlier provision of the existing law governing Rhode Island education that in
order to be certified as a school in which a child could fulfill the mandatory
school law, the private schools would be obligated to teach all the courses
mandated for the public schools and to do so in English.[14]

Mr. Peck's bill was referred initially to the House finance committee but

[12]   Letter of Dr. Charles Carroll to Gov. Emery San Souci, printed in the *Providence Journal*, April 30,
       1922; Bishop Hickey's Diary, April 9, 1922, Providence Chancery Archives Hereafter, PChA].
[13]   David Patton, *Rhode Island Story: Recollections of 35 Years on the Staff of The Providence Journal and The
       Evening Bulletin* (The Providence Journal Company, 1954), 48–50.
[14]   *The Rhode Island General Law of 1922*, Chapter 72, Section 2, Peck Education Act.

then was referred by that committee to the committee on education, which held a series of private hearings on the bill. Msgr. Peter E. Blessing, whose appointment as Vicar General Bishop Hickey had renewed, attended three of the hearings on the Peck Bill and offered several suggestions. As a result of the hearings, the committee prepared a substitute bill, which came before the House in the closing days of the January 1922 session. The bill was debated on the floor of the Republican-controlled House. Various representatives had reservations about some of the bill's provisions. The Franco Americans in the legislature had serious objections to the specification in the bill that all the courses required to qualify as an approved school be taught in English. In debate, proponents of the bill questioned why the Franco-American legislators should object to the provision when Bishop Hickey had approved it. The assertion prompted Elie Vezina, the Secretary of the Union St. Jean Baptiste d'Amerique, to send a telegram to Bishop Hickey asking if the claim was true. Bishop Hickey responded that, while he had seen the report of the Commission and suggested changes, which he was assured would be made, he had never seen or approved of the bill. Since both Republican and Democratic members of the House raised objections to some of the bill's provisions, a recess was taken so that the members of the committee on education and the opponents of the bill might have a chance to settle their differences.[15]

After the conference members agreed on two amendments and discussion on the floor was resumed, Rep. Felix A. Toupin, a Franco-American Democrat from Lincoln, sought to attach a new amendment to the bill that would remove the oversight of private schools from the authority granted the State Board of Education. Toupin expressed the fear of many Franco Americans that the Board might attack the course of study offered in Franco-American parochial schools. He felt that state supervision was uncalled for since no state funds went to the private schools. Toupin's amendment was defeated as was a similar one offered by Rep. Guillaume Myette of Pawtucket. During the course of the debate, the Democratic minority leader, Rep. William S. Flynn of Providence, asked postponement of the bill because of its complexity and the lateness at which it was brought before the House. His amendment also failed. After the two amendments agreed on during the recess were accepted, the bill passed the House on a vote of 50 to 35. The Republican-controlled Senate later concurred in passage and the bill was sent to Gov. San Souci for his signature.[16]

The passage of the Peck Act occasioned strong protests from across the spectrum of the Franco-American community. In an article, which appeared in the *Providence Journal* on April 25, 1922, Dr. F. A. Reust of Pawtucket, a national officer of the Union St. Jean Baptiste, declared that the

---

[15]   *Evening Tribune*, April 22, 1922; Robert Rumilly, *Histoire Des Franco-Americains* (L'Union Saint-Jean-Baptiste D'Amerique, 1958), p. 325.

[16]   Ibid.

Franco Americans in Rhode Island would defy any state effort to end the tradition of bilingual education that all Franco-American parochial schools followed. The same article quoted the protest of Fr. Alphonse Graton, pastor of St. Jean Baptiste Church, Pawtucket, against the bill and his rejection of any claim that the Franco-American parochial schools did not teach English properly. In a letter to Gov. San Souci also printed in the *Journal*, Charles H. Lord, the Mayor of Central Falls, which had a large Franco-American population, complained of the manner in which the legislature passed the Peck Act. Lord specifically complained that while there were private hearings on the bill there were no public hearings.[17]

The members of the Special Commission on Public Schools Finance and Administration responded to the Franco-Americans protests and their urging that Gov. San Souci veto the Peck Act by saying that the critics of the bill had misunderstood the legislation and that, even if the governor vetoed the act, the provision for teaching subjects in English would remain because it was part of the existing law. In an editorial printed in the *Providence Visitor*, the writer again denied reports that Bishop Hickey had approved the Peck Act. Rather than focusing on the threat the act posed to the tradition of bilingual education in the Franco-American schools, the *Visitor* writer's chief objection was to the act's centralizing effects. In the writer's view, the act gave "to the State Board of Education a drastic and uncalled for power over the various educational systems in towns and cities of the state." To the writer's mind, the centralization of education in the state ran counter to Gov. San Souci's stated opposition to centralization in government.[18]

On April 25, Bishop Hickey discussed the Peck Act with Gov. San Souci, Rep. John A. Hamilton, chairman of the House committee on education, Elie Vezina, Executive Secretary of the Union St. Jean Baptiste, whose organization was one of the largest and loudest voices in protest of the Act, Msgr. Blessing and William A. Needham, the governor's secretary. Mr. Vezina and Bishop Hickey had previously worked together to defeat the passage of a similar bill in the Massachusetts legislature prior to Bishop Hickey's appointment to Providence. According to his later recollection of the meeting, Vezina urged the bishop to oppose the Rhode Island legislation on the grounds that it deprived parents of their rights to choose the nature of their children's education. On his own part, Bishop Hickey did not object to the English only provision of the act, but to the fact that the substitute act had not been shown to him before being placed before the legislature. More substantially, like Mr. Vezina, he expressed his opposition to the act because the act, like the Smith-Towner Bill on the federal level, would give control of education to the State. He also believed that there had been insufficient hearings on the bill. He recommended to the governor that he veto the act. Following his meeting with the governor and

17 *Providence Journal,* April 25, 29, 1922.
18 Ibid., April 26, 1922; *Providence Visitor,* April 28, 1922.

Elie Vezina

Mr. Vezina, Bishop Hickey also met with a group of Franco-American pastors and legislators among them Messrs. Myette, Fortin, Toupin, Blais and Brazeau. Two days later, Gov. San Souci met again with Mr. Vezina and other representatives of the Franco-American societies that had protested the bill's passage in executive session at the State House.[19]

Gov. San Souci waited until May 3, 1922 to make known his decision. In his letter to the Secretary of State which was dated May 3, the governor vetoed the Peck Educational Act as it was popularly known. In his veto message, the governor made his own the basis on which Bishop Hickey had urged him to oppose the act, that it represented a fundamental and radical change in the education system of Rhode Island and that the merits of the bill had not been thoroughly considered.[20]

The citizens of Rhode Island had only given the governor the power to veto legislation in 1909 when they added Article XV to the amendments to the state's constitution. The long line of Republican governors elected since the passage of the amendment had little cause to use their new power to veto legislation passed by a legislature, which the Republican Party controlled. The amendment provided that the governor had six days (Sundays excepted) to veto and return a piece of legislation to the Assembly when it was in session and, once the legislature had adjourned, he was to have ten days to inform the Secretary of State if he chose to veto a piece of legislation. In sending his veto message to the Secretary of State on May 3, Gov. San Souci was acting on the presumption that the Sunday exception applied to the ten-day period for action after the Assembly adjourned as well as to the six-day period when the Assembly was in session.

On the day the governor's veto was made public, several lawyers questioned the validity of the governor's veto on the grounds that it had exceeded the ten-day period the constitution specified. The State Board of Education, at its meeting on May 3, voted to ask the State Attorney General to advise them as to whether the governor's veto was valid. Commissioner of Education Ranger, a member of the commission that had proposed the legislation, was quoted in the *Providence Journal* as saying that, if valid, the governor's veto of the Commission's efforts to secure more adequate

19   Bishop Hickey's Diary, April 25, 1922; *Providence Visitor*, October 15, 1925; *Evening Tribune*, April 26, 27; May 3, 1922.
20   The *Providence Visitor* printed the text of the governor's veto in its May 5, 1922 issue.

economic support for the public schools and more efficient administration of public education constituted "the severest blow ever struck at the public schools in Rhode Island." In his response to the State Board of Education, Attorney General Herbert A. Rice expressed his opinion that the governor had exceeded the specified time limit and urged him to submit the question of the validity of the law to the Supreme Court for a definitive ruling.[21]

After considering the matter for a few days more, Gov. San Souci announced on May 8 that he was having a petition drawn asking the Supreme Court to rule on the validity of his veto. In his petition, the governor asked the court to decide whether or not Sundays were included in the ten days specified by the constitution as well as to decide when the ten-day period actually began. Although the legislature officially adjourned on the Friday, April 22, the leaders of legislature, as was their practice, ordered the clocks stopped before midnight, so that the actual adjournment of the legislature occurred on Saturday morning. The lawyers for the governor argued in their petition that since the legislature did not actually adjourn until Saturday and the ten-day period could not begin on Sunday, since no legal action could be taken on that day, then Gov. San Souci did act on the last day of the period allowed by law.[22]

On receiving the governor's petition, the Supreme Court took the unusual step of ordering a public hearing on the petition on May 19 and invited all interested parties to submit briefs. At the hearing, Albert A. Baker, who served as chief counsel for the governor, argued for the veto's validity. He was supported in his arguments by Eugene J. Jalbert, president of the National Federation of French Societies; Pawtucket City Solicitor, James Connolly; and Raphael L. Daignault, who represented the city of Woonsocket in place of its solicitor, Elphege J. Daignault, who was out of state. Attorney General Rice argued against the veto's validity as did Dr. Charles Carroll and Frank H. Wildes, city solicitor of Cranston. After a week's deliberation, the Supreme Court unanimously ruled that Gov. San Souci's veto was invalid and that the Peck Educational Act was law.[23]

Prohibition Enforcement and the Textile Strikes of 1922–23 and their Impact

By itself the negative reaction of the Franco Americans and others to certain of the provisions of the Peck Act was not sufficient to cause the leaders of the Republicans Party in Rhode Island to rethink their position of support for the act as written. However, Gov. San Souci and the Republican leaders were also responsible for the passage of the Sherwood Dry Enforce-

---

[21] *Providence Journal*, May 4, 5, 6, 1922.
[22] *Evening Tribune*, May 8, 1922.
[23] *Evening Tribune*, May 19, 27, 1922; *Providence Journal*, 19, 20, 27, 1922.

ment Act, which the legislature passed at the same time as the Peck Act. Rhode Island and Connecticut were the only two states in the union that refused to pass the nineteenth amendment to the U.S. constitution, which authorized Congress to prohibit the manufacture, importation, distribution or sale of liquor. Rhode Island state officials also had challenged the validity of the Volsted Act passed in 1919. When the Supreme Court rejected the Rhode Island petition on a technicality, the Rhode Island legislature, at Gov. San Souci's urging, proceeded to consider legislation providing for the state enforcement of the liquor laws. Like the Peck Act, the validity of the Sherwood Act was also initially challenged. In the case of the Sherwood Act, lawyers for defendants arrested under the act challenged its legality on the grounds that Gov. San Souci did not have in his possession an amendment to the act passed by the legislature as well as the act itself when he signed it. While the act was eventually declared valid and in force, its enforcement soon became embroiled in Rhode Island politics and the refusal of many Rhode Islanders to abide by its provisions.[24]

In addition to the antipathy Gov. San Souci and the Republicans roused among some sections of the Rhode Island population for the passage of the Peck and Sherwood acts, many Rhode Islanders also disapproved of the manner in which Gov. San Souci responded to the labor crisis which developed in January 1923. The year before, the Rhode Island mill owners, in an attempt to roll back the gains that the workers had made during the First World War, had reduced wages in many textile plants as they had in other parts of the country by $22\frac{1}{2}$ percent. At the beginning of 1923, many mill owners announced another cut of up to 20 percent.[25]

On Monday, January 23, the weavers employed by the Royal Mills of the B. B. & R. Knight, Inc. at River Point, West Warwick, refused to start their looms and walked out in protest over the wage cuts. The next day, striking workers marched from mill to mill in the Pawtuxet Valley urging other workers to come out and intimidated those who were reluctant to join them. The instigators of the strike turned to the radical Amalgamated Textile Workers Union for help in organizing the strikers and in directing the strike. Workers in the cotton textile plants in the Blackstone Valley, who were led and organized by the more moderate United Textile workers, also joined the strike, which quickly spread to other cotton textile centers in New England.[26]

The arrest of a striker in the Pawtuxet Valley on January 31 sparked a riot the next day in front of the office of the Knight's Natick Mill. The

---

24 David Patton, in his *Rhode Island Story*, p.72, says that one of the most experienced politicians in the state told him years later that "of all the measures passed in his lifetime, this education bill was the most permanently damaging to a political party." On prohibition in Rhode Island also see Patton, *Rhode Island Story*, 63–65.
25 *Evening Tribune*, January 23, 1922.
26 Ibid.; *Providence Journal*, January 24, 25, 1922; Paul Buhle, et al., "An Interview with Luigi Nardella," in *Radical History Review: Labor and Community Militance in Rhode Island*," Spring, 1978, 153–60; Patten, *Rhode Island Story*, 50–52.

violence prompted a group of mill owners in the Valley to write to Gov. San Souci asking him to call out the state National Guard to protect property and to maintain order. Instead of the calling out the Guard, Gov. San Souci, on February 8, called the State Labor Board into emergency session to meet with him and federal mediators. The mediators were sent by the Department of Labor to offer assistance in bringing about a solution to the impasse that had develop over the question of wages and put approximately 20,000 people out of work. The Labor Board voted to set up a Board of Conciliation and Mediation charged with developing a proposal acceptable to both sides. Two days later, word spread that a Senate committee was to take up a bill that would limit the working hours of women and children to 54 hours a week. By virtue of this measure, it seemed to the workers that the mill owners were going to attempt to achieve by legislation what they could not gain by negotiation. Several thousand workers, mostly from the Blackstone Valley, then stormed the State House. They wanted a public hearing on a forty-eight-week limit for all workers as well as the provision for prohibiting night work for women and child that was included in the fifty-four-hour bill the Senate judiciary committee was to consider.[27]

Before the Board of Conciliation and Mediation could agree on a proposal to put before both sides, riots in Pontiac in the Pawtuxet Valley on February 20 and in Pawtucket on February 21 caused Gov. San Souci to send National Guardsmen first to Pontiac and Natick and then to Pawtucket as well. When word of the guardsmen's coming reached Natick in the afternoon or early evening, a crowd of about a thousand men, women and children gathered at Brown St. Square in Natick to await their arrival. At least part of the crowd gathered stones and clubs with the intention of attacking the soldiers as they had the West Warwick police earlier in the strike. When word of the gathering reached Fr. Frederick A. Tirocchi, M.S.C., the Italian-born assistant at St. Joseph's, Natick, who ministered to the Italian-speaking parishioners of St. Joseph's, Natick, he went down to the square and, in Italian, urged the people to go home. Most heeded his advice, so that when the mounted troops arrived from Pontiac, there was only a small crowd left. These dispersed when the guardsmen ordered them to go to their homes at once.[28]

In the Pawtucket riot, the Pawtucket police guarding the Jenckes Spinning Company's plant were threatened by a club wielding crowd of strikers. Fearing that their lives were endangered by the crowd, the police fired into the crowd. One man, an onlooker, Jose Assuncao of Valley Falls, was killed and six of the strikers were injured. It fell to Fr. Thomas Fitzpatrick, pastor of St. Patrick's, Valley Falls, to offer the funeral mass for Mr. Assuncao.[29]

On February 24, the day after Mr. Assuncao's funeral, the Board of

---

[27]   *Evening Tribune*, February 1, 1922; *Providence Journal*, February 1, 1922.
[28]   *Pawtuxet Valley Daily Times*, February 21, 1922.
[29]   *Providence Journal*, February 22, 24, 1922.

Conciliation and Mediation asked both sides to agree to accept Judge Jerome J. Hahn as arbitrator in their dispute over wages, a proposal, which Gov. San Souci endorsed. The offer of mediation was, however, rejected by both sides. The workers were determined not to accept the lower wages mandated by the cotton mill owners and the mill owners claimed they could not compete with southern mills if they did not reduce wages. Several individuals and groups of citizens asked the Mediation Board to continue its efforts to find a solution to the impasse. Among those who spoke on the issue were Episcopal Bishop James DeWolf Perry, who, in the first week of March, forwarded a series of resolutions adopted by the Episcopal clergy in Rhode Island at a meeting in Providence.[30]

Bishop Hickey and the Roman Catholic clergy did not speak out publicly on the issue. However, John H. Powers, a member of the executive committee of the United Textile Workers Union and one of the union's representatives at the hearings being held by the Board of Conciliation and Mediation, signed a full page advertisement printed in the *Providence Visitor* on March 10 that he presented as the basis on which the workers rested their case in the wage dispute. Mr. Powers began by quoting a statement of support by several American bishops of all legitimate efforts to fight the general post war attempts at wage reductions. He followed this with excerpts from Pope Leo XIII's, "On the Condition of Labor," and Fr. John A. Ryan's works, *A Living Wage* and "Capital and Labor," a publication of the National Catholic Welfare Council. The Jesuit monthly, *America*, in taking note of the textile strike situation in New England in its March issue, castigated the mill owners for refusing to pay their workers a living wage. When Fr. John A. Ryan came to Providence during the last week in June 1922, a reporter from the *Visitor* spoke with him. Fr. Ryan expressed his support for the workers. To his mind, the wage increases gained during the war were proper in as much they brought the workers' wages to something like a reasonable level.[31]

While Bishop Hickey did not speak out publicly in regard to the strike, he remained interested in it and was concerned about the impact the strike was having on working people. Judge Frank E. Fitzsimmons, federal Collector of Customs and a resident of Lonsdale, called on Bishop Hickey to discuss the strike in Lonsdale on March 28. Four days later, Fr. Gedeon Laverdiere, pastor of Our Lady of Good Counsel, in the Phenix section of West Warwick, called to do the same. On April 6, "some gentlemen" called on the bishop to ask if he would "become interested in bringing strike in cotton industry to a close." The bishop agreed to do so "under certain conditions." Fr. Laverdiere called again on April 7 and once more on April

---

30 *Evening Tribune*, March 9, 1922.
31 *Providence Visitor*, March 10, 24; June 30, 1922; *America*, cited in the *Providence Visitor*, March 31, 1922.

11, this time bringing with him Col. G. Edward Buxton, the head of the Knight Company operations in Rhode Island.[32]

On March 23, the Board of Conciliation and Mediation formally acknowledged the failure of its efforts at ending the strike. The mill owners resolved to try to reopen their mills with any of their former workers who wished to return and with newly recruited workers. In order to neutralize the strikers' most effective weapon, they also sought restraining orders from the courts, which banned mass picketing. When a state judge granted the injunctions against picketing, the judge's orders were carried out by the state sheriffs and their deputies. As local police forces grew stronger, Gov. San Souci gradually withdrew the Guardsmen. The troops in Pawtucket left by the middle of April; those in the Pawtuxet Valley left during July. Not all tensions ceased after the Guardsmen left. In April, when a striker in Pawtucket was wounded by a Deputy Sheriff, the strikers asked the governor to call out the Guard to protect them, but the governor refused.[33]

At some point during May, the pastors of the All Saints Church and the Swedish Lutheran Church in Pontiac together with Fr. L'Esperance, M.S.C., the pastor of St. Joseph's, Natick, and other Catholic and Protestant clergy met with union officials and mill representatives in an attempt to mediate the strike, but without success. On May 26, 1922, Fr. Thomas A. McGrath, pastor of SS. Peter and Paul Church, Phenix, and a man who sympathized with the workers and supported their strike, had a conference with Superintendent Robert N. Gee of the Interlaken Print Works in Phenix, in an attempt to mediate between Mr. Gee and the striking workers, many of whom were his parishioners. In spite of his sympathy for the workers' position, Fr. McGrath felt obligated to relay to them Mr. Gee's offer. That same evening, he went to the door of St. John's Hall, Natick, where the strikers were having a meeting. He told the men at the door that Mr. Gee had said the strikers would be welcome to return at Interlaken if they would agree to a six-months contract under which the company would guarantee to pay the same wages as just prior to the strike. Furthermore, the workers must not recognize the Amalgamated Textile Union that the Italian workers in Natick had brought in to help them organize the strike against the Pawtuxet Valley mills. The workers at the meeting did not show any indication of being willing to consider Mr. Gee's proposal. In an address that evening to the strikers in the hall, strike organizer William H. Derrick "assailed the Interlaken officials, the clergy and a certain newspaper reporter."[34]

At the beginning of June, Fr. Fitzpatrick of St. Patrick's, Valley Falls, Rev. A. M. Hilliker, rector of Grace Church, Lonsdale, former Governor Lucius

[32] Bishop Hickey's Diary, March 28; April 3, 6, 7, 11, 1922.
[33] *Providence Journal*, March 24; April 11, 15, 27, 1922.
[34] *Pawtuxet Valley Daily Times*, May 26, 1922; *Providence Journal*, July 31, 1922; Don D'Amato, "Episodes in Rhode Island History: The Strike of 1922, Part II," in *Old Rhode Island*, June 11, 1992, p. 26.

F. C. Gavin of Cumberland and Judge Fitzsimmons addressed a letter to
the Goddard Brothers, agents of the Lonsdale Company, which had mills in
Lonsdale, Berkeley and Ashton. In their letter, they proposed that the company reopen its mills on a forty-eight-hour working schedule and a wage
reduction of 10 percent with the agreements that there would be no further
cuts in 1922. The mill owners suggested initially that they would be willing
to compromise but, once again, no suitable agreement could be reached.[35]

On Saturday, July 8, the Lonsdale Company put further pressure on its
workers when it evicted the first of them from the company's tenements
because of their failure to pay their rent. The town of Cumberland put
the workers up in army tents near the grounds of Our Lady of the Valley
Monastery on Diamond Hill Road. The same afternoon the workers and
their families were evicted, Bishop Hickey, who was on his way to Worcester, stopped by their camp to view the conditions in the camp and spend
some time with the children.[36]

As the workers' frustration and anger toward the Rhode Island political
establishment, which they associated with the mill owners, grew, the Republicans in the legislature sought in March to try to appease and conciliate the
workers by passing the forty-eight-hour bill asked for by the workers. The
mill owners had said they would accept such a bill if passed by the U.S.
Congress. A forty-eight-hour bill passed the House on March 15 by a vote
of 64 to 25 with both Democrats and Republicans voting for it. A Senate
version of the forty-eight-hour bill was discussed in the Senate on March
29. Once again, as had been true when the House considered its version,
the State House was packed by strikers supporting the bill. The Democratic
senators moved that the judiciary committee discharge the bill and allow
it to come up for a vote on the floor of the Senate. Amidst the groans and
hoots of the onlookers in the gallery, the measure was voted down, 27 to 4.
As they strikers left the Senate gallery, many shouted, "We will remember
this next November."[37]

During the strike, the two union organizations which led it, each organized cafeterias or kitchens in order to feed the strikers and their families.
The money to support the relief effort came from their respective parent
unions. Samuel Gompers, the president of the American Federation of
Labor, the parent union of the United Textile Union, in order to encourage
the strikes, addressed a mass meeting in Pawtucket and then met with other
union men in Providence. Some strikers, like the French-Canadian families
in West Warwick, who had moved from Fall River and New Bedford when
strikes had closed the mills in those cities a decade or so before, returned
to their former homes at the invitation of the Fall River and New Bedford
owners whose mills were not struck. The mill owners now wished to recruit

---

[35] *Evening Tribune,* June 9, 1922; *Providence Journal,* June 10, 11, 1922.
[36] *Evening Tribune,* July 17, 1922.
[37] *Evening Tribune,* March 16, 29, 1922; *Providence Journal,* April 14, 1922; Patton, *Rhode Island Story,*
       51–52.

the "better class of workers" they formerly had employed. Other workers recognized that the future of the cotton industry in New England was not bright and found work in other fields. In early September, the Pacific Mill in Lawrence, Massachusetts, which had also been struck by its workers, announced that it would restore the 20 percent pay cut. The Rhode Island cotton mill owners followed suit and the mills slowly reopened because the workers proved reluctant to return to the mills.[38]

The Amendment of the Peck Act

As the summer of 1922 came to an end, both the Republicans and Democrats met in convention to choose their candidates for the 1922 state elections. Gov. San Souci sought his party's nomination for a second term, but the leaders of the Republican Party, fearing defeat at the polls if San Souci led the state ticket, chose to seek the nomination of former Congressman Ambrose Kennedy in his place. Since Lt. Gov. Harold J. Gross refused to step aside at the party's request and also sought nomination as governor, the Republican state convention was left to choose between three candidates. Gov. San Souci retired when the first ballot failed to choose a candidate and he threw his support to Mr. Gross, who proceeded to win the nomination.[39]

The Democrats nominated the Speaker of the House, William S. Flynn for governor and Representative Felix A. Toupin for lieutenant governor. Flynn and Toupin charged their Republican opponents with "bossism" and corruption. They castigated them for their opposition to the various political reform measures that the Democrats had long sought to see enacted and for their opposition to the forty-eight-hour bill in the last legislative session. The election ultimately turned on the votes of the Franco Americans and other ethnic groups in the Blackstone Valley. The issues generated by the recent strike turned many in the Blackstone Valley, who had formerly voted the Republican ticket, away from the Republican to the Democratic Party. Many of the Franco Americans in Woonsocket, where the majority of the mills produced woolen and worsted fabrics rather than cotton, had been relatively unaffected by the strike. However, many of them crossed party lines and voted for the Democratic candidates as a way of venting their anger toward the party which had enacted the Peck Education Act and chose to contest Gov. San Souci's veto of it. In campaigning for his own election and that of the Democratic Party before Franco-Americans audiences, Felix Toupin charged the Republicans with being prejudiced against the Franco Americans. He cited as evidence the Peck Act, the lack of Fran-

---

[38]   *Evening Tribune*, March 7, 9, 1922; Buhle, "Born Out of Strikes," 157–58; Patton, *Rhode Island Story*, p. 52.
[39]   San Souci obituary, *Providence Journal*, August 11, 1936.

co Americans on the Republican state ticket, and Elphege Daignault's defeat in the Republican legislative caucus that decided on the Republican
candidates for the Superior Court bench.[40]

On election night, William S. Flynn and Felix A. Toupin were elected by
comfortable margins over their Republican opponents. In the House elections, 48 Democrats and 2 Democratic-Independents won election as did
50 Republicans. In the Senate elections, only 20 Republicans were elected
as against 16 Democrats and 3 Democratic- Independents. In spite of the
gains of the Democrats, when the members of the legislature gathered to
organize both houses, the Democratic-Independents sided with Republicans to give them a majority in the lower house. While the Republicans in
State Senate had a clear majority, they would have to deal with the new
presiding officer, the newly elected Democratic lieutenant governor, Felix
Toupin. Although the shift of the Franco-American voters to the Democratic ticket in 1922 did not lead to an immediate Democratic triumph on
the state level, in the voting for local offices in Woonsocket, Democratic
candidates won election by margins of two and three to one over the Republicans, margins far above the state averages.[41]

The Franco Americans, who helped to hand the Republicans a decisive defeat in 1922, now looked to the new legislature for the passage of
an amendment to the Peck Education Act that would return control of
elementary schools to the local school committees and that would pre-
cisely delineate the subjects that had to be taught in English. As the Franco
Americans read the Peck Act, the State Commissioner of Education could
mandate so many subjects that there would be no time in the school day
for the teaching of religion or Canadian history. On February 23, 1922,
the day after he had spoken on the same matter before a meeting of the
Federal Council of the American Federation of Franco-American Societies, Eugene Jalbert, the federation's president, discussed with Bishop Hickey
the amendment he had drafted to the Peck Act and which had been introduced in the House by representatives Albert J. Lamarre of Pawtucket and
Edouard B. Belhumeur of Woonsocket.[42]

Mr. Jalbert prepared his amendment on the basis of Catholic doctrine,
which gave priority to the rights of parents over those of the state. Fearing
that Bishop Hickey would be opposed to his ideas since it had been asserted
during the debate over the bill in the House that the bishop had approved
the Peck Education Bill, Mr. Jalbert had sought the meeting with the bishop
in order that he might show the bishop the text he had prepared. Bishop
Hickey approved the text without asking for any changes and authorized

---

[40]   *La Tribune*, November 6, 1922; Patton, *Rhode Island Story*, 72–79
[41]   Erwin L. Levine, *Theodore Francis Green: The Rhode Island Years, 1906–1936* (Providence: Brown
       University Press, 1963), 94–95; Richard Sherman Sorrell, "The Sentinelle Affair (1924–1929)
       and Militant Survivance: The Franco-American Experience in Woonsocket, Rhode Island (State
       University of New York at Buffalo, Ph.D. dissertation, 1975), 165–66 and notes.
[42]   *Providence News*, February 23, 1923; Bishop Hickey's Diary, February 23, 1923.

Jalbert to state that he had approved it. At the hearing on the bill before the House Judiciary Committee, several of the major Franco-American organizations were represented. Mr. Jalbert, supported by Felix Toupin, argued the case for the rights of parents and for local governments having priority over those of the state. Commissioner of Education Walter Ranger and Dr. Charles Carroll argued the rights of the state.[43]

Following the House judiciary committee's consideration of the Lamarre-Belhumeur bill, Commissioner Ranger invited Mr. Jalbert to a conference in his office along with Dr. Carroll, who drafted most of the education legislation for the State Board of Education. Mr. Ranger did not raise any further objections to what Jalbert considered the major provision of the act, the returning of the control of the elementary schools to the local school committees. He did wish, however, to see changes made in the bill Jalbert had drafted in regard to

Eugene Jalbert

the various annual reports the local schools were required to send to the Board of Education. Mr. Jalbert was amenable to the changes and he and Dr. Carroll quickly reached agreement on compromise language. In later testimony before the House judiciary committee both men supported the compromise measure. The bill passed the House on April 20 on a vote of 50 to 37, with only one Republican voting for the bill. Proponents of the bill found it difficult to round up supporters for the measure in the Senate. Several women's groups, among them the State Federation of Women's Clubs, passed a resolution opposing the bill and the *Providence Journal* editorialized against it. The bill died in committee without reaching the Senate floor.[44]

Mr. Lamarre and Mr. Belhumeur reintroduced their measure in the January 1924 session of the Legislature. In an interview printed in several Rhode Island papers, Mr. Lamarre said he was introducing the measure "to remove from the statute books an evil which the majority of the citizens look upon as a menace to their liberties and an encroachment on their

---

[43]   Rumilly, *Histoire Des Franco-Americains, 347–48.*
[44]   *Providence Journal,* April 11, 21, 22, 25, 27, 1923; *Woonsocket Call,* April 21, 1922.

rights." In the interview he also charged the opponents of the bill with prejudice and had particularly harsh words for the professional women lobbyists, who did not have children, and had "the audacity to try to influence legislation pertaining to children and to try to tell the mothers of our State how they should raise and educate their children." The Lamarre-Belhumeur bill once again passed the House but the Senate, preoccupied as it was by other matters, did not take up the measure.[45]

In 1923 and 1924 the Democrats in the Senate used the power their numbers gave them and the fact that a Democrat, Lt. Gov. Toupin, presided over the Senate to force the Republicans, who controlled the Senate by virtue of one vote, to allow Democratic political reform proposals to come to the floor for a vote. By launching a filibuster early in the 1923 session, and thereby holding up the normal business of the state, the Democrats forced the Republicans to take a public stand on such reform issues as the abolishing of the property qualification for voting and the redistricting of the state to eliminate the "rotten boroughs" system that was part of the bulwark the Republicans had created at the beginning of the century to ensure their control of state politics. In the floor votes, the Republicans were forced to openly demonstrate their opposition to reform in voting down each of the Democratic-sponsored measures.[46]

In the January 1924 session, under the leadership of Lt. Gov. Toupin's and Senator Robert E. Quinn's of West Warwick, the Democrats resolved to stop all state business, including the passing of the annual budgets with appropriations, unless the Republicans again assented to a vote on the reform measures that Sen. Quinn reintroduced. The filibuster in 1924, while effective, proved unpopular among many in the state. The filibuster was finally broken on Thursday, July 19, when a Boston mobster, popularly believed to have been hired by the State Chairman of the Republican Party, exploded a bromine bomb in the Senate Chamber. The explosion allowed the Republican Senators to escape across the state line to a hotel in Rutland, Massachusetts. Without at least some of the Republicans present, the remaining Democratic and Democratic-Independents senators did not constitute the quorum necessary to conduct business.[47]

In an attempt to work out a compromise between the Democrats and Republicans in regard to their respective stands on the issue of political reform, which led to the filibuster, T. F. I. McDonnell, the president of the Providence Chamber of Commerce, appointed a committee made up of religious, education and civic leaders whose role would be to review the various reform proposals and make a recommendation as to their value. The members of the committee were Bishop Hickey; Bishop James DeWolf Perry, Bishop of the Episcopal Diocese of Rhode Island; Rev. Dr. William

[45] *Providence News,* January 3, 1924
[46] Patton, *The Rhode Island Story*, 85–87; Levine, *Theodore Francis Green*, 96–97.
[47] Patton, *The Rhode Island Story,* 101–115; Levine, *Theodore Francis Green*, 97–100.

H. P. Faunce, President of Brown University; and businessmen, William W. Moss, William L. Sweet, and James L. Jencks, along with Mr. McDonnell and the Chamber's Secretary, Ralph B. Watrous. After several meetings, the members of the civil committee unanimously recommended the adoption of many of the items on the reform agenda as a matter of justice. During the last week of July, the civic committee met with representatives from the legislature, who Gov. Flynn had appointed to a conference committee to work with the civic committee in an endeavor to arrive at a compromise, which would break the stalemate and allow the state to function properly. Two of the Republicans on the conference committee voted to reject the civic committee's recommendations and, thus, doomed any hope that the dispute over the consideration of reform measures could be ended by compromise.[48]

In September 1924, when the Democrats met to nominate their candidates for the November elections, they chose Gov. Flynn as their candidate for U.S. Senator to fill the seat of the recently deceased Sen. LeBaron B. Colt. To replace Flynn at the head of the state ticket, they chose Felix A. Toupin for governor and nominated his ally in the Senate, Robert E. Quinn, for lieutenant governor. When a day later the Republicans met in their convention, they chose former governor, Aram J. Pothier, to run for governor at the head of their state ticket.[49]

In the 1924 campaign, Mr. Toupin appealed to the emotions of his audiences more than to their intellects. In a speech given in both French and English at a Democratic rally in the Smithfield village of Georgiaville, Toupin again referred to the rejection of the American-born San Souci and Daignault by the Republicans in 1922 because in his view "these two men were not American enough." He then asked how can the Canadian-born Mr. Pothier be American enough to be governor. He questioned Mr. Pothier's readiness to protect the "future and reputation" of the Franco-Americans and later referred to Pothier's silence on question of the recall of the Peck Act. Toupin also made reference to the Democratic charges of Republican corruption in office. A week later in another speech in a heavily Franco-American area, Central Falls, Toupin said of Mr. Pothier that "he has no interest in the parochial schools. He laughs at your parochial schools." Pothier had no choice but to respond to Toupin's attacks. In a campaign speech in the village of Manville, Toupin's home, in the town of Lincoln, which he gave in both English and French, Pothier read the full text of the Peck Act to the audience and branded as a falsehood that the report spread among the Franco Americans by certain Democrats that the bill prohibited the teaching of the French language. He promised, if

---

48   *Providence News*, July 28, 1924.
49   *Providence Journal*, September 30; October 1, 1924.

elected, that he would have an amendment to the Peck Act considered "in a patriotic . . . not in a demagogic or noisy manner."[50]

Among the accusations that Mr. Toupin hurled at Pothier in his speech at Georgiaville on October 18 was that at their state convention the Republican Party had rejected former Representative Ambrose Kennedy as their candidate for governor "because he was opposed by the Ku Klux Klan, but the Ku Klux Klan wanted Pothier." Democratic campaigners frequently made the charge that the Klan exercised a strong influence in the Republican party during the campaign. The modern Klan, which had its origins in Georgia in 1915, and languished until 1920 when modern marketing techniques were used to spur membership and profits for organizers, did not begin organizing efforts in Rhode Island until 1923. In June 1924, the Providence papers reported on the initiation of several hundred Klansmen in Foster and Exeter. In that same month, the *Providence News*, which had taken on itself the self-appointed task of watchdog of Klan activities, carried an article that the Klan was conducting an intensive drive "to induce all the bigots and fanatics in this State" to register to vote in the November election.[51]

On Tuesday, November 4, the evening of the November 1924 elections, the Klan celebrated the victory of Pothier and the Republicans, who won all the state offices and substantial majorities in both houses of the legislature. Believing that their help was an important element in the Republicans' victory, Klansmen set crosses afire that evening on hills in East Providence, Warwick, East Greenwich and elsewhere. They also set one ablaze on the Providence College campus, the second one to be burned there in ten days.[52]

Edouard Belhumeur of Woonsocket, who was reelected in 1924, joined with a newly elected representative from Pawtucket, Henri Nesbit, in submitting another proposal to amend the Peck Act. Once again several women's and patriotic organizations opposed the attempt and sought to retain at least some measure of control over the local schools for the State Board of Education. The two sponsors of the bill resisted all efforts at amending their bill and they were supported by the state Republican leadership, who did not wish to further alienate the Franco Americans who strongly supported it because of Pothier. The Senate concurred in passing the bill on April 25 and Gov. Pothier signed it four days later. The two most important provisions of the amendment were the return of the power to approve private schools to the local school boards and, in view of the efforts in Rhode Island and elsewhere to prohibit the teaching of foreign languages

---

[50] *Providence Journal*, October 18, 27, 29, 1924.
[51] *Providence Journal*, June 22, 25, 1924; *Providence News*, June 27, 1924; Norman W. Smith, "The Ku Klux Klan in Rhode Island," *Rhode Island History (May 1978)*, 35–45.
[52] *Evening Tribune*, November 7, 1924; *Providence Visitor*, November 14, 1924.

as un-American, the amendment explicitly recognized the right to teach in a foreign language.[53]

The Providence College Drive
and the Expansion of the College

During his first years in Providence, Bishop Hickey chose to continue and complete the education initiatives begun by Bishop Harkins. Among the last major projects that Bishop Harkins had initiated was the founding of Providence College for which he conducted a successful drive in the parishes of the diocese aimed at raising $100,000. Bishop Harkins presided at the college's dedication on May 22, 1919. It was the last ceremony at which he would preside. When Providence College opened its doors the following September to welcome the young men who had enrolled in the college's first class, Bishop Hickey presided at the opening mass in Harkins Hall on Thursday, September 18, and delivered the sermon.[54]

Prior to the opening of the college, the Providence College Corporation held its annual meeting on July 28 in the Chancery Office on Fenner Street The members elected Bishop Hickey as a member of the corporation and then as its president in place of Msgr. Blessing, who had previously held that post. During the course of the meeting, the corporation's treasurer, Fr. Albert Casey, O.P., the president of the college, was authorized to borrow $100,000 to cover the college's debts and other expenses. As a last item of business, Bishop Hickey announced that he would establish the first scholarship for the college with a gift of $2,500. The recipient of the Bishop Hickey scholarship was to be chosen by the college in conjunction with the bishop.[55]

The need to borrow money to pay the debts of the college and to provide necessary equipment was caused in part by the increase in the price of goods created by the high demand and shortages of materials that followed on the outbreak of the first World War in 1914. The rise in construction costs had forced the corporation to scale down its plans for Harkins Hall. Prices remained high after the war due to the slowness of the American economy in reconverting to the demands of a peacetime economy. In order to place Providence College on a firm financial foundation, on March 23, 1920, Bishop Hickey invited the pastors of the diocese, together with a lay representative of each parish, to meet with him and Fr. Casey in Cathedral

[53] *Woonsocket Call*, March 27; April 13, 15, 17, 25, 29, 1925; Sorrell, "The Sentinelle Affair and Militant *Survivance*," p. 139.
[54] *Providence Journal*, September 14, 19, 1919; *Providence Visitor*, September 19, 1919. For a discussion of how many students were enrolled in Providence College's first class see Donna T. McCaffrey, "The Origins and Early History of Providence College through 1947" (Unpublished doctrinal dissertation, Providence College, 1985), p. 128.
[55] Minutes of the Providence College Corporation, July 28, 1919; *Providence Visitor*, August 1, 1919; Providence *Journal*, August 2, 1919.

Hall on Monday, April 5, to discuss a plan for raising funds to eliminate the debt on the college, provide it with scientific equipment and develop athletic facilities. What Bishop Hickey proposed to the pastors and laymen was the conducting of a fund-raising drive in the then ninety-five parishes of the diocese between May 30 and June 7 similar to those which had been conducted during the World War. The bishop set $250,000 as the total goal of the campaign. The meeting approved the bishop's plan and formally organized the Providence College Drive Association with Bishop Hickey as its president and William J. Keenan, state deputy of the Knights of Columbus, as its secretary.[56]

Bishop Hickey and Mr. Keenan prepared a series of letters, which he required his pastors to read at all the masses in the weeks before the drive. In a letter, which was also published in the *Providence Visitor* on May 14, 1920, Bishop Hickey asked each person sixteen years of age and over to donate a sum equal to at least one day's pay. Fortunately for the vast majority of Catholics in the state, hourly wages during the World War had kept pace with the rising prices. Salaries, however, had not and those on salary were less able to help with the drive. In organizing the drive, Bishop Hickey and the drive committee used the same methods that had proved successful during the large fund-raising drives during the war and carefully spelled them out in "Rule of Organization" the committee sent to each pastor. Each parish was assigned a quota of the funds to be raised. The pastors and lay chairmen organized solicitation committees in each of the parishes, which consisted of ten captains, who in turn recruited teams of men and women who would personally call on the members of their parish to solicit their donations. The Drive Committee, as an afterthought, also sent out envelopes for the use of the children of the parishes so that they too might contribute to the drive. The parish drives began with a general meeting to explain the need and stir enthusiasm.[57]

In addition to appealing to the individual Catholics of the diocese, the Providence College Drive Association also approached the twenty-one Knights of Columbus Councils in the diocese for contributions to the drive, which they made either directly or through their parishes. In addition the Drive Association addressed a letter to non-Catholic business owners in the state asking for their support in the light of the fact that Providence College was open to people of all races and creeds. Many business owners had made substantial profits during the war and were in a position to be generous. Among the Catholic businessmen who responded to the appeal was Arthur Laberte, a parishioner of St. Matthew's Parish, Central Falls, whose pastor, Fr. Joseph A. Laliberte, was a member of the Association's Executive

---

[56]   Hickey to Pastors, March 23, 1920, Providence College Archives [Hereafter, PCA]; *Providence Visitor*, April 9, 1920.

[57]   Ibid., May 14, 21, 1920; Hickey to Pastors, May 19, 1920, PCA; "Rules of Organization," PCA; Daniel J. O'Neill, "Providence College - Its Origins and Development" (Master's Thesis, Providence College, 1927), 32–33.

Committee. Mr. Laberte donated $2,000 and offered to double the largest donation made to the campaign up to $25,000. The drive proved to be a pronounced success as a total of $329,746 was collected by the time the drive closed on June 7. A week after the drive ended, Fr. Casey gave a check for $100,000 to the Industrial Trust Company to clear the indebtedness of the college.[58]

At few days later, at the ceremony which marked the end of Providence College's second year, Bishop Hickey announced that he had signed a contract for the clearing of the grounds around the college and the building of an athletic field. In order to lay out a proper baseball diamond, the corporation had purchased nineteen lots adjacent to the college on Wardlaw Avenue. Since college baseball was then among the most popular of college sports, the plans for the field included grandstands to accommodate the anticipated crowds at what would be called Hendricken Field in honor of the first Bishop of Providence.[59]

During the summer of 1921, Fr. Raymond Meagher, O.P., the Provincial of the Dominican Province of St. Joseph, who along with Bishop Harkins founded the college, secured Bishop Hickey's consent to the erecting of a small building on the Providence College grounds to accommodate the students at the college who intended to enter the Dominican's Novitiate. However, on August 16, 1921, Bishop Hickey wrote to Fr. Meagher withdrawing his consent. In explaining the reversal of his decision, Bishop Hickey gave as one of his reasons his fear that the existence of a Novitiate Preparatory Building on the grounds would alter the essential character of the college so that the college would be perceived as a Dominican institution rather than a diocesan institution. If such a perception developed, Hickey feared that "the main purpose for the college would thus be defeated and our Catholic boys ambitious of a college education would at once flock back to Brown." He also wished to leave as much room as possible in the college for the general applicants.[60]

In his response to the bishop's letter, Fr. Meagher pointed out that since he had already directed the students who were being prepared for the Novitiate to report to Providence College and, he had already assigned his personnel for the coming year, it would be impossible to make other arrangements for them at other Dominican institutions at this late date. As a compromise, he suggested that Hickey give Fr. Casey permission to rent a small house away from the college in which the order could accommodate its students for the present year. Bishop Hickey agreed to Fr. Meagher's proposal and Fr. Casey hired a house downtown near the State House from

[58] Hickey to Pastors, April 20; May 1, 6, 12, 19, 27, 29; June 2, 3, 15, 17, 1920; *Providence Journal,* May 30; June 1, 16, 1920; *Providence Visitor,* June 4, 11, 1920.
[59] *Providence Journal,* June 16, 1921; *Providence Visitor,* June 17, 1921.
[60] Raymond Meagher, O.P., to A. J. Murphy, July 25, 1921; A. J. Murphy to Bishop Hickey, July 27, 1921, PCA; Bishop William A. Hickey to Meagher, August 16, 1921, PChA.

which the students who lived there walked to the college each day as did the college's other students.[61]

Shortly after the college opened for its third year in September 1921, Fr. Casey publicly announced to the faculty and to the then almost three hundred students that ill health compelled him to resign as president of the college and pastor of St. Pius Parish. As his successor as both president and pastor, the Dominican Provincial, Fr. Raymond Meagher, O.P., chose Fr. William D. Noon, O.P., a distinguished scholar and preacher, who, at the time of his appointment, was professor of Dogmatic Theology at the Dominican House of Studies in Washington.[62]

When Fr. Meagher received Bishop Hickey's letter in which he informed him of his change of mind regarding permission for the house for the Dominican students, his first thought was to come up to Providence to speak personally with the bishop about the bishop's assertion in his letter that the college was a diocesan institution rather than a Dominican institution. When he set up the Providence College Corporation, Bishop Harkins, as was his custom for institutions that were to be open to all regardless of race or creed, sought to create a board of directors whose primary interest would be the success of the institution. According, Bishop Harkins had given the Dominicans a majority of the places on the corporate board of the college.[63]

Wishing to find support for his understanding of the nature of the college, Bishop Hickey asked Bishop Louis Walsh, a close friends and confidant of both Bishop Harkins and himself, for a statement of his understanding of Bishop Harkins' intentions when he created the college. In a notarized statement, Bishop Walsh wrote that "it was always an admitted principle and fact that the College was to be a Diocesan institution, to be owned and in all final decisions to be subject to the Bishop of Providence and his canonical Board of Consultors." He also noted that "the specific sum of money to be supplied by the Dominican Fathers was to give them an equity, create more interest on their part and promote stability in the future, since, under these conditions all question of their abandoning the work or being asked to withdraw would be much less probable. Fr. Meagher did not pursue the matter of the character of the collage. On March 14, 1922, the day on which Bishop Hickey had presided at the funeral of Fr. Bernard Logan, O.P., the founding pastor of St. Raymond's, Providence, Fr. Meagher called on the bishop later in the day and the two had, in Bishop

---

61 Meagher to Hickey, August 23, 1921, PCA; McCaffrey, "The Origins and Early History of Providence College through 1947," pp. 169–70.

62 *Providence Journal*, September 22, 1921; *Providence Visitor*, September 23, 26; October 7, 1921. It is possible that considerations in addition to his health prompted Fr. Casey to tender his resignation as president of the college. In a 1926 letter to a fellow Dominican, Fr. Casey wrote in reference to the college, "I have never attended a meeting since I left. My presence would act as a red rag to bull Hickey," Casey to Joseph M. Ripple, O.P., cited in McCaffrey, "Origins and Early History of Providence College through 1947," p. 174.

63 Hickey to Meagher, August 16, 1921, PCA.

Hickey's words, an "agreeable visit of nearly an hour" in the bishop's office on Fenner Street."[64]

Bishop Hickey's relationship with the Dominicans cooled again after Fr. William G. Moran, O.P., whom Fr. Meagher had appointed to succeed Fr. Logan resigned the parish after only three months in Providence following his election as prior and pastor of St. Vincent Ferrar's Church in New York. Fr. Meagher then chose to replace him as pastor of St. Raymond's with Fr. John A. Hinch, O.P. However, Fr. Meagher's telegram informing Bishop Hickey of Fr. Hinch's appointment arrived at the bishop's office on August 2, 1922 after news of Fr. Hinch's appointment had been announced by the *Providence News*.[65]

Since the same thing had happened when Fr. Moran was appointed, Bishop Hickey immediately wrote to Fr. Meagher informing him of his displeasure and pointing out that such a manner of appointment "discounts the episcopal authority in the eyes of the people as far as St. Raymond's is concerned." He, therefore, asked Fr. Meagher to present the name of another for the pastorate of St. Raymond's and to notify him of his recommendation "by letter, privately and before others, and not by telegram." The bishop explained that he was motivated "solely by concern for the proper order of things in the diocese" confided to his care. It fell to Fr. Noon to call on Bishop Hickey on August 4 on Fr. Meagher's behalf to discuss "matters concerning Providence College & relations between Bishop and Dominicans." While Bishop Hickey's anger flared easily, he had the welfare of the Church at heart. He privately agreed to Fr. Meagher's appointment of Fr. Hinch as pastor of St. Raymond's, but withheld official approval until Fr. Meagher sent a letter formally recommending Fr. Hinch's appointment.[66]

Fr. Noon's meeting with Bishop Hickey on August 4 was not his first experience of dealing with the bishop when he had a grievance against the Dominicans or the college. In a meeting with Bishop Hickey at the college on November 18, 1921, Fr. Noon had raised the question of a college prom, but Bishop Hickey refused to give permission. The bishop was not pleased when he read in a Providence paper on February 22, 1922, that the Providence College freshman, after a dinner in Warren, then had a dance at the Jefferson Street Armory where young ladies awaited them and expressed his displeasure at class dances in his diary. However, when a month later, Fr. Noon next called on him there is no mention of the issue in the bishop's diary entry for that day.[67]

In spite of his differences with Fr. Meagher and with Frs. Casey and Noon over the relation of the college to the diocese, Bishop Hickey continued to be the major supporter of the college. On June 17, 1921, during the

---

[64] Walsh to Hickey, December 6, 1921, PChA; Bishop Hickey's Diary, March 14, 1922.

[65] *Providence Visitor*, March 31; June 30, 1922; *Providence News*, August 2, 1922, PChA.

[66] Hickey to Meagher, August 2, 1922, PChA, Bishop Hickey's Diary, August 4, 7, 1922.

[67] Bishop Hickey's Diary, November 18, 1921; February 22; April 24, 1922.

last corporation meeting that he attended, Fr. Casey had raised the question of building a gymnasium in addition to the athletic field for which the corporation had recently purchased additional land. The original plans for Harkins Hall had provided for both a large gymnasium and an auditorium in a separate wing of building, but these features had been eliminated due to the rising costs of materials prior to the beginning of construction. The corporation members left the question of a gym to the executive committee of the corporation. On November 15, 1921, during his first private meeting with Bishop Hickey after he was appointed president of the college, Fr. Noon urged the building of a science building rather than a gymnasium. Three days later, Bishop Hickey called at the college to discuss the question of the college's needs with Fr. Noon and Fr. Michael Galliher, O.P., the college's first Director of Studies or Dean, who, rather than Fr. Noon, had a talent for academic administration. The conversation among the three ranged over various possibilities, among them a science building and an auditorium. During the meeting, Bishop Hickey apparently gave him approval to at least continued discussions of another building at the college and perhaps also recommended a Springfield, Massachusetts, architect he knew, John W. Donahue. [68]

On August 22, 1922, Mr. Donahue accompanied Frs. Noon and Galliher when they called on Bishop Hickey and discussed ideas for a new wing on Harkins Hall, which would include a "Hall, Library & Dormitory for professors." When the Providence College Corporation met at the college for the first time on September 1, 1922, Bishop Hickey, as president of the corporation, appointed a committee "to select an architect and to approve plans for a new auditorium building." On October 19, 1922, Bishop Hickey met with John W. Donahue, a Springfield, Massachusetts architect, to discuss plans for a new wing at the college. Later the next month, Fr. Noon called on the bishop to inform him that the Industrial Trust Company in Providence had agreed to extend a loan for the addition to the college.[69]

Fr. Noon's and the Dominicans' relationship with Bishop Hickey entered a crisis stage in May 1923. On May 5, Fr. Noon met with Bishop Hickey to ask permission for a field mass on the day the college's first class was to graduate during the coming June and for the purchase of a house on Eaton Street near the campus for the student candidates for the Dominican order. Fr. Noon's request for the purchase of a nearby house was prompted by the growth in the number of students in the Dominicans' preparatory program and by the disadvantages of housing them away from the college

---

[68]   Minutes of the Providence College Corporation, June 17, 1921, PCA; Bishop Hickey's Diary, November 15, 18, 1921.

[69]   Ibid., August 22, 1922; Minutes of the Providence College Corporation, September 1, 1922, PCA; Bishop Hickey's Diary, October 19; November 25, 28 1922. Cf. Sketch of proposed group of college buildings in *Providence Visitor*, June 8, 1923.

at a cost approaching $1600 a year. Bishop Hickey refused permission for both.[70]

The root cause for his refusal to grant permission for the purchase of property for the Dominican students lay in the still unresolved issue of who ultimately controlled the college. Two days after his meeting with the bishop, Fr. Noon returned to Fenner Street with a packet of documents, which he believed substantiated the Dominican's claim that Providence College was "not simply a Diocesan institution." Fr. Noon then called on the bishop the next day to discuss the matter. In a letter to Fr. Meagher three days later, Fr. Noon provided his version of what transpired during the meeting. He began by saying that "for a time it seemed necessary for me to see you tomorrow in Washington but the sky cleared a bit." The reason the meeting did not go well initially was because, in his view, the bishop "has become a maniac on the question of episcopal authority," claiming "again that this college is a diocesan institution." After looking over the documents again, however, the bishop's attitude softened, as it usually did when confronted with facts that cleared up his first impressions. Fr. Noon reported that the bishop's "last word was a request that we leave the people the impression that it is diocesan."[71]

Going on to another train of thought, Bishop Hickey suggested to Fr. Noon that he might find it necessary to reimburse the Dominicans "in some way and put us out." He included Fr. Hinch in this threat, if Fr. Hinch failed to cooperate with him in diocesan matters. The bishop revealed some of his own insecurity when he told Fr. Noon that he did not want the question taken to Washington, but rather preferred to see the question of control of the college settled by an unbiased canonist. In spite of the difficult beginning, Fr. Noon reported that, overall, their meeting was amicable and that the two parted the best of friends.[72]

The Dominicans chose not to press the issue of who controlled the college at this time. Rather, Fr. Meagher and Fr. Noon made sure that when the Providence College Corporation met, there were always enough Dominicans to constitute a majority of those present, thus ensuring that no resolution indicating that the college was solely a diocesan institution would ever pass or even be brought up. In spite of the difference of opinion in regard to control of the college, Bishop Hickey's relations with the college remained generally warm and friendly.

70   Bishop Hickey's Diary, May 5, 1923; McCaffrey, "The Origins and Early Development of Providence College through 1947," p. 212.
71   Memo, Chancery Office Files, May 7, 1923; Bishop Hickey's Diary, May 8, 1923; Noon to Meagher, May 11, 1923, PCA.
72   Ibid. A few months before Fr. Noon's meeting with Bishop Hickey, a leader of a group of Franco Americans from the diocese, who had begun to publicly criticize the English-speaking bishops in New England, had gone to see the apostolic delegate in Washington to ask him to prevent Bishop Hickey from what they regarded as "taxing" the French-Canadian parishes in the diocese in support of a drive to build Catholic high schools. Cf. Below,

Fr. Noon frequently invited the bishop, who was a sports fan, to come to PC games and important events in the life of the college and the bishop did come.[73]

In early 1926, after the number of candidates for the Dominican order, who were attending Providence College, had reached eighty-five or more, Fr. Meagher considered buying land two miles and half from the college and, in May, secured Bishop Hickey's approval of this purchase. The Dominicans were about to begin excavation work for a house on the property when the priest in charge received a phone call from Bishop Hickey that the Bradley properly, immediately adjacent to the college, could be purchased. The bishop was an astute business man and recognized that the opportunity, which he had been offered by the trustees of the Bradley property, was too good an offer to pass over. As a house for Dominican students presented the best immediate use of the property, the bishop offered to buy the property for the order and to allow the Dominicans to build a dormitory for their students on it. The Dominicans proceeded to renovate the Italianate style house on the property and to build an dormitory addition to house their students. The first students took up residence in what the Dominicans would call Guzman Hall in September 1926. During the college's commencement exercises in the month following the bishop's purchase of the Bradley Estate for the Dominicans, the college conferred on Bishop Hickey the first honorary degree it was to award. In the degree citation, the college hailed Bishop Hickey as "its greatest benefactor and most distinguished patron."[74]

Fr. Noon's health began to deteriorate at the beginning of 1926 and in June he tendered his resignation as president of the college. As his successor, Fr. Meagher chose a Woonsocket-born priest and graduate of La Salle Academy, Fr. Lorenzo C. McCarthy, O.P., who was only thirty-eight at the time of his nomination by Fr. Meagher and election by the College Corporation as president of the college. Fr. McCarthy had been part of the original faculty of the college when it opened in 1919 and had left the college in 1924 to pursue a doctorate at the University of Louvain in Belgium, which he finished in July 1926. It fell to Fr. McCarthy to continue the academic and physical development of the college begun by his two predecessors. Concerned that the college might be blacklisted because of its academic weaknesses, Fr. McCarthy, with the help of the college's Dean of Studies, Fr. Arthur H. Chandler, O.P., undertook a major reorganization and expansion of the college's curriculum with involved an increase in the size of the faculty in order to bring the college closer in line to the better colleges in the country. The fruit of their collective labors matured

---

[73] McCaffrey, "Origins and Early History of Providence College through 1947," pp. 200–01; Bishop Hickey's Diary, October 10, 1922; October 26, 1923.

[74] McCaffrey, "The Origins and Early Development of Providence College through 1947," pp. 213–17.; *Providence Visitor*, June 11, 1926.

in December 1931 when Providence College was recognized and accepted into the New England Association of Colleges and Secondary Schools.[75]

After the dispute with Bishop Hickey over who controlled the college, the Dominicans apparently realized that they could not expect Hickey to take the lead in fund-raising for any new building program at the college. In 1925, Fr. Meagher requested permission from the Dominicans' Vicar General to borrow $300,000 in order to build the addition to the college that Fr. Noon had discussed with Bishop Hickey three years earlier. Fr. Meagher had Mr. Donahue revise his previous plans. Mr. Donahue submitted the new drawings in September 1926. After consulting the Providence College faculty, Fr. Meagher discussed the plans with Bishop Hickey the following month. Hickey favored the building of a gymnasium first, after which another building could be added later to Harkins Hall in order to provide additional classrooms and faculty housing. Although no definite decisions were made at this second meeting with the bishop, at which Mr. Donahue joined them, Fr. Meagher, on his part, believed that two buildings were necessary immediately.[76]

Plans for the expansion of the college were still undecided when Fr. Meagher met with Fr. McCarthy in the spring of 1927 and urged the new president to undertake the expansion project as soon as possible. On his part, Fr. McCarthy considered Mr. Donahue's original plan, which called for separate buildings as altogether too elaborate and expensive and lamented the fact that they did not include a library, which he felt to be essential. Instead, he favored adding a wing to Harkins Hall. On July 25, 1927, Fr. McCarthy brought Mr. Donahue's sketches for the new wing to Bishop Hickey to discuss "suitable modifications." Bishop Hickey approved the plans as did the Dominicans Provincial and House Council. As he did in all cases involving a large expenditure of funds, Bishop Hickey presided at the opening of the bids submitted by the various contractors on November 18, 1927. Building operations on the four-story, one-hundred-fifty-one-foot long addition got underway that winter and was completed by the opening of the college's second semester in January 1929. Bishop Hickey blessed and dedicated the new wing on February 7, 1929. Since the issue of diocesan versus Dominican control of the college remained undecided at this time, Bishop Hickey chose not to turn over the funds that remained from the 1920 fund-raising drive for the college as part of the funding of the new building. In the end, the addition put the college $180,000 in debt.[77]

[75]   *Evening Bulletin*, June 16, 1927; McCaffrey, "The Origins and Early Development of Providence College through 1947," pp. 243–60. Fr. McCarthy was appointed president of the college only. Prior to Fr. Noon's resignation as president of Providence College, Fr. Meagher had relieved him of his duties as pastor of St. Pius Parish. In November 1926, Fr. Meagher, with Bishop Hickey's approval appointed Fr. William A. Sullivan, O.P., as the first full-time pastor of St. Pius with residence at the college.
[76]   McCaffrey, "Origins and Early History of Providence College through 1947," pp. 270–72.
[77]   Ibid., pp. 272–82; *Providence Visitor*, February 1, 8, 1929. Bishop Hickey's successor, Bishop Francis P. Keough, would not share the same sensitivity on the issue of episcopal control.

With the new addition completed, Fr. McCarthy began to lay the groundwork for the further expansion of the college's infrastructure by the building of a new science building. To his surprise, he found Bishop Hickey agreeable to the idea when he raised it with him in early April 1929. The bishop even hinted at their meeting that he would give the Dominicans some money toward the building. However, before plans for the science building progressed very far, Fr. McCarthy received word in July 1929 that the city of Providence was negotiating for the purchase of an orchard at the opposite corner of East and River avenues, opposite the college's main driveway, as the site for a public high school. Since Fr. McCarthy did not wish to see the land used for that purpose, he weighed offering to buy the land as a way to frustrate the city's plans. However, while the owner of the land was willing to sell it to the city, he was not willing to sell it to a Catholic institution. Since Bishop Hickey was also opposed to the idea of a public high school on the site, the bishop was able to use his political influence to persuade the city to choose a site on Mt. Pleasant Avenue. While Fr. McCarthy would have considered purchasing the orchard if that was the only way to frustrate the city's plans, his preference for expansion of the college's property was to purchase some seventy-eight, as yet undeveloped, lots along Wardlaw Avenue, which bordered Hendricken Field. The land had already been plotted out for house lots and their value to the college was dependent on the city being agreeable to the abandoning of the three streets, which traversed the 8.8 acres. After securing the permission of the Dominican's Provincial Council and of Bishop Hickey, Fr. McCarthy successfully oversaw the complicated effort, which resulted in his obtaining space for the future expansion of the college. With the purchase completed, Fr. McCarthy gave his attention again to the need for a new science building, which the Dominican Provincial, Fr. Raymond Meagher, OP, strongly supported.[78]

However, when Fr. Meagher's third term as provincial ended, the Dominicans chose Fr. Terence S. McDermott, O.P., to succeed him. Fr. McDermott did not share the same sense of urgency in regard to the science building that Fr. Meagher had had and was content to see the physical development of the college proceeded at a more leisurely pace. Neither Fr. McCarthy nor Bishop Hickey forgot about the project. On August 18, 1933, the *Providence Visitor* printed an announcement on its front page that work was about to begin at Providence College on a new science building designed by Ambrose J. Murphy and named in honor of Bishop Hickey. Developments reached the point where building plans were sent out to various contractors in order to secure bids. After having selected a general contractor, Bishop Hickey and Fr. McCarthy agreed to meet on October 6 to choose between the bids of the various subcontractors. Bishop Hickey

---

[78] McCaffrey, "The Origins and Early Development of Providence College through 1947," pp. 270–88.

died two days before the scheduled meeting and plans for the new science building were abruptly suspended until a successor to Bishop Hickey was chosen.[79]

Catholic Students at Non-Catholic Colleges

RHODE ISLAND STATE COLLEGE

While Bishop Hickey consistently urged the parents of Catholic high school graduates to provide their sons and daughters with an education in a Catholic college, many parents lacked the means to pay even Providence College's modest tuition, let alone the combined expenses of tuition and housing at a college out of state. Until such time as Rhode Island State College, which was founded in 1892 as the Rhode Island College of Agriculture and Mechanical Arts on the grounds of what, since 1888 had been Rhode Island State Agricultural School, expanded its curricula to include liberal arts program, few Catholics thought of enrolling there. In 1905, the total enrollment at the college was 139, of whom only 49 were college students with regular standing. The remainder were students in the preparatory program the college offered or students enrolled in other special programs. In October 1902, H. J. Wheeler, then acting president of the college, forwarded a copy of the college's latest catalogue to Bishop Matthew Harkins, the second Bishop of Providence, and, in a separate letter, called the bishop's attention to the advantages of the college for young men and women of limited means. Mr. Wheeler extended an invitation to the bishop to visit the college and to address the student body. In case the bishop was unable to accept the invitation, he asked if he might call on the bishop to discuss how the merits of the college might be best brought to the attention of the Roman Catholics of the state.[80]

Bishop Harkins elected to invite Mr. Wheeler to call on him in Providence, which Mr. Wheeler did on October 29, 1902. According to the bishop's diary, the two agreed that there was to be no coeducation at the college, that Catholics were to be part of the college corporation and hired as faculty and staff members, that there was to be no compulsory attendance at chapel exercises, and that provisions were to be made for Catholic students to attend mass. In all, Bishop Harkins found Mr. Wheeler to be "quite fair and sensible." If a Catholic student at the college wished to attend mass on Sunday, the nearest church was St. Francis in the village of Wakefield, a mile walk from the college. Since people in the early part of

[79]   Ibid., 288–93.
[80]   Charles Carroll, *Rhode Island: Three Centuries of Democracy* (New York: Lewis Historical Publishing Company, 1932) II, 976–77; H. J. Wheeler to Harkins, October 23, 1902, PChA.

the century were accustomed to walking, the trek to Wakefield would have proved no great hardship except in severe weather.[81]

Criticisms of the college prompted the Rhode Island legislature in 1908 to appoint a commission to review the college's programs, to determine its educational value to the state, and to consider ways its programs could be enhanced. In January 1909, Gov. Aram Pothier called for the separation of the Mechanic Arts from the Agricultural Program. The governor's call prompted Bishop Harkins to write a note to him expressing his support of the idea because he believed the separation would offer the young people of Providence a better opportunity to gain technical training. A month later, one of the members of commission investigating the college, Dr. James E. Sullivan of Providence, talked over the college's affairs with Bishop Harkins prior to the commission's submitting its report. In making its report to the legislature in 1909, the commission unanimously recommended the continuance of the college. After considering the report, the legislature chose to increase the state's financial support of the college and changed its name to Rhode Island State College.[82]

Bishop Harkins' concerns about the college and its Catholic students were raised again when Joseph F. Shea, who entered the college as a freshman in 1912, wrote to him about a vote of college's faculty to make chapel services compulsory. Mr. Shea reported that the services were conducted in a Protestant style and that a Protestant minister occasionally led the exercises and made a few remarks. Shea questioned whether the college's president could compel Catholic students to attend the exercises since it was a state institution. He asked Bishop Harkins to write to the Catholic students at the college forbidding them to attend. There is no indication in the records as to what Bishop Harkins' response was to the letter.[83]

The president of the college at the time Bishop Harkins received the student's letter was Howard Edwards, who had been appointed in 1905. When in August 1912, someone from the Rhode Island State College sent the *Providence Visitor* a packet of information on the college, one of the items was a copy of the *Narragansett Times* for June 21, 1912, which contained the text of the baccalaureate address Mr. Edwards gave at the college five days earlier. After reading the address, the *Visitor* took issue with Mr. Edwards' remarks and suggested that he was preaching materialism in his call for an altruistic Christianity.[84]

On his part, Mr. Edwards was anxious for good relations with all the religious groups in the state, especially the Catholics who made up the majority of the state's population by the turn of the century. In October

81   Bishop Harkins' Diary, October 29, 1902, PChA.

82   Carroll, *Rhode Island*, II, 977; Pothier to Harkins, January 15, 1909, PChA; Bishop Harkins' Diary, February 25, 1909.

83   Carroll, *Rhode Island*, II, 977; Pothier to Harkins, January 15, 1909, PChA; Bishop Harkins' Diary, February 25, 1909.

84   *Providence Visitor*, August 30, 1912.

1912, he wrote to Bishop Harkins asking if he would agree to take part in ceremonies scheduled for later in the month to mark the laying of the cornerstone of a new science building at the college. When the bishop replied through his secretary, Fr. Peter Foley, that he could not do so, Mr. Edwards asked Fr. Foley if he could suggest the name of a Catholic priest in an official position, who could represent that Catholic Church on the occasion. Edwards' note to Fr. Foley went unanswered and when the ceremony was held, no Catholic priest was present.[85]

It was not until March 8, 1924, that President Edwards addressed another request to the Bishop of Providence. This time it was to Bishop William A. Hickey. Mr. Edwards wrote to the bishop of his desire to advance the spiritual life of the students at the college without reference to creed or sect. Previously the college had anticipated that the churches in the vicinity of the college might be able to meet the religious needs of the students, who chose to stay at the college over the weekends. However, by 1924, the college had "nearly five hundred students of varying faiths . . . with a correspondingly enlarged force of faculty members and employees and their families of many religious beliefs." Mr. Edwards felt that the college was not doing its full duty unless it took some measure "to foster in larger degree, in wider scope the highest ideals and aspirations of the human soul." In order to fill the perceived need, Edwards asked Bishop Hickey's opinion of a proposal to hold a series of vesper services on Sunday evenings during the college year "at which a representative of each form of religious faith may in turn on successive Sundays conduct the service and speak to a voluntary audience." Within a few days of receiving the letter, Bishop Hickey replied that the suggestion of the vesper services gave him "great pleasure" and indicated that he would be glad to cooperate in the endeavor. He asked only that the Douay version of the Bible then used in Catholic worship be used whenever a Catholic priest presided as the services and that national hymns or hymns common to both Catholic and Protestant traditions be used on such occasions.[86]

As leaders of other religious denominations in Rhode Island also supported the idea of vesper services, Mr. Edwards was able to write to Bishop Hickey again on March 31, 1924 to inform him of the favorable consensus and to suggest that, in his view, it would be better to wait until the start of the new school year in the fall to begin the series of meetings. At the beginning, Mr. Edwards personally extended invitations to various clergymen to officiate at the services. He later asked Rev. Claude Beardslee, the minister

85 Edwards to Harkins, October 10, 1912; Rev. Peter A. Foley to Edwards, October 12, 1912; Edwards to Foley, October 15, 1912, PChA, *Narragansett Times*, October 25; November 1, 1912.
86 Edwards to Hickey, March 8, 1924; Hickey to Edwards, March 20, 1924, PChA. On Sunday, November 25, 1928, when the three new buildings built at college from the proceeds of a loan, among them Edwards Hall, a combination library and auditorium building, were dedicated, a Catholic priest, a Jewish Rabbi and a Protestant Minister were part of the program. *Narragansett Times*, November 16, 1928.

at the Kingston Congregational Church, to take charge of arranging the series of speakers which, in the first year, included Frs. David I. Quinn, the pastor of St. Francis, Wakefield, and James R. Bartley, pastor of St. Philomena [now St. Thomas More], Narragansett, among other speakers. Rev. Beardslee asked Bishop Hickey if he would preside at one of the services but the bishop declined.[87]

In choosing speakers representative of each of the religious groups in the college, President Edwards sought to apportion them according to the percentage of students of the respective faiths in the college. According to a copy of a religious census taken probably in the late twenties and sent to Bishop Hickey, there were 163 Roman Catholics in the college out of a total population of 600. Episcopalians numbered 102; Congregationalists 98; Baptists 85, Jews 53, Methodists 51 while seven other groups had twenty or less. On November 23, 1929, the *Providence Journal* carried an announcement on its religion page that Msgr. Peter A. Foley, then chancellor of the diocese, who would be the first Catholic priest to preside at the vespers service, would speak the next day on "The Place of the Bible in the Christian Church" in the recently built Edwards Hall. The article noted that 143 had attended the first meeting, 150 the second, while 183 were present the third Sunday to hear Rabbi Samuel M. Gup. The writer anticipated that more than 200 would attend Msgr. Foley's talk, among them members of the Catholic parishes in Wakefield, Narragansett, Wickford and Westerly, who had also been invited.[88]

While President Edwards saw much of his vision for the college realized during his long tenure as president of the college, he failed to persuade the state to erect a chapel on the campus, which would serve all the religious denominations represented among its students. President Edwards gave expression to his hopes during a speech to a meeting of the Lions Club in Westerly prior to an election in 1926, which included a ballot question authorizing the borrowing of money to build new buildings at the college. In addition to the college's lack of a library and a place for mass meetings of the entire college, he also stressed that there was no place for religious services at the college. Mr. Edwards clearly recognized the "dilemma," as an article in the *Providence Journal* in September 1932 put it, "of using state funds for religious purposes, on the one hand, and allowing hundreds of young men and women to lose contact with their childhood religious training while taking a four-year course at Kingston on the other." He eventually appointed a "religious director," designated as a student counselor, whose function it was to organize the series of chapel services, which sought to bring the twenty-two different religious groups on the campus together, "so that something approximating the normal religious life of the students prior

87 Hickey to Edwards, December 27, 1924; Beardslee to Harkins, February 25, 1925, PChA; *Narragansett Times*, October 2, 1925.
88 "Religious Census on Basis of 600 Students." No date, PChA; *Providence Journal*, November 23, 1929.

to their coming to the college could be pursued without serious interruption." During the interregnum following President Edwards' death on April 10, 1930, his efforts to have a campus chapel and his practice of appointing a religious director were dropped.[89]

By 1932, the continuing expansion of the college and its programs had caused the student body to increase to more than 900, of whom approximately 25 percent were Catholics. At the same time the growth of neighboring St. Francis parish had caused the church, which sat 240 in the church proper and another 60 in the gallery, to become overcrowded when the college was in session. Each Sunday, between sixty and seventy students from the college arrived for mass on a bus provided by the college. Perceiving that a new church was necessary, the pastor of St. Francis, Fr. O'Rourke purchased land in 1931 on which to build one and the parish began construction in September 1932.[90]

Although the new church could better accommodate the students at the college as well as the parishioners at St. Francis, Bishop Hickey preferred to have Fr. O'Rourke say mass for the students on the college's campus, in part to alleviate the difficulties the students might have in getting to mass. At the bishop's direction, Fr. O'Rourke conferred with the college's new President, Dr. Raymond G. Bressler, who, in a change of religious policy from that of President Edwards, advocated the appointment of denominational chaplains and affording them the use of any of the college buildings for the purpose of holding services. On Sunday, September 25, 1932, the first Sunday he went to the college for mass, Fr. O'Rourke said mass in Edwards Hall for ninety people, of whom seventy-six were students. Fr. O'Rourke heard the confessions of those who wished to receive communion prior to the mass, which at the request of the students was offered at nine o'clock. In his sermon, Fr. O'Rourke paid tribute to the cooperation he received from President Bressler in arranging for the mass and called attention to the concern of Bishop Hickey. He noted that in the years since President Edwards had died, Bishop Hickey had been concerned that the students at the college have an opportunity to profess their faith and that it was the bishop who had directed him to approach the college about offering mass on the campus.[91]

Dr. Bressler's willingness to cooperate in the offering of mass on campus and his action the previous spring of prohibiting any attempt by the students at the college to form branches of communistic or socialist societies whose literature had appeared in student mailboxes the previous March were very positive actions to the minds of Catholics. However, in reporting

[89] *Narragansett Times*, October 29, 1926; *Providence Journal*, September 24, 1932. For a review of Mr. Edward's tenure as President of Rhode Island State College, Cf. Carroll, *Rhode Island*, II, 977–79; IV, 477–80.
[90] *Providence Journal*, April 9, 1932; *Providence Visitor*, September 23, 1932; "St. Francis of Assisi Church: 100th Anniversary, April 22 – October 4, 1979" (Privately printed, 1979), p. 12.
[91] *Providence Visitor*, September 23, 30, 1932; *Providence Journal*, September 24, 1932.

High Schools and
Other Educational Resource

Catholic High Schools

Following his nomination as bishop, Bishop Hickey began asking himself why God had chosen him for the office of bishop. As he studied his new diocese looking for some work to do, he could find only one great need that was left unmet to some degree. He observed that there were not enough Catholic schools or large enough schools for all the children and young people of the diocese who sought a Catholic education.[94]

During the first decades of the twentieth century, the increasing complexity and sophistication of American commerce and industry created a need for better educated employees. As a result, demand for high school education increased as did the overall number of Catholic young men and women who sought a high school education due to the diocese's expanding Catholic population. Because the cathedral parish was not able to fund an expansion of LaSalle Academy in Providence, it had become a diocesan high school during Bishop Harkins' years. As a diocesan high school, it was open to all the young men in the diocese, who had the ability and who wished to attend. While some of the parishes in the diocese operated high schools as well as grammar schools, Bishop Hickey believed that up-to-date Catholic high schools, with all the necessary resources to meet the needs of contemporary America, could only be built and maintained by the diocese. By the end of 1922, he had reached the conclusion that the expansion of the number and size of the Catholic high schools in the diocese would be his special work.[95]

When on February 1920, Bishop Hickey addressed the annual dinner of the LaSalle Alumni Association, he spoke at length of his hopes for LaSalle and for a new building to house its students whose numbers had for some time outgrown the existing facilities in downtown Providence. The alumni association counted among its members many of the leading Catholic businessmen and politicians in the state. Following the bishop's speech, some members of the association approached the bishop with the news that they could obtain part of the old Hazard Estate on the corner of Academy Avenue and Smith Street as a site for a new academy. The land lay in the northwestern section of the city, where the last remaining large tracts of open land were to be found. They also informed the bishop that they would be willing to help pay for the property. Rather than purchase

---

[94] *Providence Visitor*, February 7, 1924.
[95] Ibid.

only part of the estate, Bishop Hickey urged the men to purchase it all. Bishop Hickey announced the pending purchase at LaSalle's graduation on June 21, 1921.[96]

James W. Donahue brought his first sketches of a new LaSalle to Bishop Hickey on February 4, 1922. On February 12, the date of the next LaSalle Alumni's dinner, which celebrated the fiftieth anniversary of the academy, Bishop Hickey spoke again of the present crowded conditions of LaSalle's buildings and of the need to build a new school that would inherit the spirit and traditions of the old. The talk of the dinner was of a campaign to raise $90,000 to cover what remained of the purchase price of the land obtained for the new school. The president of the LaSalle Alumni Association called a meeting in Cathedral Hall several weeks later to discuss what the alumni might do in order to realize their hope for a new, modern school to replace the old. William J. Keenan, who had headed the Providence College fund-raising drive and with whom Bishop Hickey had discussed the LaSalle drive prior to his address to the alumni on February 17, introduced a resolution that the LaSalle Alumni Association propose to the bishop that he hold a drive to rise $200,000 in order to build a new academy building on the Smith Street site.[97]

Bishop Hickey did not act on the LaSalle Alumni's petition immediately. He recognized that many Catholic high school age boys and girls did not chose to attend LaSalle or St. Xavier's, then the two largest Catholic high schools for English-speaking students, because of the distance between their homes and their schools. A practical solution to the problem of overcrowding at both LaSalle and St. Xavier's would not only mean the building of new facilities for both schools but the establishment of new high schools closer to the homes of students who wished a Catholic high school education.

The Million Dollar Drive

A month before the LaSalle Alumni Dinner and the subsequent petition of the association that he conduct a drive to raise funds for the school, Bishop Hickey met on January 10, 1922 with the priests who made up the Diocesan Board of Consultors. At the meeting, Bishop Hickey presented his vision of an increased number of centralized diocesan high schools and asked his priests' views on a diocesan-wide drive to raise the funds necessary to bring the vision to reality.[98]

Bishop Hickey considered the various possibilities for the next several months. During that time he made his first visit *ad limina* visit to Rome in

[96]   Ibid, June 24, 1921.
[97]   Bishop Hickey's Diary, February 4, 9, 1922; *Providence Visitor*, February 17; March 24, 31, 1922.
[98]   Bishop Hickey's Diary, January 10, 1922.

order to deliver a report on the spiritual and material well-being of his diocese. On July 11, 1922, the first day back in his office, the bishop had only one visitor, William J. Keenan, who had been a part of the official diocesan party, which had greeted him when he landed in Boston the day before. The bishop did not note in his diary what the two talked about, but since Mr. Keenan would become the lay chairman of the high school fund-raising drive that Bishop Hickey would announce the following January, it is reasonable to assume that the two talked about the drive.[99]

As was the case with Bishop Hickey's meeting with Mr. Keenan, the bishop did not mention in his diary the subject of his talk to his pastors at the second of their semi-annual meetings on November 6, 1922. However, an article that appeared in the *Providence News* on January 29, 1923 reported that the bishop had taken the opportunity presented by the meeting to discuss his idea of raising a million dollars for diocesan works. According to the article in the *Providence News*, "some of the priests at first doubted that a drive for such a large amount would be successful at this time, but when they heard his programme all expressed willingness to co-operate heartily and carry it out." Bishop Hickey was upset by the *News'* premature notice of his plans and the misinformation in the article and promptly called a representative of the *News* to his office the following day. In a subsequent article in the *News* on January 30, the paper made clear, that contrary to its previous article, the bishop's plan to raise a million dollars for the diocese was not yet fully settled either in regard to the specific purposes of the drive or in respect to the methods by which the money would be collected. Citing "high diocesan authority" as the source of its information, the article corrected the *News'* previous information that the money would be raised by an assessment on each of the diocese's ninety-six parishes and that part of the funds to be raised would go toward improvements at St. Joseph's Hospital. The article urged that the people of the diocese ignore any "previously published speculation, although coming from sources which should have been trustworthy, and wait for the official pronouncement relating to details."[100]

After the incident of the *News* article, Bishop Hickey chose not to wait any longer to announce his plans. He used an already scheduled address to the Queen's Daughters on January 30, 1923, a meeting called to mark the fiftieth anniversary of their founding, to discuss the details of the drive he was planning. Noting what he perceived to be the danger facing Catholic education as the result of the efforts of those who wished to make attendance at Catholic grammar schools illegal, the bishop told his audience that he no longer felt Catholic high schools were a luxury. Instead, he saw them as a necessity that warranted "the greatest measure of sacrifice to insure their establishment." In order to provide the young men and women of the diocese an opportunity to prepare for professional careers in a Catholic environment, he urged a million-dollar drive to expand the existing parish high schools so that they might accept students from other parishes and to build new diocesan schools in Newport and Pawtucket. The women at the meeting greeted the bishop's announcement with applause as did the LaSalle Alumni at their annual meeting when Bishop Hickey addressed them on the needs for more and larger high schools on February 11.[101]

Mr. Keenan met with Bishop Hickey on April 2, 1923 to begin making specific plans for the Drive. In a letter the bishop composed that day to the pastors of the diocese, he announced that the first step in conducting the Drive would be for Mr. Keenan and himself to meet with the pastors and two lay representatives from all the parishes in Cathedral Hall on Broad St., on Monday, April 9. In his letter the bishop stressed that the people of the diocese, conscious as they were of the dangers threatening the faith and morals of their children, wished to have the clergy lead the way to the establishment of a complete system of Catholic schools. Not knowing what would be the result of the current attacks on the elementary parochial school system, he stressed the need to have high schools to fall back on should grammar school children be compelled to attend the public schools. In this way, the American Church would not be deprived of what the Church currently relied upon in Christian education. In conducting the Drive, Bishop Hickey recognized the need for publicity. His letter of April 2 was printed as were subsequent letters in the *Visitor*. Most were also read from the pulpit at Sunday mass.[102]

Although other archdioceses and dioceses had in recent years conducted multimillion fund-raising drives and the Diocese of Providence had recently completed a successful funding-raising drive in aid of Providence College, Bishop Hickey was understandably anxious about the success of the new Drive. In his address on April 9 to the pastors and lay representatives, the bishop stressed his hope that every qualified young person in the diocese who sought admission to a Catholic high school would be accommodated. Aware that parish loyalty, particularly among the Franco Americans, had previously been more important than loyalty to the larger entity that was the diocese, Bishop Hickey urged his audience to think in terms of the diocese. At the end of the bishop's address, Frank E. Fitzsimmons introduced a resolution endorsing the bishop's proposal for the Drive. Several parish representatives spoke in favor of the resolution. Among those who rose to question the bishop was a trustee of one of Franco-American parishes. He asked if the bishop was recommending a voluntary drive or the levying of a tax on the parishes. The bishop ignored his question and asked him to sit down. At the end of the discussion, the question was moved and the pas-

---

[101] *Providence Journal*, January 31, 1923; *Providence Visitor*, February 2, 16, 1923.
[102] Hickey to Pastors, April 2, 1923, PChA; *Providence Visitor*, April 6, 1923; *Providence Journal*, April 5, 1923.

tors and laymen unanimously adopted it. Although he usually did not express his personal feelings or impressions in his diary, on the day of the meeting with the parish representatives, Hickey wrote, "Great impetus. Thanks be to God!"[103]

Bishop Hickey had reason to be concerned about the outcome of the meeting. After the *Providence News* had broken the story and he had announced his intention of holding a drive to his pastors, he had received a letter from a Woonsocket lawyer, Elphege J. Daignault. Daignault asserted that many in the diocese were deeply disturbed by the prospect of a drive in view of the already heavy debts on many parishes and also in view of the hard times and financial crisis then affecting many. He informed the bishop

Elphege J. Daignault

that he had already appealed to the Holy See against what he saw as the prospect of the bishop laying too heavy a burden on the Catholic families of the diocese.[104]

The letter to the Holy See Daignault referred to was written on November 23, 1922 and bore the names of seventeen prominent Franco Americans, Daignault's among them. The letter noted that the churches and schools of the diocese were established and supported by voluntary contributions only and that, for the most part, the parishes were heavily in debt. The letter also noted that, of the ninety-six parishes in the diocese, only forty-six had their own Catholic schools. The conclusion of the letter was that the million-dollar goal of Hickey's proposed Drive was "an exorbitant tax" that could not be met without putting the Church, schools and institutions of charity in the diocese in financial jeopardy. The letter asked for protection against the fiscal measure, which Bishop Hickey was planning to impose.[105]

In contrast to the stand of the Franco Americans Daignault represented, a larger part of the Franco-American community stood ready to support the drive. On April 12, 1923, the editor of *La Tribune*, a French-language daily published in Woonsocket, called on the bishop to place *La Tribune* at

---

[103] *Woonsocket Call*, April 10, 1923; *Providence Visitor*, April 13, 1923; Elphege Daignault, *Le vrai movement sentinellist en Nouvelle-Angleterre, 1923–1929 et* l'Affaire *du Rhode Island* (Montreal: Editions du Zodiaque, 1936), p. 131; Bishop Hickey's Diary, April 9, 1923.

[104] Daignault to Hickey, January 30, 1923, PChA.

[105] Elphege Daignault, et al., to His Holiness Pius XI, November 24, 1923, PChA.

his disposal for the Drive. Mr. Murel's visit was significant because Philippe Boucher, one of the owners of *La Tribune*, was also one of the signers of the letter Daignault sent to Rome. In addition to *La Tribune*, the Drive would also have the support of John B. S. Brazeau's *Le Jean Baptiste*, a French weekly published in Pawtucket.[106]

Bishop Hickey, who served as Chairman of the Drive's Grand Committee and Treasurer, did much of the work of organization and preparation necessary for the Drive's success. Beginning on April 11, he spent numerous hours at the headquarters of the Drive in the new Visitor Building across the street from the cathedral on Fenner Street. Along with Mr. Kennan, the Drive's Director, Bishop Hickey, on April 17, met with Frank E. Fitzsimmons and a group of selected priests and lay volunteers called the Crusaders or the Flying Squadron. According to the bishop's plan, the Crusaders would work in their assigned parishes to create enthusiasm for the Drive much as the bishop himself had done as a four-minute-man in the public fund-raising drives during the recent war. At the meeting, Bishop Hickey spoke of the encouragement and cooperation he had already received following the announcement of the Drive. The encouragement gave him the utmost confidence that the Drive would be successful. He also suggested various points the Crusaders might make in their own talks to parish groups so as to make clear the importance and necessity of Catholic high schools equipped to meet the needs of the day.[107]

As part of his preparation work, Bishop Hickey wrote out and sent to the pastors a pamphlet entitled "Rule for Guidance of Parish Organization," which were similar to those that had guided the Providence College Drive. These "Rules" for parish organization spelled out the steps the pastors were to take during the week of April 22 in order to create a parish organization to support the Drive. In his cover letter, Bishop Hickey urged his priests to stand by their bishop in the Drive and repeated what he had stressed in his address to the parish representatives in Cathedral Hall, that "In this enterprise, we must think and speak in terms of the Diocese." The bishop instructed the pastors that they must choose parish officers who would carry out every detail outlined in the "rules" he was giving them. The pastors themselves or their assistants were to make personal calls upon a number of the members of their parishes to ask their cooperation and assistance in the Drive. They were to meet with those whom they had selected and those who had volunteered in order to organize a door-to-door canvass of the parishes. Team Captains were to be appointed for each district within the parish, who would distribute Pledge Cards to their team members. The team members in turn would make the actual visits and record the pledge or the reason why it was refused. Each pastor was to appoint some mem-

---

[106]   Bishop Hickey's Diary, April 12, 1923.
[107]   *Providence Journal*, April 18, 1923; *Providence Visitor*, April 20, 1923; Bishop Hickey's Diary, April 11, 12, 16, 17, 19, 21, 1923.

ber of his parish to take care of publicity. Before the start of the Drive, the pastors or their assistants were to call upon "people of means in his parish and endeavor to secure a generous contribution from each of them." It was these parish organizational meetings that the Crusaders selected by Bishop Hickey were to address.[108]

Bishop Hickey scheduled the Million Dollar Drive to begin on May 14 and conclude ten days later on May 24. In a letter printed in the *Visitor* and read at all masses on Sunday, April 29, Bishop Hickey asked all Catholics in the diocese to wear a special campaign button, which the priests were to have passed out at each mass, as a profession of faith and, in particular, as a proof of loyalty to the principles of Catholic education. Each parish was also supplied with posters to be prominently displayed in order to call attention to the start of the Drive.[109]

Bishop Hickey took time out from his work of preparing for the Drive to attend the ordination of another Holy Cross College alumnus, Bishop Andrew Brennan, who on April 25, 1923, was ordained an Auxiliary Bishop of the Diocese of Scranton, Pennsylvania. Rather than returning directly home, Hickey went down to Washington, D.C., to make a call on the new apostolic delegate, Archbishop Pietro Fumasoni-Biondi. The delegate had apparently asked Bishop Hickey to come to see him. When Hickey arrived, the delegate handed him a letter that the delegate had received from the Sacred Congregation of the Council concerning complaints made to the congregation by Mr. Daignault concerning what he saw as the bishop's excessive demands for money. The Congregation asked the newly appointed delegate to obtain accurate information on the matter and send the information, along with his opinion, to Rome. The delegate apparently was satisfied with Bishop Hickey's response and seemingly raised no objections to the Drive. It was perhaps in light of the bishop's visit to the delegate, however, that, in addition to reading the Drive letter the following Sunday as did the other pastors of the diocese, the pastors of the French-Canadian parishes in Woonsocket stressed to their congregations that every cent contributed by the churches in Woonsocket would go toward the support of Mt. St. Charles High School, which was then under construction in Woonsocket. While the bishop's pledge that the monies raised in the drive in Woonsocket would go towards Mt. St. Charles spurred some to give, others refused to give to the drive because they believed that the school would become a diocesan school subject to a bishop who they thought wished to

---

[108] "Million Dollar Drive for Christian Education, Rules for Guidance of Parish Organization," PChA; *Providence Visitor*, April 20, 27, 1923.
[109] *Providence Visitor*, April 27, 1923.

push the assimilation of the French
Canadians into the wider American
society.[110]

In the spring of 1919, Msgr.
Charles Dauray, pastor of Woonsocket's Precious Blood Parish, had
been informed by the Woonsocket
health officials that the Academy of
the Sacred Heart, which was one of
his parish schools, was unsafe and
had to be closed. Monsignor Dauray had conducted a parish drive to
raise funds to replace the building
that was so successful that he began
to consider the possibility of building a school large enough to accommodate, not only the students of
Precious Blood Parish, but also any
day or boarding student who wished
to enroll there regardless of his parish. With the help of the Federation
of Catholic Franco-American Societies and of Fr. Georges Bedard,

Msgr. Charles Dauray

Msgr. Dauray's nephew and his assistant at Precious Blood, Dauray had
launched a drive in January 1921 with an announced goal of $500,000.
A combination of hard economic times in the textile industry and opposition within the Franco-American community in Woonsocket and elsewhere
caused the drive to fail. Some of the Franco-American priests feared that
the campaign would drain funds needed by their parishes and that Bishop
Hickey would seize control of the school. The drive raised only $45,500 in
contributions and pledges, most of that from Precious Blood Parish itself.
After the failure of the drive, Msgr. Dauray asked Bishop Hickey's advice
as to whether he should give up his dream of a larger school. The bishop
discussed the alternatives with him and Fr. Bedard. When Fr. Bedard mentioned that there was a gentleman in the parish who would guarantee the
payment of the interest on a $100,000 loan for the school, Bishop Hickey
encouraged Msgr. Dauray to go ahead with the project and have plans for
the new school drawn up. In November 1921, Bishop Hickey met first with
the Provincial of the Brothers of the Sacred Heart, who would staff the new
school as they had the old, and with Brother Josephus, the present principal
of the Academy of the Sacred Heart. Then, a few days later, he met with

---

[110] Cardinal Gaetano De Lai to Archbishop Pietro Fumasoni-Biondi, January 25, 1923, PChA;
Bishop Hickey's Diary, April 26, 1923; Woonsocket Call, April 30, 1923; Armand Chartier, *Histoire Des Franco-Américains De La Nouvelle-Angleterre, 1775–1990* (Sillery, Quebec: Les editions Septentrion, 1991) p. 143.

Msgr. Dauray and the members of the corporation of the proposed new Academy of Mt. St. Charles of the Sacred Heart. After his meeting with Msgr. Dauray, Bishop Hickey gave his permission for work. However, it would not be until November 1922, that he actually authorized the work of site preparation for the building to begin.[111]

Since Bishop Hickey had asked that details of each parish's organizational meeting be written up and sent to the local newspapers in order to publicize the diocesan Drive and had made provisions in his instructions to his pastors for reports on the Drive's progress, it was relatively easy for him to see which of his priests were following his instructions. On May 3, 1923, he wrote again to all the pastors emphasizing certain of the Drive's "Rules and Regulations."[112]

On May 7, 1923, Bishop Hickey sent individual letters to his pastors informing them of the amount or quota, which the diocesan Drive Committee felt justified in expecting from a particular parish. In determining an individual parish's quota, the Drive Committee took account of the quota assigned to the parish in the Providence College Drive and the amount actually collected by the parish. In his letter, the bishop urged on his priests the necessity of obtaining fully one-half of their quota in the first phase of the three-year Drive. He envisioned that the remainder would be pledged and collected in the two subsequent years of the Drive.[113]

The Drive itself began on Sunday, May 10, following the reading of Bishop Hickey's letter at all masses. In his letter, the bishop recalled several dioceses, which had recently conducted successful multi-million dollar campaigns. He acknowledged that he was asking the people of the diocese to make an extraordinary sacrifice. At the same time, he expressed his confidence that the people would be willing to make a sacrifice for Christian education. As was done the previous Sunday and would be done on the following, members of the parish committees passed out literature on the Drive to their fellow parishioners while they were seated. On Sunday, May 20, the bishop asked his pastors to read a letter on the Drive in which Hickey offered his thanks to those who had already contributed to the Drive and urged the Drive workers to continue their efforts in behalf of the Drive.[114]

In laying his plans, Bishop Hickey had instructed his pastors in the "Rules for Guidance" that they were to report their parish's progress toward their goals on May 16, 18, 21, and 25. Because the progress reports of the parishes were also given to the local press, each parish knew how the other parishes were progressing. The idea was to stimulate competi-

---

[111] Bishop Hickey's Diary, 10, 14, 1921; November 24, 1922; *Providence Visitor*, December 23, 1921; Ambrose Kennedy, *Quebec to New England: The Life of Monsignor Charles Dauray* (Boston: Bruce Humphries, Inc., 1948), p. 178; Yves Ruby, *Les Franco-Americains de la Nouvelle-Angleterra, 1776–1930* (Sillery, Quebec: Septertrion, 1990), p. 307.

[112] Hickey to Pastors, May 3, 1923, PChA; *Providence Visitor*, May 4, 1923.

[113] Hickey to Pastors, May 7, 1923; "Proposed Quotas To Be Used In Connection With One Million Dollar Drive," PChA.

[114] Hickey to Pastors, May 10, 17, 1923; *Providence Journal*, May 14, 1923; *Woonsocket Call*, May 14, 1923.

tion both between the various teams within the parishes, between the parishes and between pastors. Not only were the totals of the various parishes
printed in the local newspapers and in the *Visitor*, but so were the names of
the largest donors and their contributions. The manner in which the Drive
was organized and conducted did in fact stir up enthusiasm and rivalry.
When it was announced to the Drive workers of Blessed Sacrament Parish,
Providence, that the parish had exceeded its goal, the workers celebrated
by lighting a bonfire in the rear of the church following their meeting.[115]

Because he had information at hand on the progress of the Drive in each
of the parishes, Bishop Hickey was able to readily see which of his pastors
were giving the leadership in the Drive he expected of them and which
were not. He noticed immediately that the Drive in some of the Franco-
American parishes was not going well. During Bishop Harkins' years, when
the newly-established French-Canadian parishes were beginning their efforts to provide their parishioners with churches, schools and rectories, he
did not ask them to contribute substantially to the general works of the
diocese. The first time that Bishop Harkins had asked all the parishes of
the diocese, the Franco Americans included, to contribute to a diocesan
work was when he sought to raise funds to establish and open Providence
College in 1917. Bishop Hickey also expected that all the parishes of the
diocese would do their part when he launched the $250,000 campaign to
reduce the debt on the college in 1920 and again when he initiated the
more ambitious high school fund raising campaign. While some of the
Franco-American parishes had done well in the two campaigns held for the
benefit of the college, the response on the part of others had been poor.[116]

One of the parishes where the response to the High School Drive lagged
was Notre Dame Parish in Central Falls, whose pastor was Fr. Joseph H.
Beland. Fr. Beland, a native of Canada, was an ultra-nationalist on the
question of French-Canadian *survivance* and frequently voiced his convictions from the pulpit. He was also a rival of Msgr. Dauray in Woonsocket for leadership among the French-Canadian priests in the diocese. According to information in Bishop Hickey's possession, when in November
1920, the Federation of Catholic Societies had launched a fund-raising
campaign to help fund the building of the new Franco-American high
school in Precious Blood parish that would serve all of New England, Fr.
Beland's nationalism and sense of rivalry combined to prompt him and
one of his former associates at Notre Dame, Fr. Antonio Prince, to visit

---

[115] *Providence Journal*, May 15–27, 1923; *Providence Visitor*, May 25; June 1, 1923.

[116] This overview is drawn from a document concerning Fr. Joseph Beland that Bishop Hickey sent
to the Sacred Congregation of the Council on December 28, 1927, PChA.

During his years as bishop, Bishop Harkins levied assessments to support a number of diocesan
endeavors: the St. Aloysius Orphan Asylum, Cf. Circular letter, April 10, 1888; the Infirm Priests'
Fund, Cf. Circular letter, June 21, 1888; the Catholic press, Cf. Circular letter, December 1, 1908;
and the Ecclesiastical Student Fund and for the support of Missionary Work, Cf. Circular letter,
May 20, 1909, PChA. Some of these assessments might also have been laid on the French-speaking parishes as well as the English-speaking parishes.

various Franco-American pastors in New England to speak against the project. As was his custom, Fr. Beland turned over the responsibility for organizing and directing the Diocesan High Drive to one of his current assistants. Without his personal support for the Drive, collections in Notre Dame for the Drive were meager. At St. Louis, Woonsocket, where Fr. Prince was pastor, contributions to the Drive were also noticeably less than in other French-speaking parishes.[117]

While Bishop Hickey had initially announced that he did not intend to assess the parishes of the diocese to support diocesan high schools, the resistance to the drive created by Fr. Beland and others caused him to change his mind. When towards

Fr. Joseph H. Beland

the end of the Drive it became obvious that some of his priests were not supporting the Drive as he wished them to, Hickey, on May 23, 1923, sent his priests a letter reminding them of the decrees of the Third Plenary Council of Baltimore mandating Catholic Schools and of the Council's stress on high schools. He pointed out that since the individual parishes of the diocese had not been able to fulfill the Council's directives on their own, he felt it was his duty as bishop to take over the work of providing the Catholic high schools dictated by the Council. The current Drive, he said, was the first step towards fulfilling his responsibility. He went on to say:

> In order, therefore, to relieve the minds of all the faithful, hard-working Pastors and Assistants, your Bishop, having taken the advice of the Diocesan Consultors, herewith instructs you to this effect, namely, that whatever remains unpaid of the quota assigned to your Parish, over and above the amount gathered from voluntary contributions, is to be paid to the Chancery Office in three installments during this year, and the next two years following. In fact, this assessment is laid upon your parish, and is to be paid from the Parish funds now on hand or from revenues of the Parish obtained in the usual manner and by whatever entertainments or moderate collections you may be able to inaugurate.

At the end of each letter Bishop Hickey added a postscript in which he gave the amount assessed on each parish to which he sent the letter.[118]

---

[117]   Ibid.; *Le Jean Baptiste*, April 27, 1923; *Providence Visitor*, "Standing of Parishes at Close of the Drive," May 23, 1923; Sorrell, *The Sentinelle Affair*, p. 276.

[118]   Hickey to Pastors, May 23, 1923, PChA. Daignault later printed a French copy of this letter in *La Sentinelle*, October 16, 1924.

While Bishop Hickey personally believed that the need for high schools in the United States was such that an assessment on the parishes to support them was justified, there was no specific precedent for such an assessment to support high schools in the history of the Church. Hickey properly perceived that conducting a voluntary drive offered a greater chance of success. He only acted on his conviction that he could assess the parishes for support of high schools when he became convinced that a few pastors were not supporting the Drive. Since the vast majority of the parishes raised the monies contributed to the Drive through explicit contributions for high schools, the assessment only concerned the few that did not.

One of the pastors to whom Bishop Hickey sent a letter informing him of the fact that the quota given his parish had become an assessment showed the letter he received to Elphege Daignault. Through the good offices of Canon Joseph M. Gignac, a priest of the Archdiocese of Quebec and a noted canonist, Mr. Daignault had earlier asked Quebec's Cardinal Louis-Nazaire Begin for a letter of introduction to the delegate. After seeing Bishop Hickey's letter, Mr. Daignault went to Washington to call on the delegate. In his letter, Cardinal Begin praised Daignault "as an honorable man, a good father of family and as an excellent Christian." Mr. Daignault gave the delegate a letter, signed by Daignault himself and two others representing parishes in Pawtucket and Central Falls, which he had written two days before Bishop Hickey had sent his letter. In the letter, they noted that Bishop Hickey claimed the new code of Canon Law gave him authority to assess parishes on behalf of the Million Dollar Drive. However, in the view of the three men who signed the letter, the assessments he had levied were unjust and excessive and were not legitimized by the new code, which he invoked as the source of his authority. Daignault asked the delegate to instruct Bishop Hickey to publicly state that the contributions to the Drive were to be voluntary, to refrain from threatening or pressuring the faithful to respond to the appeal, and to extend his protection to the petitioners. According to Mr. Daignault's account of the meeting, the delegate received him courteously and told him to be calm about the subject. When Daignault showed the delegate Bishop Hickey's letter in regard to what was now a parish assessment, the delegate assured him that his bishop did not have the right to impose a tax on the parishes. When, according to Mr. Daignault's retelling of the meeting, he responded, "If it is not right, as you say, but he does it anyway. What are we to do? We are here to receive direction." In Daignault's version, the delegate responded, "You are a lawyer, and you know what to do." Daignault would later assert that he understood the delegate to mean that he should seek to force Bishop Hickey to refrain from taxing the parishes by having recourse to the civil courts.[119]

At the heart of the opposition to the High School Drive among some of the Franco Americans was the continued belief that parish monies were needed to support the parish schools. Alongside this conviction was the reluctance on their part to contribute monies that would pay for the education of children of other nationalities. The inherent problem behind an attitude that restricted one's help only to the members of one's national group was that it conflicted with the teaching of the Gospels and with the understanding of Church found in Canon Law. In asking the people of the diocese to think in the terms of the diocese rather than simply of the parish, Bishop Hickey was echoing traditional Church teaching. In order to adequately provide for the religious needs of the French-speaking members of his diocese, Bishop Harkins had not asked them or any other of the new immigrants groups to support diocesan works. But in Bishop Harkins' and now in Bishop Hickey's judgment, the Franco Americans were in a position to join in supporting the diocesan educational and charitable works along with the other new immigrant groups.

The Million Dollar Drive reached its conclusion on May 24. In its May 25 issue, the *Providence Visitor* announced that the Drive had exceeded its goals by $86,000. Before all the contributions were tallied, the total of pledges and contributions would reach a million and a quarter, of which nearly $575,000 was in cash. Bishop Hickey would be particularly happy to report that, in this first phase of the Drive roughly 70,000 people, both Catholics and non-Catholics, had contributed or pledged to the Drive. The people of the Cathedral Parish in Providence contributed the largest amount of any parish, while the people of Precious Blood Parish, Woonsocket, exceeded their goal by a greater amount than any other parish. In a final letter of thanks he addressed to the all those who contributed, Bishop Hickey instructed all his pastors to offer a Mass of Thanksgiving on Sunday, June 10.[120]

On June 28, 1923, Archbishop Fumansoni-Biondi wrote to Bishop Hickey asking for Hickey's reply to the letter of complaint that Mr. Daignault had sent to Rome in his own name and that of other prominent Franco Americans. There is no copy of Bishop Hickey's reply to the delegate's

---

[119] Bishop Hickey's Diary, April 26, 1923; Mr. Daignault himself gave an early account of his visit to the delegate at a meeting of the Croises. It was recorded by a then member of the Croises, Adelard Soucy, Cf. "Minutes of Croises Meeting," Wednesday, June 5, 1923, PChA.
Mr. Daignault also provided other accounts of the meeting in articles in *La Sentinelle*, January 7, 1926 and November 27, 1927. On his part, Bishop Hickey did not believe that the delegate ever said what Daignault said he did. Cf. Hickey to Gentile, February 25, 1928, PChA. A copy of the letter Daignault gave to Most Rev. Pietro Fumasoni-Biondi on this occasion is found in his "Memoire des Franco-Americains a Sa Saintete Pie XI," 1925, PChA. It is likely that Archbishop Fumasoni-Biondi urged him to appeal to Rome rather than to the civil courts because he would have been well aware of the canonical provision that a laymen needed the Holy See's permission to sue a bishop in the civil courts.
[120] *Providence Visitor*, May 24; June 1, 1923.

letter in the Providence Archives. There is, however, a list of the parishes of the diocese on which someone has noted those which were free from debt and those which were not. These notes suggest that Bishop Hickey did reply to the letter of the Franco Americans by challenging the letter's main contention that his goal of raising a million dollar was an "exorbitant assessment" which would endanger the financial stability of the diocese's parishes. In any case, he could point to the success of the Drive.[121]

Bishop Hickey set May 16–24, 1924 for the second phase of the Million Dollar High School Drive and began making preparations for it in February. On April 27, 1924, he had his pastors read the first of his letters urging the people, who had made pledges, to redeem them when the Drive workers, who again volunteered their time, called on them. He also urged those who had contributed to the Drive in its first year, but had not pledged to do so in the second and third years, to once again make a contribution. The Drive Committee set $300,000 as the diocesan goal for this second phase and, once again, the people of the state and of the diocese made the attainment of the goal possible. The final total of the second phase was almost $350,000. When a few parishes once again failed to meet their goals, Bishop Hickey, on May 26, 1924, once more wrote to the pastors who had not made their goals that they were to make up the deficiency from "parish funds now on hand." So that a pastor might not claim that parish did not have the money, Hickey also provided that the parish could borrow the money "by a note to be approved by the Bishop."[122]

In October 1924, Mr. Daignault carried his protest against Bishop Hickey's Million Dollar Drive to another forum. He was one of the directors of a new daily French language that began publication in Woonsocket as *La Sentinelle* the previous April. The newspaper did not comment on the second phase of the Drive while it was in progress, but in October it began publishing a series of articles, which set forth the core of Daignault's arguments against the Drive. Daignault continued to argue that the diocesan goal for the Drive was excessive because contributions to the bishop's drive would take money away diocese's parishes and their schools and thus endanger their financial stability. Furthermore, he pointed out that maintenance of the new high schools and the retirement of the debts incurred to buy or build them promised to be an additional burden on the parishes. He also held that the manner in which Bishop Hickey was conducting the Drive was an injustice. As in many pledge drives, Daignault foresaw that a good number of those who pledged would be unable or unwilling to pay the money pledged when it came time to collect either because their economic circumstances had changed or because they had changed their minds. Daignault realized that Bishop Hickey would not pursue individuals to force them to

---

[121] Fumasoni-Biondi to Hickey, June 28, 1923; Notes, High School Drive file, 1923.
[122] Hickey to Pastors, February 6, 28; April 21; May 1, 26, 1924, PChA; *Providence Visitor*, May 29, 1924.

pay the money pledged, he would force the parishes to take money from their own funds to make up the difference. Citing Bishop Hickey's letter of May 23, 1923, to the pastors of the parishes, which had failed to meet their goals, as his evidence, he argued that by imposing an assessment on the parishes' funds to make up the difference between the amount collected and the goal, he was diverting the parishes funds from the purposes for which they had been contributed. To his mind, parents had the primary right to decide how their children were educated. The taking of parish monies given to support parish schools was a glaring injustice which obstructed the development of the parish schools and exhausted the generosity of the parishioners. Neither *La Tribune* nor the *Providence Visitor* chose to notice *La Sentinelle's* articles. Neither did the secular press give them notice.[123]

Preparations for the final phase of the Drive began in March 1925. At the beginning of the month, Bishop Hickey wrote his priests asking that at least one sermon on Christian Education be preached during the missions given in each parish during Lent. Once again the bishop asked the pastors to organize teams to conduct a personal canvass of their parishes, this time between May 15 and May 25. During a meeting of pastors and laymen that Bishop Hickey called for April 25 to prepare for the last phase of the Drive, the bishop asked several of the pastors to say a few words. When it came his turn to speak, Fr. Peter Switala, pastor of St. Adalbert's, a Polish parish in Providence, which had just broken ground for a new church, appealed to the needs of his own parish to explain why it would be difficult for his parishioners to do anything for the Drive. According to an account of the incident that appeared in *La Sentinelle*, Bishop Hickey ordered him to be quiet and to sit down. Before he did, the Irish pastors applauded the bishop and cried, "100 percent American."[124]

In addition to the letters which he had asked to be read at all parishes masses and printed in the *Visitor* and to the talks given by the Crusaders to the individual meetings of parish workers, Bishop Hickey took advantage of an offer of free radio time made by Dutee Wilcox Flint, owner of station WDWF, to spur the campaign. On the evening before the final phase of the Drive began, Bishop Hickey made a personal and direct appeal to the people of Rhode Island for support of the Drive. In his address, the bishop, in addition to emphasizing the importance of religion for the well-being of society, stressed what the Crusaders were stressing in their addresses on behalf of the Drive, that the Catholic schools of the state were saving the state substantial monies, which he estimated at $1,800,000 a year. On its part, the *Providence Visitor* printed a special Drive Supplement on May 15.[125]

Bishop Hickey set $500,000 as the goal for the final phase of the Drive. In addressing his pastors and the lay representatives two weeks before the

[123] *La Sentinelle*, October 13, 15, 16, 17, 21, 1924.
[124] *La Sentinelle*, May 21, 1925.
[125] Hickey to Pastors, March 1, 7, 15, 23; April 13, 16, 20, 1925; *Providence Visitor*, May 15, 1925.

final phase began, Hickey expressed his concern over the high cost of construction of new schools and the continued crowded conditions of many
of the old ones. He also expressed his hope that he might also open new
schools for girls, a theme which he made a prominent part of the third
phase. Once again the Drive was successful. In all the Million Dollar High
School Drive produced $1,290,000 in contributions from some 100,000
Catholics and non-Catholics.[126]

After using the pages of *La Sentinelle* to present the arguments of those
who opposed the high school Drive, Daignault and his associates resolved
to again appeal to the Holy See, specifically against the forced assessment
or tax. Daignault asked Canon Gignac to prepare a "Memorial" in order to
present their protest to the Holy See which he, Doctor Arthur J. B. Falcon
of Pawtucket and Leopold L. Maynard of Central Falls signed. The men
engaged, Christoforo Astorri, a layman and a Roman lawyer who prac-
ticed before the Church Courts, to present their case. On April 7, 1925,
Mr. Astorri informed the three men that he had presented their Memorial
to the Signature Apostolic to ask permission to plead the case before the
Roman Rota. The Signature Apostolic decided that, since no judicial decision was involved, the question of the justice of Bishop Hickey's "taxation"
of the parishes fell under the competence of the Sacred Congregation of
the Council. Accordingly, Mr. Astorri informed his clients that he would
submit the Memorial to the Congregation when the Congregation resumed
its work after the Easter vacations. He reported to them that those with
whom he had discussed the case agreed that the bishop had overstepped
his authority in demanding payment of the quotas from parish funds and
urged that the pastors concerned flatly refuse to pay the assessment demanded of them. True to his word, Mr. Astorri submitted the Memorial to
the Sacred Congregation on April 28, 1925. On May 12, 1925, Daignault,
Falcon and Maynard, in a joint letter, informed Bishop Hickey that they
had placed his letters of May 23, 1923 and May 26, 1924 before the Holy
See and that they had been informed by their attorney that the parishes
should not pay the monies Hickey had demanded. It would not be until the
middle of July 1925, that Bishop Hickey received a copy of Mr. Astorri's
short brief from his own advocate in Rome, Msgr. Alfonso Gentile, and it
would be sometime in August before he received a copy of the actual Memorial with the Congregation's request for his response.[127]

In the end, all but three of the parishes in the diocese met or exceeded
the greater part of their goals. Most did by way of the monies collected
during the Drive itself. Some pastors, in response to Bishop Hickey's letter
authorizing them to use parish funds to make up the difference between
their goals and the monies actually collected, did pay the difference with-

126 Ibid., May 1, 1925; Hickey to Cardinal Donato Sbarretti, November 14, 1925, PChA.
127 "Memorie des Franco-Americains a Sa Saintete Pie XI," Daignault, et al., to Hickey, May 12,
1925, Gentile to Hickey, July 4, 1925,PChA; Astorri to Daignault, April 7, 1925, printed in
Daignault, *Le vrai movment sentinelliste*, 109–10; Rumilly, *Historice Des Franco-Americains*, p. 371.

out consulting their trustees, while others held corporation meetings and secured the votes to authorize their use of parish funds for that purpose. There were a few parishes that failed to meet their goals whose circumstances were such that Hickey was satisfied with what they did do. Of the two major parishes which did not meet their goals, Fr. Beland, pastor of Notre Dame, Central Falls, neither paid the whole assessment nor did he hold a corporation meeting to consider paying it. Fr. Prince, pastor of St. Louis, Woonsocket, Fr. Beland's friend and a former assistant, did hold a corporation meeting at which the trustees of the parish authorized the payment of parish funds, but no payment was ever made.[128]

In December, while awaiting the decision of the Sacred Congregation of the Council on the question of whether Bishop Hickey had exceeded his authority in the manner in which he conducted the high school drive, Bishop Hickey sent a letter to those pastors whose parishes had not met the goals assigned them to meet with him to reconsider their quota and "thus to complete the final settlement of their terms within the two weeks following Christmas Day." Neither Fr. Beland nor Fr. Prince took the bishop up on his offer to settle the question of what he considered to be the responsibility of their parishes. The pastor of the third parish did.[129]

The New High Schools

With substantial monies in hand after the first phase of the Million Dollar Drive, Bishop Hickey was able to begin implementing the plans he had discussed both for the construction of Mt. St. Charles High School in Woonsocket, whose construction was already underway, and the drawing of definite plans for a new building for LaSalle Academy in Providence. At the same time, he also undertook to establish new high schools for boys in Pawtucket and Newport.

Prior to 1923, if young men in the Pawtucket area, especially those of Franco-American background, wanted to take a "commercial course" at the high school level, they could have enrolled at the Sacred Heart Commercial High School, which Fr. Beland had established in Notre Dame parish, Central Falls, in 1910. With the prospect of Mt. St. Charles Academy, Woonsocket, opening in September 1924, the Provincial Council of the Sacred Heart Brothers, who supplied the teachers for Sacred Heart and who would also staff Mt. St. Charles, elected to close the boarding school the brothers had run in Fr. Beland's parish as the new Academy in Woonsocket offered better as well as safer living conditions. The brothers foresaw that by moving the boarding students to Woonsocket, there would be more room for day students made available in Central Falls. On his

---

[128] Memo, PChA; St. Aloysius Corporation Book.

[129] Hickey to Pastors, December 15, 1925; Hickey to Cardinal Donato Sbarretti, November 14, 1925, PChA.

part, the brother provincial insisted that the Sacred Heart Brothers would continue to staff the Sacred Heart Commercial High School, where young men of Notre Dame parish, whose parents could not afford for their sons to board in Woonsocket and take classes there, might still be able to send them to a Catholic school. With the consolidating of the two boarding schools staffed by the Sacred Heart Brothers in Woonsocket, the brothers ceased offering a classical or a scientific course at Sacred Heart as few of the day students took those courses. When in a letter to the school's director Bishop Hickey stressed that Sacred Heart accept only day students, who could not afford to pay the charges at Mt. St. Charles, the bishop opened himself up to the charge by Mr. Daignault, who echoed the thoughts of Fr. Beland, that the bishop had closed Sacred Heart to all students outside Notre Dame parish.[130]

Rather than wishing to close Sacred Heart, Bishop Hickey wished only to ensure the consolidation of the two boarding schools staffed by the brothers. Because the bishop supported the decision of the brothers' Provincial Council, Daignault concluded that it was because the bishop had made a financial contribution to Mt. St. Charles and wanted to see that school succeed. Rather than have Sacred Heart compete for students with Mt. St. Charles, Daignault charged, the bishop had "closed" Sacred Heart. Once the consolidation was achieved, the bishop readily gave his permission and his encouragement in 1926 to the parents and alumni, who expressed a desire to have the Sacred Heart Brothers in Central Falls offer a classical course as well as the commercial course.[131]

Outside of Sacred Heart College, a young man, who lived in the Pawtucket-Centrals Falls area, especially one who wanted to do his class work solely in English, had to travel to LaSalle in he wanted a Catholic high school education. Fr. Louis Deady, the pastor of Sacred Heart Parish, Pawtucket, first raised the question of establishing a Catholic high school for the English-speaking boys in Pawtucket and Central Falls in December 1915. At the end of November 1923, Bishop Hickey, who, to his surprise, had quickly found a very suitable property in Pawtucket for a high school, was able to announce the purchase of the Darius Goff estate on Wolcott St. The estate, then in the hands of Goff's granddaughter, Annie L. Adams, was situated on a large tract of land just outside the business center of the city. It contained a twenty-six-room mansion, whose upper two floors were fixed up as accommodations for the Christian Brothers, who, along with a diocesan priest-chaplain and such laymen as necessary, would staff the school. The six large rooms on the first floor were converted for use as classrooms.

[130] Brother Edouard to Hickey, August 27; September 2, 1924; June 16, 1924; Hickey to Brother Edouard, August 29; September 9, 1924; *Providence Visitor*, February 2, 1923; *La Sentinelle*, September 29, 1924.
[131] *La Sentinelle*, October 8, 9, 1924; For Bishop Hickey's response to Daignault's charges in *La Sentinelle*, see "Documents au subjet de L'Agitation Sentinelle, 1922–1927, No. 19, "Le College de Central Falls," PChA.

A garage on the property was remodeled and refitted as a laboratory. The new school welcomed its first class of freshmen on September 10, 1923. At a meeting of the pastors of Pawtucket, Central Falls, Valley Falls and Rumford called by Bishop Hickey at the school at the end of 1924 in order to prepare for its incorporation, the group decided to name the new school St. Raphael's Academy. The academy opened in September 1924 and Bishop Hickey privately blessed the school buildings on December 24, 1924.[132]

Two months after announcing the purchase of the Goff estate in Pawtucket, Bishop Hickey announced the purchase of the Weld Estate in Newport as the site of a second school for boys. The property was located on the northeast corner of Bellevue and Parker avenues in the high-class residential section of the city and contained several buildings that could be remodeled for school and residential use. Before the school, the bishop also purchased the adjoining George Peabody Wetmore and Maud G. King estates whose buildings were used for classes until renovations on the main buildings on the Weld property were finished. At a meeting of the pastors in Newport and the Christian Brothers, who were to staff this school as well, those present gave their names as incorporators of the school and suggested De LaSalle as its.[133]

When De LaSalle Academy opened on September 24, 1924, the Brothers welcomed ninety-nine freshmen and twenty-four sophomores. On November 17, only two months after school began, a spark escaping from a chimney caused a small fire. The boys quickly evacuated the building where the fire occurred, and then, when the scope of the fire was determined, returned to the building to remove the furnishings before the fire apparatus arrived. Classes were moved to one of the other buildings on the property until repairs could be made. Bishop Hickey formally dedicated the new school on March 4, 1925 in a ceremony witnessed by the students and faculty. Steady growth in enrollment and the lack of a gymnasium prompted Bishop Hickey to announce at the school's first graduation that he had authorized the construction of an addition to the main classroom building in the summer of 1927. The addition, containing a gym, additional classrooms and a cafeteria, was to be ready the following fall. It was not, however, until February 11, 1928, that the first game was played in the new gym.[134]

As a direct result of the opening of De LaSalle, St. Joseph's High School in Newport, which many of the boys in Newport had previously attended, became an all-girls school. Because of the added room in St. Joseph's, St. Mary's Academy, in St. Mary's Parish, Newport, which had served as a private grammar school and high school, was closed. Since Bishop Hickey also envisioned providing expanded opportunities for a Catholic high school

132 Bishop Harkins' Diary, December 6, 1915; *Providence Visitor*, November 29, 1923; August 28; September 12, 1924; January 2, 1925;
133 *Providence Visitor*, January 3; September 12, 1924.
134 Ibid., October 3; November 21, 1924; June 17, 1927; February 10, 1938.

for girls as well as boys, Fr. Jeremiah W. Baggott, pastor of St. Mary's, Newport, and Dr. Philip E. Clark, purchased at auction, in May 1925, the Hawxhurst Estate situated at the corner of Kay Street and Cranston Avenue in Newport with the intention that the estate would become the site of a new school for girls.[135]

Since the superiors of the Brothers of the Christian Schools received more requests from bishops and pastors than there were brothers available, Bishop Hickey did not readily obtain the brothers necessary for the opening of the two new schools when he addressed such a request to Brother Leo, F.S.C., Provincial of the New York Province of the Brothers of the Christian Schools on October 19, 1923. After consulting with his Superior General in France, Brother Leo informed Bishop Hickey that, owning to a shortage of brothers, it was impossible to provide any brothers for a new house in Pawtucket until 1925. Furthermore, the Brothers could not consider the bishop's suggestion that they transfer the brothers teaching in St. Mary's Grammar School in Providence because closing free schools to open tuition schools was contrary to the spirit of their Institute.[136]

When Brother Leo continued to insist that his Superior General would not give permission for the opening of a new house in Pawtucket before 1925, Bishop Hickey, in his reply to one of Brother Leo's letter, suggested that if the brothers persisted in their refusal, he might have to offer the school to another order. Since the chief obstacle to the new foundation was the Christian Brothers' Superior General, Bishop Hickey, on January 21, 1924 wrote to the General to plead his case directly. In his letter, he asked not for one new community but two since by that time he had also acquired the Weld Estate in Newport. As evidence of his good will and desire to aid the brothers in their good works, the bishop enclosed a check for $500 along with his letter. However, the Christian Brothers had already decided to give the bishop the brothers he wished for both St. Raphael's and De LaSalle on the day before the bishop's letter arrived in Belgium.[137]

In addition to the opening of the new high schools for boys in Pawtucket and Newport, September 1924 also witnessed the opening of the new Mt. St. Charles of the Sacred Heart High School in Woonsocket, which was built to accommodate a thousand students, half of them day students and half boarders. The boarders would come from throughout the New England states, Canada and from the Caribbean and South America. The new school was dedicated on November 11, 1924, a day, which marked the sixth anniversary of the Armistice which ended World War I and the fiftieth anniversary of Precious Blood parish, after whose pas-

---

[135] Ibid., October 3, 1924; March 6; May 22, 1925.
[136] Hickey to Brother Leo, FSC, October 19, 1923; Brother Leo to Hickey, November 25, 1923, PChA.
[137] Hickey to Brother Leo, January 9, 1924; Brother Leo to Hickey, no date; Hickey to Brother Allais Charles, Superior General, January 21, 1924, Brother Allais Charles to Hickey, February 5, 1924, PChA.

tor, Msgr. Charles Dauray, the school was named. The apostolic delegate, Archbishop Fumasoni-Biondi, presided over the celebration, which began with a mass celebrated by Bishop Hickey in Precious Blood Church. Following the mass, a parade, organized by the local American Legion Post and the members of Precious Blood parish, in which the veterans of the recent war and the various French-Canadian societies in the city marched, escorted the delegate, Bishop Hickey, the American and Canadian bishops and clergy, who were also guests on the occasion, to the grounds of the new school where the delegate laid its cornerstone and then dedicated the building. Three years later, in February 1928, the Brothers of the Sacred Heart, who staffed the new school as they had its predecessor, dedicated a new gymnasium which they had built on the west end of the new building and began using in September 1927.[138]

Demand for accommodations for girls in St. Claire's High School, in Precious Blood Parish, Woonsocket, which was staffed by the Religious of the Jesus and Mary, had also increased on the part of both day students and those who wished to board. In response to the demand, the Sisters, in July 1926, began construction of a new five-story addition to St. Claire's High School to accommodate increased numbers of boarders and day students in one wing and a new chapel for the Sisters and the students in another. The new wings were ready for use in the fall of 1927 and Bishop Hickey came up to Woonsocket on November 7, 1927 to bless the chapel and the other new facilities.[139]

The day before Archbishop Fumasoni-Biondi went to Woonsocket for the ceremonies at Mt. St. Charles on November 11, the delegate laid the cornerstone of the new LaSalle High School building in the Elmhurst section of Providence. Bishop Hickey announced the awarding of a contract for the construction of the new school just before the second phase of the Million Dollar Drive began in May 1924. In a simple ceremony attended by Gov. Emery San Souci, Mayor Joseph H. Gainer of Providence, church officials and other dignitaries, Bishop Hickey turned the first sod on May 29, 1924. The framework of the new school was already rising when, on November 9, 1924, following a service in the cathedral, a parade of Million Dollar Drive workers from most of the parishes of the diocese, LaSalle students, Crusaders and others arrived at the site of the new school for the cornerstone laying by the delegate and an address by Auxiliary Bishop John G. Murray of Hartford. That evening, the LaSalle Alumni Association hosted a reception and a dinner for the delegate in the Biltmore Hotel dur-

[138] *Providence Visitor*, August 14; September 12; October 24, 31; November 7, 14, 1924; July 29; October 14, 1927; February 10, 1928; "Dedicace du Mont St. Charles du Sacre Coeur, Woonsocket, Rhode Island, 11 November 1924"; Ambrose J. Kennedy, *Quebec to New England: The Life of Monsignor Charles Dauray*, 180–89.
[139] *Providence Visitor*, July 23, 1926; November 11, 1927.

ing which Archbishop Fumasoni-Biondi praised the efforts of the people of the diocese and their bishop in behalf of Catholic education.[140]

The new school, which cost a million dollars and could accommodate a thousand students, opened in September 1925 and was dedicated on Sunday, September 27. To mark the occasion, the sixth triennial Holy Name Parade marched to the site from downtown Providence. The parade, which consisted of 21 divisions, 101 units and 25,861 men in line, took more than two hours to pass a given point. Bishop Hickey gave the main address on the occasion.[141]

In March of the following year, work was finished on a new, three-story residence for the Christian Brothers, who staffed LaSalle, which was built adjacent to the new school. In order to complete the new complex, the LaSalle Alumni, in the same month the brothers moved into their new home, began a drive among the school's alumni in order to raise $50,000 to build an athletic field on the grounds surrounding the new school. The drive was successful and the new field was dedicated by Bishop Hickey on Thursday, October 18, 1928.[142]

The Sisters of Mercy, who staffed St. Xavier's Academy in Providence, also received more applications for admission during the 1920s than they had room to accept. In 1927, the sisters developed plans to move their novitiate from St. Xavier's Convent in Providence to Mt. St. Rita's, the name given to the former farmhouse and adjoining property that Mother Mary Alexis Donnelly had purchased in May 1912 and which had up to this time been used as a summer retreat. The proposed move allowed them to consider expanding their girls' academy on Broad St. In March 1927, a special committee of the St. Francis Xavier's Alumnae Association, known as the Loyalty Fund Committee, met at the academy to plan for the organization of a fund raising drive to help secure the necessary funds.[143]

An old building on Pine St. was demolished to make way for Academy Hall, a new L-shaped, two-story, brick building, along Claverick and Pine, with the shortest part of the L on Foster St. Together with the Convent building and Mercy Hall and an iron fence along Foster St., the new structure formed a quadrangle. The layout of the buildings resulted from a suggestion made by Bishop Hickey, who blessed the completed addition on January 3, 1929. With the added space, the sisters were able to accommodate more than eight hundred students.[144]

In 1933, the Sisters Faithful Companions of Jesus opened another high school for girls in the old St. Patrick's School, Providence, which Fr. Martin F. Reddy, the pastor of St. Patrick's, had replaced with a new building in 1928. The opening of the school was the result of a collaboration between

---

[140] Ibid., May 22; 29; October 31; November 14, 1924; *Providence Journal*, November 10, 1924.
[141] *Providence Journal*, September 28; October 4, 1925; *Providence Visitor*, October 2, 1925.
[142] *Providence Visitor*, March 26; April 9, 23, 1926; October 12, 19, 1928.
[143] *Woonsocket Call*, August 27, 1927; *Providence Visitor*, April 1, 1927.
[144] *Providence Visitor*, November 25, 1928; December 28, 1928; January 4, 1929.

Fr. Reddy; Fr. William A. Doran, pastor of Blessed Sacrament, whose parish school was the first school to be staffed by the Faithful Companions of Jesus in the diocese; and Bishop Hickey, who played a role in securing the services of the sisters at Blessed Sacrament. Since many of the Catholic elementary schools in Providence had added ninth grades to create a Junior High School program in the fall of 1929, St. Patrick's High School, when it opened, was a three-year school and welcomed its first class as sophomores.[145]

One other high school opened in the diocese during Bishop Hickey's years with his blessing but not as the result of his initiative. When Dom H. Leonard Sargent, O.S.B., founded Portsmouth Priory 1919, he envisioned that, when the Priory began to flourish, it would one day open a school for boys as other Benedictines had done. Dom Sargent's own effort at establishing the priory were not successful. However, in 1926, Downside Abbey in England, where Dom Sargent had studied in preparation for his attempt to establish a Benedictine house for Americans at Portsmouth as a daughter house of the English abbey, gave jurisdiction over Portsmouth to Fort Augustus Abbey in Scotland, an abbey within the same congregation of Benedictines. The abbot of Fort Augustus sent four members of his own community and one from St. Anselm's Priory, Washington, D.C., a daughter house of Fort Augustus, to take charge of Portsmouth Priory and to open a school there similar to the one they had established at St. Anselm's.[146]

Among the monks sent to Portsmouth from Fort Augustus was an American convert, Dom John Byron Diman, son of a Brown University professor and a former Episcopal priest. In 1896, he had founded St. George's School in nearby Middletown and served as its headmaster for twenty years before his conversion to Catholicism, his ordination as a priest of the Roman Catholic Church in 1921, and his entrance into the monastery at Fort Augustus in 1924. The monks converted the manor house on the property for school use. The school, which Dom Diman established at Portsmouth in 1926 and later served as Headmaster, was divided into six forms, only the two lowest of which were organized when the school opened on September 28 with sixteen students. Bishop Hickey solemnly blessed the new school on Monday, November 1, 1926. Bishop Hickey would return to the school again in September 1929 to bless St. Benet House, a new dormitory the monks erected to house their students.[147]

Bishop Hickey took a personal interest in the high schools enlarged or founded during his years, especially in the boys' schools, and visited them when he could. As with LaSalle, St. Xavier's, Bayview Academy, and Elmhurst Academy, he presided at the new schools' graduations and handed

---

[145] Ibid., September 8, 1933; April 21, 1938.

[146] Ibid., April 7, 1938; *Providence Journal*, April 17, 1927.

[147] *Providence Visitor*, November 5, 1926; February 25, 1927; January 9; September 26, 1931; *Providence Journal*, April 17, 1927; October 1, 1931; Geoffrey Spranger, "The Three-fold Legacy of Father Diman," in Rhode Island Yearbook: 1967, 34–37.

out the diplomas to the graduates. Among the bishop's concerns was the ability or the lack thereof of the students and their families to pay the tuition, which provided the operating revenue of the schools. In 1919, Bishop Hickey had raised the tuition at LaSalle to seventy-five dollars a year. Several times during his years as bishop, he expressed the hope that students might attend the diocesan high schools free of charge. Since he could not envision realizing that goal in the immediate future, he gave general permission to his pastors to use parish funds to pay the tuition of the students from their parishes who wished to attend Catholic high schools.

As the new high schools opened and the older ones were expanded, Bishop Hickey, in a letter sent to his pastors in August 1926, urged them of remind the parents of high-school aged children of their obligation to send their children to Catholic high schools. In his letter, he reiterated the policy that Bishop Harkins initiated in 1919 and stressed that no boy should be prevented from having a Catholic high school education through lack of funds. If need be, he said, pastors will endeavor to take this charge upon their parishes. On September 10, 1931, Hickey wrote to his pastors asking them to submit the names of those students to whom they had given scholarships to Catholic high schools. The reason behind his request was that he hoped to be able to relieve the parishes of half the burden by paying part of the students' tuition from diocesan funds. With the prospect of schools opening once again, Bishop Hickey sent a letter to all his priests dated August 11, 1932, in which he urged them to encourage all the boys and girls of their parishes to attend Catholic high schools. In the letter, he required the pastors and/or their assistants, as a pastoral obligation, to interview all the graduates of parish and public grammar schools or junior high schools or their parents within their parishes in order to encourage attendance at a Catholic high school. If a family's financial circumstances were such that they were unable to pay the full tuition required, he required the pastors to pay half of the entire amount.[148]

Elementary Schools

When Bishop Hickey took over the administration of the diocese in 1919, there were in the diocese, including the Greek-rite churches, 97 parishes with resident pastors. Of the 97 parishes, 41 had parish schools, one of the higher percentages of parish schools in the country. During the fourteen years Bishop Hickey served the diocese he created 20 more parishes, thus increasing the total number of parishes with resident pastors to 116. During those fourteen years, 18 more parish schools were built with the

---

[148] Hickey to Pastors, printed in the *Providence Visitor*, August 6, 1926; September 10, 1931; August 11, 1932, PChA.

result that the percentage of parishes with schools increased slightly from roughly 41 percent from to roughly 50 percent.

The first of the parishes that opened a school after Bishop Harkins gave over the administration of the diocese to Bishop Hickey was St. Basil's, Central Falls, in September 1920. Fr. Timothy Jock, the new pastor of St. Basil opened a school in the recently remodeled basement of the church. It was the first school of its kind opened in any Melkite parish in the United States. In addition to the usual subjects of an American school, the students of St. Basil's studied Arabic for two hours each day with Fr. Jock. The school opened with ninety-two students and a staff of four: Fr. Jock and three lay teachers. Fr. Jock supported the school for thirteen years, but was forced to close it in 1930 because of the parish's loss of revenue caused by the Depression.[149]

In September 1920, Fr. J. M. Leon Giroux, pastor of Our Lady of Victories, Woonsocket, saw his long hoped for school open in the Social Hall, which he had purchased from the Manville Company in 1910. With the future of his parish secure by July 1920, he obtained a loan of $16,000 to build classrooms on the first two floors of the building. In order to house the Sisters of the Presentation of Mary that he invited to teach in the school, Fr. Giroux purchased a house on Spring Street with his own funds and turned it over to the sisters as their residence.[150]

St. Paul's, Cranston, opened a new school building on Broad Street in September 1922, the first Catholic school south of the cathedral. To staff the new school, St. Paul's pastor, Fr. Michael McCabe, after a careful search, secured the services of the Sisters Servants of the Immaculate Conception. To house the sisters, the parish built a convent on Norwood Avenue. Since the convent was not ready at the time the school opened, the sisters lived for a time in a furnished home donated by a family in the parish for their use.[151]

A campaign to raise funds to build a school for the Italian parish of Holy Ghost, Providence, began in 1921, during the pastorate of Fr. Angelo Strazzoni, C.S. However, it was not until the pastorate of Fr. Flamino Parenti that the opening of a school occurred. Bishop Hickey took a particular interest in helping Fr. Parenti open a school. He worked with Fr. Parenti and the Fr. Peter Switala, pastor of the Polish parish of St. Adalbert's, who wished to build a new church that would be closer to where the majority of his parishioners lived. The bishop helped to arrange the sale of the first St. Adalbert's church on Ridge Street, to Holy Ghost parish. Since St. Adalbert's church had been built as a combination church and school, Fr. Parenti was able to quickly set up six large classrooms within the building. As had

149 *Providence Visitor*, November 27, 1935; "Church of St. Basil the Great, Central Falls, Rhode Island, 1975."

150 *Providence Visitor*, July 8, 1910; December 17, 1936.

151 Ibid., September 8, 1922; "St. Paul's Church, Cranston, Rhode Island, 1929–1979: 50th Anniversary" (Privately printed, 1979), 22–24.

St. Ann's parish previously, Fr. Parenti engaged the Sisters of Mercy to staff the school. Although primarily an English-speaking order, the Sisters of Mercy were able to supply sisters to conduct a class in the Italian language for the three hundred students who enrolled in the school. On October 7, the day Bishop Hickey dedicated the school, the celebration began with a mass at Holy Ghost church followed by a parade of the numerous Italian societies to the new school. Both Gov. Flynn and Providence Mayor Gainer attended the dedication exercises along with a number of dignitaries from the Italian community.[152]

It was the first pastor of St. Edward's, Pawtucket, Fr. Edward Carrigan, who first proposed building a school but it would be his successor, Fr. William Nagle, who raised the bulk of the funds and saw the task through to its completion. By 1922, Fr. Nagle had sufficient funds to go ahead and send out plans and specifications for a nine-classroom building and a convent for the school's teaching staff to bid in August of that year. Although Bishop Hickey laid the cornerstone of the new school at the corner of Hope and Weeden streets in November 1922, the need to raise additional funds to cover the rising costs of the new buildings delayed their completion until July 1924. The Sisters of Mercy agreed to staff the school and welcomed their first students in September 1924.[153]

Five new schools opened in 1925: St. Stanislaus, Woonsocket; St. Raymond's, Providence; St. Thomas, Providence; Blessed Sacrament, Providence; and St. Michael's, Providence. The pastor of St. Stanislaus, Woonsocket, Fr. Adalbert Duczmal, first wrote to the Polish Franciscan Bernardine Sisters, then under the jurisdiction of the Archbishop of Philadelpia, in 1923, to invite them to establish a school in St. Stanislaus. In 1918, the Bernardine Sisters had come to Rhode Island to staff St. Joseph's School in Central Falls. When the sisters agreed to go to Woonsocket, Fr. Duczmal, in March 1925, purchased a house at 53 Spring Street for use as a convent. Five Bernardine Sisters arrived in the city in the fall of 1925 to begin teaching classes in the renovated barn that had been part of the Greene estate when the parish purchased it. Fr. Duzmal had had the barn converted for use as a school with retractable doors dividing the classrooms.[154]

The Dominican Fathers who administered St. Raymond's Parish, Providence, broke ground for a parish school on the corner of Ninth Street and Highland Avenue in 1923 and the women's organizations in the parish began holding a series of events to raise money for the school fund. The school opened its doors to its first students in September 1925. During the

[152] *Providence Visitor*, March 11, 1921; September 6; October 8, 1923; "The Parish of the Holy Ghost, Providence, Rhode Island, 1889–1989 (Tappan, New York: Custombook, Inc., 1989), 20–21.
[153] *Providence Visitor*, September 24; December 1, 1922; April 10; July 24; August 28, 1924. *Providence Journal*, August 15, 26; September 30; November 28; December 1, 1922; January 20, 1923; April 7, 1924.
[154] "St. Stanislaus Kostka, Woonsocket, Rhode Island, 1905–1980" (Privately printed, 1980).

school's first year, the Dominican Sisters of Blauvelt, New York, who accepted the Dominican Fathers invitation to staff the school, lived on the school's top floor. During that year, the parish built a convent for them on Ninth Street, which was dedicated on Sunday, April 16, 1926.[155]

After Fr. James J. O'Reilly became pastor of St. Thomas parish in the Manton section of Providence, he undertook an extensive program of renovations and improvements. In October 1924, the parish purchased the George F. McCoy homestead on Woonasquatucket Avenue for use as a convent. In January 1925, Fr. O'Reilly welcomed the Sisters of the Immaculate Heart of Mary to the parish. In September 1925, the sisters began holding classes for the children of the parish in their convent and in rooms in the back of St. Thomas church.[156]

In November 1923, Fr. William Doran, the new pastor of Blessed Sacrament in the Mount Pleasant section of Providence, received Bishop Hickey's permission to erect a parish school "at a cost not to exceed $250,000." Bishop Harkins had frequently urged the founding pastor of Blessed Sacrament, Fr. William Simmons, to build a school, but the elderly priest had not wished to undertake another building project after having built Blessed Sacrament church. Before his death in 1921, Fr. Simmons had begun collecting money for a school, and Fr. Doran, after becoming acquainted with the parish, agreed to build an eighteen-room school and a convent for the nuns, who would teach in it. In anticipation of opening the school, Fr. Doran, with Bishop Hickey's help, secured a commitment from the Faithful Companions of Jesus, the teaching order who staffed the parish school in Gilbertville, Massachusetts, when he was pastor there. With the coming of the Faithful Companions of Jesus to Blessed Sacrament, the Sisters of St. Ursula, who had come to parish in 1911 to assist in the religious education of the children of the parish but who were unable to supply the number of English-speaking nuns necessary for the school Fr. Doran intended to build, left the parish. Blessed Sacrament school welcomed its first student on September 14, 1925.[157]

September 1925 also saw the opening of St. Michael's School on the south side of Providence. As in Blessed Sacrament, the pastors and the people of St. Michael's had perceived the need of a school. As in Blessed Sacrament too, the pastor Fr. (later Msgr.) Patrick Farrelly, believed the construction of a suitable church was a higher priority. St. Michael's new church opened in October 1915. The intervention of the First World War made it impossible to proceed quickly with plans for a school, but, in 1924, Bishop Hickey gave permission for the signing of contracts for the building of a large, sixteen class room school and a new rectory. Msgr. Farrelly natu-

---

[155] *Providence Visitor*, April 16, 1926; October 8, 1936.

[156] *Providence Visitor*, October 24, 1924; January 9, 1936.

[157] *Providence Visitor*, September 8, 1922; June 12, 1924; Charles E. Maher, *The Church of the Blessed Sacrament, 1888–1988* (Custombook: Tappan, New York, 1989), 41–51; 111–120.

rally turned to the Sisters of Mercy, who had been teaching in the parish's Sunday School since 1871, to staff the new school.[158]

In 1926, three more schools opened: Assumption, Providence; Immaculate Conception, Westerly; and St. Teresa's, Nasonville. Although the Assumption parish on Potters Avenue, Providence, was not as large as either Blessed Sacrament or St. Michael's, it shared with them the similarity that it too was an urban parish, which lacked a parochial school. Like Blessed Sacrament and St. Michael's, the pastors of the Assumption made the construction of a suitable church their first priority. The Assumption parish dedicated a new, larger church in June 1912. Following the death of the builder of the new church, Fr. John F. Haney, in September 1923, the new pastor of the Assumption, Fr. Patrick J. Sullivan, undertook the building of a school. The cornerstone of the school was laid on November 13, 1924. Bishop Hickey dedicated the completed building on May 16, 1926. Prior to the opening of the school, Fr. Sullivan had secured a commitment to staff the school from an order of sisters recently arrived in the diocese, the Sisters of the Cross and Passion, who he had previously engaged to help with the religious instruction of the children of his parish. The sisters had come into the diocese in 1924 to staff St. Gabriel's Hostel for professional women. After the Assumption School opened on February 1, 1926, St. Gabriel's Hostel closed and all the Sisters of the Cross and Passion then in the diocese eventually took up residence in the Assumption Convent.[159]

After a twelve year effort, Immaculate Conception parish, Westerly, witnessed Bishop Hickey dedicate their new school on September 5, 1926. Fr. Peter McOscar, S.M. acquired the land for a school in 1904. However, it was not until May 1922, that Fr. Thomas Larkin, S.M. began a $100,000 fund raising drive to pay for the construction of the school that there was a real prospect of having one. The fund raising drive was a success and the Sisters of Mercy sent three members of their order to staff the first grades in the new school. The sisters initially lived in a house next to the school, which the parish had refurbished for them.[160]

The third new school that opened in 1926 was St. Teresa of the Child Jesus parish in the Burrillville village of Nasonville. The school was part of a combination building, which also contained the parish hall and church. Bishop Hickey blessed the new building on Sunday, October 4, 1925. The Sisters of the Assumption from Nicolet, in Quebec Province, supplied the teaching staff.[161]

---

[158] *Providence Visitor*, September 11, 1925; "St. Michael's Parish, Providence, Rhode Island: One Hundred Years, 1859–1959" (Privately printed, 1959), no page numbers.

[159] *Providence Journal*, November 11, 1924; May 16, 1926; Mary Ann Strain, C.P., *The Women We Come From: The Sisters of the Cross and Passion in North America, 1924–1968* (Privately printed, 1998), 14–18.

[160] *Providence Visitor*, May 5, 12, 1922; Evening Tribune, September 7, 1926; "Immaculate Conception, Westerly, Rhode Island, 1886–1986" (Privately printed, 1986), 24–26.

[161] *Providence Visitor*, September 4, 1924; "75th Anniversary of St. Theresa's Shrine." The legal name of the church is St. Teresa of the Child Jesus. The shrine to St. Theresa is thought to be the first and thus the oldest in the United States.

On September 9, 1928, Bishop Hickey went over to St. Patrick's, Providence, to bless that parish's new parochial school. This was the third building built to serve the needs of the children of the parish. When he became pastor of St. Patrick's in 1915, Fr. Martin Reddy quickly perceived that the parish's school would soon be taxed beyond its capacity. Because he had first to finish the church the previous pastor, Fr. William Pyne, had begun, Fr. Reddy was not able to carry his plan for a new school into action until 1927 when the cornerstone of the school was laid. As a site for the school, Fr. Reddy had acquired the Jones' lot, which was famous on Smith Hill as "a training ground" for the youth in the neighborhood. The new $200,000 school opened in September 1928.[162]

In April 1928, Fr. James Craig, the founding pastor of St. Sebastian's on the East Side of Providence, purchased a home at 518 Lloyd Avenue for use as a convent. Although the Sisters of Mercy had long run the parish's Sunday School, it was the Sisters of the Congregation of Notre Dame who Fr. Craig was able to engage to staff the school he proposed to establish in the parish. After the newly purchased house was renovated for convent use and a chapel was added, the sisters took up residence there in the fall of 1929. St. Sebastian's first classrooms were in the convent. On October 10, 1929, former Providence Mayor Joseph Gainer, acting for St. Sebastian's, outbid two contractors in order to purchase the former public school on Slater Avenue, a two-story frame structure, the city had abandoned when it opened a new school on Sessions Street. Fr. Craig had a new boiler put in the old school and had it extensively remodeled. Bishop Hickey formally blessed the school on November 21, 1929. It initially offered a kindergarten and the first four grades.[163]

Until November 1926, the president of Providence College was also pastor of St. Pius parish. When the Dominicans, in consultation with Bishop Hickey, decided to relieve the then president of the college, Fr. Noon, O.P., of the responsibilities of pastor, Fr. William A. Sullivan, O.P., became the first full time pastor of St. Pius. On taking up his duties, Fr. Sullivan began planning for the building of a structure that would accommodate a church, eight classrooms and an auditorium on land on Elmhurst Avenue acquired from the diocese for that purpose. The new church was ready for use on Easter Sunday, March 31, 1929. The Sisters of St. Dominic from Blauvelt, New York, took up residence in the school when they first arrived until the parish was able to purchase a home for them at 44 Hilltop Avenue. The sisters opened the new school in September 1929, with five grades and one hundred ten students. Bishop Hickey formally dedicated the church and school on October 6, 1929.[164]

Also in 1929, the small, mixed French- and English-speaking parish of

[162] *Providence Visitor*, September 7, 1928; *Providence Journal*, September 8, 1928.
[163] *Providence Journal*, October 11; November 22, 1929; *Providence Visitor*, September 19, 1935.
[164] *Providence Visitor*, October 11, 1929; May 9, 1935.

the Presentation of the Blessed Virgin Mary in the Marieville section of
North Providence finally saw the opening of a school for its children. The
initial parish church was completed and dedicated in 1915 but a suitable
rectory was not purchased and paid for until 1924. It fell to the third pastor of the Presentation, Fr. Arthur Fournier, who became pastor in March
1924, to undertake the opening of a parish school. On March 5, 1928, Fr.
Fournier held a meeting of interested parishioners to ascertain their wishes
as to whether or not they were ready to undertake the work. Fr. Fournier
was authorized to call on Bishop Hickey to secure his consent and a committee undertook a canvass the parishioners to determine the number of
children who were interested in attending a parish school. On Tuesday,
March 10, 1929, several of the women of the parish met to plan a series
of social events that were to serve as fund raisers in order to secure the
necessary funds to prepare rooms in the church hall on the first floor of the
church scheduled for September. A group of the Sisters of the Presentation
of Mary came from Canada to undertake the work of teaching and lived
initially in a convent on Vincent Avenue. When a fire destroyed the church
in April 1932, Fr. Irenee Bouffard, who had been appointed pastor after Fr.
Fournier's poor health prompted him to resign his pastorate in April 1930,
had to find new quarters for the 160 children who had been attending the
school before the fire. In order to allow the children to complete the remainder of the school year under their own teachers, the North Providence
Superintendent of Schools, James L. McGuire, offered Fr. Bouffard the use
of a two-room, portable building in the rear of the old Marieville School,
which was able to accommodate between 75 and 100 children, as well as
a room in the new Marieville school. He also provided the desks needed
to set up additional school rooms in neighboring Citizens Hall, which Fr.
Bouffard would use for Sunday mass. The eighth grade continued to meet
in the convent where they met before the fire.[165]

When Fr. Bouffard met with Bishop Hickey in May to discuss plans for
rebuilding, the bishop recommended to him, in view of the relatively small
size of the parish, the hard financial times and the fact that after the fire, attendance in the temporary classrooms dropped substantially, that he rebuild
the church only. To aid the parish, the bishop informed Fr. Bouffard that he
would turn over to the parish for its own use, half the money contributed in
the parish to the Catholic Charity Appeal that year. On Sunday, June 12,
following the school graduation, Fr. Bouffard announced that he believed
that the parish could only financially afford to rebuild the church and that,
in view of the lack of proper classroom space, Presentation School would
not reopen in the fall. On hearing the news, the parishioners of the Presentation drew up and signed a petition asking that they be allowed to rebuild

[165] *Providence Visitor*, March 8, 1929; *Providence Journal*, March 20, 1929; April 19, 21, 25, 1932. A parish history published in 1963 recalls that some classes were held in private homes. Cf. "Church
of the Presentation of the Blessed Virgin Mary, North Providence, Rhode Island, 1913–1963:
Fiftieth Anniversary" (Privately printed, 1963), no page numbers

the school as well as the church. Bishop Hickey, in view of their willing-ness to make the extra sacrifice required to rebuild both, agreed to having plans drawn for a combination building, which would include a church in the central portion, a hall underneath the church and eight classrooms on either side of the hall and church, six on the lower level and two on the upper.[166]

The combining of the church and school into one building cut the costs of rebuilding both and was decisive in obtaining Bishop Hickey's consent to rebuilding the school. Although the future of the school was assured in September 1932 with the signing of a contact for the building, the deci-sion as to whether to continue Presentation School while the new building was under construction lay with Fr. Bouffard. Since Bishop Hickey's initial recommendation was that the school not be rebuilt and Fr. Bouffard an-nounced that the Presentation School would not reopen in the fall of 1932, the North Providence School Committee, during the summer months, had to make plans to accommodate the 128 students at Presentation who lived in North Providence. The challenge of accommodating the additional stu-dents was complicated by the fact that the town was already three months in arrears in paying the salaries of the public school teachers. Nevertheless, the town renovated the portable classroom building for another year's use and created a new classroom in the basement of the Marieville school to ready the three additional classrooms Superintendent McGuire predicted would be needed. The day on which he signed the contract for the new church and school, Fr. Bouffard also informed the North Providence School Committee that he would reopen Presentation School. The committee agreed to allow the parish the use of the portable school that they had had renovated. Sixty Presentation students would attend class again in Citizens Hall. Collectively, they would be taught by five sisters. The yet uncompleted Presentation church was used for the first time on Sunday, June 11, 1933. The new Presentation School opened in September 1933.[167]

Christ the King parish in West Warwick, which Bishop Hickey estab-lished in 1931, opened both a church and a school within two years, due in large measure to the efforts of its founding pastor, Fr. J. Adrien Forest, and the generous co-operation and sacrifice of his new parishioners. Christ the King School opened on September 11, 1933 on the third floor of a build-ing which also housed the parish rectory, with a staff of teachers supplied by the Sisters of the Presentation.[168]

In 1929, in view of the prospective opening of Providence's first junior high school, the Thomas H. Doyle School on Sessions Ave. in September

---

[166] *Providence Journal*, May 9; September 9, 1932; *Providence Visitor*, June 17; September 9, 1932; *Paw-tucket* Times, September 9, 1932; "Church of the Presentation of the Blessed Virgin Mary, North Providence, Rhode Island, 1913–1963: Fiftieth Anniversary" (Privately printed, 1963), no page numbers.

[167] *Providence Visitor*, June 17, 1932; June 9, 1933; *Providence Journal*, September 10, 1932.

[168] *Providence Visitor*, February 25, 1937; "Christ the King Church," 6–7.

of 1929, four Providence parochial schools, St. Joseph's, Blessed Sacrament, St. Patrick's and St. Ann's, eliminated graduation ceremonies for their eighth grade students and added a ninth grade to the existing curriculum. The other Catholic grammar schools in Providence held their eighth grade graduations as usual.[169]

When Bishop Hickey launched his education initiative in 1922, there were 23,928 students in the Catholic Schools of the diocese. This number included the students in the parish elementary schools, as well as those in the elementary schools at the Academy of the Sacred Heart, Elmhurst, in Providence; St. Mary's Academy, Bay View, in East Providence; and the Catholic Training School in Providence; as well as those in the schools maintained by the three orphanages in the diocese, St. Aloysius, Mt. St. Francis and Mercy Home and School. In October 1933, just a few weeks after Bishop Hickey died, the Catholic School Office reported that the total number of Catholic students in Catholic schools in the diocese was 27,676. The students attended 108 grammar and high schools. The total cost of their education, which was borne by their parents, the parishes and the diocese, was $2,091,044.14.[170]

Vacation Schools

Even with the best efforts of all involved in Catholic school education and the most generous spirit possible on the part of the laity, Bishop Hickey was well aware that no diocese had the financial or personnel resources to offer every child a place in a Catholic school. This was especially true after the onset of the Depression in 1929. In the years after World War One, a priest of the Archdiocese of Oregon City, Oregon, Fr. Edwin O'Hara, when confronted with the problem of providing religious education to the children in the rural sections of his large parish, began offering the children, who could not attend his parish school, an intensive, two-week period of instruction during their summer vacation. In 1923, Fr. O'Hara became the Director of the National Catholic Welfare Conference's Rural Life Bureau, which he had helped to create. O'Hara used that position to encourage bishops and pastors to organize vacation schools in the various dioceses of the United States. By September 1929, as a *Visitor* article reported, seven hundred vacation schools were being held in seventy American dioceses.[171]

In early 1930, after nine years of experience with vacation schools, the Catholic Rural Life Conference and the N.C.W.C. Rural Life Bureau jointly published *The Manual of Religious Vacation Schools*, which was an initial attempt to furnish pastors and teachers with a complete and workable pro-

---

[169] *Providence Journal*, June 19; September 18, 1929.
[170] P. J. Kenedy & Sons, *The Official Catholic Directory*, 1922, p. 547; *Providence Visitor*, October 27, 1933.
[171] Timothy M. Dolan, "Some Seed Fell on Good Ground": The Life of Edwin V. O'Hara (Washington, D.C.: The Catholic University of America Press, 1992); *Providence Visitor*, September 27, 1929.

gram for conducting religious vacation schools. The *Manual* laid out courses for the primary, intermediate junior high and senior high school levels and included a section on handicrafts, recreation and health programs. Aware that many children in urban parishes where there was no parish school, and even in parishes where there were, did not receive sufficient religious instruction, Bishop Hickey decided to introduce vacation schools to the diocese in the summer of 1930. The bishop gave three priests general supervision of the schools, among them, Fr. Cornelius Collins, an assistant at St. John's, Providence and head of the Religion and Latin Departments at La Salle Academy. Before he began his studies for the priesthood, Collins had earned a teacher's certificate while a student at St. Francis Xavier's University, Antigonish, Nova Scotia.[172]

The first vacation schools opened in Tyler School in the cathedral parish, and in Providence's Assumption and Our Lady of Mt. Carmel parishes, and in St. Cecilia's; St. Joseph's; Sacred Heart, and St. Leo's parishes in Pawtucket on July 14 and continued until August 1. The three priests, whom Bishop Hickey appointed as supervisors, were to visit the various classes several times a week to insure uniformity in teaching methods. Collectively, the schools enrolled 952 students, with the largest numbers enrolled in the Assumption parish, which had just opened a parish school four years before, and in Our Lady of Mt. Carmel and St. Leo parishes, neither of which had a parochial school. Thirty-one women were recruited from among the public school teachers in the two cities, along with three seminarians, to serve as teachers in the schools. During this first year, the pupils were divided into First Communion and Confirmation classes. The classes met from nine to twelve in the morning, and the material taught was drawn from the N.C.W.C. manual. The host pastors agreed to provide outings and picnics and assist in organizing baseball teams. In subsequent years, the monies for picnics and outings came from the Catholic Charity Fund. In the parishes that did have schools, the vacation schools were held in them. In those that did not, the classes were held in the churches. In Providence, Bishop Hickey had asked the superintendent of the Providence School System for the use of one or more of the city's public schools in which to hold the classes of the vacation schools. The superintendent declined the request on the grounds that a city ordinance denied the use of public school buildings for religious instruction. The prohibition remained until 1937.[173]

The success of the experiment in 1930 encouraged Bishop Hickey and the priests he appointed to supervise the vacation schools to expand their efforts. In 1931, four priests were assigned as supervisors and more than two thousand children attended religious education classes in sixteen schools established in Providence, Pawtucket, and Woonsocket. There were five in each city, and one in East Providence. The scope of the instruction offered

---

[172] *Providence Visitor*, April 4; August 1, 1930.
[173] Ibid., August 1, 1930; July 1, 1937.

by the schools expanded during this second year. Each school was divided into primary and intermediate grades and several offered classes to junior high school students. Sixty-seven public school teachers and seminarians were recruited to serve as teachers. During 1932, there was a slight drop in the number of students enrolled because some pastors had provided for the instruction of public school students during the school year. Over succeeding years, however, the program continued to expand.[174]

The Catholic School Office and Catholic Teachers College

Since the Third Plenary Council of Baltimore in 1884 had mandated that Catholic Schools offer the same quality of education as that available in the public schools, Bishop Harkins had created a Diocesan School Board to set policy for the schools of the diocese and had appointed priest-visitors to inspect the schools and report on their physical condition and level of instruction. In 1922, Bishop Hickey appointed Fr. Cornelius J. Holland, pastor of St. Charles, Woonsocket, Diocesan Visitor of Parochial Schools and Fr. Moise C. Leprohon, assistant at Our Lady of Good Counsel, Phenix, as Fr. Holland's assistant. In September 1922, Bishop Hickey sent Fr. Thomas V. Cassidy for graduate study at Catholic University in Washington with the intention that he take courses in Education and Social Service. When Fr. Cassidy finished his course work 1924, Bishop Hickey appointed him Diocesan Visitor of Parochial Schools. The title is the one listed in the Catholic Directory. In essence, Fr. Cassidy was the Diocesan Superintendent of Schools. Fr. Cassidy did further course work in education at Boston College and, in June 1937, he received a Doctorate in Education from Rhode Island College.[175]

Prior to Fr. Cassidy's appointment, the sister principals of each of the schools of the diocese essentially devised their own curriculum, although theoretically each school was under the control of the local pastor. Following his appointment, Fr. Cassidy conducted a survey of education in the diocese. To compile the information he needed, Fr. Cassidy visited every school in the diocese over a four-year period in order to observe teaching techniques, textbooks and courses of study. As a result of his survey, Fr. Cassidy devised a uniform curriculum that was to be adopted by all the schools of the diocese. The curriculum covered every elementary school subject in each grade and specified the matter to be covered, the objectives of instruction, teaching aids, learning experiences for the students, and suggested textbooks. The curriculum the Catholic School Board adopted in 1926 as the result of Fr. Cassidy's efforts contained progressive approach-

---

[174] Ibid., July 31, 1931; July 22, 1932.
[175] Cf. Hayman, *Catholicism in Rhode Island and the Diocese of Providence, 1886–1921*, pp. 554–55; Americo D. Lapati, "A History of Catholic Education in Rhode Island" (Ph.D. dissertation, Catholic University of America, 1958), pp. 222–23; Bishop Hickey's Diary, September 30, 1922.

es to active student participation and provision for attention to individual needs. After completing his survey, Fr. Cassidy established a Catholic School Office at 25 Fenner St. and engaged Sr. Mary Alacoque, R.S.M., as his secretary. In 1929, Bishop Hickey assigned Fr. John J. Kenny, whom he had sent the year before for graduate studies at the Catholic University at Washington, to assist Fr. Cassidy. Fr. Kenny took over the supervision of the high schools, while Fr. Cassidy continued that of the elementary schools. Among the products of the Catholic Office efforts was the preparation of a yearly census, which included the number of students and teachers, religious and lay, in each school.[176]

No one kept any systematic records of the early years of the Diocesan School Office other than statistics drawn from the yearly census. For the most part, only bits and pieces of information regarding the Catholic schools of the diocese have survived. One such bit of information comes from a letter in the Chancery Office's Catholic Schools file. In August 1926, Bishop Hickey (probably at Fr. Cassidy's suggestion) sent a letter to all the pastors of the diocese, who had parochial schools, informing them that he wished to see a course of "Physical Culture." The bishop deemed such a course "advisable and even necessary" to introduce in view of the modern development of education into the parochial schools. According to the bishop's directions, each school was required to meet the expense of such a course at the rate of twenty cents per pupil. The pastors were to forward the monies to the Chancery Office in two installments, one at the beginning of each term. The money would be used to hire a "lay teacher especially trained for this branch." The teachers hired for this purpose were to contact the various school principals to arrange for a time to conduct their classes.[177]

In 1933, Fr. Cassidy undertook to revise the 1926 curriculum by forming a committee made up of representatives of every teaching order in the diocese. The committee was divided into groups and each was assigned a subject. The result of the committee's efforts was then edited by Fr. Cassidy and approved by the priests on the Diocesan School Board before the opening of school in 1934. The Revised Course of Study was a decided improvement over the 1926 version and incorporated six major improvement and changes, all designed to improve the work of the Catholic schools and the efforts of their teachers.[178]

A second recommendation that came from Fr. Cassidy's two-year survey, as well as from the experience of the teachers at the annual Catholic Teachers Institute, which had begun in 1920, was the creation of a Catholic Teachers College. The various orders of sisters, who taught in the diocesan schools, perceived a need to provide their sisters an opportunity to obtain

---

[176] Lapati, "A History of Catholic Education in Rhode Island," 223, 226; *Providence Visitor*, November 15, 1956.
[177] Hickey to Pastors, August 10, 1926, PChA.
[178] *Providence Visitor*, October 5, 1934.

teaching certificates and college degrees. Many of the sisters had begun teaching after having finished high school and their novitiate, and lacked a college degree. The General Assembly granted a charter for the Catholic Teachers College of Providence in March 1929. The college conducted its classes in the newly completed addition to St. Xavier's Academy, Providence, in the summer of 1929, with Fr. Cassidy as Dean of the college. The diocesan normal school offered both theoretical courses, which were offered during the thirty days that the school was open during the summer, and extension courses, which began during the summer session and continued with practical work and written reports during the school year. In June 1937, the College also began offering graduate courses. Also in 1937, the College offered theoretical courses during the school year as well as in the summer. The value and usefulness of the school was recognized not only by the sisters, who taught in Rhode Island Schools, but also by sisters in the other New England states, who chose to also enroll in the college.[179]

Prior to the opening of the Catholic Teachers College, religious superiors in the diocese, who wished to see their sisters continue their education, had arranged with the Dominican Fathers at Providence College for priests of the faculty to come to particular convents to offer courses. In 1918, the Dominicans offered three courses to the Sisters of Mercy at St. Xavier's Convent and continued to do so for several years. Providence College granted its first degrees to religious women in August 1926. Beginning in June 1925, the Dominicans Fathers began offering summer courses at the college itself to a large group of religious sisters and laywomen. The offering of these courses marked the official beginning of a Sisters' College as part of the Providence College program.[180]

The *Providence Visitor* and *La Sentinella*

When in December 1918 Bishop Harkins allowed the editor of the *Visitor*, Fr. Thomas F. Cullen, to accept the invitation of Archbishop Edward J. Hanna to become the editor of his archdiocese paper, the *San Francisco Monitor*, the bishop appointed Fr. James P. O'Brien in his place. Fr. O'Brien was born in Clashmore, County Waterford, Ireland, and had come to Providence as a boy to work with his brother, Patrick, in their uncle's blacksmith shop on South Street in the cathedral parish. After graduating from LaSalle Academy, he returned to Ireland for two years to study Philosophy and Latin at Mount Melleray Seminary. He finished his studies at St. Mary's Seminary, Baltimore, and was ordained in June 1912. Following a brief assignment in East Greenwich, he was sent to Maine where he served at

---

[179] *Providence Visitor*, March 29, July 12; May 26, 1933; June 24; October 14, 1937; Lapati, "A History of Catholic Education in Rhode Island," p. 223.

[180] McCaffrey, "The Origins and Early History of Providence College through 1947," 206–09.

the cathedral and as an administrator in parishes in Bath and Winn. After returning to his own diocese, he served as an assistant at St. Joseph's, Providence, before Bishop Harkins appointed him the first full-time pastor of St. Andrew's, Block Island, in November 1916 where he ministered to the island's residents and the sailors assigned there during the First World War.

Fr. O'Brien took up his new duties at the time political developments in his native Ireland were moving towards a crisis in the aftermath of the Easter Rising in 1916 and the subsequent guerilla struggle waged by the Irish Republican Army. Under Fr. O'Brien, the *Visitor* gave considerable attention to the news from Ireland, particularly to the sufferings the Irish people experienced at the hands of the English. In his frequent editorials on the Irish struggle, Fr. O'Brien made no secret of his sympathies. The *Providence Journal*, as did other Providence papers, also carried the news of the troubles in Ireland, but contrary to the views of the editors of the *Visitor* or the *Providence News*, its editor, John Revelstoke Rothom, favored the English side and frequently denounced the Irish nationalists who sought independence. Over the years, the various editors of the *Visitor* and the *Journal* had had their differences of opinion. However, the partisanship of Fr. O'Brien and Mr. Rothom in regard to the Irish issue prompted a harsher bite to their editorials. Eamon de Valera's visit to the United States in 1920, during which he sought to collect funds to support the nationalist cause, prompted Mr. Rathom to write an editorial in the *Journal* for July 20, 1920, which he entitled "Passing the Hat for Murder." Fr. O'Brien responded three days later with an editorial entitled, "Why the Journal Hates the Irish."[181]

Shortly after this exchange, Mr. Rathom's reputation as an objective journalist was brought under public scrutiny. On October 28, 1920, the *Evening Tribune*, a paper controlled by a rival faction of the Republican party to the one that favored the *Journal*, printed a copy of the signed confession that Rathom had delivered to the Attorney General of the United States on February 12, 1916. In the confession, Rathom acknowledged that he had deliberately exaggerated his and the *Journal*'s role in exposing German subversive activities in the Unites States prior to America's entrance into the war. The publication of the letter was prompted by a public letter that Rathom printed in the *Journal* accusing Franklin D. Roosevelt, the Democratic candidate for vice president in the 1920 election, of misconduct in the course of his service as Assistant Secretary of the Navy in the Wilson administration.[182]

Given the revelation of Mr. Rathom's duplicity, the *Journal*'s reputation for objectivity, especially on the issue of the struggle in Ireland, suffered accordingly. On February 25, 1921, the *Visitor* carried copies of a series of letters sent by "A Journal Reader" to that newspaper and the paper's

[181] *Providence Journal*, July 23, 1920; *Providence Visitor*, July 23, 1920.
[182] *Evening Tribune*, October 28, 1920; *Providence Journal*, October 28, 1920; Garrett D. Brynes and Charles A. Spilman, *The Providence Journal: 150 years* (Providence: The Providence Journal Company, 1980), pp. 275–299.

explanation of why the letters were unsuitable for publication. While Fr. O'Brien let the exchange speak for itself, the *Visitor* made its position plain in the headlines it gave to the letters. The writer charged that the *Journal* collected anti-Irish opinion for its columns, but refused to publish a "Fair Statement of Ireland's Case."[183]

The spirit of animosity evident in the editorials of the *Visitor* and the *Journal* increased in March 1921 with the opening of the fund-raising drive of the American Committee for Relief in Ireland organized by its Rhode Island unit for Thursday, March 10, in Elk's Auditorium in Providence. The meeting was opened by the Rhode Island state chairman, Michael F. Dooley, and presided over by Providence Mayor Joseph H. Gainer. In addition to an address by Mayor Gainer, the meeting, which sought to raise funds to relieve the suffering of all the peoples of Ireland, regardless of religion, was also addressed by Theodore Francis Green, Rabbi Samuel Gup and by Bishop Hickey. Two weeks later, the Thomas Ashe Council of the American Association for the Recognition of the Irish Republic also held a meeting in Providence at Fay's Theater at which the main speaker was Fr. J. F. Cavanaugh, C.S.C., the president of Notre Dame University. Mayor Gainer also spoke at this meeting as did US Senator Peter E. Geary. Vicar General, Monsignor Peter E. Blessing, accompanied Fr. Cavanaugh to the platform.[184]

In response to the meetings, Mr. Rathom began writing a series of editorials that were hostile to the Irish and the Church, the first of which appeared in the *Journal* and *Evening Bulletin* on April 1. In a talk delivered at a meeting of the Thomas Ashe Council at Providence's Rialto Theater, Providence Postmaster, Dr. Charles F. Carroll, characterized Rathom's editorials as filled with "vile, lying and calumnious statements." He especially singled out Rothom's April 6 editorial as an example of the "extremes to which a newspaper will go in its departure from all sense of decency and good taste in offending citizens of Providence of Irish and German extraction." In the editorial, Rothom had again accused by Irish- and German-Americans of disloyalty during the recent war. Fr. O'Brien did not respond directly to Mr. Rathom's attacks on the Irish- and German-Americans but the *Visitor* printed Dr. Carroll's address in full. During the course of this address, Carroll made reference to the recent revelation of Rothom's 1916 confession.[185]

Two weeks before the *Visitor* printed Carroll's address, it had printed a story on its front page attacking another one of the *Journal*'s editorials, one that stated Archbishop Sebastian Messmer of Milwaukee had forbidden Catholic school children to take part in a Fourth of July pageant highlighting the Pilgrims of Plymouth Colony. The *Visitor* article contained the

183 *Providence Visitor*, February 25, 1921.
184 Ibid., March 11, 25, 1921.
185 Ibid., May 27, 1921

substance of a letter sent to a Providence attorney, Frank J. Duffy, who had asked the archbishop for a statement of his position on the pageant. In the light of the archbishop's response, Duffy characterized the *Journal*'s editorial as being "another proof of what is already well-known here: that the *Providence Journal* is always untrustworthy in any matter dealing with the Catholic Church or Catholic activity."[186]

The controversy between the two editors cooled until March 1922 when the *Journal* on March 17 printed a political carton on its front page that Rathom had the *Journal*'s cartoonist, Milton Halladay, draw. Halladay depicted Eamon de Valera as a cobra who had spawned hatred, jealousy and strife. Over the carton was written, "Another St. Patrick needed." The cartoon prompted an Oblate priest, Fr. Haley, O.M.I., who was giving a mission at St. Mary's, on Broadway in Providence, to denounce the cartoon from the altar as "a slander of our great hero." It also prompted Postmaster Carroll to introduce a resolution at the Friendly Sons of St. Patrick dinner, which was held that evening in Providence, objecting to the manner in which the cartoon had depicted Mr. de Valera and also "to the loathsome aspersion on the patron saint of Ireland," which the four hundred members of the organization gathered at the dinner adopted unanimously. Two days after the cartoon appeared, the executive board of the National Council of Catholic Women also went on record as protesting against the cartoon "from a purely religious standpoint." On his part, Fr. O'Brien wrote an editorial for the *Visitor* in which he reviewed the "blasts of bigotry let loose by the *Journal* and *Bulletin*." Fr. O'Brien placed the two papers in the same class as two well-known anti-Catholic and anti-foreigner papers, the *Menace* and *Watson's Sentinel*.[187]

The continuing animosity between the editors of the *Visitor* and the *Journal* finally prompted Bishop Hickey to intervene to try to cool the rhetoric. In 1920, Bishop Hickey had demanded a public apology from the *Journal*'s Republican rival, the *Evening Tribune*, when that paper printed a cartoon which many Catholics, the bishop included, found to be offensive. The editor of the *Tribune* quickly complied and acknowledged that the printing of the cartoon had been a mistake on that paper's part. Many Catholics, not only the Irish, also found the *Journal*'s cartoon depicting De Valera as a snake to be offensive. Bishop Hickey spoke with Fr. O'Brien about the *Visitor*'s controversy with the *Journal* on April 17, 1922 and, the next day, along with a lawyer, Patrick P. Curran, met with Mr. Rathom in Hickey's office at the Chancery for two hours. Towards the end of their meeting, the bishop called in Fr. O'Brien and noted in his diary that the meeting ended with "friendly conclusions." The exact nature of what the bishop and Mr. Rathom discussed has apparently not been recorded. However, in an edi-

---

[186] Ibid., May 13, 1921.
[187] *Providence Journal*, March 17, 18, 1922; Providence News, March 18, 1920; *Providence Visitor*, March 24, 1922.

torial he wrote for the *Visitor* on Bishop Hickey's relationship to the paper for January 24, 1924, Fr. O'Brien observed that, "The only restraint ever exercised by Bishop Hickey upon the *Visitor* was that which would induce a policy of toleration, kindliness and fair dealing."[188]

After Bishop Hickey took over as administrator of the diocese in April 1919, he was anxious to see the *Visitor*'s influence and circulation grow. It was the bishop's hope to see the *Visitor* read by every Catholic in the diocese. Fr. O'Brien directed his early efforts to expanding the paper's facilities and its size. He leased more space in the Hanley Building at 63 Washington Street, where the offices and press of the paper were then located, to accommodate the editorial and business offices and used the space vacated by the offices to enlarge the Visitor Company's printing department. Fr. O'Brien's efforts would receive a boost when the newly formed National Catholic Welfare Council established a Department of Press, Publicity and Literature Committee in 1920. The department worked in connection with the Catholic Press Association to create the N.C.W.C. News Service on the model of the commercial national and international press bureaus. The *Visitor* took a leading part in support of the plan. It became a charter member and subscriber to all its news and feature offerings.[189]

In 1921, the N.C.W.C. asked the Catholics of the United States to dedicate the month of March to the cause of the Catholic Press. On March 13, Bishop Hickey, in a sermon at the cathedral, expressed the hope of the American hierarchy, to which he gave his full assent, that there be a Catholic paper in every Catholic home in order that all might be well informed as to the doctrines and practices of their religion. To achieve the end of a Catholic paper in every Catholic home, Bishop Hickey began by asking Fr. O'Brien to visit all the parishes in the diocese in order to encourage the people to subscribe to the *Visitor*. On January 25, 1921, he wrote to all his pastors to inform them of his instructions to Fr. O'Brien and asking them to receive him cordially. In 1922, the American bishops designated February as Catholic Press Month. To mark the observance, Bishop Hickey sent a letter to his pastors and assistants in which he asked them to urge their people to subscribe to the *Visitor* as well as to provide a gracious welcome to the priests employed as canvassers for the *Visitor* when they visited the parishes. Bishop Hickey estimated that there were 50,000 families in the diocese, which meant in his mind, that the circulation of the *Visitor* should be 50,000. In his letter to the priests, he noted the number of subscriptions that there should be in that particular parish.[190]

Since Bishop Hickey was confident that the number of subscriptions would grow, he also undertook to provide better facilities for the *Visitor* so that it could become more of the positive influences and means of instruc-

---

[188] Bishop Hickey's Diary, April 17, 18, 1922; *Evening Tribune*, October 19; November 1, 1920; *Providence Visitor*, January 24, 1924.

[189] *Providence Visitor*, January 23; February 6, 1920; January 24, 1924; January 11, 1935.

[190] Ibid., March 18, 1921; Hickey to Clergy, January 25, 1921; February 10, 1922, PChA.

tion that he wanted it to be. On November 29, 1921, he held his first meeting with architect, Ambrose Murphy, about designing a new building for the Visitor Printing Company on a site at Fenner and Pond streets across from the cathedral rectory. The bishop also invited the former editor of the *Visitor*, Fr. Michael F. O'Brien and its current editor, Fr. James P. O'Brien to serve as advisors to the project. The bishop urged Mr. Murphy to provide the plans as quickly as possible. On May 19, 1922, the *Visitor* printed a sketch of the two-story brick building that Murphy designed and provided details of its proposed layout and equipment. The new building was ready for occupancy by March 1923. Over a weekend, the entire printing plant was moved from Washington Street to the new building on Fenner Street, where a new press had previously been installed on its own foundation. The new facility, which made the *Visitor* one of the few Catholic papers in the country to have its own printing plant, was formally opened the following June. The *Visitor* marked the occasion by publishing a New Home Edition on June 8.[191]

The new facilities and the additional funds available to the paper allowed Fr. O'Brien to expand the *Visitor* to a sixteen page paper in order to make use of the increased availability of material that was provided by the N.C.W.C. News Service. In order to ensure funding for the *Visitor* and to foster his goal that the *Visitor* be read by every Catholic in the diocese, the bishop, in a letter to the clergy in preparation for Catholic Press Month in 1924, announced that he was allotting a specific number of subscriptions to each parish, which each parish would be responsible for paying. In order to help the pastors collect funds to pay for the subscriptions allotted to them, the *Visitor* provided each parish with envelopes that new subscribers could use to submit their names and address and enclose the two dollar subscription price. The pastors were to take from parish funds whatever difference remained between the number of subscriptions allotted and those paid for directly by their parishioners. When on March 1, 1924, the *Visitor* printed a statement of its circulation on its front page, it noted that 10,250 copies were mailed directly to subscribers' homes while 8,350 were mailed to dealers and pastors for sale at five cents a copy on a no return basis for a total of 18,600. Both the annual subscription rate of two dollars and the per copy price of five cents represented a reduction in the price of the paper in order to make it easier to sell. The assigning of allotments proved easier to do than collecting the monies for them from the parishes. An early, undated report on the payments of the parishes to the diocese shows many of the parishes in arrears.[192]

In the same issue of the *Visitor* in which Bishop Hickey announced the campaign to place "The *Visitor* in Every Catholic Home" and which print-

---

[191] Bishop Hickey's Diary, November 29, 1921; *Providence Visitor*, May 19, 1922; June 8, 1923.
[192] Ibid., January 24, 1922; March 1, 1924. Cf. letter of Fr. Thomas E. Ryan, pastor of St. Patrick's, Harrisville, for an explanation of why it was difficult to sell the *Visitor* in his parish, PChA.

ed his letter to his clergy announcing the system of allotments to each parish, the *Visitor* carried on its masthead for the first time the statement that the *Visitor* was "America's Largest and Best Catholic Newspaper." The claim of being the largest was based simply on comparison. The claim to being the best was to be substantiated in part by the School of Journalism at the University of Notre Dame's consistent selection of the *Visitor* during the 1920s and 30s as the leading Catholic newspaper in America. The quality of the paper bore practical results. In 1933, the *Visitor* could claim that it led the Catholic field in the United States and Canada in advertising lineage for diocesan papers.[193]

The rise of the *Visitor* to the first rank of American Catholic newspapers would not have been possible without the encouragement and support of Bishop Hickey, but a great deal of the credit belonged also to Fr. O'Brien. In his early days at the *Visitor*, Fr. O'Brien not only preformed the work of an editor and business manager, but also that of a news and advertising staff and circulation manager. He wrote editorials and news stories, read proofs and designed the layout of the paper. As the paper grew, he assembled a competent staff of lay and clerical assistants to help him, many of whom had experience on daily papers before joining the *Visitor*. In July 1923, Bishop Hickey appointed Fr. James C. McCarthy, who had been contributing articles to the paper for four years, to the editorial staff of the *Visitor* and sent him to the Columbia School of Journalism to prepare for his work on the paper. Fr. McCarthy served as the paper's assistant editor until 1934, when ill health caused him to take a new assignment. In January 1926, Fr. Francis J. Deery joined the staff as assistant manager. Although Fr. O'Brien enlarged the staff, it was still insufficient to handle the task of mailing out the paper to its subscribers on press day. Fr. O'Brien and subsequent managers had to recruit a force of high school and college boys to address the papers by hand and machine. The expansion of the staff prompted an enlargement of the space occupied by the *Visitor*'s offices to the second floor of the Visitor Building at the beginning of 1933.[194]

After his battle with John R. Rathom on the Irish question, in 1924, Fr. O'Brien took up the question of Rhode Island's lax divorce laws and campaigned to have them tightened. He also championed the cause of the poor in Newport when the sale of the company that supplied water to the city threatened to cause a drastic rise in its rates. In the midst of the controversy, the *Visitor* printed a special extra edition, which was distributed in Newport. O'Brien was one of the first Catholic editors to recognize the news value of Fr. Charles C. Coughlin's radio broadcasts. Under his management, the *Visitor* became the first Catholic paper in the country to ever publish an "extra," which the *Visitor* did when Bishop Hickey died suddenly in October 1933. A few weeks after the bishop's death, the *Visitor*, on October 27,

[193] Ibid., January 24, 1922; January 27; October 27, 1933.
[194] Obituary, *Evening Bulletin*, May 29, 1937; *Providence Visitor*, December 30, 1932; February 28, 1952.

1933, observed its sixtieth anniversary by publishing its largest issue to date. In 1929, when he returned from his *ad limina* visit to Rome, Bishop Hickey recognized Fr. O'Brien's work by announcing his appointment as a domestic prelate with the title of monsignor. In 1934, Fr. O'Brien's colleagues in the Catholic Press Association also recognized his work by electing him vice president of the Association. In January 1935, failing health would force Msgr. O'Brien to offer Bishop Francis P. Keough his resignation as editor after sixteen years at the paper.[195]

Bishop Hickey well realized that the *Visitor* could only effectively serve the English-speaking part of the diocese's population. The many French Canadians in the diocese could subscribe, if they wished, to several excellent Catholic papers published in the Canadian dioceses from which they had emigrated, as well as to other French-language papers published by Catholics in the United States. The Italians of the diocese, whose number had grown rapidly in the years before the First World War, did not have the same choice as even the secular Italian papers in the United States generally and in Rhode Island in particular struggled to survive. Like other ethnic groups, Italian Catholics criticized the reporting of Church matters in both the Italian and the English local press, a point Scalabrini Father Joseph Poja, C.S., made in an article carried in *Il Corriere del Rhode Island* on November 20, 1920, during the height of a controversy between some of the parishioners of Holy Ghost, Providence, and their pastor. On February 6, 1920, Fr. Antonio Bove, the pastor of St. Ann's, Providence, began writing a column in the *Visitor* devoted to the news of the Italian parishes and the colony as a whole. He would continue writing the column until July 1925, but the column was only accessible to those who could read English.[196]

In order to provide accurate news of the Italian colonies and to offer the Italians the same opportunity to become better informed as to the doctrines of the Church, Bishop Hickey, after having discussed the matter with Fr. Antonio Bove, asked Bove to call a meeting of the Italian pastors of the diocese and several prominent Italian laymen in order to consider the founding of a Catholic Italian weekly. The group met on November 10, 1920 in St. Ann's Rectory. Although he could not be present for the meeting, Bishop Hickey gave Fr. Bove a letter expressing his eagerness to see an Italian paper established that would promote the Faith, combat error and serve the interests of the Italians. Furthermore, he promised to back the paper financially as he did the *Providence Visitor*. The clergy and laymen at the meeting agreed on details of the paper's management and among themselves agreed to purchase shares in the La Sentinella Publishing Company totaling $3,180. Other meetings followed at St. Ann's before the *Visitor* announced the incorporation of the publishing company and listed its board of directors on December 17, 1920. Fr. Bove was chosen as its man-

---

[195] *Providence Visitor*, January 11, 1935; *Star-Tribune*, May 29, 1937; *Evening Bulletin*, May 29, 1937.
[196] *Il Corriere de Rhode Island*, November 20, 1920.

ager and treasurer while Fr. Emilio Greco, who was pastor of Holy Angels, Barrington, was appointed editor.[197]

The first issue of *La Sentinella*, as the new paper was called, appeared at Christmas, 1920. Like the *Visitor*, it was a weekly and, when it made its first appearance, carried twenty columns of news. Also like the *Visitor*, *La Sentinella* started in the midst of difficult economic times caused by the adjustment of the American economy from a wartime to a peacetime economy. Nine months after the paper began, Fr. Bove wrote to Bishop Hickey in order to lay before the bishop what he believed had to be done if the paper was to survive. The paper was only bringing in $80 to $90 a week from advertising, which was its main source of income, while it was costing the company an average of $175 to $180 a week to print it. While Fr. Bove applauded Fr. Greco's work as editor, he also believed that he needed to have an assistant so that the paper would have more news and be more attractive. He proposed having a meeting with the bishop in order to decide what could be done as he was anxious to see the paper continue.[198]

As Fr. James O'Brien, the *Visitor*'s editor in 1921, was also anxious to see the paper succeed, he proposed downsizing the paper from twenty columns of Italian reading matter to six in order to reduce the cost of printing the paper. In the place of the Italian news columns, he proposed using the picture page from the *Visitor* on page three and a page of English reading material that would have been already set in print for the previous week's *Visitor*. By taking these measures, he suggested that the costs of producing the paper could be brought in line with its income. To supply that income, Fr. O'Brien estimated that *La Sentinella* had to have twelve hundred paid subscriptions. To attain that number, he suggested that the bishop mandate that each of the Italian parishes commit themselves to taking a certain percentage of the twelve hundred subscriptions, which they would pay for out of parish funds, and supply the paper with a list of parishioners' names, who were to receive the paper in the mail. On February 1, 1922, Bishop Hickey lent his support to the paper in the form of a pastoral letter sent to all the Italian parishes in which he urged the priests and people of the parishes to support *La Sentinella* by taking out subscriptions and by sending in notices of funerals, weddings and baptisms each week.[199]

---

[197] Minutes of meeting November 10, 1920, PChA; *Providence Visitor*, December 17, 1920.

[198] Bove to Hickey, September 23, 1921, PChA.

[199] O'Brien to Hickey, undated; Hickey to Italian clergy, February 1, 1922, PChA. There is not even a single copy of La Sentinella in the diocesan archives or in the newspaper collection at the Rhode Island Historical Society, so it is not possible to say if Fr. O'Brien's suggestions about the makeup of the paper were acted on.

CHAPTER II

The Sentinellist Movement

The Origins of the Sentinellist Movement

While the Americanization movement prompted many immigrants to identify more closely with their new homeland, it also caused a reaction in the hearts of others who chose to emphasize what set them apart from the American culture. The Daughters of the American Revolution, the Grand Army of the Republic and the American Legion called for laws that would prohibit the teaching of foreign languages. The stress on the use of English in both public and Catholic schools, epitomized by the Peck Education Act, caused a good number of Franco Americans to become concerned about the future of their language, race and faith. Even before the First World War quickened the flames of American nationalism, Jean Leon Kemmer Laflamme, while he was editor of *La Tribune* in Woonsocket from 1901 to 1907, had called for an organization embracing all Franco Americans dedicated to the preserving of their heritage.[1]

Mr. Laflamme's nationalism had stirred Philippe Boucher, then general treasurer of the Union St. Jean Baptiste and the organization's general secretary, Adelard Caron, to use the Union's funds to support patriotic and religious endeavors whose scope went beyond the concerns of the Union's charter interests. The nationalism fanned by Laflamme also manifested itself in criticism of the action of various New England bishops. These and other actions of the then general officers of the Union prompted a move on the part of members, who disagreed and distrusted the manner in which they conducted the Union's affairs, to organize an effort to replace them with a new slate of officers. In 1910, the disclosure of financial irregularities prompted a Rhode Island judge to call for the general officers' resignations

---

[1] Sorrell, "The Sentinelle Affair and Militant '*Survivance*'," 139–43; "Les Societe des Croisés," in "Documents au subjet de L'Agitation Sentinelle, 1922–1927." This is a collection of mimeographed materials prepared by Bishop Hickey as background reading for those in Rome interested in the Sentinellist movement.

For a short overview of the subject of French-Canadian nationalism as it pertained to the Diocese of Providence from the point of view of a respected French-Canadian historian, Cf. Yves Roby, *The Franco-Americans of New England: Dreams and Realities* (Septentrion, 2004), 241–269.

and the election of a new slate, which quickly adopted a more moderate stance on the question of nationalism. Although Mr. Boucher, the publisher of Woonsocket's *La Tribune*, in time also adopted more moderate views, the ultra-nationalists who had controlled the Union resolved to attempt to recover control over it in the years ahead.[2]

About the same time Mr. Laflamme and the officers of the Union were championing the cause of French-Canadian nationalism, a young Canadian priest of the Diocese of Nicolet, Fr. Georges Courchesne, also became interested in the nationalist cause. Courchesne became part of a group of Canadian priests who admired the work of the conservative and patriotic *L'Action Francaise* movement in France and he was one of the founders of the Canadian review, *L'Action Francaise*. In the early twentieth century, nationalism for both the French and Canadian supporters of the Action Francaise movement was a protective device used to shield their French traditions from infiltration by non-French elements into the literary, social and political life of the country. In 1915, while serving for a time in the Diocese of Manchester, Courchesne attended the meetings of the Catholic Federation of Franco-American Societies in Worcester, Massachusetts, which finalized the organization of the federation. Courchesne's view of the immediacy of the dangers that confronted the French language and traditions cherished by French-Canadian Catholics in the United States clashed with that of others at the meetings, especially with that of Eugene L. Jalbert, a Woonsocket lawyer. Jalbert did not believe that the measures aimed at conserving the faith and traditions of the French Canadians that Fr. Courchesne espoused would be welcome among the majority of the Franco Americans in the United States.[3]

In January 1919, Fr. Courchesne joined with several Franco-American priests, among whom were Frs. Achille Prince and Joseph Fautaux of the Diocese of Providence, at a meeting in Boston to form the Ligue de Ralliement français en Amérique. La Ligue du Ralliement had as its objective the preserving of the heritage and faith of the Franco Americans, particularly of their children. Like the Knights of Columbus, the Ligue offered degrees through which the members of the organization would pass as they deepened their commitment to the Ligue and its ends. Since the Ligue de Ralliement limited its activism to the publication of tracts, it did not have a

2   Cf. Hayman, *Catholicism in Rhode Island and the Diocese of Providence*, Vol. II, 153–159; *The Rhode Islander*, June 3, 1927.

3   The information on Fr. Courchesne is taken from a report on his involvement in the nationalist movement in the United States that was part of a background paper Bishop Hickey sent to Rome on February 19, 1929, PChA. For a short biography of Bishop Courchesne Cf. Adolphe Robert, *Memorial Des Acts de l'Association Canado-Americaine* (Manchester, New Hampshire: L'Avenir National, 1946), I, 280–81. For Eugene L. Jalbert, Cf. Adolphe Robert, *Souvenirs et Portraits* (Manchester, New Hampshire, 1965). Jalbert was as much a patriot as Daignault, but he was a more moderate and temperate one. Robert would write of him towards the end of Jalbert's life that he was a "Franco-American model and a model Franco-American." For information on the relationship between French and Canadian nationalism CF. Susan Mann Trofimenkoff, *Action Francaise: French Canadian nationalism in the twenties*, (Toronto and Buffalo: University of Toronto Press, 1975), 18–26.

great appeal among those who wanted to be actively and personally involved.[4]

In view of the perceived threat to private schools posed by the introduction of the Smith-Towner bill and similar legislative efforts elsewhere, a number of laymen met with Fr. Joseph D. Fautaux, one of the assistants at St. Ann's, Woonsocket, in St. Ann's Gymnasium on July 27, 1920 to discuss the formation of a secret patriotic French society in the United States. Among those who attended this first meeting was Phydime Hemond, a friend and classmate of Mr. Laflamme, and a man who shared his convictions as well as his antipathy towards the clergy. The founders of the new organization called their new society, L'Ordre des

Fr. Achille Prince

Croisés. Like the Knights of Columbus and the Ligue de Ralliement français en Amérique, L'Ordre des Croisés would have degrees of membership. Fr. Fautaux was a former pastor of St. Jean Baptiste, Warren, and a native French Canadian, whom Bishop Harkins had removed from his pastorate because of incompetence. Some years after leaving Warren, he had accepted the post of an assistant at St. Ann's. He had a talent for writing and composed a draft of the ceremonial of the five degrees or Crusades through which the members would pass as they became more committed to the order. Like the Ligue de Ralliement, the Croisés or Crusaders took as their motto, *Pour nos enfants.* Since the goals of the Croisés were similar to those of the Canadian *L'Action Francaise,* the members of the proposed new organization invited Fr. Courchesne to meet them in St. Louis Rectory, Woonsocket, where Fr. Antonio Prince was pastor, and to offer his thoughts on the drawing up of new order's constitution and degrees. The founders of the Croisés were also helped by Canon J. A. Curotte, a priest of the Archdiocese of Montreal who, while preaching a retreat in Woonsocket, was asked whether the proposed organization needed the approval of Bishop Hickey. Canon Curotte assured them that it did not.[5]

---

4   Rumilly, *Histoire Des Franco-Americains,* p. 323. A description of the objectives and organization of the Ligue de Ralliement can be found in PChA.

5   Rumilly, *Histoire Des Franco-Americains,* p. 323. In a footnote, Mr. Rumilly cites as the source of his information on the Croisés, a memorandum written by Mr. Daignault which, at the time of Mr. Rumilly's writing, was in the possession of Dr. J. B. Falcon. The emphasis on Mr. Hemond's role in the founding of the L'Ordre des Croisés is found in "La Société des Croisés," PChA. The information on Canon Curotte's role is found in a letter of Fr. Georges Bedard to Archbishop Georges Gauthier, co-adjutor Archbishop of Montreal, February 16, 1928, PChA.

I have chosen to retain the French in speaking of the members of the order as the Croisés because, to use the English translation, Crusaders, would create confusion with the Crusaders

Besides Fr. Prince, several other young priests, Frs. Ernest Morin, an assistant at Precious Blood; J. A. Forcier, assistant at St. Louis; and Henri Vincent, assistant at Holy Family, were among the initial members of the order. Father Prince sent a copy of the new order's degree ceremonies to an acquaintance of his, Canon Joseph Gignac, a professor of Canon Law at the major seminary in Quebec, for his review and also submitted them to Cardinal Begin for his approval, which he gave. In addition to the young priests, Frs. Joseph Beland, the pastor of Notre Dame, Central Falls; Joseph S. Fortin, pastor of Holy Family, Woonsocket; and Arthur F. Fournier, a former assistant at St. John the Baptist, Pawtucket, who the bishop would appoint pastor of the Presentation of Mary Parish in Marieville, North Providence on March 27, 1924, were among those who joined the order.[6]

The order's initial goals, the preservation of religious and ethnic heritage of the Franco Americans, were such to attract not only a number of priests but also a cross section of Franco-American business and professional leaders and young men just starting out in business or the professions. Among the order's first lay members were the mayor of Woonsocket, Adelard Soucy, Elphege Daignault, Stanislaus Fournier, Dr. Walter Rocheleau, Herve Lagace and Dr. Gaspard Boucher. After meeting initially at St. Ann's, the Croisés met also at the office of Dr. Rocheleau and still later in the basement of St. Louis.[7]

The Croisés played a leading role in the organizing of the public celebration of the feast of St. John the Baptist in Woonsocket in 1922 and 1923. At the public dinners, which followed the morning mass and procession, various speakers expressed concern for ethnic survival but, in these early days of the Croisés, they directed their criticism at secular Americanization movements like the Peck Education Bill rather than at New England's Irish Catholic hierarchy. Woonsocket's *La Tribune* reprinted an article, which praised the organization's activities in support of *survivance* and its financial support of ethnically beleaguered French Canadians in Western Canada. Among the early causes of the Croisés was their support of the resistance of the French Canadians in Canada's now predominately English-speaking western provinces in face of the efforts of the Irish-Canadian bishops to make English the dominant language of the Church in Western Canada in spite of the injustice such a policy was doing to the French-Canadian and French clergy there.[8]

The Order was soon large enough to rent DeNevers Hall for its meet-

---

recruited by Bishop Hickey to form a corps of speakers in support of the Million Dollar High School Drive.

6   Rumilly, *Histoire Des Franco-Americains*, 328–29; Sorrell, "The Sentinelle Affair and Militant 'Survivance'," p. 173 and note. A copy of the Les Croisés' ceremonials can be found in the Providence Chancery Archives.

7   Rumilly, *Histoire Des Franco-Americains*, 328–29.

8   Sorrell, "The Sentinelle Affair and Militant 'Survivance'," 174–75; Henry L. Wostenberg, "Exiled But Not Silent: The Factum Letter of Father Henri Voison, *Alberta History* (Spring 2010, Vol. 58,

ings. The hall's owner was a member of the order and it was conveniently located in the Social District of Woonsocket. Talks by local and visiting clergy were a prominent part of the gatherings. Among the Canadian priests who addressed various meetings were Frs. Georges Courchesne, Louis Lalande, and Arthur Curotte, a well-known canon lawyer from Montreal. They generally chose historic or patriotic subjects for their talks. A frequent subject discussed at the meetings among the Croisés was the program of Catholic schools that Bishop Hickey was developing, beginning with the building of Mt. St. Charles and continuing with the bishop's program to raise a million dollars for Catholic high schools.[9]

According to Mr. Daignault, his own anxiety and that of many who shared his concerns about the future of Franco-American families deepened with the appearance in 1922 of the N.C.W.C.'s pamphlet, "Catechism of Catholic Education," which he and other Franco Americans took as a statement of official policy of the American Church to which all bishops were bound, although the pamphlet lacked any such authoritative status. The pamphlet was written in the face of the growing movements in several states aimed as passing legislation that would require students under the working age to attend only public schools. The pamphlet urged Catholics to show their loyalty to the faith by sending their children to Catholic schools. In order to divert criticism from the Catholic schools as being foreign entities, the N.C.W.C. recommended that English quickly become the only language of instruction. The writer of the pamphlet asserted that control of the Catholic Schools in the United States lay with the bishops. Many among the Franco Americans, Mr. Daignault, included, felt that this assertion contradicted the statement of Leo XIII in his encyclical, *Saptientiae Christiane*, where the pope held that authority over the education of children lay exclusively with their parents. When Bishop Hickey announced the Million Dollar Drive in order to build new diocesan high schools, some Franco Americans saw in this decision a desire to carry out the program advocated in the "Catechism of Christian Education." In a speech to a Central Falls Circle of the Jacques Cartier Society in December 1925, Mr. Daignault would charge the N.C.W.C. with "working to deprive us of our language." He also saw in the fact that Bishop Hickey assessed each parish in the diocese a certain proportion of the monies the diocese sent to Washington to support the work of the N.C.W.C., an explicit endorsement on the bishop's part of the English-only recommendation of the *Catechism*. The fact that this assessment was to be taken directly from a parish's funds would also prove to be a cause for contention.[10]

No. 2), 17–25; Terence J. Fay, *A History of Canadian Catholics: Gallicanism, Romanism, and Canadianism* (McGill-Queen's University Press, 2002) 186–190.

[9] Rumilly, *Histoire Des Franco-Americains, 320–90.*

[10] "Catechism of Catholic Education. Why do Catholics of the United States maintain at their own expense a school system in which are instructed annually 1,981,051 pupils?" (National Catholic Welfare Council, Bureau of Education, Washington). In regard to the assessment for the NCWC,

Elphege Daignault, who would soon assert himself into a position of leadership in the Franco-American nationalist movement, was born in Woonsocket on June 8, 1879. As a boy, he attended Precious Blood School and then was sent by his parents to study at Sherbrooke, in the Province of Quebec. He later attended the Jesuit College of St. Mary's in Montreal and still later, Boston College, where he obtained a bachelor's of arts degree in 1900. Daignault went to study law at the Columbia University School of Law in New York, from which he was graduated in 1903. He was admitted to the practice of law in Rhode Island in that same year.

Also in 1903, he was elected to the General Assembly and re-elected the following year. He was later appointed a Probate Judge in Woonsocket but resigned that position when, in 1914, he became the City Solicitor in Woonsocket. As a young man, Mr. Daignault had played a prominent role in the protest movement organized in 1914 by the parishioners of his own parish of St. Ann's, Woonsocket, when Bishop Harkins planned to give responsibility of the parish to the French Marist Fathers.[11]

Although he had not played a prominent role in the protest movement against the Peck Act, Mr. Daignault accepted the leadership of the protest movement against Bishop Hickey's High School Drive because the Franco-American priests and the Canadian bishops were not in a position to do so. He took the initiative in securing the signatures of sixteen other prominent Franco Americans, many of whom were then members of the Croisés, on the letter he sent to Pope Pius XI as representatives of all the Franco Americans in the diocese. In the letter, Daignault asked the pope's protection from Bishop Hickey's fiscal measures, which he contended would endanger the financial health of the parishes of the diocese. Significantly, at the suggestion of Fr. Beland, Mr. Daignault asked a French-Canadian bishop, Joseph Halle, Bishop of Hearst in the Province of Ontario, to carry the letter to Rome in January 1923. Bishop Halle's struggle with the Ontario Provincial government to maintain the French-language schools in the Province had previously elicited the support of the Croisés.[12]

Some of the early members of the Croisés became uneasy when the more ultra-nationalistic minded of the Croisés began to publicly attack Bishop Hickey. One who dissented was Adelard Soucy, who had been present at the first meeting when the order was organized. A few weeks

cf. Hickey to Pastors, November 22, 1923, PChA; *Providence Journal*, December 7, 1925; Daignault, *Le vrai mouvement sentinelliste*, p. 51; Chartier, *Histoire Des Franco-Americains*, p. 144.

11 Obituary, *Providence Journal*, May 26, 1937; Daignault, *Le vrai mouvement sentinelliste*, p. 51; *L'Independant*, Fall River, December 16, 1929. After the St. Ann protest had achieved its purpose and Bishop Harkins appointed a Canadian-born priest as pastor, Philippe Boucher's *La Tribune* pointed out an important lesson, which was lost on Mr. Daignault, namely that the protest was successful because, with a few unfortunate exceptions, the majority of the parish had heeded the *Tribune's* call and that of the older men of the parish to conduct the protest in such a way as to remain within the limits of respect and submission to the bishop's authority. Cf. Hayman, *Catholicism in Rhode Island and the Diocese of Providence*, II, 164–66.

12 Daignault to His Holiness Pope Pius XI, December 1, 1922; Rumilly, *Histoire Des Franco-Americains*, p. 344.

after the first phase of the High School Drive ended, Mr. Soucy, along with Mr. Daignault, Dr. Gaspard Boucher and about twenty other members of the order, attended a Croisés meeting held on June 5. After a report on the well-being of the order was made, Mr. Soucy, who because of illness had not been present at the meetings of the Croisés for some time, stood to express his concern about the critical remarks certain members of the order had made about Bishop Hickey during the recent drive. He told his listeners that it was a disgrace for members of the order to advise heads of families, as some did in St. Ann's, Woonsocket and St. Louis, Woonsocket among others, not to give to the Drive. After Mr. Soucy finished, Mr. Daignault rose to answer his charges and to defend his own and the conduct of other of the Croisés. He informed Mr. Soucy that he had consulted with canonical experts in Quebec and Montreal and that they had encouraged him in his views. Although it long been a French-Canadian tradition that one did not publicly criticize their priests or their bishop, Daignault claimed for himself and others the right to disagree with their bishop since they had done so in the proper way by bringing the Croisés' case to the apostolic delegate. The constitution of the Croisés allowed only members who had been admitted to the fifth degree or crusade to have a voice in the running of the order. By 1923, Mr. Daignault had begun to use his influence over the younger members to see to it that those who shared his views on the Drive and other questions constituted a majority of the fifth degree members. After his confrontation with Mr. Daignault at the June 1923 meeting, Mr. Soucy resigned from the Order as did all the laymen and clergy who respected Bishop Hickey's authority.[13]

Mr. Soucy and others who left the Croisés with him shared many of the same values and pride of race as did those who remained with the organization. However, they did not harbor the mistrust of Bishop Hickey and the other Irish-American bishops of New England that bound Mr. Daignault with those among the Croisés who supported him. Soucy and the others who left recognized that they were part of a larger entity to which they had responsibilities alongside those they owed to their parishes. At the same time as the laymen left the Croisés, Msgr. Dauray, who might well have had reservations about the Croisés from the start, urged the French-Canadian clergy to drop their membership in the organization as well. Msgr. Dauray was in his eighties at this time and his health was poor. He had been a friend of the first two bishops of Providence and he enjoyed the respect of Bishop Hickey as well. During the High School Drive, his parish, Precious Blood, had set the standard for generosity. While most of the priests who had joined the Croisés, when asked by Msgr. Dauray, ended their association with the order, five did not. Among those who remained partisans of the Croisés and supporters of their efforts were Frs. Beland and Prince, along with Frs. Fautaux, Forcier and Fournier.[14]

---

[13] Minutes of Croisés Meeting, June 5, 1923, PChA.

[14] J. Albert Foisy, *The Sentinelliste Agitation in Rhode Island, 1925–1928* (Providence: *Providence Visitor*

Another of the Canadian priests who spoke at the meetings of the Croisés and supported their aims was a priest of the Archdiocese of Quebec, Fr. Edouard V. Lavergne. In March 1922, Fr. J. M. Leon Giroux, pastor of Our Lady of Victories Parish, Woonsocket, engaged him to preach the traditional Lenten mission in his parish. Fr. Lavergne, an associate editor of Quebec's *L'Action Catholique* and chaplain to a religious community in Quebec, was a popular and effective preacher of missions and retreats. He had a simple, down to earth style which appealed to working people. He was also a French-Canadian patriot, who used his column in *L'Action Catholique* to attack the policies of Prime Minister Alexandre Tashereau.[15]

The year after he preached in Woonsocket, Fr. Lavergne returned again to preach a retreat in St. Ann's, Woonsocket, from February 18 through March 25, 1923. It was during this time that he began attending the meetings of the Croisés and helped to develop their views on many matters. In 1925, Fr. Joseph Beland, at Notre Dame, Central Falls, had Fr. Lavergne give the Lenten mission in his parish. About the time Fr. Lavergne arrived in Central Falls, the *Providence Journal* ran a story about four Polish Catholics in Woonsocket who had broken with their pastor and the Roman Catholic Church and had begun to form an independent Polish Catholic parish. Without knowing the dispute's background and, taking Fr. Beland's word that Bishop Hickey and his policies were somehow responsible for the break, Fr. Lavergne included mention of the schism in the column, which he regularly wrote for *L'Action Catholique*. The column, which appeared on March 15, was generally critical both of the manner in which the English-speaking bishops in the United States treated the Catholics who spoke different languages and of the programs of the National Catholic Welfare Conference. While he had avoided controversial matter in preaching for Frs. Giroux and Villiard in Woonsocket, he was not so restrained in Central Falls. In his mission sermons, Fr. Lavergne criticized Bishop Hickey's administration of the diocese in a manner that caught the attention of the local press. When Fr. Lavergne's March 15 column was brought to Bishop Hickey's attention, he summoned both Fr. Lavergne and Fr. Beland to meet him at the cathedral rectory. In a letter he wrote to Cardinal Begin the same day he met with Fr. Lavergne, Bishop Hickey said Lavergne's statements had caused him pain and, believing that they were capable of creating a false impression on the readers of the column, he had invited Fr. Lavergne to his home "having in my heart to forestall a repetition of the lack of courtesy from a priest enjoying the hospitality of our diocese." The bishop reported that Fr. Lavergne showed himself unmovable and that he found Lavergne's responses insulting. In the end, Bishop Hickey removed the permission he had given him to offer

_____
      Press, 1930), 124–83; Sorrell, "The Sentinelle Affair and Militant '*Survivance*'," *175–176*.
15   Rumilly, *Histoire Des Franco-Americains,* 364–65; Hickey to Cardinal Sbarretti, Prefect, Congregation
      of the Council, January 11, 1928, PChA.

mass in the diocese and, irritated by his manner and what he regarded as his insolence, gave him twenty-four hours to leave the diocese. According to Bishop Hickey, Fr. Lavergne "left my office laughing at me." Bishop Hickey asked Cardinal Begin to call his priest home and to prevent him from using the press in order to revenge himself.[16]

In his response to Bishop Hickey, Cardinal Begin expressed his pain at hearing that one of his priests had caused Hickey difficulty and expressed the hope that the activities of which Bishop Hickey complained would soon come to an end. According to one account of the meeting, the cardinal, when he in turn called Fr. Lavergne in to discuss the matter, did not discipline him in any way, but questioned him about Bishop Hickey. On his part, Fr. Beland wrote to Cardinal Begin on April 24 to offer a defense of Fr. Lavergne's action and words. Fr. Beland characterized the article that Bishop Hickey found offensive as a call for justice for the oppressed. He sought to exonerate Fr. Lavergne of any blame and requested that the French-Canadian bishops, in view of the struggle going on in the United States between the "Saxons and Latin races," ask Rome to intervene to protect their rights, which were threatened by the Irish cardinals and bishops. In spite of Bishop Hickey having made it very clear to him that he was not welcome in the diocese, Fr. Lavergne continued to visit the Croisés in Woonsocket whenever he could and supported them through his column and personal letters.[17]

La Sentinelle

In March 1922, shortly after the first phase of the High School Drive ended, Fr. Fautaux raised the idea of founding a newspaper at a meeting of the Croisés. In Mr. Daignault's own account of the meeting, Fr. Fautaux urged the founding of a newspaper in order to provide the Franco Americans with a voice since the English papers were hostile to the cause of French-Canadian nationalism. He compared the situation in New England to that of the French schools in Ontario and in the Canadian western provinces and made the point that their struggle would have been impossible without the Canadian paper, *Le Droit*. Fr. Fautaux's argument helped to convinced those at the meeting and, shortly thereafter, Mr. Daignault and his associates initiated a drive to raise funds in both Canada and the United States for a Catholic newspaper dedicated to the defense of the rights of Franco-American Catholics and one that would urge its readers

---

[16] Memo, dated March 21, 1924, found in Fr. Lavergne's Providence Chancery Office file; Hickey to Begin, March 21, 1924; Hickey to Sbarretti, January 11, 1928, PChA. Bishop Hickey did not keep a diary during 1924.

[17] Cardinal Begin's letter to Bishop Hickey is not found in the Providence Chancery files but is referred to in Hickey's letter to Begin, July 5, 1925; Beland to Begin, April 25, 1924, PChA; Rumilly, *Histoire Des Franco-Americains,* p. 365.

to become involved in the work of the Church. Once the decision to establish a similar paper in Woonsocket, which would be named *La Sentinelle*, the new paper's board of directors hired J. Albert Foisy, the former editor of *L'Action Catholique*, the largest Catholic daily in Canada, as its first editor-in-chief. A large part of the funds that were eventually raised to support the paper came from both the Canadian and Franco-American clergy. Daignault modeled the proposed paper on both *Le Droit* of Montreal and *L'Action Catholique* of Quebec.[18]

On February 18, 1924, Mr. Daignault wrote to Bishop Hickey asking for a meeting with him and Mr. Foisy. On receiving Mr. Daignault's letter, Bishop Hickey, who knew that Daignault had written to the pope in November 1922 and probably also knew of his visit to the delegate in May 1923, composed a response promising Daignault the meeting he requested as soon his schedule allowed. In the meantime, the bishop requested of Mr. Daignault, if he wished to have his approbation for the new paper that Daignault first provide him with a statement of the new paper's "principles, program and policy." On reflection, Bishop Hickey chose not to send the letter he composed to Mr. Daignault, but rather asked his secretary, Fr. Peter Foley, to reply in his stead with the same request for a statement of the new paper's principles, program and policy signed by the paper's directors. On April 1, 1924, Mr. Daignault sent the names of the paper's directors to Bishop Hickey along with an article from the first issue of *La Sentinelle*, in which Daignault and those who supported the paper, explained their rationale for founding it and the principles which would guide it. The paper would receive congratulations from several of the French-Canadian clergy, among them Cardinal Louis Begin, the Archbishop of Quebec. Among other letters offering good wishes that appeared in the early weeks of the paper's publication were those written by Bishop Prud'homme of Prince Albert, Saskatchewan; Bishop Halle, Vicar Apostolic of Northern Ontario; and Bishop J. S. Herman Brunault, the Bishop of Nicolet.[19]

The *Providence Visitor* carried an N.C.W.C. News Service notice that the National Publishing Company in Woonsocket would begin publication of a new Franco-American daily newspaper and that the daily would be a subscriber to the N.C.W.C. News Service. Bishop Hickey did not see the *Visitor* article, but he did read the same information in the typewritten news bulletin the News Service set for release during the week of March 24. In a letter written on March 26, 1924 to Justin McGrath, the Director of the News Service, Hickey expressed his surprise that the News Ser-

---

[18]   Daignault, *Le vrai movement Sentinelliste*, 227–28. In his account, Mr. Daignault wrote that the meeting took place in 1924. According to a memoire of Daignault in the hands of Dr. J. B. Falcon and cited in Rumilly, *Histoire Des Franco-Americains*, p. 353, the meeting took place on March 22, 1922. The 1922 date fits best with other information.

[19]   Daignault to Hickey, February 18, 1924; Hickey to Daignault, February 19, 1924, (not sent); Rev. Peter Foley to Daignault, February 21, 1924; Daignault to Hickey, April 1, 1924 PChA; *La Sentinelle*, April 4, 1923.

vice would contract to sell its news "to a self-styled Catholic paper which has not obtained the written approval of the local Ordinary, no matter how many letters of encouragement may have been received by it from dignitaries in a foreign land." Mr. McGrath responded immediately with an apology for not having consulted Bishop Hickey first before listing *La Sentinelle* among the papers which subscribed to the News Service. Mr. McGrath explained that he had taken it for granted that any paper with which Mr. Foisy was associated would have the local bishop's approval. He promised to notify Mr. Foisy immediately that he would be unable to supply *La Sentinelle* with the N.C.W.C. service.[20]

Although the Croisés had discouraged contributions to the new Mt. St. Charles building fund to a significant extent, the project went ahead. Bishop Hickey challenged Fr. Georges Bedard, who was directing the drive for funds, to come up with a hundred thousand dollars more. When he did this by securing a commitment from a Woonsocket industrialist, Jacques LePoutre, that he would pay the interest on a $400,000 bank loan for construction of the college, Bishop Hickey promised to supply the remainder of the funds. Among those who were present at the dedication of the school on November 11, 1924 were the apostolic delegate, who laid the building's cornerstone, as well as the auxiliary bishops of Quebec and Montreal, who represented their ordinaries, and Bishop Fabrien Joseph Decelles, Bishop of St. Hyacinthe. In addition, several monsignori and several hundred priests from all over New England also attended. The Canadian and Franco-American priests came to the ceremony as much to honor Msgr. Dauray as to be present for the dedication of Mt. St. Charles. Following the dedication and blessing of the school, Bishop Hickey concluded the ceremonies by presenting Msgr. Dauray with the Cross of the Legion of Honor of France, an honor a committee of his friends had sought for him from the French Government. The various Franco-American societies who joined in the parade and were present at the dedication of Mt. St. Charles honored not only Msgr. Dauray, but also Bishop Hickey as well.[21]

During the first few months of its publication, *La Sentinelle* quietly fulfilled the mission its Directors had set for it in the statement of policy printed in its first issue. Mr. Foisy even commented favorably on a talk Bishop Hickey gave at the annual La Salle Alumni dinner in Providence on February 3, 1924. In his talk, Bishop Hickey had taken issue with a statement reported to have come from a state education official that the State had the first right to the education of a child. The bishop asserted his position that the natural right to the child belonged first to the parent and that the parent had the right to educate the child in any school worthy

---

[20] *Providence Visitor*, March 20, 1924; Hickey to McGrath, March 26, 1924; McGrath to Hickey, March 27, 1924, PChA; *La Sentinelle*, April 5, 19; May 3, 17, 1924.
[21] *Providence Visitor*, November 14, 1924.

of the name. The bishop's position was one that Mr. Foisy could support fully.[22]

During its first months of publication, the Directors of *La Sentinelle* found it difficult to attract sufficient readers and advertisers to meet the expenses of the paper. In Woonsocket, *La Sentinelle* was competing with an older French daily, *La Tribune*. In addition, 1924 was not an auspicious year to start any new business enterprise as the textile industry was experiencing another period of depression and many mills were again cutting wages and hours. On September 22, 1924, the Directors announced a reduction of the size of the newspaper and a change in the paper's format. The change in format placed the paper's editorials on the front page along with various controversial articles, which the paper also printed in bold type.[23]

On August 15, 1924, an article attacking Bishop Hickey and the Diocesan High Schools Drive appeared in *La Sentinelle* for the first time. With the public attack on the Drive, it was evident that a clear difference of opinion had developed in the Franco-American community in Rhode Island between those who supported Bishop Hickey in the main and those who shared the view of Mr. Daignault and the Croisés that Bishop Hickey and his policies represented a real danger to the survival of the French heritage. From this point on, it became common to refer to Mr. Daignault and his supporters as Sentinellists to distinguish their form of nationalism from the more moderate form of the majority of the Franco Americans in the diocese. If the change in the paper's tone was intended to increase circulation, the tactic did not work.[24]

Since money troubles continued for *La Sentinelle* following the November elections of 1924, during which the paper was subsidized by the Republican Party, the Directors decided that they had no choice but to cease publication of a daily paper and continue as a weekly. The paper would first appear on Fridays and, after a few months, on Thursdays. Shortly after making the decision to revamp the paper, the Directors also decided to let Mr. Foisy go as editor because they could no longer afford his services and because they blamed him for the paper's lack of financial success. The decision to end Foisy's tenure as editor was a mutual one. Mr. Foisy was uncomfortable with the articles critical of Bishop Hickey that the paper had begun printing in August. After leaving *La Sentinelle*, Mr. Foisy found other employment on *Le Bulletin*, the largest French language newspaper in Fall River. On December 15, 1924, he wrote to Bishop Hickey giving an explanation of why he left *La Sentinelle* and disclaiming responsibility for the "campaign of disparagement which had been in the newspaper for several weeks."[25]

After Foisy's departure, Elphege Daignault took personal charge of the

22 Ibid., February 7, 1924; *La Sentinelle*, April 12, 1924.
23 Ibid., September 22, 1924.
24 *La Sentinelle*, August 15, 16, 17, 1924.
25 Rumilly, *Histoire Des Franco-Americains, p. 368; Foisy to Hickey, December 15, 1924, PChA.*

overall affairs of the newspaper. Phydime Hemond served as administrator of the paper. To assist them, they hired a Frenchman sympathetic to the principles of the *L'Action Francaise* movement, Henri Perdriau, who had a background in theology and some experience working on *La Presse* in Montreal. The Directors gave him charge of the day-to-day workings of the paper. Daignault initially signed his articles with a pen name, Blaise Juillet, Hemond signed himself O. Revoir or Frontenac, while Perdriau signed his Etienne Le Moyne or Frater Stephanus.[26]

As noted above, public respect for the clergy was an integral part of French Canadian culture. While it was recognized that there were times when the clergy failed to live up to their priestly and administrative responsibility, it was understood that one did not criticize the clergy or take issue with them publically. In criticizing Bishop Hickey in the pages of *La Sentinelle*, Daignault and his associates, in essence, transferred to him and to the Irish clergy in general the animosity that French Canadians had long felt towards the Anglo-Saxon political and clerical authorities in Canada, who had sought to separate them from their French traditions. Having done this, there were then no limits to the name calling and attribution of sinister motives with which they spiced their articles to appeal to their readers.

Notre Dame Hospital, Central Falls

On November 21, 1924, *La Sentinelle* began a series of articles that focused on another project close to Fr. Beland's heart, which Bishop Hickey had prevented from developing in the way that Fr. Beland had envisioned. Back in Bishop Harkins's day, on April 9, 1910, Fr. Beland had raised the idea of a Catholic hospital in Central Falls with Harkins. The bishop told him that he could ask the Sisters of Providence in Montreal if they would be interested in staffing a hospital there, but that he was not too anxious to have a hospital in Central Falls. Fr. Beland brought up the question again three years later on April 11, 1913. This time, Bishop Harkins merely said that he would consider it. When Fr. Beland returned to Providence after two weeks had passed, Bishop Harkins told him that he could inquire of the Sisters of Providence as to the conditions they would accept a foundation in Central Falls.[27]

For reasons of his own, Fr. Beland did not pursue this first initiative, but he revived the idea in 1921 in conjunction with a group of Franco-Americans doctors, who were members of the French Medical Society of Rhode Island. The society had created a special committee, of which Dr. Florian A. Ruest of Pawtucket was chairman, to undertake planning for

---

26 Rumilly, *Histoire Des Franco-Americains*, pp. 368, 378.
27 Bishop Harkins' Diary, April 9, 1910; April 11, 25, 1913.

a Franco-American hospital in Central Falls. In 1919, Notre Dame Parish saw the completion of a new brick convent for the Sisters of St. Anne, who taught in the parish schools. In 1920, after having remodeled the sisters' old convent to serve as a rectory, Fr. Beland and his assistants moved across the street. On November 18, 1921, a month after Bishop Hickey blessed both buildings, Fr. Beland suggested to Bishop Hickey the idea of inviting the Sisters of Charity of Nicolet, who were popularly known as the Grey Nuns, to open a hospital in the former rectory. Fr. Beland proposed that he purchase the rectory, which he was already repairing, from the parish and then give it to the sisters for a hospital. That afternoon, Bishop Hickey wrote to the superior of the Grey Nuns informing her of Fr. Beland's request and asking her to consider the idea. A few days later after Fr. Beland returned to give the bishop an accounting of the money he had spent on the new convent and rectory for the parish, Bishop Hickey observed in his diary in regard to Fr. Beland and his efforts, "Good work, but too self-reliant."[28]

Fr. Beland had already made inquiries of the Grey Nuns prior to calling on Bishop Hickey and they were ready to act quickly on receiving Bishop Hickey's letter. Within a few days of receiving the bishop's letter, Sr. M. L. Carignan, the Grey Nuns' Superior General, came down to Rhode Island to visit Central Falls and Bishop Hickey. In a letter written on November 29, she thanked the bishop for his courtesy to her and asked that she be given some time to study the question before giving her answer as to whether her order would accept the invitation to establish a community in Central Falls. In light of the order's limited means, the sisters made it clear at the beginning of their conversations with Bishop Hickey that they did not wish to own the property and bear financial responsibility for it. Five days after Bishop Hickey wrote the Grey Nuns, he also wrote to the Bishop of Nicolet, Bishop J. S. Herman, to ask the bishop to approve the project. Bishop Herman, who had fond memories of Bishop Harkins, readily gave his endorsement. On December 16, 1921, the *Providence Visitor* ran an article about the proposed hospital and the expected arrival of nuns on January 1.[29]

The *Visitor* article proved more optimistic than realistic. Sr. Carignan did not secure the consent of her council to the establishment of the new foundation until the beginning of February. On February 7, 1922, she sent Bishop Hickey the names of the sisters who would be part of the civil corporation the bishop planned to set up to run the hospital and the conditions for internal administration that she wished to see inserted

---

28 Bishop Hickey's Diary, November 18, 22, 29, 1929. In his diary, Bishop Hickey notes that he sent a letter to the sisters on that same day, but there is not a copy of it in the Providence Chancery office files.
29 Sr. M. L. Carignan, Superior General, to Hickey, November 29, 1921; Herman to Hickey, December 21, 1921. Both letters are found in "Documents," PChA; *Providence Visitor*, December 16, 1921.

into the contract the sisters would sign with the bishop in establishing the new house. On receiving the sisters' consent, Bishop Hickey then asked Fr. Beland and the three other pastors in Central Falls to recommend two men from each parish, who might lend their names to the incorporation papers and serve on its board. Fr. John Sullivan of "Irish" Holy Trinity and Fr. Lawrence Malecki of "Polish" St. Joseph's quickly responded to the bishop's request as did Fr. Joseph A. Laliberte, pastor of St. Matthew's, the second of the two Franco-American parishes in the city. In his note, Fr. Laliberte wrote that, for serious reasons, which he did not elaborate, he would prefer not to have anything to do with the direction of hospital that Fr. Beland intended to open and that his parishioners, in general, felt the same way. Out of respect for Bishop Hickey, he offered the names of two possible trustees as the bishop asked.[30]

On February 16, 1922, Fr. Beland held a meeting of his parish corporation to consider and formally vote on the question of selling the old rectory to the new hospital corporation, which the Rhode Island Assembly voted to create in the middle of April. Those in the Franco-American community in Central Falls, who supported the project, referred to the proposed hospital as Notre Dame Hospital. In order to establish a tax-exempt corporation, Bishop Hickey and the other incorporators had to secure an act of incorporation from the General Assembly. Bishop Hickey at first wished to name the proposed hospital the Hospital of Our Lady of the Sacred Heart, a name that the sisters accepted willingly. But when it came time to submit the proposal to the General Assembly, he thought it wiser, in view of "the fever of Americanization which has seized upon such large numbers, particularly of those who are non-Catholics," to have the name appear on the state documents and records as St. Mary's Hospital. On April 17, with the passage of the act of incorporation immanent, Bishop Hickey went to see Fr. Beland in Central Falls to go over the proposed contract between the sisters and the diocese. Bishop Hickey had accepted all the provisions of the contract as submitted by the sisters with the exception of two minor points he wished to finalize after he had some experience of the undertaking. However, in the letter he wrote to Sr. Carignan that same day, he asked that the sisters provided for the new hospital should have a speaking and writing knowledge of English. To Hickey's mind this was necessary since the hospital was "to be a Diocesan Institution, open to the sick of all faiths and races, but particularly to those who speak English or French." Hickey suggested to the sisters that they make immediate preparations to come to Rhode Island. Although the building was not yet ready, Fr. Beland would provide rooms for them in the convent of the Sisters of St. Ann until such time as it was.[31]

[30] Sr. Carignan to Hickey, January 3; February 7, 1922; Bishop Hickey's Diary, February 11, 1922; Rev. John F. Sullivan to Hickey, February 11, 1922; Rev. L. A. Malecki to Hickey, February 11, 1922; Rev. J. A. Laliberte to Hickey, February 12, 1922, PChA.
[31] Hickey to Carignan, February 25; April 17, 1922; Carignan to Hickey, March 2, 1922, PChA.

On April 22, 1922, four days before he left on his first visit to Rome, Bishop Hickey, along with Msgr. Blessing and Fr. Beland, held the first meeting of the new corporation in order to elect officers and members and to vote the money needed to make the necessary improvements on the building. Among the business transacted at the meeting was the acceptance of the Rules and Regulations that were to govern the hospital. While acceptable to those at the meeting, the Rules and Regulations were not acceptable in their entirety to the Franco-American doctors, who had been hoping for the last twenty-five years to have a hospital under their control where they would not be subjected to prejudicial treatment. On April 25, 1922, Dr. Ruest, who thought that he and Bishop Hickey had reached an understanding concerning the nomination of Franco-American doctors to the staff of the hospital, wrote to express his surprise that there was no mention of the Franco-American medical profession in the Rules and Regulations. According to the document as adopted, the executive committee of the new hospital, who were to be elected after first being approved by the bishop, would have the right to name the members of the hospital staff for terms of one year. Dr. Ruest objected to the fact that there was no guarantee in the Rules that Franco-American doctors would be appointed to the staff and that there was no appeal against the decisions of the executive committee since it was not responsible to the corporation but to the bishop. Rather than continue to endure the discrimination, which he said, the Franco-American doctors had experienced at St. Joseph's "where the Canadians have been excluded without pity," he announced that the doctors behind the project were now resolved to open a lay Catholic hospital where he and his fellow Franco-American doctors could keep "our sick people under our own supervision."[32]

Rather than let the project as he envisioned it die, on May 11, Fr. Beland met with the Vicar General, Msgr. Blessing, who was also the diocesan director of Catholic hospitals, whom Bishop Hickey had authorized to continue negotiations after the bishop left Rome. After their meeting, Fr. Beland conveyed the import of his meeting with Msgr. Blessing to the Committee of Doctors interested in the hospital project. At this meeting, the doctors agreed that, before they would do anything in support of the hospital, Bishop Hickey would have to accept certain changes in the hospital's Rules and Regulations. In a letter that Fr. Beland sent to Msgr. Blessing on May 13, one that had the tone of an ultimatum, the doctors first demanded an increase in the number of lay members of the corporation. They also demanded a change in the way in which the executive com-

---

[32]   Bishop Hickey's Diary, April 22, 1922; Ruest to Hickey, April 25, 1922, PChA. When in March 1928, Elie Vezina wrote to Bishop Hickey inquiring what a Franco-American doctor, Walter Rocheleau, needed to do to obtain a place on the staff at St. Joseph's, Bishop Hickey replied that all he had to do was write out an application. The bishop said in reply, "As far as I can learn, no discrimination had even been exercised in selecting the staff of the hospital." Hickey to Vezina, March 23, 1928, PChA.

mittee, which appointed the medical staff, was chosen and the manner in which changes might be made in the corporation's bylaws. In both of these areas, the doctors wished to omit the provision that both the members of the executive committees and any proposed changes to the bylaws be approved beforehand by the bishop. Instead, they wished to have a physician as superintendent of the hospital. Since the hospital was to be a diocesan institution and the sisters who were to staff it were to have a contract with the bishop, Bishop Hickey was not ready to concede control of the hospital and the appointment of its medical staff to anyone. Furthermore, he had recently replaced the physician in charge of St. Joseph's Hospital because he found that having a physician as Superintendent of the hospital had caused trouble. While willing to accede to the first of the proposed changes, Bishop Hickey, in his reply to the doctors, informed them that he could not agree to any lessening of his authority over the proposed hospital, which he saw as essential to its preserving its Catholic identity.[33]

By the time Bishop Hickey returned home on July 10, the Grey Nuns themselves were having second thoughts. Bishop Hickey's letter of April 17 asking for certain minor changes in the proposed contract with the diocese and for only sisters who could speak both French and English, arrived at the sisters' motherhouse when Sr. Carignan was dying. On May 15, 1922, the assistant general of the Grey Nuns, Sr. St. Alphonse de Ligouri, wrote to Msgr. Blessing informing him of Sr. Carignan's death and of the General Council's desire to study the matter further. Within a few days, she wrote Msgr. Blessing again to say that it would be difficult for them to accept the hospital, if Bishop Hickey did not accept the contract that they had discussed with him. As to the matter of the number of sisters, who could speak and write English, she promised to send enough sisters with a command of both languages to ensure the good functioning of the hospital, but she could not promise to send only bilingual sisters. Since the matter required Bishop Hickey's input, Msgr. Blessing decided that the matter had to wait until after the bishop's return from Rome.[34]

Because Bishop Hickey had refused to accept their amendments in their entirety, the committee headed by Dr. Ruest, which included professionals and businessmen as well as doctors, obtained a for-profit corporate charter for a hospital from the Rhode Island Secretary of State. The *Providence Journal* article, which noted the issuance of the charter, also contained a

---

[33] Beland to Blessing, May 13, 1922; Amendments to Rules and Regulations of St. Mary's Hospital, Central Falls, By-Laws, a copy of this is in the Notre Dame Hospital file, with Bishop Hickey's notations of approval and rejection, PChA; *The Rhode Islander*, July 29, 1927; February 8, 1929; Foisy, *Histoire de L'Agitation Sentinelliste dans la Nouvelle-Angleterre, 1925–1928* (Woonsocket: *La Tribune* Publishing Co., 1928), 103–105; English version of this work, *The Sentinelliste Agitation in Rhode Island, 1925–1928* (Providence: *Providence Visitor* Press, 1930), 47–48. There are minor difference between the French and English texts, but no substantial ones.

[34] Sr. St. Alphonse de Ligouri to Blessing, May 15, 1922, May 21, 1922; Rev. Thomas C. Collins, to Sr. St. Alphonse de Ligouri, June 5, 1922, PChA.

great deal of inaccurate and outdated information. On the copy of the article he had placed in the files of the chancery office, Bishop Hickey wrote, "Part of the game." After reading the article, Bishop Hickey called Fr. Beland in and, according to the bishop's diary, "Warned him concerning the New Hospital affairs." Two days after the bishop asked Fr. Beland to come see him, Fr. Beland came back to Providence on anther matter. He apparently suggested that the bishop talk to Dr. Ruest, but the bishop declined to see him. The day after Fr. Beland's second visit, the *Journal* carried another article, which sought to set the record straight about the hospital. The article, citing Dr. Ruest as its source, reported that the original plan of creating a French hospital had been dropped when Bishop Hickey and the lay members of the committee "could not come to terms on the various phases of the plan." The article went on to say that, "With the withdrawal of the clergy from the project," Dr. Reust and his committee took up the project and obtained the commercial charter from the Secretary of State. Rather than use the old Notre Dame rectory as originally envisioned, the lay committee planned to buy land on which to build a hospital.[35]

In spite of what Dr. Ruest was reported to have said and done by the newspaper, at least some of the Franco Americans interested in the hospital had not given up on the idea of establishing a non-profit, Catholic hospital in Central Falls. On October 2, 1922, Bishop Hickey received a three-man committee of Franco-American doctors, who wished to speak with him about the proposed hospital. In his diary for that day, Bishop Hickey, after mentioning the call of the doctors, wrote, "Insisted on their acceptance of my terms before promising cooperation." One of the three doctors who called on the bishop was Dr. George P. Bertholet, the secretary pro tem of the Board of Incorporators set up by the charter granted by the General Assembly in April. On October 11, he submitted to the bishop a copy of the Rules and Regulations passed by some of the lay members of the corporation and their lawyer, Elphege J. Daignault, which contained several points that were essentially the same as the bishop had previously rejected. The committee asked for a response within five days. This time Bishop Hickey did not respond at all[36].

In spite of the continued reluctance to accept Bishop Hickey's terms on the part of a significant number of those interested in the hospital, the bishop continued to negotiate the terms of a contract by which the Grey Nuns would take charge of a hospital in the diocese. The acting superior of the Grey Nuns called on the bishop in Providence on November 14 to discuss their coming to Central Falls with him and a group of doctors. After the meeting, the bishop noted in his diary, "All O.K." While the sis-

---

35   *Providence Journal*, August 26, 29, 1922; Bishop Hickey's Diary, August 26, 28, 1922.
36   Bishop Hickey' Diary, October 2, 1922; Bertholet to Hickey, October 11, 1922; Foisy, *The Sentinel-list Agitation in New England*, 48–49.

ters were satisfied with the arrangements worked out with the bishop, dissension continued among the doctors and laymen. On December 4, 1922, Dr. Bertholet informed Bishop Hickey of the results of the last meeting of the Board of Incorporators. Dr. Bertholet said in his note that the board had regretfully voted to abandon the project of establishing a hospital in the old Notre Dame rectory and to proceed independently of the bishop in creating a hospital.[37]

Two days after Bishop Hickey received Dr. Bertholet's letter, he received formal word from the new superior general of the Grey Nuns that her council had approved the project and she was ready to send the six sisters, who were to make the foundation, whenever she received word from the bishop. Rather than abandon the project entirely, Bishop Hickey contacted one of the Franco-American pastors in area with the request that he suggest the names of men with whom he might speak about offering a further compromise to those interested in the hospital. The priest put the bishop in contact with Frank Dupuis, a Pawtucket businessman, a trustee of St. John the Baptist, Pawtucket, and first vice president of the civil corporation formed after the Franco-American doctors had rejected the By-Laws proposed by the bishop. Mr. Dupuis, along with Henri J. Blais, a young Pawtucket lawyer, who was a graduate of Holy Cross, Worcester, later met with the bishop to discuss the possibility of a compromise that would end the impasse that had arisen over the bishop's insistence on maintaining ultimate control. On December 18, 1922, Bishop Hickey sent Mr. Dupuis a draft of the proposed modifications the three had discussed. The bishop was willing to change the name of the hospital to Notre Dame and to have lay people make up a majority of the corporation and of the Executive Committee. He specified, however, that the elected members of the executive committee or Board of Directors had to be acceptable also to the ex-officio members, which included himself, the Vicar General, the Sister Superintendent of the Hospital and her assistant. He also specified that any amendments to the hospital's constitution and bylaws had to have the prior approval of the bishop. At a meeting of the civil corporation's Board of Trustees held on December 26, 1922, Louis Monast made a motion to accept the bylaws offered by Bishop Hickey with the suggested amendments. During the discussion that followed, there were some members of the corporation that supported the motion. However, they were in the minority. The debate over the motion went on over two days and Bishop Hickey accepted further changes that were made in the bylaws. Nonetheless, in the end, the motion failed. Following the failure of the motion, Mr. Dupuis resigned as a member of the corporation and the Board of Directors, as did Dr. Ruest, the president of the board and other

---

[37] Bishop Hickey's Diary, November 14, 1922; Bertholet to Hickey, December 4, 1922.

members of the corporation, who did not wish to see an injustice done to Bishop Hickey.[38]

After rejecting Bishop Hickey's proposals, the remaining members of the civil corporation met on Friday, January 26, 1923, to begin making plans for a fund raising drive to finance the project, which they were determined to go ahead with. More than three hundred people gathered in Notre Dame Hall in Central Falls to hear addresses by Arthur M. Suprenant, the new president of the corporation, Elphege J. Daignault, the new first vice-president, and Sen. Adelard J. Forcier of Pawtucket, who each emphasized the need for the hospital. A ten-day drive opened with a mass meeting in the Scenic Theater in Pawtucket where the speakers again emphasized the need for adequate hospital facilities close to the homes of potential donors. The drive was organized on a parish and neighborhood basis in Central Falls, Pawtucket, Manville, Woonsocket and Providence. Some donations were made in kind, while cash and pledges reached over $100,000 on the last official day of the drive. At the final meeting of the Drive's Committee, Mr. Suprenant announced the total had risen to $119,000.[39]

There was initial optimism about an early start on the construction of the new hospital. However, when plans were actually drawn for the hospital, the estimated cost was set at $200,000. Rather than begin construction immediately, the incorporators of the hospital decided to purchase the private hospital of Dr. Alphonse J. Lalonde on Brook Street in Central Falls, which had a capacity of fifty beds, to serve temporally until construction costs dropped. On June 1, 1923, the Notre Dame Hospital's trustees met at the Literary Club, on Broad Street, Central Falls, to choose a staff of physicians and nurses and to make plans for the opening of the hospital.[40]

After reducing the size of the building they hoped to build, the trustees began construction of a new, three-story, brick building on the former athletic field of Sacred Heart College, Broad Street, which was to have a capacity of fifty beds. Two houses on the property were purchased with the intent of renovating the smaller for use as an out-patient department or quarters for employees and the larger for a nurses' home. The new hospital was opened for public inspection on March 21 and welcomed its first patients during the course of the week.[41]

In a three-article series in *La Sentinelle*, which began on November 21, 1924, Daignault and his associates gave their version of the history of the hospital and charged that the reason that the Grey Nuns did not come to take charge of the hospital was because Bishop Hickey insisted on hav-

[38]   Hickey to Dupuis, December 18, 21, 1922; February 3, 1923; Dupuis to M. J. Surprenant, February 1, 1923; *Le Sentinelle*, November 21, 1924; Foisy, *The Sentinellist Agitation in New England*, 49–50.
[39]   *Providence Journal*, January 30; February 2, 3, 15, 1923; *Sunday Tribune*, February 4, 1923; *Le Jean Baptiste*, February 16, 1923.
[40]   *Evening Tribune*, February 25, 1923; *Providence Journal*, June 1, 1923,
[41]   *Woonsocket Call*, July 15, 1925; *Pawtucket Times*, March 11, 22, 25, 1926.

ing control of it. They argued that having the sisters take charge of the hospital would have guaranteed both its Franco-American and Catholic character. The writer of the series dismissed any concerns, based on past experiences of administering Catholic institutions, that the bishops of the United States had, which caused them to insist on having control. The author also dismissed the bishop's offer of a compromise so as to give the laity the majority of members on the Board of Directors, that would have cleared the way for the sisters to come, as meaningless since ultimate control would remain with the bishop. In concluding his later account of the Notre Dame Hospital's early history, J. Albert Foisy, who had access to the correspondence between Bishop Hickey and the Grey Nuns as well as other principals in the story, wrote that "The bishop was deeply humiliated by the conduct of the Franco Americans in this affair and he probably had never understood what wrong he was guilty of in acting as he did.[42]

Growing Divisions

Although Fr. Beland claimed that he did not play an active role in the organization of the Croisés, the issues Daignault and his associates at *La Sentinelle* chose to champion were predominately Fr. Beland's issues. In Bishop Hickey's view and in that shared by many during the period of the Sentinellist Controversy, Fr. Beland was at the heart of the Sentinellist movement. Although at times he stretched the limits of proper priestly conduct in regard to his bishop, Fr. Beland never publicly overstepped the bounds as did Daignault and his associates at *La Sentinelle* in their increasingly disrespectful criticism of Bishop Hickey and the other New England bishops.[43]

While Bishop Hickey had a growing number of critics within the Franco-American community, he also had his defenders. On December 15, 1924, the Federation Catholique Franco-Americaine held its annual meeting in Willimantic, Connecticut. The meeting brought together representatives of its twenty-five member societies, plus a delegation of students from Assumption College. The federation's president, Eugene Jalbert, who was also legal advisor of the Union St. Jean Baptiste d'Amerique, in giving his report for the year, deplored the federation's lack of strength due to an absence of real unity among its members. When he went on to discuss the sole accomplishment of the federation in the year, the dedication of Mt. St. Charles, for which the Federation had conducted a fund drive, Mr. Jalbert praised the contributions of Msgr. Dauray and Bishop Hickey. Rather than stop there, he went on to criticize "a certain newspaper and

[42] *La Sentinelle,* November 21, 28; December 5, 1924; Foisy, *The Sentinellist Agitation in New England,* p. 50.
[43] Cf. *The Rhode Islander,* October 25, 1929. The article reflects Bishop Hickey's view of Fr. Beland's role in the Sentinellist Affair.

certain persons more zealous than intelligent" for having attacked both the bishop and Msgr. Dauray. He expressed the hope that, at the end of the meeting when it came time for the participants to pass resolutions, the Federation would disclaim any responsibility for *La Sentinelle*'s campaign of injury and insult. Adolphe Robert, secretary of l'Association Canado-Americaine, of which Mr. Daignault was elected president in November 1922, moved to have the convention reject Mr. Jalbert's report. In the ensuing debate, Mr. Daignault called attention to the fact that Cardinal Begin and other Canadian bishops had expressed their support for *La Sentinelle*. He omitted saying that the endorsement came before the character of the paper changed. If the convention did choose to act on Mr. Jalbert's suggestion and censure *La Sentinelle*'s articles, he threatened that his association would leave the Federation. The impasse was resolved when the delegates were not asked to vote to accept or reject the report.[44]

Unlike the English language papers, the French language papers published lengthy accounts of the congress's proceedings. On reading the account in *L'Avenir National*, which was published in Manchester, New Hampshire, Georges Guertin, the Bishop of Manchester, in whose diocese the Association Canado-Americaine had its headquarters, wrote to the order's chief chaplain, Fr. L. J. A. Doucet, on January 8, demanding that the order disavow the stand taken by its officers against religious authority at the congress. When Mr. Robert and the general officers of the Association sought a meeting with Bishop Guertin, he refused to see them. On the day before the deadline Bishop Guertin set for the publication of the retraction, the Association's officers sent Bishop Guertin a statement that they would appeal to the apostolic delegate if he continued to refuse to see them. Bishop Guertin, in response, told Fr. Doucet that he had twenty-four hours to obtain and publish a retraction. When *L'Avenir National* appeared on January 17, 1926 without the retraction, Bishop Guertin removed the chaplains he had assigned and, with their removal, his recognition of the Association as a Catholic order.[45]

While Mr. Daignault would point out at various times that Bishop Hickey had a temper, which caused him to be intemperate in what he said, Mr. Daignault shared the same trait. Over the next year, Mr. Daignault wrote about thirty editorials in which he attacked Bishop Guertin for one fault or another. Some of his criticism could be justified. In the words of one historian, Bishop Guertin "remained too passive and did not do much to better the situation of French Canadians." However, the manner in which Daignault attacked Bishop Guertin's administration of the Diocese of Manchester could not be justified. Daignault made no allow-

---

44 *Woonsocket Call*, October 9, 1925; Rumilly, *Histoire Des Franco-Americains*, 372–73; Chartier, *Histoire Des Franco-Americains*, 150–51. The English language newspapers made no mention of the dispute over Mr. Jalbert's report in their reporting on the convention, Cf. *Providence Journal*, December 16, 1924.

45 Rumilly, *Histoire Des Franco-Americains*, 374–75; Chartier, *Histoire Des Franco-Americains*, p. 151.

ance for the sensitive situation in which Bishop Guertin found himself as the first Franco-American bishop in the United States. If he favored the French Canadians too much, the Irish bishops might well have complained and never allowed another Franco-American bishop.[46]

On his part, Bishop Hickey sought to avoid giving Mr. Daignault further opportunity to stir up the emotions of the Franco Americans in the diocese. As the Canadians' national feast day, that of St. John the Baptist, approached at the end of June, he asked that every Franco-American parish observe the day by celebrating a special mass rather than grant permission for a diocesan celebration. St. Ann's, Woonsocket, had hosted the main celebration of the feast in the diocese since 1922 with mass in the morning, a parade, and dinner in the parish Gymnasium. However, in 1925, unlike past years, the various St. Jean Baptiste and other societies in Woonsocket did not take part in the planning of the day, leaving any celebration of the day apart from mass to Mr. Daignault and his group. On Sunday, June 21, Fr. Villiard, the pastor of St. Ann's, announced at all the masses that mass on the feast day would be celebrated at seven rather than at nine and that he had withdrawn his permission for the committee headed by Mr. Daignault to use the parish Gymnasium for the feast's traditional dinner, speeches and entertainment. On the following day, *La Tribune* published an article listing the times for masses on the feast in all the Franco-American churches in Woonsocket and observed that the day would be celebrated in an "entirely Christian manner by the sincere Franco Americans of Woonsocket." In spite of the fact that St. Ann's Gymnasium was closed to them, Daignault and his committee held their celebration in the building anyway. Because of the withdrawal of permission to use the hall, there were no priests among the crowd of about seven hundred who attended the event. In his speech, Daignault discussed "the aims and ambitions of the Franco-American people, especially with relation to their language, their schools, and their relations with other nationalities." In an aside, he pointed out that the refusal to allow the use of the building came not from Fr. Villiard but from Bishop Hickey.[47]

On July 3, *La Presse* of Montreal printed a letter signed by "Lynnois" in which the writer asserted that Bishop Hickey had prohibited the celebration of the Canadians' national feast day. He expressed his belief that the Franco Americans in the Diocese of Providence were persecuted by their bishop and they were in revolt against him. On July 6, *La Tribune*, which represented the view of the moderate Franco Americans who supported Bishop Hickey, took issue with Lynnois' assertion. Rather then prohibit it,

---

[46] For this paragraph, I have drawn on Robert B. Perreault, *Elphege J. Daignault et Le Movement Sentinelliste a Manchester, New Hampshire* (Bedford, New Hampshire: National Materials Development Center, 1981.) While Bishop Hickey was the chief target of Mr. Daignault's criticism, Bishop Guertin was next. Cf. "Index Analytique De La 'Sentinelle' Jusqu'au 15 Septembre 1927," in "Documents au sujet de L'Agitation Sentinelliste, 1922–1927," No. 10, PChA.

[47] *La Tribune*, June 24, 1925; *Providence Visitor*, June 25, 1925; *Woonsocket Call*, June 25, 1925.

La Tribune pointed out, the bishop had encouraged the Franco Americans to celebrate their feast. What he did do, the editor noted, was prevent a small group, whose leaders had been insulting him each week in their newspaper, from using church property for their celebration.[48]

The report of the incident in *La Presse* prompted Patrick Keene, a public official and resident of Montreal, as well as a friend of Bishop Hickey and a member of the National Board of the Ancient Order of Hibernians, to write to Hickey to inquire as to the truth of the matter, as did J. J. Flaherty, of Quebec. In response to both men, Bishop Hickey sent copies of the July 6 *Tribune* article. On July 14, Lucien San Souci, an employee of *La Tribune* who served also as a local correspondent for *La Presse*, wrote to Bishop Hickey to assure him that he had nothing to do with the Lynnois letter. He assured the bishop that, when he read the letter in *La Presse* on July 6, he wrote to Oswald Mayrand, the chief editor of the newspaper, giving an accurate version of what had happened in Woonsocket, which Mr. Mayrand printed on July 10 along with *La Tribune*'s article from its July 6 issue. In his letter to Bishop Hickey, Mr. San Souci enclosed the letter he had received from Mr. Mayrand in which the editor expressed his regret for having aggravated the discontent that existed between Bishop Hickey and some of his flock. After Mr. Mayrand sent Hickey a copy of the articles he printed in *La Presse*, the bishop thanked him and gave some indication of his own thinking in regard to the Sentinellists:

> The attitude of the people, who have been airing their views in *"La Sentinelle"*, is prompted for the most part by their desire to boom their own Society, which they wished to have pose as the champion of the Franco-Americans in the United States, and to replace in that role other societies prominent in the past, societies which have merited the respect and commendation of the Bishops and Archbishops of the Church and the blessing of the Holy Father himself.[49]

While Bishop Hickey had chosen to this point to avoid scandal and not to answer *La Sentinelle*'s charges publicly, he was not a man of unlimited patience. Fr. Lavergne's name surfaced again in the program distributed to those who attended the dinner as the writer of a piece explaining the significance of the feast of St. John the Baptist and of a letter to Mr. Daignault encouraging his efforts and those of *La Sentinelle*. On July 5, 1925, Bishop Hickey again wrote to Cardinal Begin to complain of Fr. Lavergne's interference in the affairs of his diocese. Specifically, he referred to the "substantial co-operation, encouragement and advice" which Fr. Lavergne had been giving to those supporting *La Sentinelle*, whom Hickey described as "a group of malcontents who are imagining things

---

[48]   *La Tribune*, July 6, 1925; Rumilly, *Histoire Des Franco-Americains*, 381–82. Bishop Hickey was in Woonsocket on June 24 attending one of the clergy retreats that had begun to be held at Mt. St. Charles. The bishop celebrated the mass of St. John the Baptist with his clergy.

[49]   Keene to Hickey, July 8, 1925; Hickey to O'Flaherty, July 8, 1925; Hickey to Keene, July 9, 1925; San Souci to Hickey, July 14, 1925; Hickey to Editor, *La Presse*, July 14, 1925, PChA.

and inventing fancied judgements against which they pretend to stand forth as champions of the people."[50]

Bishop Hickey knew he had to be careful in writing to Cardinal Begin about *La Sentinelle*, since Mr. Daignault had printed the letter from the cardinal in the paper's first issue in which the cardinal had praised the aims of the paper. In his letter to the cardinal protesting Fr. Lavergne's activities, Hickey referred to the reliance Daignault and his associates at the paper had placed on the cardinal's letter and those of the other Canadian bishop's whose similar letters the paper had printed on its front page. He asked the cardinal, in view of the "career of vilifications, falsehood and disrespect for several members of the American hierarchy" on which the paper had embarked, if he could now write a letter Hickey could publish in which the cardinal retracted the contents of his former letter. Unfortunately Bishop Hickey's letter arrived in Quebec when the cardinal was dying. It was his auxiliary, Bishop J. Alfred Langlois, who replied to Hickey. While he assured Hickey that neither he nor the Coadjutor of Quebec, Archbishop Roy, wished to approve or support any enterprise which disregarded the respect due to the episcopacy, he was not in a position to do more.[51]

It would be ten months before Daignault and his supporters had the occasion to mount a counterattack on Jalbert, Elie Vezina, and the other officers of the Union St. Jean Baptist d'Amerique, who urged loyalty to Bishop Hickey as being in the best interest of the Franco-American cause. Not only did the various Franco-American organizations have different views on the question of militant *survivance*, the local societies that belonged to the Union also differed in their views. Daignault and Phydime Hemond, who were members of the local St. Jean Baptiste Society in the Social District of Woonsocket, were elected representatives from their council to the Union's twenty-fifth anniversary convention in Holyoke, Massachusetts, which was to begin on October 13, 1925. As did Mr. Vezina, they worked in the months before the convention to line up delegates to support the slate of officers they planned to nominate at the convention as rivals to the present officers. It was Mr. Vezina's duty as secretary of the Union's Board of Directors to make a report to the delegates regarding the condition of the Union. In a preface to his report, which took so long there was not time left in the session for him to begin reading his report, Mr. Vezina defended his stewardship of the society and denounced Mr. Daignault and Mr. Hemond for having mounted a campaign of calumny against him. That evening, the two factions within the Union, each held separate banquets. Among the thirty-five priests who were present at the Sentinellist faction dinner were Frs. Beland and Prince. They were also among the five priests who spoke at the dinner. Fr. Prince urged the delegates to elect offi-

---

50   Hickey to Begin, July 5, 1925, PChA; *La Sentinelle*, June 25, 1925.
51   Hickey to Begin, July 5, 1925; Langlois to Hickey, July 16, 1925, PChA.

cers who would oppose the "Irish" bishops and railed against parents who
sent their children to the public schools. Fr. Beland criticized Mr. Vezina
for his use of improper language in his defense of his administration and
attacked the Marist Fathers, the majority of whom were natives of France
and who did not support the Sentinellists, for thinking of themselves as
better than the French-Canadian priests.[52]

When Mr. Vezina opened the meeting the next day, he gave his report
and used the occasion to urge the members of the Union to support rather
than to defy their bishops, as Mr. Daignault had done in Providence, since
cooperation with the bishops was the best way to advance the interests
of their race. When in the afternoon session, Mr. Jalbert, the legal advisor of the Union, gave his report, he too used the occasion, with Mr.
Daignault sitting in the front row of the hall, to reply to the criticisms of
the Daignault faction and to Daignault's personal criticisms. When on the
third day of the convention the election of general officers was held, the
only close race was for secretary. The delegates cast 338 votes for Vezina
against 120 for the candidate of the Daignault faction. At the close of the
convention, the delegates adopted a resolution proclaiming their submission to the Holy See and to the bishops in spiritual matters that was introduced by Fr. Henri Vincent, an assistant pastor at Holy Family, Woonsocket. The convention also affirmed its determination to work for the
preservation of their nationality, traditions, language and faith with firmness, but with moderation.[53]

The Sentinellist Case in the Roman Ecclesiastical Courts

As Bishop Harkins had done before him, Bishop Hickey employed the
services of Msgr. Alfonso Gentile, an auditor within the Congregation of
the Council, as his agent in Rome. It was from Msgr. Gentile that Hickey
received a copy of Daignault's Memorial, which he submitted to the Congregation of the Council in behalf of the parishioners of Notre Dame and
St. Louis, along with an official letter of the Congregation. The first part
of Daignault's Memorial cited Bishop Hickey's letters of May 23, 1923
and May 26, 1924 in which he authorized his pastors to make up the difference between their parish's quota and what they collected during that
year's drive as evidence that he had taxed the parishes of the diocese. In
the second part of the Memorial, Daignault cited specific canons of the
new 1917 Code to show what kind of taxes a bishop was authorized to impose and which he was not. The Memorial concluded that the tax Bishop
Hickey had imposed on the parishes in the High School Drive was not

52 *Woonsocket Call*, October 9, 13, 14, 1925; *Providence Journal*, October 14, 1925; *Evening Bulletin*,
    October 14, 1925.
53 *Providence Journal*, October 15, 16, 1925; *Woonsocket Call*, October 15, 1925; Rumilly, *Histoire Des
    Franco-Americains*, 384–386.

authorized by Canon Law and asked the Rota to order Bishop Hickey to make restitution for the parish funds he had unlawfully taken from parish treasuries.[54]

In the cover letter that he sent Bishop Hickey on July 4, 1925, along with a copy of the Daignault's Memorial, Msgr. Gentile told Hickey that he had held onto the documents in order to discuss the case with Archbishop Fumasoni-Biondi when he came to Rome in hopes of working out a possible settlement, but that the delegate had said it was better to write Hickey directly. He asked, if Hickey was not coming to Rome for the Holy Year, that he send his response to the Memorial directly to the cardinal prefect of the Congregation. In his reply to Msgr. Gentile on July 27, Bishop Hickey informed him that he had not yet received all the relevant documents in the case, but would respond "in due season" as Gentile asked. He suggested that Msgr. Gentile could profitably speak with Monsignors Bove and Poletti, who could "tell [Gentile] the whole story," and with the Apostolic Delegate to Cuba, Archbishop Pietro Benedetti, who had assured him that he would give Gentile and Msgr. Serafini, the Secretary of the Congregation of the Council, the truth concerning the persons, the charges and the implications of this affair. When Archbishop Benedetti was appointed apostolic delegate to Mexico in 1921, he made the first of what would become regular visits to visit his sister in Woonsocket, where he stayed at Precious Blood rectory. Although an Italian by birth, he was a priest of the Congregation of the Missionaries of the Sacred Heart of Issoudun and had received his formation in French. He was sympathetic to the Croisés when he first visited Woonsocket, but, under Msgr. Dauray's influence, his views changed. Although Benedetti's influence was important, it was the American bishops who visited Rome during the Holy Year that were perhaps Bishop Hickey's most important supporters. In their conversations with Vatican officials in 1925, the bishops stressed the importance of Catholic high schools for the formation of future priests, thus justifying the stress that Bishop Hickey placed on the High School Drive.[55]

Bishop Hickey began drafting his letter to Cardinal Donato Sbarretti, Prefect of the Congregation of the Council, on July 22, 1925, but he did not finish it and send it to the cardinal until November 14, 1925. He first referred to the defeat of the Daignault faction at the Union St. Jean Baptiste d'Amerique convention in Holyoke during October as proof that Daignault did not represent the majority of the Franco-American community. He also pointed out that eight of the men whose names appeared at the bottom of the letter Mr. Daignault sent to Pope Pius XI on January 24, 1923 had since withdrawn their signatures after learning the purpose for which the document they signed was used. Hickey made the point that

[54]   Memoire des Franco-Americains a Sa Saintete Pie XI, 1925, PChA.
[55]   Gentile to Hickey, July 4, 1925; Hickey to Gentile, July 27, 1925, PChA; Rumilly, *Histoire Des Franco-Americains,* 380, 383; *Providence Visitor,* April 22, 1921.

many American dioceses had recently conducted drives aimed at raising substantial sums of money for religious, educational and charitable purposes. In regard to the Providence Drive, he stressed the fact that the monies collected were "not collected in the form of a tax." Rather, the Drive was proceeded by a meeting of the pastors and laymen of the diocese who voted unanimously to have it and who pledged to cooperate in it "by every means within their power." Hickey acknowledged that, although no one opposed the drive at his meeting with the pastors, there were some who were not able to raise sufficient funds to meet the quota given them as a goal through voluntary contributions during the course of the Drive. To help them meet their goal, if they desired to do so, he had authorized these pastors to use regular parish funds. While most parishes did meet their goals, especially after their pastors and Bishop Hickey reconsidered them, and a large majority gave more than was expected of them, only two parishes, both Franco-American, failed to do so because of their objections to the drive.[56]

Bishop Hickey further pointed out what his fellow bishops had already underlined in their conversations with the Roman authorities that, if the Congregation decided that the Drive was not of sufficient importance as to justify his asking the aid of his pastors in raising the funds for it, the decision would undoubtedly "constitute a dreadful set-back to the work of Christian education in the United States." In spite of the interference of "this small and malevolent faction of Franco-Americans," Hickey asserted that the Drive was a magnificent success. He lamented the fact that those who objected to the Drive were aided by two of his priests, Frs. Beland and Prince, who were "famous for their extreme nationalistic prejudices," and who were the pastors of the two parishes named in the Memorial. He added that he had evidence to show that both had acted irregularly in administering their parishes and asked the Congregation's advice as to what he should do in their regard. He ended by revealing something of the man he was by saying, "I feel that it is humiliating to have to answer at length the lying accusations of such a man as Elphege Daignault." He expressed the hope that the Congregation would unanimously refuse to entertain the plea "which, if favorably answered, would leave the Bishops of America disarmed and helpless in the presence of growing evils and menacing persecutions."[57]

Even before Bishop Hickey mailed his response to Cardinal Sbarretti, Christoforo Astorri, Mr. Daignault's Roman lawyer, wrote to Daignault on November 6, 1925, that Bishop Hickey had not yet sent in his response to Daignault's Memorial. He took the opportunity to inform Daignault that it was going to be difficult to sustain the main argument in his Memorial. In

---

56   Hickey to Sbarretti, July 22; November 14, 1925, PChA. In his response, Bishop Hickey certainly did not point out, as Mr. Daignault did in a review of the history of the Sentinellist movement, that this consultation hardly offered an opportunity for a frank discussion of the bishop's proposal.
57   Ibid.

view of the position that the American bishops who had visited Rome had taken in regard to high schools, Daignault's contention that Bishop Hickey had no right to tax the parishes in order to support diocesan high schools would be a hard sell. He suggested to Mr. Daignault, therefore, it would be better for him to stress two other points: that the taxes on the parishes were excessive and that instruction in English was doing damage to the Franco Americans who comprised a large part of the population of the diocese.[58]

On December 9, 1925, Msgr. Gentile acknowledged receipt of Bishop Hickey's response. He praised Hickey for stressing the fact that the monies he asked for from each parishe were not an assessment, which the parishes would be compelled to pay but the anticipated amount that the parish would raise by voluntary contributions. He emphasized in his letter that Hickey could not compel either Notre Dame or St. Louis parishes to meet the quotas assigned to them in the Drive. Since Hickey had said that there was no obligatory tax levied on the parishes, Gentile believed he could argue that there was no violation of law and thus the petitioners did not have a case. When the Congregation met on December 19, Msgr. Gentile's prediction proved true. After examining the Memorial, the Congregation of the Council responded that the Memorial was to be refused and that Frs. Beland and Prince were to be given a warning in the name of the Congregation for the part they had taken in presenting the Memorial. In conveying the good news of the Congregation's decision to Bishop Hickey, Msgr. Gentile stressed what he has said to Cardinal Sbarretti, namely, that the assigned quotas given each parish were goals rather than obligations. When Gentile asked what should be done about the two pastors, he reported that the cardinal has shrugged his shoulders.[59]

While the Sentinellists would have to wait for several weeks to learn the details of the Congregation's decision, it would seem that word of the Congregation's refusal to acknowledge that the Franco Americans had been treated unjustly did reach Mr. Daignault and the Sentinellists in late December or early January. As this attempt to have the Roman authorities intervene in the diocese to protect their parish funds seemed to have failed, pressure continued to build on Daignault to seek justice for the Franco Americans in another way. Among those who had been invited to address the Croisés in reference to the Peck Act by Fr. Prince was Bishop Joseph Prud'homme, the Bishop of Prince Albert, Province of Regina. Fr. Prince introduced him as a leading figure in the French-Canadians' struggle to retain their schools. Bishop Prud'homme spoke about the Canadians' efforts in the Province of Ottawa and urged on the Croisés similar efforts at defending their schools and their traditions. During the course of Bishop Prud'homme's visit to Woonsocket, he went to Mr. Daignault's home to bless his family and his house. While Bishop Prud'homme urged the

58 Cited in Daignault, *Le vrai movement sentinelliste*, 111–12.
59 Gentile to Hickey, December 9, 23, 1925; Sbarretti to Hickey, December 19, 1925, PChA.

Croisés to take action against the incursions of the state on their liberties, others urged the Croisés to also take action against the perceived injustices inflicted on them by the American bishops.[60]

When the Roman authorities did not render a decision on Daignault's Memorial in what they regarded as a timely manner, Daignault, Falcon and Maynard, on December 17, 1925, two days before the Congregation of the Council issued its formal response to his Memorial, wrote a letter to Bishop Hickey informing him that they had been considering for a long time taking civil action against the parish corporations whose pastors had used parish funds to meet their parish goals. "Wishing," as they said, "to act in harmony with the Church's discipline," they informed the bishop that they had asked several canon lawyers if the exemption from being taken to court that a bishop enjoyed personally in Canon Law applied in the case of moral or juridic persons such as the parish corporations. In their letter, they claimed to have a document written by a Roman canonist that a lay person could sue a parish corporation without incurring the penalty of automatic excommunication. Their letter and the declaration that they intended to pursue the question of the legality of the "taxes" imposed on the Franco-American parishes in the High School Drive appeared in the January 7, 1926 issue of *La Sentinelle*.[61]

In his *La Sentinelle* article, Mr. Daignault announced that he had sought the help of a leading law firm in Providence to prepare the court papers he needed. Anticipating the criticism that he should have waited until the Congregation ruled on his Memorial, Mr. Daignault argued that since Bishop Hickey had not heeded the statement the Apostolic Delegate made to him that Bishop Hickey did not have the right to tax the parishes, the bishop was not about to pay more attention to the pope than to his representative. Basing himself on the presumption that Bishop Hickey had not responded to the Congregation of the Council's request for an explanation to mean that the bishop did not intend to respond because he was clearly in the wrong, Daignault concluded that he had no choice but to seek justice elsewhere. In researching his case, Mr. Daignault would later relate how he consulted the works of several leading theologians and canonists, among them the work of Msgr. Louis A. Paquet, whose writing had a major influence on the *Action Francaise* movement in Canada. These authorities served to convince him, he said, that the Sentinellists were in the right when they challenged what they regarded as Bishop Hickey's taxing of parish funds for the high schools. Although he regretted the necessity of taking the parish corporations to court, he concluded that he had to act to defend the parish funds before it was too late. To support his case,

---

60 Rumilly, *Histoire Des Franco-Americains*, 338. The statement about Bishop Prud'homme's visit to Mr. Daignault's home is found in a quote of Mr. Daignault recorded in "Minutes of Croisés Meeting," PChA.

61 *La Sentinelle*, January 7, 1926; Foisy, *The Sentinellist Agitation in New England*, p. 93.

Mr. Daignault had printed, in both Latin and French, the opinion of the Roman canonist whose conclusions he relied upon to justify his action.[62]

Mr. Daignault's Roman lawyer did not learn the details of the Congregation's deliberations until several weeks after Msgr. Gentile broke protocol and conveyed them to Bishop Hickey. When he did write Mr. Daignault concerning the Congregation's decision on March 6, 1926, he expressed his belief that the Congregation's decision was favorable to his client. Since Bishop Hickey had assured the Congregation that contributions to the High School Drive were voluntary and not compulsory, Mr. Daignault, in his lawyer's opinion, had won his case. By bringing the case before the Congregation, Daignault had compelled Bishop Hickey to do what he had asked the apostolic delegate to do, force Bishop Hickey to declare that the Franco Americans were not obliged to contribute to the establishment of the high schools. In view of the fact that the most American bishops believed that high schools were indispensable for defense of the Catholic religion and Catholic morality, the establishment of the voluntary nature of contributions towards their construction was a victory for Mr. Daignault's side.[63]

In retrospect, Mr. Daignault wrote in 1936 that if he had known that Bishop Hickey had been warned to cease imposing taxes on the parishes for the building of high schools, he would probably never have brought the parish corporations to court. In reality, Bishop Hickey only "taxed" two parishes as a result of the Million Dollar Drive, his and Fr. Prince's, and he stopped before he was warned to do so. The warning, when it was given, was given unofficially by Msgr. Gentile in his December 9, 1925 acknowledgment of receipt of Bishop Hickey's response to Daignault's Memorial. The absence of a public reprimand by Rome deprived Daignault of any kind of victory celebration. If the Congregation of the Council's decision was in fact a victory for Daignault and his supporters, it was to prove a Pyrrhic victory. Once having publicly accused the bishop of illegally taking parish funds for the high schools, Mr. Daignault moved the Sentinellists' dispute with the bishop from a private Church matter to another plane. It was one thing to criticize the bishop in regard to the manner in which he assigned priests in his diocese or fault him for not creating new Franco-American parishes that the Franco Americans claimed were needed, as Daignault had done frequently in *La Sentinelle*. It was an entirely other reality to publicly accuse Bishop Hickey of illegally taking money. If Mr. Daignault would have been satisfied with his private victory, perhaps the whole affair would have been remembered as a minor incident in a

---

[62] *La Sentinelle,* January 7, 1926; Daignault, *Le vrai movement sentinelliste,* 150–151. While the canonists Daignault consulted knew Canadian Church law, they apparently did not know American church law, which reflected a different historical experience than that of the Canadian Church.

[63] Cited in Daignault, *Le vrai movement sentinelliste,* 128–30.

series of conflicts between the Franco Americans and the Irish bishops of New England.[64]

The Sentinellist Movement at its Height

In spite of the *La Sentinelle* article in which Mr. Daignault promised to file civil suits against the parish corporations, Bishop Hickey hoped that the decision of the Congregation of the Council against the Memorial had ended the matter. On Friday, January 22, 1926, Bishop Hickey met with Fr. Beland. The bishop let him read the decision of the Congregation of the Council in regard to the protest lodged by Mr. Daignault with its order that Fr. Beland be given a warning. The following day, the bishop also met with Fr. Achille Prince, the pastor of the other parish named in Daignault's petition, and conveyed the congregation's warning to him as well. The two then had a long talk.[65]

Another voice calling for an end to the controversy was heard at the end of January 26, 1926. On that day, the *Woonsocket Call* reprinted in translation an article written by J. B. Couture, the editor of Lewiston, Maine's *Le Messager*. Mr. Couture was one of the Franco Americans excommunicated as result of a controversy with Bishop Louis Walsh of Portland in 1911. Couture had long since been reconciled with the Church. In his article, Couture called on the Franco Americans in Rhode Island to end their warfare against Bishop Hickey and seek other means to secure justice as the Franco Americans of Maine had done.[66]

Mr. Daignault and his associates, however, did not choose to remain quiet and seek other means. They continued to attack Bishop Hickey and the other Irish bishops in New England in the pages of *La Sentinelle* for what they saw as abuses of Franco-American rights. *Le Sentinelle* was urged to continue their struggle by at least one Canadian bishop and several priests. In a letter to Mr. Daignault on February 13, 1926, Bishop Joseph Halle, of Hearst, Ontario, who asked Mr. Daignault not to use his name (a request that Mr. Daignault respected as he did in the case of all the bishops who supported him), encouraged Daignault to continue to send Memorials to Rome signed by important people with their titles and proof of the authenticity of their signatures. He told him he would not get a response but when Rome received five or six of them, the Holy See would secretly investigate the complaints. Mr. Daignault took Bishop Halle's advice and sent off another Memorial in the name of the Franco-American Catholics of the Diocese of Providence, whom he said were experiencing

---

[64] Ibid.
[65] Bishop Hickey's Diary, January 22, 23, 1926.
[66] *Woonsocket Call*, January 23, 1926. Cf. *La Sentinelle*, January 28, 1926 for a response.

trials because of their attachment to their native language. The Memorial, which was signed by Daignault, Dr. J. B. Falcon of Pawtucket, and Leger Morissette of Central Falls, asked that the Holy See investigate the situation that existed in the diocese.[67]

Fr. Lavergne was one of the priests who, in person and by letter, urged the Sentinellists to continue their struggle. *La Sentinelle*, in its March 4, 1926 issue, printed a letter of Lavergne thanking the Croisés for a check compensating him for his services to the order on a recent visit to Woonsocket. The article in which Fr. Lavergne's letter appeared prompted Eugene Jalbert to send a copy to Auxiliary Bishop J. A. Langlois of Quebec. Along with the article, Jalbert sent a letter in which he expressed his dismay that a priest who Langlois had warned not to come to the diocese, had done so. Jalbert said he wrote out of concern for the reputation of the priests of Quebec less they be seen as interfering in the affairs of another diocese and out of concern also that Bishop Langlois not be seen as being mixed up in the Daignault's struggle against Bishop Hickey. He found Fr. Lavergne's continued support of the Sentinellists disturbing in the light of Mr. Daignault's announcement in *La Sentinelle* that he intended to take civil action against the parish corporations.[68]

While the words of support from the Canadian bishops and clergy, as well as from the Franco-American priests who encouraged the Sentinellists, were appreciated, money was also needed if the Sentinellists hoped to receive what they saw as justice. However important it was for the Sentinellists to have a voice, the founding of *La Sentinelle*, at a time when there was not a sufficient a number of subscribers and advertisers to support a weekly, let alone a daily newspaper, created great difficulties. In *La Sentinelle*'s December 10, 1925 issue, Henri Perdriau wrote an article addressed to the paper's "fifteen to twenty thousand" friends and readers. In order to sustain the Sentinellists' struggle, he asked each *patriot* to contribute a dollar. The paper urged the need for its financial support many times but in its March 4, 1926 issue, the directors of the paper made an especially earnest appeal for *Le Dollar du Patriot* in view of the fact that a $1,200 debt was coming due in fifteen days and they lacked the funds to pay it off. In the course of an overview of the agitation, which he would later send to Rome, Bishop Hickey observed that, in order to stimulate contributions for the paper's support, *La Sentinelle* had to stir up the nationalist sentiments of its supporters, "without shame."[69]

La Sentinelle continued to carry articles on what the Sentinellists considered abuses of their rights and threats to their traditions from through-

---

67 Bishop Halle's letter is cited in Rumilly, *Histoires Des Franco-Americains*, p. 391; the Memorial is found in Daignault, *Le vrai movement sentinelliste*, pp. 133–40.

68 *La Sentinelle*, March 4, 1926; Jalbert to Langlois, March 10, 1926, PChA; Rumilly, *Histoire Des Franco-Americains*, p. 390.

69 *Le Sentinelle*, December 10, 17, 24, 1925; March 4, 1926; "Documents au sujet de L'Agitation Sentinelliste, 1922–1927," PChA.

out New England. The French-Canadians' traditional celebration of the feast of St. John the Baptist would provide the next occasion for confrontation between the Sentinellists and Bishop Hickey. In *La Sentinelle's* June 24 and July 1, 1926 issues, Mr. Daignault discussed the difficulties Bishop Hickey caused the Sentinellists when they sought to organize their traditional celebration of the feast of St. John the Baptist that year. On April 25, 1926, Henri Messier, chairman of the Committee of Arrangements, wrote to Fr. Foley, the diocesan chancellor, asking if Bishop Hickey would receive a delegation from two Central Falls councils of the Union St. Jean Baptiste d'Amerique, who were making plans for a state celebration of the feast in Central Falls on Sunday, June 27, and who had invited representatives from other groups to join them in the preparations. Bishop Hickey approved of their plans, which called for a mass in Notre Dame, a street parade and a dinner in the evening to which the organizers invited both Bishop Hickey and Gov. Aram J. Pothier. On receiving his invitation, Bishop Hickey replied that he would attend the celebration if he was not too late in returning from the Eucharistic Congress that was being held in Chicago that year.[70]

Two days after the *Woonsocket Call* printed an article on the arrangements being made for the celebration of the feast in Central Falls, Mr. Daignault wrote to Bishop Hickey in the name of a group of Franco Americans in Woonsocket, who he said represented "all the national Franco-American societies established in the United States," to ask permission to have a mass in St. Ann's Church, Woonsocket, on June 24, "with an appropriate sermon by a priest of our choice, agreeable to Your Excellency." Bishop Hickey, who did not wish to deal with Daignault, had his secretary, Fr. Thomas C. Collins, respond to Daignault that the only way in which the bishop could deal with the various societies was through their chaplains or their chaplain general. In reply, Daignault wrote to Bishop Hickey pointing out that the Irish committee who planned the state celebration of St. Patrick's Day did not have a chaplain, since the committee came together only for the purpose of planning the event, and concluded that Hickey's refusal to deal with his committee could not legitimately rest on the fact that his committee did not have a chaplain. What was really the issue was that in framing his answer as he did through Fr. Collins, Bishop Hickey had underlined the fact that the Canado-Americaine Association, of which Mr. Daignault was president, was without chaplains.[71]

Since Bishop Hickey would not even discuss the question of allowing Daignault's group to sponsor a mass, Daignault was forced to hold his celebration of the feast in Harris Hall, Woonsocket. The main speaker of the evening was Aurelien Belanger, a deputy in the Canadian National As-

70 Henri Messier to Foley, April 25, 1926; Edgar A. Langlois to Hickey, May 28, 1926; Hickey to Langlois, June 3, 1926, PChA; *Woonsocket Call*, June 7, 1926.
71 Daignault to Hickey, June 9, 1926; Collins to Daignault, June 11, 1924; Daignault to Hickey, June 16, 1926, PChA.

sembly from Ottawa, with whose struggle for bilingual schools Mr. Daignault's group had long identified. In announcing the arrangements for the
feast day in Woonsocket in his June 24 article in *La Sentinelle*, Daignault
printed his letters to Bishop Hickey and Fr. Collins' response to his initial
one. The article also noted that Bishop Hickey had asked that high masses
be celebrated in all the parish churches. To Daignault's mind, the reason
the bishop had asked for the masses was because he did not wish the Franco Americans to have a "patriotic sermon." He ignored the fact that the
bishop had granted permission for a mass and sermon during the celebration arranged by the committee headed by the Union St. Jean Baptiste in
Central Falls.[72]

The Central Falls celebration of the feast day took place on Sunday,
June 27, in order to allow Franco Americans from all parts of Rhode
Island, as well as delegations from Massachusetts and Connecticut, to take
part. Gov. Pothier and two of his aides attended the high mass in Notre
Dame at 11:30 and, after dinner in the rectory, the governor rode in the
parade of 4000 Franco Americans, which some 20,000 people assembled
to watch. Following the parade, the crowd gathered for speeches on the
grounds of Notre Dame School. The day's festivities closed with a banquet
in the evening in St. Joseph's Gymnasium at which Elie Vezina was the
main speaker. The committee, which planned the celebration, invited the
various Franco-American organizations to delegate a representative to give
one of the various toasts that came at the end of the meal. Mr. Daignault
delegated himself as the representative of the Canado-Americaine Association. When it came time for him to toast the ladies, he used the occasion to charge the American hierarchy with being the chief obstacle
to the development of the Franco Americans in the United States. As an
example of the obstacles the bishops had created, he cited the closing of
the boarding school at Sacred Heart Academy in Central Falls, the refusal
of Bishop Hickey to allow nuns to staff Notre Dame Hospital and the use
of parish funds without the consent of the parishioners and in defiance
of civil and canon law. His remarks provoked several in the audience to
challenge him publicly. One of them, Guillaume L. Desaulniers, a trustee
of Precious Blood, Woonsocket, and a member of the Mt. St. Charles
Corporation, got up and walked out of the dinner when the crowd booed
his interruption.[73]

During the course of the summer of 1926, Mr. Daignault sought to
resolve the doubts that existed as to whether the canonical privilege of a
bishop's exemption from suits applied to parish corporations of which the
bishop was president. He sought out the advice of Fr. Albert Vermeersh,
a Belgian Jesuit, who was a professor at the Jesuits' Gregorian University
in Rome and an expert in Moral Theology. Fr. Vermeersh, who served as

---

72 *La Sentinelle,* June 24, 1926.
73 *Pawtucket Times,* June 28, 1926; *La Sentinelle,* July 1, 1926.

an occasional consultant at the Vatican, was in United States during the summer of 1926. On hearing of Fr. Vermeersh's meetings with Daignault, Bishop Hickey wrote to Vermeersh asking him about them. On September 20, 1926, shortly before he returned to Europe from New York, Fr. Vermeersh replied to Bishop Hickey that he had met Mr. Daignault several times and found him "personally well disposed." According to information in the hands of one historian, Fr. Vermeersh supposedly reassured Daignault that the privilege of exemption from being cited before the courts applied only to a bishop personally and not to moral persons such as parish corporations.[74]

On October 30, 1926, Mr. Daignault wrote once more to Archbishop Fumasoni-Biondi. In his letter, Daignault reminded the delegate of what he recalled the delegate had said to him during their first meeting in May 1924, namely that Daignault "was a lawyer and should know what to do." Daignault suggested that he understood the delegate's response to mean that he should file suit against Bishop Hickey. Daignault noted that he had consulted a "Roman canonist," whose opinion Daignault enclosed with his letter. In spite of the canonist's favorable opinion, Daignault told the delegate he had heard that his bishop would excommunicate him and his associates if they dared to start civil proceedings against him as head of the parish corporations. He therefore asked the delegate for a meeting to obtain the delegate's "benediction and protection in the procedure we are about to take for safeguarding the rights we consider sacred."[75]

After receiving Daignault's letter, the delegate wrote to Bishop Hickey informing him of the letter and asking what the result of the case presented by Mr. Daignault to Rome had been. Bishop Hickey sent him a copy of the congregation's decision, along with a letter in which he observed that he found it impossible to take Daignault's threat seriously. The bishop believed that Daignault's letter asking for the delegate's protection was "merely a subterfuge employed to throw back upon the Delegate's Office the responsibility for the nonfulfillment of a menace which he has repeatedly and publicly made both by word of mouth and in his weekly newspaper." He informed the delegate that Daignault had told a crowd in Central Falls that he did not expect a favorable reply. He added his assessment that Daignault "was now thoroughly discredited by 99 per cent of the Catholics of his own race in this Diocese, and is no longer taken seriously here." In acknowledging the receipt of Hickey's letter, Msgr. Paul Marella, the delegation's auditor, assured Hickey that the delegation was not taking Mr. Daignault seriously. When on November 19, 1926, the delegate answered Mr. Daignault's letter, he wrote that he had read it with displeasure and that it was a matter of surprise to him that Daignault could claim to be a good Catholic and still be an active participant in the

---

[74]   Vermeersch to Hickey, September 30, 1926, PChA; Rumilly, *Histoires Des Franco-Americains*, p. 395.
[75]   Daignault to Fumasoni-Biondi, October 30, 1926, PChA.

agitation against his bishop. He told Daignault that it was high time that he abandoned his uncatholic agitation and in a spirit of true and practical loyalty that he give his bishop the support he deserved in furthering the cause of the Holy Faith.[76]

In making their assessments of the situation, both Bishop Hickey and the apostolic delegate believed that they could appeal to Mr. Daignault's and his associates' loyalty to the Church. However, the Church to which Mr. Daignault and his associates were loyal was the Church in which the lay person had far more influence than in the United States. On Sunday, November 7, 1926, supporters of Daignault passed out circulars at the doors of Notre Dame, St. John the Baptist, and Our Lady of Consolation churches in Pawtucket, and perhaps others as well, announcing a meeting the following evening in Notre Dame's St. Joseph's Gymnasium to mark *La Sentinelle's* second anniversary. Inside Notre Dame church, Fr. Beland made note of the meeting and urged his parishioners to attend. An account of the meeting, which appeared in *La Sentinelle* on November 11, prompted Elie Vezina to write a letter to Bishop Hickey expressing his dismay that the meeting was held on parish property and that pastors of the diocese had allowed the circulars, advertising a meeting in which religious authority was scorned and Bishop Hickey insulted, to be passed out at the doors of their churches and to thus tacitly give encouragement to the "fomenters of discord and insulters of the Catholic clergy." In his letter he also mentioned that Frs. Beland, Prince, Lavergne and a young priest of the Archdiocese of Boston, who had grown up in Woonsocket, Fr. Georges Duplessis, an assistant at St. Joseph's, Salem, attended the recent celebration of the Canado-Americaine Association's thirteenth anniversary in Manchester, in spite of the fact that Bishop Guertin had removed his chaplains from the organization. In his mind, the presence of priests at such meetings diminished the laity's respect for their bishops when priests they respected and love defied the bishop's authority.[77]

At the request of Msgr. Dauray, on December 3, 1926, Mr. Vezina addressed a similar letter to Archbishops Joseph M. Emard of Ottawa, Georges Gauthier of Montreal and to the newly appointed Archbishop of Quebec, Raymond M. Rouleau, O.P. In each, he called the archbishop's attention to *La Sentinelle* and the repeated attacks of its editor, Mr. Daignault, on the authority of Bishops Hickey and Guertin. He noted that Daignault had made frequent trips to Canada to visit various priests, who had contributed to the financial support of the paper, and, although Daignault had announced his intent to "arraign the Bishop of Provi-

[76] Fumasoni-Biondi to Hickey, November 5, 1926; Hickey to Fumasoni-Biondi, November 11, 1926; Marella to Hickey, November 15, 1926; Fumasoni-Biondi to Daignault, November 19, 1926, PChA.

[77] *La Sentinelle*, November 11, 1926; Vezina to Hickey, November 19, 1926, PChA; Wilfrid H. Paradis, *Upon This Granite: Catholicism in New Hampshire* (Portsmouth, New Hampshire: Peter E. Randall, 1998), 144–145; Chartier, *Histoire Des Franco-Americains*, 151–152.

dence before a public tribunal," these priests continued to contribute to his cause. The result, he suggested, was that the public would conclude that "all episcopal authority had no weight before the opposition of certain priests and the audacity of a few laymen." Mr. Vezina included with his letter a copy of the decree of the Congregation of the Council in which the Congregation rejected Mr. Daignault's Memorial and Archbishop Fumasoni-Biondi's letter to Daignault dated November 19, 1926. While Bishop Hickey had not chosen up to this time to publish the congregation's decree, he had given Vezina permission to show it to anyone interested in the question. In his letter to Archbishop Rouleau, Mr. Vezina made note of Fr. Lavergne's presence, along with that of Frs. Beland and Prince at the thirteenth anniversary celebration of the Canado-Americaine Association at Manchester. He said he found Fr. Lavergne's participation disturbing in light of the fact that Mr. Daignault was reputedly preparing to take Bishop Hickey to court. While Archbishop Gauthier had previously spoken out against those who criticized episcopal authority, Archbishop Rouleau, when Bishop of Valleyfield, had been one of the Canadian bishops who wrote in support of *La Sentinelle* when it first appeared and who had previously expressed his support for the Action Francaise movement in Canada. The archbishop had his secretary acknowledge the reception of Mr. Vezina's letter in a three-line note.[78]

The gathering *of La Sentinelle's* supporters in Central Falls was a prelude to a yet larger gathering at the Joyland amusement hall on Cumberland Hill Road in Woonsocket. On Sunday, December 13, 1926, nearly 1500 Franco Americans from all parts of New England assembled to celebrate the second anniversary of *La Sentinelle's* appearance as a weekly. The main speaker of the evening was Samuel Genest, president of the Commission of Separate Schools in the Province of Ontario. Mr. Daignault acted as master of ceremonies. In the course of his remarks, Daignault charged that two years ago, at the same time *La Sentinelle* first appeared, the Franco-American clergy in the Diocese of Providence was diminishing in numbers, in part, because many Franco-American young men were being refused admission to the diocesan clergy. After making reference to the difficult financial straits the paper had faced two years ago, he expressed his pleasure with the number of people then supporting his paper in spite of the criticism of it.[79]

Prior to introducing the main speaker, Daignault invited Fr. Duplessis, who was one of those seated at the main table, to make a few remarks. Fr. Duplessis quoted Archbishop William Cardinal O'Connell of Boston as urging the support of Catholic newspapers, but stopped short of saying O'Connell supported *La Sentinelle.* He did, however, say that Cardinal

---

[78]   Vezina to Arcbbishop Joseph M. Emard, Georges Gauthier, and Raymond M. Rouleau, December 3, 1926, PChA; Archbishop Rouleau's response is noted in Rumilly, *Histoire Des Franco-Americains*, p. 398.

[79]   *Woonsocket Call*, December 13, 1926; *La Sentinelle*, December 15, 1926.

Begin of Quebec had supported the paper "in its fight against error." He characterized *La Sentinelle* as the most Catholic paper in New England. When it was the main speaker's turn to address the crowd, Fr. Lavergne was greeted with cheers and applause. Lavergne likewise defended *La Sentinelle*, against those who held that the paper lacked charity, attacked authority and caused scandal. He compared *La Sentinelle*'s struggle with one for "Christ and his race." During the course of his remarks, he accused the American bishops of trying to deceive Rome and of conspiring against those who sought to challenge Irish dominance. Although not at the head table, Fr. Beland was among the crowd seated at the banquet tables, having come to the dinner with about three hundred of his parishioners. The dinner and the speeches at it prompted another letter from Mr. Vezina to Bishop Hickey. In it, he again asked the bishop for permission to print the Roman decision issued the previous December as well as the apostolic delegate's letter to Daignault in his organization's bulletin.[80]

Vezina's letter arrived at a time when Bishop Hickey was already thinking about publishing the Congregation's letter. Up to that point he had been reluctant to bring the whole controversy out into the open. His reluctance was motivated, in part, by his hope that Daignault himself would make the congregation's letter public and, in so doing, accept the decision of the Congregation that the bishop had acted correctly in regard to the funds of the parishes. The bishop informed Vezina that he would make his decision on the Congregation's letter in a week or two.[81]

To build up the readership base of *La Sentinelle*, the "Amis de La Sentinelle" continued to organize meetings in various places at which Mr. Daignault was the featured speaker. A second meeting for that purpose took place the St. Joseph Gymnasium, in Notre Dame Parish, on Monday evening, January 24, 1927. Mr. Daignault quickly reviewed the various grievances of the past, which continued to rankle the French Canadians but focused mainly on the current struggle with Bishop Hickey. He spent considerable time discussing his attempts to persuade the apostolic delegate to intervene. He correctly surmised that the delegate and Bishop Hickey had discussed his most recent letter because, in his words, the delegate's response was not written in the ordinary style of a diplomat but in that of a "'policeman' particular to a certain Irish bishop." He ended by announcing that he was ready to seek the justice denied by Rome through the civil courts.[82]

Even before he read of the Sentinellist meeting in Central Falls, Bishop Hickey had reached the conclusion that the agitation would only persist if he continued to ignore it, as Daignault was not about to undercut his support by accepting Rome's decision. On December 5, 1926, Bishop Hickey had written to the apostolic delegate asking for permission to print the dele-

---

[80] Ibid.; Vezina to Hickey, December 20, 1926, PChA.
[81] Hickey to Vezina, December 28, 1926, PChA.
[82] *La Sentinelle*, January 27, 1927.

gate's October 30 reply to Daignault in a French newspaper. After the delegate replied that he would leave the matter to Hickey's prudence, Hickey wrote to him on December 17 with certain materials he wished him to look over before he had them published. The delegate quickly returned them with the hope that their publication would accomplish the purpose Hickey intended.[83]

While copies of Bishop Hickey's December letters to the delegate are not in the Providence Chancery Office files, it is a reasonable surmise that Bishop Hickey sent the delegate a draft of the pastoral letter he was preparing to issue on the Daignault-led agitation. After finishing his draft of the letter on January 18, 1927, Bishop Hickey talked over the letter with Brother Josephus, the director of Mt. St. Charles, and with Fr. Georges Bedard, Msgr. Dauray's nephew and one of the assistants at Precious Blood (Fr. Bedard in effect ran the parish due to Msgr. Dauray's age and poor eyesight). Not having a French-speaking secretary, Bishop Hickey apparently made use of Fr. Bedard's language skills to either translate his English letters into French or edit the bishop's French text. Bishop Hickey's pastoral letter appeared in the *Providence Visitor*'s February 4, 1927 issue. It included in the pastoral's text a copy of Cardinal Sbarretti's letter giving the Congregation of the Council's response to the Daignault Memorial as well as the apostolic delegate's October 30 response to Mr. Daignault. The same day as the *Visitor* appeared, Bishop Hickey also sent copies of his pastoral to the priests of the diocese and to various members of the American hierarchy.[84]

In his pastoral letter, his first since he became bishop, Bishop Hickey spoke of his hope that, in the months since the Congregation of the Council had reached its decision in regard to Daignault's protest, "the fruits of prayer and reflection would have brought the leaders thereof, and their comparatively few followers, to clearer views and more Catholic sentiments." Having waited patiently for Daignault to announce to his supporters Rome's reply, Hickey said he felt it necessary for him to print the reply, as well as that of the apostolic delegate, with his admonition that Daignault cease his agitation against his bishop. The bishop urged those who had allowed themselves to become involved in the agitation against their bishop "through a baseless fear concerning rights which they justly hold dear" to heed the delegate's admonition. In concluding his letter, Bishop Hickey spoke of his confidence that his prayer to the Holy Spirit, that he might enlighten the minds of "these victims of dissension," had been heard and again voiced his hopeful view of the situation that the "contagion seems to have been checked." Bishop Hickey asked his pastors to read the letter or have it read at all masses on Sunday, February 6 "in the language best known to the people of the parish." The day before the

---

[83]   Fumasoni-Biondi to Hickey, December 10, 20, 1926, PChA.
[84]   Bishop Hickey's Diary, January 28; February 4, 1927; *Providence Visitor*, February 4, 1927.

letter was to be read, Hickey held a meeting of all the Franco-American clergy in the diocese to explain to them what to do with the letter.[85]

While Daignault had been publicly criticizing Bishop Hickey and other bishops for their alleged infringements on the rights of Franco Americans, the English language press had for the most part ignored the whole agitation. The silence of the local newspapers ended with the printing of the bishop's pastoral. Not only did the Rhode Island papers print the pastoral, but the *New York Times* ran a small article on the controversy in the second section of its Sunday edition on February 6. Three days after Bishop Hickey's pastoral was read in all the parishes, Ernest Boddington of *Commonweal*, then a relatively new Catholic journal, called on the bishop to obtain background information on the agitation. Before joining *Commonweal*, Mr. Boddington had been press director for the National Catholic Welfare Conference. His article on the Daignault movement appeared in *Commonweal*'s March 2, 1927 issue.[86]

On the Friday that the bishop's letter appeared in the *Visitor*, the *Providence Journal* sent a reporter to get Mr. Daignault's reaction to it. Daignault said that, while his Memorial seeking recourse against what he called the "taxes" and what the bishop would call "a quota or a goal" that had been imposed by the bishop on the parishes was signed by only a few Franco Americans, those few represented all the Franco Americans in the diocese. Rather than being convinced by the bishop's letter to end his struggle, he continued to promise that he would file suit against the parish corporations, which had sent funds to the bishop without the permission of the people.[87]

The priests of the diocese dutifully read the pastoral letter as asked by the bishop. One, Fr. Alphonse Graton, the pastor of St. John the Baptist, Pawtucket, broke down while reading the letter and wept. When he attempted to comment on the letter, all he could say was, "It is regrettable," and then could not continue. Most priests chose to let the letter speak for itself and not comment on it. That was the case in Notre Dame, Central Falls. Most of those who did comment on the letter pointed out that the question had been brought before the highest authorities in the Church and, since the Memorial had been refused, acceptance of the decision was the only thing a good Catholic could do. In St. Ann's, Woonsocket, where Mr. Daignault attended mass, Fr. Villiard urged his people to follow the bishop's directions and added, "It would be a danger for the faith if the people were led astray." One of the most forceful comments on the letter was given by Fr. Napoleon Plasse, an assistant at St. Louis's, Woonsocket, whose pastor, Fr. Achille Prince, was a known supporter of the Sentinellists. Fr. Plasse warned his congregation that Daignault and his followers

---

85   Ibid.; Bishop Hickey's Diary, February 5, 1927.
86   *New York Times*, February 6, 1927; Bishop Hickey's Diary, February 9, 1927; *Commonweal*, March 2, 1927; *Providence Visitor*, March 4, 1927.
87   *Providence Journal*, February 5, 1927.

faced excommunication if they pursued the civil suits against the parish corporations as Daignault had promised. While unreported by the press, several of the bishops to whom Bishop Hickey sent copies of his pastoral, among them Archbishop Austin Dowling of St. Paul and Auxiliary Bishop Emmanuel A. Deschamps of Montreal, sent letters of support.[88]

The publication of Bishop Hickey's pastoral letter provided justification also for a change in policy on the part of *La Tribune*, *La Sentinelle*'s rival in Woonsocket. After Guatave Hurel, the editor in chief of *La Tribune*, died the day after the Union St. Jean Baptiste Convention ended at Holyoke, the owners of the paper hired Albert Foisy, the former editor of *La Sentinelle*, to replace him. Mr. Foisy, who, as editor of the *Le Bulletin* in Fall River, had already written in defense of Bishop Hickey's administration of the diocese and his pastoral care of the Franco Americans, was seen as a traitor to their cause by those associated with *La Sentinelle*. On March 8 and 9, Foisy announced in *La Tribune* that henceforth his paper would give its version of events that *La Sentinelle* reported. In the months and years that followed, *La Tribune* offered numerous articles, many of which were reprinted in the *Providence Visitor*, in which the paper attacked the Sentinellists and their methods. Mr. Foisy's mentor and guide in the controversy with *La Sentinelle* was Fr. Georges Bedard, Msgr. Dauray's nephew, and the priest to whom Bishop Hickey turned for information and assistance more than any other during the course of the struggle.[89]

In addition to writing the pastoral letter, Bishop Hickey, on Saturday, January 29, 1927, summoned Fr. Beland to a meeting with him in his office. In the presence of Fr. Peter A. Foley, the chancellor, and Fr. Thomas C. Collins, the assistant chancellor, Bishop Hickey read to Fr. Beland a list of charges against him and his administration of Notre Dame. Among them, Bishop Hickey accused him of conspiring "with French-Canadians doctors to defeat the Bishop's desire to be the responsible head" of Notre Dame Hospital and of aiding and abetting "a conspiracy of laymen to nullify a collection in favor of Catholic High Schools." The bishop also faulted him for allowing his parish hall to be used for the November 8, 1926 meeting in support of *La Sentinelle*, and for the meeting of "discontents" on January 24, 1927 at which Mr. Daignault presided. He further expressed his displeasure that Fr. Beland was present at the banquet in honor of *La Sentinelle*'s second anniversary at the Joyland in Woonsocket. The bishop allowed Fr. Beland to read the list of particulars after which he imposed a penance of ten days retreat at the Recollects in Canada.[90]

88   *Providence Journal*, February 7, 1927; *Pawtucket Times*, February 7, 1927; *Woonsocket Call*, February 7, 1927.
89   *La Tribune*, March 8, 9; April 9, 23, 1927; Rumilly, *Histoire Des* Franco-Americains, pp. 388; 391–92; Richard S. Sorrell, "*La Sentinelle* and *La Tribune*: The Role of Woonsocket's French Language Newspapers in the Sentinelle Affair of the 1920s," in Claire Quintal, ed., *Steeples and Smokestacks: A collection of essays on the Franco-American Experience in New England* (Worcester, Mass.: Institut francais, Assumption College, 1996), 342–356.
90   Statement in Beland file, Sentinellist Papers, PChA.

A few days before his meeting with Fr. Beland, Bishop Hickey received a note with enclosures from Cardinal Rouleau of Quebec. After the banquet marking *La Sentinelle*'s second anniversary, Mr. Vezina, as noted above, had again written to Cardinal Rouleau protesting Fr. Lavergne's presence and his remarks. The enclosures Bishop Hickey received concerned an inquiry the cardinal's secretary had made into Fr. Lavergne's presence at the *Sentinelle* celebration in Woonsocket on December 12 and as to whether or not Lavergne gave the speech attributed to him in *La Sentinelle*'s December 16 edition. Fr. Lavergne acknowledged that he had been in Woonsocket and that the first part of the speech attributed to him was accurate, but that the latter part was not, since it was lacking the nuances and the qualifications he had made. He explained to the priest making the inquiry that Cardinal Begin had given him written permission to leave the diocese whenever he was invited to speak. In his letter to Fr. Lavergne after reading his response, Cardinal Rouleau informed him that since he was now a pastor, the former permission he had received was no longer valid. Furthermore, he expressed his regret that a priest, especially a stranger, should publicly attack a bishop of another country.[91]

On February 10, four days after Bishop Hickey's pastoral letter was read from the pulpits of the diocese, Mr. Daignault printed a front page editorial in *La Sentinelle* in response to the pastoral. Since Bishop Hickey's letter had made the controversy more public than it was, Mr. Daignault had now to reconcile certain apparent contradictions in the statements he had made. In his editorial, Daignault says he did not make the response of the Sacred Congregation of the Council to his Memorial public because he believed such matters were to be kept quiet. Daignault devoted the bulk of his editorial to the delegate's November 19, 1926 letter, which charged him with conducting an "uncatholic agitation." Since he had previously suggested that it was the delegate who had implied that he should file suit against Bishop Hickey, he had to explain the delegate's change of attitude. He included in his editorial a letter that he wrote to the delegate on February 8, 1927 in which he protested that the delegate's letter had in no way replied to his and that the delegate's view of his conduct was based on misinformation. (He did not suggest at this time that it was Bishop Hickey who supplied the misinformation but he would do so later.) In continuing to promise to bring suit against his bishop, he asserted that he was only doing his duty, as an American citizen, to see that laws were respected. He continued to assert that his intentions were honorable and in accordance with the dictates of his conscience. He further placed the blame for what would follow on Bishop Hickey for his failure to formulate a plan that would protect the interests of the Franco Americans. To support this statement, he quoted from a letter he had received from Rome in November

---

91   Rouleau to Hickey, January 25, 1927, with enclosures, PChA. The reference to Vezina's letter to Rouleau, December 22, 1926, is found in Rumilly, *Historie Des Franco-Americains*, p. 400.

1925 informing him that the bishop had been advised to formulate such a plan. He ended by once more appealing to the opinion of the canonist, whose views he had cited in *La Sentinelle* previously, that the privilege of exemption from suit applied to the bishop personally and not to the bishop as head of the parish corporations, in order to justify his course of action in "serving the cause of the church and the cause of our race."[92]

In retrospect, it seems clear that Mr. Daignault had made the threat to take his case to the civil courts primarily as a way of convincing the authorities in Rome that they had to take the initiative in the working out of a settlement of the dispute over the use of parish funds acceptable to both sides and, secondarily, as a way of sustaining the enthusiasm of his followers. As a lawyer, he knew that the Rhode Island law governing the parish corporations had been written in such a way as to favor the bishop's authority. He also knew that several American canonists had disputed the advice his Canadian canonist had given. While he assured his readers and the audiences he addressed that he would win his case if he did bring it before the courts, as a Catholic he was reluctant to take the step since he was convinced that Bishop Hickey would seek to have him excommunicated, regardless of what the canonists whom he had consulted told him. On November 21, 1926, he had again written to Canon Gignac to ask his advice. Fr. Gignac assured him that a bishop was not able to declare those who filed suits excommunicated *ipso facto*. A bishop might threaten excommunication but the petitioners had a right to appeal to the Holy See, during which time the sentence would be suspended. With the reading of the Bishop Hickey's pastoral, Daignault felt he now had no choice but to file the suits as he had been promising to do. The consequence of not carrying through on his promise would have been the loss of his credibility as a leader in "the struggle."[93]

The Filing of the Suits

When *La Sentinelle* appeared on February 3, 1927, the day before Bishop Hickey's Pastoral Letter appeared in the *Visitor*, as a way of explanation for the lack of any articles on the controversy, it carried a notice on its front page that Mr. Daignault was devoting himself exclusively to preparing the civil cases he intended to file against the Franco-American parish corporations. On Saturday, February 12, Henry M. Boss, Jr., a Providence lawyer who was an associate in the law firm of Curtis, Matteson, Boss and Letts, filed bills of complaint in the Superior Court in Providence against ten of the parishes. Each of these bills was signed by five members of the parishes

---

92   *La Sentinelle*, February 10, 1927; *Providence Journal*, February 10. 1927, reprinted Daignault's letter
      to the delegate in English translation.
93   *La Sentinelle* discussed the law under which the diocese was incorporated in its June 30, 1927 issue.
      Gignac's letter to Daignault is printed in Rumilly, *Histoire Des Franco-Americains*, 401–02.

cited. The bills named the trustees of each parish, among them Bishop Hickey, as president of each corporation, as defendants in the suits. A week later, two more bills were filed for a total of twelve out of the sixteen Franco-American parishes in the diocese. Except for the names of those involved, the bills were exactly the same. They charged the defendants with a violation of the bylaws of the church corporations by diverting money from the parish's funds to build schools outside of the parish, to support the *Providence Visitor* and to fund the National Catholic Welfare Conference. The bills asked that the court summon the respondents so that they may be made to give an accounting of the funds of the various parishes.[94]

Bishop Hickey addressed the question of the suits at the eleven o'clock mass in the cathedral on the day after the bulk of the suits were filed. Before reading the gospel, he advised the people of the cathedral and, through them, of the diocese to await calmly the outcome of the suits in equity against the parish corporations. He emphasized in his remarks that he did not want to see the men who had signed their names to the complaints excommunicated. But he went on to say that the decision, as to whether or not a person was excommunicated in such cases, was not up to him. Under canon law any person who prosecuted a suit against the Church in the civil courts stood excommunicated, *ipso facto*, just as soon as the case was carried through to a conclusion. He expressed his belief that the "wayward children of the church" who had brought the suits were few in number and they were identified with organizations which themselves represented only a small proportion of the parishes to which they belonged. He concluded that the people of the diocese needed to take no counter or public action, but to rely on the justice and good sense of the state courts and on God.[95]

A few weeks after the suits were filed, a *Providence Journal* reporter, who wished to know more about the threat of the excommunication that Daignault and the other signers of the suits faced, arranged an interview with the bishop. Following the filing, Bishop Hickey wrote to Msgr. Paul Marella, the Apostolic Delegation's Auditor, informing him of Daignault's action and asking his opinion of Daignault's present church standing in regard to the *privilegium fori*. He told Marella that he did not wish to excommunicate anyone "as this would only perpetuate present conditions." Marella consulted with Msgr. Filippo Bernadini, a canon lawyer at Catholic University, and relayed his response to the bishop. Drawing on this expertise, Bishop Hickey explained to the reporter, as he had to the cathedral

---

94   *La Sentinelle*, February 3, 1927; *Woonsocket Call*, February 12, 1927; *Providence Journal*, February 12, 13, 1927. The parishes cited in the suits were St. John the Baptist, Arctic; St. Matthew's, Central Falls; St. James, Manville; St. Cecilia's, Pawtucket; St. John the Baptist, Pawtucket; Our Lady of Consolation, Pawtucket; Our Lady of Good Counsel, Phenix; Our Lady of Victories, Woonsocket; Precious Blood, Woonsocket; St. Louis, Woonsocket; and St. Ann's, Woonsocket; Holy Family, Woonsocket.

95   *Pawtucket Times*, February 14, 1927; *Providence Visitor*, February 18, 1927.

congregation, that, while a person was liable to excommunication when he cited a bishop before a civil court, the penalty was not incurred until the offending party pushed the case to a conclusion.[96]

After Daignault filed the suits, Bishop Hickey immediately proceeded to hire legal counsel to defend himself and the parishes. The seriousness with which he took the suits was indicated by the fact that he engaged three lawyers from three different law firms, Patrick P. Curran, John P. Deagan, and John H. Slattery, to undertake the legal defense of the diocese. He met with the three lawyers he engaged on Monday, February 14, to begin discussion of the suits. In addition to the lawyers the bishop also accepted the volunteered services of two Franco-American lawyers, Eugene Jalbert and Adonat J. Demers. Each of the individual parishes named in the suits also had to hire counsel. In order to hire counsel and authorize the payment of their fees from parish funds, each corporation had to hold a special meeting. These meetings took place in the chancery office on February 17 and 18.[97]

Bishop Hickey did not choose to discuss the motivation for the suits other than to say that he believed that there was "a great deal of animosity" connected with their filing and that the suits had their origin in "personal disappointment." However, an unnamed diocesan authority, in an interview with the *Providence Journal*, declared that "one of the motives prompting Mr. Daignault's suits was resentment on the part of the Woonsocket lawyer that Bishop Hickey had not helped him secure a position on the Superior Court bench at the time there was a judgeship vacant and at which time Judge A. A. Capotosto was appointed to the post." He said that he believed Daignault was extremely resentful of the fact that the Bishop of Providence was of Irish descent, and not a prelate of French extraction and that he was "one of those Frenchmen who believe that the French parishes and the French schools of the diocese are a separate entity." He further added that "Daignault is hitting directly at the Bishop of the diocese because he believes that the diocesan head has stood in his way in many things." On his part, Daignault called the diocesan official's statement that he had sought the bishop's help "absurd" and took issue with other parts of the official's statement.[98]

Fr. James P. O'Brien, the editor of the *Providence Visitor*, who had to respect the bishop's wishes in regard to what appeared in the paper and the subject of his editorials, expressed his relief, in speaking of the Daignault suits, that he had no longer "to suffer in silence the avalanche of abuse and libel which this irresponsible, fanatical, and intolerant individual had

---

[96]   Hickey to Marella, February 12; March 3, 1927; *Providence Journal*, March 6, 1927.
[97]   *Providence Visitor*, editorial, February 18, 1927; Bishop Hickey's Diary, February 14, 15, 17, 1927; *Providence Journal*, February 18, 1927.
[98]   *Pawtucket Times*, February 14, 1927; *Providence Journal*, February 15, 16, 1927. Mr. Daignault did acknowledge that two Irish pastors in Woonsocket supported him when he was a candidate for the judgeship.

heaped upon the chief pastor of the diocese." He said that Bishop Hickey had chosen not to speak out in his own defense up to the present because he did not want to make Daignault a hero in the minds of "the professional and avowed defamers of everything Catholic." Fr. O'Brien asserted, however, that bishop's primary motive for not speaking out against his detractors was that, as the pastor of all in the diocese, he did not want to "fan the flames of rebellion in their hearts." He too found the root of the attacks on the bishop in personal animosity harbored by Mr. Daignault against him.[99]

Eugene Jalbert, who had frequently opposed Mr. Daignault's views in regard to the relation of the Franco Americans and their bishops, issued a statement, which was printed in *La Tribune* on March 2. He remarked that it apparently had taken many of the Croisés by surprise that the Franco-American parishes cited by Daignault had chosen to defend themselves "accustomed as they are to seeing their Grand Master speak and act with no one to contradict him." He found the civil suits a calamity. To his mind, all that Daignault had accomplished by his agitation was to deepen the split that existed in the ranks of the Franco-American laity.[100]

One of the Franco-American priests who chose to speak on the issues raised by Bishop Hickey's pastoral was Fr. Napoleon Plasse, who had been, up to the time of the publication of the bishop's pastoral, one of the strongest in his condemnation of the agitation against the bishop. Because of his comments from the pulpit, Fr. Plasse received a phone call the next day in which the caller threatened "to get him." He challenged the caller to carry out his threat in his sermon delivered on February 21 and charged Daignault with attacking the character of priests who opposed him and with falsifying statements they made. He returned to the same theme on the following Sunday after Mr. Daignault replied to his comments through the pages of *La Sentinelle.*[101]

While Daignault and his associates expected that Bishop Hickey and some of the Franco-American clergy would challenge and criticize their actions, they were surprised when some of the French-Canadian papers supported Hickey, while the rest remained silent. *La Presse* of Montreal and *Le Devoir* both printed Bishop Hickey's pastoral letter, and both refused, as did all the other French-Canadian Catholic papers, to print a response which Daignault sent them. Following the filing of the suits, *La Tribune* of Woonsocket and *L'Avenir National* of Manchester, both of which had defended bishops Hickey and Guertin against attacks on them in *La Sentinelle*, challenged Daignault's claim that he had support among the French-Canadian bishops as did *La Patrie*, another Montreal paper. In an article in *La Sentinelle*, Daignault listed the "desertion" of the French-Canadian

[99] *Providence Visitor*, February 18, 1927.
[100] *La Tribune*, March 4, 1927.
[101] *Providence Journal*, February 21, 28, 1927; *La Sentinelle*, February 17, 1927.

cause by the Canadian newspapers, proven by their "conspiracy of silence" in not printing his reply to the pastoral letter, as one of the many
causes of his sadness in the wake of the filing of the suits. Later in a speech
on March 8, he dismissed the action of the Canadian papers as being of
little importance.[102]

Mr. Daignault did not remain quiet in the face of criticism. Even before
the suits against the parish corporations were filed, he gave the *Providence
Journal* a copy of the legal opinion by the Roman canonist that he had
previously printed in *La Sentinelle* as justification for what he was about
to do. On February 14, the same Sunday that Bishop Hickey made his
comments on the suit in the cathedral, Mr. Daignault and his supporters held a rally in Joyland hall, which drew a crowd, which the *Journal*
estimated at 3,000 people, the *Woonsocket Call* at 4,000, and *La Sentinelle* as
being almost 5,000. By this time in the agitation, the leaders of the struggle
against Bishop Hickey had formed a Committee of the National Cause in
order to direct the effort. Daignault, who was to be the principal speaker
at the Joyland rally, received a warm welcome from the crowd, which had
come from New Hampshire and Massachusetts as well as Rhode Island.
Daignault began his address by making a profession of faith in the Catholic Church to make it clear that his cause was not anti-Catholic. Turning
next to the letters he and Mr. Astorri had exchanged over the last few
years, Mr. Daignault acknowledged that he was aware of Bishop Hickey's
willingness "to discontinue the method of campaigning for funds followed
in the great drives for Catholic diocesan high schools." However, since the
Roman courts had not ruled on the legality of the bishop imposing "a
direct tax upon the parishes," he saw nothing improper in asking for a
hearing of the question before the civil courts. He even thanked the bishop
for being a booster of his cause by citing the fact that within five or six
week of the Federation Catholique Franco-Americaine convention at Willimantic, the circulation of *La Sentinelle* had an increase of 2,000 and that,
since last Sunday, circulation of the paper had increased from 10,000 to
15,000. The last speaker of the evening, Dr. C. T. Mathieu, gave a short
history of the oppression experienced by the French Canadians over the
last three centuries. In response to Bishop Hickey's published statements
that the supporters of Daignault's cause were few in number, he warned
Bishop Hickey not to think of those who were campaigning for what they
saw as their rights as only "a handful of kickers."[103]

Mr. Daignault was not the only Sentinellist to be applauded that evening. When Fr. Beland returned to Central Falls after his retreat in Canada, a large number of his parishioners gathered in the church for the Ves-

---

[102] *Providence Journal*, March 9, 1927. The *Providence Visitor*, on February 18 and 25, 1927, carried
excerpts from the articles of the various French newspapers. Cf. also Rumilly, *Histoire Des Franco-
Americains*, p. 410–11.

[103] *Providence Journal*, February 8, 14, 1927; *Woonsocket Call*, February 14, 1927; *Pawtucket Times*,
February 14, 1927; *La Sentinelle*, February 17, 1927.

pers service. A committee of women had canvassed the parish in order to raise funds for a purse and gifts, which they planned to present Fr. Beland in honor of his thirty-fourth anniversary of ordination. Since Bishop Hickey had made it clear to Fr. Beland that he did not want the parish's facilities to be used for large gatherings, the committee and the parishioners who wanted to honor Fr. Beland attended the Vespers service. At the close of the service, they presented him with a purse of $3,500 in gold, a silver loving cup and a large bouquet of roses. After leaving the church, the committee held a reception for Fr. Beland in the rectory in order to accommodate the hundreds of parishioners who wished to pay their respects to their pastor. Dr. Arthur J. H. Falcon, one of the speakers at the rally in the Joyland Hall later that same evening, recounted the details of the reception in his address to the crowd at the Joyland.[104]

The rally at the Joyland was followed by a similar one in Manville that took place after Mr. Daignault returned from a trip to Canada. Mr. Daignault was again the main speaker at a rally held in the Music Hall on March 8. In the week before the rally, the acting pastor of St. James, Manville, Fr. Francois Desmarais, had castigated Daignault and the Sentinellists as outsiders who came to Manville to "act against the Church, the Bishop and regularly constituted authority after they had been denounced by the Church, by the people and the Canadian press, and the national societies." Mr. Daignault made it his first order of business to deny Fr. Desmarais' charge that his movement was "diabolical" because it had been denounced by the Church and by the people. As proof of the last, he pointed to the more than six hundred who had crowded the Music Hall to hear him. He also denied the charge made earlier by Fr. Napoleon Plasse that he had made his recent trip to Canada to consult with the Canadian bishops as to whether he should continue the suits he had filed. He related that, while on the train to St. Hyacinthe, he had met with a Canadian bishop who assured him that the Canadian episcopate was altogether with him in the fight. He went on to criticize Bishop Hickey, whose plan to build high schools in the diocese was "coarse theft," and the apostolic delegate for his failure to respond to the Sentinellists complaints.[105]

Mr. Daignault was not back in Woonsocket from his trip to Canada but a few days when his court case suffered a setback. On March 1, 1927, Henry W. Boss, Jr., the co-counsel he had engaged to help him in the filing suit against the twelve parish corporations, withdrew from the case citing personal reasons. According to Mr. Daignault, Mr. Boss returned the $2,500 retainer Daignault had given him because he had been threatened and because he believed they could not win the case if Irish Americans were a part of the jury. In making his announcement of the filing of the suits in the cathedral, Bishop Hickey has said that those seeking equity

---

104 *Pawtucket Times,* February 14, 1927.
105 *Providence Journal,* March 7, 9, 1927.

before the courts were "being represented by a well-known firm of non-Catholic lawyers. You know the names of the lawyers, and you know them well." Eight days after he made this comment, Vincent McMahon, called on Bishop Hickey to assure him that Mr. Letts, another of the partners, would not participate in the proceeding Daignault had initiated. When a week after Mr. McMahon's visit, Mr. Boss announced his withdrawal as co-counsel, he said that his action had been actuated solely "by personal reasons, the principal being the fact that certain of the members of the law firm with whom I am associated are opposed to my continuance in the case." He prefaced his remarks by saying that his action should in no way be construed as an expression of opinion regarding his client's case. The *Providence Visitor*, however, observed that the position of the "Crusaders" was generally believed to be weakened by Mr. Boss' withdrawal. Rather than engage other counsel, Mr. Daignault would tell an audience of 3,000 in the West Warwick village of Arctic the following Sunday, that he felt confident in his ability to take care of the cases by reason of twenty-five years of practice.[106]

Both the supporters of the Sentinellists and of Bishop Hickey would find that there was a price to be paid for their loyalty. The printing of Bishop Hickey's pastoral letter in the pages of *L'Union*, the publication of the Union St. Jean Baptiste d'Amerique, prompted some individual members of the society to resign their membership. One of those who chose to do so was Fr. Louis E. Raymond, chaplain of Sacred Heart College, Sharon Heights, Massachusetts, who had been one of the priests at the head table in Joyland Hall the previous December. In an open letter to Mr. Vezina, which was printed in the *Providence Journal* among other papers, Raymond submitted his resignation and announced his intention of joining the Canado-American Association. Another of the priests who attended the anniversary dinner at the Joyland and one of the speakers of the evening, Fr. Georges Duplessis, submitted his resignation a week later. In addition to the printing of the bishop's pastoral, other members of the Union objected to Eugene Jalbert, the Union's legal advisor, taking on the responsibility of defending several of the Woonsocket parishes cited by Mr. Daignault and his continuing vigorous denunciation of the Sentinellists in the pages of *La Tribune* and elsewhere.[107]

Both Mr. Jalbert and Mr. Vezina defended themselves against the accusations of the Union's dissident councils and those of Daignault. In an interview given to the *Providence Journal*, Mr. Vezina charged Daignault with unethical conduct in advising members of the society to resign and affiliate with the Canado-Americaine Association of which he was president.

---

[106] *Pawtucket Times*, February 14, 1927; *Providence Journal*, March 2, 7, 1927; *Providence Visitor*, March 4, 1927; Bishop Hickey's Diary, February 22, 24, 1927; Daignault, *Le vrai movement sentinelliste,*, 153–54.

[107] *Providence Journal*, March 3, 1927; *Providence News*, March 11, 1927; *La Tribune*, March 2, 1927; *Providence Visitor,* March 4, 1927.

He further justified his decision to print the pastoral in *L'Union*, for which he had authorization in advance from the organization's executive committee, both in his interview with the *Journal* and in the February number of *L'Union*. He said that it was the decision of that society's executive committee that the better course of action was "to follow the example of the Franco-American priests rather than support the President of the Canado-Americaine Association in his mad defiance of religious authority.[108]

The supreme officers also had their defenders and supporters among the various councils. As the number of councils of the Union who voted to censure its supreme officers grew, the Union's Board of Directors met for a special meeting in the Union's headquarters in Woonsocket on March 29 to consider the charges and formulate a response to them. After reviewing the movement initiated by Mr. Daignault and hearing from Jalbert and Adonat J. Demers as to their reasons for accepting the charge of defending the Franco-American parishes in Woonsocket against the suits, the directors voted to endorse the policies pursued by the executive officers of the Union and endorse Jalbert's and Demers' decision to aid the parishes sued. In large part, because of the stand taken by its supreme officers, membership in the Union, which stood at around 52,000 before the Congress at Holyoke in October 1925, fell to 51,669 on January 1, 1927, to 50,945 on June 1, 1927, and then to less than 50,000 by the end of the month. But, there were also rewards for loyalty. Following the Union's Holyoke convention in 1925, Bishop Hickey had helped Mr. Vezina obtain a special papal blessing for the order, which had pledged its devotedness to the Church at the close of the convention.[109]

Criticism of Vezina and the Union's other officers was but one of the initiatives on the part of the committee that had undertaken the direction of the struggle against Bishop Hickey. Their main effort was the organization of a series of meetings, which began in Providence on March 17 and extended to most of the places in Rhode Island where there were large numbers of Franco Americans, as well as to Massachusetts and New Hampshire. At each meeting, there would be a core of Sentinellists to ensure that the speakers and their message were enthusiastically received. The ostensible reason for undertaking this series of rallies was to afford Mr. Daignault and his associates the opportunity of explaining why they had taken the radical step of charging the parish corporations with violations of the law before the courts. The rallies also had the practical purpose of helping to raise funds to support the committee's efforts in Rhode Island. In a rally at Worcester, on April 3, 1927, Fr. Duplessis gave a résumé of the Sentinellist doctrine in four points: The inviolability of parish funds; the continuing need for new national parishes; opposition to the opening of

---

[108] *Providence Journal*, March 12, 1927.
[109] *Woonsocket Call*, March 11, 12, 16, 26, 29, 30; April 7, 1927; *Providence News*, 12, 24, 1927; Rumilly, *Historie Des Franco-Americains*, p. 414.

bilingual schools without respect for the rights of parents in the matter of education; and opposition to Americanization in the sense advocated by the National Catholic Welfare Conference. As the series of meetings continued, various speakers also sought to arouse their audiences with comparisons to the past struggles of the Canadians for their rights and liberties. A favorite recollection in word or song was the Papineau revolt against the British in Canada in 1837. The speakers followed these reviews of the past with a call to the Franco Americans to defend their liberties anew against the many transgressions by the Irish-American bishops. The meetings of the "Friends of *La Sentinelle*" attracted large crowds. At Lowell, Massachusetts, on May 15, a crowd of between six and seven thousand people assembled to hear the speakers.[110]

After having received reports on the Sentinellists' meeting in Worcester, Elie Vezina made another attempt to have the priests of Cardinal O'Connell's diocese silenced. After the Sentinellist meeting at the Joyland in December 1926, Vezina had sent copies of the newspaper account of Fr. Duplessis' remarks regarding Cardinal O'Connell's alleged sympathy for the Sentinellist movement to the cardinal. Bishop Hickey would leave such correspondence with Cardinal O'Connell to laymen because of the tensions that existed between the majority of the bishops in New England and the cardinal. A serious rift had developed in 1921 between the majority of the New England bishops and the cardinal in reaction to the manner in which Cardinal O'Connell had handled a scandal involving his priest nephew, James P. E. O'Connell. At the same time that Bishop Hickey was seeking to bring an end to the Sentinellists' agitation by publishing Rome's response to Daignault's Memorial and the apostolic delegate's letter urging him to cease his agitation in his pastoral letter, Mr. Vezina asked Fr. Rodolphe Fortier, pastor of St. Anne's church, Salem, Massachusetts, and chaplain of the Franco-American Catholic Federation, to call on Cardinal O'Connell to ask him not to allow his neighbor, Fr. Duplessis, to leave the Diocese of Boston "to stir up trouble among the Catholics of Rhode Island." After the Sentinellists' Worcester meeting at which Duplessis, whom the cardinal in the meantime had transferred to Lowell, was again a featured speaker, Vezina again asked Fr. Fortier to call on the cardinal to complain of the conduct of Fr. Duplessis as well as that of Fr. Joseph D. Binette, who had also addressed the Worcester rally. After his meeting with the cardinal, Fr. Fortier reported to Vezina that the cardinal had reprimanded the priests, but that no further action would be taken. He also noted that the cardinal "entertained the hope that the movement would quiet down if one ceased to feed it with replies and discussion." Vezina made another attempt to persuade the cardinal to personally intervene

---

[110] Accounts of the out of state rallies can be found in *La Sentinelle:* Fall River, March 24; Worcester, April 7; Lowell, May 19; Nashua, May 26; Berlin, June 2; Dover and Salem, June 9, 1927; Rumilly, *Histoire Des Franco-Americains,* pp. 409, 413.

when on April 13 and on May 11, 1927, he wrote him "on behalf of Msgr. Dauray" to ask the cardinal to denounce the revolt directed by Daignault "with the moral and financial support of several of the priests of your diocese." The cardinal did not send a reply. When Fr. Duplessis was again a featured speaker at the St. John's Day celebration in Fall River in June, Mr. Vezina once more asked Fr. Fortier to call on the cardinal to register yet another protest.[111]

The collections to support the cause that were taken up at each of the rallies offered the Sentinellists' opponents an opportunity to turn the tables on Mr. Daignault. Writing in *La Tribune* in 1926, Mr. Jalbert had begun asking Daignault for a similar accounting of the monies contributed to the cause that Daignault was asking of Bishop Hickey. When *La Tribune* intimated that the money raised in the "Dollar for the Patriot" drive was to be used to pay legal fees, Mr. Daignault had countered the charge by first threatening and then actually suing the paper for $100,000 in damages, a tactic common among Rhode Island politicians. In the April and May 1927 issues of *La Sentinelle*, the paper began acknowledging contributions "for the suits," a development noted and commented on by *The Rhode Islander*.[112]

The chief remedies that Daignault offered to redress the grievances of the Franco Americans were the exposure of those injustices in the pages of *La Sentinelle* and the pursuit of justice through the civil suits. On June 2, 1927, his colleague, Henri Perdriau, in a front page article in *La Sentinelle*, offered another. In Perdriau's view, the ultimate remedy for the grievances of the Franco Americans was for Rome to create a separate ecclesiastical province for the Franco Americans in New England headed by a French-Canadian bishop with jurisdiction over all the Franco-American parishes. The idea was not original and was one that the American bishops had consistently rejected over the last fifty years. It had resurfaced in an article written by Msgr. Paquet, in an October 1926 issue of *La Canada Francais*, which *La Sentinelle* reprinted in two installments in December of the same year.[113]

Although Mr. Daignault and the committee in charge of organizing the various rallies continued to hold meetings to explain why Mr. Daignault had put himself and those who signed the complaints against each of the parishes at risk of excommunication, Daignault allowed the February 26 date, which he specified in his suit as the date on which those cited would

---

[111] Rumilly, *Histoire Des Franco-Americains*, 400; Mr. Vezina's letters are also cited in Rumilly, 402–03; 410, 411, 415. Fr. Duplessis's change of assignment does not appear to have been a punishment. For the rift between the New England bishops and Cardinal O'Connell see James M. Toole, *Militant and Triumphant: William Henry O'Connell and the Catholic Church in Boston, 1859–1944* (Notre Dame: University of Notre Dame Press, 1992), pp. 195–196.

[112] *Rhode Islander*, May 20, 1927.

[113] *La Sentinelle*, December 2, 9, 1926; June 2, 1927. On the idea of national dioceses, Cf. Rory T. Conley, "Simon Peter Cahensly," in Michael Glazier and Thomas J. Shelley, *The Encyclopedia of American Catholic History* (Collegeville, MN: The Liturgical Press, 1997), 183–184.

have to appear in court to answer the complaint, to pass without arranging with a sheriff to serve the bishop and the other officers of the parish corporations with summonses. Daignault claimed that his failure to have the subpoenas served was due to the withdrawal of his counsel. The failure to arrange for the serving of the summonses, however, prompted Eugene Jalbert to write an article that appeared in *La Tribune* on April 12, 1927, charging that the suits were a "monumental bluff." He declared that Daignault "sits back and laughs and mocks those who applaud him." Believing that the agitation was a ploy to secure money for his newspaper, he said, "Daignault and his followers continue to hold meetings while dollars are coming in by the thousands." By delaying the cases, Mr. Daignault ensured that they could not possibly come up for a hearing during the current court session since the bishop's attorneys could be expected to file a demurrer. As one observer noted, this then gave Mr. Daignault all summer to continue to put pressure on Bishop Hickey for some sort of compromise.[114]

When on April 19, the Catholic Club and the Catholic Woman's Club honored Bishop Hickey at their annual reception for him, the Catholic Club's president, Charles H. Kiernan, expressed to the bishop the readiness of both clubs to support the coming Catholic Charity Drive. The bishop had previously announced that the new drive would be held in May to aid the various works and institutions of charity in the diocese. He promised he would see it through to a successful termination regardless of the "peculiar crisis in the diocese." In his response to Mr. Kiernan's remarks, Bishop Hickey thanked the two clubs for the cooperation they had given him during his eight years as bishop and gave a rare glimpse of his own personal view of the agitation:

> Whatever is going on in the diocese, I am sure it is passing. It was all due to a misconception, a misunderstanding.
>
> But we cannot go out into the streets or into the newspapers and say that this is wrong, that is a misunderstanding, and the other is due to a misconception. To do so would be only to cheapen ourselves . . .
>
> Such a crisis is not confined, in its action, to a certain class. Some of it is in a particular group. Some in those whose longing for worldly grandeur or political preference surpasses the goodness of their hearts.
>
> I believe that those who stir up agitation are sometimes negative instruments in the hands of God. We were in danger of growing proud and puffed up; of attributing to ourselves our accomplishments.

The large crowds attracted to the Sentinellists' out-of-state meetings would

[114] *La Tribune*, April 12, 1927; *Providence News*, April 13, 1927; *The Rhode Islander*, August 19, 1927.

show that the optimism that Bishop Hickey expressed at the reception as to the early end of the agitation was unfounded.[115]

On May 3, 1927, Mr. Daignault announced that he was giving the summonses he had promised to a Woonsocket Deputy Sheriff for immediate service. The sheriff served the first summonses, which had a return date now of May 20, on Bishop Hickey and Msgr. Blessing, as they were part of each parish corporation. The law provided that, after the defendants filed their answer to the complaint on May 20, they then had thirty days in which to file a demurrer or response to the complaints filed. On June 1, seven lawyers, Patrick P. Curran, John B. Beagan, John H. Slattery, Eugene L. Jalbert, Adonat J. Demers, Henry J. Blais, Jr., and Edward De V. O'Connor, notified the Superior Court that they would appear for the defendants. Rather than force an early hearing of the case, the bishop's lawyers decided to take as much time as they deemed necessary to prepare their response to Daignault's complaints. After several preliminary meetings, the lawyers gathered on June 11 to consider and approve a final draft of their response. Bishop Hickey then convened a meeting of the twelve pastors involved in the suits at the Chancery Office to have the pastors sign the Demurrer. The bishop's lawyers filed their Demurrer, which had thirty-two points, on June 19. The case was given to Judge Willard B. Tanner, the same judge who had presided over the case charging the previous general officers of the Union St. Jean Baptiste with infractions of the society's charter of incorporation in 1910. On July 2, Judge Tanner met with the lawyers for both sides and, since the court was about to rise for its summer vacation, the bishop's lawyers asked for a date in the next session of the court. Judge Tanner agreed to the request and set September 19 for a hearing of the case.[116]

Beginning in February 1927 and for the next two years, Fr. Georges Bedard's name appears in Bishop Hickey's Diaries as having met with the bishop more than any other Franco American. Brother Josephus frequently accompanied Fr. Bedard when he met with the bishop, and Fr. James P. O'Brien, the editor of the *Visitor*, was often at the meetings as well. These three, along with the bishop, orchestrated the diocese's response to the continuing agitation.[117]

Since there were many among both the Franco-American clergy and

---

[115] *Providence* News, April 20, 1927; Providence *Journal*, April 20, 1927; *Woonsocket Call* April 20, 1927; *Providence Visitor*, April 22, 1927. Articles in *The Rhode Islander*, July 8, 15, 1927 continued to exhibit the same optimism. The author cites numerous cases, similar to Daignault's, where the courts ruled in favor of the Church.

[116] *Woonsocket Call*, May 3, 6; June 18, July 5, 1927; *Providence Journal*, May 6; June 19, 1927; Curran to Hickey, June 8, 23, 1927, PChA.

[117] Bishop Hickey's Diary, February 15, 22, 24, 26; March 3, 6, 7, 9, 10, 11, 31; April 9, 11, 18, 29; May 3, 13, 27; June 7, 18, 22; July 11, 15, 21, 31; August 4, 19, 23, 30; September 9, 10, 16, 19; October 1, 3, 1927. There are no entries in Bishop Hickey's Diary after October 9 for the remainder of 1927. Fr. Bedard's name continues to appear among the few entries Bishop Hickey made in his diary in 1928.

laity who believed that the tack taken by the Sentinellists was wrong and hurtful to the Church, conscience moved many to keep Bishop Hickey reasonably well informed about what was happening among the Sentinellists. On December 13, 1926, Bishop Hickey summoned Fr. Achille Prince to his office in order to ask him whether it was true or not that he had furnished Fr. Lavergne hospitality on the night he attended and spoke at *La Sentinelle*'s second anniversary dinner. The next morning he was said to have allowed him to say mass in St. Louis "even though it was common knowledge that Fr. Lavergne did not enjoy the faculties of the Diocese." Fr. Prince admitted that he had done as the bishop said.[118]

On March 15, 1927, after having had reports that laymen were taking up a special collection in Notre Dame church for the building of the new church Fr. Beland had planned and was depositing the money in an account which they controlled, Bishop Hickey called Fr. Beland in and asked him for an explanation. Before the meeting ended, the bishop secured his consent to preach "on the supremacy and authority of the Holy See, and hence on the authority of the Episcopate in the diocese." After his meeting with Bishop Hickey, Fr. Beland made a deliberate effort to avoid any further confrontations with his bishop.[119]

Mr. Daignault, who had claimed he was acting in the name of the Franco-American clergy, continued his attacks on the Church of Providence. In an April 14, 1927 article in *La Sentinelle*, he advised the Franco-American Catholics in the diocese not to contribute to the first Catholic Charity Drive, which Bishop Hickey had scheduled to begin on May 16. Fr. Beland and the two trustees of Notre Dame had been present at the general meeting to organize the Charity Drive on April 6 and supposedly voted along with the other pastors and trustees to hold the Drive. During the month of May, Daignault returned to the subject twice more in *La Sentinelle*. Like the Catholic High School Drive, the Charity Drive was to run for ten days. Daignault pointed out that the Franco Americans in the diocese constituted five-elevenths of the total Catholic population, and that there were only two specifically Franco-American charitable institutions in the diocese out of twenty-four. If distributed proportionally then, much of the money that the Franco Americans would give would go to non-Franco-American institutions. This was something that he was personally opposed to.[120]

The Catholic Charity drives were organized in the same way as the previous diocesan drives, except that this time, no specific goal was set for the diocese or for the individual parishes. On May 2, when Notre Dame Parish held a meeting in the parish hall to select a general committee and

[118] Memo, Fr. Prince's file, PChA.
[119] Bishop Hickey's Diary, March 15, 1927.
[120] *Evening* Bulletin, 7, 1927; La *Sentinelle*, April 14, 1927; May 5, 12, 1927; *La Tribune*, April 21, 22, 25, 26, 1927. The *Worcester Sunday Telegram* noted that all the pastors and trustees of the French-speaking parishes in the diocese supported holding the Charity Drive, April 10, 1927.

organize the teams that would do the actual collecting, Fr. Beland was sick and was unable to attend. His three assistants represented him. When the lay president of the meeting asked for general comments, some among the parishioners announced that they would not give to the drive because their subscriptions toward their new church had sufficiently taxed their finances. A motion was made from the floor that the members of Notre Dame take no active part in the drive and was carried by a large majority. Following the meeting, some parishioners began circulating two petitions. The first said that the signers would do nothing to support the charity drive, and the second said that the signers were ready to support their pastor in his protest against the closing of Sacred Heart College and in his desire to have a Catholic hospital in the parish conducted by Catholic nuns. Despite the reported two thousand signatures on the two petitions, Fr. Beland announced on Friday, May 6, that the Catholic Charity Drive would be held in the parish.[121]

Although one of the larger parishes in the diocese, the contributions of the parishioners of Notre Dame were relatively few so that the parish was not even acknowledged in the final report of the Drive. Although the bishop optimistically hoped to see the drive top $500,000, a sum which would have supplied funds to replace inadequate and outdated structures, Bishop Hickey found the $347,361.12 contributed to the Drive and to the Easter Collection in the various parishes, which also went to the Charity Fund, to be sufficient to meet the current needs of the diocesan institutions. In the May 26 issue of *La Sentinelle*, Mr. Daignault called the Drive a "fiasco" when compared to the sums realized by other recent Catholic and Protestant charitable drives in the state. He saw two benefits coming out of the drive's failure: one, that the Franco-American institutions would once again be able to conduct their own fund-raising drives, and second, that the lack of success would serve to convince Bishop Hickey to stop the financial measures which were ruining the diocese.[122]

On June 4, 1927, the bishop met with Fr. Prince again and asked him, as he had of Fr. Beland, to speak to his people on their duty to respect episcopal authority. He specified that Prince was to inform them that the Daignault agitation was "unhealthy" and that they were "on the wrong track following those agitators." He was to do this in a sermon of at least four typewritten pages, which he was to submit to the bishop. Since a prominent member of his choir, Theodole Hemond, the brother of Phydime Hemond, frequently sang at the meetings of the "Friends of the Sentinelle" between speeches, the bishop also told Fr. Prince that Mr. Hemond was no longer to be given solos. Since it was a matter of considerable prestige to sing solos, the bishop added, "If [Mr. Hemond] is not satisfied, let him leave the choir." A short time earlier, Bishop Hickey also informed Fr.

---

121 *Woonsocket Call*, May 6, 1927.
122 *Providence* Visitor, May 27, 1927; La *Sentinelle*, May 26, 1927.

Camille Villiard, the pastor of St. Ann's, that he was to dismiss his organist, Emile Brunelle. Mr. Brunelle had been traveling with Mr. Daignault to play the piano and accompany singers, like Mr. Hemond, between the speeches given at the Sentinellists' rallies.[123]

The tension that existed between Frs. Beland and Prince and their bishop came to a head at the end of the first session of priests' retreats that since 1925 were held at Mt. St. Charles. On June 25, the last day of the retreat, all the priests were to receive communion at the mass offered by Bishop Hickey. Both Fr. Beland and Fr. Prince chose not to do so. When asked by the bishop why they had acted as they had, they explained they intended to say mass in their parishes when they got home. Bishop Hickey informed the two that since they had not sought permission from him, he regarded their actions as "a continuance of their insubordination to authority" and that he was suspending them from all priestly ministry for one month.[124]

Part of Bishop Hickey's concern about the fact that Frs. Beland and Prince wished to say mass in their parishes was perhaps motivated by a desire to see the feast of St. John the Baptist pass without providing any occasion for Mr. Daignault to again use a church celebration as a forum for his criticisms. Mr. Daignault and his associates marked the observance of the feast on Thursday, June 23, with a banquet and speaking program at the Joyland Ballroom. Although no priests of the diocese were present at the dinner, two Canadian priests from the Diocese of Nicolet were seated at the speakers table and four priests from the Archdiocese of Boston were there as well. Among those present was Fr. Duplessis, who gave the talk in honor of St. John that evening. Mr. Daignault was again among the featured speakers. In his remarks, Daignault reiterated his intention of pursuing the suits he had filed against the twelve parishes in order to force them to account for all parish monies. He also made reference to Fr. Villiard's "release" of his organist, Mr. Brunelle, and urged his fellow parishioners of St. Ann's to refrain from contributing to the parish to protest Fr. Villiard's action.[125]

Word of Fr. Beland's and Fr. Prince's suspension spread quickly through their respective parishes and the Franco-American community. The *Woonsocket Call* ran a story about the suspension of the two priests in its Monday, June 27, edition and the *Providence Journal* ran one that focused on Fr. Beland's suspension on Tuesday. In both newspaper accounts, the reporters noted the speculation current in the community that the priests were sus-

[123] Bishop Hickey's Diary, June 4, 1927; Memo, June 4, 1927, PChA; Paul A. Bourget and Donald L. Hoard, *Towers of Faith and Family: St. Ann's Church, Woonsocket, Rhode Island, 1890–1990* (State College, PA: Jostens Printing and Publishing, 1990), p. 67.
[124] Memo, Frs. Beland's and Prince's files, PChA.
[125] *Woonsocket Call,* June 24, 1927; *Providence Journal,* June 24, 1927; *Providence News,* June 24, 1927. For a discussion of Mr. Daignault's charges concerning Mr. Brunelle and Fr. Villiard, Cf. *La Sentinelle,* June 9, 16, 1927 and *Rhode Islander,* June 17, 1927.

pended because they had "lent their influence to the spread of the movement led by Mr. Daignault" and because of "the poor showing made by
Our Lady of the Sacred Heart and St. Louis parishes" in the Charity
Drive. Both articles reported also that Fr. Beland and Fr. Prince planned
to appeal their suspension to the apostolic delegate. The delegate was not
in Washington when the two priests called during the second week in July.
They were received by Msgr. Marella, the delegation's Auditor. After hearing them out, Msgr. Marella advised them to go home and apologize to
their bishop for what they had done. Both priests, however, continued to
insist they had done nothing wrong and informed Msgr. Marella that they
had each appealed their suspension to Rome, which they did in a letter to
Pope Pius XI signed on July 4, 1927. Like the news of their suspension, a
report of their appeal to the delegate and Msgr. Marella's reply also became public information by early September at least.[126]

On Thursday, June 30, a crowd of nearly seven hundred women from
the five Franco-American parishes in Woonsocket gathered in DeNevers
Hall to consider a response to Fr. Beland's and Fr. Prince's suspensions.
Herve J. Lagace presided at the meeting and Phydime Hemond was the
main speaker. Before introducing Mr. Hemond, Mr. Legace spoke of the
suspension of the two priests and urged the women not to contribute to
any of the collections in their parishes as a protest against the suspension.
Mr. Hemond reviewed the history of the Franco-American parishes in
Woonsocket and stressed the conditions, which he asserted led to the filing
of the church suits. In his remarks, he recalled the efforts of the parishioners of St. Ann's in 1914 to keep the Marist Fathers from taking charge
of that parish, which had included a pew-rent strike, which, he claimed,
had led to Bishop Harkins' giving them the French-Canadian priests they
demanded. Mr. Legace presided at a second meeting in DeNevers Hall a
week later at which Mr. Daignault was also one of the speakers. He spoke
of his plans for yet another series of meetings, this time to protest the
suspension of the two priests, which would start in two weeks. He urged
his listeners not to give a cent to the church "without knowing where our
money goes."[127]

At one of the meetings promised by Mr. Daignault held in Woonsocket,
nearly a thousand people, according to the *Woonsocket Call*, representing
twenty-two parishes in the diocese, gathered in DeNevers Hall in order to
organize the protest against the suspensions. The representatives agreed to
form parish committees to decide from week to week what course of action they would take. While the majority favored continuing the contribution strike until such time as Bishop Hickey altered the policies to which

---

[126] *Woonsocket Call*, June 27, 1927; *Providence Journal*, June 28; September 5, 1927; Prince and Beland
to Pope Pius XI, July 4, 1927; J. A. Basinee, S.S. to Hickey, August 3, 1927. Fr. Basinee gives
Hickey information about the visit of Frs. Beland and Prince to the delegate after having had a
conversation a few weeks later with Msgr. Marella.

[127] *Woonsocket Call*, July 1, 1927; *Providence News*, July 1, 8, 1927.

the Sentinellists objected, at least some at the meeting favored continuing the contributions strike until such time as Bishop Hickey was removed from the diocese.[128]

The protest meetings reached a kind of climax on Sunday, July 24, 1927. A crowd of "several thousand" people gathered around the bandstand in Cass Park, Woonsocket, for a mass meeting sponsored by Mr. Daignault and the Sentinellists. Laure Lussier reviewed the list of the Sentinellists' grievances, which now included the suspensions of Fr. Beland and Prince, the "supplanting" of Emile Brunelle as organist at St. Ann's and the withdrawal of permission from Theodule Hemond to have solos in St. Louis. Because of the condition of his voice, Mr. Daignault did not give one of the main addresses, but he read the Franco-American Catholic Manifesto, which he had prepared for the meeting. The manifesto reviewed the condition of the Franco Americans in the diocese from the Sentinellist perspective and called on the Franco Americans "to abstain completely from turning money into parish funds, either by paying pew rent, or contributing to collections or other parochial organizations." After reading the manifesto, Mr. Daignault evoked a storm of approval when he stated that "a radical change was needed in the diocese and that it could come only with the removal of the present bishop." Mr. Daignault then asked the crowd if they approved the manifesto. After a "roar of assent" followed the question, the manifesto was declared adopted as representing the attitude of the twenty-two Franco-American parishes of Rhode Island.[129]

The Sentinellists held their meeting in Cass Park on the day that they did to counteract the impact of the dedication of the new headquarters of the Union St. Jean Baptiste. On July 24, 1925, three bishops—Bishops Hickey and Guertin and Auxiliary Bishop Alphonse Emanuel Deschamps, Auxiliary Bishop of Montreal—honored the Union St. Jean Baptiste by their presence at the dedication of the organization's new national headquarters building on Monument Square in Woonsocket. The day began with a parade from the new building to Precious Blood church, where Bishop Deschamps celebrated mass while Bishops Hickey and Guertin sat in the sanctuary and state and local dignitaries joined the congregation. Msgr. Victor Primeau, a chaplain of the order from Illinois, preached at the mass and he pleaded for concord and unity among the Franco Americans. During the course of the mass, in what was in those days an unusual feature for a layman, Mr. Henri T. Ledoux, the president of the order, mounted the steps of the altar and, after disavowing the action of the two thousand members who had recently left the order in what he saw as an attack on Bishop Hickey, he pledged obedience, fealty and devotion from every member of the order. Several thousand people gathered in Monu-

[128] *Woonsocket Call*, July 19, 1927; *Providence News*, July 19, 1927.
[129] *Woonsocket Call*, July 25, 1927; *Providence Journal*, July 25, 1927; *La Sentinelle*, July 28, 1927.

ment Square for the dedication of the new building and the speeches by
church and civil officials that accompanied it. In the evening there was
a fireworks show followed by an outdoor dinner, which the Union's officers hosted, on the grounds of Mt. St. Charles. At the dinner, all three
of the bishops present for the dedication spoke. Bishop Hickey began his
address by saying that he did not fear schism among the Franco Americans because he was confident that they "were too devoted to their religion to allow [them]selves to be drawn away from the religion of Franco-
Americans." He also praised the leaders of the Union for the success of
their society. Bishop Guertin, in turn, urged respect for episcopal authority
as did Bishop Deschamps.[130]

It might well have been the coincidence of the protest meeting that
prompted Philippe Boucher, one of the owners of *La Tribune* and its publisher, to persuade Bishop Hickey to hold a press conference at five o'clock
on the same afternoon as the mass celebrating the dedication of the new
headquarters of the Union St. Jean Baptiste. While Bishop Hickey had up
to this time refused to reply to the specific complaints of Mr. Daignault
and the Sentinellists, he agreed to take questions from the dozen reporters who gathered for the conference, some of whom had been present
at both the dedication of the Union's headquarters and the rally in Cass
Park. With Bishops Guertin and Deschamps and Msgr. Dauray present,
Bishop Hickey, in response to the reporters' questions, denied, among
other things, any discrimination on his part against the Franco-American
community in the diocese or any hostility toward them in relation to the
closing of the boarding school at Notre Dame, Central Falls, and the circumstances surrounding the failure of the Notre Dame Hospital in Central Falls to secure nuns to run that institution. Bishop Hickey also took
issue with the census figures cited by Daignault and others to stress the importance of the Franco Americans in the state. While Daignault put their
number at 120,000 and claimed that they constituted a majority of the
Catholic population of the state, Bishop Hickey asserted that there were
80,000 French Canadians and Franco Americans, while English-speaking
Catholics alone numbered 130,000. In response to the charge that he had
ordained only two Franco-American priests for the diocese, which was
taken as proof of his prejudice against the Franco-American clergy, Bishop
Hickey responded that twelve had been ordained and that he had more
Franco-American priests than he had parish assignments in which to place
them. When one reporter asked Bishop Deschamps how many Canadian
bishops approved of Daignault, Bishop Deschamps replied that there were
none to his knowledge.[131]

The Sentinellists could not let the Bishop Hickey's statements go un-

---

[130] *Providence Journal*, July 25, 1927; *Woonsocket Call*, July 25, 1927; *Providence Visitor*, July 29, 1927.

[131] *Providence Journal*, July 25, 1927; *Woonsocket Call*, July 25, 1928; *La Sentinelle*, July 28, 1927; *The Rhode Islander*, August 5, 1927.

challenged. Since Mr. Daignault continued to give his time to the preparation of the civil cases, it fell to Henri Perdriau to compose *La Sentinelle*'s response. Mr. Perdriau was a better polemicist than a reporter. In challenging Bishop Hickey's statement that he had never attempted in any way, however slight, to interfere with the teaching or use of French, Perdriau charged that, while pastor in Gilbertville, Hickey had replaced the Sisters of St. Anne with the Sisters of Mercy, "an Irish community, who have never wished to teach a word of French." A simple phone call to Gilbertville or a consultation of a Catholic directory would have elicited the information that Hickey had asked an international order, the Faithful Companions of Jesus, whose members were fluent in both French and English, not the Sisters of Mercy, to replace the Sisters of St. Anne when they left. In fact, three of the five sisters who came to the parish were French Canadians. In like fashion, Perdriau used the rest of the article to offer evidence to disprove Bishop Hickey's other statements, which, to his mind, were also suspect as to their veracity or at least open to dispute. At the end of his article, he addressed Bishop Deschamps' statement that he did not know of any bishops in Canada "who approved of Daignault." Mr. Perdriau responded that more Canadian bishops supported Mr. Daignault than those who did not. However, on this point where he was on solid grounds, the force of his response suffered because discretion prevented him for using the names of specific bishops.[132]

For completely other reasons, Mr. Perdriau refused to use the name of the reporter who posed the questions at the news conference to Bishop Hickey so that he would not "soil" the pages of his paper. The reporter Perdriau referred to was Jean Sabate, who worked for the new weekly publication *The Rhode Islander*, which made its appearance on Friday, May 6, 1927. Beginning with the paper's second issue, Mr. Sabate had subjected the Sentinellists to an ongoing criticism of their aims and deeds. In the first of the articles he wrote on the Croisés, he asserted that "representative men of the French race" had no sympathy with the Croisés, and used the comparison, which had first appeared in an editorial in a Franco-American newspaper, that the Croisés were modeled after the Ku Klux Klan since the Croisés wished to preserve Canadian religion in the same way that the Klan sought to preserve American religion. He furthered asserted that the Sentinellists did not represent the sentiments of the majority of Franco Americans in New England. This last point was an important one. If the Sentinellists were to convince Rome to force a settlement on Bishop Hickey as they firmly believed Rome would, it would be because they represented a majority of the Franco Americans in New England rather than a rebellious faction. In only a few months, Sabate's articles, offering English translations of *La Sentinelle*'s articles and coming as they did

---

[132] *La Sentinelle*, July 28, 1927.

the day after *La Sentinelle* appeared, had already caused a deep rift between himself and the Sentinellists.[133]

On July 31, the first Sunday following the adoption of the Franco-American Catholic Manifesto with its call to abstain from contributing any monies to the Franco-American parishes, Fr. Gedeon Laverdiere, the pastor of Holy Family Church, Woonsocket, who was one of the younger pastors in the city and who had publicly spoken out against the Sentinellists, elected to change the way seat money was collected in his church. Rather than have himself, his assistants or designated collectors take up the collection during the mass as was traditional in the Franco-American parishes, he had the fifteen-cent seat money collection taken at the doors of the church. Any who refused to pay were not admitted. There were also policemen at the doors to keep order. Between fifteen and seventeen people were turned away when they refused to pay.[134]

When the parishioners of Holy Family left church that Sunday, they could easily see a hand-painted sign across the street on the lawn of Dr. A. H. Monty's home, announcing a meeting at two o'clock in nearby Fairmount Park, to hear "protests against the present abusive regime." When the first speaker, Dr. A. J. B. Falcon of Pawtucket, began his remarks, there were about 300 or 400 people gathered in front of a flatbed truck, which served as speakers' platform. Fr. Henri Vincent, one of the assistants at Holy Family who had strongly criticized the Daignault group in his sermon, pushed his way to the front of the milling crowd and began to challenge the speaker. Dr. Falcon responded by saying that they had a priest there who was "Irish and not Franco American," a frequent rebuke addressed at the bishops and clergy who opposed the Sentinellists. When he went on to say, "There are cowards among the clergy, and here is one," his remark was met by calls to cease talking, while others cheered. Fearing for Fr. Vincent's safety as some continued to boo and hiss and others clapped, the police who were at the rally shoved their way through the crowd and stood around Fr. Vincent. When Dr. Falcon tried to continue his speech, Fr. Vincent's partisans continued to interrupt him. After Dr. Falcon gave up his attempt at speaking, Mr. Daignault climbed up on the truck bed and likewise attempted to speak. His speech was interrupted and kept short by both Fr. Vincent and his fellow assistant, Fr. Joseph Baril, who harried him with questions. At this juncture, another of the Sentinellists, Herve Lagace, arrived with a permit for the meeting in the park. When he asked the police to "put the priests out," the policemen refused to put their hands on a priest. Fr. Vincent continued to challenge the statements of both Legace and Phydime Hemond when each of them took a turn at speaking. All

---

133 *The Rhode Islander*, May 13, 1927 and subsequent weeks. The following month Mr. Sabate filed a libel suit against Daignault, Perdriau and *La Sentinelle* after Perdriau indirectly charged that Sabate had been writing articles opposing Mr. Daignault's campaign that appeared in *La Tribune*. Cf. *Woonsocket Call*, June 23, 1927; *Providence Journal*, June 24, 1927.

134 *Providence Journal*, August 1, 1927.

during the exchange between the speakers and the priests, various voices in the crowd also were heard supporting either the priests or the speakers. In the opinion of the *Woonsocket Call*, it was only the presence of the police officers at the rally that prevented serious trouble.[135]

The following Sunday, August 7, the Sentinellists held another protest meeting, this time on the Fournier Plat, near Park Square. The meeting attracted a crowd, which a reporter for the *Providence Journal* estimated at about 1200. The same reporter noted that the crowd was made up both of supporters of the Sentinellists and others who came "merely to see the fun." Although a deputy chief had said earlier in the week that he expected that the law-abiding citizens at the meeting would help to keep order, policemen were stationed around the grounds to keep order if necessary. To the probable disappointment of some, only one dissenting voice was heard from the crowd, which was otherwise content to let the speakers have their say. When a *Woonsocket Call* reporter later asked Holy Family's Fr. Laverdiere about the legality of his action, Laverdiere removed one cause of discontent when he decided, in the light of the small number who had refused to pay, that the collection of seat money at the door was not necessary and returned to the traditional method of taking the collection on the following Sunday.[136]

At the beginning of September, Bishop Hickey provided yet another cause for Sentinellist protest, when he relieved Fr. Prince of his duties as pastor of St. Louis, Woonsocket. After Bishop Hickey had taken away his authority to celebrate the sacraments for one month on June 24, 1927, Fr. Prince had met with Bishop Hickey on July 19 to discuss the conditions on which the bishop would remove the suspension. He urged Fr. Prince to publicly condemn and denounce Daignault, Hemond and Legace. Furthermore, he urged him to resign his parish and to go back to Canada. When Fr. Prince declined to do so and said he was ready to again take an oath of obedience, Bishop Hickey gave him specific directions as to what he wished to see Fr. Prince do about the people associated with him in his parish whom the bishop knew to be Sentineliists or sympathetic to their cause. Bishop Hickey spoke with Fr. Prince again on August 19 to once more admonish him and give him direction.[137]

Despite his willingness to accede to most of what Bishop Hickey asked, Fr. Prince remained committed to the Sentinellist cause. By calling for a halt in contributions to the Franco-American churches, Mr. Daignault had

[135] *Woonsocket Call*, August 1, 1927; *Providence Journal*, August 1, 1927; *Providence News*, August 1, 1927.

[136] *Woonsocket Call*, August 4, 8, 1927; *Providence Journal*, August 8, 1927; *Providence News*, August 8, 1927; *La Sentinelle*, August 11, 1927. Both the *Call* and the *News* said that there was a large crowd present. *La Sentinelle* gave 10,000 as the estimated number of those present.

[137] Bishop Hickey's Diary, July 19, 23, 1927; Fr. Prince File, PChA. Rumilly, *Histoire Des Franco-Americains*, p. 410, notes that, during this time, Fr. Prince consulted with Canon Gignac and wrote to Fr. Vermeersh in Rome, and that he also went to see Cardinal O'Connell, who afforded him a "sympathetic welcome." He cites a letter of Fr. Prince to Fr. Vermeersch, dated July 17, 1927 that he found in the private archives of Antonio Prince as his source.

created financial problems for both friendly and hostile pastors. In the face of the strike, Fr. Prince grew concerned that he would not have enough money to pay the interest on his parish's outstanding bank loans and that his failure to pay the interest would give Bishop Hickey further cause of complaint against him as a poor administrator. Fr. Prince's solution to his difficulty was to reincorporate the *Institut St. Joseph,* which had formerly existed in the parish, and to place it under a treasurer who was to take charge of the money collected at every mass by a group of forty collectors. By reviving the *Institut,* Fr. Prince hoped that the people would give to help support the church and yet be assured that Bishop Hickey would not get his hands on the money. Fr. Prince announced his collection plan at the masses on Sunday, August 28, and said that women of the parish, who would be canvassing the parish selling tickets for a clambake, would provide more information for those who wanted it. The clambake Fr. Prince spoke about was to be held on Labor Day on the grounds of the new Our Lady of the Assumption parish, which Cardinal O'Connell of Boston had created a few weeks before in the southern part of Bellingham and appointed as pastor Fr. Joseph-Donat Binette, a priest who had long been a public supporter of the Sentinellist cause. The parish included many families among its parishioners, who had previously worshiped at St. Louis. The clambake was to be a thank you to the people of St. Louis for the help they had given to the parishioners of the new parish in the past. Fr. Prince announced from the pulpit that the proceeds from the one dollar ticket for the clambake were to go to St. Louis's St. Vincent de Paul Fund. However, it was widely believed that half the proceeds would go to *La Sentinelle.*[138]

Fr. Prince's announcement about the revival of the *Institut St. Joseph* and the collection of funds created a crisis of conscience for his assistant, Fr. Napoleon Plasse. Fr. Plasse had already announced his stand on the Sentinellist issue when he publicly criticized the Sentinellist agitation after reading Bishop Hickey's pastoral letter. However, concerned that Bishop Hickey would take his silence to mean agreement with Fr. Prince's plans, Fr. Plasse felt obliged to write to Bishop Hickey on September 1 to report what had been said in church. Fr. Plasse also reported that he had heard that in many sections of the parish the women collectors were being rebuffed by the same people who had rebuffed the collectors for the Charity Drive. Some reportedly told the ticket sellers for the clambake that, if the people could not trust the bishop with their money, they also could not trust the man Fr. Prince had placed in charge of the St. Vincent de Paul Society.[139]

Partisans of the Sentinellist movement would charge that Bishop Hickey had placed priests like Fr. Plasse in parishes to spy on the Sentinellists. In the case of Fr. Prince and his plan to follow Fr. Beland's example

---

[138] Napoleon J. Plasse to Hickey, September 1, 1927, PChA.
[139] Ibid.

in the creation of a fund controlled by laymen and separate from the parish, Bishop Hickey was already aware of Fr. Prince's announcement of the plan before Fr. Plasse wrote his letter. The day before Fr. Plasse wrote, Bishop Hickey had again called Fr. Prince to his office, a meeting to which he invited his Chancellor and Assistant Chancellor as witnesses. The diversion of funds to a separate account outside the bishop's control constituted a serious violation of Church law covering the administration of parishes. The *Institut St. Joseph* was the first item Bishop Hickey brought up with Fr. Prince and it was, in his mind, the last piece of evidence he needed to justify demanding Fr. Prince's resignation. Bishop Hickey went on to detail other reasons for asking for Prince's resignation. The bishop gave him three days to comply with his request for his resignation or to send a letter giving reasons why Prince could not do so.[140]

When he did not receive either Fr. Prince's resignation or his defense of his actions, Bishop Hickey let two days pass before, on September 5, he appointed Fr. Ernest Morin, the senior assistant at Precious Blood, to act as the temporary administrator of St. Louis. The Chancellor, Fr. Peter A. Foley, delivered the letter of appointment to Fr. Morin and delivered a second letter to Fr. Prince notifying him of his removal and the appointment of Fr. Morin as administrator. When he read the bishop's letter, which declared the pastorate of St. Louis vacant, Fr. Prince's first response was to telephone Canon Gignac in Quebec for advice. Canon Gignac evidently urged him to accede, under protest, to the bishop's wishes and surrender control of the parish's affairs. Adelard Soucy, who was a trustee of St. Louis, also was at the rectory at this time. He too urged Fr. Prince to surrender control of the parish.[141]

Fr. Prince, accompanied by Fr. Beland, left the next day for Quebec to consult with Canon Gignac personally. During that day he also wrote a letter to Bishop Hickey in which he declared that the bishop had no reason to remove him. On Wednesday, September 7, Prince sent telegrams to several Rhode Island newspapers containing a letter addressed to his parishioners announcing that Bishop Hickey had declared the pastorate of St. Louis vacant and that his only recourse was to appeal to the Holy See. On Thursday night, a number of the parishioners of St. Louis gathered at the home of Theodore Talbot on Social St. to discuss the situation and lay plans for a protest. The committee arranged for the stationing of automobiles on Privilege St. and in front of the U.E.R. car barn on Social St. to transport any parishioners of St. Louis who wished to boycott masses in their own church to the new Assumption Church in South Bellingham. Members of the committee stationed themselves at the doors of St. Louis to direct those who wished to participate in the boycott to the waiting cars.

---

[140] Bishop Hickey's Diary, August 31, 1927; Memo, August 31, 1927, Fr. Prince File, PChA.
[141] Bishop Hickey's Diary, September 5, 1927; *Woonsocket Call*, September 6, 8, 12, 1927; *The Rhode Islander*, September 16, 1927, provides details of Fr. Prince's suspension and its aftermath.

As a result of the boycott, only a relatively small number of parishioners attended mass at St. Louis. The parishioners of St. Louis found additional grounds for grievance when Fr. Prince returned to St. Louis from Canada. Fr. Morin had moved into the rectory and removed Fr. Prince's belongings from his room. When Fr. Prince protested, Bishop Hickey reportedly threatened to call the police if he did not leave the rectory.[142]

The protest movement gained momentum when the committee welcomed several thousand parishioners and sympathizers to a meeting planned for the St. Louis Plat, but actually held on the neighboring St. Louis baseball grounds on Diamond Hill Road, which was parish property. One of the principal speakers was Antonio Prince, Fr. Prince's nephew, who spoke in defense of his uncle and his administration of the parish. Mr. Daignault also addressed the meeting. He dismissed as a subterfuge the charge that Fr. Prince had mishandled the finances of the parish. To his mind, the real reason for Fr. Prince's removal was his support of the Sentinellists. He claimed that the expulsion of Fr. Prince was "the culminating point of a regime of tyranny and terror which has never yet been seen in the history of the Catholic Church in the United States." To his mind, Fr. Prince enjoyed the status of a permanent pastor at St. Louis, who could not be moved without his consent or a clerical trial. Other of the Sentinellist leaders also addressed the meeting, during which the members of the committee who organized the protest took up a collection that amounted to $720, to defray the costs of Fr. Prince's appeal of his removal to Rome.[143]

The protest continued the next week, when it was estimated that more than half of those who usually attended St. Louis on a given Sunday chose to avail themselves of the transportation provided by the leaders of the protest movement and attended mass at the Assumption church, where Fr. Binette added extra masses to accommodate them. The committee also organized a second protest meeting on the St. Louis plat and its ball field. At this second meeting, seven speakers, including Mr. Prince, addressed a crowd estimated at 10,000, the largest to have ever attended a Sentinellist meeting. As it was important to show the size that the support of their cause commanded, the organizers supported their estimate by counting the cars parked at the ball field and on adjacent streets and announced that there were 2,504. Mr. Prince charged that Bishop Hickey had removed his uncle without making any provisions for his support. What he was not aware of at the time was that on September 10, 1927, Bishop Hickey appointed Fr. Prince administrator of Our Lady of Good Help parish in Mapleville. Bishop Hickey's letter of appointment did not reach Fr. Prince quickly because the bishop did not know where he went after

---

142   *Woonsocket Call*, September 8, 10, 12, 1927; *Providence Journal*, September 9, 1927. Prince's letter to
       Hickey is cited in Rumilly, *Histoire Des Franco-Americains*, p. 420.
143   *Woonsocket Call*, September 10, 12, 13, 1927; *Providence Journal*, September 12, 1927.

he left Woonsocket. Fr. Prince would refuse to accept the new assignment since Our Lady of Good Help was a smaller parish than St. Louis. In light of his uncle's lack of an assignment at the time he spoke, Mr. Prince once again urged those present to support his uncle financially and urged them to contribute toward the goal of $25,000 the committee hoped to raise to support his appeal to Rome.[144]

The Civil Trials

Having unsuccessfully sought justice in the Church courts and having had only a degree of success in the court of public opinion, Elphege Daignault focused his attention on the church suits scheduled to be heard when the courts came back from the summer break. On Tuesday, September 13, 1927, as he had arranged the day before, Daignault went to the Providence office of Patrick P. Curran, lead counsel in Bishop Hickey's defense against Daignault's suits. Mr. Curran agreed to see him on condition that there was to be no discussion between them as to a continuance of the church cases, which were assigned for hearing in six days. Realistically, Daignault knew that the 1869 law of incorporation, which was the basis on which the individual parish corporations were set up, favored the bishop's position and not his. In spite of what he had told his followers about his confidence that the civil courts would support his charge that Bishop Hickey acted illegally, his best hope of achieving his stated goals continued to be some kind of negotiated settlement with the bishop, who he thought would want to avoid the scandal of the lawsuits and Daignault would be spared the threat of excommunication.[145]

Mr. Daignault, however, failed to understand the kind of man Bishop Hickey was, if he thought the bishop could be intimidated or cowered. Bishop Hickey might have had a quick temper and had an autocratic and abrasive style of administration, but he did not lack courage. After a year of Mr. Daignault's charges, the bishop's patience was exhausted and he was determined to see the agitation brought to an end the only way he could, by establishing in the courts that he had acted properly in asking that the parishes of the diocese contribute toward the building of diocesan high schools. Daignault began his conversation with Mr. Curran by asking him if there was any truth to the rumor circulating in some circles, that the bishop was ready to settle the church cases out of court. Since Daignault

---

144 *Woonsocket Call*, September 19, 1927; *Providence News*, September 19, 1927; *Providence Journal*, September 19, 1927; Hickey to Prince, September 10, 1927, PChA.

145 Memorandum of interview between Elphege J. Daignault and Patrick P. Curran, Tuesday, September 13, 1927, PChA. For insight into Mr. Daignault's thinking, Cf. *La Sentinelle*, September 22, 1927. For the threat of excommunication, Cf. the statement of Fr. John Sullivan in *The Rhode Islander*, September 2, 1927.

himself would have had to be part of any settlement, the question rose from a hope that Rome might be pressuring Bishop Hickey to make some concessions to the Franco Americans rather than risk the possibility of large scale defections from the Church on the part of the protestors or provide the enemies of the Church in the United States with cause to criticize it. Later in the conversation, Daignault said that, on one occasion in the past, a priest had come from Rome and talked with him and Bishop Hickey. The priest suggested to both that they meet to settle their differences. As Daignault related the initiative, Bishop Hickey had agreed to meet with him only on the condition that Daignault confess that he was in error and publicly express his sorrow for the campaigns he had conducted. Daignault refused to do so on principle, he said, because he believed that the people of a parish had a right to a voice in the management of their churches, an opinion in which a canonist he had consulted at Boston College concurred. Mr. Curran quickly assured him that there was no talk of a settlement.[146]

After satisfying Daignault on this point, Curran told him frankly he did not see any possible chance of Daignault's winning the cases he had brought against the bishop and the parish corporations and that continuing to prosecute them would only do harm to himself, his party and the Church. Mr. Daignault explained that his reason for bringing the suits initially was that he was afraid the large expenditures that appeared to be contemplated for the support of high schools might bankrupt the diocese. He admitted that his opposition and that of his associates had been based on a vision of the worst possible result from the bishop's plans, which had not in fact developed.[147]

When Mr. Curran pressed him further as to whether he had any hope of winning the cases, Mr. Daignault mentioned some legal precedents in New York. Curran then asked him if he had prepared a brief and Daignault admitted that he had not. As Daignault was evidently in a difficult position, Mr. Curran suggested a way out. In view of the participation of some of the Franco-American clergy in Daignault's agitation and of Fr. Prince's removal from his parish, he said that Daignault could very well abandon the suits "upon the grounds that to continue the agitation would jeopardize the position" of other priests who, like Fr. Prince, had supported and encouraged Daignault. Daignault replied that while he personally was very reluctant to go on with the agitation and the trials, he could not abandon the cause now or his followers would "kill him." Since Daignault could not drop the suits and Bishop Hickey would not meet the Sentinel-

---

146 Memorandum of Interview. Mr. Daignault's point about the people of a parish having a right to a voice in the management of their parish was true of the particular law of the Church in Canada. It was not true of American particular law.
147 Ibid.

lists' demands, Curran and Daignault agreed that there was nothing left to be done but to meet next in court.[148]

Before he left Mr. Curran's office, Daignault returned once more to the hope that the Roman authorities would in fact intervene to force Bishop Hickey to make the concessions demanded of him by the Sentinellists. He told Mr. Curran that he was thinking of asking for a continuance of three months so that he could go to Rome to try to get a hearing there, as he believed that the threat of intervention by the court in Church affairs was "just the thing to get him a hearing in Rome." Curran responded that neither he nor any of the other counsel the bishop had engaged had any authority to even talk about a continuance and that the only way to avoid the coming hearing on Monday was for Daignault to go to see Bishop Hickey and make his peace with him. Daignault again declined to do so, if it meant he had to acknowledge that he had been wrong.[149]

Since there was to be no pretrial settlement, Mr. Daignault and the seven lawyers who appeared as counsel for the bishop and the ten parishes first cited by Daignault appeared as scheduled in the court of Presiding Superior Court Justice Willard B. Tanner on Monday, September 19, 1927 to make their opening arguments. Every seat in the court room was filled by an interested audience, which included a few women as well as men. Mr. Curran began the argument as to why the court should dismiss Daignault's suits against the parishes. In the course of two hours, he made three main points. As a matter of due course, he argued, the whole case was an internal affair and belonged solely to the Church courts. Without saying that it would refuse to accept the court decision in the matter, Curran stated that, as a lawyer for the bishop, he was obliged to remind the court that the Church had it own courts with the power to judge and enforce its decisions in all matters. On February 12, 1927, when Bishop Hickey informed Msgr. Marella at the Delegation in Washington that Daignault had filed citations in the court of equity, he commented that he believed that, on the basis of civil law by which the diocese was incorporated, the courts would be obliged to throw out Daignault's case. The same opinion was echoed by a chancery official in an interview with the *Providence Journal* on February 15.[150]

As his second point, Mr. Curran argued that, even if the court decided that it had jurisdiction, the plaintiffs' status as parishioners, communicants and contributors did not give them the right, under Church law, to bring suit against the parish corporations. Although Bishop Hickey was initially confident that the court would decline to accept jurisdiction in what he

148 Ibid. Mr. Daignault later said the same thing publicly when addressing a gathering in New Bedford in January 1928, Cf. English transcription of meeting of January 25, 1928 in New Bedford, MA., dated January 26, 1928, PChA.
149 Memorandum of Interview.
150 Hickey to Marella, February 12, 1927, PChA; *Providence Journal*, February 15, September 20, 1927; *Providence News*, September 19, 1927; *Providence Visitor*, February 18; September 23, 1927.

saw as a Church-State case, the bishop's lawyers well knew that the state courts had jurisdiction over legal entities that the state had created and that the judge would most likely rule that the complainants did have the right, under state law, to bring suit. They were confident, however, that Judge Tanner would agree with their third argument, which was the heart of their case. In this third argument, Curran held that all the acts complained of by complainants were perfectly within the rights given to parish corporations by their charter and, consequently, perfectly legal.[151]

Before he allowed the other lawyers for the bishop to speak, Judge Tanner gave Mr. Daignault a chance to present his case so that he might decide if it were necessary for the other lawyers to address the court. Daignault began what would be a seven-minute presentation by arguing that parishes were incorporated for the benefit of the parishioners rather than for the bishop. To support his position, he cited a New York State decision that held that parishes were incorporated to hold property in trust for the members of the parish in general, and not for the bishop. Since Judge Tanner was not familiar with the case, he asked to see a full report of it. The bishop's lawyers were familiar with the case and Mr. Jalbert objected that the New York case was decided under an old statute and not the current one, which was similar to the statute incorporating the Diocese of Providence. After reading the case, the judge agreed with Mr. Jalbert. When Daignault resumed his argument, he contended that the law of incorporation did not mean anything if the court did not have jurisdiction. He expressed his concern that, according to Mr. Curran's reading of the law, Bishop Hickey was free to distribute parish monies to whomever he desired, while he contended that parish monies might only be used for diocesan purposes under canon law. He insisted that his clients were within their rights to ask for an accounting of parish funds and that Bishop Hickey had violated the law in using parish monies for unauthorized purposes. At the conclusion of his argument, Daignault asked for ten days to file a brief. Although the bishop's lawyers, anxious as they were to have the case tried, contended that Daignault had had more than enough time to prepare his case, Judge Tanner granted the continuance to September 30.[152]

While Bishop Hickey had confidence in the justice of his cause and the abilities of his lawyers, he also sought divine assistance in his efforts to restore peace to the diocese. In a pastoral letter, which was printed in the *Visitor* on Friday, September 23 and read from the pulpits in English or French on the following Sunday, the bishop asked for a special prayer during the customary October devotions that:

> These misled and mistaken members of the Church of Jesus Christ may be brought back to their full measure of respect, confidence and allegiance to their divinely ac-

151 *Providence News*, September 19, 1927; *Providence Journal*, September 20, 1927; *The Rhode Islander*, September 23, 1927.
152 Ibid. *The Rhode Islander*, September 30, 1927 gives Mr. Daignault's argument verbatim.

credited leaders, and that thus the most dreadful spiritual consequences of wilful persistence along forbidden paths may be averted.[153]

Mr. Daignault filed his brief in response to Mr. Curran's arguments at three o'clock on September 29. The heart of his argument was that, according to the Act of Incorporation of 1869, which formed the basis for the incorporation of the individual parishes in the diocese and according to the bylaw adopted afterwards, "the Board of Trustees in each parish were trustees for the congregation and must not disburse moneys except for the benefit of the congregation."[154]

In rendering his decision the next day, Judge Tanner disappointed Bishop Hickey by asserting the court's right to jurisdiction and did so without bothering with legal citations. The judge also rejected Mr. Curran's argument that followed upon the first, that the petitioners had no standing before the court. However, he accepted Mr. Curran's main argument that the parochial funds of the parish church corporations had not, as charged, been misapplied since such funds could "be expended not only for the benefit of the local church but for the educational or charitable institutions of the church as a whole." To support this part of his decision, Judge Tanner cited a Massachusetts Court decision in *Enos* vs. *St. John the Baptist Church*, which the *Visitor* had discussed on March 11, 1927, after some of Daignault's supporters cited it to defend their position. In rendering his decision, Judge Tanner referred to the vagueness in the wording of the bills of complaint, which Mr. Curran had pointed out in his argument before the court. For the sake of justice, he afforded Mr. Daignault the chance to either amend the bills or take the matter directly to the Supreme Court on appeal.[155]

When interviewed by a reporter for the *Providence Journal* on the evening of the decision, Mr. Daignault claimed victory on two of the three points Judge Tanner had ruled on, namely, as he heard the ruling, that the civil courts had jurisdiction in the matter complained of and that contributors to parish funds had a right to an accounting. He acknowledged that the court had not found Bishop Hickey guilty of any violation of the law and that Judge Tanner had ruled against his view of Church as meaning parish. However, Daignault did not accept that the decision meant the end of his cause. Rather he said, "This decision is only the beginning of our action in the matter."[156]

Daignault's nemesis, *The Rhode Islander*, quickly challenged his version of the judge's ruling. Quoting from the decision itself, the author of *The Rhode Islander* article on October 7 argued that Daignault had misread Judge Tanner's ruling and that the judge had not ruled that contributors to par-

153 *Providence Visitor*, September 23, 1927.

154 Daignault Brief, as quoted in *Providence Journal*, September 30, 1927.

155 *The Rhode* Islander, June 10, 1927; *Woonsocket Call*, October 1, 1927; *Providence Journal*, October 2, 1927; *Providence Visitor*, October 7, 1927.

156 *Providence Journal*, October 2, 1927. For *La Sentinelle*'s response to the ruling cf. *La Sentinelle*, October 6, 1927, "The Death of Our Parish Institutions."

ish funds had a right to an accounting of the parish funds, in general, or to those parish funds contributed to the high school drive. *The Rhode Islander* saved its harshest criticism for a parody of Bishop Hickey's peace pastoral that Mr. Perdriau had written for *La Sentinelle*'s September 29 issue. The *Rhode Islander* called it "the height of mendaciousness," and observed that "Nothing like it was ever written in the most bigoted anti-Catholic sheet." Mr. Foisy and *La Tribune* also failed to find Perdriau's parody amusing. Foisy wrote that, to his mind and perhaps to the minds of many others, Perdriau had gone beyond the line that a self-respecting Christian should not pass.[157]

Judge Tanner's decision on the crucial question of the meaning of Church in the Act of Incorporation of 1869 was consistent with the American tradition of church property holding wherein complete control of church property was placed in the hands of the bishop as head of the local Church. The understanding of Church was developed in the various meetings of the Provincial Councils of Baltimore when they took up the trustee problem, which had arisen in the first half of the nineteenth century, and offered remedies for it. Since the American solution to the problem of trusteeism was consistent with universal Church law, Rome had approved and supported the legislation of the Baltimore councils.[158]

In French Canada, a different tradition had developed following the adoption of the 1791 Canadian Constitution wherein lay trustees had a significant voice in parish affairs, unlike their American counterparts. In practice, most French-Canadian and Franco-American pastors acted as buffers between the two traditions. Most French pastors tended to give the laity in their parishes a greater say in parish affairs than most other pastors. The majority of the parishioners in the Franco-American parishes in the diocese were content with the status quo. Daignault and his supporters' rejection of the American traditions was an expression of their extreme nationalism. What they were insisting on was that their Canadian traditions, although historically conditioned, were the only legitimate form of church governance.

On his part, Mr. Daignault waited until October 15, the last day of the ten day period allotted him by Judge Tanner, to file his amended bills of complaint. In the bills, Daignault provided the clarity and specifics whose absence Mr. Curran had complained of. In spite of the judge's ruling on the meaning of Church, Daignault continued to maintain in the amended bills that, outside of the cathedraticum, a tax a diocese traditionally imposed on all parishes to support the cathedral and the chancery office, which he conceded in his initial bill was legitimate, parish funds could only be used for parish needs and that any other use was illegal.[159]

---

157 *La Sentinelle*, September 29, 1927; *La Tribune*, October 1, 1927; *The Rhode Islander*, October 7, 1927.
158 On the question of trusteeism, Cf. Patrick W. Carey, *People, Priests and Prelates: Ecclesiastical Democracy and the Tensions of Trusteeism* (Notre Dame, Indiana: Notre Dame University Press, 1987).
159 *Woonsocket Call*, October 15, 1927; *Providence Journal*, October 16, 1927.

In order to file the amended bills, Daignault had to once again obtain the signatures of parishioners of each parish cited. Most of those who signed the original bills also signed the amended ones. However, three of those who signed the original bill against St. Matthew's, Central Falls, did not sign the amended ones, and one of the signers of the bill against Our Lady of Victories in Woonsocket did not sign the second one. In the case of the bill against St. John the Baptist Church in Pawtucket, only Dr. J. B. Falcon signed both bills. One of the four parishioners who did not sign the amended bill was former state representative Albert J. Lamarre, who did not do so because he was not asked to sign. Although reports circulated in the press of a split in the ranks of Daignault's supporters, both Daignault and Lamarre took the trouble to deny the report. The differences between the two would be only be made public later.[160]

Bishop Hickey's attorneys duly filed their demurrer in response to the new bill of complaint. In their brief, the attorneys, for principle's sake, again reiterated the claim that the State courts had no jurisdiction in the case. They then proceeded to give reasons why the allegations contained in the bills of complaint were defective and ended by saying that the distribution of parish funds for the support of diocesan high schools did not need the approval of the trustees and, if they did, that approval was duly given. On receipt of the demurrer, Judge Tanner set Saturday, October 29, as the date on which he would hear arguments on it.[161]

At the beginning of the Saturday court session, Mr. Daignault moved to put off the hearing of the case until some time in January. He told the court that he wished to be away from the court's jurisdiction from November 1, 1927 until January 20, 1928. He explained later that he asked for the continuance in order to bring his case before the authorities in Rome. The bishop's attorneys strongly objected to a continuance because of the length of time the case had been before the public and urged that the case should be settled promptly. Judge Tanner delayed ruling on either request until the next Tuesday, at which time he promised to either grant the continuance Daignault sought or order the attorneys to proceed.[162]

Before court reconvened on the Tuesday, Judge Tanner met with both sides in his chambers. During the conference, Mr. Daignault acknowledged that there was practically no difference between the original bills of complaint and the amended ones. Accordingly, when the parties returned to open court, Judge Tanner, as expected by most court onlookers, entered a decree rejecting the suits Daignault had brought. The judge, however, granted Mr. Daignault's request that he be excused from attendance in

---

160 *Woonsocket Call*, October 18, 1927; *Providence Journal*, October 19, 25, 26, 1927.
161 *Woonsocket Call*, October 26, 1927; *Providence Journal*, October 27, 1927.
162 *Woonsocket Call*, October 29; November 1, 1927; *Providence Journal*, October 30, 31; November 2, 1927.

Superior Court for the time he had requested and granted him a delay of thirty days for filing an appeal with the Supreme Court.[163]

On September 13, 1927, the same day on which Mr. Daignault had met with Mr. Curran, Bishop Hickey met with the apostolic delegate, Archbishop Fumasoni-Biondi, and Msgr. Marella, the delegation's auditor. The bishop was in Washington to attend the meeting of the National Conference of Catholic Bishops on September 14 and 15 and took advantage of his time in the city to meet with the delegate. During his meeting with the two men, Hickey reviewed all that he had done in regard to the Daignault and the Sentinellists. Hickey reported in his diary that the delegate, who had previously urged Mr. Daignault to cease his agitation and submit to his bishop, supported the actions he had taken so far and urged him to condemn *La Sentinelle* and declare the complainants in the church cases excommunicated.[164]

There is no copy of a letter from Bishop Hickey to Rome in the Providence Chancery Archives asking if he could proceed to declare excommunicated those who had cited him before a civil tribunal. However, Cardinal Gasparri, the Vatican Secretary of State, refers to one in a cablegram sent to the delegate, in which the cardinal gives Bishop Hickey the authority he asked for. The contents of the cardinal's cablegram was conveyed to Bishop Hickey by Archbishop Fumasoni-Biondi in a letter dated October 20, 1927. The bishop had the delegate's letter, with the content of the cardinal's telegram, printed on the front page of the *Providence Visitor* on Friday, October 21. The secular press reprinted it the following day. The publication of Rome's response to Bishop Hickey's inquiry appeared too late to influence the decision of most of those who signed the amended version of the bills of complaint filed by Daignault on the twenty-sixth. However, its publication did disturb the conscience of a few. When a reporter for the *Providence Journal* asked Phydime Hemond, one of the leaders of the Sentinellists, for his reaction to the cardinal's cablegram on the day it appeared in the *Visitor*, Hemond expressed himself as not worried, because advisers in Rome had assured the Sentinellists that, if they were not satisfied with Bishop Hickey's administration as president of the parish corporations, they could sue him. However, when a reporter for the same paper sought the reactions of four of those who signed the citation against Precious Blood, Woonsocket, Adolphe E. Simard, one of the four, asserted that he had never expected that the matter would go so far and probably would not have signed the citation if he had. Ovila Lavoie, another of the signers, urged that Bishop Hickey and Daignault "get together and settle it" and added, "If we are wrong, of course, we have got to submit." The other two interviewed, former councilman, Louis T. Allard and

163 Ibid.
164 Bishop Hickey's Diary, September 13, 1927.

Mathias Thibeault, expressed no regret for their actions or fear of the consequences.[165]

Mr. Daignault gave his own response to the cablegram in an article in *La Sentinelle* on Thursday, October 27, 1927. While he acknowledged that Rome had the right to excommunicate anyone who cited his bishop before the civil courts, he asserted that the Sentinellists' case was different. Like Mr. Hemond, he appealed to the opinion of the Roman canonist Daignault had first mentioned in a letter to Bishop Hickey on December 17, 1925, a letter that he had printed in *La Sentinelle* on January 7, 1926, along with his letter to Bishop Hickey. Having undertaken the agitation at the behest of the Franco-American priests and the Canadian bishops, he had never considered himself to be personally responsible for the agitation. Now with the possibility of excommunication facing him, he asserted that "If anybody is to blame, it is the Roman lawyers whose direction we are following. If, unfortunately, excommunication strikes us, we will hold them responsible." In regard to the fact that, in spite of his Roman lawyers' opinion, he did stand under the threat of excommunication, Daignault again expressed himself as not being concerned. He attributed Cardinal Gasparri's action to the cardinal's having been deceived by Bishop Hickey as to the nature of his suits and expressed confidence the bishop's deceit would be uncovered.[166]

Throughout the controversy, Mr. Daignault consistently asserted that he was acting "in good faith," and that, in his conscience, he did not believe that there was anything wrong in what he was doing. In law, acting in good faith did mitigate the culpability of one's action and in this case protected anyone who summoned a bishop to court without papal permission, if he did not know such permission was required. As Daignault had consistently argued that he was citing the president of the parish corporations, not the bishop as a person, he could argue, as he did, that he was acting in good faith. However, Bishop Hickey, for one, both publicly and privately, doubted that Daignault could justly claim to be acting in good faith. When the question of excommunication was first raised in March 1927, Bishop Hickey held that Daignault's motive in attacking diocesan management appeared not to be "one of good faith" but of a selfish nature based on economic rather than spiritual salvation. Good faith on Mr. Daignault's part would have meant that he seriously considered the possibility that Bishop Hickey was himself acting in good faith in his administration of

---

165 *Providence Visitor*, October 21, 1927; *Providence Journal*, October 22, 1927; *Providence Journal*, October 23, 1927; *Woonsocket Call*, October 22, 1927.

166 La *Tribune*, March 2, 1927; *Providence Visitor*, March 4, 1927; *La Sentinelle*, January 7, 1926; October 27, 1927. An English translation of part of Daignault's article appeared also in the *Providence Journal*, October 28, 1927. In a speech he gave in Woonsocket, on February 7, 1927, Daignault showed the crowd the letter from the canonist whom he said was "one of the greatest canon lawyers living today." Although Daignault told the crowd he was forbidden to give the canonist's name, he said "the style of the opinion would lead anyone to believe that it comes from an expert in these matters." *Providence Journal*, February 8, 1927.

the diocese. It would also have meant that Daignault had seriously considered the fact that his authorities were not in agreement with the view of the apostolic delegate, who supported Bishop Hickey, and, after the publication of Cardinal Gasparri's letter, with the Roman authorities. In reality, the longer he chose to contest the case, the less he could claim to be acting in good faith.[167]

In addition to seeking authorization to have those who signed the bills of complaint excommunicated for the scandal they had given, Bishop Hickey also sought to have *La Sentinelle* placed on the Index or list of forbidden works. In order to do that, canon law required that the bishop of the diocese where the newspaper was printed had to warn the principals at the paper (Daignault, Phydime Hemond and Henri Perdriau) to discontinue printing articles on religion and morals and from printing attacks on the Church and its clergy. It also required two other similar warnings, after which, if they were not heeded, the bishop, in his capacity as judge, could forbid the people of his diocese to read the paper. Bishop Hickey sent the required canonical warnings on October 6, 13, and 26. In an open letter to the bishop printed in *La Sentinelle*, Mr. Daignault asked him to specify which articles he objected to. He apologized for any rudeness on the paper's part in criticizing ecclesiastical officials but, appealing to his rights as a journalist, promised to continue his campaign in behalf of the cause. However, he did agree to drop the word Catholic from the subtitle of the newspaper. While Bishop Hickey did not take up publicly the challenge of specifying objectionable articles, Jean Sabate and *The Rhode Islander* did. (Bishop Hickey would later supply the Roman authorities with a very detailed list of the names of the bishops and priests attacked in various articles in *La Sentinelle*.) On his part, Bishop Hickey prepared a pastoral letter in which he prohibited the reading of *La Sentinelle*, but he never sent the letter to his priests because he preferred that a ban be issued by all the bishops of New England, if that was possible, since support for *La Sentinelle* came from several of the New England dioceses.[168]

On November 4, 1927, Bishop Hickey sent a draft of an Episcopal Ordinance forbidding Catholics to support and read *La Sentinelle* to all his fellow bishops in New England, which he hoped they would agree to have read in all the churches in New England on November 13, three days before Daignault's announced departure for Rome. Hickey asked his fellow

---

167 *Providence Journal*, March 6, 1927; *Providence Journal*, October 22, 1927.

168 Hickey to Daignault, Phydime Hemond, and Henri Perdriau, October 5, 13, 26, 1927; Hickey to Pastors, November 4, 1927, PChA; *La Sentinelle*, October 20, 1927; *Providence News*, October 20, 1927; *Providence Journal*, October 21, 1927; *The Rhode Islander*, October 28, 1927; Documents au sujet de L'Agitation Sentinelliste, 1922–1927, Number 10, Index general de la "Sentinelle," PChA. Bishop Hickey also prepared an extensive document detailing the dogmatic errors, which had appeared in *La Sentinelle*. In keeping with his policy of seeking not to inflame the situation, Hickey never publicly accused *La Sentinelle* of heresy. But, he did send the list of errors to Rome to support his request that Rome intervene to forbid the reading of the paper. Among the articles listed under "Injury and Outrage" was Perdriau's parody of the Peace Pastoral read on September 25.

bishops to sign the document so that it might have greater force when issued by them all. While several of the New England bishops did sign the document, Cardinal O'Connell sent it back on November 14 unsigned with a letter expressing his hope the "this very disagreeable situation should be terminated as quickly as possible" and noting that, in his opinion, the matter was best handled by Hickey himself. As a final thought, he added that if copies of *La Sentinelle* had been sent to him, he had not seen them, nor had he read them. When Bishops Nilan of Hartford and Rice of Burlington also declined to sign the document, Hickey abandoned the idea. Bishop Nilan expressed concern that a condemnation might provoke similar groups to open rebellion in Hartford, while Bishop Rice had consulted with three different sources familiar with "Canadian doings" in his diocese and found that there were "very, very few subscribers" of the paper in his diocese. Those who did subscribe did so out of curiosity rather than sympathy.[169]

Although the majority of the signers of the bills of complaint against Bishop Hickey professed themselves unfazed by the threat of being excommunicated for having cited their bishop before the civil courts, many leaders of the Franco-American community in New England and elsewhere were upset by the growing animosity between the Sentinellists and their bishop. The same leaders were also concerned that unrest and animosity was being spread to other dioceses, as Daignault and his supporters held fund-raising meetings in many other New England cities where there were large Franco-American communities. On November 4, 1927, three prominent Franco-Americans, J. Henri Gillet, Joseph A. Legace and Telesphore Desrosiers, wrote to Bishop Hickey informing him that they had been appointed by the Federation Catholique Franco-Americaine, as impartial and discreet men as well as men prominent in the Franco-American community, to attempt to see if they could help "abate and terminate" the differences between Hickey and the supporters of Daignault. There is but the one letter from the committee in the Providence Chancery Office files, suggesting that nothing came of this attempt at mediation.[170]

On Tuesday, November 2, the evening that Judge Tanner's decision was announced in the newspapers, the Franco-American Social Club, an organization that supported the Sentinellist movement, held a meeting in Jacques Cartier Hall in Pawtucket. During the course of the meeting, Albert Lamarre, who was president of the group and head of its executive committee, engaged in an argument with Dr. J. B. Falcon over the manner in which the local organization was being run. In the course of their exchange, Lamarre professed faith in Mr. Daignault's leadership of the

169 Hickey to O'Connell, November 4, 1927; Hickey to Bishops Nilan, Feehan, O'Leary, Guertin, Rice and Murray, November 12, 1927; O'Connell to Hickey, November 14, 1927; Nilan to Hickey, November 15, 1927; Rice to Hickey, November 18, 1927, PChA.
170 J. Henri Guillet, Joseph A. Legace and Telesphore Desrosiers to Hickey, November 4, 1927, PChA.

cause, but held that the court might have ruled differently "if the matter had been more forcefully brought to its attention" in the briefs Daignault had submitted. He told the gathering that Judge Tanner had handled the church suits fairly. Unlike those who professed to hold out hope that the Rhode Island Supreme Court would rule in their favor, Lamarre was realistic enough to see that the chief obstacle to victory in their cause lay in the way the 1869 Act of Incorporation was written so as to favor the bishop. He believed that only by "finding some men of courage" who would introduce a law to amend the church corporation act of 1869 so as to incorporate the Sentinellists' understanding of Church could they hope to prevail. To his mind, any appeal to the Supreme Court was "a waste of time." Although Daignault did not drop the idea of the suits, he did include Mr. Lamarre's suggestion in the list of possible remedies he intended to pursue in the speeches he made during the week that followed.[171]

While Daignault had failed to prove by any objective standard that Bishop Hickey had been guilty of injustice against the Franco-American parishes, he knew he would face enormous political difficulties if he undertook an effort to have a revised law of incorporation passed without the cooperation of Bishop Hickey. However, he continued to hope that Rome would impose a solution to the impasse the Sentinellists had created in their dealings with Bishop Hickey. Daignault did not publicly confirm that he intended to go to Rome until Sunday, October 30, when, as president of the Canado-Americaine Association, he presided at the installation exercises of Courts Napoleon and Villa Marie in DeNevers Hall in Woonsocket. He told his audience, composed of members of the Association from Connecticut, Massachusetts as well Rhode Island, that he was going to Rome on November 16, "to make a last and honest effort to settle this matter out of the civil courts. . . . In Rome, I will expose the question of parochial funds and explain how our maternal language is in danger of being lost." In order to continue the threat of continued legal action against Bishop Hickey while he was in Rome, Daignault filed his appeal of Judge Tanner's ruling to the Rhode Island Supreme Court on November 14. *The Rhode Islander* and other partisan and neutral observers of the controversy offered a second explanation for Daignault's wishing to continue his legal action against Bishop Hickey. Without continuing to stir the emotions of the Franco Americans, the Sentinellists' cause would cease to command attention outside of their own circles and the flow of "patriot dollars" to support the movement would dry up.[172]

Several thousand supporters filled the Joyland Ballroom in Woon-

---

171 *Providence Journal*, November 2, 3, 1927; *Providence News*, November 2, 3, 1927. Although a more realistic a way to achieve the Sentinellists' ends, any attempt to revise the 1869 Act of Incorporation without the bishop's consent would not have succeeded. Cf. the example of a similar attempt in Maine, *Catholicism in Rhode Island and the Diocese of Providence*, II, 152–163.

172 *Providence Journal*, October 31; November 2, 1927; *Providence News*, October 31; November 2, 1927; *Rhode Islander*, November 4, 1927.

socket to capacity on Sunday, November 13, 1927 to give Daignault a sendoff. Dr. J. Gaspard Boucher presided at the meeting and, in his opening remarks, in which he appealed for funds to support the movement, he repeated an accusation the Franco Americans had often made in the past to explain why their cause had not been heard in Rome. He told the audience, "I know that you will give the money necessary to help [Mr. Daignault] with his trip, to open doors over there. I am sorry to say it, but in Rome one must have money to make himself heard." The second speaker of the evening, Adolphe Robert, general secretary of the Canado-Americaine Association, offered a realistic appraisal of what Daignault's supporters could hope from the trip. "We do not expect you to bring back a victory, but we believe that in your asking for justice it will be already a great step in the solution of our difficulties. After your trip we expect we will have to continue."[173]

When Mr. Daignault addressed the meeting, he asserted that none of the funds used to support *La Sentinelle* would be used to pay for his trip. Rather he claimed the bulk of the funds he would use came from the contributions of a group of New England pastors who, he said, along with members of the laity, asked him to undertake the trip "for the race." He again rejected the idea, as he had in the past, that Rome had ruled against his claim that Bishop Hickey has acted unjustly in seeking parish funds to support the building of diocesan high schools. He then elaborated on what he had said was the purpose of the trip when he first announced he was going. "[Rome does] not like the cases before the courts. We will stop them if Rome declares formally that the taxes are illegal and gives us the pleasure of removing the man who does not listen to Rome and send him somewhere else." In order to underline their demands for justice and to put pressure on the Roman authorities, Daignault urged his audience not to contribute to their churches. According to information that Bishop Hickey had, it was Fr. Beland who raised the $7,000 Daignault needed to make the trip. He did so by personally visiting pastors in his own and neighboring dioceses to ask them to donate $500 each. He appealed by letter to those he did not visit personally. Bishop Hickey was aware of at least one priest who received such a letter.[174]

Two priests of the Archdiocese of Boston, Fr. Binette, pastor of the new Assumption parish in Bellingham, Massachusetts, and Fr. Duplessis, of Lowell, were on the dais that same evening. Fr. Duplessis also urged the Catholics in Rhode Island to refrain from financially supporting their parishes until the question of the control of parish funds was resolved. While Fr. Binette was not scheduled to speak, someone in the audience called for him to say a few words after Dr. Boucher had formally closed the meeting.

173 *Providence Journal*, November 14, 1927; *Woonsocket Call*, November 14, 1927; *Providence News*, November 14, 1927; *La Sentinelle*, November 17, 1927.
174 Ibid.; "Exposé of the Facts concerning Fr. J. H. Beland," December 28, 1927, PChA.

In the course of his remarks, Fr. Binette said that Cardinal O'Connell "approves the fight that we are waging." The English-language press found Fr. Binette's remark particularly newsworthy and sought confirmation of his statement from the cardinal. Cardinal O'Connell did not issue any statement on the matter, but he did speak with Fr. Binette on the day the newspaper carried the story of the Sentinellist meeting. On the day after he spoke with the cardinal, Fr. Binette issued a statement to the press denying that he had involved Cardinal O'Connell in the controversy by saying that he approved of the agitation in any way. *The Rhode Islander* could not let Fr. Binette's denial go unchallenged. It sought out three reporters who had been at the meeting and compared their notes, one to the other. All three agreed that Fr. Binette had said what he was quoted as saying. Rather than approving of Daignault's stand, Cardinal O'Connell, as he noted in his response to Bishop Hickey on the subject of a New England-wide condemnation of *La Sentinelle*, had not read a great deal about the whole matter.[175]

As he had announced, Mr. Daignault sailed for Europe on November 16, 1927. During his absence, Daignault's associates continued to stir emotions and raise expectations in a series of meetings they held in Central Falls, Pawtucket and Woonsocket. Five days before his departure, Bishop Hickey wrote to Msgr. Gentile to inform him of Daignault's intention of going to Rome and to provide him with information on Daignault's background. He identified him as an agitator and demagogue who had incited "a certain number of Franco-Americans to revolt, on false issues, against the diocesan administration." He also noted that he was the lawyer who had cited him into the courts and, by so doing, had incurred excommunication, which Hickey had not pronounced, because the bishop's lawyers had advised him not to do so until the court proceedings were finished. Daignault was going to Rome, he said, "expecting another hearing on the case already decided by the Congregation of the Council and to help Fr. Prince who was appealing his month's suspension by Bishop Hickey." Hickey warned Gentile that if Daignault gained "any kind of an entree in Rome, the impression here would be disastrous."[176]

Prior to leaving for Rome, Mr. Daignault secured several letters of recommendation and support from priests in Canada, Canon Gignac among them. In his 1936 account of his first trip to Rome, Daignault described his meeting with Msgr. Gentile, who as the auditor attached to the Congregation of the Council, was the official who prepared the business of the American dioceses for presentation at the congregation's general sessions. When Daignault, accompanied by his Roman lawyer, called on Gentile, Gentile, in the course of their meeting, labeled Daignault as a rebel against authority and produced a copy of *La Tribune* to justify the charge. During

---

175 *Woonsocket Call*, November 14, 15, 1927; *Providence Journal*, November 16, 1927; *The Rhode Islander*, November 18, 1927.

176 There are accounts of these meetings in the Providence Chancery office files; Hickey to Gentile, November 11, 1927, PChA.

the meeting, Msgr. Gentile advised him, that if he wanted to be heard at Rome, he had to cease his agitation and refrain from making public statements. Daignault correctly surmised that Bishop Hickey had supplied the information at Msgr. Gentile's disposal on which he based his judgment of Daignault. After sending Msgr. Gentile warning of Daignault's coming, Hickey had prepared an extensive series of documents in French which he had mimeographed and bound in a volume entitled, "Documents au subjet de L'Agitation Sentinellist." He sent two copies of the volume to Msgr. Gentile and asked him to advise him as to whom else he might send a copy. While Bishop Hickey had prepared his defense, Mr. Daignault had not taken the same care to prepare his case. According to Bishop Hickey's information, his lawyer, Mr. Astorri, advised him to return home to prepare one.[177]

Frustrated by Msgr. Gentile in his attempt to reopen the case he had previously submitted against Bishop Hickey, Mr. Daignault did succeed in having a meeting with Cardinal Pietro Gasparri, the Vatican Secretary of State. On his way to Rome, Mr. Daignault had stopped in Paris to visit with his brother-in-law, Alphonse Gaulin, who was the American Consul General in Paris. With his brother-in-law's help, Daignault secured from Louis Canet, an advisor on religious affairs in the French Ministry of Foreign Affairs, an introduction to France's ambassador to the Vatican, Mr. Doulcet. Daignault told the ambassador that, because his concerns went beyond the routine matters considered by the Congregation of the Council, he wished to discuss them with Cardinal Gasparri. According to Daignault's account, when the two met, the cardinal allowed him to give a complete account of the questions which brought him to Rome.[178]

While Mr. Daignault was in Rome, the English-language newspapers speculated about the purpose of the trip. According to *The Rhode Islander*, which might well have been repeating speculation current in many circles, Daignault went to Rome to speak with Pope Pius XI in order to make known to the pope the religious situation that prevailed in New England and to ask him to reverse the adverse decisions of the Sacred Congregation of the Council. He also hoped to ask the pope to remove Bishop Hickey. When Mr. Daignault arrived back in Woonsocket on January 4, 1928, he told the reporters who sought him out, that the machinery had been set in motion to bring about "a favorable change." He added that he probably would have to return to Rome before a satisfactory understanding could be brought about. He also expressed his conviction that Bishop Hickey would not proceed with the excommunication of himself and the sixty-four Franco Americans associated with him since the bishop had been given permission to pronounce sentence but had not done so.[179]

177 Ibid., December 28, 1927; Hickey to Sbarretti, December 12, 1929, PChA; Rumilly, *Histoire Des Franco-Americains*, p. 425; Daignault, *Le vrai mouvement sentinelliste*, 167–174.

178 Ibid.; *Woonsocket Call*, December 29, 1927.

179 *The Rhode Islander*, November 4; 18; December 9, 1927; *Woonsocket Call*, January 5, 1928; *Providence*

Daignault gave a fuller report of his trip to Rome before a capacity crowd at the Joyland Hall in Woonsocket on Sunday, January 8, 1928. The reporters who covered Daignault's meetings on Sunday at the Joyland and later that evening in Arctic Center in West Warwick heard him give various versions of what happened in Rome. The version Daignault stood by was that "he was approached in Rome and asked what were my terms of settlement and if I would drop the civil cases if the Rev. Fr. William [sic] Prince was given back his parish and the bishop ceased to oppose Rev. Fr. Beland." Daignault said he replied that he would not stop the suits on such easy terms.[180]

In the course of his remarks, Daignault told the crowd that nationalism was not in favor in Rome at the moment. On December 20, 1926, Pope Pius XI had formally banned Catholics from adhering to the program or the ideas of those in the *L'Action Francaise* movement, which placed party interests before religion and which made use of religion for political ends. Daignault assured his audience that their agitation was not a national agitation such as that condemned by the pope but "a family question, the right of a parent to give to their children the culture they see fit." In order to achieve their ends, Daignault proposed the drafting of a "circular explaining that question and containing the principles involved; the drawing up of a document covering the administration of the Diocese of Providence over the last few years; and the signing of a petition by a number of Catholics large enough to get Rome's attention asking that an inquiry be held into the affairs of the diocese." Although Daignault did not see a similarity between his movement and that of *Action Francaise*, the Roman authorities apparently did.[181]

Two priests, by their presence, once again lent a degree of legitimacy to the meeting, but this time they were Canadian priests, Fr. Charles Ouellette of St. Francois de Assise, Quebec, and Fr. Edmond J. Tremblay, formerly of Fall River, but teaching at that time at a Jesuit School in Montreal. Both of the priests addressed the meeting and, like the lay leaders, they urged the Franco Americans not to contribute to the financial support of their parishes until their rights were acknowledged.[182]

Since *The Rhode Islander*, among others, had suggested that Mr. Daignault had gone to Rome to present the Franco Americans' case before the Pope, he was specifically asked by reporters after his return whether he had seen the pope. Daignault replied that he had attended two general audiences, but that he did not have a private audience with the pope. In his speech at the Joyland Ballroom, Daignault denied that he had ever said he

---

News, January 5, 1928.

180 *Providence Journal,* January 9, 1928; *Providence News,* January 9, 1928; *Woonsocket Call,* January 9, 1928. According to *La Sentinelle,* not less than ten thousand people assembled at the Joyland to welcome Daignault home, *La Sentinelle,* January 12, 1928.

181 Ibid.; Trofimenkoff, *Action Francaise,* 99–100.

182 Ibid.

was going to see the pope, but that he was going to Rome to consult with
advisors who would direct him. Significantly, Mr. Daignault did not mention in his public statements that he had met with Cardinal Gasparri.[183]

Because the English-language papers gave varying reports as to what
Mr. Daignault said in his speech at the Joyland and also differed with the
account of the talk that appeared in *La Sentinelle*, it is quite possible that
Bishop Hickey engaged the services of a stenographer to record exactly
what Daignault said at a second reception for Daignault on January 15,
1928, in the Comic Theater, New Bedford, at which Daignault was the
main speaker. In his speech at the Joyland, Mr. Daignault had prefaced
his remarks by saying that he had been told in Rome that he needed to
be discreet in his remarks. Perhaps, because he was speaking in another
diocese or perhaps because he got caught up in the excitement of the moment, he was more forthright about what had transpired in Rome than
he was in Woonsocket. In the course of recounting the events of his trip,
he expressed his anger that the nationalism of the Franco Americans had
been compared to that of the French of *Action Francaise*. To counter what
he saw as Rome's lack of understanding of the nature of Franco-American nationalism, he promised once again to prepare and send to Rome
a memorandum on the subject. He told his audience who, like himself,
hoped to see Bishop Hickey removed from his diocese, that he "was told in
certain Congregations that one should not expect a public condemnation"
of Bishop Hickey. He noted that Roman officials were aware that Hickey
was temperamental, but that Rome would remove him only if the Franco
Americans did not publicly find fault with him. To assist the Roman authorities, Daignault announced that he had prepared a second memorandum listing all their grievances.[184]

Following the singing of two songs by Theodule Hemond, the president
of the meeting introduced Fr. Duplessis of Lowell as the "chaplain of the
Sentinelle." Although Fr. Duplessis had previously denied that he had said
Cardinal O'Connell supported the Sentinellists, on this occasion, he told
the audience that the cardinal knew he was going to New Bedford and also
what he was going to say. He further said that the cardinal would never
stop his priests from assisting at the meetings of the Sentinellists as Bishop
Hickey had. When in the course of his speech he got to the question of
the parish collections, he acknowledged that he was the one the *Providence
Visitor* had referred to when it said a certain priest was teaching erroneous
doctrine on the question of the people's obligation to contribute to their
parishes. He continued to urge the people in the Diocese of Providence
not to give a red cent to the Offertory collection.[185]

183 Ibid.
184 "Meeting of January 15, 1928 in New Bedford, Mass," PChA.
185 Ibid., Bishop Hickey sent a verbatim copy of what each speaker at the New Bedford meeting said
along with an analysis of the meeting to the Congregation of the Council on January 26, 1928,
PChA.

Mr. Daignault's lack of apparent success in Rome encouraged his opponents to greater efforts toward bringing his agitation to an end. At the beginning of January 1928, Msgr. Charles Dauray, who because of his ill health had played a behind the scenes role in the controversy to date, gathered together the Franco-American pastors and administrators of the diocese who supported Bishop Hickey to decide on what course of action they would follow. One reason Mr. Daignault had enjoyed a degree of success was that up to this point the priests had not taken any unified action against his agitation. One action on which they were unanimous was to draft a letter to Bishop Hickey, which they all signed, urging him to take steps to prevent priests of their own or other dioceses from speaking in public meetings against ecclesiastical authority. Since Bishop Hickey had already taken steps to discipline the priests of his diocese who supported the Sentinellists, the bishop would concentrate his efforts on the priests of other dioceses who had been speaking at the Sentinellists' meetings.[186]

Among the most notorious of the priests of other dioceses who supported the Sentinellist was Fr. Duplessis, who had told the crowd gathered in New Bedford that he took particular pride in being introduced as the chaplain of the *La Sentinelle*. On reading the newspaper accounts of Fr. Duplessis' talk, one of Msgr. Dauray's parishioners and a parish trustee, Mr. Joseph Roy, wrote to Cardinal O'Connell protesting the fact that a priest of his diocese would support the Sentinellists' claim that Catholics were not required to financially contribute to the maintenance of their parishes.[187]

Although Bishop Hickey had not personally written to Cardinal O'Connell to protest the intervention of Boston priests in his diocese, Fr. Duplessis's remarks at New Bedford so aggravated the situation that Bishop Hickey felt that he had to do something. On January 25, 1928, Bishop Hickey sent the apostolic delegate copies of the documents the Franco-American pastors of the diocese had drawn up to make clear their attitude toward the Sentinellist agitation. He also pointed out that the pastors explicitly asked him to prevent Fr. Duplessis from coming to the diocese and making inflammatory speeches. In the letter, Hickey asked the delegate if he would send word to Cardinal O'Connell about Fr. Duplessis. In his response to Bishop Hickey dated February 6, the delegate found it "deplorable to see priests from outside the diocese of Providence . . . interjecting themselves into the internal affairs of [Providence] and abetting those who are striving to obstruct the peaceful exercise of ecclesiastical authority." The apostolic delegate did write to Cardinal O'Connell to express his dismay over the actions of Fr. Duplessis. On March 5, 1928, the cardinal replied that he had spoken with Fr. Duplessis and that Fr. Duplessis denied

186 Charles Dauray et al., to Hickey, January 14, 1928. Fr. Fournier was the only pastor who did not sign this letter.
187 Joseph Roy to O'Connell, week of January 15, 1928, PChA.

any intent of showing contempt toward Hickey's ecclesiastical authority. Duplessis did, however, write a letter of apology to the delegate and promised to abstain from all connections with the Sentinellists. Not satisfied with only the letter as a punishment, Cardinal O'Connell later transferred Fr. Duplessis from Lowell to Amesbury, Massachusetts, as far away from Rhode Island as the cardinal could possibly send him.[188]

As the Franco-American pastors also asked Bishop Hickey to prevent Canadian priests from coming to the diocese to encourage the Sentinellists in their opposition to the bishop, Bishop Hickey, in his January 25 letter to the delegate, asked him to write to his counterpart, the apostolic delegate to Canada, for his aid in the matter. Archbishop Fumasoni-Biondi shared Bishop Hickey's concern and that of his Franco-American pastors about the confusion and dismay of the people of the diocese created by the interference of priests of other dioceses in the affairs of Providence. As the delegate's urging, Bishop Hickey himself wrote to Archbishop Andrea Cassulo, the apostolic delegate to Canada, on February 14, 1928, and enclosed with his letter, at Fumasoni-Biondi's suggestion, a packet of documents which provided the delegate with background information on the Sentinellist agitation. Hickey pointed out that the Canadian priests who had been supporting the Sentinellists were potentially causing incalculable harm to the faithful and damaging respect for legitimate Church authority. He singled out Fr. Edouard Lavergne, who he reported was with Fr. Beland in Rome, as the principal cause of the difficulties in Rhode Island.[189]

Two days after Bishop Hickey wrote to Archbishop Cassulo, Fr. Georges Bedard wrote, at Hickey's request, to Archbishop Georges Gauthier, the coadjutor Archbishop of Montreal, to bring him up to date regarding the state of the agitation in Rhode Island and to bring to the archbishop's attention the degree that one of his priests, Canon Joseph-Arthur Curotte, a canon lawyer, who was then in Rome, had been involved in the affair. Bedard informed the archbishop that Canon Curotte had met with the leaders of the Croisés when they were in the process of forming the society when he was in Woonsocket to preach a retreat. According to Bedard, Curotte had assured the leaders that a society like the kind they proposed did not need the approbation of the local bishop. Furthermore, he suggested that Curotte was the canonist whom Daignault had initially consulted when he was first considering filing a civil suit against Bishop Hickey. Since Bishop Hickey was planning to write the Roman authorities concerning Curotte's role in the Sentinellist agitation and he did not wish to provide Rome with inaccurate information, Bedard relayed Bishop Hickey's query as to whether Fr. Curotte had gone to Rome on his own or as a representative of the archbishop. Archbishop Gauthier supplied the information

---

188 Hickey to Fumasoni-Biondi, January 25, 1928; Fumasoni-Biondi to Hickey, February 6, 1928; March 5, 1928, PChA; *The Rhode Islander*, March 16, 1928.
189 Hickey to Cassulo, February 14, 1928, PChA.

requested, for which Bishop Hickey sent him a thank you note on February 26.[190]

Bishop Hickey also wrote to Cardinal Rouleau in Quebec for a similar reason. Hickey was aware that Fr. Lavergne had sailed for Rome at the same time as Fr. Beland and that he had played the role of peacemaker at Rome when he persuaded Frs. Beland and Prince to sign the formulas of submission that Msgr. Gentile had sent to Bishop Hickey earlier. However, rather than going home to Quebec on his return from Europe, Bishop Hickey reported that Fr. Lavergne's first concern was to visit Woonsocket, where he attended a secret meeting at which Mr. Daignault had gathered the leaders of the agitation from all over New England. At the meeting, Fr. Lavergne had given an address urging those at the meeting to continue the struggle. Hickey informed Cardinal Rouleau that he had hoped that the Daignault affair would end without his having to invoke the censures of the Church. However, he feared that the encouragement given by Fr. Lavergne and other priests from outside the Diocese of Providence would bring about a "renewal of ardor among the Sentinellists" and their words might serve to justify the stance taken by Daignault in *La Sentinelle* in which Daignault had implied at times that Cardinal Rouleau was hostile to the Bishop of Providence. Under the circumstances, Hickey told the cardinal, he felt obliged to write to Rome concerning Lavergne's visit to Woonsocket, but did not want to do so without first informing the cardinal. In his reply to Bishop Hickey, Cardinal Rouleau cautioned him not to take at face value the reports regarding his supposed sympathy for the Sentinellists movement, which had appeared in *La Sentinelle*. The cardinal assured Hickey the articles were distorted and pure fantasy.[191]

The controversy initiated by the Sentinellists did nothing to dissuade Bishop Hickey from doing what he believed to be right and his duty. If Daignault and his supporters thought they might intimidate the bishop by their threats and their negative rhetoric, they badly misjudged the man. After making his position clear in the pastoral letter he wrote in February 1927, Hickey for the most part ignored the rhetoric of *La Sentinelle*. There were times however, such as the press conference that followed the dedication of the new home office building of the Union St. Jean Baptiste in July 1927, when the bishop did publicly seek to refute certain charges made by the Sentinellists. Another occasion presented itself in October 1927, when Bishop Hickey went to Holy Family Parish, Woonsocket, on Sunday, October 16, to preside at the ceremonies celebrating the parish's twenty-fifth anniversary. In response to an address of welcome read to him by State Senator Wilfrid Mathieu, Bishop Hickey began by congratulating the people of the parish for what they had accomplished and by stressing that it was belief in a doctrine and submission to a manner of thinking

190 Bedard to Gauthier, February 16, 26, 1928, PChA.
191 Hickey to Rouleau, January 26, 1928; Rouleau to Hickey, March 1, 1928, PChA.

and acting in conformity with the Church that made one a Catholic rather than a member of a race. In response to one of the main points of Daignault's criticism that the use of parish funds for purposes other than parish needs endangered the Franco-American parishes, the bishop asserted, with a care to make a distinction that Daignault ignored, that it was the duty of the parish to participate, insofar as it is possible without detriment to its parish works, in the works of the universal Church and of the diocese. In an indirect reference to the agitation, Hickey recalled the parable of Christ about the wheat and the weeds and the gospel's attributing the weeds to the work of an enemy. He ended by saying that he wanted the people to have confidence in their bishop "who in his administration is a Catholic bishop and nothing else. He is for everybody."[192]

On Monday, November 7, 1927, the dedication of new additions to Woonsocket's Jesus-Marie Academy and Convent staffed by the Religious of Jesus and Mary in Precious Blood Parish afforded another opportunity for Bishop Hickey to respond to his critics against the background of a positive example of his concern for the Franco Americans. In response to the addresses read to him on the occasion, Bishop Hickey, in referring to the civil suits against the parishes initiated by Daignault, expressed his conviction that the good sense of the majority of the Franco Americans in the diocese would prevail in the end and that the strife of the past few months would soon cease.[193]

Bishop Hickey offered one of his most detailed and specific responses to the charges made against him in *La Sentinelle* concerning his administration of his parish in Gilbertsville; the administration of Notre Dame Hospital, Central Falls; and St. Joseph's School in Natick, Rhode Island, in his response to a letter which R. G. de Tonnancour, editor of the Fall River *Herald News*, wrote to him on November 14, 1927. In his letter, which was printed in the *Providence Visitor*, as was Mr. de Tonnancour's, Bishop Hickey sought to set the record straight about what actions he did or did not take in all three matters, rejecting in the process any bias on his part against Franco Americans with which *La Sentinelle* had charged him.[194]

When on Monday, December 7, 1927, Bishop Hickey returned to Woonsocket once more to bless the cornerstone of the new convent and annex to the school that Msgr. Dauray was building in Precious Blood Parish, the occasion allowed his supporters an opportunity to turn out in large numbers to demonstrate their support. In his address to Bishop Hickey, Guillaume Desaulniers, one of the parish trustees, in a pointed rejection of the rhetoric of *La Sentinelle*, thanked the bishop for the many proofs of his love for the Franco Americans and for his support of the educational institutions the Franco American held so dear. In his response to the ad-

192 *Woonsocket Call*, October 17, 1927.
193 Ibid., November 5, 8, 1927.
194 *Providence Visitor*, December 2, 1927.

dress, Bishop Hickey made a point of stressing that both the Academy of Jesus-Marie and Mt. St. Charles Academy were bilingual schools, which both supported the faith of their students and prepared them for success in the world.[195]

Also, in December 1927, Bishop Hickey took advantage of his being in Woonsocket on Sunday, December 18, to bless the cornerstone of a new church for the Italians, St. Anthony's, on Greene Street, to announce the allocation of funds from the Catholic Charity Drive to Jesus-Marie Academy ($25,000 to be used in paying for the new addition), to L'Hospice St. Antoine ($10,00 toward a building fund to replace the existing building), and to St. Francis Orphanage ($5,000). In denouncing the Charity Drive, Daignault had charged that the bulk of the Charity Fund monies would go to "Irish" institutions rather to Franco-American ones and that the Franco-American institutions would receive less money than they would if they retained their own fund-raising drives. Since there were more "Irish" charitable institutions than French, the charge was valid. But in announcing the contributions, Bishop Hickey wished to show that the French institutions would receive their share and more.[196]

Since *La Sentinelle* and its supporters had undermined Bishop Hickey's authority in his administration of the diocese, the Franco-American priests of the diocese who stood with the bishop had also seen their authority questioned. On January 11, 1928, a committee drafted a collective letter, which twenty of the twenty-one priests who were pastors or administrators of the Franco-American parishes, along with Fr. Elphege Caron, chaplain at Hospice St. Antoine and spiritual director for many of the French clergy and religious, signed at a meeting with Bishop Hickey on Saturday, January 14, 1928. The clergy read their letter to their congregations on Sunday, January 15. In it, the Franco-American clergy praised the "vast majority" of the French-speaking Catholics in the diocese who "remained loyal to the past and to their duty." While they had hoped that "the authors of the current trouble" would have at length "stopped their agitation, regretted their errors, and returned to a sane appreciation of the facts," the fact that leaders of the movement seemed to give it a new impulse each day caused them, they said, to unite their efforts in a concerted action to warn their parishioners of the dangers contained in the Sentinellists' doctrines. Specifically, the priests urged their people to avoid the Societe des Croisés, which, while it had a good purpose initially, had embarked on a "path that leads directly to schism." Secondly, they warned their parishioners against *La Sentinelle* because its policy, "based on a misconstrued nationalism," prompted its editor and writers not only to unjustly attack Bishop Hickey

---

195 *Woonsocket Call*, December 8, 1927; *Providence Visitor*, December 11, 1927. Mr. Desaulniers was himself a patriot, but a moderate one. In 1922, he edited a collection of articles aimed at encouraging Franco Americans to be loyal American citizens as well as to remain loyal to their French Catholic heritage. Cf. his *Precieux pele-mele franco-americain*, Woonsocket, R.I., 1922.

196 *Woonsocket Call*, December 20, 1927.

but also to hold "doctrines that [were] opposed to the teachings and discipline of the Church." Finally, they urged all to avoid the public meetings organized by the Sentinellists "in which speakers strive with craft and artfulness, sometimes, unfortunately with success," by playing on patriotic feelings, to persuade their hearers to approve and applaud statements that no honest and sincere Catholic would accept. In essence, the pastors said, the Sentinellists and their doctrines, contrary to their claims that they were merely attacking the administration of the diocese, represented a danger to the faith of the Franco Americans. They specifically repudiated the Sentinellists' claim that the Franco-American priests of the diocese were in favor of the movement and called on the people to witness that, rather than seeking to repress their traditions and religious institutions, their bishops had been doing everything they can to promote them.[197]

The Rhode Islander had turned to the subject of the impact of the Sentinellist agitation in its November 11, 1927 issue. The writer of the article observed, "The most important and at the same time the most regrettable result of the Daignault campaign has been the loss of prestige the Franco-American people of Rhode Island have suffered." The writer observed that the campaign had been about an unfortunate division among the Franco-American people, "a division which is responsible for the present lack of political influence that element had in the State several years ago." He found it the same in the religious life of the Franco Americans. To substantiate this last statement, he recalled an observation made by the apostolic delegate when he visited Woonsocket in 1924 in regard to criticism that Bishop Guertin was receiving from the Sentinellists when he asked, "What encouragement has the Holy Father to appoint another Franco-American Bishop in New England?"[198]

One major obstacle to the Sentinellists' abandoning their campaign was that they would have to admit that they were wrong in regard to their views and their actions. The reverse was that they would also have to acknowledge that those who remained loyal to their bishop and to the majority of their priests would have been right. The difference of opinion among the Franco Americans in the diocese in regard to the existence or the extent of any attempt on the part of their bishop to suppress their language and traditions aggravated the already existing divisions within Rhode Island's Franco-American communities as *The Rhode Islander* article observed. With the exception of the 1922 election, most Franco Americans had supported the Republican Party because the party had done more than the Democrats to court the Franco Americans by offering them prominent places on the party's tickets. However, the 1920s saw serious differences appear in the ranks of the state's Republicans, and the Franco-American ranks split

197 Msgr. Charles Dauray, et al., to "Dear Brethren," January 11, 1928, PChA; *Providence Journal*, January 16, 1928; For the Sentinellists' response to the letter Cf. *La Sentinelle*, January 19, 1928. *La Sentinelle* reprinted the latter in its pages.
198 *The Rhode Islander*, November 11, 1927.

as they supported different factions within the party. Many of the same men whose names have been mentioned above as partisans or opponents of Bishop Hickey also vied with each other for political office or for the satisfaction of seeing their candidate elected to political office.[199]

When in January 1928, the Republicans began talking about the possibility of increasing the number of Superior Court judgeships by two, the Republican Party's Woonsocket city committee, which was chaired by Eugene L. Jalbert, met on January 16, 1928, to endorse the candidacy of Twelfth District Court judge, Guillaume Myette, for a post on the Superior Court. Representatives of four of the five ward committees joined in the endorsement, but the Fifth Ward, where many of the supporters of Daignault's agitation lived, did not. The prospect of a seat on the Superior Court once again enticed Mr. Daignault to declare himself a candidate for a judgeship if the new posts were created. On Saturday, January 21, he declared that, if he was not elected to the Superior Court, he would be a candidate for the United States Senate. Since Daignault did not have any intra party organization that could support his candidacy, the political reporter for the *Providence Journal* interpreted Daignault's announcement of his candidacy for the senate as a ploy to force consideration of his aspirations for the Superior Court bench. In announcing his candidacy, Daignault tied his political hopes to the Sentinellists' cause. In a statement to the *Woonsocket Call*, he said, "We are only seeking recognition" and that "We are fighting for certain principles that we want recognized."[200]

Given the notoriety he had created in the course of his agitation and the evident partisanship he had shown, Elphege Daignault's chances of being elected were non-existent, for it was evident that he did not possess the qualities of fairness desired in a judge. State Sen. Mathieu, leader of the bloc of Franco-American legislators who supported Myette's candidacy and who had worked hard in behalf of Daignault's candidacy for the court in 1922, now backed Myette rather than Daignault because he had found that Daignault had even less chance of being elected in 1928 than in 1922. Sen. Mathieu made his comments about the various candidates for the proposed judgeship on the day after the Providence newspapers carried a story that Gov. Pothier [like Eugene Jalbert, a supporter of Bishop Hickey and an avowed opponent of Daignault's cause] had met with sixteen of the eighteen Franco Americans in the General Assembly and agreed to support Judge Myette. In the end, the Republican Party decided not to create any new judgeships. Any hope that Gov. Pothier might have had of using the Franco-American bloc to persuade Republican leaders to

199 Cf. Patrick T. Conley, "Ethnic Politics in Rhode Island: The Case of the Franco-Americans" in *Rhode Island in Rhetoric and Reflection: Public Addresses and Essays* (East Providence: Rhode Island Publications Society, 2002), 285–292.
200 *Providence Journal*, January, 17; 22, 23, 28, 29, 30, 1928; *Woonsocket Call*, January 31, 1928

agree to the creation of more judgeships and to electing Judge Myette to one of them ended when he died suddenly on February 4, 1928.[201]

On the day before Gov. Pothier died, *The Rhode Islander* published an excerpt from a document that it claimed it had obtained from an un-impeachable Roman source. According to the document, Rome had already sent to the delegate, Archbishop Fumasoni-Biondi, authorization for Bishop Hickey to pronounce Mr. Daignault and all the signers of the church suits excommunicated for having caused scandal and for having caused a large number of the faithful to lose their faith. The excommunication supposedly applied with equal force to the clergy in league with them. Bishop Hickey neither confirmed nor denied the truthfulness of *The Rhode Islander*'s document as he had no intention of proceeding with any declaration of excommunication until after the civil proceedings before the courts were ended.[202]

On February 6, 1928, one of the bishop's attorneys, John H. Slattery, appeared in the Supreme Court along with Mr. Daignault to set a date for the court's hearing of the diocese's motion that the Mr. Daignault's case be dismissed and Daignault's appeal of Judge Tanner's ruling. Mr. Slattery argued that it would be best if both motions were heard on the same day. As Mr. Daignault agreed, the court agreed to hear both motions on March 12. In the February 16, 1928 issue of *La Sentinelle*, Daignault returned, after a three-month absence, to writing his weekly article. In his article on the sixteenth, Daignault, overlooking the fact that it was he who had initiated the suits and then appealed Judge Tanner's ruling to the Supreme Court, claimed that the blame for bringing church matters before the civil courts lay with Bishop Hickey. The alternative would have been to reach some compromise with Daignault out of court as Daignault asserted the Congregation of the Council had asked the bishop to do.[203]

In anticipation of the final act in the legal drama in the church suits, Bishop Hickey resolved to make one last appeal to the Sentinellists to end their legal action short of a final judgment and thus avoid excommunication. On January 30, the bishop sent the apostolic delegate a draft of a pastoral letter addressed to the Franco-American priests who had sought in their own letter to call their parishioners back to obedience and respect for the Church. The delegate returned the letter with his suggestions on February 6 and added a letter of his own that Hickey could publish if he wished.[204]

Bishop Hickey had his letter and that of the delegate printed in the *Providence Visitor* on February 17, 1928 and read in either French or English in all the parishes on the following Sunday. In his letter, Hickey particu-

---

201 Ibid.
202 *Rhode Islander*, February 3, 1928.
203 *Woonsocket Call*, February 6, 1928; *La Sentinelle*, February 16, 1928; *Rhode Islander*, February 17, 1928.
204 Msgr. Paul Marella, auditor, to Hickey, February 6, 1928, PChA.

larly praised and thanked his priests for their efforts over the past year "in preaching the doctrine of the Church on the question of the retention of seat money and Offertory collection," which he noted had been attacked and contradicted. The sixth Commandment of the Church, a doctrine regularly taught in catechism classes, stated that the faithful had the duty of providing for the materials needs of the Church, each according to their means. In was in the light of this Church teaching that Fr. Villiard and other pastors had spoken out against the Sentinellist-inspired strike in their parishes. In was in the light of this teaching that Bishop Hickey wrote:

> "This 'strike' is a conspiracy against the very existence of the Church and its neces-
> sary institutions, and the leaders who are organizing this conspiracy, preaching and
> trying to spread it among the flock, must be considered as enemies of the Church.
> Therefore, all those who extol it, encourage it and who, by their refusal to pay their
> seat money, contribute to its progress, are guilty of a grave sin and must be treated in
> the confessional as recidivists, as obstinate sinners."[205]

This was not the first time the French Canadians had tried to force the bishop of the diocese to accede to their wishes by refusing to contribute to their parish until their demands were met. Daignault and many others could remember the pew rent strike in St. Ann's in 1914 and a few could remember the strike in Notre Dame, Fall River in 1885–86, while a very few might even remember the strike in Precious Blood in 1875. The pew rent and Offertory strike initiated by the Sentinellists began in a small way in late 1925 with a few refusals and had increased slowly in 1926 and 1927. In February 1926, La Sentinelle reported that a selective boycott was taking place in St. Ann's, Woonsocket. Parishioners there contributed to the weekly collections, which went to the parish, but some refused to contribute to the Offertory collection since part of it went to the diocese. The strike picked up strength in July 1926, which caused Fr. Villiard at St. Ann's to warn the strikers from the pulpit to desist. The seat money strike reached a high point in August and September 1927, when Fr. Prince was removed from St. Louis. As noted above, the majority of the Franco-American priests had spoken out against the strike and disturbances that followed. The boycott of seat money and the Offertory collection was particularly effective in St. Louis Parish, but had a lesser effect in the other parishes. Although speaker after speakers in the Sentinellists' rallies from August 1927 on urged their audience not to contribute to their parish churches until justice was done to them, La Tribune on February 10, 1928 declared that the strike was a complete failure as it has failed to intimidate Bishop Hickey or persuade him in any way to make concessions to the Sentinellists. Even worse, the refusal to contribute pushed parishes like St. Louis into a severe financial crisis.[206]

205 *Providence Visitor*, February 17, 1928.
206 For this overview of the pew rent and Offertory strike I have used Sorrell, "The Sentinelle Affair

Daignault, Perdriau and Fr. Duplessis each in turn had pointed out that
the obligation to support the Church was not an absolute one. Furthermore, Mr. Daignault and the Sentinellists argued that, unlike Canada,
where tithing to support the churches was mandated by law, all contributions in the United States were voluntary. The bishop and his priests readily
agreed that those who lacked the means to contribute were not obligated
to do so and that in the United States all church contributions were voluntary. Where they disagreed with the Sentinellist was whether one could
morally withhold one's support of the Church for political reasons. To the
bishop's mind, to conspire to conduct a "financial strike," as the Sentinellists were doing, for the purpose of coercing those in authority into doing
something they were bound in conscience not to do, was a grave sin. As the
bishop would point out to the authorities in Rome, Daignault's question-
ing and criticism of episcopal authority echoed that of the *L'Action Francaise*
movement.[207]

In Precious Blood Parish, Woonsocket, Msgr. Dauray supplemented the
appeal of Bishop Hickey and the apostolic delegate with a written appeal
of his own. This was the first time Msgr. Dauray has spoken publicly on
the controversy, although his opposition to the movement was well known.
He too deplored the Sentinellist movement as a menace to the faith and
threat to the existence of the Church. While he acknowledged that there
may have been some who initially supported the movement in good faith,
there could be no doubt in the light of the bishop's letter and that of the
apostolic delegate that "good faith no longer exists."[208]

On Monday, February 20, 1928, *La Tribune* added its voice to the call
to the Sentinellists to give up their cause. The writer of the *La Tribune* article might well have been voicing the view of the majority of the Franco
Americans in the diocese when he wrote:

> The agitation which has been carried on, especially in the last few months, is not only
> anti-Catholic and irreligious, it is anti-American. The good sense and spirit of toler-
> ance of the better Protestant element in this country, is disgusted with the campaign
> of odious defamation which is conducted under the pretext of *preserving the mother tongue
> in a milieu where no one is attacking it, under the pretext of obtaining justice where no injustice has
> been committed* (emphasis mine).

A few months earlier, Daignault's English-language antagonist, *The
Rhode Islander,* had offered another negative assessment of the Sentinellist
movement:

> Intelligent persons who have endeavored to analyze the Daignault racial and religious
> campaign and have tried to ascertain its causes have been compelled to admit that

and Militant *Survivance*," 282–85.
207 "Synthesis of Principals of the Sentinellist Agitation, January 5, 1929, PChA.
208 *Providence Visitor*, February 17, 1928; *Woonsocket Call*, February 18, 20, 1928; *Providence Journal*,
    February 20, 1928.

it has no jurisdiction in fact, that it is based wholly upon false premises and that its leaders have depended for their success upon the credulity of many together with the ignorance of the real situation and the prejudice of their followers.[209]

For all the charges made and repeated, the *Tribune* writer suggested that the Sentinellists had failed to persuade either the Church courts, the civil courts, or the court of public opinion, that Bishop Hickey had done them any injustice or wished to curb the use of the French language in any way. In addition to lessening respect for the teaching and authority of the Church, both within and without the Church, the writer held, as had the writer in *The Rhode Islander*, that the agitation was disastrous "because it sets [the Franco Americans] back fifty years and it puts us back in the class of "foreigners" incapable of understanding American institutions and adjusting our life to them." The writer ended with a final appeal: "Franco-Americans who love your race and who love the Church, abandon this agitation founded on passion which had produced nought but evil and could not on the face of it ever do any good."[210]

When Mr. Daignault was approached by a reporter for the *Woonsocket Call* on the day Bishop Hickey's and the delegate's letters appeared in the *Visitor*, he told the reporter he had "absolutely nothing to say." However, at a Sentinellist meeting in Emmett Hall on Manton Avenue in the Olneyville section of Providence, Daignault responded to the letters by saying that he rejected the idea that not contributing to the support of the Church was a sin. He urged his audience to continue the strike. For the Sentinellists, it was essential to their cause that they create a crisis in order to force Rome to intervene. Daignault added, "We depend on an authority that is too far away." Recognizing as he had in his speech in New Bedford in January that Rome consistently supported the bishops in any confrontation with the laity when it was a matter of discipline, he argued that it was "necessary to continue the strike. Don't give to the church, and I promise that in three months we will witness the disappearance of our bishop." He repeated much the same message in his article in *La Sentinelle* on February 23.[211]

Whatever hope that the Sentinellists had in securing what they saw as justice lay in the petition Daignault had drafted asking the Holy See to send a special emissary to investigate the complaints outlined in the petition. They hoped to get a majority of the Franco Americans in Rhode Island to sign after they began circulating it at their meetings following Daignault's return from Rome. However, the reporter who covered the meeting in Olneyville for the *Evening Bulletin* observed that only some at the meeting signed it, while others left the hall when it was sent around. Two

---

209 *La Tribune*, February 20, 1928. The article was reprinted in translation in the *Providence Visitor*, February 24, 1928; *The Rhode Islander*, November 25, 1927.
210 Ibid.
211 *La Sentinelle*, February 23, 1928; *Providence Journal*, February 20; March 5, 1928; *Evening Bulletin*, February 28, 1928; *Woonsocket Call*, February 18, 20, 1928.

weeks later, at a Sentinellist meeting in Jacques Cartier Hall in Warren, Mr. Daignault sought to support the call for initiating the offering strike by saying that the canonists he had consulted had advised the Sentinellists to stop paying the pew rent.[212]

Daignault repeated much of his criticism of Bishop Hickey's pastoral letter in a front-page article in *La Sentinelle* on February 22. As was his custom, he did not deny that it was a grave sin not to contribute to the support of the Church. Lawyer that he was, he justified not heeding the teaching of the letter because the letter failed to specify what kind of sin one committed by not contributing. Daignault made the apostolic delegate's letter the subject of his article published on March 1. In the article, he asked whether the writer of the letter was truly an apostolic delegate or an Irish bishop, since the he found the letter repugnant to the diplomatic tradition of the Church. He also found fault with the delegate, as he often did with other bishops and clergy who opposed his movement, for using language "devoid of charity and religion."[213]

The day after the Olneyville meeting at which Mr. Daignault gave his public response to the bishop's and delegate's letters, Bishop Hickey wrote the delegate in order to elaborate on the reasons why he had not declared the signers of the church suits excommunicated as Rome had authorized him to do. He gave five reasons why it would be better if Rome issued the decree. First, the Sentinellists had declared that they would disregard any excommunication coming from Hickey and that would have required him to issue a second censure, etc. Secondly, he had delayed action until the "public mind" seemed better prepared for it. He told the delegate he now believed that the people were actually expecting the penalty and asking that it be pronounced. Thirdly, he wished to forestall "any accusation of precipitancy due to racial prejudice or hatred." Fourthly, his lawyers had asked him to defer any condemnation of *La Sentinelle* or excommunications until after the Supreme Court heard and decided the case, lest action on the bishop's part provoke an endless series of recriminations in the court for contempt or damages. Lastly, in view of the fact that the agitation had spread to the Fall River and Springfield dioceses, Hickey believed that it was much better for Rome to pass sentence once and for all and that Rome wait to take this action at least until after March 12, when the church case would be heard by the Supreme Court. Along with his letter Hickey sent newspaper clippings of the Olneyville meeting and suggested that the only explanation of the "closest and best informed observers" for Daignault's continuing the agitation was the "probable existence of large financial obligations undertaken long since for the conduct of his paper, *La Sentinelle* . . . coupled with some unsound advice from a prelate in Rome." Hickey identified the prelate as Msgr. Curotte, who was also the advisor to

---

212 Ibid. A copy of the petition is found in *La Sentinelle*, February 23, 1928.
213 *La Sentinelle*, February 22; March 1, 1928.

Frs. Prince and Beland. He suggested to the delegate that, if some word would arrive from Rome that Daignault would not be received when he made his promised return visit to the city, "it would be a good thing."[214]

The day after he wrote to the delegate, Hickey sent another letter informing the delegate that, after meeting with his Board of Consultors and some of the "French pastors best acquainted with the situation," he had decided to wait two or three weeks before making it a reserved sin to participate in the strike. The priests at the meeting agreed that, if Rome declared the excommunication following the Supreme Court judgment, it would be far more effective than if it came from Hickey himself. As the delegate agreed to pass on Hickey's request, Hickey spent the next few days writing his letter to the Congregation of the Council and assembling the names of those who had incurred the censure. In addition to the names of the men who signed both the original church suits and the amended versions, Hickey also asked that Henri Perdriau and Antonio Prince be included among those to be censured because of their roles in the agitation and explained why he made the request. Furthermore, he asked that Rome also condemn *La Sentinelle* and forbid the faithful from reading it.[215]

While the Sentinellists' response to Bishop Hickey's pastoral and the delegate letter's helped to strengthen the resolve of their supporters to continue the struggle, the words of defiance only served to reinforce Bishop Hickey's argument that the time had come for Rome to act in a definitive way. As was his custom, Bishop Hickey sent copies of the newspaper articles describing Mr. Daignault's response to the pastoral and the delegate's letter to Rome. He also sent a letter in which he pointed out the inherent contradiction in Mr. Daignault's drafting a petition asking Rome to send a papal investigator at the same time that the Sentinellists continued to reject Hickey's own authority and that of the delegate. He labeled Daignault's new petition as yet another "insult to the Pope after all that has been said and all that has been written against the religious authorities." When on March 1, 1928, *La Sentinelle* published a reply to the delegate's letter, Hickey sent a copy of it along with another letter in which he wrote, "It is obvious that the goal of this impudent reply is to ruin, in the spirit of this newspaper, the authority of the representative of the Holy See in this country."[216]

While Bishop Hickey's pastoral letter on the sinfulness of refusing to support the Church lessened support for the strike movement in Woonsocket, it did not do so everywhere. On March 4, the Sunday following the reading of the letter, Fr. Mathias Hebert, the pastor of St. Cecilia's Church, Pawtucket, took up the seat money collection during the ser-

---

214 Hickey to Fumasoni-Biondi, February 20, 1928, PChA.
215 Hickey to Fumasoni-Biondi, February 21, 1928, PChA.
216 Hickey to Sbarretti, February 25; March 5, 1928,PChA.

mon of his curate as was the custom in Franco-American parishes. When
he came to the bench where a seventeen year old young man, Herman
Lallier, was sitting, Lallier, rather than rub his hands over his knees as the
supporters of the pew rent strike had been doing to show their opposition
to it, displayed a white card with the single word "Justice" on it, which the
Sentinellists had been passing out. Since Fr. Mathias Hebert had previously told the young man not to show the card again or he would have to
keep him out of the church, he reminded him of what he had said. When
Lallier replied that the church was a public place and that, as long as he
did not create a disturbance, he had a right to remain there, Fr. Hebert
asked one of the ushers to put Lallier out. When Lallier refused to go, the
usher, who was a special policeman on the Pawtucket force, went out to get
a regular Pawtucket policeman, who was doing traffic duty in the square
outside. The police officer also asked Lallier to leave as Fr. Hebert was
within his rights to ask him to do so. When the young man again refused,
the usher and officer forcibly ejected him. The incident attracted considerable attention and, when the young man was ejected, about three hundred
others worshipers also left the church.[217]

On March 10, two days before the scheduled hearing of the appeals
in the church suits, Mr. Daignault telephoned the bishop's lead counsel,
Mr. Curran, to suggest a two-day postponement of the hearing date. Mr.
Daignault's suggestion was prompted by the announcement that a prominent Franco-American priest, Fr. Joseph Bourgeois, pastor of St. John the
Baptist, Arctic, West Warwick, had died on March 7 and his funeral was
to be on the 12. Mr. Curran readily agreed to the delay as did the court.
When the case was called in March 14, Mr. Daignault was the first to
speak and took about a half hour to make his argument. He centered his
argument on Judge Tanner's ruling that the funds of the churches could
be used for educational and charitable purposes of the Church as a whole.
He argued that, if large sums of money could be diverted from the funds
of the parish corporations and used for purposes not connected with
them, such as to aid diocesan high schools and for support of the *Providence
Visitor* and National Catholic Welfare Conference, then the bishop and
trustees could apply parish funds "to the election of public officers and the
donors of these funds would have no redress." The bishop's attorneys, Patrick Curran and John Slattery, asked for two hours to argue their case, but
were limited to an hour and a half. They again argued Catholic doctrine
that the civil courts had no jurisdiction in the case since the question in
dispute was an ecclesiastical one. However, Chief Justice Sweetland intervened to rule that the question of jurisdiction was not at issue. When Mr.
Curran then sought to pursue the point by asking the court to dismiss Mr.
Daignault's suit on the grounds that the court did not have jurisdiction,
Justice Sweetland replied that he should have appealed Judge Tanner's rul-

217 *Providence Journal*, March 5, 1928.

ing. When Justice Chester W. Barrows agreed with his colleague on the question of jurisdiction, Mr. Curran went on to his other arguments, the chief of which was that Daignault's amended bill had failed to state what the general laws, doctrine, discipline and ritual of the Roman Catholic Church were, so far as they are related to the question before the court, and that the amended bill also failed to show that the complainants had already brought their appeals to the tribunals of the Church. After hearing both sides, the judges then reserved decision.[218]

With the hearing over, Mr. Daignault sailed for Rome on the voyage he had promised he would make after he returned from his first trip there. As they had done before, his supporters met at the Joyland Ballroom in Woonsocket to give him a send-off. While ten thousand had gathered at Joyland in January to hear his report of his first trip, about two thousand gathered on Sunday, March 11, 1928. Showing that he was well aware of the anti-nationalist sentiments in Rome, Daignault told those who gathered to see him off again that authorities in Rome "frowned upon the 'strike' and the civil suits. Because of their attitude it can be construed that they want to see this fight ended as soon as possible." He declared that the Sentinellists had a twofold purpose in calling the meeting: to obtain signatures on the petition Daignault was to bring to Rome and to show that the Sentinellists were "united in desiring the triumph of the cause we represent."[219]

Throughout the agitation, both sides had paid attention to the number of people attending the Sentinellists' rallies and both sides had come up with different numbers at the same events. For the Sentinellists, it was vital for their cause to show that they represented the majority or at least a substantial part of the Franco-American population in New England. It was just as important for their opponents to show that they did not. One scholar, Richard Sorrell, who has sought to answer the more limited question of how strong were the Sentinellists in Woonsocket, concluded that the Sentinellists "failed to win the consistent support of a majority, even a large minority, of the masses of Franco-Americans in Woonsocket." Mr. Sorrell notes there were times in August and September 1927, in the aftermath of Fr. Prince's removal as pastor of St. Louis, "when thousands boycotted their parishes, attended rallies, and contributed money." Granting that Daignault had only four weeks to circulate his petition to the Holy Father asking that a papal official come to investigate the spiritual condition of the Franco Americans, 15,000 signatures on it are significant, but

218 Curran to Hickey, Statement of Professional Services rendered, June 12, 1928, PChA; Woonsocket Call, March 14, 1928; *Providence Journal*, March 15, 1928.
  Cf. *Providence Visitor*, March 23, 1928 for a reprint of the argument of the bishop's attorney's before the court. The day before Fr. Bourgeois, who had been emphatic in condemning the Sentinellist movement, suffered the shock which caused his death, he had been the subject of an attack in *La Sentinelle*. *The Rhode Islander* in an article on March 16, 1928 noted that Fr. Bourgeois was believed to be another victim of the Sentinellist controversy.
219 *Providence Journal*, March 12, 1928.

not particularly impressive, since the signatures were gathered at rallies in Rhode Island as well as outside the state. At the time Daignault was gathering signatures on the petition, Bishop Hickey was writing Cardinal Sbarretti via the apostolic delegate that he believed Daignault's followers numbered not more than a thousand out of Rhode Island's more than 80,000 French-speaking Catholics.[220]

As he had prior to Mr. Daignault's first trip to Rome, Bishop Hickey wrote to the apostolic delegate of Daignault's planned visit so that the delegate could inform the Roman Congregations. He began his letter by noting that he heard "from an authorized source that the Supreme Court will confirm the decision of the Superior Court, declaring the case in favor of the Bishop of Providence." While Mr. Daignault would complain to his followers that those who opposed his movement poisoned the minds of the Roman authorities by sending them copies of Woonsocket's *La Tribune*, the fact of the matter was that copies of *La Sentinelle*, which Bishop Hickey sent with a commentary on the articles Daignault wrote, were more influential than those of *La Tribune*. In his cover letter to the delegate dated March 20, Bishop Hickey sent an extensive account of what Daignault had said and done since December 29, 1927, when he last left Rome. Using Daignault's own words, the bishop pointed out how Daignault had tried to use the threat of court action to "obtain the settlement of our difficulties through the intervention of the Roman authorities," which the civil courts would then have recognized. In a second part of his letter, Bishop Hickey discussed the Sentinellists' offerings strike. Again quoting Daignault's own words, this time from the speech he gave when he returned from his first trip to Rome, Bishop Hickey sought to show the strike's origin and ultimate purpose. "In Rome, one does not like the offerings strike; but certain Canadian bishops have told us that it was useless to address ourselves to the apostolic delegate or to Rome because we would not obtain anything without undertaking the offerings strike." On the question of nationalism, Hickey quoted from a speech Daignault gave in New Bedford on January 15, 1928, to show that Daignault had mocked what he saw as the Congregation of the Council's ignorance in regard to the question of nationalism, because the members of the Congregation did not see a difference between the Sentinellists' form of nationalism and that which Rome had condemned in speaking out against the *Action Française* movement.[221]

What Mr. Daignault did not know when he left for Rome on March 24, 1928 was that the Roman authorities had already decided to act on Bishop Hickey's request that Rome declare all the signers of the Church suits, along with Henri Perdriau and Antonio Prince, excommunicated. When Bishop Hickey's news that the court would decide in his favor reached

220 Sorrell, "The Sentinelle Affair and Militant *Survivance*,", 273–320; Hickey to Sbarretti, March 5, 1928, PChA
221 Hickey to Fumasoni-Biondi, March 20, 1928, PChA.

main outside during the funeral mass. Following the mass, she was buried in Precious Blood Cemetery.[234]

Within a year of Rose's death, a small pamphlet appeared, which gave a very short biography of Rose and included a prayer for her intercession. Following the publication of Fr. Boyer's *She Wears a Crown of Thorns* in 1948, interest in the cause of Rose Ferron sharply increased. Shortly after his ordination as Bishop of Providence in July 1948, Bishop Russell J. McVinney asked Fr. (later Msgr.) Arthur Geoghegan to investigate the case of Rose Ferron. Because Fr. Boyer's book had prompted many letters to the diocese and to Rome seeking to promote Rose's cause, Bishop McVinney anticipated that the Roman authorities would eventually ask for details of Rose's life and for the bishop's opinion of the authenticity of the spiritual phenomenon Fr. Boyer associated with her. He asked Fr. Geoghegan to interview the lay people who best knew Rose before they died. Because of the thoroughness with which Fr. Geoghegan conducted his interviews and the time constraints under which he worked, he only conducted six interviews. When he realized he would not be able to do the work in a timely fashion, he asked to be replaced as investigator. Subsequently, Bishop McVinney asked Fr. (later Msgr.) William McKitchen, the pastor of Sacred Heart Parish in Woonsocket, to undertake the work. Before his appointment to Sacred Heart, Fr. McKitchen had worked in the Diocesan Marriage Tribunal. The care with which he did his work convinced Bishop McVinney he would be the best individual to complete the investigation. Because Fr. McKitchen, like Fr. Geoghegan, asked specific questions of the people he interviewed and then prepared a typed copy of both his questions and their answers for the witnesses to sign, he too found the task time consuming. Altogether, the number of those interviewed by both priests was relatively small. Their interviews, however, were quiet detailed and revealed no substantial evidence to cause Bishop McVinney to alter the negative evaluation of the case made by Bishop Hickey. On January 9, 1964, Bishop McVinney issued a degree in which he officially responded to those who had asked him to promote the cause of Rose Ferron before the Sacred Congregation of Rites. The bishop wrote, "With deep regret we conclude that any further action to promote the cause of Rose Ferron is not warranted. We urge all who have manifested an interest in this cause to discontinue their activity and to pray with us that this pious soul may be permitted to find her place among the myriad unheralded saints who enjoy the Beatific Vision in heaven."[235]

---

234 *News-Tribune*, May 15, 1936; *Woonsocket Call*, May 15, 1935.

235 In his letter to Bishop Hickey on August 18, 1933, Fr. Boyer correctly identified the testimony of Fr. Baril and the two women, who had helped Mrs. Ferron care for Rose, as that which convinced Bishop Hickey that there were other explanations for the marks that Fr. Boyer had identified as spiritual phenomena. Since that time, advocates of Rose Ferron's cause have sought to discredit the testimony of the three. Fr. Palm devoted his third volume of testimonies and letters to this effort. Unlike the interviews conducted by Frs. Geoghegan and McKitchen, which specifically addressed the question of the authenticity of the spiritual phenomena identified by Fr. Boyer,

question in a letter he sent to Msgr. Marella to thank him for sending the telegram. In the letter, he also asked how he should proceed in the matter as he was desirous of announcing the excommunications in the most solemn manner in each of the parishes affected. Msgr. Marella noted in his reply that the full text of the interdict and excommunication would be printed in the *Acta Apostolicae Sedis* that he expected would arrive in about ten days. Without the text of the interdict and excommunication in hand, the *Providence Visitor* for April 13, 1928, printed the telegram from Msgr. Marella and an explanation of excommunication. On the following Sunday, the pastors of all the Franco-American churches announced the ban and the excommunications at all the masses. The announcement of the excommunications and ban on reading *La Sentinelle* was the death knell for the Sentinellist movement, at least within the Diocese of Providence.[236]

The Excommunications and the Rhode Island Supreme Court's Final Judgment

It fell to Archbishop Fumasoni-Biondi, the apostolic delegate, to determine how those excommunicated were to be notified. Although Bishop Hickey had had Fr. Georges Bedard prepare a list of names and addresses to include with Bishop Hickey's letter to the Congregation of the Council asking that the Congregation declare the men excommunicated, the bishop sent a letter to each of the pastors where the men lived asking for a list of the names and addresses of those who signed the original bills of complaint and those recruited to sign the amended ones. The delegate then sent a personal letter, dated May 11, 1928, to each of the signers officially informing them that they had incurred the penalty of excommunication. The delegate also sent a different letter to Perdriau and Prince calling on them to renounce their part in the agitation and to declare their readiness to obey their bishop within one month or be placed under personal interdict and denied the reception of the sacraments if they did not. As the delegate specified that each of the letters was to be delivered by

---

Fr. Palm allowed those giving testimony to say what they wished. The result was that not all the questions at issue were addressed and many remained unresolved.

236 Hickey to Marella, April 9, 1928; Marella to Hickey, April 12, 1928, PChA; *Providence Visitor,* April 13, 1928; *Providence Journal,* April 16, 1928; *Woonsocket Call,* April 16, 1928.
The Rhode Islander in its April 13, 1928 issue claimed that it had learned from an authoritative source outside of the Diocese of Providence that "the degree of excommunication against Elphege J. Daignault and the leaders of his group, together with the interdiction of his newspaper, *La Sentinelle,* . . . was hastened by an appeal sent to the Vatican by the archbishops and bishops of the Province of Quebec, who repudiated the Daignault agitation in most emphatic terms and indignantly resented Daignault's repeated assertion that they were giving him their moral support. Archbishop Gauthier of Montreal is said to have headed the signers of the protest to the Pope."

hand, Bishop Hickey assigned the task to the pastors of the men. On May 18, 1928, the *Visitor* printed a copy of the delegate's letter and a list of the names and addresses to whom the letters were sent.[237]

In his 1936 narration of his second trip to Rome, Mr. Daignault said he arrived in Rome on Holy Thursday, April 5, 1928. He went to confession on Holy Saturday and received communion on Easter Sunday to fulfill his Easter duty before he learned of his excommunication, news of which was published in Easter Sunday's *Osservatore Romano*. However, during the struggle itself, he said he knew of the excommunication before it appeared in the paper and before he went to communion. He would relate that he was angry when he first heard of it, thinking for the moment that he was the only one excommunicated. When Mr. Hemond telegraphed him asking if he should continue to publish *La Sentinelle* in spite of the ban, Daignault replied in the affirmative. In publishing news of the paper being placed on the Index, Mr. Perdriau wrote, "If our Holy Father, the Pope, demands the death of *La Sentinelle*, as faithful sons of the Church, we will offer it on the altar of sacrifice. Even so, the truth will come to life."[238]

On Friday, April 13, Daignault met with a reporter from the Associated Press. Daignault reiterated his intention of pursuing his appeal to the Holy See. He also said that, as a Catholic, he would submit to all the decisions of the Church. Daignault continued to plead good faith as his excuse for persisting in his pursuit of what he saw as justice and once again said his decision to act as he had was based on the "advice of persons well versed in ecclesiastical legislation." He asserted that, if he had gone to the civil courts, it was only to protect the rights of a Catholic citizen from an evident abuse of power. Although in the course of several of his later addresses, he promised his supporters he would never agree to stop the suits, on this occasion, he went on to claim that, in 1927, when he first visited Rome, he had been "summoned" there and that he had agreed with those who had summoned him to suspend the civil cases he had brought before the court. [In his petition to the Sacred Congregation, he added that he promised to "suspend" the civil proceedings "until the Holy See pronounced itself."] To explain why the case had remained before the courts, he pointed out that it was the bishop's attorneys who had insisted the proceedings continue. He acknowledged that he had heard from an American lawyer in Rome, who had himself heard it from a good source, that the Supreme Court would reject his appeal and wondered how the "bishop of Rhode Island received this assurance." As to the difficulties he anticipated in having his case heard, he again attributed the Congregation of the Council's disinterest in hearing his appeal, not to the members of the congregation itself, but to a "subordinate advisor" who was working against

237 Hickey to Fumasoni-Biondi, May 5, 1928; Fumasoni-Biondi to Hickey, May 12, 1928, PChA; *Providence Visitor*, May 18, 1928.
238 *Providence Journal*, April 13, 1928; *La Sentinelle*, April 12, 1928.

the interests of the French Canadians. [This charge originated with Daignault's lawyer, Mr. Astorri, who accused Msgr. Gentile with frustrating his
client's appeal.] Bishop Hickey also pointed to this last remark in his comments on Daignault's interview when writing to Cardinal Sbarretti.[239]

Not only would Daignault's hopes for any kind of an interview with the
Congregation of the Council languish during the five weeks he spent in
Rome, but his hopes for another meeting with Cardinal Gasparri were also
frustrated because of the death of Mr. Doulcet, the French Ambassador to
the Vatican, who had helped arrange the previous meeting with Cardinal
Gasparri. Mr. Doulcet had died several weeks before Daignault arrived in
Rome and no successor had yet been named. While he was unsuccessful in
securing a personal meeting with the officials of the Sacred Congregation
of the Council, Mr. Daignault had his lawyer submit to the Congregation
a long letter dated April 14, in which Mr. Daignault professed his submission, in spirit and heart, to the decisions of the Sacred Congregation.
The main intent of his letter was to offer an explanation of his past conduct. In order to have the Congregation of the Council accept the letter,
Mr. Daignault had to sign a statement disavowing his action of bringing
suit against the bishop in contradiction to the laws of the Church and to
pledge to do everything in his power to end the pew-rent strike as well as
the "meetings to which Catholics are invited to discuss matters reserved to
ecclesiastical authority." He likewise pledged to neither write nor publish
anything about these same matters. As Director of *La Sentinelle*, he signed a
second document that condemned and disapproved of everything in that
newspaper contrary to the discipline of the Church and offensive to the
members of the Catholic hierarchy. Before leaving Rome, he also sent a
telegram to his fellow Directors at *La Sentinelle* that they were not to publish
any more articles on Franco-American religious affairs, a copy of which he
sent to Cardinal Sbarretti on May 6, 1928.[240]

The announcement of the banning of *La Sentinelle* and the excommunication of Daignault and his followers did a great deal toward ending the
controversy in the parishes. According to a report in the *Providence Journal*
on April 16, the day after the French clergy confirmed the announcements
from Rome, many parishioners in Woonsocket resumed paying the seat
money. While some of those who had been sympathetic to the Sentinellist
cause might have been persuaded by the excommunications to drop their
support of the Sentinellists, not all were. When Phydime Hemond was
asked about the *Journal* report on the excommunications' effect, he replied,

239 *Woonsocket Call*, April 12, 14, 1928; *Providence Journal*, April 14, 1928; *Providence News*, April 14,
    1928; Daignault, *"Le vrai movement sentinelliste*, 177–87.
240 Ibid. Mr. Daignault printed copies of his letters to the Sacred Congregation in *La Defense*,
    January 10, 1929. Copies of formulas for the Censure and for *La Sentinelle*, n.d., are found in the
    Providence Chancery Archives. In a letter to Archbishop Fumasoni-Biondi, Bishop Hickey quoted
    from a speech given by Daignault on June 25 that he signed the formula in order to be able to
    present his case, Hickey to Fumasoni-Biondi, July 1, 1928, PChA.

"Far from dropping the struggle our friends seem to be more animated that ever before." Mr. Hemond's comment echoed the sentiments of those who attended a meeting in Artisans Hall, Woonsocket, on the previous Friday evening. The meeting was addressed by Herve Legace, Dr. Falcon and Antonio Prince. Mr. Legace continued to cast doubt on the reliability of the story of the excommunications and promised that victory would soon come. He too held to his lack of responsibility by saying that it was priests who had advised them to strike as the only way that would gain the victory that they sought over Bishop Hickey, who should be held responsible.[241]

The banning of *La Sentinelle* and the excommunication of Mr. Daignault and the other signers of the suits caused them to be hailed as martyrs or champions of the cause of liberty by the ultra nationalist Franco Americans and even by some of the moderate nationalists whose basic source of information about the struggle was *La Sentinelle* or a French newspaper sympathetic to its cause. They were also hailed as martyrs or champions of the cause of liberty by the extreme nativists of the Ku Klux Klan. In 1927, the Klan's official organ, *The Fellowship Forum*, in its July 4 issue, had discussed the church suits as evidence of the oppressive and dangerous character of the Catholic Church in the United States. On Friday, April 13, 1928, Democratic Sen. Thomas Heflin of Alabama, a Klan supporter and an avowed opponent of Gov. Alfred Smith's aspirations to become the Democrats' candidate for president in November 1928, avoided the attempts of his senate colleagues to keep him from speaking and delivered a speech in a mostly empty Senate. In the course of his speech, he referred to a *New York Times* article of April 8 reporting the banning of *La Sentinelle* and the excommunication of Daignault and his supporters. In his interview with the Associated Press, Daignault had justified his bringing suit against Bishop Hickey as his right as a citizen who felt injustice had been done. Acknowledging an incomplete familiarity with the facts of the case, Heflin defended Daignault's right as a citizen to sue the bishop for an explanation of how parish funds were used. While the United States government had found no cause to stop the publication of Daignault's paper, he charged that the "Roman Catholic Government" in Rome had undertaken to disgrace Daignault and his supporters and destroy their business. He ended by asking why Gov. Smith had not "said a word of protest against this denial of American rights and liberties to American citizens." In the course of a letter to Msgr. Gentile in Rome, Bishop Hickey later referred to Mr. Daignault's claim that he was excommunicated for having exercised the rights of French-speaking Catholics as American citizens. To the bishop's mind, Daignault was only seeking to place the Church law and State law in opposition to each other. He cited Heflin's Senate speech as proof that that was what Daignault intended to do.[242]

241 *Providence Journal*, April 16, 1928; *Woonsocket Call*, April 14, 1928.
242 *The Fellowship Forum* is quoted in Foisy, *The Sentinellist Agitation in New England*, 73; *Providence Journal*,

Hoping to exploit the anger among Daignault's supporters created by the Sentinellists' excommunication, the Ku Klux Klan invited Sen. Heflin to deliver a speech at the Klan's regular meeting place at Grant's Field on the Stillwater Road in the Smithfield village of Georgiaville. Rather than setting up the speaker's rostrum in the valley at the western end of the grounds where they usually did because of the secrecy afforded by the slope of the land, the organizers put a platform up at the center of the seven-acre field to afford a chance for as many people who wished to pay the fifty cents admission fee to hear the speaker. About six thousand people from Connecticut and Massachusetts as well as Rhode Island paid to hear Heflin speak, while another two thousand gathered on the road outside of the grounds. Those who anticipated that Heflin would attack Gov. Smith were disappointed, as Heflin avoided any direct reference to him. He did, however, attack the Roman Catholic Church's "political program" through which the Church sought to manipulate the American government to serve its ends. After he reviewed the French-Canadians suits against Bishop Hickey and Daignault's excommunication, he said if he were president, "I would issue a proclamation that no where under the shining sun should any foreign potentate have jurisdiction over any American citizen."[243]

A few days after news of the condemnation of *La Sentinelle* and the excommunications reached Rhode Island, the Catholic Club and the Catholic Woman's Club held their annual reception for Bishop Hickey at the Biltmore Hotel on Wednesday, April 18, to mark the ninth anniversary of his ordination as bishop. Ordinarily the affair was confined to the Catholic clubs that sponsored it, but, in planning for the 1928 reception, the two clubs decided to invite anyone who wished to honor Bishop Hickey to join them at the affair. More than seven hundred people gathered in the main ballroom at the Biltmore, six hundred to dine, while the remainder, who could not be accommodated at dinner, waited outside until after the dinner before they entered the room to take a seat. Besides the addresses by the presidents of the two clubs, Gov. Norman Case praised the bishop for what he had accomplished in his nine years in Providence. In the main address of the evening, State Senator Wilfred Mathieu made a vigorous plea for harmony among Catholics and stressed their common love of their country and of their Church. State Democratic Chairman Luigi DePasquale brought the greetings of the Italian people of the diocese. He expressed their appreciation of his efforts on their behalf and spoke of their affection for him. In his response to the addresses, Bishop Hickey declared, in view of the charges raised by the prospective presidential candidacy of Gov. Smith, that the Catholic Church had no political program which it was trying to carry through and no part in politics. While saying that the Church had no political ambition, he applauded the ambition of individual Catholic men who, in the face of public opposition to them simply because they were Catholic, sought to exercise their rights as a citizen. He urged solidarity among Catholics "not for political or professional purposes, but that they may know each other better and appraise each other at the proper value, give each one their due, and understand the sources of inspiration as Catholics and true Americans." Touching on what he called the "very troublesome period" made so by those "not guided by principles of justice," he called for unity among Catholics in matters of religion as well as in other concerns.[244]

Buoyed by the affirmation of good will and support provided by the Catholic clubs' reception, Bishop Hickey was also relieved of any anxiety he might have had about the church suits when the Supreme Court, as expected, rejected Mr. Daignault's appeal of Judge Tanner's reading of the incorporation law of 1869. Mr. Daignault had argued in his appeal only against Judge Tanner's understanding of the words "that church" in section 3 of the law, holding that it meant a particular parish church rather than the universal Church, when the law authorized the use of funds and property for the support of educational and charitable institutions. The judges of the Supreme Court ruled that Judge Tanner's reading of the law was correct. The court also agreed with the contention of the attorneys for the bishop that Mr. Daignault had not specified how and by whom his clients had been injured and thus rejected his appeal entirely. At the same time, the judges also rejected the bishop's attorneys' appeal of Judge Tanner's ruling that the court did have jurisdiction in the matter of the church suits. Whereas Judge Tanner had not offered a defense of his ruling on the question of jurisdiction as the court was the only judge of its jurisdiction, Justice J. J. Barrows, in the opinion he wrote for the court, pointed out the clear fact of the matter. Since the Roman Catholic Church, as other churches, had sought the protection of the state in the holding of its property by seeking an act of incorporation to protect that property from the greedy and unscrupulous, the court had the right to judge the meaning of the charter. Such an exercise of jurisdiction, Justice Barrows contended, did not constitute interference with the internal management of the corporation as Mr. Curran had contended.[245]

On the day the Supreme Court issued its decision, Mr. Curran wrote to Bishop Hickey congratulating him on the outcome. The *Visitor* applauded the courts for maintaining and upholding the rights of the bishop in regard to the funds of the Church and frustrating the attempt of the men who summoned the bishop to court "to hamper the Episcopal functions

244 *Providence Journal*, April 19, 1928; *Providence News*, April 19, 1928; *Providence Visitor*, April 20, 1928.
245 Edward C. Stiness, reporter, *Rhode Island Reports*, (Providence: E. L Freeman, Co., 1929), Vol. 49, 269–276.

and to break down the loyalty of the laity." On its part, *La Sentinelle* did not discuss the decision but, in an article written by Henri Perdriau, reviewed all the Sentinellists' grievances in an effort to show, once again, that Rome had made a terrible mistake in condemning the movement."[246]

On receiving the news of the court's decision from Mr. Curran, Bishop Hickey immediately cabled the good news to Cardinal Sbarretti in Rome. On April 27, he followed up the cable with a copy of the decision translated into French, with which he enclosed a commentary. The bishop reported that the leaders of Rhode Island, both Catholics and non-Catholics, were pleased that the civil and Roman authorities were in accord in condemning the Sentinellist movement, which the bishop called "a disgrace and a source of all sorts of abuse." While the Roman authorities were inclined to look at the question of civil jurisdiction over local churches from the point of their European experience with hostile secular governments, Bishop Hickey took pains to explain to the Congregation that the attitude of the court "showed its real respect for the rights of the Church" and stressed the part of the Supreme Court decision where the judges were explicit in saying that they did not wish to meddle in the internal affairs of a church corporation. He also pointed out the section in the Supreme Court's decision specifying that the bishop could appeal the question of jurisdiction if he felt the rights of the Church had been violated as proof of his contention that the court took great care to show its respect for Church rights.[247]

Unfortunately, the bishop had not heard the last of the church suits. When he learned of the Supreme Court's decision, Mr. Daignault cabled from Rome to Everett L. Walling, a Protestant attorney who had defended the National Publishing Co. against the libel suit brought against it and *La Sentinelle*'s editors by Jean Sabate, to ask for another hearing of the case by the Superior Court. On his return to Rhode Island, Daignault arranged for a meeting with the chief justice of the Supreme Court and tried to obtain a dismissal by which the whole matter would be dropped without prejudice to the complainants and returned to the Superior Court under another form. The justice scheduled a session before the full court at which the bishop's counsel was also to be present to consider Daignault's request. However, before the scheduled meeting with the full court, Daignault called on Mr. Curran and, without reference to the court's decision, proposed an out of court settlement in order to avoid another round of argument in the courts. According to Bishop Hickey, when he wrote of the meeting in a letter to the apostolic delegate, an out of court settlement "would be the equivalent to an acknowledgment on the part of the bishop's lawyers that the defense had as much interest in a settlement as the plaintiff." Such an agreement would have given Daignault an appear-

246 *Woonsocket Call*, April 25, 1928; *Providence Journal*, April 26, 1928; *Providence Visitor*, April 27, 1928; *La Sentinelle*, April 26, 1928; Curran to Hickey, April 25, 1928, PChA.
247 Hickey to Sbarretti, April 27, 1928, PChA.

ance of victory by setting aside the court's judgment against him by way of a withdrawal by both parties. Mr. Curran, who had been convinced from the beginning that the bishop would prevail, rejected the idea. When Mr. Daignault failed to show for the scheduled session, the justices then ordered the court's judgment registered as final.[248]

The Aftermath of the Excommunications and Censure of La Sentinelle

After his return from Rome, Daignault and his fellow directors ceased publication of *La Sentinelle* with its May 24 issue. However, on June 7, they began publishing *La Verite*. Unlike its predecessor, the directors did not print their names on the masthead or sign their articles. While in its first paragraph *La Verite* claimed that it was the successor and heir of *La Sentinelle*, its writers initially set a softer tone than that of its predecessor. By publishing the paper under a new name, Daignault and his associates technically enabled its readers to avoid incurring mortal sin as they would if they continued to subscribe to or read the paper under the name of *La Sentinelle*. The new paper was welcomed by some of the Canadian and Franco-American papers whose editors were sympathetic to the Sentinellist movement, but there were no episcopal endorsements as had appeared in the early issues of *La Sentinelle*.[249]

True to his word, Mr. Daignault did not make any public statements or call any public meetings during the first weeks following his return from Rome. However, the Croisés continued their regular meetings. On Sunday, June 3, Mr. Daignault was at the Croisés meeting held that evening. While he declined to speak to the general meeting, he told those present he would speak to the five members who made up the society's governing council, who could if they chose, relay what he said. According to the report of this private or secret meeting which Bishop Hickey passed on to the apostolic delegate, the members of the council told the general meeting that it was impossible to reveal the serious things that Daignault had brought from Rome, but they could say that the bishop "would soon leave on a long trip and he would never come back. Therefore, one thing most important than all and that is to continue the resistance: victory, complete victory, was in sight."[250]

---

248 Hickey to Fumasoni-Biondi, June 9; July 1, 1928; "List of dates in the civil process", PChA; *Rhode Islander*, July 27, 1928. On June 12, 1928, Mr. Curran submitted a bill encompassing all the charges and expenses for services he and his associates had rendered to the bishop from February 7, 1927 to May 7, 1928. The total bill was $15,299.96, PChA.

249 Copy of Formula of Submission, n.d., PChA; *La Verite*, June 7; June 14, 1928; *Rhode Islander*, June 1, 8, 1928; Bishop Hickey took note of the new paper in a letter to Archbishop Fumasoni-Biondi, June 2, 1928, PChA.

250 Hickey to Fumasoni-Biondi, June 9, 1928, PChA; A reporter from *The Rhode Islander* checked with

When *La Verite* appeared for the second time on June 7, its main concern was with plans the Croisés had made for the celebration of the annual feast of St. John the Baptist at a banquet in the Joyland Ballroom at which Mr. Daignault was to be one of the main speakers. In its June 14 issue, *La Verite* noted that the Croisés had expanded on their plans by arranging for a solemn high mass celebrated outdoors on the grounds of the newly dedicated church of the Assumption in South Bellingham, of which Fr. Binette was pastor. Fr. Louis Raymond, chaplain of the College of the Sacred Heart, Sharon Heights, Massachusetts, was to be the celebrant and Fr. Duplessis was to preach the sermon. According to the announcement, the mass was to be sung at the request of the Directors of *La Verite* and the friends of the newspaper. On June 22, *The Rhode Islander* headlined the news of the planned mass as a "Defiance to Decree of Holy See."[251]

One who took offense at Fr. Binette's agreeing to say mass for the excommunicated directors of *La Verite* was G. L. Desaulniers, the trustee of Precious Blood parish in Woonsocket, who had welcomed the bishop to Precious Blood in December 1927. He wrote Cardinal O'Connell on Precious Blood parish stationary to protest Fr. Binette's encouragement of the Sentinellist movement and the scandal he gave by agreeing to say the mass. Whether it was Mr. Desaulniers' letter or the call or letter of someone else that was the immediate cause, Cardinal O'Connell withdrew his permission for the outdoor mass. When reporters asked Fr. Binette for an explanation when he canceled the outdoor mass, Fr. Binette told them that a special messenger brought a letter from the cardinal on Friday, June 23 in which the cardinal asked him to cancel the mass because of the misunderstanding that might result. Also in order to avoid misunderstanding, the cardinal requested that Fr. Binette preach at a mass in the church and send him a copy of his sermon. Fr. Binette emphasized that it was the cardinal's desire not to become involved in the Rhode Island trouble in any way whatever. In his statement to the press, Fr. Binette claimed that the idea for the mass was his alone. On his part, Mr. Daignault denied that he had anything to do with the mass arrangements, a claim which Bishop Hickey, for one, did not believe. As directed by Cardinal O'Connell, Fr. Binette read from his prepared text at the mass. However, before reading his sermon, Fr. Binette made his sympathies known when he said, "Unfortunately some of our people have been excommunicated, but they are as much Christians as I am. Their excommunication will not last long." Bishop Hickey found these words of Fr. Binette scandalous since they raised doubts about the seriousness of the Roman censures. On his part, Fr. Duplessis gave the text of the sermon he had prepared to *La Verite*,

        postal officials and found that the same men, who had previously applied for mailing privileges for
        La Sentinelle, also had applied for mailing privileges for *La Verite*.
251 *La Verite*, June 7, 14, 1928; *The Rhode Islander*, June 22, 1928. Cf. also Bishop Hickey's comments on
    this issue in his letter to Fumasoni-Biondi, June 16, 1928, PChA.

which printed it in its July 5 edition along with an account of the mass and the dinner at the Joyland.[252]

Mr. Desaulniers wrote to Cardinal O'Connell again on June 30, 1928 to thank him for his reply, which clarified the question of the cardinal's support, and for the cardinal's intervention in South Bellingham. Desaulniers took the opportunity to point out the sympathy and support both Fr. Duplessis and Fr. Binette showed in regard to the Sentinellists in general and, in particular, to Daignault and those excommunicated with him. He noted that Fr. Binette had opened his doors to two Providence priests, Frs. Fautaux and Forcier, whose services Bishop Hickey had dispensed with because of their Sentinellist views; that a large number of the cars parked at the Joyland had Massachusetts plates; that between five and six thousand copies of *La Verite* were mailed each week to readers in Massachusetts; and that *La Verite* had asserted in its last number that Cardinal O'Connell "had been forced to act in the way that he did by one higher than him." Mr. Desaulniers observed that, while the Sentinellist movement was dead in Rhode Island, he was concerned that Frs. Binette, Raymond and Duplessis were attempting to resurrect it in the dioceses in Massachusetts. On July 6, 1928, *The Rhode Islander* printed an article which expressed the same concerns and which voiced the opinion that Cardinal O'Connell was not aware of how his name was being used by the Sentinellists.[253]

On the night of the dinner, about 2,500 people crowded the Joyland Ballroom and overflowed into the streets. Partisans of the bishop counted the cars from out of state and found that 117 came from Massachusetts and thirty-seven from New Hampshire, while a large number came from different parts of Rhode Island. They estimated that less than 1,000 people came from the Woonsocket area. Dr. Gaspard Boucher was the first speaker. He noted how Fr. Binette had been forced to abandon his plans for the outdoor mass. When he alluded to Fr. Binette's remarks, he said, "You know how he submitted," the audience applauded. When Mr. Daignault stood to speak before the main speaker, Paul Mercier, a member of the Quebec legislature, he related some details of his trip to Rome and mentioned how he had received communion on Easter Sunday before word spread of his excommunication which, according to Mr. Daignault, prompted someone in Rome to remark that "It was a dirty Yankee trick." He disclosed that he had promised the Congregation of the Council, as a condition of his reinstatement, not to write for the newspaper, hold public gatherings, or speak about the offering strike. He simply said he "will

---

252 The Diocese of Providence Archives only has Mr. Dasauliniers' cover letter to Archbishop Fumasoni-Biondi, June 16, 1928, which he wrote when he sent a copy of his letter to Cardinal O'Connell to the delegate; *Woonsocket Call*, June 23, 1928; *Providence Journal*, June 24, 1928; *La Verite*, July 5, 1927; Hickey to Fumasoni-Biondi, June 26, 1928, PChA. *The Rhode Islander* also had its doubts about the veracity of Daignault's denial of involvement in planning for the mass, cf. July 6, 1928.
253 Desaulniers to O'Connell, June 30, 1928, Archdiocese of Boston Archives; *The Rhode Islander*, July 6, 1928.

not give another cent to the church." He promised that the fight was only starting and that they would be victorious. Before ending, he hinted that certain "developments" in the last few days were all that had prevented "a member of the clergy" from being present.[254]

In making his now weekly report to the apostolic delegate about the state of the agitation in the diocese, Bishop Hickey pointed out that to his mind three things might be gathered from what Daignault said:

> First, his determination to carry on the agitation, notwithstanding the promises he made in Rome; second, his wish to compromise the Roman authorities and the Bishops in the minds of his followers; and third, his connection with *La Verite.*

As partial proof of his view, the bishop cited Daignault's own words:

> They wanted *La Sentinelle* to disappear. That was easy. We brought forth *La Verite* . . . . We are asked not to hold public meetings. Today is a public meeting, but a meeting in honor of St. John the Baptist . . . . I was asked not to write any more. I do not object, as I am lazy when it comes to writing . . . . Support *La Verite* as you did *La Sentinelle.* You will recognize my articles."[255]

Bishop Hickey treated the whole matter of the mass, banquet and speeches in a fuller context when he discussed them in a letter that he sent to Cardinal Sbarretti on July 13, 1928. In his letter Bishop Hickey sought to show why it was necessary to have Fr. Beland acknowledge his errors and repudiate his connection with the Sentinellist movement by pointing out how Daignault and his associates were trying to deceive their followers as to the seriousness of the censures that Rome had imposed. Hickey referred to an article in *La Sentinelle,* which appeared on April 12, in which Perdriau questioned whether Mr. Daignault and the others were really excommunicated since the censures were imposed by the Sacred Congregation of the Council and not by the Holy Office. In Bishop Hickey's view, the celebration in Bellingham, in which Frs. Duplessis and Raymond as well as Fr. Binette took part, was organized to demonstrate, by the fact of the participation of these three priests, "that the Church was not rejecting the movement and that the censures were not serious." He made particular note of Daignault's "stubbornness" when he urged his associates to remain united and promised that they would all be absolved at the same time. Daignault had remarked that he could have been absolved at Rome after he had made his submission, but chose not to and urged them "to await the arrival of an Apostolic Visitor" who would come from Rome to settle the affair.[256]

The reference to an Apostolic Visitor was prompted by a report that the Sentinellists had heard during the second week of July that Cardinal Luigi

---

254 *Woonsocket Call,* June 25, 1928; *Providence Journal,* June 25, 1928; *Providence News,* June 25, 1928.
255 Hickey to Fumasoni-Biondi, July 1, 1928. Cf. also Hickey's second letter to Fumasoni-Biondi on this date in which he analyses the June 28, 1928 issue of *La Verite* and points out the discrepancies between Daignault's remarks at the banquet and the claims made in *La Verite,* PChA.
256 Hickey to Sbarretti, July 13, 1928, PChA.

Sincero was to leave the French port of Le Havre on his way to Canada to visit the institutions directed by the Sisters of the Holy Names of Jesus and Mary and the Sisters of St. Ann of Lachine. They concluded from this that the cardinal was a secret envoy sent from the Vatican in response to their petition to investigate the religious situation in New England. Before the story of the cardinal's visit appeared in the newspapers, Elie Vezina, general secretary of the Union St. Jean Baptiste, had thought of inviting the cardinal to come to Woonsocket during the Union's semiannual meeting of its Board of Directors, so that they could meet the cardinal and talk about the religious situation in the diocese and New England. After the articles concerning the cardinal's visit appeared, he wrote to Bishop Hickey asking him if he thought it would still be a good idea. Bishop Hickey's response was noncommital and Mr. Vezina decided not to invite the cardinal.[257]

While *La Verite* had initially discussed the religious situation in New England in more moderate tones than *La Sentinelle*, the tenor of its articles began changing back to the old ways of *La Sentinelle* after a few issues. One of the editors' chief targets for their criticism continued to be Mr. Vezina and the current general officers of the Union. After the news of Mr. Daignault's excommunication, the Union's executive committee had sent a letter to each of those excommunicated who was a member of one of the union's local councils. The letter reminded them that, since the rules of the society required that its members be Catholics in good standing, they had until July 15 to rectify their status or face expulsion from the society. Several members of the society feared a mass exodus from the local councils if the society expelled those excommunicated. In his opening address to the general board's semiannual meeting on July 23, Msgr. Dauray, the Union's Supreme Chaplain, who was then ninety years old and who had come to the meeting at the executive secretary's request, deplored the impasse and asked the directors of the Union, in view of *La Verite*'s attacks, "not be troubled with the wrongs that are done to you. Without doubt you must uphold your customs, your honor and your society in the usual course." Rather than move to expel those who had been excommunicated, the executive board decided it could take no action because the bylaws of the society provided that it was the responsibility of the individual council to pass on the qualifications of the members of the society. Only if the local society refused to expel the accused could the general board intervene.[258]

The Canado-Americaine Association, of which Mr. Daignault was president and a candidate for reelection to that post, also had a provision in its bylaws that a member had to be a Catholic in good standing, but

257 Vezina to Hickey, July 14, 1928; Hickey to Fumasoni-Biondi, July 17, 1928, PChA; Rumilly, *Histoire Des Franco-Americains*, p. 442.
258 *Providence Journal*, July 23, 24, 27, 1928; *La Verite*, July 5, 11, 21, 1928; Rumilly, *Histoire Des Franco-Americains*, 437–38.

never took up the matter when it gathered for its quadrennial convention in Quebec City at the end of July 1928. Daignault and the members of his executive committee had carefully chosen Quebec City because they expected a friendly reception there by a clergy that was supportive of the Sentinellist movement and because 3,700 out the Association's 14,571 members lived in the Province of Quebec. As noted above, Bishop Guertin of Manchester, in January 1925, had removed the chaplains assigned to the Associations' courts and villas within his diocese. In the program for the convention, there was no mention of any opening mass although past conventions always had one. However, Fr. Edouard Lavergne, who was a member of one of the local societies, arranged before the convention to celebrate mass for the delegates, Mr. Daignault among them, in his parish church, Our Lady of Grace. At the banquet that same evening, Daignault sat between Fr. J. D. Binette and Jules Dorion, the editor of the Quebec Catholic paper, *L'Action Catholique*, who welcomed the delegates and congratulated them on the struggle they were making to ensure the survival of the French language in New England. During the course of the convention, Mr. Daignault was unanimously reelected as president when rumored opposition to his candidacy failed to materialize.[259]

The Canadian press gave the convention wide coverage and the Associated Press carried a report on its wire of the opening mass at Our Lady of Grace and of Daignault's reelection. The Press dispatch, which was picked up by the *Providence Journal*, noted that the Association differed from the Union St. Jean Baptiste in that it was more nationalistic. The writer of an article printed in *The Rhode Islander* observed that most members of the Canado-Americaine Association remained attached to the land of their birth and lived in hope that they would ultimately return to their homes in the province of Quebec and that many of them were not citizens of the United States.[260]

In its August 9 issue, *La Verite* presented the words and actions of Fr. Lavergne and Mr. Dorion as proof of the official support the Sentinellist movement enjoyed in Quebec. *La Verite* even suggested that the Cardinal Archbishop of Quebec, Archbishop Rouleau, had given his tacit, even perhaps, his formal approbation of the Association and its leaders. However, *The Rhode Islander*, after reading the Quebec and Montreal newspapers, offered the suggestion that Cardinal Rouleau was absent from the city at the time of the convention and that the religious ceremony was held without his knowledge or consent.[261]

---

259 *Providence Journal*, August 2, 1928; *The Rhode Islander*, August 3, 1928; Hickey to Sbarretti, August 18, 1928, PChA. For the Canado-Americaine Association's own account of the convention at Quebec Cf. Robert, *Memorial de l'Association Canado-Americaine*, I, 272–76; Rumilly, *Histoire Des Franco-Americains*, 438–39, also gives an account of the convention and notes some of those excommunicated in Rhode Island went to confession in Quebec City and others in Chicoutimi.
260 Ibid.
261 *La Verite*, August 9, 1928; *The Rhode Islander*, August 10, 1928.

The publicity that surrounded the convention and *La Verite*'s insinuation that Daignault had the support of Cardinal Rouleau was, however, to backfire on Daignault and the Sentinellists. In view of the disappointment he felt that the general board of the Union St. Jean Baptiste had not expelled Daignault and the other members who had been excommunicated, Msgr. Dauray wrote a letter to Bishop Hickey with the intention that he send copies of *La Verite* for July 19 and 26 to "the highest authorities in the Church" in order to show that the Sentinellists had returned to "their former method of attacking the religious authorities, of fostering opposition to episcopal directions and of undermining the respect for priests." In the course of his letter he related reports he had received of the support of the Sentinellists on the part of priests and others in the various New England dioceses as well in the Province of Quebec. To his mind the agitation was gaining ground because of "the prevailing uncertainty" outside of Rhode Island "concerning Rome's official condemnation of the movement." For him, the remedy was clear: the Roman sanctions needed to be officially made known outside of the diocese.[262]

Complaints about the interference of priests from outside the diocese in the affairs of the diocese had been for the most part voiced in private letters between the clergy and laity of the diocese and Bishop Hickey, who in turn took up the matter with the apostolic delegate. While a sizeable majority of the Franco-American clergy stood with Bishop Hickey in the Diocese of Providence, in the Archdiocese of Boston, Fr. Binette believed that 52 out of 55 sympathized with the Sentinellists, while in the Diocese of Manchester, 28 out of 34 supposedly did. On October 19, 1927, *La Tribune* publicly raised the issue of outside clerical interference in a front-page article. *La Tribune*'s article focused on the letters, reputedly from priests, which *La Sentinelle* regularly published in its pages. While some were signed, most were printed as "X . . ., priest." The writer of the *La Tribune* raised the question of whether the letters signed with an X were authentic letters, since priests took vows of obedience at their ordinations and knew that the greatest form of scandal was that caused "from above." He also wondered, in view of the fact that Sentinellists claimed that the Canadian bishops supported their cause, why was it necessary for Canadian priests to withhold their identity, if there was nothing wrong about their supporting the Sentinellists.[263]

Msgr. Dauray requested that Bishop Hickey send copies of his letter protesting the actions of priests outside of the diocese who continued to support the Sentinellists to Archbishop Cassulo, the apostolic delegate to Canada, and to the Canadian hierarchy. Rather than send the letters by mail, Msgr. Dauray's nephew, Fr. Georges Bedard, agreed to deliver them personally. Fr. Bedard's companion on his three week journey through

---

262 Dauray to Hickey, July 27, 1928, PChA
263 Rumilly, *Histoire Des Franco-Americains, 391, 404; La Tribune*, October 19, 1927.

Canada was Archbishop Pietro Benedetti, who had come from Rome to visit his ailing sister in Woonsocket. Archbishop Benedetti's visit to the city had initially fueled the Sentinellists' hopes that Rome was to intervene on their behalf, since he had visited Daignault in Rome and had sought then to work out some kind of compromise with Bishop Hickey. Prior to leaving for Canada, Fr. Bedard met twice with Bishop Hickey to talk matters over.[264]

La Verite took notice of the trip. The paper referred to Fr. Bedard as a *putois*, a skunk, and mistakenly thought he was the author of a recently printed French-language history of the Sentinellist agitation. In its October 25 issue, it reported, on the basis of word that the editors had received from Canada, that Fr. Bedard and Archbishop Benedetti had not been warmly or kindly received by some of the bishops of Canada. As was their practice, the editors withheld the names of the bishops in describing how they received the two travelers.[265]

Bishop Hickey's understanding of Fr. Bedard's and Archbishop Benedetti's trip and the reception they received was quite different from that of *La Verite*. On August 18, 1928, Bishop Hickey prepared a packet of documents for Cardinal Sbarretti, with a cover letter to Msgr. Gentile, in order to bring the Congregation of the Council up to date on what had happened since the Congregation had pronounced the interdict of *La Sentinelle* and the excommunications. Among the documents were excerpts from Canadian newspapers reproduced by *La Verite* which suggested, at least to Bishop Hickey, that Mr. Daignault and his colleagues were ceremoniously received in Our Lady of Grace by Fr. Lavergne and were present at the mass during which Fr. Lavergne preached. Bishop Hickey spent a considerable portion of his report on the Canado-Americaine Association convention in Quebec and particularly on the speech that Mr. Daignault gave at the convention to show that Mr. Daignault was deliberately lying about his role in the agitation and was trying "to discredit the Roman congregations in the most Catholic center of North America." Hickey included in his letter to the congregation a request by the general officers of the Union St. Jean Baptiste that the religious authorities end their "persistent silence" on the condemnations that Rome had passed on the Sentinellist movement. In the same packet, Bishop Hickey asked the congregation to forbid the reading of *La Verite* for the same reasons it had *La Sentinelle*.[266]

On September 20, 1928, during the time Fr. Bedard and Archbishop Benedetti were in Canada, Bishop Hickey also wrote to Cardinal Rouleau to express his concern that priests of the Quebec archdiocese were still encouraging the Sentinellists. He suggested that the silence of the Cana-

---

264 Dauray to Hickey, July 27, 1928, PChA; Bishop Hickey's Diary, September 6, 8, 1928.
265 *La Verite*, October 4, 25, 1928. The work referred to was J. Albert Foisy's, *Histoire de L'Agitation Sentinelliste dans la Nouvelle-Angleterre, 1925–1928*. It was published by La Tribune Publishing Company in 1928.
266 Hickey to Sbarretti, August 18, 1928; Hickey to Gentile, August 18, 1928, PChA.

dian bishops on the Sentinellist agitation had created the impression that
the Canadian bishops approved of the struggle against ecclesiastical authority in the United States, an impression made more persuasive by the
recent events surrounding the Canado-Americaine Association convention
in Quebec. Having read in the newspapers that the bishops of Quebec
province were planning to meet at the end of September, Hickey asked
Cardinal Rouleau to discuss the Sentinellist agitation with them and to ask
them to make their thoughts on the subject known.[267]

Cardinal Rouleau replied to Bishop Hickey a week later and told him
that the Canado-Americaine Association's convention made little local impression and "was only of importance far away in consequence of the false
accusations and exaggerated passions of the struggle." The cardinal found
echoes of those inaccuracies in Hickey's letter in the presumption that
the cardinal supported the movement in any way. He made clear that one
could never argue from the silence of the Canadian bishops that they approved a movement condemned by the Holy See. If the Canadian bishops
had not said anything on the matter, it was because they were absorbed in
the administration of their dioceses, where there was no enthusiasm for
the movement.[268]

On October 16, 1928, Bishop Hickey wrote again to Cardinal Sbarretti
to convey what he regarded as "the happy turn of events" that had developed in the diocese since the excommunications and interdict had been
announced. He was most happy to report that, as a result of his letter
to Cardinal Rouleau and Fr. Bedard's and Archbishop Benedetti's visit to
Canada, his doubts on the subject of the attitude of the religious authorities in the Province of Quebec had "entirely disappeared and the spirit of
the most cordial cooperation and the most sincere friendship" again existed between the members of the hierarchy of the two countries. Bishop
Hickey particularly praised the efforts of Archbishop Benedetti "as an en-
lightened and disinterested visitor" who was able to dispel the doubts and
misunderstandings that existed in the minds of the Canadian bishops."[269]

Among the questions Archbishop Rouleau would discuss with the
Canadian bishops was that of nationalism, particularly the form of nationalism that the Pope had condemned when he condemned the *Action
Francaise* movement. The dual condemnations of the French *Action Francaise* and then of the Sentinellists had created an uneasiness among those
in Canada who were partisans of Montreal's *Action Francaise*. One Canadian scholar has written in a study of French Canadian nationalism in the
1920s:

Nationalism as a protective device for a minority culture became suspect; so too did

267 Hickey to Rouleau, September 20, 1928, PChA.
268 Rouleau to Hickey, September 27, PChA.
269 Hickey to Sbarretti, October 16, 1928, PChA.

any criticizing of the political status quo. Even the intimate association of religion and nationalism became risky.

The *Action Francaise* movement in Montreal had pondered what to do for a year after the papal condemnation of the French movement before changing its name to Action Canadienne-francaise in January 1928. The strong language of *La Sentinelle* in its public and legal challenge to ecclesiastical authority had also made some Canadian bishops uneasy and caused them to be more sympathetic towards and supportive of Bishop Hickey and wary of the partisans of Action Canadienne-francaise.[270]

After receiving Bishop Hickey's summary of the events surrounding the Canado-Americaine Association convention in Quebec, the Congregation of the Council also wrote to Cardinal Rouleau on November 30, 1928, asking the cardinal to convey certain concerns that the congregation had to Fr. Lavergne and Mr. Dorion. In his reply to Cardinal Sbarretti, Cardinal Rouleau asserted that the facts surrounding the convention had been "exaggerated, distorted and even made up." He denied the report that Bishop Hickey had made to the congregation, part of which he derived from the newspaper accounts of the convention reproduced by *La Verite*, that Mr. Daignault had attended the mass Fr. Lavergne offered at the beginning of the convention or that Daignault has been the object of numerous marks of esteem by Fr. Lavergne or Mr. Dorion. To demonstrate that he and his archdiocesan newspaper had not been silent on the question of the Sentinellists' agitation, he enclosed a marked copy of *L'Action Catholique* for May 23, 1928 in which the paper printed an exact translation of the condemnation of *La Sentinelle* and the excommunication of Mr. Daignault and the others taken from the *Acta Apostolicae Sedis*. At the request of Archbishop Cassulo, the apostolic delegate to Canada, the ban on buying and reading *La Sentinelle* and all the publications that replaced it, was again printed in the Canadian diocesan and other newspapers.[271]

As the season of Advent approached, Bishop Hickey prepared another pastoral letter in which he called on those who had incurred excommunication to reject their error and return to the Church. In all, the number excommunicated had reached sixty-three. Following Antonio Prince's and Henri Perdriau's receipt of a letter from Archbishop Fumasoni-Biondi informing them that they had one month to renounce the part they had taken in the agitation and declare their readiness to obey the directions given by Bishop Hickey or be placed under personal interdict and denied the reception of the sacraments, neither Mr. Prince nor Mr. Perdriau chose to submit and thus each incurred censure along with those who signed the church suits. On his part, Perdriau sent the letter he received from the delegate back to him with a request that he communicate with him in

270 Trofimenkoff, *Action Francaise*, 99–104.
271 Rouleau to Sbarretti, December 27, 1928, a copy of the letter is in the PChA. Cf. Montreal's *La Semaine Religieuse*, January 10, 1929 and *Le Devoir*, January 11, 1929.

French. He made a point of informing the local press that he had insisted that the apostolic delegate send notice of his excommunication to him in French so that there could be no ambiguity. Believing that Perdriau knew sufficient English to understand the letter he received, the delegate ignored the request. Because Hemond, Perdriau and others had questioned the authenticity of the newspaper reports of the excommunications and of the apostolic delegate's telegram to Bishop Hickey, Hickey had a copy of the official letter announcing the excommunications that he received from the Congregation of the Council and the text of the *Acta Apostolicae Sedis* of May 4, 1928 printed in the *Providence Visitor* on May 25 and had his French pastors read the letter and the acts to their congregations.[272]

While sixty-two men signed the church suits and did not repudiate their signatures, only sixty-one had been excommunicated. One of the signers of the bill of complaint against Precious Blood church, Adolphe E. Simard, became gravely ill at the end of March. According to the account that appeared in the *Providence Journal*, Mr. Simard, who had previously expressed his regret that the church suits had gone so far, welcomed one of Msgr. Dauray's assistants when the priest came to visit him. He then made his confession and received absolution. The *Journal* article also noted that Msgr. Dauray later called on him as well and the two talked over Mr. Simard's part in the affair. As Msgr. Dauray was convinced that Mr. Simard did not appreciate the significance of his signing the bill, Msgr. Dauray wrote to Bishop Hickey on March 27, after Simard died, to ask that he be allowed to bury him publicly from Previous Blood. Since, in his reply, Bishop Hickey left the matter of Mr. Simard's funeral entirely in Msgr. Dauray's hands, Mr. Simard was given a church burial. To forestall any confusion about the matter, both Bishop Hickey's and Msgr. Dauray's letters were read at the mass and printed in the papers. However, there were those at the time of Simard's death and funeral, including members of his own family, that did not believe he had repented. Worcester's *L'Opinion Publique* printed a story that in fact Mr. Simard refused to repudiate his signature and that his family denied that he had expressed regret for his action.[273]

One of the sixty three who were formally excommunicated, Jerry Breault, a parishioner of St. John the Baptist Parish, Pawtucket, also became seriously ill in the latter part of May. On May 20, Bishop Hickey sent a night letter to the apostolic delegate asking what the man needed to do to be reinstated in the Church. The delegate responded by telegram and followed it with a letter, pointing out the place in Canon Law that covered the situation and subdelegating Hickey to absolve from censure

272 Perdriau to Fumasoni-Biondi, May 18, 1928; Hickey to Fumasoni-Biondi, May 21, 1928; Fumasoni-Biondi to Hickey, May 22, 1928; Dauray to Hickey, June 14, 1928, PChA; *Providence Journal*, May 18, 26; June 18, 1928; *Providence Visitor*, May 25, 1928.
273 *Providence Journal*, March 31, 1928. A summary of the *L'Opinion Publique* article is found in Rumilly, *Histoire Des Franco-Americains*, 430–31.

those to whom the delegates had sent letters dated May 11, 1928. Breault recovered sufficiently to acknowledge the scandal he had created by signing the church suits in a letter to Bishop Hickey on June 25 and to promise to relinquish "any and all connection with any society whose members are at present resisting the authority of the Church." Fr. Alphonse Graton, the pastor of St. John's, as he was required to do, had the letter publicly read in St. John's Church at all the masses by one of his assistants. In view of the public retraction, Mr. Breault was absolved and readmitted to the Church. According to the *Providence Journal*, which, together with the other local papers, reported the retraction, Mr. Breault told Fr. Graton that he did not realize at the time that he was a party to an action which would bring the Bishop of Providence into the civil courts. He said that he thought that he was citing the presidents and members of the various church corporations mentioned in the Daignault suits. Mr. Breault died on July 6. Believing it important to once again undermine the impact of Breault's retraction, *La Verite*, in Bishop Hickey's words, "cast contempt and derision upon the submission of a dying man" and questioned the value of an excommunication coming from the Congregation of the Council rather than from the Holy Office in its comments on the account of Breault's funeral that appeared in *La Tribune*.[274]

On June 2, Bishop Hickey received a telegram from one of the more prominent Sentinellists, Dr. J. Gaspard Boucher, who had been on vacation in Quebec and did not learn about the excommunications until several weeks after they were announced. Confusing his own case with that of Perdriau and Prince, who were given a month to end their agitation or face excommunication, Dr. Boucher thought, when he heard of the excommunications, that he had only one month to make his submission, which he made in his telegram to the bishop. The bishop never mentioned Dr. Boucher's telegram publicly and Dr. Boucher took a less prominent role in the agitation over the next few months.[275]

While Mr. Daignault urged his supporters to stick together in order to ensure victory in their struggle, he himself was a cause of division within the ranks of his supporters. During the Canado-Americaine Association convention in Quebec, Daignault created something of a sensation when at the opening dinner he predicted the victory of Herbert Hoover in the November presidential elections and declared that the French voters in the East would overwhelmingly support the Republican candidate. In a front-page editorial in the September 19, 1928 edition of *La Verite*, Daignault declared his support of Hoover for president and Judge Felix Hebert for U.S. Senator. In the article, Daignault indulged in a long attack on the Irish in the Democratic Party. He gave as his one of principle reasons for

---

274 Hickey to Fumasoni-Biondi, May 20, 1928; July 17, 1928; Fumasoni-Biondi, May 22, 1928, PChA; *Providence Journal*, July 2, 1928; *Providence News*, July 2, 1928; *Woonsocket Call*, July 6, 1928; *La Verite*, July 11, 1928.
275 Telegram, Boucher to Hickey, June 2, 1928, PChA.

supporting Hoover and Hebert rather than Smith and incumbent Senator Peter G. Gerry the fact that the Democratic candidacies were "glutted by representatives of that race which for 50 years has never ceased to mock our rights and trample our liberties." By urging his supporters to vote for Hoover and Hebert as a means of advancing the interests and promoting the aims of the Sentinellist movement he sought to connect his political campaign with his religious one. "So much the worse for Senator Gerry [who was not Irish], if he is a political ally of Smith and Bishop Hickey." When a *Providence Journal* reporter brought Daignault's article to the attention of Judge Hebert at a Republican campaign rally, Judge Hebert replied, "I can't help it. If he wants to support me, I can't help it." When Eugene Jalbert, head of the Republican Party in Woonsocket, was asked for a comment, Jalbert regretted Daignault's interjection of the religious issues into politics.[276]

Daignault's article in *La Verite* angered both Herve Legace, who was the Democratic candidate for mayor in Woonsocket, and Antonio Prince, who was also an active Democrat. Although both men has long been allies of Daignault, Prince accused Daignault of not turning over all the money collected to support the appeal of his uncle, Fr. Achille Prince, and of accepting $100,000 from the Republicans to work for a Hoover victory. As in the religious dispute, the charges were either made up or based on misleading information. Political passions ran high among Smith's Franco-American partisans. When, on November 2, Daignault and Phydime Hemond sought to speak at a Republican rally in the Opera House, Manville, the very real threat of their being pelted with eggs caused them to forgo their speeches and leave the village in a hurry. After this and other incidents, the heads of the Republican State Committee ordered Daignault not to take part in any more campaign rallies. Shortly after the election, the Franco-American Social Circle of Pawtucket, of which Albert Lamarre, another of Daignault's prominent supporters, was president, voted unanimously to repudiate and condemn Daignault for his activities in the past political campaign.[277]

Bishop Hickey's Advent pastoral in which he urged those who had fallen under the censures of the Church to repent and to return appeared in the *Providence Visitor* on November 23, 1928. In his pastoral, the bishop asked that those who had been excommunicated not harden their hearts, neglect the practice of their faith or engage in a fictitious submission. At the urging of Archbishop Gauthier of Montreal and with the permission of the cardinal, Hickey printed Cardinal Rouleau's letter within the body of his pastoral. He also included the formula of submission that Daignault and the others would be asked to sign. As he had secured the Congregation of

---

276 *Providence Journal*, August 2, 1928; September 2, 1928; *La Verite*, September 19, 1928.
277 *Woonsocket Call*, September 21; November 2, 1928; *Providence Journal*, November 2, 3, 15, 1928; Rumilly, *Histoire Des Franco-Americains*, 440–41.

the Council's approval to publicly condemn *La Verite*, Bishop Hickey formally advised the clergy and laity that reading *La Verite* was forbidden. At
Precious Blood, Msgr. Dauray, in a written message, again added his own
voice to that of the bishop as did other pastors. Bishop Hickey sent a copy
of his Advent pastoral to all the American bishops as well as to the bishops
of Quebec Province. A dozen or so of the American bishops took the time
to praise it and congratulate Hickey on it. In taking these steps, Hickey was
following the advice sent to him by Archbishop Benedetti.[278]

Among those who took a negative or hostile view of the Advent pastoral letter was Henri Perdriau, who had ridiculed Bishop Hickey's previous
pastoral in September 1927. When asked for a statement, Perdriau declared that he would never make his peace with the Church on the conditions laid down in the letter by the Congregation of the Council. As
Daignault would reveal in another editorial, Perdriau chose to read Cardinal Rouleau's letter as dismissing the whole matter of the objections raised
regarding the Canado-Americaine Association's convention in Quebec
without passing judgment upon the merits or demerits of the case. After
Bishop Hickey's announcement that *Le Verite* was banned as was its predecessor, the directors of the Daignault newspaper suspended publication
for a week. However, on November 29, 1928, the same company that had
published *La Sentinelle* and *Le Verite* began to publish *La Bataille* in the same
style as its predecessors.[279]

Only one issue of *La Bataille* ever appeared. Due to the illness of Mr.
Hemond during November and the frequent absences of Mr. Daignault
from Woonsocket for one reason or another, the greater part of the editorial duties fell to Henri Perdriau. About the end of November, Mr. Perdriau
received a visit from a fellow Frenchman, Casimir Durand, a New York
resident who claimed to be a bishop in the Latin Orthodox Church. Durand stayed at Perdriau's home at 209 Harrison Street for two weeks and
during that time celebrated mass daily in the Polish National Church on
Arnold Street, at which some forty or fifty Franco-Americans assisted.
During the time of Durand's visit, Mr. Perdriau wrote or completed work
on a forty-four-page pamphlet, "Fiat Lux – Common Sense and Logic"
by "A Catholic who wishes to become a better Catholic." On the inside
cover, Perdriau included the traditional statement found in Catholic works
that there was nothing heretical in the work. The "Nihil Obstat" as well
as an "Imprimatur" [Let it be printed] was signed "Casimir, Episcopus."
The text of the pamphlet attacked first, the primacy of St. Peter in the
Church; secondly, the extravagant living of priests, the notion of priestly celibacy, and the hypocrisy of the Roman Curia; and thirdly, praised
the American Catholic Church (or the Orthodox Latin Church as he also

278 *Providence Visitor*, November 23, 1928; *Woonsocket Call*, November 25, 1928; *Providence Journal*,
     November 24, 26, 1928; Memorandum of Benedetti, n.d, PChA.
279 *La Sentinelle, 28, 1927; Woonsocket Call*, November 24, 1928.

called it) wherein "parish finances were controlled by and administered by the faithful." At the end of the pamphlet, all those interested in obtaining information on the American Catholic Church were invited to write to Casimir Durand, D.D., P.O. Box 108, Woonsocket, R.I. Excerpts from the pamphlet were apparently included in the second issue of *La Bataille*, which was never distributed.[280]

Mr. Perdriau had ten thousand copies of the pamphlet printed on the presses of Daignault's National Printing Company. At the time Perdriau was entertaining Durand and writing "Fiat Lux," Mr. Daignault was in Sherbrooke, Quebec taking a rest after the presidential and state political campaigns. After one of Daignault's associates, who knew he would never countenance any movement which would lead to the establishment of a schismatic church, obtained a copy of the pamphlet, he sent word of it to Daignault. Daignault immediately cut short his vacation to return to Woonsocket. He arrived in Woonsocket before the second issue of *La Bataille*'s came off the press and ordered it stopped. He also ordered all the copies of "Fiat Lux", which Perdriau had intended for distribution at Christmas time, to be burned. According to an article in the *Woonsocket Call* on December 5, 1928, after the publication of the first issue of *La Bataille*, Perdriau decided to take a vacation. Both Daignault and Perdriau denied rumors of a rift between them when asked about the rumors by the *Call*'s reporter. In the pages of yet another reincarnation of *La Sentinelle*, *La Defense*, which appeared for the first time on December 13, 1928, Mr. Daignault informed the paper's readers that Perdriau had been discharged as editor.[281]

In spite of the promise he had made at Rome that he would cease writing for his newspaper, after firing Perdriau, Mr. Daignault again began writing editorials. While Mr. Daignault signed his own name to his editorials, articles in *La Defense*, which discussed the Church and the rights of the Canadians in it, were signed with a pen name, Armand-Jean Richelieu. When Daignault at last decided to cease publishing the newspaper with its February 14, 1929 issue, the paper's and the Sentinellist movement's obituary was written by "Richelieu." He praised the men who had conducted the struggle as "men of courage, disinterested, generous in their sacrifices, desirous of defending their brothers." For him, the struggle was about the securing the well-being of the Franco-American parishes and, in preserving them, preserving also their French-Canadian heritage. He scorned those who had abandoned the struggle, which he described as one

---

280 *Woonsocket Call*, December 5, 1928; *The Rhode Islander*, December 28, 1928; Hickey to Fumasoni-Biondi, December 21, 1928, PChA. The analysis of "Fiat Lux," which Hickey sent to the delegate, is reproduced in Foisy, *The Sentinellist Agitation in New England*, 200–208; Rumilly, *Histoire Des Franco-Americains*, 445; Daignault, *Le vrai movement sentinelliste*, 38–40, says that four thousand copies of "Fiat Lux" were printed..

281 *Woonsocket Call*, December 5, 1928; *The Rhode Islander*, December 28, 1928; *La Defense*, December 27, 1928; Hickey to Sbarretti, December 14, 1928, PChA.

fought with unequal resources. He did not believe that the struggle had been in vain because it had prevented the bishops in other dioceses from placing intolerable taxes on their Franco-American parishes. He depicted the excommunications as having come as a great surprise since the signers had had no intention of bringing Bishop Hickey before the civil courts, but only the corporate entity, Bishop of Providence, and he compared the sufferings of those excommunicated to those of Christ. The future he left in the hands of God.[282]

Bishop Hickey initially thought that Perdriau was the writer of the Richelieu articles, but Perdriau himself was to disclose on February 29, 1929 that the writer of the articles signed Armand-Jean Richelieu was Fr. Georges Duplessis. Fr. Duplessis's renewed intervention in the diocese prompted Bishop Hickey to make him the subject of a letter he sent to the apostolic delegate on March 4, 1929. He thought that after Cardinal O'Connell had admonished him several months ago that Duplessis would have stayed in the background. With the new evidence that Perdriau had provided, Hickey felt obliged to protest again about his interference. He signaled out Duplessis' "apologia" as demonstrating that the Sentinellists "regret nothing, and that they glorified themselves in a campaign which has been in progress for five years and that all of the accusations and calumnies had to be maintained. On March 21, 1929, the auditor at the delegation forwarded Bishop Hickey's complaint about Fr. Duplessis to the Sacred Congregation of the Council.[283]

On his part, Bishop Hickey initially had his doubts that Perdriau's discharge was a real one, since he believed that Daignault was committed to supporting Perdriau and saw the report of the separation and their later hostile exchange of words as a ploy intended to safeguard appearances. While Bishop Hickey at first doubted the reality of the break between Daignault and Perdriau, others recognized it as a real one, which, at its heart, was occasioned by an attempt on Perdriau's part to seize control of the Sentinellist movement. Daignault not only fired Perdriau, but read him out of the Sentinellist cause. Unlike the Frenchman, Perdriau, Daignault knew that the strong attachment of the Franco Americans to the Roman Catholic Church was not something that one could even suggest was at risk without losing the support of the French-Canadian bishops and priests. In spite of his attacks on the manner by which the Irish bishops of New England administered their dioceses, Daignault and the Sentinellists were committed to the doctrines of the Roman Church as they understood them and persisted in seeing themselves as good Catholics, even when under the threat of excommunication. With his support waning in Rhode Island and wavering in Canada and elsewhere, Daignault

282 *La Défense*, February 14, 1929.
283 Hickey to Sbarretti, March 4, 1929; Marella to Hickey, March 21, 1929, PChA; *Le Cahier / The Book*, February 28, 1929. Mr. Perdriau's statement that Fr. Duplessis is the Richelieu of *La Défense* is found in his "Commentaires de la Semaine."

realized that Perdriau's appeal to schism, if it received wide circulation, could mean the withdrawal of support on the part of some of his strongest remaining supporters. In spite of his efforts to destroy the pamphlets, at least one copy found their way into Elie Vezina's hands and he passed a photographic copy of the pamphlet to Bishop Hickey.[284]

Elie Vezina also sent a copy of "Fiat Lux" to Henri Bourassa, editor of *Le Devoir*, which was published in Montreal. Bourassa was a champion of bi-cultural Canadian nationalism and was seen by the Franco Americans in New England as a defender of *survivance* although he had his differences with the supporters of *Action Francaise* in Canada. On November 18, 1926, when Bourassa was in Rome, Pope Pius XI had sent for him. For an hour, the pope spoke on the question of nationalism and its relation to the Church. The Pope reportedly told him, "That at the present hour, the principal obstacle to the work of the papacy and the Church in the world, was the predominance of the racial feelings in your country, the substitution of nationalism for Catholicism." In the course of five articles, which appeared in *Le Devoir* from January 15 to 19 and which were reprinted in Woonsocket's *La Tribune*, January 18–23, Bourassa reviewed the history of the Sentinellist agitation and charged the Sentinellists with undermining the principles of order and discipline in their campaign,, which put nationality over religion. Getting to the heart of the matter in an article in which he cited Perdriau's "Fiat Lux," Bourassa charged the Sentinellists with supporting a new form of Gallicanism in which each national church and even each parish would be virtually autonomous. In another article, in which he argued that the Sentinellists had not understood the principle of authority, he undercut their assertion that they had acted in good faith by pointing out that five different ecclesiastical and civil jurisdictions (their bishop, the Congregation of the Council, the apostolic delegate, the pope and the Rhode Island superior and supreme courts) all had ruled that what Bishop Hickey did was within his authority as bishop. Several pro-Sentinellists newspapers at the time protested that Bourassa "had printed only a caricature of the Sentinellist movement and reduced the quarrel to a question of money." Mr. Daignault later took Bourassa to task for labeling all the Sentinellists with the charge of advocating schism.[285]

A month and a half before the "Fiat Lux" incident, the Congregation of the Council took up the "Providence matter" on November 17, 1928. Prior to the meeting, the Secretary of the Congregation had sought out

---

284 Hickey to Sbarretti, December 14, 1928, PChA; *The Rhode Island*, December 28, 1928; *La Tribune*, January 14, 1929; Sorrell, "The Sentinelle Affair and Militant 'Survivance,'" p. 254.

285 *Le Devoir*, January 15–19, 1929. These articles were also reprinted in pamphlet form, a copy of which is in the PChA; Pope Pius' statement is found in Rumilly, *Histoire Des Franco-Americains*, p. 397.
  For the reaction of pro-Sentinellists, Cf. Daignault, *Le vrai movement sentinelliste*, 236–44. For a more recent critique of the Bourassa articles, Cf. Chartier, *The Franco-Americans of New England*, 162–164. In writing this paragraph I have made use of Sorrell, "The Sentinelle Affair and Militant 'Survivance,'" 254–56 and notes.

Archbishop Benedetti and discussed the Providence situation with him. Before the congregation met, Benedetti asked the congregation's permission to submit his thoughts in writing, which was granted. Cardinal Sbarretti conveyed part of what the congregation discussed when he wrote to Archbishop Cassulo and the Canadian hierarchy, on November 30, asking them to make the censures the congregation had issued against the Sentinellists known, so as to undermine the support they continued to receive from the French-Canadian clergy. Also on November 30, the congregation ordered that those who had incurred censure should be warned that if, by Easter 1929, they had not repented, they would be suspect of heresy and forbidden to enter any Catholic Church. Archbishop Fumasoni-Biondi prepared the notices and sent them to Bishop Hickey to have them delivered. Bishop Hickey mailed the notices on January 8. At least two of the letters were refused by the addressee and returned to the bishop. On January 11, 1929, the *Providence Visitor* printed copies of the delegate's letter to Bishop Hickey informing him of the decision of the Congregation of the Council and of the letter the delegate sent each of those excommunicated calling on them to repent.[286]

Believing that the crisis was near its conclusion, Bishop Hickey gathered all the Franco-American pastors and administrators in the diocese together for a meeting in Providence on January 18, 1929 to discuss how they could go about bringing an end to the agitation in their respective parishes once Daignault and the others submitted. He explained to the priests the procedures they were to follow when those excommunicated came to them to seek reconciliation with the Church. During his talk, he reemphasized what he had said the previous December about the obligation of all parishioners to pay seat money and to contribute to the Offertory collection. He made it clear that all those who systematically refused to give became guilty of mortal sin and were to be denied the sacraments. Aware that in the retreats given in some of the Franco-American parishes during the Lenten season the previous year, certain of the preachers disputed this doctrine, he warned the pastors that during the retreat, preachers in the coming year must either follow it or refrain from preaching. Finally, he stressed that the people needed to be reminded that buying the Sentinellists' newspapers encouraged the movement and reading them, which caused the "bad spirit to spread," was forbidden.[287]

After dealing with the crisis occasioned by "Fiat Lux," Mr. Daignault returned to Canada to speak with Bishop Georges Courchesne, the same

286 Gentile to Hickey, November 6, 1928; Fumasoni-Biondi to Hickey, January 2, 1929, PChA; *Providence Visitor*, January 11, 1929; *Providence Journal*, January 12, 1929. The delegate also informed Bishop Hickey that the Congregation of the Council was considering sending a document discussing the whole Sentinellist question to the bishops of New England and Quebec, which the congregation would ask them to publicize. Hickey supported the idea and sent suggestions as to what such a letter should cover. Fumasoni-Biondi to Hickey, January 2, 1929; Hickey to Fumasoni-Biondi, January 5, 7, 1929, PChA.
287 "Directions of His Grace to the Clergy of the French Language," PChA.

Georges Courchesne who had encouraged him and the other Franco-Americans in Woonsocket to found La Société des Croisés. Courchesne had been ordained Bishop of Rimouski, another of the dioceses in the Province of Quebec, in May 1928. Daignault wished to know if the Canadian bishops could do anything to have the conditions for the removal of the excommunication modified somewhat. On December 31, 1928, Bishop Courchesne called at the apostolic delegation in Ottawa to discuss the Daignault affair with the delegate. Courchesne told the delegate that Daignault was arriving that day on the train at noon and that he hoped to have some news for him later in the day as to his submission. At 3:30 Bishop Courchesne returned to the delegation, bringing Mr. Daignault with him. The delegate spoke first with Courchesne, who told him that Daignault was ready to sign an act of submission, to desist from any action against his bishop, and to do his best to rectify the situation. However, according to Courchesne, Daignault feared that the act of submission would cost him dearly because the formula required him to pay damages. Furthermore, he felt it prudent to hold off a bit so see whether he could persuade his associates, especially the most tenacious and daring, to go along with him. Before ending their conversation, the delegate and Bishop Courchesne agreed that Daignault and his followers would have to present themselves to Bishop Hickey to make their submissions. Following the meeting with Bishop Courchesne, the delegate spoke briefly with Mr. Daignault, who urged the delegate to write the American delegate, Archbishop Fumasoni-Biondi, to tell him that he would be very willing to go to Washington in order to put an end to the agitation. Before his two visitors left, Archbishop Cassulo promised, that after Daignault's submission, he would write to Rome to ask an indulgence in favor of those excommunicated. Either before or after his meeting with Bishop Courchesne, Daignault also met with Canon Gignac at Quebec and another canonist, Canon Dusablon, at Louiseville, who gave him the same advice as Bishop Courchesne.[288]

In addition to his personal wishes to be reconciled with the Church, Mr. Daignault had to take into consideration a resolution of the High Court of the Canado-Americaine Association, adopted by a vote of ten to four at its meeting in Manchester on January 30, 1929, that Daignault and others who been excommunicated had to be reconciled with the Church or face expulsion from the Association. At the beginning of January 1929, Archbishop Fumasoni-Biondi notified the Canado-Americaine Association that a society that had a president and members who were excommunicated could not be considered a Catholic society. The delegate's notice prompted the Association to consult a canon lawyer, Fr. Edmour Hebert, who advised the Association that Mr. Daignault should free himself of excommunication quickly or be removed as president and that the other

288 Cassulo to Fumasoni-Biondi, January 1, 1929; *Woonsocket Call*, February 11, 1929; Rumilly, *Histoire Des Franco-Americains*, p. 446.

members of the Association who had been excommunicated should also be warned to free themselves from excommunication by Easter or face expulsion. By their vote on January 30, the High Court accepted Fr. Hebert's advice and agreed to send the necessary notifications to Daignault and the others concerned.[289]

In view of Bishop Courchesne's longstanding support of the Sentinellists before he became bishop, Bishop Hickey continued to have suspicions regarding the role he was playing in the Sentinellist agitation. In actuality, Bishop Courchesne was working with other Canadian priests to persuade Mr. Daignault to remain within the Church, even if the cost was submitting to his bishop. In a letter to Daignault at this time, Bishop Courchesne suggested that the Canadian bishops who had been supporting him might have personal motives in urging him to make his peace with his bishop. In 1929, both the Canadian and American bishops would be going to Rome for their *ad limina* visits. The bishop well knew that Bishop Hickey and perhaps other of the American bishops had informed Rome of the degree of support that a few Canadians bishops and many Canadian priests had been giving Daignault and the Sentinellists. On February 16, at the urging of Archbishop Fumasoni-Biondi, Bishop Hickey sent a long report on the state of Church affairs in Rhode Island, in which he gave considerable space to what he saw as Bishop Courchesne's role in the agitation. The Canadian bishops might also have heard through other sources what Cardinal Cerretti, the former apostolic delegate to Washington and more recently Papal Nuncio to France, had said to Elie Vezina when Vezina met him in New York. Vezina reported to Henri Bourassa that Cerretti said to him, "The movement of revolt would have no importance if priests and certain bishops had not encouraged it and at times sustained it as other French priests and bishops did in the *Action Francaise* affair.[290]

On his return from Canada, Mr. Daignault called a secret meeting of the men excommunicated at the usual meeting place of the Societe des Croisés, DeNevers Hall, Woonsocket, on February 10, 1929. The meeting lasted three hours. At the beginning of the meeting various individuals rose to have their say. Some of them charged Mr. Daignault with insincerity for having previously insisted that none submit to the demands made on them by Congregation of the Council. Several others supported

---

289 Mr. Daignault would again be reelected president of the Association in its 1932 convention. In 1936, the Association's General Secretary, Mr. Robert, wrote to Bishop Guertin's successor, John R. Peterson, concerning the reappointment of chaplains. Bishop Peterson replied that because the Association had not repudiated Daignault's election and because it retained an excommunicated Catholic as a member, he would not appoint chaplains until it did. When the Association held its convention in Boston, Mr. Daignault, who was recovering from an attack of paralysis caused by a cerebral hemorrhage, was bypassed and the convention chose Adolphe Robert as its president. Bishop Peterson reappointed chaplains soon after. Robert, "Memorial de l'Association Canado-Americaine," I, 282–284, 339–343.

290 Rumilly, *Histoire Des Franco-Americains*, 449,450. Rumilly quotes from letters of both Bishop Courchesne and Fr. Charles Charlebois, a hero of the Franco-Ontario struggle; Hickey to Sbarretti, February 16, 1929, PChA.

his stand. After all had their chance to speak, Mr. Daignault rose and explained in detail how he had been finally persuaded to repent and to advise his companions to do likewise. Expecting resistance to his call for submission, Daignault had invited Fr. J. Albert Forcier and, more importantly, Fr. George Duplessis, the movement's "chaplain" to address the meeting. Of the two, Duplessis was the stronger in recommending submission. Phydime Hemond, whom Bishop Hickey thought would find it the most difficult to submit, objected that he was unwilling to submit right away and declared he was prepared to wait until May 17 before he made his decision. Daignault then read a letter from Bishop Courchesne expressing the hope that the Canadian bishops might be able to intervene with the Holy See. Before the meeting ended, Daignault asked who favored submission. All but seventeen at the meeting did. As part of his submission, Mr. Daignault agreed to end publication of La Defense, the last issue of which appeared on February 14.[291]

Following the meeting at which Daignault announced his decision to submit and urged the others who were excommunicated with him to do so as well, the six men who belonged to St. James, Manville, and the five who were members of St. John the Baptist Parish, Arctic, West Warwick, went immediately to their parishes to sign their acts of submission. Within a week, a total of fifty-three had signed the acts. Mr. Daignault signed his on February 13. As a public penance, those who had been excommunicated were required to attend a parish mass at which their letters of submission were read. After the reading, their pastors were authorized to absolve them "in the external forum." They were also required to make a private, personal confession. Antonio Prince also signed an act of submission shortly after the February meeting and was absolved privately. Between February 23 and March 15, two more signed.[292]

The Providence Visitor carried the news of the meeting of those excommunicated and its result on February 15, 1929. A Visitor editorial expressed a sense of satisfaction and thankfulness that the editor believed all Catholics felt in seeing their bishop vindicated. The editor praised Bishop Hickey for his patient firmness and for the fact that "No word of harshness, no enmity, fanned the fires of rebellion, no wavering, or compromise gave hope of ultimate success to those who erred." Daignault likewise was hailed by Fr. Duplessis, writing in the last issue of La Defense under the pen name of Armand-Jean Richelieu, as a hero for having put an end to the terrible taxes and having created a magnificent national revival. In the same issue of La Defense, Daignault wrote, "We have drunk to the dregs the chalice of humiliation for the privilege of remaining children of the Roman Catholic Church." In response to Daignault's statement, Bishop Courchesne com-

291 Providence Journal, February 10, 11, 1929; Woonsocket Call, February 11, 1929; Rumilly, Histoire Des Franco-Americains, 450–51; Acts of Submission, PChA.
292 Acts of Submission, PChA; Providence Journal, February 12, 14, 1929.

mented, "Your declaration is perfect, very dignified, very catholic. Not a word to take back." Canon Curotte wrote from Rome to applaud his "heroic gesture."[293]

Whether Bishop Hickey would have in fact imposed "terrible taxes" on the two parishes whose pastors did not give him the kind of cooperation he had expected of them in the High School Drive is a matter for speculation. It is true that the attempt on the part of the ultra-nationalist clergy and laity to force Bishop Hickey to continue the past policy of exempting the French Canadians from having to do their share in the support of diocesan drives and institutions failed. The national revival of which Fr. Duplessis also spoke in his last *La Defense* article certainly caused many Franco Americans to rally to the defense of their language and customs challenged by the Americanization campaign spurred by the United States participation in the First World War. However, in the words of *The Rhode Islander*'s Jean Sabate, one of Daignault's and the Sentinellists' most persistent critics, Daignault "divided his people in New England into two bitterly antagonistic parties, this division setting his race in this country back at least 50 years." While Mr. Daignault admitted in his address to the Sentinellists on February 10 that he had seen the folly of the attempt to have an accounting made of the parish funds, he would not let go of the conviction that the Irish were and would continue to be prejudiced against the Franco Americans. For him, as for Fr. Duplessis and the other Franco-American and French-Canadian priests who had been the core of his support, to use Fr. Duplessis' words, the Franco Americans "had to be ready to put a stop to any repetition of the situation created in Providence in other dioceses."[294]

On the day that he signed his letter of submission before his pastor, Fr. Camille Villiard, at St. Ann's, Woonsocket, Mr. Daignault expressed a desire to have a meeting with Bishop Hickey. The bishop and his assistant chancellor, Fr. Thomas Collins, agreed to meet with Daignault, who came to the bishop's office with Fr. Villiard on February 18, 1929. During the meeting Daignault expressed the conviction that all the men who had been excommunicated would sign the letters of submission in a few days, with the exception of Mr. Phydime Hemond and Henri Perdriau. He believed that Mr. Hemond would be the first of the two to give in once he had established he was not being influenced by Daignault. As for Perdriau, he believed he was a stubborn individual who would follow his own whims. When Bishop Hickey advised him that he had committed a grave sin, which required both the external as well as internal contrition, Daignault responded that internal contrition was "an affair of conscience," a response Bishop Hickey presumed was suggested by Daignault's "ecclesiastical sympathizers." The bishop then pressed Daignault to explain why

293 *Providence Visitor*, February 15, 1929; *The Rhode Islander*, April 27, 1928;
294 *La Defense*, February 14, 1929; *Providence* Journal, February 10, 1929; *The Rhode Islander*, April 27, 1928. Jean B. Sabate sued Daignault and the National Publishing Co. for libel and won.

he had charged him with being unjust to the Franco Americans when the grievances Daignault had complained of were not supported by facts. The bishop gave a defense of his actions and suggested at the end that he believed that Daignault "would have never gone so far in this movement if you had not been egged on by Fr. Prince and Fr. Beland, whose mouthpiece you were." When Mr. Daignault did not deny this assertion, the bishop took his silence as confirmation of his statement. Towards the end of the meeting, Bishop Hickey asked Mr. Daignault for a copy of the Croisés' constitution and bylaws in order to fulfill a request from the Congregation of the Council that he send a copy to Rome. Mr. Daignault promised to secure one if possible when the Société des Croisés next met on February 20, at which time those members who had already signed their letters of submission planned to insist that Mr. Phydime Hemond and those who had not signed theirs either do so or resign from the society. While Mr. Daignault did finally admit publicly what Patrick Curran had told him privately in their conversation before Daignault filed the church suits and the courts would affirm, that it was folly to proceed with the suits when the law was clearly on Bishop Hickey's side, he would never have admitted personal responsibility for challenging the bishop's authority.[295]

The divisions within the ranks of the Croisés were also present in the ranks of the thousands of people who supported them. It is evident from the responses that the various signers of the church suits gave to the newspaper reporters that they were not all totally committed to what Daignault did or, more so, to what he said in his attacks on the New England bishops, the clergy, among them the Franco-American clergy who supported Bishop Hickey, and the Irish in general. While a few publicly broke with Daignault when they refused to sign the amended church suits, others chose to remain in the ranks rather then risk the taunts of coward and traitor. One such individual, Emile J. Brunelle, the former organist at St. Ann's, Woonsocket, wrote a personal letter of apology to Bishop Hickey on September 10, 1932. He told the bishop that he had been dragged into the movement without knowing the real aims of the organizers, that he was kept in it by a lot of promises and menaces and that when, on two different occasions, he expressed a desire to cease all activities, "there resounded against him a chorus of charges."[296]

295 "Interview of Mr. Daignault with Bishop William A. Hickey, February 18, 1929, PChA. The document contains Bishop Hickey's questions, Mr. Daignault's answers and the bishop's later commentary on the purpose of his questions and on Daignault's answers.
296 Emile J. Brunelle to Hickey, September 10, 1932, PChA.

The Submissions of Frs. Beland and Prince

If Elphege Daignault was the public face of the Sentinellist movement, Fr. Joseph Beland was its heart. From the very beginning of the agitation, Fr. Beland, pastor of Notre Dame, Central Falls, and Fr. Achille Prince, pastor of St. Louis, Woonsocket, were closely associated with Daignault and were the two most prominent clerical supporters of the Sentinellist movement in the diocese. Several other priests, who were priests of the Diocese of Providence or priests of Canadian dioceses who were serving in Providence, encouraged Daignault and his associates in their campaign. Each would pay a price for their encouragement and support of the Sentinellists.

Fr. Prince was born in St Gregoire, Conte Nicolet, in the Province of Quebec on September 27, 1872. He had studied for the priesthood at the Grand Seminary at Montreal and was ordained for the Diocese of Nicolet on December 23, 1900. His first assignment after ordination was as an assistant to Fr. Beland at Notre Dame, Central Falls. He remained at Notre Dame until March 1914, when Bishop Harkins appointed him pastor of St. Louis (St. Aloysius in English). His mentor, Fr. Beland, was born on July 3, 1857 in St. Maurice, Quebec. He was ordained on December 23, 1883 for the Diocese of Three Rivers. As a young priest he served in Duluth, Minnesota, and, after a few years, he was admitted to the Diocese of Providence and served in New Bedford, Fall River, and Manville before Bishop Harkins appointed him pastor of Notre Dame, Central Falls, a parish in which the pastor was an "irremovable rector," in February 1894. The older man was to have a great influence on the younger.[297]

After Bishop Hickey removed Fr. Prince as pastor of St. Louis in September 1927, Prince went to Quebec to consult with Canon Gignac, with whom Fr. Beland had also consulted in the past. Shortly thereafter, Fr. Prince, on September 9, 1927, sent a letter to Cristoforo Astorri, the same church lawyer Mr. Daignault had engaged in 1925 to present his Memorial to the Congregation of the Council, asking Astorri to represent him before the competent congregation or tribunal. On September 15, 1927, Fr. Prince sent a formal letter to Pope Pius XI alleging that Bishop Hickey had removed him from St. Louis without legitimate cause and without following proper procedure. To support Fr. Prince's claims in his letter to the pope, Canon Gignac prepared "an exposition of the facts" which he sent to Rome. After having removed Fr. Prince from St. Louis, Bishop Hickey, on September 10, 1927, appointed Fr. Prince administrator of Our Lady of Good Help, Mapleville. Because Fr. Prince was away in Canada, he did not receive the bishop's letter of appointment until after he returned to the diocese. On October 4, the day before he was to take up the new position, Fr. Prince wrote to Bishop Hickey to inform him that he could not accept

297 Obituary, *Providence Journal*, October 24, 1929; September 26, 1936.

the appointment because he was leaving for Rome on October 12 in order "to defend his cause at Rome."[298]

The following month, Bishop Hickey met with Fr. Beland at the Chancery Office on Friday, November 25. The main topic of their meeting was the collection being taken up in Notre Dame parish by the committee in charge of raising funds for finishing the interior of the new church. The committee deposited the monies collected at mass in a bank account set up in 1925 at a credit union that Fr. Beland had helped found, that was run by an ex-trustee of the parish, Leger Morisette. Fr. Beland had free access to the account to pay the expenses of construction. Since the account was not in the name of the parish corporation, the procedure was in violation of American Church law. At their meeting, Bishop Hickey warned Fr. Beland that, if the practice of keeping the separate account continued, he would declare Beland incapable of running his parish or else close the parish school and place the church under an interdict. On his part, Fr. Beland responded that, if he changed the collectors and put out "the refractory crowd" as the bishop wished, the people would not give and they would apostatize. Bishop Hickey was not fazed by the threat and responded that, if the people apostatized, then the conspiring priest who scandalized them would be to blame. The bishop ordered Fr. Beland to preach the correct doctrine in regard to the authority of a bishop, to counter what *La Sentinelle* had been preaching. If he did not, Hickey promised that he would appoint an administrator. If the people then refused to financially support the church, he would close it. The bishop gave Beland until the following Sunday to get things in order.[299]

On the Wednesday of the following week, November 30, Fr. Beland wrote to Bishop Hickey that he was ill and, on the advice of his doctor, he was obliged to absent himself from his parish and take a rest. He also said that he needed to see his legal advisor about the suit he and Fr. Prince had filed protesting their suspension in June 1927 at the end of their retreat. Fr. Beland's note arrived at the bishop's office on Friday, December 2. The bishop phoned Notre Dame rectory and sent a special delivery letter to Fr. Beland asking for a "satisfactory report" that Beland's health required his absence and refusing him permission to be absent from his parish until after New Year's Day. Two weeks later there was another exchange of notes, when Fr. Beland asked for a "celebret" for use during the vacation he was obliged to take on the advice of his doctor. In his response, Bishop Hickey reminded him that Sacred Congregation of the Council had recently required that priests inform their bishop of the time of their departure and return and the places they intended to visit. When next Fr. Beland wrote on December 27, he informed the bishop that he was going

298 Prince to Astorri, September 9, 1927; Prince to Pope Pius XI, September 15, 1927; Hickey to Prince, September 10, 1927; Prince to Hickey, October 4, 1927, PChA.
299 "Memo," November 25, 1927, Beland File; Hickey to Sbarretti, "Exposition of fact on Fr. J. H. Beland, December 28, 1927, PChA.

to Rome since he had been notified by his procurator in Rome that his case was to go before "the competent office" and that his presence was required. He also told the bishop that, because of all the vexation to which he had been subjected by Hickey, his doctor had ordered him to take a long rest before returning to the work of his parish. Later, Bishop Hickey learned that Fr. Beland announced his departure for Rome at Notre Dame before asking for permission to be absent from his parish.[300]

While Frs. Prince and Beland had been consulting first with Canon Gignac and then Mr. Astorri in the preparation of their appeals before the Sacred Congregation of the Council, Bishop Hickey had also been drafting his response to the statement of facts the two submitted to support their claims that Hickey had acted unjustly against them when he suspended them for a month. In addition to the specific responses the congregation's procedures required of him, in December 1927, Bishop Hickey prepared an overview of the issues raised by the Sentinellists and included copies of Frs. Prince and Beland's petitions and his responses to them, along with documents that supported his reasons for his actions. In a note he sent to Msgr. Gentile, enclosing two copies of the documents that he had prepared in French for the convenience of the congregation and had mimeographed and bound "for the private information of those most interested in the Sentinellist disturbance," he asked Gentile to give him the names of anyone in Rome to whom he should send a copy.[301]

As events developed, Frs. Beland and Prince were persuaded to seek an "out of court" settlement with Bishop Hickey, which, on their part, they worked out with Msgr. Gentile. Both agreed to sign an act of submission to the authority of their bishop and accept in advance whatever decision he would make in their regard. In the formula which both signed, they acknowledged that the movement set in motion by the Societe des Croisés and *La Sentinelle* was disastrous for the faith of the faithful and contrary to the interests of the Church. In Prince's case, he denied any responsibility for encouraging the Sentinellist movement. In Beland's case, he also denied responsibility for encouraging the Sentinellists, but acknowledged that he did do some of the things Bishop Hickey considered contrary to ecclesiastical discipline, although he did not think they were. Nonetheless, he regretted them and promised to do better in the future. Msgr. Gentile, who arranged the signing of the submissions, wrote to Bishop Hickey that he was quite pleased with them. He believed that, because the congregation had shown leniency to the two priests, they could be more severe with Daignault and the Sentinellists whom he considered the most guilty of all.[302]

Bishop Hickey, however, did not share Msgr. Gentile's view. He con-

---

300 Beland to Hickey, November 30; December 2, 19, 20, 27, 1927; Hickey to Beland, December 2, 20, 1927, Beland File, PChA.
301 Hickey to Gentile, December 28, 1927, PChA.
302 Gentile to Hickey, February 6, 1928, PChA.

sidered both priests, but Fr. Beland in particular, to be at the heart of the agitation against him. Hickey was adamant that the two be forced to acknowledge their responsibility for the agitation in the diocese. The bishop pointed out that each of the submissions ignored the more serious charges Bishop Hickey had brought against them. To the bishop's mind, if he accepted the submission of the two priests as worked out at this time, they would be considered as innocent and he would stand guilty in public opinion for having wrongly accused them. Furthermore, he believed that if the two were let off, the leniency of the Church would renew the life and ardor of the revolt by glorifying the two priests who identified themselves with resistance to the bishop. To the bishop's mind, acceptance of the documents would confuse and discourage the majority of the Franco Americans, who had remained loyal to the Church. For him, there was no middle ground. He was convinced that Frs. Prince and Beland had to recognize that they had been at fault, if the Sentinellists were ever to cease using their priestly authority to slander the other priests of the diocese and to mock himself and the apostolic delegate.[303]

To further substantiate his stand for declining to accept the acts of submission as written, Bishop Hickey informed Gentile that Fr. Lavergne, who played the role of a peacemaker in encouraging Frs. Beland and Prince to sign the acts, rather than go directly home from Rome, went to Woonsocket, where he spoke at a meeting of Sentinellist leaders on February 22. The meeting was called to encourage the Sentinellists to remain firm in the face of the Bishop Hickey's February pastoral in which he supported the letter of his priests who had reinforced the Church's teaching on the obligation to financially support the Church. According to the information in Bishop Hickey's possession, Fr. Lavergne had encouraged the Sentinellists to continue to withhold their financial support of the Church. He asked Msgr. Gentile whether he thought Lavergne's action was in keeping with his words in Rome. Hickey also reported to Gentile that, after the bishop had sent Fr. Prince a *celebret* when Gentile asked him to do it as a favor to him, Prince had written to his Sentinellist friends to urge them to continue their struggle as victory was close because the bishop had been obliged to send the *celebret*. After offering these two incidents as reasons why he doubted the sincerity of Prince's and Beland's submissions, as a counterproposal Hickey included in his response to Msgr. Gentile a formula of submission, which he felt responded to the gravity of the situation.[304]

At the same time in November 1927 that Bishop Hickey confronted Fr. Beland in regard to the manner in which he administered his parish, he also confronted two other priests in the diocese who had also identified themselves with the Sentinellists, Frs. Joseph A. Fautaux and J. Albert Forcier. Bishop Hickey removed Fr. Fautaux from his position as chaplain

---

303 Hickey to Gentile, February 24, 1928, PChA.
304 Ibid.

at the Cenacle in Newport and Fr. Forcier from his position as an assistant in St. John's, West Warwick. Both were priests who were ordained
for Canadian dioceses and had been incardinated into the Diocese of
Providence. Fr. Fautaux appealed his removal to the apostolic delegate,
while Fr. Forcier did not. The apostolic delegate supported Bishop Hickey's
action in removing Fr. Fautaux, who later signed a letter of submission
and apology after he returned to Canada, as had Fr. Forcier previously.
The fifth priest of the diocese who supported the Sentinellists, Fr. Arthur
F. Fournier, the pastor of the Presentation of the Blessed Virgin Mary,
North Providence, had not taken an active role in the agitation. As a result,
Bishop Hickey did not take action against him. However, when Fr. Fourni-
er submitted his resignation as pastor of the Presentation of Mary Parish
in North Providence on April 11, 1930 because of poor health, Bishop
Hickey accepted his resignation on the same day.[305]

Following their signing of their acts of submission, Frs. Beland and
Prince went to the Holy Land, partially on the advice of Fr. Beland's doctors, who advised him to go to a warmer climate. The two returned to
Rome before Easter and were in the city when Mr. Daignault arrived there
on April 5, 1928. While Daignault was unsuccessful in securing a meeting
with the Congregation of the Council, Frs. Beland and Prince, together
with Frs. Adrien Verrette and Josee Vachon, priests of the Diocese of
Manchester who had been suspended by Bishop Guertin for their involvement in the Sentinellist cause, were able to present their individual cases
to the congregation.[306]

On May 7, 1928, Fr. Prince signed a letter of submission at the office
of his lawyer, in which he denied any part in the founding of the Societe
des Croisés or in the founding or editing of *La Sentinelle*. He also denied
that he ever sought to undermine the authority of Bishop Hickey and renewed his profession of respect and obedience to the bishop. Fr. Beland
also signed a letter of submission, which he sent to the Congregation of
the Council. Shortly after signing the letters, the two left Rome along with
Mr. Daignault to take a Cunard liner for America. When Msgr. Gentile
forwarded the two letters to Bishop Hickey, he again found them unsatis-
factory. Since Fr. Prince had denied any wrongdoing and Fr. Beland, in his
letter, failed to make the kind of complete submission that Bishop Hickey
wanted, he told Msgr. Gentile that he feared that their supporters would
expect that both would be restored to their parishes. The bishop was particularly concerned about Fr. Beland's parish, Notre Dame, since it was
the only parish where there had not been a significant change for the better following the public announcement of the excommunications. In large
measure, many of the parishioners of Notre Dame remained defiant of

305 Hickey to Fumasoni-Biondi, December 15, 1927; Hickey to Fautaux, December 6, 24, 1929;
    Fournier to Hickey, April 11, 1930; Hickey to Fournier, April 11, 1930, PChA; *Providence News*,
    November 10, 1927.
306 Rumilly, *Histoire Des Franco-Americains*, 431, 432, 434–45.

the bishop's authority because Fr. Beland had written to one his chief supporters in the parish, Leger J. Morissette, to assure him that he was coming
back to take charge of the parish as before. Mr. Morissette read the letter
at a parish meeting in the presence of the priests of the parish. In a letter
to Archbishop Fumasoni-Biondi shortly after receiving Msgr. Gentile's regarding Fr. Beland submission, Bishop Hickey expressed his surprise that
the two had returned to America "before their complete surrender to the
authority of their bishop."[307]

Fr. Beland and Fr. Prince did not come directly to Rhode Island from
the ship on which they crossed the Atlantic. Because Fr. Beland's health
continued to be poor, they took a train for his native diocese, Trois-
Rivières, in Canada. On June 19, 1928, Fr. Beland wrote Bishop Hickey
from St. Joseph's Hospital in Trois-Rivières to inform him that he was late
in returning from his vacation in Europe and, since his health was no better, it would probably be several weeks before he could return. Fr. Prince
stayed with Fr. Beland in Trois-Rivières for three months. According to the
information Bishop Hickey received concerning them during this time,
the two priests continued to claim, as did the Sentinellist leaders, that the
Congregation of the Council did not have the authority to excommunicate the Sentinellist leaders and that the congregation's decision would be
reversed when the pope sent a representative to investigate the matter. A
nun, the sister of Fr. Henri Vincent, an assistant at Holy Family, Woonsocket, wrote to Elie Vezina of her distress at hearing Fr. Prince say that
the whole matter was scandalous and at hearing him criticize her brother.
While Fr. Beland was in Canada, his lawyer in Rome continued to defend him before the Congregation of the Council. In his own defense, Fr.
Beland swore that he had always been opposed to the revolt against Bishop
Hickey's authority. On July 13, 1928, Bishop Hickey sent the congregation
a document in which he challenged Fr. Beland's profession of innocence
and offered evidence to the contrary.[308]

On August 14, 1928, the *Woonsocket Call* published an article that said
Fr. Prince would return to the diocese on the following day and be given
charge of another parish somewhere in the diocese. The *Call* report proved
only partially true. Fr. Prince returned to the United States, but since his
case was still unresolved in Bishop Hickey's mind, he went to live with Fr.
Binette in East Bellingham, where Binette had previously offered hospitality to Frs. Fautaux and Forcier. On September 8, 1928, Prince's Roman
lawyer, Mr. Astorri, sent a letter on Prince's behalf to the Congregation
of the Council explaining that Fr. Prince was not able to accept the parish
of Our Lady of Good Help, Mapleville, that Bishop Hickey had offered
him when he was removed from St. Louis, because the parish had scarcely

307 Ibid., p. 434; Hickey to Gentile, May 22, 1928; Hickey to Fumasoni-Biondi, June 2, 1928, PChA.
     Hickey received the information on the return of the three from an official of the Cunard line.
308 Beland to Hickey, June 19, 1928; Hickey to Gentile, August 18, 1928; Hickey to Sbarretti, July 13,
     1928, PChA.

one-fourth the population of St. Louis and his appointment would be seen as a clear and explicit punishment. Such an action would be unjust, he contended, since no serious charges had been made against him, much less proved. To Bishop Hickey's mind, his charges against Fr. Prince had been proven and the proof was found in the documentation he sent to the Congregation of the Council. On October 29, 1928, Cardinal Sbarretti wrote to Bishop Hickey asking his opinion of the petition submitted to the congregation on Fr. Prince's behalf and for a formula of retraction and submission that Hickey would accept.[309]

Fr. Beland's church lawyer, Canon J. A. Curotte, also continued to pursue his case before the congregation. On June 18, 1928, Canon Curotte wrote to Msgr. Gentile to thank him for sending the formula of submission that Bishop Hickey had sent in order to cover all the points the bishop believed to be important. Since Canon Curotte took Fr. Beland at his word when he said he had always been against the "movement of insurrection" and that he never wrote letters from Rome encouraging the people of Notre Dame to support the offering strike, Msgr. Curotte believed that Beland would readily sign the document that he forwarded to him at Trois-Rivières. On July 16, 1928, Fr. Beland signed the formula of submission that Bishop Hickey had sent him and mailed it back. Bishop Hickey received word of Fr. Beland's signing of the document from Msgr. Gentile in a letter dated September 9, 1928. In his response to Gentile on October 16, 1928, Hickey asked him to forward the original as soon as possible. Although his case before the congregation was still unresolved, the death of one of his brothers prompted Fr. Beland to return to Rhode Island during the middle of October.[310]

Before Fr. Beland left Notre Dame in December 1927 for his "vacation" in view of his poor health, Bishop Hickey had appointed Fr. Normand Meunier to serve as administrator of Notre Dame during Fr. Beland's absence. In the continuing tug of war between the bishop and Fr. Beland, Beland accepted Fr. Meunier as administrator, but did not turn over to him the combination of the safe where the corporation records of the parish were kept along with all the keys and books of the parish. After Fr. Beland left, Fr. Meunier discovered and reported to the bishop that $95,000 had been taken from parish funds and placed in the lay corporation of which Fr. Beland was the treasurer.[311]

When Fr. Beland come back to Rhode Island, he called on Bishop Hickey. The two talked for a while and Fr. Beland promised to return a

309 *Woonsocket Call*, August 14, 1928; Cristoforo Astorri to Msgr. Serafini, September 8, 1928; Sbarretti to Hickey, October 29, 1928, PChA.
310 Curotte to Gentile, June 18, 1929; Letter of submission addressed to Sacred Congregation of the Council, July 16, 1928; Gentile to Hickey, September 9, 1928; Hickey to Gentile, October 16, 1928, PChA.
311 Hickey to Sbarretti, addendum to Beland fact sheet, February 1928; Hickey to Msgr. Paul Marella, Auditor, February 25, 1929, PChA.

few days after his brother's funeral. He returned to Providence two weeks later, on October 29, and expressed a desire to take back his parish. Bishop Hickey was not willing to let him do that. He did, however, allow him to take up residence in Notre Dame Rectory on certain conditions. The bishop insisted that no further work could be done towards finishing the interior of the new church until the bishop had received the act of submission from Rome that Beland had signed and until all the parish money then in the Credit Union in Central Falls was placed in the name of the Church of Notre Dame. Furthermore, Fr. Beland was not to say mass in the new church until it was ready and blessed by Bishop Hickey. Finally, Fr. Meunier was to remain at Notre Dame for the present. Fr. Beland fulfilled part of what the bishop required on the day after he saw the bishop. On October 30, 1928, Leger J. Morissette, who was Treasurer and General Manager of Credit Union Central Falls, sent Bishop Hickey a letter notifying him that the name of the church had been added to the New Church account at the Credit Union.[312]

Bishop Hickey's meeting with Fr. Beland prompted him to write to Archbishop Fumasoni-Biondi on the following day to ask the delegate to secure for him from Rome the power to divest the parish of Notre Dame of the character of Irremovable Rectorship, a faculty that Hickey would use "only in case of persistent refusal or neglect on Father Beland's part to fulfill the conditions of his signed submission." In his response, the delegate noted that, since the promulgation of the Code of Canon Law in 1917, the process of removing an irremovable pastor was only slightly different from that of removing any pastor. On receiving this information, Hickey asked the delegate not to pursue his request for an indult.[313]

As requested by the bishop, Fr. Beland went to Bishop Hickey's office on November 9 to sign a second "Formula of Submission" in the presence of Fr. Foley, the Chancellor, and Fr. Thomas C. Collins, the bishop's secretary. Since he would ask of the laymen under excommunication that their letters of submission be read publicly at a parish mass, Bishop Hickey asked Fr. Beland to announce his submission to the bishop's authority and his condemnation of the revolt against it at the parish masses on November 11. Rather than read his act of submission as the bishop required him to do on Sunday, November 18, 1928, Fr. Beland, on November 10, wrote to the bishop, that "the death of his brother, annoyances of all sorts, and the milieu in which he was obliged to live since his return, plus the need to regain his health," forced him to again leave the parish. On the advice of his doctor, he asked permission to be absent for two or three months. Fr. Beland's note crossed paths with a letter expressing his submission and a commentary on the letter, which Bishop Hickey had prepared and expect-

---

312 Memorandum, Beland File, October 29, 1928; Leger to Hickey, October 30, 1929, PChA.
313 Hickey to Fumasoni-Biondi, October 30; November 9, 1928; Fumasoni-Biondi, November 2, 1928, PChA.

ed him to read. On November 13, Fr. Beland wrote a short note to Bishop Hickey that he had read the letter and commentary very carefully, but found them impossible to sign. Fr. Beland left the parish without waiting for the permission he asked for and went first to Lynn, Massachusetts and then to the hospital in Trois-Rivières. Before he left, Fr. Beland shared his reasons for leaving with some of his parishioners. On Thursday, November 15, the day after he left Central Falls, his parishioners filled the Casino Theater on Broad Street, Central Falls, under the auspices of Cercle Notre Dame, an organization created to protest Fr. Beland's perceived removal from the parish, where they listened to Leger Morissette and others urge them not to contribute to the building fund.[314]

When on Sunday, November 25, 1928, the priests at Notre Dame, as in the other Franco-American parishes, were to read Bishop Hickey's pastoral letter setting forth the conditions whereby the followers of Mr. Daignault might be reinstated by the Church, crowds of parishioners gathered around the church before the masses. When asked by a reporter why they had booed a priest who had come from the Old Folks' Home in Pawtucket to say mass, one member of the crowd said they objected to the reading of the bishop's letter since there were no excommunicates in the parish and the publishing of the letter was not considered necessary. At the nine o'clock mass, some two hundred church goers got up and left the church when the priest began reading the letter and returned for the ten-thirty mass to do the same again. All during the morning, a detail of police kept order outside the church.[315]

On November 30 and again on December 7, *The Rhode Islander* carried stories that suggested that Fr. Beland had signed a letter of submission when asked to by Bishop Hickey, but that he had refused to read the letter out loud in Notre Dame as the bishop asked as a penance. Someone at Trois-Rivières who had read *The Rhode Islander* showed the two references to his having signed an act of submission to Fr. Beland. Fearing that he would be discredited in the eyes of his parishioners, Beland denied having signed any papers and attributed the report to an adversary. Whether he intended his denial to be made public is not clear. In any case, the gentleman, Henri Jodoin, who asked about *The Rhode Islander* articles, wrote to Daignault, who was now publishing his newspaper under the name of *La Defense,* in order to let the friends of the Sentinellists know the truth of the matter. *La Defense* published Jodoin's letter in its December 20, 1928 issue. Before he left Canada to return to the United State, Daignault had Fr. Beland sign an affidavit denying that he had signed anything and affirming his allegiance to the cause. One of Daignault's first acts on returning from Canada was to read a copy of Fr. Beland's affidavit at a meeting of

314 Beland File, Letter and Commentary, n.d.; Beland to Hickey, November 10, 13, 1928; Hickey to Marella, February 25, 1929, PChA.
315 *Providence Journal,* November 16, 26, 1928.

Notre Dame parishioners in Gagnon's Hall in Central Falls on February 1, 1928.[316]

For Bishop Hickey, the incident strengthened his doubts about the sincerity of Mr. Daignault's rumored repentance. It also confirmed his resolve to force Fr. Beland to publicly acknowledge his submission to the bishop's authority and his complicity in the Daignault agitation as well as to secure his resignation or removal from Notre Dame. On February 1, 1929, Henri Bourassa wrote to Elie Vezina with a request that he pass the information on to Bishop Hickey that he had heard from two ordinarily reliable sources in Rome that the Roman authorities thought that Bishop Hickey was asking too much in terms of retraction and reparations from Frs. Beland and Prince. Regardless of Rome's attitude, Bishop Hickey was determined to force Fr. Beland to resign or to remove him because he considered him and Fr. Prince to be "the chief originators of the opposition" to his authority as bishop. In their resistance to episcopal authority, he believed that "they had both committed acts of grave disobedience, for which they had been censured, and, contrary to the interests of the Church, "they had spread among the French Canadians the false accusation that the Bishop of Providence persecuted the French language." In commenting on Fr. Beland's denial of having signed an act of submission in a letter to Archbishop Fumasoni-Biondi, Bishop Hickey observed that, "One can hardly expect submission on the part of the laity as long as priests set the example for revolt and obstinance." In an earlier letter to the apostolic delegate, Bishop Hickey pointed out that, while Fr. Beland had declared in Rome that he had had nothing to do with "the cause of Daignault," he said in the affidavit that Daignault read that he supported "the cause." Hickey saw in this episode, he told the delegate, further reason why Fr. Beland was not suited to return to his parish.[317]

In order to clarify the situation concerning Fr. Beland, Bishop Hickey sent a copy of the newspaper article in which Mr. Daignault claimed he had an affidavit signed by Fr. Beland disclaiming having signed an act of submission, to Tampa, Florida, where Fr. Beland was staying in a Jesuit house. He asked him, in his own name and that of the apostolic delegate, to sign an affidavit declaring Daignault's affidavit to be false and acknowledging that he had freely signed an act of submission. On February 16, 1929, Fr. Beland replied from Tampa that he refused to sign the affidavit because, in doing so, he would be contradicting himself, since he had already signed an act of submission the previous December.[318]

316 *The Rhode Islander*, November 30; December 7, 1928; *La Defense*, December 20, 1928; *Pawtucket Times*, February 2, 1929.

317 Rumilly, *Histoire Des Franco-Americains*, p. 450; *Providence Visitor*, "Brief History of the Sentinellist Agitation," February 15, 1929. Bishop Hickey made essentially the same charges in his responses to the petitions of both Fr. Beland and Prince; Hickey to Fumasoni-Biondi, February 6, 1929; Hickey to Sbarretti, February 5, 1929, PChA.

318 Hickey to Beland, February 9, 1929; Beland to Hickey, February 16, 1929. Fr. Beland would later say that, in denying he had signed a letter of submission, he was referring to the documents

While Daignault's submission and that of the majority of his supporters put an end to the laymen's legal challenge to the authority of the bishop in the Church and civil courts, which was at the heart of the Sentinellist agitation in Rhode Island, it did not put an end to the challenge to the bishop's authority raised by Frs. Beland, Prince, Fautaux and Forcier, whose appeals against the action taken against them by Bishop Hickey were still pending. In a report Bishop Hickey sent to Rome on March 4, 1929, Bishop Hickey told the Congregation of the Council that only the four priests remained obstinate in their revolt. Of the four, Bishop Hickey singled out Frs. Beland and Prince as being the most responsible for it. In the history of the Sentinellist movement that appeared in the *Providence Visitor*, the same issue in which the *Visitor* announced the end of Mr. Daignault's campaign against the bishop, the writer of the history stated that Fr. Beland and Fr. Prince had been "the chief originators of the opposition to the Bishop, the chief promoters of the Daignault agitation" and that they had "spread among the French Canadians the false accusation that the Bishop of Providence persecuted the French language." The two priests sent a joint letter to the editor of the *Visitor* on April 1, 1929, in which they denied the charges in the *Visitor* article. Rather than answer their letter in the pages of the *Visitor*, Bishop Hickey included the letter and the proof he had of the charges the *Visitor* history contained in a dossier he sent to Rome.[319]

To Bishop Hickey's mind, Notre Dame, Central Falls, was the center of the first challenge to his authority in the course of the agitation and it would be the focus of the last. Even before Mr. Daignault actually closed down *La Defense*, Perdriau announced his intention of publishing a new newspaper to continue the struggle in Central Falls. In the last issue of *La Defense*, Daignault, believing that he would be attacked by Perdriau and Phydime Hemond, who was to join Perdriau in the venture, disclaimed all responsibility for what the two were planning to do. On February 29, 1929, the first issue of Perdriau's French-English weekly, *The Book of the Statements of the Truth* or *Le Cahier des Communiques de-la-Verite*, appeared. The paper listed its editorial and administrative office as being at 713 Broad Street, Central Falls.[320]

The first issue of Perdriau's and Hemond's paper carried an editorial, "Still on the Firing Line," that served as the paper's manifesto. Perdriau wrote that he had been induced by "a group of militant champions of the cause" to remain in the struggle. In an article that appeared in the *Woonsocket Call* on February 25, 1929, which Perdriau reprinted in his first issue,

Bishop Hickey sent him after he signed a second act of submission in December which contained notes for a letter he was to write to the bishop after making a public announcement of his submission in Notre Dame church, Memorandum, August 22, 1929, PChA.

319 *Providence Visitor*, February 15, 1929; Hickey to Sbarretti, March 4, 1929; Beland and Prince to editor, April 1, 1929, PChA.
320 *La Defense*, February 14, 1929.

Perdriau explained that he was presenting the new paper as a bilingual paper for the benefit of the Franco Americans who "have lacked the opportunity to learn the language of their fathers" and "the American people who speak only English," so that they might become conversant with the facts. On April 11, 1929, Perdriau changed the name of the publication to *L'Intransigeant* or *The Intransigent*, in response to an expressed desire on the part of his financial backers that he choose a name "less complicated and less learned." A supporter of Bishop Hickey sent copies of the new publication and an analysis of its article sometime in April 1929.[321]

Perdriau and Hemond sought to exploit the unrest in Central Falls created by what some parishioners saw as the bishop's abominable abuse of his authority and the unmerited punishment inflicted upon Fr. Bedard. After Fr. Bedard left the parish to pursue his appeal against his month's suspension in June 1927, Fr. Meunier, at Bishop Hickey's direction, appointed two new trustees to fill the vacancies created when Bishop Hickey did not confirm Fr. Beland's renomination of Leger J. Morissette and Philias Chartier. When Fr. Meunier announced the names of the trustees appointed in their place on Sunday, May 6, 1928, the supporters of Morissette and Chartier called a parish meeting in St. Joseph's Gymnasium, at which George Huot presided while Fr. Meunier and this two assistants were seated on the platform. Rep. Leopold L. Maynard defended the cause of the two deposed trustees. At the close of the meeting, those present voted unanimously to demand the two new appointees resign but at the same meeting also voted to dismiss the building fund committee established six years ago to raise money to buy furnishings for the new church the parish was building.[322]

Affairs in the parish entered a new crisis phase when Mr. Daignault and other Sentinellists announced their submissions to the authority of Bishop Hickey. During the week of February 17, the committee that was collecting funds for the new church called for a general strike against all contributions of any kind in order to protest the bishop's having taken the administration of the parish away from Fr. Beland, his closing of their college, his refusal to allow the Grey Nuns to take charge of Notre Dame Hospital and "a thousand annoying incidents' of which they had been the object on the part of authority. The strike call circulated in the form of a printed appeal on the part of the committee to all parishioners of Notre Dame. On the following Sunday, Fr. Meunier, who had been personally attacked in the circular, warned that plotting against the parish would not be tolerated. To forestall any protest in the church itself, Fr. Meunier suspended the building fund collection. On the Sunday on which Fr. Meunier warned the plotters, the parishioners responded by giving more in the col-

321 Interview of Mr. Daignault with Bishop William A. Hickey, February 18, 1929, PChA; *Le Cahier / The Book*, February 28, 1929; "Analysis," PChA.
322 *Providence Journal*, May 11, 1928.

lections taken up that day than before, indicating to Bishop Hickey's mind
that they were tired of the struggle and wished to manifest their loyalty
to the Church. On Thursday of the following week, some two hundred
parishioners sought to disrupt a meeting Fr. Meunier was holding in St.
Joseph's Gymnasium to organize a whist party to be held for the benefit of
the church. A detail of police was called out to maintain order and keep
them out of the building.[323]

When on February 5, 1929, Bishop Hickey had asked Fr. Beland to sign
an affidavit that he had indeed signed an act of submission, the bishop
also sent several checks on the new church account in the Credit Union
Central Falls that he asked Fr. Beland to sign so that Fr. Meunier might
be able to withdraw the funds and put them into the regular church accounts. In the light of what had ensued in regard to his claim that he had
not signed an act of submission that the bishop had in his office, Fr. Beland
knew that, if he hoped to return to his parish, he had to do something to
remove the most serious of the charges that the bishop had made against
him, his irregular handling of the funds for the new church. He sent back
the blanks, which would authorize Fr. Meunier to withdraw the funds for
the new church, unsigned. He told the bishop that the matter was delicate,
since he was not the only one interested in the funds. He asked for time in
order to convince the members of the committee to turn over the funds as
it would be much easier for him to do it than for the bishop to persuade
them.[324]

Fr. Beland was true to his word. On March 16, 1929, Leger Morissette
called on Bishop Hickey to work out the details for the transfer of the
funds. Bishop Hickey had exchanged letters with Morissette and, after a
face to face meeting with him the previous year, Mr. Morissette had accused the bishop, in a letter sent after the meeting, of having demanded a
$15,000 commission for agreeing to allow Notre Dame parish to take out
a loan to complete the church. The bishop's lawyer had sent Morissette a
letter on May 21, 1928, demanding that he not repeat the libelous charge
or he would be called into court to prove it. Mr. Morissette apologized to
the bishop in writing for all that he had said and done against him and
promised to do all in his power to reestablish in Notre Dame "the order
and peace, the respect and obedience to ecclesiastical authorities." Three
days later, several "collectors of the Voluntary Collection" wrote to Bishop
Hickey asking for an appointment. Bishop Hickey agreed to see them if
they informed him in advance what they wished to discuss and sent a letter
of recommendation from Fr. Meunier. Presumably, the matter of the funds
was straightened out shortly thereafter, because work on the new church
was resumed by the end of April.[325]

323 *Woonsocket Call*, February 28, 1929; "Parossiens de Notre Dame;" Hickey to Sbarretti, March 4,
    1929, PChA.
324 Hickey to Beland, February 5, 1929; Beland to Hickey, February 16, 1929, PChA.
325 Patrick P. Curran to Morisette, May 21, 1928; Morissette to Hickey, March 16, 1929; Louis

On March 8, 1929, Bishop Hickey announced, through the pages of the *Providence Visitor*, that he had decided to make his *ad limina* visit to Rome in the spring of the year. On April 6, the bishop, accompanied by Fr. Georges Bedard, who had played an important role in coordinating the diocese's response to the Sentinellist movement, sailed for Rome on board the *S.S. Biancamano* from New York. One of Bishop Hickey's aims while in Rome was to secure the Holy See's recognition of the priests and laymen who supported him and the authority of a bishop in the Daignault agitation.[326]

Elie Vezina, who had stood by the bishop personally and as the representative of the Union St. Jean Baptiste, also continued to seek papal recognition and support for his society to underline the differences between Union St. Jean Baptiste and the Canado-Americaine Association, of which Daignault was president. Vezina was aware that his ideological opponents were organizing another attempt to oust him and the general officers who supported him. Prior to Bishop Hickey's sailing for Rome, Mr. Vezina had sent his pastor, Fr. Gedeon Laverdiere of Holy Family, Woonsocket, to Rome, where he would work with Archbishop Benedetti to promote the cause of the Union St. Jean Baptiste and the Franco Americans in general. Vezina was aware that Mr. Daignault was planning to return to Rome and wished to ensure that the views of the moderate Franco-American nationalists were heard at Rome as an antidote to his. Both Fr. Laverdiere and Henri Bourassa pointed out in separate letters to Vezina at this time that they believed Rome should not to permit either the Irish or the Canadians to be ultra-nationalists. Like Fr. Bedard and the laymen who supported him, Vezina wished to see his pastor have the greatest possible latitude in administering parish affairs and to see funds contributed directly to a parish remain there. However, he did recognize the need for the bishop to provide for institutions that the parishes could not and, unlike Fr. Bedard and Mr. Daignault, he believed Bishop Hickey when he said he loved the Franco Americans and had their best interests at heart.[327]

By the time Bishop Hickey reached Rome, only seven of those who had been excommunicated remained unreconciled with the Church. According to the newspaper reports, during his meeting with the Congregation for the Propagation of the Faith, to which he gave a report on the spiritual state of his diocese, he mentioned the Franco-American situation in the diocese only briefly because it was considered a closed incident. According to the same reports, when he and Fr. Georges Bedard, who had accompanied him to Rome, met with Pope Pius XI, one of Hickey's first acts was to report that peace was once again established in the diocese. On the first Sunday after his return from Rome, Bishop Hickey gave a brief summary of his visit in his sermon in the cathedral. He told his people that Pope

---

Provencher, et al. to Hickey, March 19, 1929; Rev. Thomas C. Collins to Provencher, March 23, 1929, PChA; *Woonsocket Call*, April 29, 1929.

326 *Providence Visitor*, March 8, 1929.

327 Rumilly, *Histoire Des Franco-Americains*, 453–55.

Pius had approved "every move taken by your bishop during the recent unfortunate dissension in the diocese."[328]

Mr. Daignault, who also traveled to Rome in the spring of 1929, arrived in Rome after Bishop Hickey had left. He had once again stopped in Paris on his way to Rome to call on Mr. Canet at the French Foreign Ministry to obtain a letter of introduction to the new French ambassador at the Vatican, the Count of Fontenay. Through the good offices of the French ambassador, Mr. Daignault met with Cardinal Sbarretti on April 30. He submitted the petition he had hoped to present on his second trip to Rome before he learned of his formal excommunication. According to his account of the meeting, he had a long conversation with the cardinal in regard to the controversy with Bishop Hickey. At the end of meeting, the cardinal asked him to prepare a statement on the condition of the Franco Americans in the diocese.[329]

Daignault prepared the memorial for the next meeting with the cardinal on May 6. In the memorial, he complained explicitly about the tone of the account of the Sentinellist movement printed in the *Providence Visitor* on February 15, which he felt treated himself and the Sentinellists harshly and did not make any concessions to the good faith Daignault continued to maintain had animated his actions. In the memorial he returned again to his original charge, which he now believed to have been proven, that the diocesan collections mandated by Bishop Hickey had undermined the financial base of the diocese and the parishes. He claimed that the great majority of the faithful in the diocese no longer had the confidence in their bishop necessary for the good spiritual and temporal functioning of the diocese. Once again, he cited population figures for the Franco Americans in the diocese that gave an exaggerated importance to Franco Americans, as the figures were over forty thousand higher than those reported by Bishop Hickey. As was common in his addresses during the agitation, he continued to assert as incontrovertible facts and information that were inaccurate or only partially true. During his May 6 meeting with the cardinal, Daignault also touched on Bishop Hickey's relations with the four priests who had supported the Sentinellists, whose cases still remained unresolved, one of whom, Fr. Forcier, was in Rome at the time. Before he left Rome, he also had a meeting with Msgr. Serafine, the secretary of the Congregation of the Council, whose knowledge of Franco American affairs impressed him. When asked by reporters in New York on June 8, while his ship waited in quarantine, if he had any comment to make, Mr. Daignault replied that the only thing he could say was "that the one thing that has been settled in Rhode Island's controversy is the question of excommunication."[330]

---

328 *Providence Journal*, April 24, 1929; *Woonsocket Call*, April 24; June 13, 1929; *Providence Visitor*, May 3; June 17, 1929.
329 Daignault, *Le vrai movement sentinelliste*, 187–201.
330 Ibid.; *Providence Journal*, June 9, 1929; Rumilly, *Histoire Des Franco-Americains*, 455–56. If parish finances suffered during the controversy, they suffered more because of the offering strike

By the time Bishop Hickey returned home, six more of those excommunicated, among them both Phydime Hemond and Henri Perdriau, had made their submission to the Church. Only Ovila Morgeau, who had pointedly refused to accept the letter from the delegate, informing him he had until Easter to repent, for reasons of his own still remained unreconciled. Mr. Morgeau would wait until March 15, 1932 before he signed his letter of submission.[331]

On June 14, 1929, the *Providence Visitor* officially announced the rewards for loyalty during the Sentinellist controversy. Fr. Peter A. Foley, diocesan chancellor and rector of the cathedral, Fr. John F. Sullivan, pastor of Holy Trinity, Central Falls, and Fr. James P. O'Brien, editor of the *Providence Visitor* and pastor of St. Agnes, Providence were raised to the rank of monsignor. Msgr. Dauray was raised in rank to Protonotary Apostolic in recognition of his support and the assistance of his nephew, Fr. Georges Bedard. In a move calculated to emphasize the kind of leadership Bishop Hickey expected, Fr. Joseph A. Laliberte, the pastor of St. Matthew's, the second Franco-American parish in Central Falls, was also made a Domestic Prelate. Msgr. Laliberte and the majority of his parishioners had enthusiastically supported the Million Dollar High School Drive and, during the period of time that Daignault claimed Bishop Hickey's diocesan collections were undermining the finances of the parishes, Msgr. Laliberte and his parishioners replaced their original wooden church with a new stone structure, which Bishop Hickey would dedicate on December 8, 1929.[332]

In addition to the priests honored by Rome, eight Franco-American laymen were made Knights of the Order of St. Gregory for their moral support of the bishop in the controversy and also for their financial support of Catholic endeavors. The men honored as knights were Philippe Boucher, president of La Tribune Publishing Company; Guillaume Desaulniers, trustee of Precious Blood Parish and ex-president of Cercles Lacordaire and Ste. Jeanne d'Arc; Norbert Descelles, official representative in New England of the Society of French-Canadian Artisans; Jacques Lepoutre, a Woonsocket industrialist and a distinguished benefactor of Catholic institutions; Wilfrid J. Mathieu, now former Senator and secretary of the Franco-American Foresters; Joseph Roy, another trustee of Precious Blood Parish and president of the St. Vincent de Paul Society of Woonsocket; former Mayor Adelard Soucy, a trustee of St. Louis Parish; and Elie Vezina, supreme secretary of the Union St. Jean Baptiste, whose recognition was also due to the efforts of Archbishop Benedetti on his and the Union's behalf. For his services to the cause, J. Albert Foisy, whose *Histoire*

---

championed by the Sentinellist in order to create a crisis than they did from funds collected in the parishes in response to diocesan drives.

331 *Providence Journal*, June 3, 1929; *Woonsocket Call*, June 3, 1929; *The Rhode Islander*, June 7, 1929. The newspaper gave the most attention to Perdriau's submission. Prior to his submission he ceased publication of his newspaper.

332 *Providence Journal*, June 14, 1929; *Woonsocket Call*, June 15, 1929.

de l'Agitation Sentinelliste dans la Nouvelle-Angleterre, 1925–1928 was written at the behest of Bishop Hickey and published in 1928, was rewarded with an Apostolic Benediction and papal medal. In honoring Mr. Decelles, former Sen. Mathieu and Mr. Vezina, the Holy See also took official cognizance of the support the societies they represented gave to the bishop during the controversy. Percival De St. Aubin of Providence was also made a Knight of St. Gregory at this time, but for reasons apart from the Sentinellist controversy.[333]

While the public challenge to Bishop Hickey's authority had officially ended, the whole matter could not be put to rest until the cases of the four priests whom Bishop Hickey had disciplined were settled. While he was in Rome for his *ad limina* visit, Bishop Hickey had asked Cardinal Sbarretti what he should do in Fr. Beland's case. The cardinal advised him to write the priest a kindly letter referring to his age, his long illness, and his extended absences from his parish and ask him, for those reasons, to retire on a pension. On June 20, 1929, Bishop Hickey sent Fr. Beland the kind of letter the cardinal had advised. Fr. Beland, who had come back from Florida in May, replied on June 26 that he refused to resign. On June 28, Msgr. Blessing went to Notre Dame Rectory in Central Falls, where he found Fr. Prince staying with Fr. Beland after coming back with him from Florida. Msgr. Blessing gave Fr. Prince a letter from the bishop and told him to come to the Chancery Office at 11:30 that morning. Msgr. Blessing spoke with Fr. Beland and once again urged him to retire on pension. Fr. Beland, however, repeated his determination not to resign. Msgr. Blessing then laid out the conditions on which the bishop would allow Fr. Beland to remain at Notre Dame Rectory. Fr. Meunier was to remain in charge of the parish, and the religious sisters, who served in the rectory, were to be under his direction. Fr. Beland was not to say mass publicly or function in any public capacity.[334]

When Msgr. Blessing returned to Providence to meet with Fr. Prince, he told him that the bishop required him to sign a formula of submission, which proved to be the same one he had signed in Florida and sent back to his lawyer in Rome. After Fr. Prince agreed to do so, Msgr. Blessing stated that he was not to return to Notre Dame Rectory. After writing to Bishop Hickey for an appointment, Fr. Prince returned to the Chancery Office on July 15 to sign the formula of submission the bishop handed him. After that, to his surprise and consternation, Bishop Hickey told him that, in view of the public scandal that he continued to hold Prince and Beland responsible for, Fr. Prince had best look for another bishop who would receive him. The bishop gave him a week to think the matter over. When Fr. Prince called the following week, he waited over an hour but the bishop

333 Ibid.; *Providence Visitor*, June 21, 1929 gives short biographies of each of the laymen honored as Knights of St. Gregory.
334 Memorandum, June 28, 1929, Beland File, PChA; Rumilly, *Histoire Des Franco-Americains*, p. 458. Rumilly cites letters form Antonio Prince's private archives.

was not able to see him. Fr. Prince left the bishop's office with a *celebret*, but nothing more. Unable to stay at Notre Dame, Fr. Prince found a welcome with Fr. Stephen Grenier, pastor of Our Lady of Good Counsel in Phenix, who had served with him as an assistant at Notre Dame. On August 31, 1929, Fr. Prince wrote to Bishop Hickey to officially inform him that, after consulting with his Roman attorney, he would not seek another diocese.[335]

After Fr. Beland again refused to resign, Bishop Hickey, on July 19, 1929, wrote to Archbishop Fumasoni-Biondi to bring him up to date with what had occurred in Fr. Beland's case. He reported that, on July 11, 1929, he had written to Fr. Beland again, now calling for his resignation for canonical reasons and that once more Fr. Beland had refused, but, in the bishop's view, without answering in the manner canon law required. Furthermore, he reported that Fr. Beland had allowed himself to be elected a Daignault delegate to the upcoming Union St. Jean Baptiste convention where Daignault would make another try to remove Elie Vezina from the office of supreme secretary. Hickey asked the delegate's advice as to whether or not he had followed proper procedure before he formally declared Notre Dame parish vacant. Since the delegate was away from Washington, Msgr. Marella answered that in his view Hickey had done all that was required. After receiving Msgr. Marella's reply, Bishop Hickey went to Notre Dame on July 29 to speak with Fr. Beland once more. The bishop laid out his reasons for asking for his resignation, which to the bishop's mind were more than sufficient to support his request. When Fr. Beland again refused to resign, Bishop Hickey, on July 31, 1929, formally declared the parish vacant.[336]

Since it would have been against his nature to go quietly, Fr. Beland, through his Roman attorney, Canon Curotte, filed an appeal with the Congregation of the Council on August 8, 1929. Fr. Prince's lawyer, Mr. Astorri, also filed an appeal on his behalf on August 12. Bishop Hickey once more compiled long dossiers challenging the points made in each appeal and included supporting documentation. How much longer this test of wills between Bishop Hickey and Fr. Beland would have gone on is unclear. While Fr. Beland's will was strong, his heart, at age 72, was not. Although Bishop Hickey at times questioned the seriousness of his reported ill health, Fr. Beland did suffer from heart problems and anemia. His health continued to fail after he returned from Florida and finally it forced him to enter Notre Dame Hospital, where he died on October 23, 1929. An obituary notice in the *Woonsocket Call*, a paper that had no particular bias but reported the various incidents in the Daignault agitation with objectivity, summed up Fr. Beland's role in the Sentinellist movement well: "Always jealous of the prerogatives of the Franco-American element

---

335 Hickey to Prince, June 24, 1929; Prince to Hickey, n.d., Prince to Sbarretti, August 12, 1929; Prince to Hickey, August 31, 1929, PChA.

336 Hickey to Marella, July 13, 26, 1929; Marella to Hickey, July 15, 23, 1929; Hickey to Fumasoni-Biondi, July 19, 1929; Curotte to Sbarretti, August 8, 1929. PChA.

and fearful lest some efforts might be made to halt its development along national lines, Fr. Beland saw in the Daignault movement what he, according to his lights, thought was a worthy movement, and he gave it his support."[337]

Shortly after Fr. Beland's death, Fr. Prince made his peace with Bishop Hickey. Hickey believed that Fr. Prince had been misled by Fr. Beland and, when Prince apologized for his actions, he changed his mind about forcing Fr. Prince to find another diocese and instead allowed him to assist priests in the diocese who needed help. At the beginning of 1930, Hickey appointed him an assistant at Our Lady of Lourdes, Providence. The bishop did not rule out reappointing him as a pastor after a suitable period of time had passed. However, shortly after his appointment to Our Lady of Lourdes, Fr. Prince was stricken with a throat ailment that caused the temporary loss of his voice. After an extended rest in Canada, Bishop Hickey appointed him as an assistant to his cousin, Fr. Henri Vincent, pastor of St. John's, Arctic. Limited by his throat problems as to the work he could do in the parish, Fr. Prince devoted himself particularly to the care of the poor. On September 25, 1936, while driving a three-year-old child to the St. Francis Orphanage in Woonsocket, he was forced to stop at a house on Greenville Avenue in Johnson to seek aid. The occupants of the house called their pastor and a doctor. The priest arrived first and administered the last rites. When the doctor arrived, he found Fr. Prince beyond medical aid. He died shortly thereafter.[338]

In a private letter that Archbishop Benedetti wrote to Bishop Hickey in November 1929 to acknowledge a gift he had received from Hickey, Benedetti took a moment, as a brother, to repeat to Hickey a piece of advice that he had passed on in the past when the two had discussed the bishop's dealings with his priests and which Cardinal Sbarretti had asked him to convey to Hickey privately: "To temper the manner of your relations as superior especially with the priests." The archbishop went on, "What can I say? Sometimes a direct and forceful manner spoils the best causes. It is essential, Bishop, that your priests love you as much as respect you. It will not require a great effort on your part."[339]

337 *Woonsocket Call*, October 23, 1929; *Providence Journal*, October 24, 1929; *Providence Visitor*, October 25, 1929; *The Rhode Islander*, October 25, 1929, which was not known for its objectivity, described Fr. Beland as "the real originator and financial backer of the racial and religious agitation conducted in this State during the past five years by Elphege J. Daignault."
338 Hickey to Sbarretti, February 27, 1930; Prince to Hickey, December 10, 1929; Hickey to A. P. Desrochers, December 10, 1929, PchA; *Providence Journal*, September 26, 1936; *Pawtuxet Valley Daily Times*, September 26, 1936.
339 Benedetti to Hickey, November 8, 1929, PChA.

The End of the Affair

Although Bishop Hickey had declared the controversy surrounding Daignault's challenge to episcopal authority a closed matter, Mr. Daignault himself was not ready to cease his advocacy of what he regarded as the rights of the Franco Americans. At a yet another banquet held at the Joyland Ballroom in Woonsocket to mark St. John's Day, this one on June 23, 1930, Mr. Daignault was again the principal speaker. His speech at the Joyland, his first since his return from Rome, addressed Bishop Hickey's recent account of his visit to Rome at the cathedral by saying that he too had been well received at Rome, when he arrived after the bishop. Furthermore, after he had had the opportunity to explain matters to the Roman authorities, "the sentiment was certainly not in favor of the bishop." His claim that "The fight had only started" prompted a great outburst of applause from the 1,500 people from all over New England who gathered for the event, and further applause followed when he declared, "If you are ready to keep up the good work, I am also."[340]

Mr. Daignault directed the body of his speech to what he saw as the threat to the proper education of French-Canadian children presented by recent changes in the school programs in St. Matthew's, Central Falls, and St. Cecilia's Pawtucket as well as the presence of a Catholic priest, Fr. Adelard Laliberte, on the Woonsocket School Committee, an issue first raised by Perdriau in the March 6 issue of *La Verite*. The dinner at the Joyland followed a mass celebrated in Fr. Binette's Assumption Church, South Bellingham, by Fr. J. F. Fautaux at which Fr. Louis E. Raymond served as deacon. Fr. Georges Duplessis gave the sermon on St. John as well as an address at the banquet that evening in which he defended the right of the Franco-American churches to use French and defied anyone to call it un-American.[341]

Although his many confident predictions of victory in the struggle on the part of the Franco-American had failed to materialize, neither Mr. Daignault nor his hard core of supporters were ready to give up their struggle. On September 15, 1929, Daignault's group sponsored what they called the first annual outing of the French-speaking people in New England at the Lincoln Woods State Reservation in the Saylesville section of Lincoln. According to a report in the *Providence Journal*, more than two thousand automobiles occupied every available parking space adjacent to the recreation field. The *Journal* reporter estimated the crowd as being more than 6,000. The day was devoted to an extensive sports program, but included a band concert and a speaking program. Among those who addressed the crowd were Laure B. Lussier, Dr. J. B. Falcon and Mr. Daignault. The *Journal* account did not report the remarks of any of the

340 *Providence Journal*, June 24, 1929; *Woonsocket Call*, June 24, 1929.
341 Ibid.

speakers, but the *Worcester Daily Telegram* did. According to its reporter, Mr. Daignault told the gathering on that particular afternoon that "the 'movement' seemed rosier than ever before" and that he expected the 'cause' to result in victory for him and his followers before long. The writer referred to Mr. Daignault as "the former stormy petrel of the diocese" and said that "he and his henchmen would for the time being abide by the mandate of those who have decreed that he cease publishing the paper, of which [he] was reputed to be the power." Furthermore, he reported that Daignault informed his audience that "in the near future another publication would be in circulation thereby giving the French-speaking people an opportunity to be posted on the vital issues in their language." Daignault carried out his plan by sending a subscription blank to the former subscribers to *La Sentinelle*, inviting them to sign up for his new publication, *L'Etendard Franco-Americain*," which he proposed to begin publishing during the first week of January 1930. Apparently the response from the former subscribers was not such that he was able to raise the funds to begin the venture.[342]

On October 8, 1929, the *Providence News* reported that "the publication of a new French language weekly in Central Falls under the aegis of Elphege J. Daignault" was momentarily expected, but the announcement was merely a rumor without apparent foundation, as *The Rhode Islander* was quick to show. Rather than devoting his efforts during the first weeks of October to the starting of a another newspaper, Mr. Daignault and his partisans were more concerned with the prospect of unseating Mr. Vezina and the current general officers of the Union St. Jean Baptiste when it met in its twelfth quadrennial convention in Burlington, Vermont. The year before, at the September convention of the Franco-American Order of Foresters Convention in Hartford, Daignault's supporters had sought to unseat State Senator Wilfrid Mathieu from his post as Financial Secretary as well as the Foresters' other general officers, who had supported Bishop Hickey but had been defeated. It became evident from the votes taken on procedural matters such as the seating of delegates, that the Daignault faction again lacked the votes to unseat Mr. Vezina and the Union general officers who had also backed Bishop Hickey. When the time came for the balloting on the officers for new terms, Daignault's candidates were soundly defeated. The leader of the insurgent slate, Edouard J. Lajoie of Fall River, was quoted as saying at the conclusion of the balloting that the struggle to unseat the current officers that Mr. Daignault had initiated had "come to a definitive end."[343]

The investiture of the new monsignors and the Knights of St. Gregory named by Pius XI during Bishop Hickey's *ad limina* visit in April during

342 *Providence Journal*, September 16, 1929; *Worcester Daily Telegram*, September 16, 1929. The *Daily Telegram* article is found among the Sentinellist Papers in the Chancery Archives as is Daignault's circular for his new paper.
343 *Providence News*, October 8, 1929; *The Rhode Islander*, September 7, 1928; October 11, 25, 1929; *Providence Journal*, October 16, 17, 18, 1929.

the weeks after his return prompted feelings of pride among the partisans of those honored and resentment on the part of Daignault's partisans. The same was true of the appointment of Fr. Camille Villiard as pastor of Notre Dame following Fr. Beland's death at the end of October. Having been frustrated in all but his initial attempt to defend what he saw as the rights of the Franco Americans in the Church, Mr. Daignault continued to refuse to give up. He organized yet another meeting at the Joyland Ballroom on Sunday, November 10, 1929 that attracted a crowd of 3,000 (Mr. Daignault's figure), 2,500 people (the newspapers' figure) or 1,500 to 1,800 (Elie Vizina's figure). Advertised as a meeting of the Franco-American Fathers and Mothers, Mr. Daignault gave the main address during what was a three-hour speaking program. According to a *Providence Journal* reporter, Daignault rehearsed the grievances of his followers since he and the others who were excommunicated were readmitted to the Church. In the course of his address, Mr. Daignault gave a lengthy account of the part Fr. Beland had played in the movement, something he was free to do now that the priest was dead. Chief among Daignault's new complaints, according to the reporter, were "the promotion of young priests by the Bishop to reward them for service to the episcopal cause" and "the bestowal of the Order of St. Gregory upon many of [the bishop's] adherents through the Providence prelate's influence." Daignault also brought out all the old grievances. At the end of the speaking program, Daignault proposed a series of eleven resolutions encompassing both the old and the new grievances, which, after being adopted by voice vote, he promised to present to the pope. He also again promised to begin the publication of a new newspaper, if he received the necessary financial backing.[344]

In his letter to the apostolic delegate that Bishop Hickey wrote the next day concerning the meeting, the bishop regretted that the English language newspapers had given the meeting more importance and more space than it deserved. According to his information from reporters who were there, half the audience abstained from any manifestation of approval and three fourths of them came from outside the city. He found that there was nothing new in the eleven resolutions except the criticism about the recent pastoral appointments and the questions raised by the speakers about the presence of a Catholic priest on the Woonsocket School Board. The fifth resolution adopted at the meeting contrasted the practice of priests of the Archdiocese of Boston, who threatened parents who sent their children to the public schools with the refusal of absolution in confession, with the situation in Woonsocket, where Fr. Adelard Laliberte, an assistant at St. Ann's, was chairman of the Woonsocket School Commit-

344 *Providence Journal*, November 11, 1929; *Woonsocket Call*, November 11, 1929; *L'Etoile*, November 13, 1929. *L'Etoile* was printed in Lowell, MA. A copy of the article on the Woonsocket meeting is found in the Chancery files; *The Rhode Islander*, November 15, 1929. According to the *Rhode Islander*, the majority of those present at the meeting were from Massachusetts; Vezina to Hickey, November 13, 1929, PChA.

tee. The resolution suggested that his presence on the School Committee furnished many parents with a pretext for sending their children to the public schools. Bishop Hickey explained to the delegate that Fr. Laliberte, as had other priests, first had stood for election to the School Committee in 1918 at Bishop Harkins' request. Bishop Harkins asked his priests to become involved in school affairs because it was the various school committees who, among other duties, chose the textbooks used in the schools. As many of the available texts were anti-Catholic, the presence of a priest on the boards worked to prevent the Catholic children who attended the public schools from being exposed to religious bias. In concluding his letter, Bishop Hickey expressed his own conviction that Mr. Daignault's attempt to revive the agitation would fail.[345]

Bishop Hickey wrote to the delegate again five days later and sent him fuller copies of the speeches given at the Joyland than had appeared in the newspapers. He also sent a copy of a recent letter he received from Mr. Vezina in regard to the Daignault meeting. In his letter, Vezina complained of the continued support Daignault was receiving from priests in all the New England states, except Maine, and particularly from priests of the Archdiocese of Boston. Bishop Hickey cited Vezina's letter to support his own view that Daignault's agitation would die without the support it was receiving from the clergy. Hickey suggested to the delegate that the agitation would end if each of the bishops whose priests were supporting Daignault would send a letter to then "declaring that any priest taking part in the Daignault movement . . . would incur 'ipso facto' the censures of the Church." On his part, Hickey singled out the role played by the priests from Boston as being "the preponderant one in the renewal of the sentinellist agitation." In his reply, the delegate urged Hickey, if he had not already done so, to send a copy of the letter Hickey had sent him to the Sacred Congregation of the Council to keep them informed, and offered to forward any materials Hickey might have.[346]

Mr. Daignault's next move was to hold a meeting in Amiot Hall, Fall River, under the auspices of the Canado-Americaine Association. He invited his Sentinellist supporters to attend along with the members of the Association. Less than five hundred people attended the meeting and there were, this time, no clergy among them. Mr. Daignault was one of four speakers that afternoon. In his talk, he freely recounted that he had undertaken his agitation at the request of the Franco-American priests and the Bishops of Canada, who, he reminded his audience, could not put themselves in the forefront. Although he had previously told an audience in Fall River that, if he had not pursued the civil suits against Bishop Hickey he would have been shot, he told this meeting that he did not regret having

345 Hickey to Fumasoni-Biondi, November 12, 1929, PChA.
346 Vezina to Hickey, November 13, 1929; Hickey to Fumasoni-Biondi, November 17, 1929; Fumasoni-Biondi to Hickey, PChA.

filed them. As to his excommunication, he told the audience he felt it was unjust because he had been assured by priests and bishops that he would not incur any censure. He went on to recall the struggle of the Canadians in Fall River during Bishop Hendricken's years and in Danielson, Connecticut, during Bishop McMahon's time. He then compared these struggles to his own. He rejected the idea put forth by the English-language press that his talk at the Joyland in Woonsocket was an attempt to restart his revolt against episcopal authority in Rhode Island. His intent, he contended, was simply to protest against the system of teaching the catechism in English in certain Franco-American schools and the recent prestigious appointments of priests in the Diocese of Providence because of their loyalty to Bishop Hickey during the recent struggle.[347]

After this second meeting, Bishop Hickey was less confident that Daignault's agitation was dead and could not be revived. In his previous letters, he had speculated that one way to put an end to his renewed efforts, in the face of Daignault's failure to live up to the promises he had made when he was readmitted to the Church, would be to reimpose the censures. In the two letters he wrote to the delegate on the Fall River meeting, Hickey returned to the idea of reimposing the censures on Daignault with more emphasis. Putting him again under censure, he pointed out, would have the effect of forcing his removal from the presidency of the Canado-Americaine Association, which he was exploiting as his platform for renewing this struggle for the cause.[348]

The Sacred Congregation of the Council took up the matter of Daignault's apparent renewal of his criticism of episcopal authority at a meeting during February 1930. On February 28, the secretary of the Congregation wrote to the apostolic delegate, who had written a long letter on the matter, asking him to pass on the Congregation's decisions. It asked first, that Bishop Hickey and his Curia should summon Mr. Daignault to enquire whether on June 24, 1929 he had declared that the struggle was not yet ended and on November 10, 1929 whether he had presented resolutions to be sent to the Holy See in which the authority of his bishop and his bishop's administration were again brought into discussion and subjected to criticism. Since there was ample evidence that Daignault did do these things and that he would admit to them, the congregation advised that Bishop Hickey was to admonish him and, if he did not desist from the agitation, Hickey was to declare that the censures were reimposed. As to the priests who continued to support Daignault, the congregation postponed action until it received further information from Bishop Hickey, especially about Daignault's response to the bishop's admonition.[349]

By the time Bishop Hickey received the congregation's directive, the

---

347 *L'Independant*, Fall River, December 16, 1929; Hickey to Sbarretti, December 26, 1929, PChA.
348 Hickey to Fumasoni-Biondi, December 16, 28, 1929, PChA.
349 Marella to Hickey, March 18, 1930, PChA.

situation had changed dramatically. On March 25, 1930, Bishop Hickey wrote to the delegate that:

> Of late, Mr. Daignault appears to have had a change of heart: he has resumed his place in the parish church as an active, contributing member; there is absolutely no agitation at present, and he has publicly abandoned his announced purpose of establishing a newspaper. He has also advised those holding out in the pew rent strike to begin to pay.

In view of these changes for the better, Bishop Hickey informed the delegate, he wondered if "it would not be better to let sleeping dogs lie." The delegate's auditor, who answered the letter, agreed.[350]

Although the bishop was content to let the question rest, there were some matters that still had to be addressed. A small but important one was who controlled the monies that had been collected for a new church in Notre Dame parish and deposited in the Central Falls Credit Union. On March 11, 1930, at a parish meeting, the members of the parish authorized their new pastor, Fr. Villiard, to withdraw the remaining $27,000 in the account. In April 1930, lawyers hired by Fr. Villiard went to court to force the Credit Union to turn over the remaining monies to himself as treasurer of the parish corporation. The Cercle Notre Dame, whose members controlled the account, announced that it was willing to see the money turned over, provided that Fr. Villiard give the committee that had collected the money the authority to determine the legitimacy of the bills. Fr. Villiard rejected, on principle, the idea of giving the building fund committee a voice in the matter. The impasse persisted for another year. Finally, in February 1931, three members of the building committee vagreed to turn over the funds without restriction. To settle the matter legally, the officials of the Credit Union asked a judge to determine to whom they should hand over the funds. In April 1931, the judge ruled in favor of Fr. Villiard, naming the church the trustee of the fund and ordering the Credit Union to disburse the fund on orders signed by Fr. Villiard.[351]

A question of even greater significance in Bishop Hickey's mind was how was he to set the record straight since his integrity had been publicly questioned by the church suits. In October 1927, on the Sunday after Judge Tanner handed down his initial ruling in favor of the bishop and dismissed Daignault's suits, Bishop Hickey told his congregation at the cathedral that he was considering suing Mr. Daignault for libel since Daignault had charged that he had taken money illegally from the parish corporations.[352]

Since a libel suit would have damaged the prestige of his episcopal office as much as his choosing to answer the particular charges against him

---

350 Hickey to Fumasoni-Biondi, March 25, 1930; Marella to Hickey, March 27, 1929,PChA.
351 *Providence Journal*, April 8, 18, 1930; March 20; April 28, 1931.
352 *Providence Visitor*, October 7, 1927; *The Rhode Islander*, December 30, 1927. In this article *The Rhode Islander* reviewed the status of the six libel suits that the agitation had generated. All of the suits eventually died for lack of prosecution.

in the public press, Bishop Hickey decided to set the record straight by commissioning a historical study of the agitation in which he could present his side of the story. When the French version of the study commissioned by the bishop appeared in late 1928, it drew nothing but scorn from Perdriau and *La Verite*, both of whom mistakenly believed it was written by Fr. Georges Bedard and that no one would read it. An English version of the work, which was in fact written by J. Albert Foisy and translated by the staff of the *Providence Visitor*, appeared in late 1930.[353]

When the editor of *Le Progres* in Manchester, who was sympathetic to the Sentinellist cause, examined the translation and compared it to the French original, he concluded that the translator had taken certain liberties to picture Daignault and his supporters in the worst possible light. He found the work an unchristian trampling on one's adversaries, who had been guilty only of defending their traditions. The editor's thoughts were echoed in the same issue by J. L. K. Laflamme. Neither thought of acknowledging the lack of charity on the part of the Sentinellists.[354]

On his part, Mr. Daignault waited until 1936 to publish his version of what had transpired. He introduced his book at a reception to which he invited his "compatriots" by means of a printed circular. In his *Le vrai mouvement sentinelliste*, he reprinted the various memorials and other documents that he wrote at the time of the controversy. The work also included Fr. Duplessis' obituary for the movement that appeared in the final edition of *La Defense*. In a concluding chapter, Daignault took issue with Henri Bourassa's judgment on the Sentinellist movement, which had proved so devastating at the time, in part because of Bourassa's labeling all the Sentinellists as schismatics. He does acknowledge at the beginning of this last chapter that *La Sentinelle* made some mistakes, thereby echoing the apology he made in *La Sentinelle*'s October 20, 1927 issue. However, he does not respond to any of the rebuttals in Foisy's book that challenged his own version of the events.[355]

Although Daignault was himself unsuccessful in establishing another newspaper to continue to support the cause of Franco-American nationalism, one of his former associates at *La Sentinelle*, Wilfrid Beaulieu, who was excommunicated along with Daignault, succeeded in finding support for the publication of *La Travailleur*, whose first issue appeared on September 10, 1931. Mr. Beaulieu announced that *Le Travailleur* would be "a militant newspaper, whether some like it or not." One who did not like it was Fr. Georges Bedard, who on the appearance of the paper, sent a letter to Archbishop Fumasoni-Biondi alerting him to the fact of *Le Travailleur*'s appearance and to the fact that Mr. Beaulieu stated in the paper that he

353 *La Verite*, October 25, 1928; [Foisy], *Histoire de L'Agitation Sentinellists* (1928); Foisy, *The Sentinellist Agitation in New England*, (1930).
354 *Le Progres*, September 26, 1930. A copy of these articles is in the Providence Chancery Office archives.
355 Daignault, *Le vrai Movement Sentinelliste*, Cf. particularly, The Conclusion, p. 227 and fl.

Rome, the authorities decided to act without waiting for the formal decision. Rome would issue the decree of excommunication at the same time it
issued a second decree in which the faithful were forbidden to subscribe to
or to read *La Sentinelle*, because of the support it gave to "the unwise agitation of a group of French-Canadians, based on unjustified motives, against
ecclesiastical authority in New England and especially in the Diocese of
Providence, with evident spiritual loss and scandal to the people." [222]

Bishop Hickey learned the news of the excommunication of Daignault
and his followers from a telegram sent to him by Msgr. Marella, the auditor at the apostolic delegation in Washington, at 7:00 P.M. on Saturday,
April 7. On that same day, the *Woonsocket Call* carried a dispatch from the
Rome bureau of the Associated Press relaying a story from the Vatican
newspaper, *Osservatore Romano*, that *La Sentinelle* had been placed on the
Index and its director, Mr. Daignault, and those who had brought suit
against Bishop Hickey had been excommunicated. The *Providence Journal*
printed a story based on the Associated Press dispatch, which included
comments from Bishop Hickey and from Daignault's associates in Woonsocket. In his comment, the bishop emphasized that, since the Congregation of the Council had declared Daignault excommunicated, it alone
could grant a dispensation from it. [223]

When a *Journal* reporter asked Phydime Hemond for his response, Mr.
Hemond declared that the excommunications would not stop the church
suits. He said that the excommunications were regrettable but that the
Sentinellists were prepared to fight to the end as there was no bishop who
could scare them. In subsequent comments, Mr. Hemond began casting
doubt on the reliability of the AP report. In an article written for the first
issue of *La Sentinelle* printed after the announcement of the ban, Henri
Perdriau, after saying that *La Sentinelle* would be sacrificed if that was what
the pope wanted, also cast doubt on the reliability of the reports from
Rome. In a manner then typical of the Sentinellist attitude toward religious authority, which first challenged rather than accepted any authority
that was not French, he expressed his confusion on reading the reports as
to whether the report said that excommunication was actually declared or
simply threatened. [224]

On his part, Bishop Hickey had no doubts about the accuracy of the
AP dispatch, but was anxious to know if Henri Perdriau and Antonio
Prince had been included among those excommunicated. He raised the

---

222 Cardinal Sbarretti, prefect, to Fumasoni-Biondi, apostolic delegate, March 24, 1928, PChA.
223 Marella to Hickey, April 7, 1928; *Woonsocket Call*, April 7, 9, 12, 1928; *Providence Journal*, April 8,
     1928; *Providence News*, April 9, 1928; *La Tribune*, April 9, 1928.
224 *Providence Journal*, April 8, 1928; *La Sentinelle*, April 12, 1928.

Marie Rose Ferron

In 1948, Fr. O. A. Boyer published *She Wears a Crown of Thorns: Marie Rose Ferron (1902–1936), The Stigmatized Ecstatic of Woonsocket, R.I.* In his book, Boyer links Rose Ferron, the invalid daughter of a Woonsocket blacksmith, whose patience in the midst of her suffering had won for her a reputation for sanctity with the Sentinellists. Fr. Boyer, whose sister lived in Woonsocket, related that Bishop Hickey visited Rose at a time when the Sentinellist movement was at its height in Woonsocket. In Fr. Boyer's recounting of the visit, Hickey asked the bed-ridden young woman, who suffered an illness that confounded the doctors of her day, to offer her suffering for the Diocese of Providence, for its priests and for those the bishop was obliged to excommunicate. She agreed to do so immediately. However, the bishop asked her to take a few minutes to consider the question and left the room, apologizing as he did so to Rose's mother for the tears he shed. When he returned to the room, Rose again agreed to offer her suffering for the peace of the diocese and the return of those excommunicated.[225]

Marie Rose Ferron was born on May 24, 1902, in St. Germain de Grantham, Quebec, the tenth of fifteen children. In the spring of 1907, her father, Jean-Baptiste Ferron, moved his large family to Fall River as had many French Canadians before him. The family settled in a tenement house on Tremont Street, near St. Roch church, where the assistant, Fr. Adrien Gauthier, became well acquainted with the family and with Rose. As was the case among immigrant families, the Ferrons would move frequently as better apartments became available. While in Fall River, they moved from Tremont to Seventeenth St. Rose was a very bright and intelligent child and, early in her life, had great devotion to St. Anthony and later to St. Gerard Majellan. Like her other family members, Rose also frequently prayed the rosary and made novenas. At about five or six years of age, she became seriously ill for the first time and at six or seven she was diagnosed as having rheumatism. In time, her health failed to the point that her family sent for Fr. Gauthier to anoint her with the oil of the sick. Her sister, Rose DeLima, later recalled that during her illness, she prayed to and conversed with St. Gerard and with Jesus to whom she was very devoted.[226]

---

225 O. A. Boyer, *She Wears a Crown of Thorns: Marie Rose Ferron (1902–1936); The Stigmatized Ecstatic of Woonsocket, R.I.* (New York, etc.: Benziger Brothers, Inc., 1948), 52–53. Cf. also Jeanne Savard Bonin, "A Stigmatist Marie Rose Ferron," Paulist Press, 1987.

226 Cf. The testimony of Rose's older sister, Mrs. Alberic (Rose DeLima) Francoeur, Palm Testimonies, PChA.
Among the most ardent promoters of the cause of Rose Ferron beginning in the late 1940s was a Jesuit priest, Fr. John Baptist Palm, S.J., who was a missionary in China until his expulsion by the Communist Government in August 1953. In 1960–61, he tape-recorded and later had translated and transcribed the testimony of all those he could locate who knew Rose Ferron. Fr. Palm sent

While living in Fall River, Rose was hospitalized three times. During her first hospitalization at St. Anne's, a Catholic hospital in Fall River, she underwent electric treatment for nerves. The experience left her black and blue. When she was twelve, she was well enough to seek work in order to assist her family financially and, for about a year, she cared for a lawyer's children. During this time, she became ill again. She later recovered, but her right hand and left foot were paralyzed and she had to use crutches to get about. After repeated novenas in honor of St. Gerard, she recovered the use of her hand. At fifteen or sixteen, she underwent an appendectomy and, shortly after, exploratory surgery occasioned by menstrual problems. During the years the Ferrons lived in Fall River, Fr. Gauthier visited Rose often. When her suffering did not cease, he urged Rose to accept her suffering as the will of God and her sickness as a way of life. None of her doctors, either in Massachusetts or Rhode Island, were able to do a great deal to help. Since they were not able to understand the cause of her disability, they were only able to treat the symptoms. To relieve her pain, they prescribed drugs, among them doses of morphine. When in May 1925, her father decided to move his family to Woonsocket where his brother lived, Rose had been confined to her bed for two years and was transported to her new home in the back seat of large car owned by the husband of her older sister, Irene Lagasse.[227]

In Woonsocket, the Ferrons lived first in a second floor tenement on West Street in the Fairmount district. After a year, the family moved to another second floor tenement on Asylum Street After seven years, they moved again to Ballou Street, and finally to a first floor tenement on Providence Street, all within the confines of Holy Family parish. In 1926, Rose was strapped to a board to prevent curvature of the spine. When the family moved to Providence Street, she was carried on a board by several men. During the season of Lent in 1927, Fr. Henri Vincent, one of the assistant pastors at Holy Family, who was her confessor, had by this time made the judgement she should receive communion every day. During his visits, he noticed stripes on Rose's arms. Fr. Gauthier had noticed marks on Rose's arms years earlier, but he urged her mother not to say anything about them "lest people will think it is a disease and your daughters will have difficulty finding husbands."[228]

Among the priests who visited Rose during Lent in 1927 was Fr. O. A. Boyer, a priest of the Diocese of Ogdensburg, New York, who was visiting his sister at the time. Fr. Boyer had an interest in the mystics and the mysti-

copies of these transcriptions to the bishops of Providence and they can be found in the Providence Chancery Archives. These testimonies are what are referred to as Palm Testimonies.

227 Ibid.; Boyer, *She Wears a Crown of Thorns*, 42–44, 172–79. Fr. Gauthier, who later became pastor of St. Hyacinth, New Bedford, continued to visit Rose Ferron each Monday after the Ferrons moved to Woonsocket.

228 Testimony of Mrs. Rose DeLima Francoeur, Mrs. Jules Guerin, Leo Desrosiers, etc., Palm Testimonies, PChA.

cal experience and interpreted the marks on Rose's body in that light. In a letter to Bishop Hickey in 1931, he described himself as Rose's protector, who for some years covered her expenses. After Fr. Boyer, other visitors also testified that they observed wounds on Fridays, which they too associated with the wounds or stigmata of the suffering Christ. On Fridays, Rose's mother kept the door to Rose's room locked as Rose did not wish to make an exhibit of herself. Her mother did allow a few people into Rose's room on Fridays and some, when admitted, fainted at the sight of Rose. These incidents of fainting caused Rose's mother a great deal of worry. To relieve her mother of anxiety, Rose related that she prayed to Jesus for the removal of the outward signs of the stigmata. Her prayer was not answered right away. In addition to the phenomena of the stigmata, those who knew Rose also related that she experienced visions of Jesus, Mary and her particular saints.[229]

Bishop Hickey first heard of Rose Ferron in August 1927. Her pastor, Fr. Gedeon Laverdiere, wrote to the bishop on August 6 to ask permission for Rose's cousin, Fr. Philippe Auger, a priest of the Diocese of St. Hyacinth, Quebec, who was visiting his relatives in Woonsocket, to say mass in the Ferron home since Rose had not been able to go to mass for a long time. In March 1928, there appeared a story in both the English and French language press recounting Rose's sufferings and noting the attention she was receiving. The article observed that on Sunday, "upward of a hundred people visit her home." As Rose's fame spread, the number of visitors increased. As noted above, Bishop Hickey was among those who visited Rose in 1928, and did so several times. On December 8, 1928, with Bishop Hickey's permission, Rose was allowed to take her vows as founder of the "Sisters of Reparation of the Sacred Wounds of Jesus." Among the many priests, brothers and sisters who came to see Rose was Brother Andre Bessette of Montreal, to whom Rose gave her beloved statue of Jesus. Fr. Vincent, who in July 1929 had become pastor of St. John's, West Warwick, brought Brother Andre to see Rose during a time when the brother was visiting relatives in West Warwick after his superior had written to Bishop Hickey to ask the bishop's permission for him to do so.[230]

In the years before the Second Vatican Council, as Jay Dolan has observed in his *The American Catholic Experience*, the fascination with the mi-

---

229 Boyer to Hickey, February 7, 1931, PChA.; Boyer, *She Wears a Crown of Thorns*, 59, 71, 94–153; 236–37.
During her visions, Rose said that Jesus conveyed to her messages for others. On one occasion during the Sentinellist agitation, she is reported to have sent Bishop Hickey a message, reminding him to treat all his priests alike, regardless of their opinions. In Fr. Boyer's work, she is reported to have told a Canadian priest, Fr. Emile Leonard, "The people do not know Bishop Hickey; I know him, he has a good heart. And Mr. Daignault is a good Catholic. Both mean well. Out of this conflict, both sides will reap good fruits, and, with Jesus, I rejoice." *She Wears a Crown of Thorns*, 55–56.
230 Laverdiere to Hickey, August 6, 1927; L'Etoile, March 27, 1928; Boyer, *She Wears a Crown of Thorns*, 57, 94–110.

raculous was a distinctive trait of the devotional Catholicism of the time. At the same time as the reputation of Rose Ferron was growing, the more famous case of Therese Neumann, a German girl who lived in the Bavarian town of Konnersreuth, Germany, also attracted the attention of many. As was true also of Rose Ferron, there had been claims made that Therese abstained from all food and drink. While similar stories circulated about Rose, her family reported that they fed Rose, but that she was not able to tolerate much food. In order to discover the truth of the claims in Therese Neumann's case, her father had allowed her to go to a hospital for a period of observation. While Fr. Vincent initially was convinced of the authenticity of the spiritual phenomena associated with Rose, his fellow assistant at Holy Family, Fr. Joseph Baril, was not. He had brought communion to Rose a few times each week and had doubts about the authenticity of the phenomena associated with her. He also believed that, because of her willingness to have visitors, she was placing too great a burden on her parents who had to deal with them. In November 1930, Fr. Baril, who believed that Rose was mentally unbalanced, challenged Fr. Vincent to secure Bishop Hickey's permission for Rose to be taken to St. Joseph's Hospital in Providence where she could be observed as Therese Neumann had been. Fr. Vincent obtained Bishop Hickey's consent for Rose to go by ambulance to Providence, where she would be cared for by two sisters while she was there. Although Rose agreed to go, when Fr. Vincent presented the plan to Rose's father, Mr. Ferron angrily refused to allow his daughter to go because, to his mind, it would mean more agony for his daughter. After Rose's last hospitalization while the family was in Fall River, a doctor had advised the Ferrons not to allow any further examinations of Rose since they would only cause her suffering. Fr. Vincent was deeply hurt by Mr. Ferron's response to his offer, when he said, "You are not seeking my daughter's cure or health, but your own ideas." He did not return to visit the Ferrons for a long time.[231]

At the same time as Fr. Vincent was seeking to arrange to take Rose to St. Joseph's, the outward appearance of what was seen as stigmata by Fr. Boyer and others disappeared at the beginning of August 1930 with the exception of the marks on her head. Rose believed the bleeding stopped and the wounds disappeared in answer to her prayers that God might relieve the anxiety of her mother. The disappearance of the wounds did not diminish the number of people who came each Sunday and even during the week to see Rose; rather the number continued to increase. The crowds coming to see Rose also began to disturb Fr. Vincent, who con-

---

231 Jay P. Dolan, *The American Catholic Experience: A History From Colonial Times To the Present* (Garden City, New York: Doubleday & Company, 1985), p. 235; Testimony of Fr. Joseph Baril, and Mrs. Jules Guerin, Palm Testimonies, PChA.
   Fr. Vincent was dead when Fr. Palm made his recordings. Therese Neumann's story was carried in the religious press. Cf. *Providence Visitor*, September 30; October 21, 1927; February 3; November 24, 1933.

tinued to visit Rose after he went to West Warwick, as well as Fr. Baril. After replacing Fr. Vincent as Rose's confessor, Fr. Baril began to question whether Rose was receiving communion worthily since she went into "ecstacy" immediately after receiving. The morning before Christmas in 1930, after observing her closely, he expressed his concerns to her family and informed them that he was not going to continue bringing her communion. One of the women who helped Mrs. Ferron care for Rose went to see Bishop Hickey to complain of Fr. Baril. On the afternoon of December 24, Bishop Hickey and his chancellor, Msgr. Peter Foley, came up to Holy Family rectory to inquire about Fr. Baril's reasons for his refusal. After seeing Fr. Baril, they intended to go on to console Rose. Fr. Baril's explanation of his actions convinced Bishop Hickey that he had acted properly and the bishop returned to Providence without stopping at the Ferrons. Before he left, the bishop instructed Fr. Baril to give Rose a series of instructions on the spiritual life. Fr. Baril later testified that he gave the first of the instructions asked of him on December 27, 1930. During the course of one of these instructions on January 8, 1931, Fr. Baril related that Rose admitted to him that the "extraordinary favors" that she had allegedly received were fraudulent. In time, Fr. Baril's relationship with Rose became more positive and friendly.[232]

Fr. Baril shared the responsibility of bringing Rose communion with his fellow assistant, Fr. Henry Brouillette, who came to Holy Family after Fr. Vincent left in 1929. Neither priest ever saw the wounds described by other visitors, even though they started visiting the Ferron home before the external manifestations of the wounds disappeared. During Holy Week of 1933, the two women who had been assisting Mrs. Ferron in taking care of Rose went to Fr. Baril to apologize for having opposed him for not believing in Rose and offered evidence to discount Fr. Boyer's interpretation of Rose's sufferings. On August 18, 1933, Fr. Boyer wrote Bishop Hickey to challenge the testimony of the women and to suggest ulterior motives for their witness. Bishop Hickey replied that, because of the information he had received, he found it advisable to ask Fr. Boyer "and, in fact, to advise [him] earnestly and authoritatively, to pay no more visits to Miss Ferron without special permission."[233]

Rose Ferron died on May 11, 1936. Nearly 15,000 people signed the guest book placed in her home on Providence Street where she was waked and thousands more came in without doing so. Between three and four thousand people gathered for her funeral. Because there was not space in the church for more than 1500, the majority of them were forced to re-

---

232 Boyer, *She Wears a Crown of Thorns*, 86–93, 151–53; Boyer also complained to Bishop Hickey about Fr. Baril, Bishop Hickey's Diary, February 7, 1931; Baril to Bishop Russell J. McVinney, January 8, 1950; Baril Testimony, Palm Testimonies, PChA.
233 Baril to McVinney, January 8, 1950; Testimony of Fr. Baril, Palm Testimonies; Boyer to Hickey, August 18, 1933; Hickey to Boyer, August 26, 1933, PChA.

CHAPTER III

Institutional Growth

Diocesan Charitable Efforts

The Diocesan Charities Bureau, the Catholic Charity Fund Drive and the Expansion of Diocesan Institutions

At the end of the nineteenth and the beginning of the twentieth century, Catholics seeking to alleviate the plight of the poor and the needy began to recognize the advantages of better training of charity workers and greater cooperation and coordination between social agencies. Catholic social workers also recognized the need for greater cooperation with public and private non-denominational service agencies. Bishop Harkins had sent three priest-delegates to the first National Conference of Catholic Charities that was held in Washington, D.C., in 1910. While Providence did not initially follow the lead of other dioceses, who sought to better coordinate diocesan social services and update the training of the priests and lay people involved in social work, Bishop Hickey, in late 1921, began to organize a Diocesan Charities Bureau. In January 1922, he announced his intentions to his clergy in a notice that he was initiating an assessment on each parish of ten dollars a year for the support of a diocesan bureau.[1]

Planning for a Diocesan Charities Bureau proceeded slowly, as Bishop Hickey elected to make the establishment of new Catholic high schools his first priority. In July 1925, he contacted Fr. John O'Grady, Secretary of the National Conference of Catholic Charities, to solicit his advice on how to proceed. Fr. O'Grady suggested that the first step the bishop should take was the selection of a competent priest who could be properly trained to direct the social work undertaken in the diocese. Secondly, he urged that the bishop authorize a study of the social institutions in the diocese, which he volunteered to undertake, but suggested that ideally the priest the bishop would designate to direct any diocesan social bureau should be

---

[1]   *Providence Visitor*, September 23, 1910; Hickey to Pastors, January 15, 1922, PChA.

involved in the study. Along with his letter to Bishop Hickey, Fr. O'Grady included a memorandum in which he set forth the rationale for a central organization of Catholic charities.[2]

In his report to Bishop Hickey, Fr. O'Grady suggested that one of the possibilities for financing Catholic Charities would be a "concerted annual appeal made under the direction of the bishop." The argument for a single yearly appeal aimed at raising funds to support all the charitable institutions, which had previously conducted their own fund raising appeals, was a persuasive one. This was particularly true in the light of the fact that many of the public and private social agencies in Providence had elected to create a community chest organization, which held its first united drive for its member agencies in October 1926.

The idea for a united effort to raise funds for the many charitable groups headquartered in Providence arose among the members of the Providence Chamber of Commerce, which formed a special committee among its members to study the idea. In December 1925, the committee extended invitations to twenty-three organizations that had agreed in advance to conform to the rules governing the fund, to join what was to be a charitable corporation for the collection of funds known as the Community Chest of Providence. Many of the organizations that joined in the united Community Chest appeal had also agreed to be a part of the Council of Social Agencies of Providence, which was organized in 1923. By the time the drive for funds began, the number of member organizations had risen to twenty-five.[3]

The Providence Community Chest launched its initial fund raising campaign on October 18, 1927, after many months of preparation. It was to be the biggest fund raising campaign in Providence since the bond drives of World War I. A pledge card was prepared for each potential donor by combing the records of the member agencies for people who had given more than a dollar to past campaigns. The central organizing committee divided the city into seventeen districts, each with their own district chairman, who then recruited captains and solicitors. Each of the districts was assigned a particular sum as its part of the $425,000 goal set for the campaign. All solicitation was to be done at the potential donor's business or place of employment, with the object of encouraging each donor to contribute the equivalent of a day's pay. When the drive closed on October 25, the two thousand solicitors had just about made their goals.[4]

During the time in December 1925 that the Chamber of Commerce's committee was exploring the idea of a Community Chest campaign and the criteria for participation in it, representatives of the committee approached Bishop Hickey about the possibility that the Catholic institu-

2   O'Grady to Hickey, July 22, 1925, PChA.
3   *Providence Journal*, December 21, 1926; October 10, 17, 1926.
4   Ibid.

tions in Providence might join the effort. During a talk Bishop Hickey gave
to the members of the St. Vincent de Paul Society in the diocese at their
annual outing in July 1925, he expressed his belief that it would be wiser
for all institutions under religious auspices to keep separate from the civic
agencies and to continue seeking financial support in the usual manner.
For much the same reason, he had decided against St. Joseph's Hospital
joining the Council of Social Agencies when the hospital was invited to
join that group. After the special committee of the Providence Chamber
of Commerce had formalized their plans for a Community Chest appeal,
Bishop Hickey brought up the possibility of the Catholic institutions par-
ticipating in the coming campaign at a meeting of the Diocesan Board
of Consultors on January 2, 1926. The consensus of the consultors was
against joining with the other charities in the city in their campaign, but to
hold a separate but united campaign for the Catholic charitable agencies
in 1927. Bishop Hickey offered the rationale behind this decision in an address he gave to the clergy at their annual retreats in 1929. In referring to
the Community Chest, he said, "You would not want the Church to be in
a position to beg from lay persons who are not of our faith to obtain the
funds to sustain our works and our institutions." Furthermore, the church's
charitable institutions were diocesan in scope, while the Community Chest
focused on charities that served the needs of the people of Providence.
While social workers employed by non-sectarian agencies supported by
the Community Chest or paid by the city had of necessity to refrain from
concerning themselves with the religious welfare of their clients, Catholic
social workers as well as the members the St. Vincent de Paul societies that
also served the needy believed that addressing the question of religious
practice was part of their work.[5]

Bishop Hickey made the first announcement of his plan to hold a separate drive to support Catholic charities at the annual dinner of the Knights
of Columbus held on October 12, 1927, in the ballroom of the Narragansett Hotel. With the start of the first Community Chest campaign only
five days away, the bishop again offered his reasons for keeping diocesan
charities separate from the Community Chest. He told the Knights that
for Catholics:

> The only right thing to do seems to be to keep our charitable institutions solely and
> exclusively within the atmosphere of Christian charity, that they may never lose their
> individuality, and that gifts, and the grace of God that accompany them, might go
> direct from giver to receiver.

He wished the organizers of the Community Chest well and announced

---

5   *Providence Visitor,* July 24, 1925; April 11, 1933; Bishop Hickey's Diary, January 2, 1926;
     "Directions Given by Bishop Hickey during the retreat, July 5, 1927," PChA.

that within a year he hoped to "centralize our efforts and to consolidate our charities and do our charitable work by ourselves."[6]

Bishop Hickey returned to the topic of his plans for a Catholic Charity Fund Drive in a talk to the Queen's Daughters, on Tuesday evening, January 28, 1927, the same forum in which he had first announced his intention to hold the High School Drive. In surveying the needs of the various Catholic social agencies, he noted that two different concerns confronted the diocese. The first was the question of operating expenses. Bishop Hickey estimated the annual cost of funding the twenty-two Catholic charitable agencies at roughly $600,000, of which only $200,000 was generated by fees paid to the agencies themselves. In addition to operating expenses, certain of the institutions were faced with the need for raising funds to finance new construction to alleviate unsafe, outdated or overcrowded conditions. In view of the need of generating both adequate operating funds and monies to finance new construction, Bishop Hickey told another audience at the annual St. Vincent de Paul Infant Asylum benefit concert on February 6, 1927, that "almost $500,000 will be needed for relief of want and for the development of our present institutions."[7]

Bishop Hickey organized the Catholic Charity Fund Drives in the same manner as he did the High School Drives, with the exception that for the Charity Drive, there would be no diocesan or parish quotas. During the campaign, various speakers did suggest the same criteria for giving, a week's pay, as the promoters of the Community Chest had suggested. The bishop called an initial meeting of the pastors and two lay representatives of the parishes for April 6, 1927, in Cathedral Hall, Providence. He again presided at the meeting and delivered the main talk in which he urged the necessity of the Drive. As was the case with the previous drives, the bishop recruited a layman, this time Judge Frank E. Fitzsimmons of Cumberland, to serve as lay chairman. It was Judge Fitzsimmons who introduced a motion at the meeting that the pastors and lay representatives agree to support the proposed Drive which was to be held between May 16 and 26.[8]

Once again the responsibility of organizing the individual parishes to support the Drive fell on the pastors and to a greater or lesser degree on the lay chairman that they selected. As they had done previously, the pastors, assistants or lay chair people recruited team captains, who in turn re-

---

6   *Providence Visitor*, October 15, 1927.
7   *Providence Visitor*, January 28, 1927; *Providence Journal*, February 7, 1927. The twenty one agencies for whom the first Charity Drive was organized included: The Rhode Island Catholic Orphan Asylum, St. Vincent de Paul Infant Asylum, House of Good Shepherd, St. Joseph's Hospital, Carter Day Nursery, St. Ann's Day Nursery, St. Bartholomew's Day Nursery, St. Raphael's Industrial School, St. Dorothy's Home, the Rhode Island Home for Working Boys, and Tower Hill House, all of which were either in Providence, or administered from Providence; Home for the Aged and Holy Ghost Convent, in Pawtucket; Mt. St. Francis Orphanage, Hospice St. Antoine, Woonsocket; Mercy Home and School, St. Clare's Home, in Newport; Villa St. Rose, Greenville; St. Francis Home for Consumptive, Hillsgrove; the Home for Retreats, Cistercian Fathers, Cumberland; Poor Missions; Charities Bureau.
8   Bishop Harkins' Diary, March 15, 1927; *Providence Visitor*, April 6, 1927; *Providence Journal*, 9, 1927.

cruited solicitors who would make the actual calls on parishioners to invite them to contribute to the Drive. The names of the parish chair people, as well as those of the captains and workers were subsequently printed in both the *Visitor* and local papers. Also, the organizers of the Drive sought and obtained the cooperation of the print and the radio media to make Rhode Islanders aware of the needs of the state's Catholic charitable institutions. Drive headquarters furnished information about the various institutions that would be helped by the Drive and photos of them. Particularly appealing were the stories and photos of the orphans and children in the various nursery schools. The Sunday before the Drive began, its organizers held a mass meeting for campaign workers at LaSalle Academy, at which each of the 105 parishes of the diocese were represented. The gathering would prove to be one of the larger gatherings of Catholics the state had seen. Bishop Hickey spoke at the meeting but the main address was given by Rev. Dr. William J. Kerby, professor of sociology at Catholic University and acting director of the National Catholic School of Social Service. That same Sunday, priests were assigned to speak in designated churches to set out the needs of the Catholic institutions and to stress the demands of Christian charity.[9]

Three weeks before the Drive actually began, Drive headquarters began receiving reports from the Olneyville section of Providence, that unauthorized solicitors were approaching residents of that section asking for contributions to the Drive. Those in charge of the Drive issued a warning through the newspapers that no one was authorized to collected funds until the start of the Drive on May 16. When the Drive did begin, all the parish volunteers were supplied with authorization cards. In a letter dated May 17, which appeared in the *Providence Visitor* on May 20, Bishop Hickey directed his pastors to make a special plea to those whose means allowed them to make a larger contribution than most Catholics. The bishop's letter was prompted by the large number of textile workers, who were currently out of work in Woonsocket and Manville, and the significant number of Catholics whose incomes did not allow them to make a contribution. Unlike the Community Chest campaign, the Catholic Charity Fund Drive did not ask for pledges, which a significant part of those who pledged did not fulfil, but for one time, cash contributions. In order to encourage generosity, each contribution of five dollars or more was acknowledged by printing the contributor's name in the *Providence Visitor* and the names of the contributors of ten dollars or more names were also printed in articles in the secular press. While Bishop Hickey publicly expressed his confidence that the Drive would be a success, privately he was anxious. His anxiety increased when the first returns from the parishes failed to meet expectations. In spite of the hard times and the Sentinel-

9   *Providence Visitor*, May 6, 13, 1927; *Providence News*, May 14, 1927 *Providence Journal*, May 15, 16, 1927; *Providence Tribune*, May 16, 1927.

list opposition to the Drive, however, the final total of the 1927 Drive was $296,484.32. Bishop Hickey would express his thanks and satisfaction with the amount he received. When the total of the Easter Collection in the parishes of the diocese, which traditionally went to charity, was added together with the interest accumulated by the funds, the final total for the year was $347,361.12.[10]

The parishioners of the thirty parishes in Providence contributed more than half of the monies collected. Pawtucket parishes contributed $42,024; the Woonsocket parishes, $39,801; the Newport parishes, $18,658; the South County parishes, $6,103; and the Central Falls parishes, $5,656. The parishioners of the Cathedral parish contributed the largest sum, followed by the parishioners of St. Mary's and St. Michael's in Providence; Precious Blood, Woonsocket; St. Joseph's, Providence; St. Joseph's, Pawtucket; and St. Charles, Woonsocket. The largest single contribution, besides that of Bishop Hickey himself, to the initial campaign, $2000, came from the Bouvier-Brien Construction Company of Woonsocket. The only expenses of the campaign were for the pamphlets describing the work of the agencies that were to be helped by the Drive and for the printing of the letters and the postage of the letters sent out by the Drive Committee to prospective donors.[11]

The Catholic Charities Bureau

During the first few days of the Charity Appeal, Bishop Hickey announced that he was planning to establish a Catholic Charities Bureau. In the summer of 1925, Bishop Hickey had asked Fr. Charles C. Curran, who had returned to the diocese in July after serving for six years as vice rector of the American College in Louvain, to serve as the diocese's first head of the Bureau of Catholic Charities. The purpose of the bureau was to unite, supervise and supplement the work being done by the existing Catholic charitable institutions and organizations. The bureau was to also act as a clearing house for Catholic agencies in their relations with other private charitable organizations and with city and state authorities. As Fr. O'Grady had suggested, the bishop sent Fr. Curran to the Catholic University in Washington for a year of graduate courses in sociology and social work. After receiving his M.A. degree in May 1926, the bishop appointed him an assistant at St. Anthony's Parish, Providence. He served in St. Anthony's until September 1930, when he was transferred to St. Mary's, Pawtucket. As Fr. O'Grady had suggested to Bishop Hickey, Fr.

---

10 *Providence Visitor,* April 22; May 20, 27, 1927; "Directions Given by Bishop Hickey during the Retreat, July 5, 1929.
11 *Providence News,* May 27, 1927.

Curran spent his first year, after getting his degree, in studying the social services of the diocese and the best means of financing them.[12]

Following on the success of the first Charity Drive, Bishop Hickey went ahead with his plan and officially established the Catholic Charities Bureau with Fr. Curran as its director. Fr. Curran established his office in the Visitor Building on Fenner Street. With the establishment of the bureau, people, particularly people with children, needing aid applied there rather than to the individual institutions. During 1929, the first year for which there is a published report, Fr. Curran's office handled some 352 cases, some of whom came to him directly, others by referral from parish priests, Catholic institutions, or by state, city or private agencies. One of Fr. Curran's primary goals was to keep families together. Whenever a parent asked to have a child admitted to one of the diocesan institutions, Fr. Curran investigated the case to determine the extent of the need. It was the bureau's policy not to accept children if the mother was working. When they could, Fr. Curran and his staff called upon the assistance of relatives, the Director of Public Aid in Providence and other cities, the Domestic Relations Officer of the Probation Department or some other social agency to assist so that families were not split up unnecessarily. If the illness or absence of a mother was the occasion for the request for aid, rather than take children out of their home environment, the bureau recruited, trained and paid housekeepers to live in with the families until such time as their services were not needed. Another of Curran's responsibilities was to verify the marriage record of the parents and the baptismal record of the children the parents wished to place in the Catholic agencies so that the spiritual needs of the people seeking help were not neglected. In addition, Fr. Curran also supervised the children who were placed out in foster homes from the Catholic institutions. This work involved a monthly visit to some ninety children, who had not yet been legally adopted.[13]

Because of the success of the 1927 Charity Drive, Bishop Hickey was also able to announce to a meeting of the Union of Holy Name Societies in Cathedral Hall in March 1928, that the diocese was going to do away with a number of collections during the course of the year. If the people of the diocese continued to be generous to the Charity Drive, he foresaw the elimination of other of the calls he made each year on the parishes to support various charities. In 1928, the Charity Drive was held between May 14 and 24. Bishop Hickey inaugurated the Drive by taking advantage of the offering of free air time on station WJAR to appeal, not only to Catholics, but to all the people of the state to support the agencies in whose name he was speaking. In his talk, the bishop made reference to the fact that several other groups were also holding drives at the same time as

---

[12]   *Providence Journal*, May 18, 1927; *Woonsocket Call*, May 18, 1927.
[13]   *Providence Visitor*, January 24, 1930; Joseph J. Lamb and Edward J. McGovern, "The Diocesan Bureau of Social Service: An Historical Sketch," (Privately printed, 1966).

the Catholic Church was so that they did not conflict with the Community Chest appeal in the fall. He did not see any sense of rivalry or indifference in the coincidence of the various drives, but discerned the fact as "an indirect tribute to the loyalty and practical interest of those upon whom we chiefly and most confidently rely for our success." Once again the initial returns of the 1928 Drive were disappointing. Drive officials began speculating that it might be necessary to go back to the older methods of fund raising to supplement the funds collected during the Drive. While the total from the 1928 Drive proved to be somewhat less than the previous year's total, when the Easter Collection and interest was added, the final total for 1928 was $303,396. Bishop Hickey was again pleased with the result, since the Sentinellist agitation continued to be a factor, as did the difficult economic circumstances many in Rhode Island were experiencing, especially those who worked in the textile industry.[14]

Two years of experience with the Charity Drive convinced Bishop Hickey of the effectiveness and utility of the idea of a general appeal. Because of the Drive, the directors of the various institutions funded by it could count on a given revenue each year and plan accordingly. Rather than see monies expended on a celebration of his tenth anniversary, Bishop Hickey asked that contributions to the 1929 Charity Drive be the diocese's only observance of his anniversary. The pastors and laymen who collectively made up the general committee held their meeting for the 1929 Drive in the Cathedral Hall on April 15. In the absence of Bishop Hickey, who had left for his second *ad limina* visit to Rome, the Vicar General, Msgr. Blessing, chaired the meeting along with Judge Frank E. Fitzsimmons, who served as lay chairman for the third time. Msgr. Blessing urged his audience to make the 1929 appeal an acknowledgment of Bishop Hickey's devotion to the service of the church and to alleviation of the distress of the poor and the afflicted. The people of the diocese and their generous neighbors responded by contributing a sum of $321,010.11.[15]

In his address to the clergy and laity at the beginning of the 1928 Charity Drive, Bishop Hickey had acknowledged that some of his pastors were "not overjoyed at the prospect of a drive, anytime, anywhere." He returned to the question of the Drives and the work that pastors had to commit to them if they were to be successful, when he addressed his clergy at the end of their retreats in June and July 1929. He praised those pastors and parishes where up to sixty percent of those who could, did contribute to the Drive. In regard to those parishes where the response was only twenty percent or even only four percent, he said that he had to acknowledge that the parishes did not make the needed effort. He asked his pastors

<hr />

[14] *Providence Visitor*, March 30, 1928; *Providence Journal*, May 14, 21, 1928; *Providence News*, May 22, 1928.

[15] *Providence Journal*, April 12, 16; May 12, 1929; *Providence Visitor*, May 3, 10, 1929.

to consider the possibilities if, in each parish, sixty percent of those capable
of giving did so:

> Instead of $321,000, we would have a million yearly. We could create an institution
> a year and, in a short time, all the obligations of all the parishes of the diocese would
> disappear.

To those who were hoping that the Drives would cease, he responded that
the Drives would continue as long as the Community Chest campaigns
did.[16]

When on April 14, 1930, the pastors and the lay representatives of the
parishes gathered at the Cathedral Hall to inaugurate the 1930 Charity
Fund Appeal, they did so in the aftermath of the financial collapse of the
stock market and in the midst of a deepening crisis occasioned by layoffs
of larger and larger numbers of people. In his address, Bishop Hickey
praised the people of the diocese for their generosity of the past and urged
them to maintain their reputation for generosity in view of the still greater
present need. Although the number of people who gave to the 1930 appeal rose by roughly 20,000 over the number who gave to the 1929 appeal, the final total realized by the campaign, $307,790, was almost four
thousand dollars less. Over the next two years, the increasing number of
unemployed continued to reduce the number of those able to contribute
to the Charity Fund or to contribute the amount they had in the past. In
1932, the total would drop to $276,159, and in 1933, to $252,172.69.[17]

New Construction

With the monies from the first Catholic Charity Drive in 1927, Bishop
Hickey was able to begin to address some of the pressing needs of the
agencies for whom the monies were collected. Because St. Joseph's Hospital never refused care or treatment to anyone in need, demand for admission had reached the point where the hospital was overcrowded and needed to expand. A week after the first Charity Drive closed in May 1927,
Bishop Hickey announced plans to build a six-story, one-hundred bed
addition facing Peace Street. While the monies collected by the Charity
Drive would not meet the $500,000 cost of construction, they were suffi-
cient to meet the interest payments on the construction loan he took out to
build the new building. Plans for the addition were ready for bid in March
1928 and ground was broken for the building a year later in March 1929.
Before breaking ground, Bishop Hickey had first to secure a commitment
from the Sisters of St. Francis of Glen Riddle, who ran the hospital, that

---

[16] *Evening Tribune*, April 18, 1928; "Directions given during the retreat, July 5, 1929, PChA.
[17] *Providence Visitor*, April 18, 1930; March 15, 1931; April 15, 1932; April 11, 1933; April 13, 1934.

they would supply additional sisters to meet the expanded staffing needs that the new addition would create. While the superior of the Sisters of St. Francis would not commit to meet the level of staffing Bishop Hickey requested, she was able to assure him that she would provide some additional sisters.[18]

With construction of the new hospital underway, Bishop Hickey authorized an appeal to all the people of the state for additional funds in November from the twenty-third to the twenty-eighth. Prior to the Building Fund Drive, St. Joseph's Hospital mailed out a circular noting the number of patients the hospital had cared for in the thirty-seven years of its existence. In its appeal to the wider community, the Building Fund Drive circular broke down the hospital's patient census by religious affiliation. Of 317,536 patients cared for since the hospital opened in 1892, 55 percent of the in-house patients were Catholics, 20 percent Protestants, and 25 percent Jews. Of the out-patients cared for, 60 percent were Catholics, 13 percent Protestants, and 27 percent Jews. The hospital's appeal raised $45,500 towards construction of the addition.[19]

The hospital received a major setback on Sunday morning, February 23, 1930, when a fire broke out shortly after 6:00 a.m. in a waste bandage chute that ran from the basement to the roof of the five story building that had been opened in 1895. All the sisters and nurses who were not on ward duty were at mass when the fire was discovered. With the help of the police and firemen, who arrived in answer to the alarm, as well as that of passersby who lent a hand, all 148 patients, including 14 infants, were rescued from the burning building. The mothers and new-born children were taken to the Nurses' Home nearby. The other child patients were transported to Rhode Island Hospital, and the adult patients to the Homeopathic Hospital, St. Xavier's Convent and Lying-In Hospital. Evelyn Welch, the student nurse who discovered the fire while on duty at the telephone switchboard, stayed at her post throughout the morning as she had done previously during a fire in Fall River in 1928. Bishop Hickey arrived at the hospital at 10:00 and conferred with the hospital's Superintendent, Sr. Plautilla. Later in the day, the bishop issued a statement praising the firemen and policemen who took part in fighting the fire and rescuing the patients and the many institutions that offered to receive the patients who had to flee the hospital.[20]

On the day after the fire, Bishop Hickey announced that he would start reconstruction of the hospital at the earliest possible moment. To assist in the task of rebuilding the hospital, Providence mayor James E. Dunne

---

[18] *Providence Visitor*, May 13, 27, 1927; *Providence Journal*, March 4, 1928; March 20, 1929; Mother M. Kilian, O.S.F. to Hickey, December 12, 1928, PChA..

[19] *Providence Journal*, November 20, 1929; *Providence Visitor*, December 6, 1929.

[20] *Providence Journal*, February 24, 1930; *Providence Visitor*, February 28, 1930. This was the first hospital fire in the city of Providence. On March 25, 1924, a similar fire had forced the patients at the State Infirmary in Cranston to flee their beds in the dead of night.

created a rehabilitation fund for the hospital and appealed to the community at large for help to rebuild it. He also urged that the city appropriate $25,000 to help with the reconstruction. On Friday, March 28, Mayor Dunne handed Bishop Hickey a check for $31,373 representing the money the rehabilitation fund had received from private sources up to that time. Other monies came from the insurance on the building. The remainder of the $200,000 it would cost to renovate the hospital came from increasing the size of the loan taken out to build the new wing of the hospital. Workmen put a new roof on the building and laid new tile floors. They completed sufficient work on repairing the damage for the accident rooms and outpatient department along with the children's and maternity wards to reopen on March 19, the feast of St. Joseph. In the renovated hospital, the children's ward was relocated from the fifth floor to the first and the maternity ward from the fifth to the fourth floor. Bishop Hickey formally dedicated St. Joseph's Hospital's new wing on October 1, 1930. The two wings of the hospital provided space for three hundred beds, together with the necessary operating rooms, laboratories and other facilities a modern hospital needed.[21]

In 1925, Bishop Hickey received the first of two letters from the Inspector of Buildings in Providence in reference to conditions prevailing at the House of the Good Shepherd on Eaton Street. The inspector informed the bishop that the Fire Commissioners' Office had found many safety deficiencies in the course of its inspection of the buildings and urged the bishop to remedy the prevailing situation. The Sisters of the Good Shepherd were well aware of the deficiencies and had commissioned a fund raising company to conduct a study of their buildings and of the possibility of conducting a successful campaign to raise monies for a new building. While the report on the potential for a successful campaign was positive, Bishop Hickey decided against holding one. Instead, he made the needs of the House of the Good Shepherd a focus of the 1929 Charity Fund Appeal. Several of the pieces written for the newspapers stressed the larger demands placed on the services of the Sisters of the Good Shepherd by the increasing number of broken homes. While many families experienced conflict and the first generation of all immigrant groups experienced problems of adjustment, *The Rhode Islander* pointed out in a rejoinder to Elphege Daignault's opposition to Franco-American support of the Charity Drive, that "more than 40 per cent of the inmates of that life-saving institution are girls of French-Canadian birth and more than half of the 40 per cent are girls from Woonsocket."[22]

21 *Providence Journal*, February 25; March 29, 1930; *Providence Visitor*, March 21, 28; October 3, 10, 1930.
22 Spencer C. Hopkins to Hickey, May 13, 1925; Captain James W. McKenzie to Board of Fire Commissioners, February 25, 1926; Thomas M. Finn to Rev. Mother M. St. Francis Elliot, May 26, 1925, PChA; *Providence Visitor*, April 23, 1926; *Providence News*, April 18, 1927; *The Rhode Islander*, May 27, 1927.

The 1927 Appeal's success had enabled Bishop Hickey not only to announce plans for a new wing at St. Joseph's but, at the beginning of July, 1927, to also announce plans to erect a group of new buildings for the House of the Good Shepherd. Work began in the spring of 1928 on the first of the buildings, a four-story Juveniles Building, which would allow the sisters to separate the girls twelve to eighteen from the older women. The House of the Good Shepherd provided a large part of its operating revenue. As with the new wing at St. Joseph's hospital, Bishop Hickey used the monies raised by the Catholic Charity Drives to pay the interest on the loans which were taken out to pay for the construction of the new building. Bishop Hickey blessed the new building on January 26, 1929.[23]

New Works of Charity

Because of Bishop Harkins' zeal in the past, the diocese was well organized to assist the Catholics of the diocese and the people of the state in dealing with the challenges and emergencies of life. There were some needs, however, that still needed to be addressed when Bishop Hickey assumed responsibility for the diocese. Although immigrants had been entering the United States from the Azores and Cape Verde islands on the packet ships that had long made the dangerous journey to and from these islands each summer, the beginning of regular sailings of Fabre Line ships from Italy to Providence by way of the Azores in 1911 brought a larger influx of Italian and Portuguese immigrants into the city. In 1917, the parents of two young Portuguese girls, who lived in Pennsylvania, failed to reach Providence in time to meet their daughters when the ship on which they were traveling docked in the city. Left without assistance, the two young girls vanished. Soon after Fr. Antonio Rebello succeeded Fr. Serpa as pastor of Holy Rosary in 1918, he called a meeting of his parishioners to discuss the conditions existing at the state pier in Providence where the passenger ships docked. Those present at the meeting decided that Fr. Rebello should appoint two women from the parish to meet every Fabre Line ship in order to offer assistance to the women and children who had nobody to meet them. Later, the Providence Red Cross took over the task and the women from the parish became workers for that organization.[24]

In 1924, Fr. Rebello and Bishop Hickey discussed the situation. Fr. Rebello proposed opening a house in his parish where the immigrants, who had to wait a day or longer for someone to meet them or for a train or boat connection to their ultimate destination, might wait in comfort and safety or be put up for as long as they needed. Bishop Hickey readily

---

23 *Providence Journal*, April 22, 1928; *Providence Visitor*, April 22; July 1, 1927; January 18; February 1, 1929.

24 Bishop Hickey's Diary, November 4, 1921; *Providence News*, February 27, 1928.

agreed to support the work with diocesan funds and, in February 1924, wrote to the Provincial of the Sisters of St. Dorothy, who had a convent in Holy Rosary parish, to ask if the sisters there might assist in the planned work. Originally, Fr. Rebello thought of buying a separate house, but changed his mind when he had the opportunity to buy a large, three story tenement at the corner of Wickenden and Benefit. As he re-envisioned the project, the new house would provide larger quarters for the Sisters of St. Dorothy as well as a waiting room, cafeteria and sleeping quarters for the immigrants in need of assistance. Bishop Hickey dedicated the new convent and immigrant home on Sunday, November 3, 1924. In addition to the help Fr. Rebello received from the diocese, the Ladies' Welfare Council of Providence also assisted in arranging the new quarters. The women who met the ships on their arrival did not limit their care to Portuguese women and children only, but offered help to all women and children in need.[25]

In January 1926, Bishop Hickey was approached by Miss Agnes Storer, the daughter of Dr. Horatio Robinson Storer of Newport, with the idea of opening a rest or convalescence home for women in Newport. Dr. Storer, who died in Newport in 1922, was a convert to the faith, along with his daughter, and a benefactor of his adopted city. Since her father was well known for his concern for the health of women, Miss Storer proposed offering a house at 91 Washington Street on Newport harbor to the Sisters of the Holy Ghost for the purpose of establishing the home. As a result of the meeting, Bishop Hickey agreed to write to the White Sisters, as they were popularly known, to invite them to accept Miss Storer's offer. The White Sisters agreed to the idea at a meeting with Bishop Hickey on February 16, 1926. Bishop Hickey officially opened the new home, which was called Stella Maris and had space for sixteen guests, on July 16, 1926. The new home proved to be especially popular with vacationers during the summers.[26]

In May 1931, Bishop Hickey announced the purchase of the Trinity Club property on Blackstone Street in Woonsocket. The Trinity Club was the leading Catholic women's group dedicated to the welfare of Catholic women and children in the northern part of the state. The club would continue its social and charitable activities and make use of the large auditorium it had built in 1923, but no longer had need of the living accommodations in the building. Bishop Hickey acquired the property in order to open a residence for the elderly run by the Franciscan Sisters of Allegany whose rates would be kept within the means of their guests. The home was intended to round out the services offered by the diocese. Relying on the Catholic Charity Fund for support, Bishop Hickey authorized

[25]   Sr. Olga Zama to Hickey, March 3, 1924; Hickey to Zama, March 29, 1924, PChA; *Providence Journal*, November 3, 1924; August 8, 1925; *Providence Visitor*, November 7, 1924.

[26]   Bishop Hickey's Diary, January 4; February 15, 1926; *Providence Visitor*, July 9, 16, 1926; April 9, 1936; *Newport Daily News*, July 16, 1926.

the construction of a three-story, u-shaped, brick building with fifty rooms for guests and ten rooms for the sisters. The Trinity Club's auditorium was retained as the basement floor of part of the building. Bishop Hickey blessed the new facility on Wednesday, October 4, 1933, the Feast of St. Francis, under whose patronage the new institution was dedicated.[27]

New Parishes and Missions

The First World War severely hindered immigration from eastern Europe, Italy and Portugal. Although there was a surge of new immigration from Europe after the war, nativist sentiments moved Congress in the 1920s to pass a series of restrictive immigration laws, which served to slow immigration from southern and eastern Europe. After Bishop Harkins handed over the administration of the diocese to Bishop Hickey in May 1919, Bishop Hickey established two new parishes for the Italians, Our Lady of Mt. Carmel, on Federal Hill, Providence, in December 1920, and Our Lady of Loreto in East Providence. Our Lady of Loreto was established as a mission of Holy Ghost, Providence, in 1921. These two parishes, as well as St. Casimir's, which Bishop Hickey created for the Lithuanian Catholics in the Providence area, were created under the provisions of the new universal code of canon law that had been promulgated in 1917. Under the new code, a bishop had to obtain an indult from Rome for each new ethnic parish he wished to create.[28]

For the Italians

ST. ANTHONY, *Woonsocket*

By 1924, a census of the Italian population in Woonsocket revealed that it had grown to between three and four hundred families. Prior to 1924, the priests at St. Charles took responsibility for ministering to them. As in other communities, the early Italian immigrants to Woonsocket had formed a mutual help society, but the society did not embrace the entire community. In June 1912, Fr. James FitzSimon formed a Holy Name society for the Italians in the city to counteract the influence of the Socialists among the Italians, but it too attracted only some of the immigrants. Like the Italians in many other Rhode Island communities, the Italian families in Woonsocket emigrated from a variety of towns and districts in Italy.[29]

By the late summer of 1924, enough of the Italian families in Woon-

---

27 *Providence Journal*, May 9, 1931; October 7, 1933; *Providence Visitor*, May 11, 1932; November 11, 1932; August 11, 1933; April 9, 1936.
28 Hayman, *Catholicism in Rhode Island and the Diocese of Providence*, II, 190–91, 290.
29 Ibid., 700–701.

socket had indicated their willingness to support a parish of their own for
Bishop Hickey to appoint Fr. Emilio Greco, formerly an assistant at Holy
Angels, Barrington, pastor of the Italians in Woonsocket. Fr. Greco offered the first mass for his new parishioners in the basement chapel of St.
Charles church on October 26 at 10:00 a.m. Within two weeks, Fr. Greco
was offering two Sunday masses, one at 8:45 and the other at 10:00 as well
as a daily mass at 7:00. On November 6, Fr. Greco gathered a group of his
new parishioners together at the home of Joseph Cavedon on Verry Street
to discuss how they should go about raising funds to buy land and build a
church of their own. Within a month of this first meeting, Fr. Greco had
arranged for the purchase of the Aldrich place on Greene Street as the
site for a new church, which would be dedicated to St. Anthony. Fr. Greco
would use the cottage at the rear of the property as a rectory and the barn
as a meeting place.[30]

On January 11, 1925, members of the new parish met in Harris Hall
to launch a campaign to raise $100,000 to build their new church. Several
speakers addressed the meeting and team captains were chosen to recruit
workers to canvass the parishioners for the needed funds. Before a church
could be built on the Greene Street site, the cottage that stood at the front
of the property had to be torn down. During July 1925, after work was
done in the mills and before it got dark, Fr. Greco and some of the men
of the parish undertook the task of removing the house. With his hat and
coat off and, at times, with his Roman collar removed, Fr. Greco labored
alongside the men. Fund raising for the new church took the form of con-
certs, entertainments and dances. Fr. Greco had Ambrose Murphy draw
the plans for the church which he presented to Bishop Hickey for his approval on November 22, 1926. At the beginning of December, Fr. Greco
broke ground for the new church, which was to be a red-brick church in
the Italian Renaissance style, that was to seat six hundred people.[31]

In 1920, while pastor of Holy Angels in Barrington, Fr. Greco had also
taken on the editing of *La Sentinella*. After that paper ceased publication,
he began editing *La Vita Nova*, a bilingual magazine in English and Italian. By July 1927, he was involved with yet another Italian publication, *Il
Grimole d'America*. During July and August, Greco met with Bishop Hickey
several times to discuss the situation in his parish and the financial difficulties of the newspaper he was editing. It was evident by the time that the
bishop talked with Fr. Greco that the initial enthusiasm of the Italians in
Woonsocket to have a church of their own had given way to disillusion-
ment and a lack of confidence. Few of the people were attending mass
and there was no religious life or activity apart from mass. At the end of
August, Bishop Hickey gave Fr. Greco a leave of absence from the parish

---

30   *Providence Visitor*, October 24; November 7; December 5, 1924; *Providence Journal*, December 6, 1924.
31   Bishop Hickey's Diary, November 22, 1926; *Woonsocket Call*, July 25, 1926

equal to that he took from the newspaper. To replace him in Woonsocket, the bishop appointed Fr. Beni DiMascolo, an Italian immigrant, who had come to the United States with his parents when he was eight. He had attended the Webster Avenue school in Silver Lake and had graduated from La Salle Academy in 1915. After two years at St. Charles College, Baltimore, he studied at St. Bernard's, Rochester, New York, for four years and then spent his final two years of theology at St. John Lateran Seminary in Rome. He was ordained a priest in Rome on March 23, 1923. Following his return to the United States, Bishop Hickey had appointed him an assistant at St. Ann's, Providence, under Fr. (later Msgr.) Bove.[32]

Fr. DiMascolo re-energized the efforts of the small group of Italians that had undertaken the building of the church. On Sunday, December 18, 1927, Bishop Hickey came up to Woonsocket to bless the cornerstone of the new building and to praise the sacrifices of the parishioners. Within a few months, construction of the church was far enough along for Fr. DiMascolo to begin offering mass in the basement. On Easter Sunday, May 13, 1928, even though it was not yet complete, Fr. DiMascolo celebrated mass in the church proper for the first time. Bishop Hickey came up to Woonsocket again on Sunday, September 30, 1928, to dedicate the then completed church. In addition to completing the church, Fr. DiMascole, during his five and a half years in Woonsocket, bought the house and property adjoining the church at 128 Greene Street, which he used as a rectory, and formed a number of parish societies.

THE CHAPEL OF THE SACRED HEART, NATICK, *West Warwick*

In the Pawtuxet Valley, St. Joseph's, Natick, which had originally been established in 1875 through the combination of an Irish and a Canadian congregation, had by the mid-1920s become a parish in which there were now Italians and Italian-Americans. The Italians in Natick had come primarily from Fornelli, Province of Isernia, in the Molise Region of Southern Italy and from Grazzanise, Province of Caserta, in the Campania Region, as well as from other towns in southern Italy. In 1899, Bishop Harkins had given charge of the parish to the Missionaries of the Sacred Heart, an international order of priests and brothers, because he believed they could supply priests fluent in the languages of the parishioners. As the Sacred Heart fathers assigned to St. Joseph's at the turn of the century were Frenchmen, they initially relied on the assistance of Italian priests who belonged to the diocese to minister to the Italians of the Valley, particularly when they celebrated their local feasts.[33]

Regardless of where in Italy they came from, the Italians were occasion-

32   Bishop Hickey's Diary, July 8, 19, 22; August 26, 29; September 2, 1927; Ubaldo U. M. Pesaturo, *Italo-Americans of Rhode Island* (Providence, 1936), p. 44; Carroll, *Rhode Island: Three Centuries of Democracy,* IV, 368–69.
33   Hayman, *Catholicism in Rhode Island and the Diocese of Providence,* II, 15; 196–97.

ally insulted or chose to take offense by words and actions of both their French-born clergy and their French Canadians fellow parishioners, who at the turn of the nineteenth century made up the majority of St. Joseph's parishioners. The Canadians made fun of the Italian women because they wore a shawl on their heads in church. Not having a tradition of pew rent in Italy, the Italians did not understand the American custom whereby certain pews were reserved for the person who "rented" it. As a result, they felt insulted when they were asked to move and were directed to the back of the church where there were pews open to everyone. In their view, they were "thrown out of the pew and confined to the back of the church because [they] stunk."[34]

It was partly to avoid this abuse and these insults that in 1902 the Italians in Natick asked to have an Italian-speaking priest assigned to St. Joseph's so that they could worship apart from the Canadians and the Irish in the basement of the church. At the request of pastor at that time, Fr. Daniel Lehane, M.S.C., the provincial of the Missionaries of the Sacred Heart sent Fr. Jean B. Guillarme, M.S.C., who spoke Italian, to St. Joseph's. In 1911, Fr. Guillarme gave way to Fr. Frederick Achille Tirocchi, M.S.C., a newly-ordained priest of the order's Italian province. Fr. Tirocchi served in Natick for two years until he was transferred in October 1913 and Fr. Alvaro Santolini, M.S.C., arrived to replace him. Under Fr. Santolini steps were taken toward erecting a separate church for the Italians, but America's entrance into World War I interfered and the idea was dropped for a time. Fr. Santolini, like his Italian parishioners, occasionally clashed with the Canadians in the parish and with his French fellow-religious, particularly Fr. Pierre L'Esperance, M.S.C., who succeeded Fr. Lehane as pastor in 1904 and quasi-provincial in 1912. When in 1917 Fr. L'Esperance sent Fr. Santolini to another parish, the move occasioned a vigorous protest on the part of the Italians in the Valley. In spite of the protest, Fr. L'Esperance refused to reconsider. Shortly thereafter, Fr. Santolini left the Missionaries of the Sacred Heart and joined the clergy of the Diocese of Hartford.[35]

After Fr. Santolini left Natick, he was replaced by Fr. Tirocchi, who was able to get along more easily with his French co-religious. The 1922 strike against the B. B. & R. Knight Company mill severely disrupted the community. Since the strike proved to be a long and bitter one, it took some time before the majority of those involved had recovered financially from the loss of income. Fr. L'Esperance revived the idea of creating a separate congregation of Italians in Natick when he brought it up in a meeting with Bishop Hickey on May 4, 1923. Rather than give an answer at that time, the bishop promised to drive down to Natick and look over the situation.

<hr>

[34] Committee for the Italian Community of Natick to Archbishop Giovanni Cicognani, September 10, 1936, PChA.
[35] Hayman, *Catholicism in Rhode Island and the Diocese of Providence*, II, 196–97.

In a letter to Fr. Tirocchi dated January 28, 1924, Hickey agreed to the idea of a division of St. Joseph's and granted Fr. Ticocchi "the personal privilege of the title of 'Parroco' and empowered him to stand in that relation towards the Italians, who belonged to St. Joseph's. By 1926, the Italian congregation at St. Joseph's had grown to about three thousand or to the point where they now constituted the majority of the parishioners of St. Joseph's. The increase was such that the leaders of the Italian community began once again considering building a church. During the summer of 1926, Archbishop Pietro Benedetti, the Apostolic Delegate to Cuba, who visited Rhode Island each summer, paid a visit to the fellow members of his order in Natick. Prior to his recruitment into papal service, Benedetti had been general director of the Missionaries of the Sacred Heart. Fr. L'Esperance talked over the Italians' desire to have their own church, separate from St. Joseph's, with the delegate and some of the leaders of the Italian community. Archbishop Benedetti convinced the Italians of the uselessness of having two separate churches in a small town like Natick. He proposed, instead, that the Italians, who were in the majority, should take control of the parish with Fr. Tirocchi as their pastor. When the French Canadians heard of the suggestion, they quickly organized a demonstration against the idea and threatened Fr. L'Esperance. In the face of the French-Canadians' opposition, Fr. L'Esperance dropped the idea and agreed to building a separate chapel for the Italians. His first step was to purchase from the Knight Corporation a piece of land on Providence Street, only a short distance from St. Joseph's. In June 1928, Fr. Tirocchi broke ground for a Spanish Mission-style church, with a seating capacity of about six hundred, that was to be finished with stucco on the outside. Bishop Hickey laid the cornerstone of the new building on October 7, 1928 and Fr. Ticocchi said the first mass in the new church on Christmas Eve. Bishop Hickey came down to the valley on a hot day in September 1929 to dedicate the church to the Sacred Heart, bless its bells, and to confirm two hundred of the Italian children of the parish.[36]

After the opening of the church but prior to its dedication, Fr. Tirocchi, aware of his congregation's feelings towards the French Canadians and the French clergy who staffed St. Joseph's, raised the idea with the provincial of the Missionaries of the Sacred Heart's Italian Province that Sacred Heart be separated from the jurisdiction of the order's American Providence and be placed under the jurisdiction of its Italian Province. The Italian provincial, Fr. Pierre A. Pillarella, M.S.C., brought up the idea to Fr. L'Esperance in a letter. On June 15, 1929, Fr. L'Esperance replied, that after having consulted with the members of his provincial council, and especially after having discussed the idea with Bishop Keough, the consensus

---

[36]   Bishop Hickey's Diary, May 4, 1923; Hickey to Tirocchi, January 28, 1924, PChA; *Providence Visitor,* October 5, 1928; September 6, 1929; April 8, 1937; Committee for the Italian Committee of Natick to Archbishop Cicognani, September 16, 1936, PChA.

was that Sacred Heart chapel ought to remain under the jurisdiction of the American Province.[37]

In addition to overseeing the building of a church, Fr. Tirocchi organized a number of parish societies, among them the St. John's Dramatic Club, the Mt. Carmel Society, Children of Mary Sodality, Third Order of St. Francis, and the St. Aloysius Society. Besides the religious groups attached to the parish, Fr. Tirocchi also recruited and directed successful baseball and football teams, which won not only Pawtuxet Valley championships but also State championships. In 1920, he organized the first Catholic troop of Boy Scouts among the boys of his parish. Initially independent of the national scout organization because of Bishop Hickey's concerns about it, the troop would not be affiliated to the national group until the 1930s. Because of Fr. Tirocchi's deep involvement in the social as well as the religious life of the valley, his sudden death from a heart attack on March 6, 1935 came as a shock to the community. His funeral was attended by about a hundred priests and a equal number of civil officials as well as by thousands of his parishioners.[38]

HOLY CROSS, *Providence*

In Providence, the Italians who lived in the Hartford Avenue district of St. Bartholomew's parish had to walk a considerable distance to attend mass in Silver Lake. As early as 1924, the idea of a chapel in the district that would bring the mass closer to their homes was discussed. When in 1926, Fr. Peter Gorret, C.S., the pastor of St. Bartholomew's, finished the census of the district, he found that there were then 110 families with 284 adults and 326 children there. After a meeting with the heads of the families in the area and after having secured Bishop Hickey's permission, Fr. Gorret purchased five lots on the corner of Hartford Avenue and Stella Street as a site for the proposed chapel. Work on the building began on May 27, 1926 and Fr. Gorret celebrated the first mass in the chapel on November 27. A year later, on Sunday, November 11, 1927, Bishop Hickey blessed the building and its new bell and dedicated it under the title of the Holy Cross.[39]

[37] Pillarella to Keough, October 22, 1936, PChA.
[38] *Providence Journal*, March 7, 1935; *Pawtuxet Valley Daily Times*, March 11, 1935; Hayman, *Catholicism in Rhode Island and the Diocese of Providence*, II, 612–14.
[39] *Providence Visitor*, November 9, 1927; *Providence Journal*, November 10, 12, 1927.

The Attempt to Build a Church in Eagle Park, Providence

St. Bartholmew was not the only Italian parish in Providence that experienced a substantial increase in its parish population in the 1920s. St. Ann, in the North End, experienced a similar increase both in the Eagle Park section of the parish and in the Woodville section in North Providence. On Sunday, April 21, 1929, representatives of the 700 families who lived in that section met with Msgr. Antonio Bove, the pastor of St. Ann's, to discuss a proposal to build a chapel on Douglas Avenue and Columbus streets, for which four lots had already been donated to Eugenio Addeo, the founder and president of the Society Maria Santissima Della Carita, by former Senator Jesse H. Metcalf. At the meeting, Msgr. Bove read a letter from Bishop Hickey giving his approval of the project. The proposed chapel was to be named in honor of Our Lady of Charity. Msgr. Bove informed the parishioners interested in the project that, for their dream to become a reality, they needed to raise between forty and fifty thousand dollars to finance the chapel's construction. The idea of building a chapel in honor of Our Lady of Charity originated with the society of the same name that Mr. Addeo helped organize in 1913 and which held a yearly feast in May. A shrine was erected on the proposed site and the church was incorporated in April 1924, but the chapel was never built.[40]

THE MISSION OF ST. ANTHONY, *North Providence*

A week before the people of the Eagle Park section met with Msgr. Bove to discuss building a church, Msgr. Bove held a similar meeting with the people of the Woodville section of North Providence, which was bounded by Woodward Road, Mineral Spring Avenue and Douglas Avenue Msgr. Bove explained to those at the meeting what steps were necessary to start a new parish and stressed that the co-operation of all in the section was necessary if the project was to succeed. At their next meeting, Msgr. Bove was able to tell the people of the Woodville section, as he had those of Eagle Park, that Bishop Hickey approved of their project as well. During this second meeting, Msgr. Bove announced that those interested in having a church built in Woodville had taken an option on the site they had decided on, eighteen lots on Woodward Road near where it intersected with Mineral Spring Avenue He also announced that work on the proposed church would not start until $15,000 had been raised. In order to raise the money, an executive committee was set up at the meeting to organize a canvass of the two to three hundred families who would be served by the proposed

---

[40] *Providence Visitor*, June 2, 1922; April 26, 1929; May 23, 1935; *News-Tribune*, July 17, 1936; Pesaturo, *Italo-Americans of Rhode Island*, p. 36.

church, which shortly thereafter it was decided to place under the patronage of St Anthony.[41]

A little better than a year after these initial meetings, on Sunday, August
10, 1930, nearly fifty men of the new St. Anthony's mission laid the foundation for their church. During their spare time, men of the parish had
already dug out the foundation for the 33 by 97 foot, two-story building,
that was to have a brick first floor, where religious education classes were to
be held and a wood frame second floor where mass would be celebrated.
On Thursday, December 11, 1930, the Bonatelli Construction Company
began work on the church itself, which was projected to cost $20,000 and,
by the following June, the congregation of the new mission celebrated the
feast of St. Anthony with the consecration of a bell in honor of the saint.
The following day, June 14, 1931, Msgr. Bove blessed the statues of the
Blessed Virgin and St. Anthony, which were carried into the new church
prior to its blessing.[42]

ST. MARY, Knightsville, Cranston

South of Providence, immigrants from Itri, a town in the southern Italian province of Latina, began settling in the Knightsville section of Cranston about the turn of the twentieth century. By 1905, their numbers were
large enough for them to organize an American version of the feast of the
Madonna della Civita, which they had long celebrated in their native land.
As was true of all Italian communities, immigrants from other Italian villages and towns who also lived in Knightsville or in other Italian colonies
gladly joined the natives of Itri in celebrating the feast. Initially, the celebration of the feast received little attention outside of Knightsville because
it was overshadowed by the feast of Our Lady of Mt. Carmel, which was
celebrated at the same time in Providence. The celebration of the feast of
the Modonna della Civita was suspended after the outbreak of the First
World War, but, in the July following the Armistice in November, 1918, the
Monte Civita Society, which had begun the feast, once again arranged for
its celebration. In that year, the streets around the first Cranston City Hall
were festooned with colored lights and various decorations for the band
concert which opened the feast. The next day, the community celebrated
the usual mass in honor of their patroness at St. Rocco's in Johnston. As
was the custom, the mass was preceded and followed by a street parade
during which the men of the Monte Civita Society carried the statue of
the Virgin through the streets of their community, and, in the evening,
there was another band concert and the usual fireworks display.[43]

In April 1904, the increasing number of Italians in Cranston had

41 *Providence Visitor*, April 29, 1929; *Providence Journal*, April 15, 1929.
42 *Providence Journal*, August 11; December 12, 1930; June 10, 15, 1931; *Providence Visitor*, July 3, 1931.
43 *Evening Bulletin*, July 21, 1919; Bernadette Conte, *Eviva Maria*: Madonna della Civita (Exlibris,
    2014).

prompted Fr. Domenico Belliotti, C.S., then an assistant at Holy Ghost parish in Providence, to discuss with Bishop Matthew Harkins the possibility of having a mission for the Italians in Cranston. The year before, the Scalabrini Fathers at Holy Ghost had opened the mission chapel in the Thornton section of Johnston dedicated to St. Rocco for the convenience of the Italians who lived in Johnston and Cranston. Many of the Knightsville Italians, like other immigrants, did not attend the "Irish" church, St. Ann's, because of the differences of language and culture. Missions were an important tool apostolic-minded priests used, in all communities, to awaken religious traditions and practices. At the time of Fr. Belliotti's visit, Bishop Harkins promised he would speak with Fr. John Tully, the new pastor of St. Ann's. After November 1902, the Italians living in the Auburn district of Cranston further to the East could also go to St. Matthew's, the newly opened mission church of St. Ann's, which Bishop Harkins set off as a separate parish in October 1905. Depending on where they lived in Cranston, the more devout or the more nationalistic-minded might make the trip to St. Rocco's or to Providence to attend Holy Ghost or St. Batholomew's, which was opened in the Silver Lake district of Providence in 1907. Some at least chose to attend St. Ann's or St. Matthew's, both of which offered an occasional mission in Italian.[44]

While the organization of the feast of the Madonna della Civita in 1905 and its yearly celebration in the years following helped to fulfill the religious needs of the many Italians residents in Knightsville, the ultimate goal of the organizers of the feast was to see a church built in honor of the Madonna della Civita. There was no progress toward that goal until January 1922, when Fr. Antonio Bove, the pastor of St. Ann's, Providence, who often assisted English-speaking pastors in ministering to the Italians in their parishes, called on Bishop Hickey with the proposal of sending an Italian priest to Cranston. At the time, Fr. Bove was anticipating the arrival of two young Italian priests from Italy, who would initially serve as his assistants at St. Ann's. His current assistant was Fr. Cesare Schettini, an Italian-born priest who had come to the United States in 1919. Fr. Schettini had worked for a few months in a parish in New York City before coming to Providence, where, in November 1919, Bishop Hickey sent him to assist Fr. Bove. Aware of the desire of the Italians in Cranston to have a church of their own, Fr. Bove suggested that the bishop send Fr. Schettini to St. Ann's, as an assistant to Fr. Thomas Tiernan. As Fr. Tiernan's assistant, Fr. Schettini could make the pastoral care of the Italians his special apostolate. Bishop Hickey agreed to the proposal and on the following day, January 18, 1922, gave Fr. Schettini his new assignment.[45]

Fr. Schettini was born in Vicovaro, one of the towns near Rome, on August 15, 1884. He spent five years in the public schools of Vicovaro

---

[44]   Bishop Harkins' Diary, April 8, 1904; September 17, 1912.
[45]   Bishop Hickey's Diary, January 17, 18, 1922.

and four in the schools at Tivoli. After a year in the Apollinare College at Rome, he entered the diocesan seminary at Tivoli, where he spent seven years prior to his ordination on June 18, 1905 at the age of twenty. Because he was not of the canonical age required for ordination, his ordination required a special papal dispensation. After a year's further study, his bishop appointed him a professor at the Tivoli Seminary, where he served until he was appointed pastor of Our Lady of Victories Church in 1908. During this time, he returned to the Apollinare for a course on sacred eloquence, following which he joined the Diocese of Tivoli's mission band. At this time, he took a prominent part in the Catholic Action movement directing Catholic youth clubs in Tivoli and Rome and organizing rural banks. With the outbreak of World War I, he enlisted as a chaplain and served in the military hospital at Celio and later in the General Inspectortate of the Army in Rome. With the war's end, he applied for missionary work among the Italians in the United States and was sent to New York City.[46]

On taking up his new duties, Fr. Schettini began offering two masses each Sunday for the Italians in the basement of the new, but yet unfinished, St. Ann's Church. Three months after Fr. Schettini took up his duties at St. Ann's, a committee representing the Italians who lived in the Auburn section of Cranston and who were regarded as parishioners of St. Bartholomew's parish, asked Bishop Hickey that they be included in the "proposed Italian congregation to be established in the Print Works Section," and, pending the organization of a new Italian parish, that they be allowed to assist at the masses celebrated by Fr. Schettini at St. Ann's. Almost a whole year passed before Bishop Hickey took up the Italians' requests with Fr. Tiernan of St. Ann's and Fr. Gorret of St. Bartholomew's. At a meeting with the two priests on April 6, 1923, an agreement was reached between them for a change in the parish lines separating St. Ann's and St. Bartholomew's parishes in regard to the care "of parishioners of Italian birth, tendencies, sentiments, etc." In addition to announcements regarding the change made in St. Ann's and St. Bartholomew's, the change of jurisdiction was announced in St. Matthew's parish by the pastor Fr. John Sullivan. Bishop Hickey also conveyed the news in a letter to the members of the committee who had written to him.[47]

Fr. Scettini's appointment as an assistant at St. Ann's spurred the hopes of the Italians in Cranston that they might soon have a parish of their own. His appointment also moved representatives of the Italians who lived

[46] *Providence Visitor*, March 22, 1951; "St. Mary's Church, Cranston, Rhode Island: Christian Love and Unity, 1925–1975 (So. Hackensack, N.J.: Custombook, Inc., 1975), p. 5.

[47] Domenico Vallone, et al., to Hickey, April 17, 1922; Hickey to Tiernan, April 6, 1923; Alexsondro Sepe, et al, to Hickey, no date; Bishop Hickey's Diary, April 6, 1923. Although Fr. John Tully had succeeded in building a new church in 1909 to replace the wooden one built in 1860, the parish lacked the funds to complete the upper church. The task of finishing and furnishing the upper church fell to Fr. Tully's successor, Fr. Tiernan. It was not until November 25, 1928, that Bishop Hickey came to bless and dedicate the newly completed structure.

in the Auburn section to write to Bishop Hickey asking to be included in the proposed Italian congregation at St. Ann's. When the bishop granted the requested permission, representatives from the several Italian neighborhoods in Cranston formed a committee to organize a lawn festival on the Haven plat at the corner of Haven Avenue and Cranston Street as a fund raiser for a future Italian parish. The festival opened on August 21, 1922 and ran for a week. On October 6, 1922, Fr. Schettini, who was the treasurer of the Italian Committee, brought Bishop Hickey the proceeds in the form of a check. When added to the funds already placed in the bishop's keeping for the purpose, the combination amounted to four thousand dollars.[48]

When in April 1923, a farmhouse and fifteen lots on Cranston Street across from Haven Street and bordering on the St. Ann's cemetery property, was offered for $10,000, the Italian Committee wrote to Bishop Hickey to ask him to come out to Cranston to see the land, which they proposed buying as a site for a parish. On April 28, 1922, Fr. Schettini called on Bishop Hickey to discuss the same question. At the time, Bishop Hickey's attention was focused on the upcoming Million Dollar High School Drive and the bishop made no immediate response to the Committee. Impatient with the bishop's delay in responding to their request that the bishop look at possible sites for a church, the Committee wrote to Bishop Hickey on May 8, urging the need for a parish to care for the religious needs of the "500 Italian families in Cranston," who collectively comprised over 3000 people. Specifically, the Committee asked, once again, that the bishop come out to Cranston to look at a parcel of land they hoped to purchase. The committee expressed the belief that the land was a "splendid buy financially." They promised the bishop, in the name of the Italians in Cranston, that they were ready to make any sacrifice "with either money or work" to achieve their goal. Unfortunately, the letter went on to describe their condition under their present pastors as one of "slavery" and "continuous persecutions" on the part of the "American priest." Bishop Hickey's preoccupation with the Drive and the tone of the committee's letter combined to ensure that again there was no response on the bishop's part.[49]

To compound the situation, an article appeared in the *Providence Journal* on Sunday, May 20, 1923, concerning the Italians' determination to build a church on the Cranston Street site, hopefully with Bishop Hickey's permission. In the eventuality the bishop did not give the requested permission, the Committee declared itself determined to go ahead with their plans "because necessity forces us to immediate action." The decision to go forward with their plans was made at a meeting of "many prominent

---

[48] *Providence Journal*, August 20, 1922; Bishop Hickey's Diary, October 6, 1922.
[49] Bishop Hickey's Diary, April 28, 1923; Luigi Vallone et al., to Hickey, May 8, 1923, PChA. Rather than being directed at Fr. Tiernan, the complaint was most likely directed at Fr. John F. Sullivan, the Irish-born pastor of St. Matthew's

parishioners who were invited to be present," in the office of Luigi Vallone, "a Cranston contractor," and spokesman for the committee. The
vote on whether to proceed was reported to have been unanimous. As laid
out for the *Journal* reporter, "the men of the parish would do the excavation and foundation work themselves and much of the other construction," but other than determining that the structure would be simple, no
specific type of building was agreed on.[50]

The committee waited until May 22 before they wrote to Bishop Hickey
again. They informed the bishop that the Italian people of Cranston had
to have their own church "at any price," even if it meant building one
independent of the bishop's authority. They placed responsibility for any
troubles that would cause scandal on the bishop for not having responded
to their request. They again asked for permission to build a church or, as
an alternative, for the bishop to give them back the monies they had already raised and which Fr. Schettini, as treasurer of the committee, had
passed on to the bishop. Although 152 signatures accompanied the letter,
the Italians would learn what both the French-Canadian ultra-nationalists
and the Portuguese in West Warwick would later learn: Bishop Hickey
could not be moved by threats. Once again, the bishop ignored the committee's letter.[51]

While the committee had an agreement to purchase the land that they
believed was suitable for a church, they lacked the money to pay for it. On
Saturday evening, July 14, 1923, a week before the now traditional celebration of the feast of the Madonna, Mr. Vallone and five or six others set
up a four by six signboard near St. Ann's church that announced that the
committee had bought the land in question in behalf of the Italian people
and appealed to the Italian community for the funds to pay for it when
money was due on August 20. The appeal concluded with the admonition
that the appeal should be heeded lest they make their neighbors laugh at
them. The posting of the appeal was duly reported to Bishop Hickey by
Fr. Tiernan.[52]

Fr. Schettini found himself in the middle between the Cranston Italians and Bishop Hickey. As a native-born Italian, he was aware that local
customs in Italy gave the laity a greater role in parish affairs than in the
United States. As a priest who had spent time with Fr. Bove, he also knew
that American traditions placed control of parish affairs almost exclusively
in the hands of the bishop and pastor. He had, of course, encouraged the
Italian Committee in their desire to see an Italian parish created in Cranston and supported their fund-raising activities. Although he was on retreat
when the notice was printed, Fr. Tiernan reported to Bishop Hickey that
he had seen Fr. Schettini talking with a few Italian men in front of the sign

50   *Providence Journal*, May 20, 1923.
51   Luigi Vallone et al., to Hickey, Mat 22, 1923, PChA.
52   Tiernan to Hickey, July 16, 1923, PChA.

between masses on Sunday. He also reported that Fr. Schettini had suggested that he, as pastor of St. Ann's, ask the bishop's permission to hold the annual procession with the statue. Tiernan thought that Fr. Schettii asked him to make the request so that any refusal would put Fr. Tiernan in a bad light.[53]

While the Italian Committee announced its intention to build a church independent of the bishop's authority, it is doubtful that the Italian community in Cranston as a whole supported such action. Without the financial support of the entire community, there was little prospect that the Committee would even be able to raise the funds necessary to purchase the land on Cranston Street Some form of a compromise was necessary. On July 21, Bishop Hickey met with the Italian Committee. Although there is no extant record of what was said at the meeting, the bishop evidently assured the Committee that he would create a parish for the Italians of Cranston when they fulfilled certain conditions that he laid down, among them the conveying to the Bishop of Providence the deed to any land purchased for a church. With the threat of an independent parish removed, ten men and women interested in seeing an Italian parish created in Cranston agreed to loan the Committee a total of $3,500 with which to purchase the land, on condition that the Committee would pay back the loans once it had the funds to do so. On November 22, 1923, Fr. Schettini wrote to Bishop Hickey assuring him that the Committee was willing to convey to the diocese the deed to the property they had purchased. Father Schettini suggested that the Committee might use the money already collected for the parish that was in the bishop's hands to pay back the loan. Bishop Hickey, however, believed that the better course was to continue fund raising and use the new monies to pay those who had loaned the money for the land. It took the Committee over a year to accomplish the task the bishop set for it, but on February 9, 1925, the Committee informed the bishop that all the notes issued to buy the land had been paid. In contrast to the Committee's other letters, which had gone unanswered, Bishop Hickey wrote back on February 11 in order to congratulate the Committee for the good work they had done. Ten days later, February 21, 1925, the bishop appointed Fr. Schettini pastor of the new parish of Santa Maria Della Civita.[54]

In setting off St. Mary's (as the parish is known in the English-speaking community) from St. Ann's, Fr. Tiernan agreed to rent the old wooden

---

53 Ibid.
54 Luigi Vallone, et al., to Hickey, August 15, 1923;. Schettini to Hickey, November 23, 1923; Luigi Vallone, et al., to Schettini, January 4, 1924; Angelo Saccaccia to Hickey, February 12, 1924; Saccaccia et al., to Hickey, February 9, 1925; Hickey to Italian Committee, February 11, 1925; Fr. Schettini's personal file, PChA. The committee attempted to write a clause into the deed by which they conveyed the land to the bishop so as to restrict the use of the land as "a site for a projected new church." However, the real estate agent who handled the transfer assured Bishop Hickey that the clause had no legal standing and the bishop did not make an issue of it. John J. Sullivan to Hickey, February 7, 1924, PChA

St. Ann's to the new parish for $500 a year. The people of St. Ann's had moved from the old church to the basement of their new one in April, 1909, and the old church had been used as a parish hall since. The renting of the old church met an immediate need and Fr. Schettini was able to scrap the plan for a church that he had submitted to the bishop in November 1923. His original thought had been to construct a simple building with a flat roof that could be used as a school when a proper church was built. With the organization of the new parish, the land at Cranston Street and Haven Avenue became the focal point for the annual celebration of the feast of the Madonna della Civita.[55]

Several weeks after receiving his appointment as pastor, Fr. Schettini moved into the old farmhouse at 1521 Cranston Street that was on the property bought for the new parish. Prior to the move, he had had the house repaired and provided with a heating system at the cost of more than $1,500. He also arranged for the reconversion of the old St. Ann's to a church by having a wooden altar constructed and second-hand pews installed. He first celebrated mass there for his new parishioners on Easter Sunday, April 12, 1925. Significantly, on forming the parish corporation, Fr. Schettini chose two prominent members of the Italian Committee, Luigi Vallone and Antonio B. Cardi, as the parish's first lay trustees.[56]

As pastor of a new parish, it was Fr. Schettini's responsibility to organize the parish religious societies that were the marks of a vibrant parish life in any parish of that time. In the absence of a parish school, he also had to organize religious education classes for the hundreds of children in the parish. In addition to his duties as spiritual leaders, he had now to take the lead in the continued fund raising that was necessary if the parish was to have a proper church. Carnivals, bazaars and socials continued to be important fund-raising events as well as social occasions. During 1927, Fr. Schettini invited architects to present proposals for a new church. The plan selected was drawn by Ermino Migliori and was based on the church of Santa Maria Della Civita known to many of the immigrants from Itri. In the fall of 1927, Mr. Migliori was invited to speak at a meeting which launched a fund-raising campaign to build the proposed church. In order to canvass the entire parish, Fr. Schettini recruited volunteers to go out in pairs on monthly visits to all prospective donors to the church building fund. Each donor was provided with a pass book wherein his or her monthly donation was recorded and, at the end of each month, certificates bearing a picture of the proposed church were awarded. Although the Great Depression did not hit the country until 1929, Rhode Island's economy was plagued with weakness throughout the 1920s. The greater

[55] Schettini to Hickey, November 23, 1923; *Providence Visitor*, May 6, 1937; *Providence Journal*, July 18, 21, 24, 1927.
[56] *Providence Visitor*, May 6, 1937; "St. Mary's Church, Cranston, Rhode Island," p. 5.

part of the monies contributed on a monthly basis were coins. As a result, the building fund grew slowly.[57]

In March 1928, after approximately $20,000 had been collected, Fr. Schettini announced that ground would be broken for the new church in the following July. In making the announcement, he was being overly optimistic. The actual beginning of construction was contingent upon the raising of another $15,000. When July came, the parish celebrated the feast of its patroness as usual, but there was no ground breaking that year. The onset of the Depression in fall of 1929 added to the challenge. The parish revenue dropped to the point where Fr. Schettini let certain bills go unpaid. In November 1932, the credit manager of the candle company that supplied St. Mary's with candles, wrote to Msgr. Peter A. Foley, the chancellor of the diocese, asking for his assistance in persuading Fr. Schettini to pay something each month towards the parish's debt to the company.[58]

By 1933, some at least of the parishioners grew tired of waiting for Fr. Schettini to begin construction of the new church as he continued to promise. In August 1933, Nicola Tatangelo gave voice to the impatience of a certain faction within the parish by writing a letter to the Apostolic Delegate, Archbishop Ameleto Cicognani, in which he complained about the delay in the start of construction and the poor and unsafe conditions of the old church the parish continued to use. As was the delegate's usual practice, Archbishop Cicognani sent the letter to Bishop Hickey, who in turn, asked Fr. Schettini to reply to the complaints in Mr. Tatangelo's letter. In his reply, Fr. Schettini informed the delegate that Mr. Tatangelo had come to live in the parish only in the last two years and was not a regular contributor to the parish or diocesan collections. He was, however, a personal friend of the architect, whose design had been chosen for the church. Furthermore, Fr. Schettini suggested that, from the style and language of the letter, it was not likely that Mr. Tatangelo was its author. In his cover letter with which he replied to the delegate, Bishop Hickey praised Fr. Schettini as a "very good, hard working and devoted priest." The bishop assured the delegate that he was very much interested in the parish and that, when the proper time came to build, he would see to it the parish's choice of an architect would be in the parish's best interest.[59]

The impatience of the parishioners to see the proposed church built motivated a movement of another kind less than two years later. On December 31, 1934, the Societa Religiouse Pellegrinaggio Itrano applied for a building permit to build a private chapel on Vervena Street, a short distance from the site of the proposed church. The proponents of this idea claimed that wished to see the image of Mary, Maria Santissima della

57 Nicola Tatangelo to Archbishop Ameleto Cicognani, August 31, 1933, PChA; "St. Mary's Church, Cranston, Rhode Island," 7–8.
58 *Providence News*, March 28, 1928; Anthony N. Markert to Foley, November 31, 1932, PChA.
59 Tatangelo to Cicognani, August 31, 1933; Cicognani to Hickey, September 8, 1933; Schettini to Hickey, September 19, 1933; Hickey to Cicognani, September 22, 1933, PChA.

Civita d'Itri, honored in their new home as Mary was in Italy. Since nothing had been done about a new church, the society, which sought to build the private chapel, justified their action by appealing to their Italian traditions where private chapels served as places where the women of the neighborhood could go each evening to recite the Rosary and other common prayers. When a committee representing the society called on newly installed Bishop Francis Keough, Bishop Hickey's successor, to seek his permission to build the chapel, which would have been less than a mile from the site of the proposed church, the bishop made it clear to them that, if they went ahead with their plan without his permission, he could never consider accepting the chapel as an official place of worship. In a candid letter to an Italian religious who interested herself in the case, a representative of the society acknowledged that many of the men who belonged to the society did not attend religious services. However, he claimed that under the men's indifference there still burned the everlasting flame of the religion they were taught in Italy.[60]

When Fr. Schettini learned of the society's plan, he successfully sought to persuade the donor of the land on which the society planned to build the chapel to withhold his donation. When the potential donor withdrew his support, another stepped forward to make a similar donation of land on C Street. In spite of Bishop Keough's opposition to their efforts, the society resolved to go ahead with their plan. The men of the society worked on the building on the weekends and after returning from their jobs. In 1937, after finally completing the chapel, they too would write to the apostolic delegate to plead their cause. In his reply to the auditor of the delegation, Msgr. Vagnozzi, Bishop Keough explained the motives and politics that he believed lay behind the society's action and his reasons for refusing to accept the chapel as a place for worship. In turn, the Delegation urged the letter writers to join in the support of their proper parish church.[61]

Whether the action of the society forced Fr. Schettini's hand or not is not clear, but on February 7, 1935, Fr. Schettini, through the *Providence Visitor*, announced that architectural plans for the new church would be ready "in about a month." The plans for St. Mary's were drawn by Ambrose J. Murphy, a prominent architect, who designed many churches in the diocese. Murphy's design was based loosely on Andrea Palladio's 1565 church of San Georgio Maggiore in Venice. According to its original description, the church, which was to cost $100,000, would have a seating capacity of 725. Fr. Schettini arranged for the ground breaking for the new church on Palm Sunday, April 14, 1935. The day began with a street parade, which

60   Building permit application; Societa Religiouse Pellegrinaggio Itrano, to Rev. Mother, January 14, 1935; Keough to Msgr. Egidio Vagnozzi, auditor, February 12, 1937, PChA.

61   Schettini to Rev. Mother, January 4, 1935; Societa Religiouse Pellegrinaggio Itrao to Rev. Mother, January 14, 1935; Mother Teresa Saccucci to Keough, January 23, 1935; Rev. Francis E. Hyland, Secretary to the Delegate, February 16, 1937, PChA; *Providence Journal*, April 13, 1936.

formed on the church property, and, headed by local bands, the various societies of the parish marched through the Knightsville and Chestnut Grove sections of the parish, before returning to building site where the ground breaking took place. The day ended with Benediction in the old St. Ann's. In order to accommodate the construction of the church, the builders had first to remove a wing of the old farmhouse rectory.[62]

Mr. Murphy oversaw the bidding process on the part of the contractors who were anxious to have the work. Aware of the undercurrents active in the parish, Bishop Keough allowed a number of local contractors, about whose ability to carry out the proposed work there were doubts, to bid on the job. On Mr. Murphy's advice, Fr. Schettini awarded the building contract to the A. C. Construction Company of Providence, of which Alfred Cardi was president. The parish celebrated the completion of the exterior of the church at a dinner in the church's basement on Sunday, November 24. The hall was filled to capacity by members of the parish who gathered to hear speeches by prominent Italians from all over the state.[63]

Fr. Schettini celebrated the first mass in the basement of still uncompleted church on Easter Sunday, April 12, 1936. In order to prepare for the first mass in the church, all the shrines and furnishings that had been in the old St. Ann's were removed from the church and set up in the basement of the new church. The start of construction on St. Mary's prompted a new round of contributions from the parishioners. Among the more prominent gifts was the marble main altar, carved in the studio of Angelo Lualdi in Florence, that was the donation of Luigi and Libera Vallone in honor of Mr. Vallone's parents. The side altar dedicated to Our Lady of the Valley was donated by parishioners who came from Monticelli, in the Province of Esperia. The altar dedicated to Santa Oliva was donated by parishioners whose birthplace was the town of Santa Oliva in Pontecorvo. Over a hundred families who came from Itri contributed money for the communion rail. Bishop Keough blessed the cornerstone and formally dedicated the new church on Sunday, July 3, 1938. The Sunday following the dedication, the parishioners celebrated the event with a dinner tendered to Fr. Schettini that was held in the church hall.[64]

For the Portuguese

THE CONTINUING DEVELOPMENT
OF ST. ANTHONY, PORTSMOUTH

Just as the Italians spread out from the places where the first immi-

---

62   *Providence Visitor*, February 7; April 11, 1935; *Providence Journal*, April 8, 15, 1935.
63   *Providence Visitor*, April 25, 1935; *Evening Bulletin*, November 20, 1935; *News-Tribune*, November 25, 1925.
64   *Providence Visitor*, March 25, 1937; June 30, 1938; *Providence Journal*, March 27, 1937; July 4, 1938.

grants had settled and created new Italian colonies, so did the Portuguese. According to the 1905 State Census, of the 5,293 Rhode Island inhabitants who declared mainland Portugal, the Azores, or the Cape Verde islands as their place of birth, slightly less than half lived in Providence. The other cities or towns with significant numbers of Portuguese-born residents in 1905 were Bristol (659), Portsmouth (537), East Providence (403), Newport (256), Warwick (243), Middletown (237), and Tiverton (219).[65]

Bishop Harkins had established St. Anthony's, Portsmouth, in 1906 as a mixed-ethnic and territorial parish. During the summer months, St. Anthony's served a large English-speaking population of summer visitors, but, during the rest of the year, a high percentage of the parishioners of St. Anthony's were Portuguese or their American-born children. Realizing this, and having sought Portuguese-speaking diocesan priests to serve in his diocese with only limited success, Bishop Harkins sought out a religious order whose apostolate included work among the Portuguese-speaking in other parts of the world. In 1907, Harkins appointed Fr. Christopher Rooney, C.S.Sp., a Holy Ghost Father, the first pastor of St. Anthony's. Two other Holy Ghost Fathers came to the parish in 1909 and 1910 to live with Fr. Rooney at Portsmouth and to serve the mission churches attached to St. Anthony's. The second of these priests was Fr. Manuel Barros, C.S.Sp., who, during his years at St. Anthony's, had particular charge of St. Catherine's, the parish's mission church in Little Compton, which had many Portuguese among those who went to mass there. Fr. Barros was born in Vilas Boas, Portugal, in 1881 and had been ordained a priest on October 28, 1904. Following the Republicans' rise to power in Portugal in 1910 and the overthrow of the Portuguese monarchy, Fr. Barros, along with other religious, was forced to leave the country.[66]

After Fr. Rooney became ill in 1919, he left the parish on a trip to Ireland to try to recover his health. When he died ten days after landing in Ireland, it fell to Bishop Hickey to choose his successor from among the two Holy Ghost Fathers then serving as assistants, Fr. Cornelius D. O'Rorke, C.S.Sp., who had come to St. Anthony's in 1916, after a time as assistant pastor in Wisconsin and who Fr. Rooney had placed charge of St. Anthony's during his absence, and Fr. Barros. O'Rorke was Irish-born and educated. Following his ordination in 1891, he had been assigned to teach in an Irish college run by the Holy Ghost Fathers. Poor health eventually forced his temporary retirement from the classroom. He recuperated in Portugal and, while there, learned to speak Portuguese. He later resumed his work as teacher and taught in Trinidad and in the United States before going to Wisconsin. When he came to Portsmouth, Fr. Rooney put him in charge of St. Christopher's, the parish's mission in Tiverton, before he

[65]   *Providence Journal*, July 25, 1907. Figures for the *Journal* article were obtained from the
        Commissioner of Industrial Statistics.
[66]   *Providence Journal*, May 9, 1937.

assumed the duties of acting pastor. While the bishop was considering his decision, Fr. O'Rorke wrote to him to counteract a petition in support of Fr. Barros's appointment, in which disparaging statements had been made about him. O'Rorke pointed out that if the bishop made Fr. Barros pastor, he would be "giving [the parish] over to the Portuguese, the majority of whom contributed nothing to building of the church & very little to its support for the last twenty years." Furthermore, he noted, if Fr. Barros was appointed pastor over him, the change would go to prove the charges against him were true. Of the two men, Fr. O'Rorke was the better administrator. For reasons Bishop Hickey did not share with posterity, he chose to accept the arrangements the Holy Ghost fathers had worked out and confirmed Fr. O'Rorke as pastor.[67]

Since the overall population of St. Anthony's had grown since the church was constructed in 1901, the church had become crowded. After becoming pastor in 1919, Fr. O'Rorke created more space by adding transepts to the original building. In order to better accommodate the summer visitors who vacationed at Sakonnet Point in Little Compton, Fr. O'Rorke, with Bishop Hickey's help, acquired a building site and built a small church there, which was first used during the summer of 1926. The church at Sakonnet was placed under the patronage of St. Teresa of the Child Jesus and was attended during the summer months by the priest, who served at St. Catherine's in Little Compton.[68]

HOLY GHOST, *Tiverton*

During Fr. O'Rorke's years as pastor of St. Anthony's, the Church of the Holy Ghost, North Tiverton, another mission of St. Anthony's, was set off and made a separate parish. The initiative for the change came from the parishioners of Holy Ghost themselves. After consulting Fr. O'Rorke, representatives of the Irish, French Canadian and Portuguese populations in the parish presented a petition to Bishop Hickey outlining their reasons for asking his permission that the mission might build a rectory so that a priest could be assigned to the parish on a full time basis. They gave as their reasons for making the request the number of families attached to the mission (301), and its total population (1,589); the fact that the mission was free of debt; and that the daily travel to the parish and the time involved in doing so took its toll on the priest's health who made the trip. Although the resources of the parish were limited, Bishop Hickey agreed to set the mission off and appointed Fr. Joseph Boehr, C.S.Sp., an Alsatian-born priest, who spoke Portuguese and English as well as his native French, as Holy Ghost's first pastor in November 1923. Fr. Boehr had come to St.

---

[67]   O'Rorke to Hickey, no date, PChA..

[68]   *Providence Visitor*, February 11, 1937. The Holy Ghost Fathers first arranged for a mass at Sakonnet in 1913.

Anthony's in 1909. The first charge given him by Fr. Rooney was that of
St. Catherine's, Little Compton. When Fr. Barros arrived, Fr. Boehr took
charge of St. Christopher's until 1918, when Fr. Rooney, who had himself
been serving Holy Ghost, then gave responsibility for St. Christopher's
to Fr. Boehr. At Holy Ghost, Fr. Boehr preached each Sunday in English
and French. Although Fr. Boehr received Bishop Hickey's approval for the
rectory plans he submitted in December 1923, it would be almost a year
before construction of the rectory at 117 Hooper Street began and January
1926 before he moved in.[69]

ST. CHRISTOPHER, *Tiverton*

Although Fr. O'Rorke proved a good administrator, his health and age
was such that by 1925, it was evident that he could no longer continue at
St. Anthony's. Accordingly, Bishop Hickey, early in 1925, appointed him
pastor of St. Christopher's, Tiverton, and made Fr. Louis J. Ward, C.S.Sp.,
who had been appointed an assistant at St. Anthony's after Fr. Barros left,
pastor of St. Anthony's. Fr. O'Rorke appointment to St. Christopher's
came also as the result of the initiative of the people who attended that
church. Eighty-five families, who lived near the Tiverton end of the Stone
Bridge, made up the permanent nucleus of the parish. As was true of the
people of Holy Ghost, North Tiverton, the people of St. Christopher's
were anxious to have a priest residing in their midst. Fr. O'Rorke's first
concern as pastor of St. Christopher's was to provide a rectory for the new
parish. At the time, the Giezok Estate at the corner of Main Road and
North Avenue was for sale. The parishioners of St. Christopher's urged Fr.
O'Rorke to inquire about purchasing the estate even though it was a small
distance from the church. After approaching Bishop Harkins on the matter, the bishop had architect Ambrose Murphy inspect the property and
prepare a report for him. The property was large enough for the parish to
move the church to the estate, if they so chose, and to accommodate any
future needs of the parish. On the basis of Mr. Murphy's report, Bishop
Hickey gave Fr. O'Rorke permission to buy the property in August 1925.
Fr. O'Rorke took up residence in the house, which its previous owner had
been renovating, in December.[70]

ST. MADELEINE SOPHIE, *Tiverton*

Because of Fr. O'Rorke's age and poor health, he was limited in the
ministry he could do. By the 1920s, there was a significant number of
both English and Portuguese-speaking Catholics in the Four Corners
section of Tiverton, which was part of St. Christopher's. Because of Fr.

---

[69]   Henry Perrault et al. to Hickey, January 22, 1923; Bishop Hickey's Diary, November 23;
      December 14, 1923; *Providence Visitor*, February 18, 1937.
[70]   Murphy to Hickey, May 26, 1925, PChA.; *Providence Visitor*, March 4, 1937.

O'Rorke's limitations, Fr. Emil Knaebel, C.S.Sp., Fr. Ward's assistant at St. Anthony's, who had taken over the care of the St. Catherine's mission, Little Compton, in 1924, eventually assumed responsibility for the spiritual care of the Catholics at the Four Corners as well. In December 1926, Bishop Hickey bought property on Lake Road, a mile and a half from Tiverton Four Corners. The property included an old school house. Fr. Knaebel used the school house as a place for mass on Sundays and Holydays until 1927, when he negotiated a favorable price with the Circle A Products Corporation for a prefabricated church which he had erected on the land. When the building was finished, he dedicated the new church to St. Madeleine Sophie. The old school continued in use as a parish hall.

ST. CATHERINE, *Little Compton*

In June 1930, Bishop Hickey set off St. Catherine's, Little Compton, as a separate parish, from St. Anthony's. When he did so, St. Madeleine's became a mission of St. Catherine's. In anticipation of the change, Fr. Knaebel began building a rectory next to St. Catherine's on Willow Street in Little Compton, in September 1929. When the new parish was formally erected and Fr. Knaebel was made its pastor, he moved into the new rectory on June 2.[71]

The Increasing Need for More Portuguese Parishes

On Sunday, May 14, 1919, after it was announced that Fr. O'Rorke was confirmed as pastor of St. Anthony's over Fr. Barros, Manuel S. Lopes of Newport and three other Portuguese members of St. Anthony's parish wrote to Bishop Hickey to express their sadness that the bishop had chosen to appoint as pastor a priest who did not understand a word of Portuguese, the language of "95 per cent" of his parishioners. When the Holy Ghost Fathers transferred Fr. Barros from St. Anthony's in late 1921, his departure prompted another petition from Mr. Lopes, who wrote the bishop again in November 1921, lamenting the fact that there was then "no priest in Newport or in this vicinity, who speaks or understands the Portuguese language." According to the petition, the result was that the Portuguese were unable to go to confession in St. Anthony's or an adjacent parish; that there had been a falloff in attendance at mass and the sacraments; and that there was much dissatisfaction among the parishioners. Fr. Barros' return to St. Anthony's sometime after February 1922 helped to alleviate the situation for a time, but, by this time, he was considering leaving the Holy Ghost Fathers. When he eventually did leave the order and the parish, his departure prompted another petition for a Portuguese priest in May 1923.

---

71 *Providence Visitor*, February 25, 1937; Arthur MacDonaldson to Rev. Peter A. Foley, April 2, 1927; Arthur MacDonaldson to Knaebel, April 4, 1937, PChA.

Although Fr. Louis J. Ward, who had become pastor of St. Anthony's after Fr. O'Rorke, had learned some Portuguese while working as a missionary in Africa, the petitioners complained that Fr. Ward had only a limited speaking knowledge of the language. On June 4, 1923, Bishop Hickey replied to Mr. Ferreira, the chairman of the committee that had sent the May 1923 petition. The bishop expressed his regret that he did not have a Portuguese priest to serve and that he had no immediate prospect of securing one. He asked for patience until such time as he could find a suitable replacement for Fr. Barros.[72]

Among the "detrimental spiritual conditions" within the Portuguese communities, which Mr. Ferreira and those who also signed the June 1923 petition referred to, was the fact that the contemporary Portuguese government's attack on the Catholic Church in Portugal was having an impact on the Portuguese in the United States as well. In September 1922, a Baptist minister and his colleagues began circulating pamphlets in Providence, Pawtucket, Warren and Bristol, and the Riverpoint section of Warwick, attacking Catholic beliefs and inviting anyone interested in hearing the true gospel to a meeting on October 1 at the Union Baptist Church at the corner of East and John streets in Providence's Fox Point section. In June 1923, Baptists went door to door in Fox Point distributing a flyer inviting all interested to a series of talks to be given by Joao G. Loja of Cambridge, Massachusetts, in the same church. When Fr. Rebello's assistant at Holy Rosary, Fr. Alberto Duarte wrote a series of "Religious Chats," which appeared in a local newspaper, Mr. Loja responded by challenging Fr. Duarte to a debate on a series of questions that he proposed. At least two of the lay leaders of the Portuguese communities sent copies and translations of the various pamphlets and leaflets to Bishop Hickey.[73]

In the other parts of the state where the Portuguese population was growing, Bishop Hickey would have to rely mainly on Portuguese-born priests, recruited primarily from the Azores, to serve the needs of the Portuguese people. While Newport and West Warwick had sizable and growing Portuguese populations as early as 1905, Bishop Hickey would create the first Portuguese parish under his administration in Pawtucket. According to the 1905 census, only fifty-four persons of Portuguese birth lived in Pawtucket. The first Portuguese to settle in Pawtucket settled in the area of Pleasant Street, on the west side of the Pawtucket River, in one of the older sections of St. Mary's Parish. Others settled in a scattered pattern through the Woodlawn and Fairlawn sections in the newly created St. Edward's parish. A particularly large concentration of Portuguese settled near Power Road. The nearest Catholic church to their homes was the

---

72   Manuel S. Lopes et. al. to Hickey, May 14, 1919; November 19, 1921; Frank E. Ferreira et al., to Hickey, May 29, 1923; Hickey to Ferreira, June 4, 1923, PChA; *Providence Visitor*, February 11, 1937.
73   Charles A. Sylvia to Hickey, June 21, 24, 1923; Humberto T. Amaral to Hickey, December 8, 1924, PChA.

French-speaking parish in Marieville, the Presentation of the Blessed Virgin Mary. By 1915, the number of Portuguese in the city had risen to 379 and grew yet larger as the result of a shift in population caused by the First World War. The onset of the war in Europe in 1914 led to a substantial increase in orders from the allied nations for a variety of American-made products. America's own entrance into the war in 1917 further increased the demands for industrial production.[74]

ST. ANTHONY, *Pawtucket*

By September 1918, the number of Portuguese who had settled in Pawtucket was such that Bishop Harkins sent Fr. Alfred U. Jette to St. Mary's, Pawtucket, where he was given the responsibility of caring for the spiritual needs of the Portuguese in that parish. Fr. Jette was one of two French-Canadian seminarians whom Bishop Harkins had sent to the Portuguese National College in Rome in order to learn Portuguese. Through some mixup, his name was not on the register of the college when he arrived and there was no room for him. After consultation with his contracts in Rome, Bishop Harkins found a place for him in the Pio Latino, the Latin American Seminary, in Rome, which also offered Portuguese studies. Following his ordination in August 1917, Bishop Harkins had assigned Jette temporarily to St. Cecilia's Parish, Pawtucket, before appointing him as an assistant at St. Mary's. Fr. Jette offered mass for the Portuguese in the basement church in St. Mary's. After only a year at St. Mary's, Fr. Jette was appointed an assistant at Notre Dame in Central Falls. Despite his studies in Rome, Fr. Jette had not acquired a sufficient command of the language to preach effectively, although he could read the traditional announcements at mass and preach simple sermons. After moving to Central Falls, his service to the Portuguese was limited to visiting the sick.[75]

Whatever language difficulties Fr. Jette had were complicated by the fact that, like the French Canadians before them, the Portuguese preferred to have priests of their own language and culture. Like the French-Canadian bishops, the Portuguese bishops did not have an abundance of clergy that they could make available to the American bishops who asked for their assistance. In February 1920, at the request of Fr. Francisco Vieira, pastor of St. Elizabeth's, Bristol, who was anxious to have an as-

---

[74]   E. James Aissis, "Immigration to Rhode Island, 1898 to 1972: The Major Trends," (Seminar paper prepared for Dr. Patrick T. Conley, 1973). In 1920, 2,127 Portuguese immigrants listed Rhode Island as their destination and, in 1921, 2,569 gave Rhode Island as their destination. In 1922, the number fell to 148. Cf. M. Rachel Cunha, Susan A. Pacheco, and Beth Pereira Wolfson, "The Portuguese in Rhode Island: A History," Providence: Rhode Island Ethnic Heritage Pamphlet Series, 1983, Table II, 8. Cf. also, Louise Lamphere, *From Working Daughters of Working Mothers*, 165–68. The first Portuguese to settle in the Blackstone Valley was Joseph Gumano, who moved to the valley from Fox Point shortly after 1888. Cf. *Providence Journal*, March 30, 1938.

[75]   *Providence Visitor*, September 3, 1936; "St. Anthony's Church, Pawtucket: Seventy-Fifth Anniversary, 1926–2001" (Privately printed, 2001), 17–18.

sistant, Bishop Hickey wrote to Bishop Manuel Damasceno de Costa, the Bishop of Angra, Terceira, Azores, asking him to release one of his priests, Fr. Francisco Vaz Diniz, for service at St. Elizabeth's. Bishop de Costa granted Bishop Hickey's request. Fr. Vaz Diniz was almost sixty when he came to Bristol and unfortunately died suddenly of complications following a heart operation in December 1922. In his letter to Bishop da Costa asking for Fr. Vaz Diniz's services, Hickey stressed the need he perceived for securing Portuguese-speaking priests to serve the growing Portuguese population in the diocese. Like Bishop Harkins before him, Bishop Hickey stressed to his episcopal colleague the need not only for sufficient priests but for good priests.[76]

The problem of finding suitable priests to serve the Portuguese population of the state would only compound the problem of building a church for them in Pawtucket. If the Portuguese families living in the vicinity of Power Road wanted to go to mass in a Portuguese church, they had to walk to the corner of Mineral Spring and Smithfield avenues in order to catch a trolley to go in Providence and attend mass at Holy Rosary in Fox Point. Along the way, they would be joined by a group of Portuguese who lived on Seneca Avenue, at the Providence-Pawtucket line. On March 27, 1922, when he met with Bishop Hickey in regard to repairs to Holy Rosary church, Fr. Antonio Rebello, the pastor, brought up the matter of the Portuguese living in St. Mary's and St. Edward's parishes. Following Fr. Rebello's visit, Bishop Hickey wrote in his diary, "Pawtucket Portuguese census after Easter in St. Mary's & St. Edward's."[77]

Within three days of Fr. Rebello's visit, a Portuguese priest, Fr. Francis Vincent, who wished to leave the Friars of the Atonement at Graymoor, New York and join a diocese, met with Bishop Hickey to apply for admission into the Diocese of Providence. While he considered the matter, Bishop Hickey sent Fr. Vincent to live with Fr. Jose Lopes at St. Francis Xavier parish in East Providence. When Fr. Lopes and Fr. Vincent called on Bishop Hickey a few weeks later on April 21, Bishop Hickey asked Fr. Vincent to take a census of the Portuguese families living in Pawtucket, Central Falls and the Cumberland community of Valley Falls. Fr. Vincent returned to the bishop's office on July 25 with his report.[78]

In the end, the initiative for a Portuguese parish in Pawtucket came from neither Fr. Rebello nor Bishop Hickey but from the Portuguese in Pawtucket themselves. On a Sunday in 1923, several of the heads of the Portuguese families who lived in area of Power Road, agreed that the Portuguese families in the area were numerous enough to have their own church, which would spare them the ride into Providence. They agreed to meet the following Sunday to discuss the matter. While only twenty-eight

---

[76]   Hickey to de Costa, February 18, 1920, PChA; *Providence Visitor*, December 1, 1922.
[77]   "St. Anthony's," p. 19; Bishop Hickey's Diary, March 27, 1922.
[78]   Bishop Hickey's Diary, April 21; July 25, 1922.

people attended the initial meeting, their enthusiasm was such that they agreed to each contact other Portuguese families to stir up their interest and gain their support. To attract the attention of families that they did not know personally, the instigators of the idea placed an ad in English in the *Pawtucket Times* and one in Portuguese in a Portuguese paper announcing their intentions. Those at the meeting agreed that they needed to consult with Fr. Rebello to secure his support. After many more people showed up for a second meeting on the question of a parish, those present at the meeting agreed to ask Fr. Rebello to write to the bishop to request a meeting with representatives that they chose to present a petition for a parish of their own. Bishop Hickey agreed to the idea of a meeting and Bernardino Ramos of Atwood Avenue and Antonio de Melo of Mineral Spring Avenue, along with Pedro Pimental, a brother in law of Mr. Ramos, who, as a college student, was fluent in English as well as Portuguese, went to Providence to present the bishop with the list of names and donations that they had collected. At the end of the meeting with the three men, Bishop Hickey agreed to the formation of the new parish, which would be dedicated to St. Anthony. However, one final part of the establishment needed to be worked out. Bishop Hickey had to find a priest to undertake the work of establishing the parish.[79]

The problem of staffing a new Portuguese church in Pawtucket was solved when Fr. Barros decided to leave the Holy Ghost Fathers. Barros had met with Bishop Hickey in July 1922 to discuss the possibility of joining the Diocese of Providence. When in February 1923, Fr. Barros was still resolved to leave the order, although reluctant to leave the congregation at Portsmouth, Bishop Hickey gave him two more months to think over his decision. Barros took only two weeks. On February 19, 1922, Hickey appointed him assistant at St. Elizabeth's, Bristol. When in July 1923, Bishop sought to honor the request of the Portuguese in Pawtucket and Central Falls for a new parish, he chose to give the task of forming it to Barros and formally appointed him a pastor on August 6. A week later, after he had met with Fr. Rebello, Bishop Hickey expanded the mission to also include the Portuguese in the Valley Falls section of Cumberland.[80]

As had Fr. Jette before him, Fr. Barros found in Fr. John C. Tennian, the pastor of St. Mary's a generous supporter of his work. Once again, Fr. Tennian made available to him, as he had to Fr. Jette, the use of the basement church at St. Mary's and invited him to stay at St. Mary's rectory while he was organizing the new parish. In addition to the help he received from Fr. Tennian, Fr. Barros also turned frequently to Bishop Hickey for advice. As early as September 15, 1923, he met with the bishop to discuss the question of acquiring a church and a rectory and did so again on

79 "St. Anthony's," p. 19.
80 Bishop Hickey's Diary, July 24; September 12, 1922; February 6, 19; July 24; August 11, 1923; Hickey to Barros, August 6, 1923, PChA.

November 9. Fr. Barros's first task was to take a census of his new parishioners. The work took him a year. In a letter to Bishop Hickey dated September 22, 1924, he reported that there were 321 Portuguese families in Pawtucket or 1,648 souls. Of this number approximately 1,300 came from Portugal itself, while between 350 and 400 came from the Azores. The immigrants from the Azores lived mainly in the area of Power Road, while the immigrants from Portugal itself, the Continentals, lived throughout the city. As other Portuguese priests attested, the Continentals, who lived closest to St. Mary's, did not regularly attend mass, while the Azoreans, who lived the farthest from St. Mary's, did. In spite of his best efforts, Fr. Barros confessed that he was not able to immediately change the situation. Since it was difficult and expensive to find a suitable site for a church in the built up areas where the Continentals lived, Fr. Barros asked the bishop's permission to search for a site further out from the core of the city that would be about half-way between the homes of the Continentals and those of the ninety or so Azorean families that did attend mass.[81]

After Bishop Hickey agreed to the plan, Fr. Barros eventually secured a small site on Lawn Avenue in Pawtucket's Woodlawn section, which was a short distance from the intersection of Mineral Spring and Lonsdale avenues, and thus convenient to the trolley lines. Under Bishop Hickey's direction, Fr. Barros engaged architect John F. Hogan to design a church that combined Gothic and Roman features, with a capacity of four hundred, and was to be built of brick, tile and stucco. While Mr. Hogan prepared the plans, Fr. Barros and his parishioners continued their fund-raising activities. Two of their major projects were a bazaar for the benefit of the new parish in the basement of St. Mary's church in November 1923 and a concert in the State Theater in Pawtucket, which the parish presented in October 1925. Both of these events were well supported by the Catholics of other nationalities in Pawtucket.[82]

Fund raising was not one of Fr. Barros' talents. On November 1, 1925, he wrote to Bishop Hickey that the committee he had placed in charge of another parish bazaar had recently told him that they could not continue to work on it, as they could not get the support of the majority of the parish. Barros suggested that Bishop Hickey rethink the organization of the parish and, rather than a separate entity, it might become a mission of St. Francis Xavier Parish in East Providence, which was in a flourishing condition, or some other parish. However, Bishop Hickey was not to change his mind. He was in a better position to provide funds than priestly personnel. The bishop used diocesan funds to purchase the site for the new church on Lawn Avenue and took out a building permit in his own name. Ground was broken for the new church on December 15, 1925. Shortly

81   Bishop Hickey's Diary, September 15; November 9, 16; December 11, 1923; Barros to Hickey,
     September 22, 1924, PChA.
82   *Providence Visitor*, November 29, 1923; October 16, 1925.

after the new building was ready for use, Bishop Hickey dedicated it under the protection of St. Anthony, on Sunday, September 19, 1926, in a ceremony during which seven hundred people squeezed into the building and three hundred more stood outside. In addition to the church, the parish acquired a three-tenement house adjoining the building site, which was renovated to serve as a rectory.[83]

OUR LADY OF FATIMA, *Cumberland*

Until 1933, the 100 Portuguese families living in Central Falls and the 200 in Valley Falls had to come to Pawtucket to hear mass in Portuguese. On October 22, 1933, Fr. Barros's successor, Fr. Albino Marques Martins, began offering a mass on Sundays in a rented hall in a three-story building at the corner of Broad and Meeting streets in Cumberland, just across the Blackstone River from Central Falls. The mission was dedicated to Our Lady of Fatima, the first mission dedicated to Our Lady under that title in the United States.[84]

ST. ANTHONY, *Riverpoint, West Warwick*

While St. Anthony's, Pawtucket was the first parish created under Bishop Hickey to serve the Portuguese, the Portuguese families in the Pawtuxet Valley had anticipated them by several years in asking for a parish of their own. While he was at St. Anthony's, Portsmouth, Fr. Barros had made regular visits to the Portuguese in the Pawtuxet Valley, who petitioned Bishop Harkins for a separate parish on March 6, 1915. In February 1918, Bishop Harkins sent the second of the two French-Canadians priests whom he had sent to Rome to learn Portuguese, Fr. Ovila Brouillette, to serve as an assistant at St. James, Arctic, in the recently created town of West Warwick. Fr. Brouillette's particular assignment was to serve the needs of the Portuguese in the Valley. Although Fr. Brouillette read the announcements at St. James in Portuguese as well as English, he regularly preached only in English, since most of his congregation would have been English-speaking. In June 1920, the Portuguese in the Riverpoint section renewed their petition to have a parish of their own in order that the majority of the Portuguese, who did not understand the English sermons, might enjoy the benefit of a Portuguese priest. The three petitioners were members of a committee delegated for the purpose of making the petition by the Holy Ghost Society in Riverpoint. They informed the bishop that, if he granted the petition

---

83 *Providence Visitor,* January 1; August 6; September 17, 1926; *Pawtucket Times*, September 18, 20, 1926; "St. Anthony's Church," 21–23.

84 *Providence Visitor*, September 3, 1936.

they made in the name of the Portuguese of Riverpoint, they would immediately take steps for the erection of a church.[85]

While there is no mention in the petition of the name of the organization which delegated the three men who made up the committee, Bishop Hickey was kept well informed about the Portuguese community in West Warwick by Fr. William J. Keefe, the pastor of St. James and St. Mary's, Arctic and Crompton, and by Fr. Thomas McGrath, the pastor of SS. Peter and Paul, Phenix. He properly deduced that the petition was instigated by the local Holy Ghost Society. The experiences that many of the Portuguese priests in the diocese had had with the various Holy Ghost Societies had not been all positive. Fr. Barros, for one, believed that the men who made up the leadership of the societies in Rhode Island had been influenced by the same currents of thought that were circulating at that time in France and Portugal, where the lay governments were seeking control "of the church property, of church activities and influence for their own personal benefit [to the exclusion of the clergy]." Writing in 1926, Fr. Barros compared the aims of the leaders of the Holy Ghost fraternities with what he perceived to be those of the Sentinallists. To his mind, they wanted "to bring their Bishops and Pastors under their control in financial and other matters." On his part, Bishop Hickey, as he frequently did in similar circumstances where the petitioners had not followed the proper protocol which required that they go first to their parish priest, chose not even to respond to the petition.[86]

In the early spring of 1922, the same three gentlemen went to Providence to renew their petition. The priest who received them at the Chancery Office suggested that they put their request for an interview with Bishop Hickey in writing. Since Bishop Hickey had left for Rome on April 26 and did not return until early July, they believed it better to wait a few weeks before they sent their letter. Since they recognized their limitations as writers of English, one of the three asked his neighbor, Patrick Quinn, a local lawyer and political leader, to write the letter of request for them. Apparently the gentlemen signed the letter without reading it closely. The committee's interview with Bishop Hickey did not go well. Unknown to them, Bishop Hickey, at the time of their meeting, was in the midst of his dealings with the French Canadians, who wished to see a Catholic Hospital opened in Central Falls under their rather than the bishop's control. Since the Portuguese delegation's first petition in 1920 had hinted at lay control of any prospective church in Riverpoint and, since they were most likely unaware of the difficulties the American Catholic Church had experienced during the nineteenth century with the Trustee Movement, they were "dumfound-

---

85   Bishop Harkins' Diary, March 6, 1915; Frank Costa, Antonio Miller and Frank J. Medeiros to Hickey, June 14, 1920. The citizens of Warwick approved the division of their town into Warwick and West Warwick in 1912 and the General Assembly chartered the Town of West Warwick in 1913.
86   Barros to Hickey, April 20, 1926, PChA.

ed" [their word] by Bishop Hickey's attitude towards their petition. Since the nineteenth century, the common practice — at least in the dioceses of Hartford and Providence — was for the bishop to purchase the site for a new church in consultation with the laity, as was the case in the creation of St. Anthony's in Pawtucket. In their response to the bishop on September 25, the West Warwick committee attributed the bishop's rejection of their petition to the manner in which Mr. Quinn had put forward their request in the letter he had written for them. They explained the circumstances under which they had asked Mr. Quinn to write the letter and apologized for any affront they had unintentionally caused the bishop.[87]

In spite of the fact that Bishop Hickey refused to give the committee of the Holy Ghost Society permission to proceed with the acquisition of a site for a church out of the funds the society had been collecting since they first approached Bishop Harkins, the members of the Holy Ghost Society believed that it was their right to have a Portuguese church and pastor. They formed a new committee, whose spokesperson was Humberto F. Amaral, a Phenix merchant, who lived in Riverpoint. Mr. Amaral made another call on Bishop Hickey on October 31, 1922. Like the previous delegation's, Mr. Amaral's experience was not a pleasant one. Among at least one segment of the Portuguese people in the Valley, Bishop Hickey was later referred to as "William the Terrible, Bishop of Providence." When Mr. Amaral was also unsuccessful in securing the bishop's permission for Holy Ghost Society to proceed with their proposal, the society elected to go ahead on its own. Acting as trustees of the Holy Ghost Society, the three gentlemen who first approached Bishop Hickey with a petition for a church, purchased two lots for a building site at the corner of Maple Avenue and Pleasant on November 20 and 21, 1922.[88]

After having had an unpleasant experience when he called on Bishop Hickey in October, Mr. Amaral, as secretary of the committee of the Holy Ghost Society charged with seeing a church built, chose to write to the bishop to renew the society's request for a parish, a request they now had been making for nine years. As Mr. Amaral believed the bishop knew, the committee was ready to proceed with the laying of a foundation for the new church during the next month. He asked the bishop to send them a Portuguese priest to take charge of the funds they had collected for the building. Amaral wished the bishop success in his fund raising drive for Catholic high schools and prayed that he might grant them the happiness of seeing their hopes realized. In closing, he related that, because of the stand he and the committee had taken, he personally had been accosted on the street by one of the two local pastors and threatened. Nevertheless, he was determined to persist, because like the bishop, he felt he was doing

[87] The Committee: Antonio Miller, Frank Costa, John King to Hickey, September 25, 1922, PChA.
[88] Bishop Hickey's Diary, October 31, 1922; Copies of the deeds as recorded in the Warwick Land records are found in the Diocesan Archives; Amaral to Keough, February 20, 1939; Antonio P. Chadinha to Bishop Francis P. Keough, February 5, 1940, PChA.

God's work. When his first letter went unanswered, Amaral wrote again at the end of May. In this letter, he reported that the Portuguese in River-point were coming to the opinion that "Church authorities don't consider the Portuguese race respectable to deal with" and once again asked for a response.[89]

The frustration of Amaral and the other trustees of the Holy Ghost Society was further underlined in the following month when the French-Canadian parish in Arctic (or Jericho, the alternate name for the village) celebrated its fiftieth anniversary as an ethnic parish. Since Bishop Hickey continued to refuse to respond to their request for permission to begin work on a church, the trustees decided to proceed with the work without his permission. Mr. Amaral would characterize their motives as enthusiasm or zeal to have a church of their own, but to others, the committee's action constituted defiance of authority. Before they did commit themselves to undertaking the construction of the church, the committee in charge of the project made one last effort to secure Bishop Hickey's consent. In the face of a rumor that the Portuguese in West Warwick were divided as to whether or not they wanted a church of their own, those who favored a parish circulated a petition, which several hundred of the Portuguese of West Warwick signed. The committee submitted the signatures on the petition along with another letter restating their request. In their letter, the committee referred to the fact that they had signed a contract for the build-ing of a 40 by 100 foot church on the land they had previously bought. When there was once again official silence, the contractors began work on the church. On October 3, 1923, Bishop Hickey drove down to Phenix to inspect the "so-called Portuguese church" and the next day had a conver-sation about the situation with Fr. McGrath.[90]

In their letters to Hickey, the Portuguese committee continually repeated their offer to turn over the land they had bought and the funds they had collected to any priest that Bishop Hickey appointed as their pastor. During the course of October 1923, Bishop Hickey did lay out the conditions on which he would accept the land owned by the Holy Ghost Society when a group of Portuguese attempted to act as intermediaries. Nothing substan-tial resulted from the discussions held.[91]

While Bishop Hickey was quite willing to see ethnic parishes created, his hesitancy in the case of the request of the Portuguese in West Warwick was prompted, first of all, by the lack of Portuguese clergy and, secondly, by his unwillingness to allow a group of Portuguese to dictate diocesan policy any more than he was willing to allow the Sentinellists to do so. Contrary to the suspicions of the many of the Portuguese in West War-wick, Hickey did have their best interests at heart. On March 28, 1924,

---

89   Amaral to Hickey, May 7, 28, 1923, PChA.
90   Amaral et al. to Hickey, August 11, 1923, PChA; Bishop Hickey's Diary, October 3, 4, 1923.
91   A copy of the bishop's terms is dated October 22, 1923 and is found in the Diocesan Chancery Archives.

Bishop Hickey met with Fr. Thomas McGrath, pastor of SS. Peter and Paul, within whose parish boundaries about 800 of the Portuguese of the valley lived. The two sought a way resolving the impasse that had developed. In April 1922, as the result of their meeting, Bishop Hickey appointed Fr. Francisco Vincent, the former Graymoor friar, whom he had appointed as assistant at Holy Rosary, Providence, assistant to Fr. McGrath at SS. Peter and Paul, with the specific responsibility of caring for the Portuguese of the parish "until further notice."[92]

The trustees of the Holy Ghost Society took Fr. Vincent's appointment as a positive sign. On April 11, 1924, they signed a mortgage note with the Centreville Savings Bank for $10,000 in order to raise funds to finish the church they had begun building. The committee also sent representatives to Washington to lay their petition before Archbishop Fumasoni-Biondi, the Apostolic Delegate. In May 1924, they engaged a Portuguese-American lawyer, Joseph S. Neves, to undertake, in Neves's words, "an honest endeavor to persuade [Bishop Hickey] to create a separate parish for [them] and to accept the Church which they had built." As he later told Bishop Hickey, Neves recognized "that they had seriously blundered when they purchased their land and contracted for the building of a church in willful disobedience to the Bishop." But he also recognized that "a pernicious campaign was being waged by enemies of the Roman Catholic Church to persuade these people to desert their Faith and declare themselves an independent Church. He resolved his hesitancy at acting as their lawyer by exacting from them a solemn promise that they would never desert their Faith nor entertain any thought of an independent Church.[93]

On his part, Fr. Vincent, who was anxious to be appointed a pastor, also encouraged Mr. Neves to represent the Portuguese of West Warwick and not to charge the committee for his services. He promised him, that if he was appointed pastor of the new church, he would regard his bill as a debt owed by the church. Vincent advised him not to go to Bishop Hickey but to the Apostolic Delegate in Washington. According, Mr. Neves also went to Washington to plead the Portuguese case with the delegate. On May 24, 1924, as was his custom in such cases, Archbishop Fumasoni-Biondi wrote to Bishop Hickey to inform him of the visits he had received. He acknowledged that the Portuguese were at fault for defying Hickey's authority, but asked if something might be done, especially in the light of fact that the Portuguese might be "drawn into an heretical sect." In his reply to the delegate, Bishop Hickey asked him if he might forward a copy of the assertions made by the representatives of the Portuguese in Riverpoint, together with the signatures attached, so that he might respond to the specific points. In his response, Hickey assured the delegate that there was no

---

[92] Hickey to McGrath, March 28, 1924, PChA.
[93] A copy of the promissory note endorsed by the committee is found in the Diocesan Chancery Archives; Neves to Hickey, November 7, 1925, PChA.

real danger whatever of heresy. In his view, it was "merely a question of whether a few business leaders can force upon the Bishop a debt they contracted in a spirit of defiance, mortgaging their own property to do so." He further assured the delegate that the religious needs of the Portuguese in Riverpoint were already being met by two priests, one who was Portuguese and the other, a man who spoke Portuguese fluently. As the delegate had no documents to send Hickey, he expressed his gratitude to learn that there was no danger of the Portuguese being drawn away and conveyed his confidence that Bishop Hickey would do all that was possible for their welfare.[94]

Mr. Neves' trip to Washington and pressure from other sources had their impact. When, during the first week in November 1924, the delegate came to Rhode Island to lay the cornerstone of the new La Salle Academy, he met with Mr. Neves along with Mr. Amaral, at Providence College. At the meeting, the delegate assured the two men that Bishop Hickey was going to accept and bless the new church at Riverpoint. However, he asked the two, in Mr. Amaral's recollection of the meeting, "to promise not to reveal that the Bishop was forced to accept the church," but to say that the Bishop "had come to the conclusion that the time was ripe and the faith of our people had convinced him that the best thing to do was to give us a parish." Within a few days of the delegate's visit to Providence, Bishop Hickey received a letter from Cardinal Gaetano DeLai, the Secretary of the Congregation for the Council, informing Hickey that the Congregation had received information that the Portuguese in Riverpoint were without spiritual assistance and that Hickey had prevented them from building a church.[95]

On December 2, 1924, as Canon Law required him to do, Bishop Hickey asked the diocesan consultors for their opinion on the advisability of establishing a Portuguese parish at Riverpoint. The consultors agreed to support any action that Hickey thought advisable. As the situation was delicate one, the bishop's first step towards establishing a parish was the appointment of Fr. Vincent as a trustee of the Catholic Bishop of Providence with the authority to collect funds on behalf of the proposed parish. The bishop asked Frs. Keefe and McGrath to make the announcement of Fr. Vincent's appointment at all the masses on Sunday, December 21.[96]

Fr. Vincent was born in Boston of Portuguese immigrant parents in February 1888 and had studied for the priesthood in the Azores and in the United States. He was ordained a priest in St. Patrick's Cathedral, New York, for the Graymoor Friars, on May 29, 1920. Fr. Vincent's appointment as trustee did not meet with the approval of all the Portuguese of

[94] Fumasoni-Biondi to Hickey, May 24, 1924; Hickey to Fumasoni-Bioindi, May 27, 1924; Fumasoni-Biondi to Hickey, May 29, 1924, PChA.
[95] Amaral to Keough, February 20, 1939; DeLai to Hickey, November 12, 1924, PChA.
[96] Diocesan Consultor Minutes, December 2, 1924; Hickey to Vincent, December 19, 1924; Hickey to Keefe and McGrath, December 19, 1924, PChA.

the Valley. Three days after the announcement of Fr. Vincent as trustee was made in the Valley, twelve people signed a letter to Hickey informing him of their reservations about having Vincent as their pastor. They were concerned about his limited knowledge of Portuguese, which caused him to say things that were unintelligible and incomprehensible. More seriously, they informed the bishop that Fr. Vincent, even before he had been appointed to SS. Peter and Paul's, had urged the Portuguese of the Valley to create a public scandal in order to force Bishop Hickey to meet their request for a parish. After arriving in Phenix, they asserted, he had sought to settle the conflict by attempting to persuade Mr. Amaral and the trustees of the Holy Ghost Society to sell the building that they had built to Fr. McGrath for use as a parish center, an action the writers saw as a betrayal of the Portuguese people. The trustees of the Holy Ghost Society, however, were not inclined to sell. If the building would not be used as a church, they would use it as hall dedicated to St. Michael.[97]

Bishop Hickey might have had his own reservations concerning Fr. Vincent, if only in view of his relative inexperience. In reply to another letter from the delegate, dated Dec. 31, 1924, in which the delegate again called Hickey's attention to "the matter of the Portuguese of Riverpoint" and in which he suggested the names of two bishops to whom Hickey could write in order to secure the assistance of a Portuguese priest, Hickey responded that he had already written to the Bishop of Angra, the Azores, inquiring about two priests, who had indicated that they were willing to go to the United States. He told that delegate that the bishop's first reply was not favorable, but he hoped for a more positive response to his second letter. Hickey also conveyed to the delegate, in his response on January 3, 1925, the news that the trustees of the Holy Ghost Society had turned over the deed of the property they had bought to the diocese and that Fr. Vincent was collecting the balance due on the debt.[98]

Anxious as he was not to suggest that the leaders of the movement for a Portuguese church in Riverpoint had "conquered authority by diplomacy," Bishop Hickey waited until May 1925 before appointing Fr. Vincent, not pastor, but "Administrator of the established Mission of St. Michael's at Riverpoint, R.I." Since he had few other options and because of the pressure put on him to establish a Portuguese parish in Phenix, Bishop Hickey had little choice but to name Fr. Vincent to the new parish. Fr. Vincent labored along with his parishioners in preparing the building built by the Holy Ghost Society for its new use. Vincent offered mass in the new church for the first time on June 14, 1925.[99]

On the day the new church opened, Fr. Brouillette received a telephone

[97]   Maria E. Mancinha et al. to Hickey, December 24, 1924; Affidavit of Joseph E. Nune, November 11, 1925, PChA.
[98]   Fumasoni-Biondi to Hickey, December 31, 1924; Hickey to Fumasoni-Biondi, January 3, 1925, PChA.
[99]   *Providence Visitor*, June 12, 19, 1925.

call asking him to go over to Riverpoint. As he was approaching the River-point Congregational Church, he noticed a large group of people gathered there along with a band. Led by the band, the crowd accompanied Fr. Brouillette to Odd Fellows' Hall on Bridge Street, where they held a reception to thank him for his eight-years-service to the Portuguese of Riverpoint and presented him with a watch, fountain pen, shaving set and clock.[100]

As was true in Pawtucket, funds to pay off the remaining debt on the new church in Riverpoint came from a variety of sources. In July 1925, the Portuguese Club of Riverpoint donated the proceeds from its annual lawn festival to help complete the church and, in July 1926, Fr. Vincent organized a very successful social and entertainment in Forester's Hall. On the first Sunday of August 1925, the Portuguese Society, which announced as one of its goals the raising of a fund to erect a statue in the new church in holding their recent festival, held its first procession associated with the church. During his first few months as pastor, Fr. Vincent continued to live in SS. Peter and Paul rectory, until the parish purchased a house at 27 Woodside Avenue and renovated it for rectory purposes. Bishop Hickey dedicated the new church on Armistice Day, November 11, 1926, not under the title of St. Michael's, but under the title of St. Anthony's.[101]

Much of what transpired in the movement to establish St. Anthony's, Riverpoint, might have remained a private parish matter. However, after he had succeeded in his goal of being named pastor, Fr. Vincent began to shun the trustees of the Holy Ghost Society, who had been the driving force in pushing for the parish. When he first came to the Valley, Fr. Vincent had ignored Bishop Hickey's advice to stay away from Mr. Amaral and the other trustees. Instead, he had encouraged them in their campaign for a church and urged them and their lawyer, Mr. Neves, to send as many letters as possible to Bishop Hickey with copies to the Apostolic Delegate. Following his appointment as administrator in December 1924, however, Fr. Vincent, from the pulpit, took the sole credit for the success of the effort to create a parish in the Valley. When he refused to honor his word to pay Mr. Neves for his legal services to the Holy Ghost Society, the Society voted to pay Mr. Neves from the funds it had collected. After Fr. Vincent blocked the payment of the money, the president of the society sued the Centreville Savings Bank for the sum the society had designated. In view of the pending case, Mr. Neves wrote to Bishop Hickey on November 7, 1925, to ask his permission to defend himself. The bishop met with Mr. Neves. While he defended Fr. Vincent, Bishop Hickey offered Mr. Neves the opportunity to confront Fr. Vincent in a face to face meeting. Mr. Neves agreed to the meeting, but, in fairness to Fr. Vincent, prepared an affidavit detailing his complaint against him that Fr. Vincent might read in

100 *Pawtuxet Valley Daily Times,* June 16, 1925.
101 *Providence Visitor,* July 24, 31, 1925; November 5, 1926; April 29, 1937; *Pawtuxet Valley Daily Times,* June 8, 1925; November 12, 1926.

advance. There is no indication in the records that a meeting took place. As for the court case, both sides in the dispute filed papers, but the case never came to trial.[102]

Mr. Neves was not the only one who had complaints to make about Fr. Vincent. Mr. Amaral and other of the business leaders of the community had theirs, but, since their pleas had been ignored by Bishop Hickey in the past, they kept them to themselves. While he had his critics, Fr. Vincent also had his supporters and admirers. However, even priests who were familiar with Fr. Vincent's administration of St. Anthony's sympathized with the complaints of the parishioners. When one of them conveyed his concerns to Bishop Hickey, the bishop reportedly silenced him with the retort, "That's enough. They wanted a church. They have got it. Never mind the priest."[103]

JESUS SAVIOR, *Newport*

By 1919, the leaders of the Portuguese in Newport began organizing their countrymen there in hopes of persuading Bishop Harkins to establish a Portuguese parish for them. On April 11, 1921, a delegation of Portuguese from Newport called on Bishop Hickey with such a request. As with the Portuguese communities elsewhere, the chief obstacle to a favorable answer was the lack of a Portuguese priest to undertake the work of forming a parish. On December 2, 1924, at the same meeting during which he raised the question of establishing a Portuguese parish in West Warwick, Bishop Hickey also asked the consultors about the advisability of establishing a Portuguese parish in Newport. As they did with the West Warwick situation, the consultors consented to any action the bishop deemed advisable.[104]

In the summer of 1925, Bishop Hickey asked Fr. Antonio P. Lopes, the brother of Fr. Jose P. Lopes, the pastor of St. Francis Xavier, East Providence, where he was serving as an assistant, to take a census of the Portuguese Catholics in Newport and Middletown. Fr. Lopes first went to see Fr. Edward Higney, pastor of St. Joseph's, Newport, in whose parish the majority of the Portuguese in the Newport area lived. Fr. Higney introduced Fr. Lopes to the leaders of the Portuguese community, who then assisted Fr. Lopes in locating the Portuguese. They also began taking up a collection to support a new parish. Bishop Hickey challenged those who had asked for the parish to raise $25,000 as evidence that they could support one. The funds were raised in just a few days. By the end of October, Fr. Lopes, as representative of Bishop Hickey, had practically finished negotiations for the purchase of the former Keeson estate at the corner of

[102] Neves to Hickey, November 7, 11, 1925, PChA.
[103] Amaral to Keough, February 20, 1939, PChA.
[104] "Jesus Savior Parish, 75th Anniversary: 1926–2001 (Privately printed, 2001, 10; Bishop Hickey's Diary, April 11, 1922; Board of Consultor Minutes, December 2, 1924, PChA.

Broadway and Vernon avenues. On November 1, 1925, Fr. Lopes invited all the potential parishioners of a new parish to a meeting in the hall that the Portuguese Beneficent Association of Newport had built in 1920 on Fenner Avenue[105]

The members of the Portuguese Beneficent Association proved to be important benefactors of the new parish when they later voted unanimously to allow the new parish to use their hall free of charge. With the guidance of Joseph Venancio, members of the parish built pews and altars to furnish the hall. Mr. Venancio himself donated the main altar. Fr. Lopes celebrated mass in the hall for the first time on December 24, 1926. It would take the parishioners of the new parish three years before they were able to raise sufficient funds, in addition to the $25,000 they originally raised, in order to pay off the cost of the land Fr. Lopes had arranged to buy, and to build up enough monies to persuade Bishop Hickey to grant permission for Fr. Lopes to proceed with his plans for a church. The monies came from the usual collections and from such functions as suppers, card parties, and bazaars, which served the social as well as the financial needs of the parish. As the first step towards building the new church, Fr. Lopes had the house on the former Kesson property moved back along Vernon Avenue to provide a suitable building site on Broadway. After moving the house to its new location, Fr. Lopes had the building renovated for use as a rectory during the spring of 1927.[106]

Ground was broken for an Ambrose Murphy-designed church before the end of 1928. It was ready for use by Christmas Eve in 1929 so that Fr. Lopes celebrated midnight mass in the new church, three years after he first celebrated mass in the temporary one. Approximately 700 people crammed into the building for the first mass, while another 500 were unable to gain admittance. Bishop Hickey laid the cornerstone and blessed the new, red-brick building under the title of Jesus Savior on Sunday, July 13, 1930.[107]

The Frustration of the Hopes of Some of the Portuguese for a Second Parish in Portsmouth

While the establishment of Jesus Savior in Newport satisfied the desires of the Portuguese in Newport and Middletown, the ambition of the Portuguese in Portsmouth to have a Portuguese priest in their parish remained unfulfilled. On November 9, 1929, Jose de Arruda, of Glen Street, Portsmouth, wrote to Archbishop Fumasoni-Biondi as spokesperson for twenty-seven other parishioners of St. Anthony's, Portsmouth, asking

---

[105] "Jesus Savior Parish," 10–11; *Providence Visitor*, October 30, 1925; November 5, 1936.
[106] *Providence Visitor*, November 5, 1936.
[107] *The Newport News*, December 25, 28, 1929; July 14, 1930; *Newport Herald*, July 14, 1930.

the delegate's help in securing for a priest of Portuguese descent for their parish. In his letter, Arruda pointed out that, of the 305 families in St. Anthony's, 257 were of Portuguese descent. While he praised Fr. Ward as a good pastor whom all admired and respected, Arruda told the delegate that he and those he represent wished to have a priest whose Portuguese was better than Fr. Ward's, whose sermons in Portuguese they found difficult to understand. With the opening of the new Portuguese church in Newport, Arruda was concerned that many of the Portuguese in Portsmouth would choose to attend mass in a church where the pastor was one of their own.[108]

Archbishop Fumasoni-Biondi, who by now had a close relationship with Bishop Hickey, forwarded Mr. Arruda's letter to Bishop Hickey for his comments on the matter. In turn, Bishop Hickey forwarded Arruda's letter to Fr. Ward. In his December 2, 1929 reply to Bishop Hickey, Ward pointed out that the majority of the Portuguese in St. Anthony's did not share Mr. Arruda's point of view. Of those who signed the letter that Mr. Arruda sent to the delegate, Ward noted that most did not attend mass on a regular basis or contribute to the church's support. When Fr. Ward asked Mr. Arruda what about the younger generation among the Portuguese who spoke Portuguese poorly and who were unable to understand a sermon in the language, Mr. Arruda clarified his request by saying that what he wanted was a Portuguese assistant, who would act as Fr. Ward's assistant and preach to the older people. Fr. Ward pointed out, that he could, if he thought it prudent, preach longer sermons in Portuguese but, if he did so, his English and French-speaking parishioners would grow restless. As it was, the majority of the Portuguese people of the parish attended church regularly and none of them had signed Mr. Arruda's letter. Bishop Hickey forwarded Fr. Ward's explanation of the situation in St. Anthony's to the delegate. On December 11, 1929, the delegate replied to Mr. Arruda assuring him of Bishop Hickey's and Fr. Ward's concern for his spiritual welfare and asking him to co-operate loyally and whole-heartedly with his bishop.[109]

In July 1933, a few months after Archbishop Fumasoni-Biondi was named Cardinal Prefect of the Propaganda and his place as delegate was taken by Archbishop Amleto Cicognani, another of the parishioners of St. Anthony's, Jose da Costa Dias, wrote to the new delegate again asking the delegate's assistance in obtaining a Portuguese-speaking priest for the parish. He once more expressed admiration for Fr. Ward, but complained that "many of the parishioners" were attending churches in Newport and Fall River where there were Portuguese priests. He added that he feared that the faith of the Portuguese people in Portsmouth was being endangered by

[108] Arrude to Fumasoni-Biondi, November 9, 1929, PChA.
[109] Fumasoni-Biondi to Hickey, November 23, 1929; Ward to Hickey, December 2, 1929; Hickey to Fumasoni-Biondi, December 5, 1929; Fumasoni-Biondi to Hickey, December 11, 1929; Fumasoni-Biondi to Arruda, December 11, 1929, PChA.

the fact that the Baptists had set up a mission in Portsmouth with "a resident minister speaking the Portuguese language." Reportedly, he said, this mission had already done "great damage to our people." With his letter to the delegate, Mr. Dias enclosed copies of a circular the Baptists were passing out in Portsmouth.[110]

Although Mr. Dias' letter was similar to that of Mr. Arruda's, his inclusion of the threat to the faith of the Portuguese posed by the Baptist mission prompted Archbishop Cicognani to call the enclosure to Bishop Hickey's attention. Once again, Bishop Hickey turned to Fr. Ward for an explanation of the situation. In his response to Bishop Hickey, Fr. Ward asserted that the Baptist minister in question lived in Fall River, not in Portsmouth, and came to the town only on Sundays. It was true, he said, that when the mission began a few years ago, a few Portuguese families joined it. Those who did, with the exception of one person, had not been coming to church. Since that time, one of the families had expressed a desire to return to the Church and the vast majority of the Catholic population felt compassion for those who had left. As to Mr. Dias's assertion that there was no priest in St. Anthony's to care for the spiritual interests of the Portuguese in their own language, Fr. Ward vehemently rejected such a claim and pointed out that he had been preaching on Sundays and hearing confessions in Portuguese for ten years without complaint of the people with the exception of Mr. Dias.[111]

Overview

During Bishop Hickey's years, only one Portuguese community, the Portuguese colony in Warren, did not see its request for a priest and parish honored by Bishop Hickey in some way. On April 8, 1927, a Portuguese committee from Warren called on the bishop. Other than his diary entry, there is no information as to what transpired at this meeting. In looking at an overview of Bishop Hickey's relations with the Portuguese Catholics of his diocese, it is evident that Bishop Hickey was genuinely concerned about the spiritual welfare of the Portuguese as he was with that of all in the diocese. As he apparently informed Archbishop Fumasoni-Biondi when the two discussed the matter during the delegate's visit to Providence in November 1924, he would have done more in response to the various requests of the Portuguese for parishes and priests of their own nationality if he had had an adequate number of Portuguese priests. Although Hickey urged the various committees who called on him to be patient while he sought out clergy to aid them, the same strong spirit of nationalist pride

[110] Dias to Cicognani, July 15, 1933, PChA.
[111] Cicognani to Hickey, July 19, 1933; Hickey to Cicognani, July 28, 1933; Ward to Hickey, October 3, 1933; Msgr. Peter E. Blessing to Cicognani, October 28, 1933, PChA.

felt by all ethnic groups and a sense of disrespect they believed was harbored by those in authority in the United States made patience a difficult virtue to practice. In the case of the Portuguese, Bishop Hickey harbored his own suspicions about the true motives of the men who represented the various communities. While bishops with other temperaments might have made it a point to respond in some way to letters asking for Portuguese priests, if they had received the number that Hickey had, Hickey increased the frustration of those whom he asked to wait patiently by choosing not to respond to individuals whose motives were suspect.[112]

For the French Canadians

CHRIST THE KING, *Centreville, West Warwick*

In January 1922, Providence's *Sunday Tribune* carried an article written by its Pawtuxet Valley correspondent reporting on a movement among the French Canadians in the Centreville section of West Warwick, who wished to see a new French-Canadian parish created near their homes. The promoters of the idea suggested that the Archambault place on Warwick Avenue would well serve as a site for any new church. The idea apparently never progressed beyond the talking stage at this time, for, although the promoters of the idea debated forming a committee to call on Bishop Hickey, they decided against the move at that time. The idea of creating a new parish in Centreville did not surface again until after the death of Fr. Joseph Bourgeois in March 1928. Bourgeois was pastor of St. John's for thirty years. He was followed as pastor by Fr. Henri Vincent. By Fr. Vincent's time the population of St. John's was such that the masses were crowded. At Vincent's urging, Bishop Hickey, in October 1931, after obtaining the necessary indult from Rome to establish a new national parish, set off the section of St. John's to the south of the Pawtuxet River, which he named in honor of Christ the King. To head the new parish, which consisted at its beginning of about 316 families, Bishop Hickey appointed Fr. J. Adrien Forrest, the pastor of St. Ambrose, Albion.[113]

Fr. Forest was born in Lachine, Quebec, on February 12, 1883. He received his early education in his parish grammar school and then spent nine years at L'Assomption College in Lachine before deciding to study for the priesthood. He entered the Major Seminary at Montreal and was ordained on July 26, 1907 in Joliette, Canada. After ordination, he served two years in his native diocese before coming to the Providence diocese where he was appointed an assistant at Our Lady of Victories, Woonsock-

---

[112] Bishop Hickey's Diary, April 8, 1927.
[113] *Sunday Tribune*, January 22, 1922; *Providence Visitor*, October 30, 1931; Hickey to R. Cardinal Rossi, November 24, 1931; Joseph A. Cichon, Jr., "St. John the Baptist Church: Faith and Sacrifice Build a Parish" (South Hackensack, N.J.:Custom Book, Inc., 1974), p. 25.

et. He served at Our Lady of Victories from 1909 until his appointment as pastor of St. Ambrose in February 1930.[114]

Fr. Forest first met his new parishioners when he offered mass for them in the basement of St. John's, on Sunday, November 8, 1931. In anticipation of creating the new parish, Bishop Hickey had had Albert Coutu place a binder on a large parcel owned by the Knight Finance Corporation, which faced on Warwick (now Legris) Avenue. There was a large barn on the property along with three tenement houses. The bishop also arranged for the purchase of a three-story, brick building at the adjacent corner of Warwick Avenue and New London Turnpike from Yvon Archambault, which Mrs. Archambault had also purchased from the Knight Finance Corporation. Although Christ the King was established in the midst of the Depression, Fr. Vincent gave the new parish $12,500 in recognition of the support the people of the new parish had given to St. John's. The sum would be augmented by the proceeds of a number of suppers and whist parties the ladies of the parish organized. With the monies, Fr. Forest engaged the Brien Builders of Woonsocket to execute a design of Walter F. Fontaine & Son for the renovation of the main part of the barn into a church. The same company also converted the first floor of the brick store into a rectory for Fr. Forest and the second floor into a parish hall. Work on the renovations began in March 1926 and was finished in only six weeks. On Sunday, May 1, 1932, following a street parade that consisted of children, local veteran's organizations, and the newly-formed parish societies, Bishop Hickey dedicated the new church, which could accommodate 450 people.[115]

In October 1932, Bishop Hickey sent Fr. J. George McCra to assist Fr. Forest. The two worked together toward the fulfillment of Fr. Forest's second main goal after seeing the church opened, the creation of a parish school. The parish sexton, Charles Turgeon, with the help of numerous volunteers, undertook the renovation of the third floor of the brick building where the two priests lived into a parish school. Frs. Forest and McCra went door to door throughout the new parish to raise funds for the school. Christ the King School opened on September 11, 1933, with a staff of teachers supplied by the Sisters of the Presentation. Initially the sisters commuted from St. John's Convent, but in April 1936, Fr. Forest rented a house at 44 New London Avenue for use as a convent. When Fr. Forest later bought the large superintendent's house on the west side of the parish property, he and Fr. McCra moved into it, after it was renovated, and the six Sisters of the Presentation took up residence on the first floor of the brick building where the priests had initially lived.[116]

---

[114] *Providence Visitor* Biographical Form, PChA.
[115] *Providence Visitor*, November 14, 1931; March 25; April 16; May 6, 1932; "Christ the King Church: A Half Century of Love and Labor" in "Christ the King Church, West Warwick, R.I. (South Hackensack, N.J.: Custombook, Inc., 1981), 4–5.
[116] *Providence Visitor*, February 25, 1937; "Christ the King Church," 6–7.

New Mixed French-English Territorial Parishes

ST. THERESA OF THE CHILD JESUS, *Nasonville, Burrillville*

The population expansion in various parts of the state during the 1920s created pressure for the creation of new territorial parishes. While Bishop Hickey would appoint French-Canadian priests as pastor of three of the new parishes he created, they were created to serve all the Catholics who lived within their boundaries. The pastors of the new parishes were expected to preach and minister the sacraments in both English and French. By 1923, the various pastors of St. John's, Slatersville, had been saying mass on Sundays in the mill village of Mohegan, in Burrillville, for many years. In August 1923, Bishop Hickey separated the villages of Mohegan, Nasonville, Mount Pleasant and Tarkiln from the care of the pastor of St. John's and created a new parish with Fr. Adolphe Phillipe Desrochers, than an assistant in Notre Dame, Central Falls, as its first pastor.[117]

Fr. Desrochers was born in Princeville, Arthabaska County, Quebec, on November 1, 1870 and was ordained a priest of the Diocese of Nicolet on July 31, 1898, after studying in the minor seminary at Nicolet and the major seminary at Montreal. He served in two parishes in his native diocese before coming to Rhode Island in 1910, where his first assignment was as an assistant at Precious Blood, Woonsocket. After Precious Blood, he was an assistant at Notre Dame, Central Falls, for nineteen years. [118]

On receiving his appointment, Fr. Desrochers went by trolley to Mohegan to make arrangement for a place to say mass and to live. For several years, the Wanskuck Company, which owed a mill in the village, had been allowing Fr. Frehill, the pastor of St. John's, Slatersville, to say Sunday mass in a former schoolhouse the company used as a recreation hall for its workers. The company now allowed Fr. Desrochers and his parishioners to continue using the building. On Sundays, the parishioners turned around the benches in the building and set up an altar on the back wall. The Wanskuck Company also agreed to rent Fr. Desrochers one of its duplexes for use as a rectory. Besides making these arrangements, Fr. Desrochers spent his first week in Mohegan making the acquaintance of some of the 159 families and 628 souls who were his new parishioners. He celebrated the first mass in the hall on Sunday, August 26, 1923.[119]

His trips by trolley to and from Mohegan brought Fr. Desrochers past a hillside at the Mohegan-Nasonville line that he perceived would make an excellent site for a church. Since Fr. Frehill had given the new parish $21,000 from St. John's, Fr. Desrochers was able to approach Bishop Hickey on September 14 with a proposal that the parish buy the part of

---

[117] *Providence Visitor*, August 23, 1923.

[118] Ibid.

[119] Ibid.; "75th Anniversary of St. Theresa's Shrine, 1923–1998," p. 3; *Providence Visitor*, March 18, 1937.

the Fayette-Bartlett farm that had attracted his attention. The bishop came out to Mohegan the next day to see the site Fr. Desrochers suggested for the combination of buildings he envisioned would rise there and gave his approval for its purchase. The following month, when Fr. Desrochers again called to see him, he suggested to Fr. Desrochers that he engage Walter F. Fontaine to design the new buildings he envisioned.[120]

Rather than address the needs of the new parish in separate building campaigns, Fr. Desrochers had Mr. Fontaine draw plans for three different buildings. The central structure was to be a combination: hall, church and school; the one to the east of the school building was to be a convent, and the one to the west, a rectory. Fr. Desrochers reserved a corner of the property for a separate church he hoped would rise there one day. Work on the complex began during the first week of September 1924 and proceeded rapidly. Bishop Hickey blessed the new church and school on Sunday, October 4, 1925, and placed them under the protection of St. Theresa of the Child Jesus, who had just recently been proclaimed a saint. Bishop Hickey had suggested the possibility of dedicating the parish to St. Theresa to Fr. Desrochers when the parish was created. The new school, which was on the third floor of the central building, opened in September 1926, following the arrival of the Sisters of the Assumption from Nicolet, Quebec Province, on July 15.[121]

The steady progress of the new parish was interrupted on Holy Saturday morning, April 3, 1926, when the parish's sexton, James Murphy, spotted smoke coming from the church and school building while he was on his way to work. He immediately notified Fr. Desrochers, who rushed to the church to save the Blessed Sacrament. Even before Fr. Desrochers arrived, another parishioner, Wilbur George, went into the church with the same intent. Mr. George reached the altar first and was on his way out of the building when he collapsed due to the smoke. Fr. Desrochers, who also succeeded in reaching the altar and had carried out other sacred objects, took the ciboria from Mr. George's hands while others carried him out of the church. Firemen from both Woonsocket and Pascoag responded to the fire, but they were hindered in their efforts by the lack of water pressure due to the fact that the buildings were set on a hill. To supply the water they needed, they connected their pumpers to the W. and K. Mill, whose pumps were capable of pushing water up the hill. Before the firemen were able to finally extinguish the fire, flames had succeeded in reaching the school rooms on the third floor and the roof above them. When he assessed the situation, Fr. Desrochers concluded that the fire had been accidently caused by someone who had broken into the building to steal monies from the votive offerings. Although discouraged by the tragedy and its

---

[120] Bishop Hickey's Diary, September 14, 15, 1923; Carroll, *Rhode Island*, IV, 438–39.

[121] *Providence Visitor*, September 4, 1924; "75th Anniversary of St. Theresa's Shrine." The legal name of the church is St. Teresa of the Child Jesus. The shrine to St. Theresa is thought to be the first and thus the oldest in the United States.

presumed cause, Fr. Desrochers and his parishioners determined to rebuild their church.[122]

Fr. Desrochers used the convent for Easter Sunday masses but soon began saying mass in the basement hall of the combination building while workmen repaired the damage to the church and the school floors above. Repair of the building progressed rapidly. Fr. C. J. Holland, the pastor of St. Charles, Woonsocket, blessed the restored church on Sunday, August 15, 1926, and gave the sermon on the occasion. On that same day, a statue of St. Theresa, the gift of Mr. and Mrs. Gustave Friedrichs of Woonsocket, was unveiled by their two daughters. From his first days as pastor, Fr. Desrochers encouraged devotion to St. Theresa. Even before the new church and a proper shrine to St. Theresa were built, pilgrims came to the church hall to venerate a relic of the saint that Fr. Desrochers had secured for the parish. Fr. Desrochers' successors as pastor of St. Theresa also encouraged devotion to the saint and pilgrimages to her shrine.[123]

ST. JOSEPH, *Woonsocket*

Also in northern Rhode Island, there was an evident need in the Woonsocket area for new parishes as the French-speaking population of Woonsocket had spread out from the core of the city. In 1925, Catholics in the Chipman's Corner section of Woonsocket held meetings and appointed a committee to represent them in asking Bishop Hickey to establish a parish in that section for the parishioners of St. Anne's who lived there. Two members of the committee, City Solicitor Ovila Lambert and Mederic Gaulin, wrote to Bishop Hickey to present their request. Bishop Hickey replied that he was willing to look into the matter and would take such action as would appear desirable. The committee heard nothing more from the bishop. However, in April 1926, the *Woonsocket Call* reported that representatives of the diocese were seeking a suitable site in East Woonsocket for a possible parish. In July, the same paper reported that the diocese had concluded negotiations for a six-acre parcel at Chipman's Corner. A few days later, the *Providence Visitor* ran a brief story confirming the *Call* story.[124]

Bishop Hickey, evidently, did not believe the time was right to proceed with creating a new parish in Woonsocket while the Sentinellist Controversy was at its height. At the end of May 1929, those interested in the creation of a parish in the eastern part of Woonsocket organized a drive to secure over a thousand signatures on a petition to the bishop asking him to

---

[122] *Woonsocket Call*, April 3, 8, 1926.

[123] *Providence Journal*, July 18, 1925; October 11, 1930; *Providence Visitor*, August 20, 1926; March 18, 1937.

[124] *Woonsocket Call*, April 21; July 28, 1926; *Providence Visitor*, July 30, 1926. Not everyone agreed that the Jillson property was the best site for a church. At least one potential parishioner wrote to Bishop Hickey in 1927 and again in 1931 to argue that the Coutu property at the corner of Elm and Cass avenues was preferable. George M. Heroux to Hickey, April 21, 1931, PChA.

create one, which would have its church on the land he had purchased at Chipman's Corner. On July 12, 1929, the *Providence Visitor* published a list of new appointments of French-speaking priests, one of whom was Fr. J. F. Dumont, then assistant at St. Ann's, Woonsocket, who was "to take charge of the new parish to be established in the neighborhood known as Chipman Corner, Woonsocket." Although Fr. Dumont was French-speaking as were most of his new parishioners, the parish was established as a territorial, not a national parish.[125]

Following Bishop Hickey's announcement of his appointment, Fr. Dumont and his new parishioners laid plans for the erection of a temporary chapel on the land the diocese had acquired. Work on the one-story, 80 by 30 foot chapel began on Tuesday, July 16. Fifty men worked under the direction of Aime Lefebvre to build the new structure. They had made sufficient progress by the following Sunday for the first mass to be celebrated in the chapel, which was to be dedicated to Fr. Dumont's patron, St. Joseph, on July 21, 1929. Funds to support the new parish came from collections and from a series of whist parties and such other activities as children's plays, dramatic productions at St. Ann's Gymnasium, raffles, bean suppers and baseball games. Initially, about five hundred families living along Mendon Road, Cass Avenue, Elmer Ballou Meeting House Road and Diamond Hill Road and in the Cumberland Hill road district as far as the Cumberland-Woonsocket line, formed the nucleus of the new parish. While he was organizing his new parish, Fr. Dumont continued to live at St. Ann's rectory. He later rented a house at 1229 Mendon Road, which served as the parish rectory until a substantial brick building on Mendon Road designed by Walter F. Fontaine & Son was finished in 1933.[126]

St. Joseph's first pastor, Fr. Joseph Francois Dumont, was born in St. Henedine, Dorchester County, Quebec, on March 17, 1856. After completing his studies at the College de Levis and Major Seminary at Quebec, he was ordained a priest for the Archdiocese of Quebec on May 25, 1902. Fr. Dumont spent his first five years as a priest teaching English at the College de Levis. In 1906, he spent the summer at St. Ann's, Woonsocket. In 1907, he returned to Woonsocket to serve full time as an assistant in the parish. In June 1912, his archbishop, Cardinal Begin, agreed to release him and Bishop Harkins incardinated him as a priest of the diocese. After twenty-two years as an assistant at St. Ann's, Fr. Dumont and the majority of his new parishioners were well acquainted.[127]

The new parish celebrated its first anniversary on Sunday, July 20,

125 *Woonsocket Call*, June 1, 1929; *Providence Visitor*, July 12, 1929.
126 *Woonsocket Call*, July 18, 1929; *Providence Journal*, July 29, 1926; Raymond 1H. Bacon, "A Fifty-Year History of St. Joseph's Parish, Woonsocket, R.I., 1929–1979," in "St. Joseph's Parish, 50th Anniversary" (Privately printed, 1979), 20. The biographical information on Fr. Dumont comes from his biographical form on file in the Chancery Office.
127 *Providence Journal*, May 25, 1907; Bishop Harkins' Diary, July 12, 1907; June 22, 1912.

1930. The focal point of the day was the blessing of a bell that formerly had hung in the tower of Woonsocket's Boyden Street School. The growth of the parish during its first year was such that in November 1930, Fr. Dumont hired some unemployed carpenters to construct a twenty foot addition to the original church. In September 1930, Fr. Dumont opened a school that offered only the first two grades, on the first floor of a rented tenement at 83–85 Kenwood Avenue. Volunteers from the parish provided transportation to the two Sisters of the Presentation of Mary from St. Ann's Convent, who came over to the school each day to instruct the children. The new school enrolled 106 — 59 in the first grade and 47 in the second grade. Initially, the older children in the new parish continued to attend other parochial schools in Woonsocket or the Woonsocket public schools.[128]

Fr. Dumont served the new parish until February 1936, when he was transferred to St. Jean Baptiste Parish, Warren, and the pastor of St. Jean Baptiste, Fr. Ovide J. Plasse, became the new pastor of St. Joseph's. On Wednesday, May 12, 1937, a fire broke out in the church an hour after the sexton locked the building following the evening's May devotions and Benediction. About 8:30 a.m., an explosion in the church blew out its windows and flames could be seen in the interior. Fr. Plasse tried to enter the building in order to remove the Blessed Sacrament, but the flames prevented him from doing so. When the firemen arrived, an assistant chief and a captain, accompanied by one of the parishioners, managed to reach the altar through the dense smoke and remove the Blessed Sacrament from the tabernacle. In spite of the best efforts of the firemen, the interior of the church suffered substantial damage.[129]

On the Sunday after the fire, the parishioners of St. Joseph's gathered for mass on the ground floor of the nearby Fairmont Worsted Company mill on Mendon Road that was owned by Laurent Jarrett. Since Mr. Jarrett hoped to find other uses for the mill, Fr. Plasse, in August 1937, announced to the people of St. Joseph that work would begin as soon as possible on the construction of a new church on the site of the temporary chapel. The chapel itself was moved from its original site and placed on a new foundation. It was then renovated in anticipation of being used as a parish school, and the priests of St. Joseph began saying mass again there while the work progressed on the new church. In September 1937, Fr. Plasse was named pastor of Our Lady of Good Help Parish, Mapleville, and Fr. J. Adrien Forest, the founding pastor of Christ the King Parish, West Warwick, was made the new pastor of St. Joseph's.[130]

Fr. Forest celebrated mass in the basement of the new St. Joseph's for the first time on Sunday, June 26, 1938. With Bishop Keough's permission,

---

[128] Bacon, "A Fifty-Year History," 19–20.
[129] *Providence Visitor*, February 27, 1936; *Providence Journal*, May 13, 1937; *Woonsocket Call*, May 13, 1937.
[130] *Providence Visitor*, May 13; September 30; November 23, 1937.

Fr. Forest blessed the new church on Sunday, July 17, 1938, when mass
was first celebrated in the church proper. The new building was designed
by Walter F. Fontaine and Son in colonial style to harmonize with the rectory the parish had built on Mendon Road. The new building was constructed of red brick trimmed with limestone and was intended to seat 590
people. Bishop Keough solemnly blessed the new building on September
25, 1938.[131]

On becoming pastor of St. Joseph's, Fr. Forest promised his new parishioners that he would make it his first concern to create a parish school for
their children. Even though the work on the church was not finished, Forest bought the Fairmont Worsted Mill and had it renovated for temporary
use as a parish school building to accommodate six elementary grades.
The work on a new school next to the church was finished in time for the
opening of the school year in September 1938. Bishop Keough blessed the
new school on the same day he blessed the church.[132]

ST. JOAN OF ARC, *Cumberland*

On the same day, July 12, 1929, that he announced the establishment
of St. Joseph's, Bishop Hickey also announced that he was setting off the
northern part of Cumberland as a new parish. The move did not come as
a surprise to many. Bishop Harkins had turned over the keys to the former
Episcopalian mission chapel on Cumberland hill overlooking Manville to
Fr. Jeremiah Baggott, the pastor of St. Joseph's, Ashton, on June 21, 1912.
Thereafter, Fr. Baggott began saying mass in the chapel, which was known
as St. Mary's, every other Sunday. There was no heat in the chapel, but
the hardship of attending mass there was offset by the shortening of the
distance the English-speaking Catholics in the northern part of Cumberland had to travel to attend a mass where the sermon would be in English.
In September 1912, Fr. Baggott raised the question with Bishop Harkins
"with regard to division of Cumberland Hill." He discussed the Cumberland Hill mission again with the bishop in May 1917. Providence's *Evening
Tribune*, on December 21, 1917, carried notice of a rumor that Bishop
Harkins was about to set off the Cumberland Hill section of St. Joseph's as
a separate parish, but it proved to be just a rumor.[133]

In July 1921, Bishop Hickey appointed Fr. Baggott pastor of St. Mary's,
Newport, and sent Fr. Joseph P. Gibbons to be the new pastor of St.
Joseph's, Ashton. A year later, in June 1922, Fr. Gibbons bought the house
and land adjoining the chapel on Cumberland Hill and, in February 1927,
he purchased a much larger parcel from the estate of Dr. Thomas Hague,
which had a large farmhouse on it. As early as January 1922, Bishop

---

[131] *Providence Journal*, June 20; July 18, 1938; *Providence Visitor*. July 14; September 23, 29, 1938.
[132] *Providence Journal*, September 7, 12, 1938.
[133] Bishop Harkins' Diary, June 21; September 14, 1912; May 18, 1917; *Providence Evening Tribune*,
December 21, 1917.

Hickey had received a letter from a number of French-speaking Catholics, who lived within the confines of Woonsocket and Cumberland, asking if they might write to him to explain why they would like to have a parish closer to their homes in order to ease their difficulty in getting to mass. But the bishop was not ready to alter the situation in Cumberland yet.[134]

Like St. Joseph's, the new parish on Cumberland Hill was established as a territorial parish, which embraced not only the Irish who had long attended mass in St. Mary's Chapel, but also the Poles in the area, who were comfortable with English or who did not wish to make the long trip to St. Stanislaus in Woonsocket, as well as the French-speaking Catholics who lived in the vicinity. The new parish was bounded by Mendon and Diamond Hill roads on the west, by Pound Road and the Woonsocket border on the south and on the north, and by the Massachusetts border on the east. It embraced Grant's Mills, Sheldonville, Abbot Run, and all the territory of Diamond and Cumberland Hills. After taking charge of St. Joseph's, Fr. Gibbons, who spoke French fluently and had visited France shortly after Joan of Arc was canonized in 1920, suggested to Bishop Hickey a change in the name of the mission in order to honor the new saint, a suggestion which the bishop approved.[135]

St. Joan's founding pastor, Fr. David Barthelmy Brunelle, was born in Joliette, Province of Quebec, August 13, 1875. He attended the parish school in Joliette and the College de Joliette before going on to the Major Seminary at Montreal. He was ordained for the Archdiocese of Montreal on December 17, 1898, one of five brothers in the same family ordained to the priesthood. After ordination, he taught at the College de Joliette for five years before coming to the Diocese of Providence, where he served as an assistant at St. John's, Arctic from 1902 to 1923 and at St. Louis, Woonsocket, from 1923 until his appointment as pastor in 1929.[136]

Fr. Brunelle took up residence in the farmhouse on the Hague place and proceeded to get to know his new parishioners. During the first two weekends Fr. Brunelle served his new parish, it became immediately evident that his command of English was poor and that he was uncomfortable speaking the language. While Fr. Dumont, the new pastor of St. Joseph's, served mostly a French-speaking population, the majority of Fr. Brunelle's new parishioners were English-speaking. During the 1920s, Bishop Hickey had relatively more French-speaking priests than English-speaking priests. His reluctance to ordain more was one of the complaints made by the Sentinellists. Bishop Hickey had presumed that Fr. Brunelle had a sufficient command of English to effectively minister to both his English-speaking as well as his French-speaking parishioners. However, the bishop's presump-

---

134 Louise Lind, "St. Joan's Church: Its People, Its History and Its Faith," in "St. Joan's Church, Cumberland Hill, Rhode Island" (South Hackensack, N. J.: Custombook, Inc., 1980), 11–12; Joseph Bergeron et al. to Hickey, January 9, 1922, PChA.

135 *Woonsocket* Call, July 13, 1929; Providence *Visitor*, July 16, 1936.

136 Biography, *Providence Visitor* files, PChA; *Woonsocket Call*, July 13, 1929.

tion proved to be wrong. After Fr. Brunelle's second Sunday in the parish, a number of his English-speaking parishioners held a meeting and those present appointed a committee composed of parishioners who had worshiped at Cumberland Hill for a long time. On July 26, 1929, the members of the committee wrote Bishop Hickey to ask for an appointment with him so that they might express their concerns in regard to their spiritual welfare. Bishop Hickey saw the committee on the following Monday. As they had in their letter, the committee expressed their desire to continue to have an English-speaking priest because they believed that the French-speaking people in their area would likely choose to go to St. Joseph's. Bishop Hickey told them to be patient and "to continue as good, submissive Catholics" and "let the Good Lord take care of the future."[137]

On September 12, the gentlemen who called on the bishop and a few others signed another letter to Bishop Hickey in order to acquaint him "with certain facts regarding the conditions existing in the parish." Specifically, they reported that they could not understand the announcements when they were given in English, that Fr. Brunelle read his English sermons from a book in such a manner that they found it almost impossible to "fully appreciate and understand the significance of the lesson taught," and that the English-speaking people of the parish found it absolutely necessary to go out of the parish to confession. In the light of the Sentinellist agitation, those who signed the letter disclaimed any desire to promote agitation or to question the bishop's judgment in the appointment of the pastor. They asked only to be able to describe the situation in the parish as it existed at the present time. On receiving the letter, Bishop Hickey sent Fr. Brunelle a copy of it and asked him to come to Providence so that he might talk over the situation with him.[138]

After waiting eight months for things to change, on May 8, 1930, three women parishioners of St. Joan's wrote to Bishop Hickey to express their dismay that, since Fr. Brunelle's appointment, they and their children had not had instruction in a manner that they could comprehend. As a result many of the parishioners were bringing their children to other parishes to hear a sermon in English. They expressed their frustration that, while St. Joan's was established as a "mixed" or territorial parish, it was in reality a French parish since "no prayers are offered up in our language." Their frustration was underlined by the fact that the English-speaking parishioners had been and continued to be the main financial supporters of the parish. While being careful to once again disclaim any intention of causing "a similar uprising" as some of the French-speaking had done, the parishioners ended by reminding the bishop of what he had said to them when the committee representing the English-speaking parishioners had called

[137] Timothy Murphy et al. to Hickey, 26, 1929, PChA. Hickey's notes on his meeting with the committee are found on their letter.
[138] Patrick F. Casey et al. to Hickey, September 12, 1929, PChA. Cf. Hickey's note on the action he took, which he wrote on the letter.

on him the previous July: "Have patience and something will be done." In contrast to the manner in which he responded to other groups, Bishop Hickey replied to the three ladies that he had not forgotten what he had promised and invited the committee they represented to call on him if they wanted to discuss the matter further.[139]

Fr. Brunelle's difficulty in effectively serving both his English and French-speaking parishioners took a toll on him. He admitted to many of his parishioners that he was a failure. The psychological strain might well have complicated the physical strain in ministering to a country parish. For a period of a few months at the beginning of 1931, Fr. Brunelle was unable to attend to his duties and Fr. John Fahey, a priest whose own health prevented him from having a regular assignment, filled in for him. Aware of his English-speaking parishioners' disappointment with his inability to minister to them, Fr. Brunelle engaged another French priest to prepare the young people of his parish for confirmation. At times his own frustration surfaced, as when he reportedly proclaimed from the pulpit that he was "a Frenchmen and have no apologies to make." Following Bishop Hickey's visit to St. Joan's on June 4, 1931, the three ladies, who wrote to him previously, again expressed their "disappointment and chagrin" in a second letter dated August 8, 1931. In their letter, the ladies once more felt the need to disclaim any anti-French feelings. They asked not for the restoration of "an all American parish," but for "a pastor with the healing quality of friendliness and understanding."[140]

The division of St. John's, Arctic, and the creation of the new parish of Christ the King, in Centreville, West Warwick, gave Bishop Hickey the opportunity to effect the change in pastor at St. Joan's that he had been anticipating since Fr. Brunelle was unable to effectively minister to the larger part of his parish. On October 29, 1931, after appointing, Fr. J. A. Forest, the pastor of St. Ambrose, Albion, pastor of Christ the King, Bishop Hickey transferred Fr. Brunelle to St. Ambrose and appointed Fr. Moise Leprohon, the assistant at Our Lady of Victories, Woonsocket, the new pastor of St. Joan of Arc. Under Fr. Leprohon, the parishioners of St. Joan's again united behind their pastor and, in spite of the hardships created by the continuing economic depression, the development of the parish was renewed. On March 19, 1931, the three ladies who had written him before addressed a final letter to Bishop Hickey thanking him for his "diplomacy for having selected for [them] a capable pastor."[141]

[139] Mrs. James A. Mulcahey et al. to Hickey, May 8, 1930; Hickey to Mulcahey, May 14, 1930, PChA.
[140] Ibid.; Hickey to Brunelle, April 6, 1931; Mulcahey to Hickey, August 8, 1931, PChA.
[141] *Providence Visitor*, October 30, 1931; Lind, "St. Joan's Church," 13–15; Mrs. D. J. Murphy to Hickey, March 19, 1932, PChA.

All English-speaking Territorial Parishes

ST. TERESA OF THE CHILD JESUS, *Darlington, Pawtucket*

In addition to the territorial parishes which served a mixture of ethnic groups using both French and English, Bishop Hickey would also create three territorial parishes where English was the only language used. Because Bishop Harkins had provided for the people of his diocese so well, Bishop Hickey did not create an exclusively English-speaking territorial parish until July 1929. On Friday, July 26, 1929, the *Providence Visitor* announced the establishment of two new parishes, one each in Pawtucket and Providence. In Pawtucket, the bishop set off the Beverage Hill Avenue section of St. Joseph's parish, which was also known as the Plains or Darlington section, as a new parish to be formed by Fr. Eugene V. Hughes, who had served as an assistant at St. Joseph's since 1910. Fr. Hughes anticipated the *Visitor*'s official announcement of the creation of a third church dedicated to St. Teresa of the Child Jesus, on Sunday, July 21, when he bade his former parishioners at St. Joseph's goodbye and, in so doing, confirmed a rumor that had been circulating in the parish concerning its division.[142]

Fr. Hughes was born in Fall River, Massachusetts, on October 8, 1887. When he was a child, his family moved to Bristol, Rhode Island, where he attended the public schools. After two years at Holy Cross College, Worcester, Bishop Harkins sent him to the American College, Louvain, Belgium, to study philosophy and theology. Fr. Hughes was ordained in Louvain on July 10, 1910. After returning to the United States, he spent a few weeks at St. Joseph's, Pascoag, before being appointed an assistant at St. Joseph's, Pawtucket.[143]

Fr. Hughes celebrated mass for his new parishioners for the first time on Sunday, July 28, 1929, in the Clubhouse of the Pawtucket Public Golf Course on Manton Street, whose owner, William Lynch, made the building available to the new parish. The owners of the neighboring What Cheer Airport allowed the use of their field for parking cars. The chairs used on the occasion were provided by the Novelty Park Club. Over 900 people reportedly attended the first masses. In view of the number of people who attended the masses at the golf club, Fr. Hughes realized larger quarters were going to be needed and secured the use of the Italian Dramatic Club at the corner of Berkeley and Sharon streets, which the parish began using on September 1 for Sunday mass. Within two weeks of his appointment, Fr. Hughes moved into a rented house at 64 Benjamin Street

---

[142] *Providence Journal,* July 22, 27, 1929; *Providence Visitor,* July 26, 1929.
[143] Providence Chancery Office, Biographical Record, PChA.

that would serve as a rectory and as a place for daily mass. In September 1930, Fr. John J. Salesses came to St. Teresa's as Fr. Hughes's assistant.[144]

While Fr. Hughes was organizing his new parish, Bishop Hickey finished negotiations with the Bridge Mill Power Company for the sale of a site for the new church. The land the bishop bought was on Newport Avenue between Smith and Dwight streets, opposite the rear entrance of Slater Park. To create a proper building site, Fr. Hughes successfully petitioned the Pawtucket Board of Aldermen for the abandonment of part of Worcester Street (now Williston Way) that intersected the plots the bishop bought. As in other parishes, fund raising to repay the cost of the land and to raise funds for the construction of a church for the new parish would be made more difficult by the onset of the Depression in the month following the establishment of the parish. On October 27, 1929, Fr. Hughes announced to his parishioners that the monthly collection for October, $295.50, was less than that for September. The collections for the support of the church were supplemented by the usual variety of fund-raising socials and entertainments. The first bazaar held in the parish in October 1929 netted $1,700. On January 12, 1930, Fr. Hughes introduced the use of budget envelopes.[145]

Fr. Hughes and his Building Committee, with Bishop Hickey's approval, elected to begin construction of their new church by building a basement which the parish would use for mass until such times as the parish collected sufficient funds to build an upper church. Work on the basement began on October 28, 1929, and it was used for the first time on Easter Sunday, April 20, 1930. On the day the church opened, Fr. Hughes announced at all the masses that Fr. John F. Sullivan, the pastor of Holy Trinity Church, Central Falls, had given the new parish a relic of St. Teresa and that a friend of the pastor's in Belgium had also sent the parish a relic. Bishop Hickey blessed the new church on Sunday, September 28, 1930. With the basement church finished, Fr. Hughes next oversaw the building of a red brick rectory on the side of the church which was ready for occupancy in March 1931.[146]

ST. AUGUSTINE, *Fruit Hill, Providence*

Bishop Hickey established the second of the two new parishes he announced on July 1929 in the Fruit Hill section of Providence. The northwest corner of the city was the last to be developed. In the early part of the century, there were still a number of farms in the section of Providence that bordered on North Providence. For a number of years, the residents

[144] *Providence Visitor*, May 25, 1939; *Pawtucket Times*, July 29; August 6, 1939; "St. Teresa's: A Trilogy," in "St. Teresa's Church, 50th Anniversary, 1929–1979 (Privately printed, 1979), p. 2.

[145] *Pawtucket Times*, August 3, 1929; "St. Teresa's: A Trilogy," 2–3.

[146] *Pawtucket Times*, April 21; September 29, 1930; *Providence Journal*, September 29, 1930; *Providence Visitor*, October 3, 1930; "St. Teresa's: A Trilogy," 3–4.

of Fruit Hill had been hoping for a church closer to their homes so as to reduce the walk to St. Lawrence in Centredale. As founding pastor of the new parish, which would initially serve about 210 families, Bishop Hickey appointed an Irish-born priest, Fr. Thomas A. Robinson.[147]

Fr. Robinson was born June 17, 1880 on Boa Island, County Fermanagh, and received his early education in the National Schools. He came to the United States with his parents in 1892 and settled in Central Falls. At the start of his road to the priesthood, he went to the preparatory school at St. Charles College at Ellicott, Maryland, and then pursued a college course at St. Michael's College, Toronto, Canada. After studying philosophy for two years at St. Jerome's, Berlin, Canada, he went to St. Mary's Seminary, Baltimore, Maryland, for theology. Robinson was ordained to the priesthood by Cardinal Gibbons on December 19, 1908. His first assignment was as assistant at St. Edward's, Pawtucket. In January 1915, he was transferred to the Immaculate Conception Parish in Providence.[148]

Among Fr. Robinson's first actions as pastor was the purchase of a house on the corner of Buena Vista Avenue (later Mt. Pleasant Avenue) and Homefield Avenue as well as an adjacent lot on the corner of Buena Vista and Elmcrest in the Westerleigh Plat, which began to be developed about 1917. On August 4, 1929, Robinson celebrated the first mass for the new parish in the auditorium of the new La Salle Academy. About six months later, at the end of January, Bishop Hickey, whose own middle name was Augustine, announced that the title of the new parish would be St. Augustine's, whose fifteenth-hundredth anniversary was to be celebrated that year by the holding of a Eucharistic Congress at Carthage, North Africa. On May 5, the parish broke ground for a temporary church on the site next to the rectory. Architect John Hogan designed a reinforced concrete structure, 60 by 80 feet, with a seating capacity of 450, which would serve as the parish's first church. Mr. Hogan envisioned that the structure would one day serve as the auditorium of the parish school. In Robinson's mind, a new church would rise on the opposite side of Elmcrest Avenue. Fr. Robinson first celebrated mass in the new church at midnight on Christmas Eve in December 1930. Bishop Hickey formally blessed the new church on Sunday, November 29, 1931.[149]

ST. WILLIAM, *Norwood, Warwick*

Before he dedicated a church under the protection of St. Augustine, Bishop William Augustine Hickey, in April 1926, had dedicated a mis-

---

[147] *Providence Visitor*, July 26, 1929; February 6, 1936; *Providence Journal*, July 27, 1929.

[148] *Sunday Tribune*, December 20, 1908; Providence Chancery Biographical Record, PChA.

[149] *Providence Journal*, February 1; December 22, 1930; November 14, 27 30, 1931; *Providence Visitor*, June 13; December 19, 1930; November 21; December 4, 1931; Thomas E. Greene, "A History of Saint Augustine Parish," in "St. Augustine Church Golden Jubilee, 1929–1979" (Privately printed, 1979).

sion chapel in St. Matthew's Parish, Cranston, to St. William. As early as December 1913, Fr. Sullivan, the pastor of St. Matthew's, had submitted a report to Bishop Harkins on the number of people living in the Norwood section of Warwick. At that time, he found fifteen English-speaking families and fourteen French-Canadian families, all of whom spoke English. The Italians who lived in the area told him they attended mass at the Sacred Heart Fathers' mission in Hillsgrove. In October 1922, when Fr. Sullivan and his assistants reported to Bishop Hickey the results of the latest parish census, Fr. Sullivan noted that the number of families living south of the Pawtuxet River had grown to 110. At the time of the census, one of the Catholics in Norwood promised to contribute five hundred dollars towards the construction of a chapel there, which would alleviate the need of traveling the two miles to St. Matthew's. A chapel in Norwood would also help ease the crowded conditions at St. Matthew's.[150]

On January 25, 1922, Fr. Sullivan purchased the Commonwealth Plat, containing some 11,000 square feet, which was bounded by Perry, Imperial and Majestic avenues. On January 11, 1926, he broke ground for the construction of a 54 by 30 foot wooden chapel with a seating capacity of four hundred. Although finished in March, the blessing of the chapel, which was to be dedicated to St. William, was delayed until the streets around it could be properly graded. Bishop Hickey solemnly blessed the new chapel on Sunday, April 11, 1926.[151]

When the population of the Norwood section continued to grow, Bishop Hickey, in September 1933, set off St. William's as a separate parish and appointed Fr. Joseph M. Walsh, the senior assistant at Sacred Heart, Pawtucket, as its first pastor. Fr. Walsh was born in Central Falls. He attended the Broad Street Grammar school in his native city and graduated from Mt. St. Charles Academy, Woonsocket, before taking up the study of Philosophy at St. Charles College, Ellicott City, Maryland, and Theology at St. Mary's Seminary, Baltimore. After his ordination on June 21, 1911, he served for a brief time in St. Edward's, Pawtucket, and St. Joseph's, Ashton, before being appointed to Sacred Heart in January 1912. Following his appointment as pastor, Fr. Walsh oversaw the renovation and enlargement of St. William's and its rededication on Sunday, November 10, 1935.[152]

ST. PETER, *Pawtuxet, Warwick*

At the same time he set off St. William's, Bishop Hickey also created a new parish in Warwick's Pawtuxet section, which was experiencing an increase in population. Besides Pawtuxet, the new parish was to serve War-

---

[150] Sullivan to Harkins, December 15, 1913; Report of Census of 1922, PChA.
[151] *Providence Visitor*, April 9, 16, 1926.
[152] *Providence Visitor*, September 22, 1933; November 30, 1934; October 31; November 7, 1935.

wick Downs, Gaspee Plateau, Spring Green, Lakewood, Palace Gardens, Dryden Heights and the Silver Hook areas. Previously, these areas of War- wick had been sparsely inhabited, except during the summer, when many city dwellers took up summer residence to take advantage of the cooler temperatures at the shore. However, increasing numbers of the summer residents were choosing to live in Warwick year round and commute to work in the city.[153]

Before Bishop Hickey decided to create a new parish in Pawtuxet, the area was part of St. Paul's Parish in Cranston. For many years, a priest from St. Paul's offered mass during the summer in the Casino at Warwick Downs. As he had in other instances, Bishop Hickey chose the assistant at St. Paul's, Fr. Patrick W. McHugh, to be the first pastor of the parish creat- ed out St. Paul's southern section. Born in Providence on October 6, 1883, Fr. McHugh had attended the Federal Street Grammar School, La Salle Academy, and the College of the Holy Cross, Worcester, before beginning his studies for the priesthood at the Grand Seminary, Montreal, where he studied Philosophy, and at Mt. St. Mary's Seminary, Emmitsburg, Mary- land, where he studied Theology. After his ordination on June 18, 1912, he served for short periods at Our Lady of Mercy, East Greenwich and Holy Name, Providence, until he was sent to St. Francis, Wakefield as an assistant. In May 1915, he was transferred to St. Joseph's, Newport and in September 1923, he was appointed to St. Paul's.[154]

Following his appointment, Fr. McHugh offered the first mass for the new parish in Warwick Downs Casino on Sunday, October 1, 1933. When he took the census of his parish for the first time, Fr. McHugh counted 370 families. On the day following his first mass in his new parish, Fr. McHugh began saying mass in the Lakewood Volunteer Fireman's Memorial Hall on Atlantic Avenue in Lakewood, which was to be the regular place for the parish masses while he searched for a site on which to build a church. The search took him until May 1935. He chiefly considered two sites, the first at Warwick and Atlantic avenues, which was favored by many, but, since Fr. McHugh wished to have a larger site, he chose instead to purchase two and a half acres on Fair Street, between Pawtuxet and the Gaspee Plateau section, where development had begun in 1912. McHugh announced the location of the site he had acquired and explained why it was selected to his new congregation at mass on Sunday, June 2, 1935. In anticipation of building a church on Fair Street, Fr. McHugh acquired a house at 112 Fair Street for use as a rectory.[155]

Besides saying mass in Lakewood, Fr. McHugh, after surveying the needs of his parish during his first summer there, began saying mass in the summer of 1934 in a tent at Gaspee Point. When Fr. McHugh visited

[153] *Providence Visitor*, September 22, 1933; *Providence Journal*, September 23, 1933.
[154] *Providence Visitor*, March 29, 1951.
[155] Catherine M. Miller, "Together Faithfully for 50 years: A History of St. Peter's Parish" (Privately printed, 1984), *News-Tribune*, May 31; June 3, 1935.

the colonists at Gaspee Point at the beginning of the season, he found a substantial number of Catholics there who found it difficult to get to mass on Sundays because they had to travel a mile or more over poor roads before reaching a paved one, or row across to Gaspee Plateau or down to Conimicut and then walk to mass. Fr. McHugh reported the situation to Bishop Hickey's successor, Bishop Keough, who gave him permission to celebrate mass at Gaspee Point. Each Sunday, those wishing to go to mass brought their own chairs to the tent, which lacked any seating. During the week the residents of the Point used the tent for bridge and bingo parties and children's entertainments. During the summer of 1935, the Catholics and non-Catholics at the Point built a community hall, which they would use for social gatherings as well as for religious services. Fr. McHugh offered mass in the new hall during the summer of 1936.[156]

While Fr. McHugh was seeking out and arranging for the purchase of a site for a church, the Woman's Club, organized in October 1933, was sponsoring suppers, strawberry festivals, dances and card parties as fund-raisers to supplement the monies the parishioners contributed directly towards the amount needed for the purchase of the land and building of a church. Beginning in 1934, the parish began holding an annual carnival as a fund raiser. Once the site was selected, Fr. McHugh turned his attention to securing a bank loan. Because of the hard times, he was unable to procure a loan from a Rhode Island bank and had to look to Boston before he was able to persuade a bank to loan the parish the money needed. On April 26, 1936, the parish broke ground for a red brick, colonial style church designed by Ambrose Murphy to seat 525 people. The actual construction of the church began on May 10, 1936 and progressed sufficiently so that it was ready for midnight mass on December 24, 1936. Bishop Keough laid the church's cornerstone and blessed the new building on Sunday, October 24, 1937.[157]

ST. ANDREW, *Block Island*

In addition to establishing two parishes in Warwick in September 1933, Bishop Hickey also announced that he was appointing Fr. John W. Marren, the senior assistant at St. Joseph's, Newport, as pastor of St. Andrew's, Block Island. During the First World War, Bishop Harkins had sent a priest, Fr. James P. O'Brien, to Block Island to serve the Catholic servicemen stationed on the island and the few Catholics who lived there year round. When at the war's end, the bishop transferred Fr. O'Brien to St. John's Providence and later made him editor of the *Providence Visitor*, St. Andrew's reverted to mission status. Following Fr. O'Brien's reassignment,

---

[156] *Providence Visitor*, July 3, 1935.

[157] *Providence Journal*, May 2, 1936; October 25, 1937; *News-Tribune*, October 5, 1936; *Providence Visitor*, December 17, 1936; October 14, 1937.

St. Andrew's became a mission of the cathedral. Among those cathedral priests who served on Block Island was Fr. Thomas J. McKitchen, who offered mass on the island for fifteen years during the summer and who occasionally visited the island during the winter. In November 1931, Mrs. Alfred Petitpas wrote to Bishop Hickey in behalf of the fifty or more Catholics who lived on the island throughout the year, asking if the bishop might send a priest to the island once a month during the winter months. The bishop replied that, weather permitting, a priest would begin coming to the island one Sunday a month during the off season.[158]

The first pastor of St. Andrew's, Fr. Marren was born in Pawtucket, November 7, 1884. He attended St. Mary's Grammar School and Pawtucket High School before going on to St. Charles College, Ellicott City, Maryland, and finally to St. Mary's Seminary, Baltimore. He was ordained on June 21, 1911. After a summer assignments at Our Lady of Mercy, East Greenwich, and in Hallowell, Maine, he studied at the Catholic University in Washington for two years. On his return to the diocese, he served as an assistant at Sacred Heart, Pawtucket, from September 1913 to June 1916. He next went to the cathedral where he helped out while teaching at La Salle Academy. In 1918, he was assigned to St. Joseph's, Newport.[159]

There were about sixty Catholics who were permanent residents of Block Island when Fr. Marren took up residence in the rectory on Spring Street that Fr. O'Brien had bought. During his first winter on the island, Fr. Marren found it impossible to heat the church properly, but not one Catholic missed mass that winter because of the cold church. Recognizing that he could not adequately winterize the church, Fr. Marren elected to rent a bungalow near the church the following winter as a place to offer mass during the cold months.[160]

OUR LADY OF PRUDENCE, *Prudence Island*

Although legally a part of the Town of Portsmouth and thus part of St. Anthony, Portsmouth, Prudence Island was more easily accessible from Bristol, from which a ferry ran to the island, than from Portsmouth itself. As early as the 1860s, a few Catholic families had built summer homes on the island and, according to a tradition recorded in the 1920s, a priest first said mass for the summer residents there in the 1890s. Until the 1920s, however, when summer visitors on the island from Providence, Pawtucket and Attleboro went to Sunday mass, they had to take the ferry over to St. Mary's, Bristol. Although he was not in a position to send one of his own priests to Prudence, as pastor, Fr. O'Rorke's permission was needed for

[158] *Providence Visitor,* July 23, 1936; Petitpas to Hickey, November 19, 1931; Hickey to Petitpas, November 20, 1931, PChA; Robert W. Hayman, "The History of the Catholic Church on Block Island" (Privately printed, 1979).
[159] *Providence Visitor,* December 29, 1943.
[160] Ibid., July 23, 1936.

other priests to do so. On July 27, 1923, Fr. O'Rorke gave that permission during a meeting with Bishop Hickey. In 1919, Bishop Hickey had sent a chaplain to say mass for the naval boy scouts encamped at Fort Sims. In 1923, the Catholic summer residents on the island formed the St. Joseph's Catholic Club and arranged for various priests to say mass for them and their guests during the summer of 1923. In that same year, they asked Bishop Hickey to build a chapel there. In 1924, a priest from the cathedral regularly went to the island and said mass in the Casinos at Sandy Point and Homestead Point on the eastern side of the island. Julia Herreshoff, a Bristol resident whose family had owned land on the island since 1621, donated a site for a chapel between Sandy Point and Homestead Point, which Bishop Hickey himself chose. During the late fall of 1925 the bishop also arranged with the Circle A Products Corporation for the purchase and installation of a pre-fabricated building capable of seating 150 people. The building had two sacristies, one of which was fitted up to serve as a residence for the priest from the cathedral parish, who would come out to say mass there on Sundays. The church was ready for use in the spring of 1926. Bishop Hickey went to the island on July 18, 1926, to bless the new chapel and dedicate it under the title of Our Lady of Prudence. The major fund raising event in support of the new chapel was the annual lawn fête and supper, which the Catholic Club on the island held annually. At the beginning of the summer season in 1927, Bishop Hickey altered the staffing arrangements for the mission and gave Fr. Thomas F. Gillan, the pastor of St. Mary's, Bristol, responsibility for providing a priest to say mass on the island during the summer.[161]

Catholics of Other Rites

ST. ELIAS, MELKITE RITE, *Woonsocket*

Syrian immigrants began settling in Woonsocket in the first years of the twentieth century, as did the Syrians and Lebanese who settled in Providence, Pawtucket and Central Falls. Many of those who made their homes in Woonsocket did so because, due to the French influence in Syria, they spoke French rather than English as their second language. As they were immigrants from the cities of Syria, where many had worked in the silk industry, they sought work in the city's textile mills. The number of Syrians in Rhode Island jumped slightly at the end of the First World War and the breakup of the Turkish Empire. During the 1920s, Fr. Timothy Jock, the pastor of St. Basil's, Central Falls, began offering mass several times a year in the basement of Precious Blood Church for the twenty-

---

[161] Bishop Hickey's Diary, July 27, 1923; May 28, 1927; *Providence Visitor*, November 27, 1925; July 16, 23, 1926; *Providence Journal*, November 27, 1925; *Providence News*, August 9, 1928.

five Syrian families of the Melkite Rite who lived in the city. In July 1931, the community expressed the desire to have a church of their own where mass could be celebrated on a more regular basis. After several meetings, a substantial start was made towards having a church when Louis and Mary Salome donated a building site on Hamilton Street. On August 6, Fr. Jock signed a contract with Albert Ferrier for the building of a 53 by 33, wooden church. Work began immediately, and the new building was ready for its dedication on Sunday, December 20, 1931, when Fr. Jock offered mass in it for the first time following its blessing by Bishop Hickey. The church, which was to be a mission of St. Basil's, was dedicated to St. Elias.[162]

ST. MICHAEL UKRAINIAN CATHOLIC CHURCH, *Woonsocket*

Also in Woonsocket, the Ukrainian Catholics, who worshiped according to the Greek Rite at St. Michael's, built a new church at 396 Blackstone Street. The building of the church was accomplished only with difficulty. Between the departure of Fr. Basil Turula in 1920 and the dedication of the new church, six different priests served St. Michael's. The constant misunderstandings between the members of the congregation and the priests assigned to the parish caused a delay in the building of the church and continuing tensions. The new church was dedicated on August 24, 1924 by Bishop Constantine Bohachevsky, whom the Holy See had appointed on May 20, 1924 as bishop for the Ukrainians from Galicia. Bishop Bohachevsky was ordained a bishop in Rome on June 15, 1924, along with Bishop Basil Takach, who was appointed bishop for the Ukrainians from Tanscarpathia, Slovakia, Hungary and Yugoslavia. The change in the organization of the Ukrainian-rite diocese, which was created in 1907 to serve the Ukrainians in the United States, came about as a result of tensions created by the differences in the political and cultural backgrounds from which the Ukrainian immigrants came. The dedication day of St. Michael's began with a street parade to the old church on West School Street, where Bishop Bohachevsky had celebrated mass earlier in the day. The parade stopped for a brief service at the old church, after which the various societies, whose members formed the parade, escorted Bishop Bohachevsky, who carried the Blessed Sacrament, to the new church. Bishop Hickey and other clergy were guests at the celebration. The old church was subsequently sold and the money used to reduce the mortgage on the new church. A year later, on Sunday, March 1, 1925, Fr. Humphrey Kowalsky, the pastor who saw the completion of the church

---

[162] *Providence Journal*, September 26, 1931; *Woonsocket Call*, December 19, 1931; St. Elias Melkite Greek Catholic Church, Woonsocket, Rhode Island, Golden Jubilee, 1931–1981."
During the early years of the diocese, St. Basil's, Central Falls, and its mission, St. Elias was not officially part of the Diocese of Providence, but rather fell under the jurisdiction of a bishop of the Melkite Rite or his delegate. However, in the absence of a fully developed Eparchy in the United States, the pastors of St. Basil's regularly looked to the Bishop of Providence for guidance.

and its dedication, blessed the first of what was to be four bells, which the congregation planned to hang in the tower of the new church.[163]

Shortly after Fr. Kowalsky blessed the bell, Bishop Bohachevsky sent him to serve the Ukrainians in Boston. As his replacement, the bishop appointed Fr. Gleb Werchowski as the new pastor of St. Michael's. Although Fr. Werchowski spoke Ukrainian well, he was a Russian by birth. In December 1925, at least one of the lay trustees of the parish wrote to Bishop Bohachevsky asking the bishop to remove Fr. Werchowski because, in the view of many of the parishioners, he did not speak their language and they had difficulty understanding him. While the Ukrainians' request might possibly have had a basis in fact, it was certainly colored by Ukrainian nationalism. During the chaos created by the Bolshevik Revolution in Russia in 1917, the Ukrainians had declared their independence of the Russians. However, the Ukrainian attempt to recover their independence from Russian control was eventually crushed by the Bolshevik forces. The defeat only served to increase nationalist feelings among the Ukrainian immigrants in America. Although Bishop Bohachevsky understood that there could be tension between Fr. Werchowski and his parishioners, he also did not have another priest he could send to Woonsocket, who might be able to deal with the tensions that had been created there.[164]

Among the first responsibilities Bishop Bohachevsky charged Fr. Werchowski with was the securing of a charter of incorporation from the Rhode Island General Assembly similar to the one the Assembly had passed in order to incorporate the Diocese of Hartford, which was amended when the Diocese of Providence was created. On March 26, 1926, Bishop Hickey wrote to Governor Theodore Francis Green, the Secretary of State and the General Assembly asking them to consider favorably the petition of Bishop Bohachevsky, which Fr. Werchowski submitted in the bishop's name. Although the legislature passed the charter as requested, the leaders of the parishioners opposed to Fr. Werchowski declared that the lay trustees of the parish would not sign the charter, which would have recognized Bishop Bohachevsky's legal claims to the parish.[165]

During the course of the various disputes with the priests who served the parish between Fr. Turula and Fr. Werchowski, the leaders of the opposition created what they called the Autocephalic Orthodox Church or the Independent Orthodox Church to underline their independence from Rome and from the authority of the bishops sent by Rome. The leaders of the opposition to Fr. Werchowski claimed that their "church had been

[163] *Woonsocket Call*, August 23, 25, 1924; March 2, 1925; *Providence Visitor*, August 28, 1924; "St. Michael's Ukrainian Catholic Church, Woonsocket, R.I.: 50th Anniversary, 1908-1958 (Privately printed, 1958).
    Although St. Michael's was properly a parish first of the Eparchy of Philadelphia and later of Stamford, Connecticut, it is included here because of its local ties.

[164] *Providence Journal*, May 6, 1926.

[165] Ibid.; Hickey to Green, et. al, March 26, 1926.

wholly independent of the Roman church and that the parishioners had voted it should always be." In April 1926, the leaders of the faction opposed to Fr. Werchowski organized a boycott of church services in order to force Bishop Bohachevsky to remove him. Although the police were called to the church in order to prevent any disturbance, none developed, as all but a dozen of the seven hundred parishioners of St. Michael's refused to defy those who picketed the church. Fr. Werchowski suspected that the strategy of those who claimed that the church was independent of Rome and Bishop Bohachevsky was to bankrupt the church and then to buy the property back at auction.[166]

Bishop Bohachevsky came to Woonsocket during the second week of May and spoke with Fr. Werchowski, Ambrose Kennedy, a Woonsocket lawyer, and Fr. Georges Bedard, the pastor of Precious Blood. At the meeting, Mr. Kennedy proposed that the impasse might be resolved if he were to go to see one of the strikers' lawyers, Judge John F. Higgins, to suggest that if the trustees accepted the new charter and paid all the monies that were owed by the parish, Bishop Bohachevsky might in response remove Fr. Werchowski. Fr. Bedard objected that a bishop did not have the right to remove a priest without cause. Bishop Bohachevsky assured Fr. Werchowski that he would leave the matter in Fr. Werchowski's hands. Later, at Fr. Bedard's insistence, Mr. Kennedy wrote to the bishop withdrawing his proposition. When after seven weeks, neither Bishop Bohachevsky nor Fr. Werchowski made any gesture towards meeting their demands, the supporters of the dissidents met in the parish hall and voted to take legal action to force Fr. Werchowski from the parish rectory and to remove Bishop Bohachevsky's name from the parish board of trustees.[167]

Although St. Michael's fell under the jurisdiction of the Ukrainian Catholic Church and Bishop Bohachevsky, Bishop Hickey followed the developments in St. Michael's carefully, if only because they might set a precedent for action taken by the French Canadians he knew were involved in legal action against him in the Church courts. Also, it was difficult for Bishop Hickey not to be interested in the St. Michael's affair because it was chronicled in the local newspapers. In view of the threat of legal eviction, Hickey advised Fr. Werchowski to solicit the help of Mr. Kennedy. On July 13, 1926, Fr. Werchowski wrote to Bishop Hickey that he had been unable to speak to Mr. Kennedy because he was on vacation with his family and was not expected back until September. His main concern in writing Bishop Hickey, however, was to convey the news that those opposed to his continuance at St. Michael's had arranged with a Ukrainian priest who had recently been hired to serve the Orthodox Ukrainian parish in Manville, to offer mass in St. Michael's on the following Sunday.[168]

[166] *Providence Journal*, May 6, 8, 1926.
[167] *Providence Journal*, May 8, 24, 1926; the incident of the meeting is recalled in Werchowski to Hickey, July 19, 1926, PChA.
[168] Werchowski to Hickey, July 13, 1926, PChA.

The Orthodox priest did not appear as Fr. Werchowski feared, but on Wednesday, July 14, 126 members of the parish met to vote on an amendment to the church charter, which would remove Bishop Bohachevsky and the current officers of the church corporation and replace them with new ones. Those at the meeting claimed that they had no knowledge of a previous amendment to the church charter that was filed with the Secretary of State's Office on February 16, 1924, embracing the actions taken at a meeting which supposedly had taken place on June 3, 1923. Those at the meeting in July also voted to authorize the new officers of the corporation to engage counsel and "to take such steps as necessary to retain for the members the full and undisputed right, title and management of the church corporation."[169]

On July 19, Fr. Werchowski again wrote to Bishop Hickey to explain why, in his view, it was important for him to remain in Woonsocket until the Catholic charter for his parish was accepted. He expressed the belief that there was a minority within the parish that were for the bishop and himself but who, at the moment, were intimidated by the majority, who would label them as strikebreakers or traitors. He recounted the details of his meeting with Bishop Bohachevsky, Fr. Bedard and Ambrose Kennedy in May and assured the bishop that this was not the first time since the Russian Revolution that he had been attacked. If his fellow priests in Woonsocket continued to provide him with dollar mass stipends, he would be able to remain there as long as necessary.[170]

After several weeks of rumors that the trustees were planning to have a priest say mass in St. Michael's, Maxim Maruschak did so on Sunday, July 25, 1926. During the week after the mass, the lawyer for the trustees approached Patrick P. Curran, a Providence lawyer associated with the firm of Green, Curran and Hart, whom Bishop Hickey had engaged as counsel for Bishop Bohachevsky and Fr. Werchowski in order to obtain a restraining order against the trustees' use of the church, for the purpose of proposing a settlement. The trustees offered not to have the "schismatic priest" say mass in the church if those Mr. Curran represented would agree not to seek an injunction against the priest and the trustees. After Mr. Curran inform Fr. Werchowski of the proposal, Fr. Werchowski wrote Bishop Hickey to urge the bishop not to agree to it because it would not settle anything. Essentially, the trustees had either to turn the bishop out or accept his authority, which meant practically, they had to accept the new charter passed by the legislature. Either that or the situation would remain as before, when they were trying to starve the priest out, abuse the bishop and declare that the schism was voluntary from the first.[171]

Since any of the parishioners who sided with the bishop would expose

[169] *Providence Journal*, July 18, 1926; Minutes of meeting of St. Michael's Ruthenian Greek Catholic Church, June 3, 1923, PChA.
[170] Werchowski to Hickey, July 19, 1926, PChA.
[171] Werchowski to Hickey, July 30, 1926, PChA.

themselves to the real risk of personal injury if one of them signed a petition for an injunction, Mr. Curran, on July 28, suggested that Bishop
Hickey write to Bishop Bohachevsky asking him to serve as the complainant in the case. Bishop Hickey did as Mr. Curran asked and Bishop
Bohachevsky agreed to sign the complaint. Mr. Curran notified the trustees' counsel that he would file a bill asking for a restraining order on August 9 in Superior Court before Judge Walsh. When the counsel for the
trustees did not appear, Mr. Curran made an oral statement as to the facts
supporting his request. He also asked Judge Walsh to broaden the requested injunction to cover the accosting of people going to or returning from
the church as well as any interference with them while attending church
services. The additional actions covered by Mr. Curran's request were
prompted by the fact that, when Fr. Werchowski went to St. Michael's on
August 8 to say mass, he found that the chalice and vestments had been
removed and that the bell had been tied so that he could not ring it. He
also found a group of about twenty women at the church, who told him
that he ought not say mass because he was Russian. After a discussion with
the women, he walked out only to have about a dozen eggs thrown at him,
four of which hit him.[172]

Since the trustees' lawyer did not appear for the hearing, Judge Walsh
granted a temporary injunction against the use of St. Michael's by the
trustees and against any further inference with Fr. Werchowski and those
who remained loyal to him and Bishop Bohachevsky. Mr. Curran had subpoenas served on all the trustees but not on the priest, Maxim Maruschak,
for whom he did not have an address. He also had a copy of the judge's
order printed in the *Woonsocket Call* on August 12, 13 and 14. Under
Judge Walsh's order several Providence County deputy sheriffs went to
St. Michael's on Sunday, August 15, to ensure that there was no repetition
of the disturbances that had occurred in the church the previous Sunday.
The Woonsocket police also sent officers to the church for the same reason. The sheriffs informed the parishioners loyal to Bishop Bohachevsky
and Fr. Werchowski, who lived in Lapham Court, that they would ensure
their protection. Only six persons appeared for the mass Fr. Werchowski
said that day.[173]

Prior to going to court to seek an injunction against the trustees, Bishop
Bohachevsky offered the trustees a compromise. If the dissenting parishioners would go church and attend the services peacefully; go to confession to Fr. Werchowski; organize in harmony as before; and agree to conform to the Ruthenian rite, he would then remove Fr. Werchowsky and
appoint a new pastor. Rather than accept the bishop's offer, on August 19,
1926, the dissidents had their counsel file a request for a restraining order
against Bishop Bohachevsky. Superior Court Judge Herbert L. Carpenter

---

[172] *Providence Journal*, July 18; August 27, 1926; Curran to Hickey, August 16, 1926, PChA.
[173] *Woonsocket Call*, August 12, 16, 1926; Curran to Hickey, August 16, 1926, PChA.

chose to consider both parties' requests for a restraining order at the same time. The hearing of the case took a full week of overtime sessions. In rendering his decision, Judge Carpenter rejected Mr. Curran's argument that St. Michael's was founded by priests united with Rome and accepted the trustees' argument that the church was and had always been independent of Roman authority. Judge Carpenter was swayed by the fact that the trustees represented ninety percent of the congregation of St. Michael's, who had contributed a large part of the monies to build the new church. He therefore ordered the dissolution of the restraining order granted by Judge Walsh and awarded control of the church property to the trustees and the corporation. When asked by a reporter from the *Woonsocket Call* for his reaction to Judge Carpenter's ruling, Bishop Hickey replied that "the basic trouble with the church [was] racial and political, Bolshevistic and highly colored with the Ukrainian dream of complete independence." He acknowledged that it was unfortunate that the pastor, Fr. Werchowski, was a Russian, and, "therefore, racially in discord with his parish."[174]

On the day Judge Carpenter rendered his decision, Mr. Curran announced that Bishop Bohachevsky would appeal the judge's ruling to the Rhode Island Supreme Court. Accordingly, Mr. Curran prepared a brief which he submitted to the court for consideration during its winter term. On February 7, 1927, Bishop Hickey wrote to Bishop Bohachevsky in confidence that he feared that the court's decision would be unfavorable, but that he would do his best to have the announcement of the decision postponed as long as possible. In the meantime, he recommended that Bishop Bohachevsky remove Fr. Werchowski and appoint another priest of the same race as the people of Woonsocket in his place in the hope that such a priest might bring about a peaceful resolution of the situation.[175]

While Bishop Bohachevsky was willing to do as Bishop Hickey suggested, as he had indicated earlier to the trustees, he was only willing to remove Fr. Werchowski if the trustees agreed to his conditions. As he lacked an adequate number of priests to serve all the Ukrainian communities that were asking for one, he was willing to send another priest to Woonsocket if there was a real hope for reconciliation. Fr. Werchowski complied with the court's ruling and left the rectory next to the church, but he did not leave Woonsocket. He found lodging elsewhere in the city and rented Trinity Hall in the city as a place for saying Sunday mass for the few families that had remained loyal to their bishop. Some of the loyal families chose to go to the Latin Rite churches close to their homes. Other families continued to attend the services offered by Fr. Werchowski. This small group dedicated their new parish under the title of SS. Peter and Paul's. Even though

Mr. Curran continued to seek a legal remedy, Fr. Werchowski and his parishioners began collecting funds to build another church.[176]

Fr. Werchowski left Woonsocket in the fall of 1929 for another parish in Pennsylvania. Believing that the community he had served was too small to support a priest, Bishop Bohachevsky did not immediately assign another. The nearest priest in union with Rome to Woonsocket was Fr. Jaroslaw Strotsky, pastor of St. John Ukrainian Catholic Church in Fall River. After a while, the people in Woonsocket asked if Strotsky might be appointed to take charge in Woonsocket. Initially, Bishop Bohachevsky was reluctant to agree to the proposal because Fr. Strotsky's did not have a reputation as a prudent administrator. Bishop Bohachevsky finally relented and, in September 1929, gave Fr. Strotsky, who, like the people of Woonsocket, was a Ukrainian from Galicia, charge of Woonsocket as well as Fall River. For the first three weeks he served in Woonsocket, Fr. Strotsky said mass, as had Fr. Werchowski, in Trinity Hall and opened a Ukrainian Catholic school at 160 Blackstone Street. As Bishop Bohachevsky feared, Fr. Strotsky also arranged to buy the former St. Michael's rectory and church on West School Street, which had not been used as a church since the new St. Michael's was dedicated in 1924. On Fr. Stortsky's advice, several parishioners mortgaged their homes to aid in the purchasing of the property.[177]

On his part, Bishop Bohachevsky did not agree to accept the church property which the parishioners had brought at Fr. Strotsky's urging because of his reservations about the financial wisdom of such a transaction. Apparently, someone asked Bishop Hickey if he might write to Bishop Bohachevsky in behalf of the Ukrainians in Woonsocket. On May 6, 1930, Bishop Hickey did send a letter to Bishop Bohachevsky urging him to accept the property in order to prevent those who bought it from "becoming the laughing-stock of those schismatics who have thus far succeeded in depriving them of the beautiful new church which they helped to build." Hickey also feared that, if they failed to secure Bohachevsky's support, they might turn to "schism, heresy or unbelief." In reply to Bishop Hickey, Bishop Bohachevsky related what had happened in Woonsocket after Fr. Werchowski left and the reasons for his reluctance to accept the church property.[178]

On Saturday, January 24, 1931, a Ukrainian priest who was married, Rev. A. Ulanitsky, called on Bishop Hickey to present him with a petition signed by the Ukrainians in Woonsocket, asking that they might be affiliated to the Diocese of Providence. Unsure how to proceed in the matter, Bishop Hickey on the same day wrote to the Apostolic Delegate, Archbishop Fumasoni-Biondi, to present the case to him and to ask his advice. The

---

[176] *Woonsocket Call,* January 25, 1927; "St. Michael's Ukrainian Catholic Church: 50th Anniversary."
[177] *Woonsocket Call,* October 4, 1929; Bohachevsky to Hickey, May 21, 1930, PChA.
[178] Hickey to Bohachevsky, May 6, 1930; Bohachevsy to Hickey, May 21, 1930, PChA.

delegate, as was his custom in such matters, wrote to Bishop Bohachevsky to ascertain his position in the matter. In his response, Bishop Bohachevsky reviewed the situation as he understood it. He continued to decline to accept financial responsibility for the property the Ukrainians in Woonsocket had bought and the "independent" priest they had found to minister to them. As to the peoples' petition, he had no objection to the Ukrainians joining the diocese if Bishop Hickey would accept them. The delegate sent a copy of Bishop Bohachevsky's letter to Hickey. In his letter, the delegate raised the question of whether Bishop Hickey's acceptance of the Woonsocket Ukrainians would mean a change of rite for them. In the light of this question, he advised Hickey to write to the Sacred Congregation for the Oriental Church to determine whether the delegate could empower an entire congregation to switch rites. While the Ukrainians were anxious to preserve their Catholic faith by seeking Bishop Hickey's financial and moral backing for their parish, they also wished to preserve their Ukrainian liturgical heritage and thus were not seeking to change rites.[179]

A critical point in the history of the parish was reached in January 1932 when Bishop Bohachevsky came to Woonsocket to conduct a three-day mission. Only nineteen families made the mission but, at its conclusion, Bishop Bohachevsky promised to send them another priest. Within a few weeks of his visit, Bishop Bohachevsky sent a newly ordained priest, Fr. Basil Tremba, to reform the parish and to do what he could to bring those who had rejected the bishop's authority back to the Church. Shortly after coming to Rhode Island, Fr. Tremba, on February 12, called on Bishop Hickey to introduce himself. Eleven days after his meeting with Hickey, Fr. Tremba wrote to thank him for his kind reception and to give Hickey a report on the situation as he found it in his new parish. To his mind, the key to the welfare of the parish was the stabilizing of its finances. The thirty-three families who then composed the parish were struggling to pay the parish debt. Many had already contributed considerable monies to the church and many others, because of the Depression, were unable to contribute anything at all. On his parish visits, Tremba found the people lighting their homes with kerosene lamps because they did not have money to pay electric bills. Specifically, he asked Bishop Hickey if the bishop could find someone to loan the parish $8,000 interest free so that the parish could get on its feet and cut expenses. His entire weekly collection on Sunday, he noted, was $11.26. He also asked if Hickey would allow a collection for his parish in the churches of the diocese as though for a mission church.[180]

Fr. Tremba, newly ordained and inexperienced, found himself in a very difficult situation. As a first step in pursuit of his objective of recovering

[179] Bishop Hickey's Diary, January 24, 1931; Hickey to Fumasoni-Biondi, January 24, 1931; Bohachevsky to Fumasoni-Biondi, January 30, 1931; Fumasoni-Biondi to Hickey, February 6, 1931, PChA.
[180] Tremba to Hickey, February 23, 1932, PChA.

St. Michael's church, Fr. Tremba worked to restore the original Rhode
Island charter, which the trustees had allowed to lapse in 1928, after obtaining a new one of their own. While the trustees had earlier refused to
sign the charter of incorporation Bishop Bohachevsky had secured from
the legislature, now Bishop Bohachevsky, on his part, refused to sign the
revived charter until such time as the Ukrainians in Woonsocket under
Fr. Tremba's care had paid off the first mortgage on the church they had
bought. As Fr. Tremba explained to Bishop Hickey in a letter on April
9, 1932, the bishop's stance was based on his conviction that the parishioners, who had supported the trustees and who had begun worshiping
again with those who had remained loyal to the bishop, would be bound
to the church if they had invested money in it and less likely to return to
the independent church. Fr. Tremba knew from his meeting with Bishop
Hickey that the bishop wished to see an end of the schism in Woonsocket.
Caught as he was between the demands of his bishop and the lack of resources of his people, Tremba once again asked Bishop Hickey for financial aid. Although Bishop Hickey received many such requests at this time,
he helped to the degree that he could.[181]

In his first letter to Bishop Hickey, Fr. Tremba also informed him that
he had heard that there was a possibility of regaining possession of the
cemetery the parish had bought in Blackstone, Massachusetts in 1914
and incorporated in 1915. In view of that end, Fr. Tremba engaged counsel to seek the return of the cemetery property by bringing suit in the
courts of Massachusetts. As had the Rhode Island courts, the Superior
Court in Worcester and the Massachusetts Supreme Court decided the
case in favor of those who claimed that the church had been independent
of any episcopal authority from its beginnings. While disappointing, the
litigation prompted the gathering of witnesses and documents that had
not been available to the lawyers who had previously brought suit in behalf of Bishop Bohachevsky in the Rhode Island courts. On January 7,
1935, a second bill of equity was filed in the Superior Court in Providence
on behalf of Bishop Bohachevsky. The trial before Judge Alexander L.
Churchill lasted from April 2 to June 13, 1935. The collection of testimony
took twenty-six days and filled fourteen hundred typewritten pages. However, on October 22, 1935, to the great disappointment of Fr. Tremba and
his congregation, Judge Churchill again ruled in favor of the trustees. The
case was once again appealed to the Rhode Island Supreme Court. The
court that heard the St. Michael's case on appeal was substantially a different court than that which had heard the first appeal. In 1935, the Democrats had gained control of the State Senate as well as the House and the
governor's office. The first bill passed by the General Assembly after the
Democrats gained control over the state vacated the office of the Providence County Sheriff and the second vacated the five judgeships of the

---

[181] Tremba to Hickey, April 9; June 2; July 6, 1932, PChA.

Supreme Court. The Democrats then proceeded to elect their own slate of judges to the Supreme Court. It was the new court that heard Bishop Bohachevsky's appeal. On January 25, 1938, the court unanimously over-ruled Judge Churchill and restored the St. Michael's church and rectory to Bishop Bohachevsky. On Monday, Janaury 31, 1938, the trustees turned over the keys to the church and rectory to Fr. Tremba as well as the par-ish's books and records. The litigation cost both sides over $15,000. On February 6, 1939, Fr. Tremba offered mass for the first time in the newly reconsecrated church. Fr. Tremba served St. Michael's until October 1949, when he was succeeded by Fr. Joseph Galysh.[182]

Fr. Galysh was married with three children. Along with his family and the other villagers in his parish, he had been arrested in 1944 by the Nazi Gestapo in the western Ukraine and sent to a labor camp near Vienna and later moved to a second camp in Stuttgart. All during the time of confinement, he was not allowed to say mass. The camp he was in was liberated by American troops in 1945. On coming to the United States, he was given charge of St. Nicholas Ukrainian Church in Muskegan Heights, Michigan. Fr. Tremba took his place in Michigan when Bishop Bohachevsky sent him to Woonsocket.[183]

Schism Within the Polish Parishes

Nationalism and personality conflicts also played an important role in the continuation of the divisions that arose within St. Joseph's Parish, Cen-tral Falls, which Bishop Harkins had created for the Polish Catholics there in 1906. Tensions that had existed in the parish from its inception were aggravated under the administration of Fr. Francis Kluger, the first pas-tor of St. Joseph's. On December 16, 1917, those opposed to Fr. Kluger created an independent parish under the title of Our Lady of Perpetual Help, which they placed under the authority of an Old Catholic bishop in Chicago. In the 1920s, a split developed within the independent parish and the parish's affiliation was switched to the Polish National Church. The congregation's one-story brick church at the corner of High and Clay streets was built with the proceeds collected from the purchase of shares of stock sold at fifty dollars each. In February 1929, one of the stockholders brought suit against the corporation in an effort to recover the money he had invested. As a result of the suit, the church was placed in the hands of a receiver. When the court ordered the property sold, the loyal parish-ioners bought it and changed the official name of the church to the Pol-ish National Catholic Church of the Holy Cross. A similar split occurred

---

[182] "St. Michael's Ukrainian Catholic Church: 50th Anniversary;" *Providence Journal*, January 26; February 1, 1938; *Woonsocket Call*, January 26, 1938.
[183] *Providence Journal*, October 29, 1949.

within St. Stanislaus Parish, Woonsocket, in February 1924, when nearly four hundred members of that parish left to organize a parish whose official name is the Polish National Catholic Church of Our Savior.[184]

Other Administrative Challenges

At the end of 1921 and during the first two months of 1922, several churches and rectories in the dioceses were robbed. At the end of January, a robber broke into the Assumption rectory in Providence and robbed the pastor at gunpoint. In addition to concern for the physical welfare of the priests whose homes were being burglarized and the security of the funds of the churches and of the sacred vessels used in divine worship, Bishop Hickey also became concerned about the threat of desecration of the Eucharist. In the neighboring Diocese of Fall River, thieves entered St. Anne's Church, Fall River, pried open the tabernacle and threw the Blessed Sacrament on the floor so as to steal the ciboria kept there. To deal with the threat, Bishop Hickey gathered the clergy of the diocese together in the cathedral hall on Wednesday, February 22, to discuss what could be done.[185]

The pastors at the meeting decided to employ night watchmen, who would also be special constables, to guard their churches, and in some cases, to hire a private detective to work with the police. Among those who addressed the meeting was an expert on burglar alarms, who explained the various types. Two days before the meeting, a burglar alarm in St. Patrick's Church, Providence, which the pastor, Fr. Martin F. Reddy, had installed after a series of attempted and successful robberies of the church, alerted Fr. Reddy to yet another attempt in progress. Fr. Reddy called the police who, after their arrival, found the potential thief hiding behind an altar with a complete set of burglary tools. In addition to these measures, Bishop Hickey urged his pastors to correct the public impression that there was anything of extraordinary value in the rectories and churches of the diocese. In parishes that did have valuable chalices, he emphasized for the benefit of the press, that such vessels were generally kept in safety deposit vaults and used only on special occasions, while any large church collections were deposited in the banks before nightfall.[186]

In addition to protecting the churches of the diocese from theft, Bishop Hickey was also concerned with protecting them from fire. On October 17, 1918, fire destroyed St. John the Baptist Church, one of the two French-

[184] Hayman, *Catholicism in Rhode Island and the Diocese of Providence, 1886–1921*, 270–71, 282–83; William Wolkovich-Valkavicius, "A Glimpse at the Origin of the Polish National Catholic Church in Central Falls, Rhode Island, PNCC Studies, Vol. 20, 1999/2000, 69–86.
[185] *Providence Journal*, February 2, 21, 1922; *Evening Tribune*, February 1, 20, 21, 22, 1922; *Providence Visitor*, February 24, 1922.
[186] Ibid.

Canadian parishes in Pawtucket. The church had only recently been re-paired after being struck by lightning the year before. Four years later, on December 22, 1922, fire heavily damaged St. John's Hall that the par-ish began using after the 1918 fire. During the night of November 10, 1919, St. James' Church, Manville, was completely destroyed by fire. On Sunday, December 28, 1924, during the children's mass, a fire began in Sacred Heart church, Woonsocket, causing substantial damage that forced the parish to replace the building. In the early morning of August 6, 1926, fire destroyed the roof of St. Mary's, Crompton, then a mission of St. James, Arctic. On Holy Saturday morning, April 3, 1926, as noted above, fire heavily damaged the new combination church-school-hall building in Nasonville that Bishop Hickey had dedicated to St. Teresa of the Child Jesus only in October 1925. On Saturday, April 16, 1932, fire devastated the Church of the Presentation of the Blessed Virgin Mary and several other buildings in North Providence. Finally, on Monday, May 16, 1932, a fire struck and destroyed St. Mary's, Carolina, a mission of Immaculate Conception, Westerly.[187]

Bishop Hickey stopped to inspect the ruins of the Presentation on the day following the fire as he was on his way to dedicate the newly rebuilt church of St. James in Manville. As he usually did, Bishop Hickey shared with the congregation of St. James the thoughts that had occupied his mind over recent days. At the banquet following the dedication, the bishop gave voice to his concerns raised by the recent rash of church fires. He urged his pastors and others in charge of diocesan institutions to keep a strict watch over all parochial and diocesan property because he believed that someone "with a mania for fires" was at work.[188]

While no one was seriously injured in the various fires that struck the churches, a fire in St. Mary's rectory, Newport, on January 7, 1921, claimed the life of Ellen Rush, who worked in the rectory as a housekeeper. The pastor of St. Mary's, Fr. James T. Ward, and his two assistants got out of the rectory safely and Miss Rush's sister was saved by the firemen who responded to the emergency. Fr. Ward suffered emotionally from the expe-rience and the fire was a factor in his death on June 30, 1921.

---

[187] *Providence Visitor,* November 14, 1919; August 6, 1926; May 20, 1932; *Woonsocket Call,* December 29, 1924; April 3, 8, 1926; Edward G. St. Godard, *St. John's Parish, Pawtucket, R.I., 1884–1978* (Privately printed, 1978), 28–30.

[188] *Providence Visitor,* November 14, 1919; August 6, 1926; May 20; April 22, 1932.

New Religious Orders
and Spiritual Movements

Bishop Hickey's commitment to expanding the number and scope of the Catholic Schools in the diocese had to deal with the reality that religious orders were experiencing difficulties responding to all the requests pastors and bishops were making of them to supply teachers for the schools they hoped to build. The shortage of teachers in relation to the demand was greater in the case of the English-speaking schools than the French-speaking. Because of the continuing and expanding need for teaching sisters, between 1922 and 1933, three new religious orders of women entered the diocese: the first two, the Sisters of the Immaculate Heart of Mary came to St. Paul's, Cranston in September 1922 and the Faithful Companions of Jesus came to Blessed Sacrament, Providence, in 1925, to teach in the parish schools.[189]

Sisters of the Cross and Passion

The third order that came during Bishop Hickey's years engaged in a variety of ministries. In 1921, the newly appointed pastor of St. Margaret's, Rumford, East Providence, Fr. Peter A. Hanley, wrote to Bishop Hickey concerning his search for a religious order that would be willing to come to his parish to assist in the work of the parish. As the bishop had predicted in a conversation the two had had earlier, Fr. Hanley reported that it was very difficult to secure the services of sisters because of the many demands for them. However, he reported that he had assurances that the Sisters of the Cross and Passion, an Order established in England in 1851, were interested in coming to the United States. He sent some printed material on the order and asked for a meeting with the bishop to discuss the possibility of inviting the sisters.[190]

The apparent source of Fr. Hanley's information regarding the Sisters of the Cross and Passion was a Passionist priest, Fr. Felix Ward, C.P., with whom Fr. Hanley was acquainted. Fr. Ward also wrote to Bishop Hickey in December 1921 about establishing a community of the sisters in Fr. Hanley's parish. In his reply to Fr. Ward, Bishop Hickey raised some question as to whether establishing a community in St. Margaret's might present "the prospect of future growth" desired by all religious orders, but

---

[189] *Providence Visitor*, September 8, 1922; Charles E. Maher, *The Church of the Blessed Sacrament, 1888–1988* (Custombook: Tappan, New York, 1989), 111–12.

[190] Hanley to Hickey, December 7, 1921, PChA.

assured him that there would be a "a field for them in the Providence Diocese among the works of charity called nowadays social welfare." In order to gain a closer acquaintance with the sisters and they with the diocese, Hickey suggested that a delegation of the sisters might come for a visit to Providence. At the same time Bishop Hickey responded to Fr. Ward, he also wrote to the Superior General of the Sisters of the Cross and Passion, Mother Gerard (Dunn). Mother Gerard waited to respond to the bishop's letter until she had some concrete information to give. On August 1, 1922, she conveyed the news that her General Council agreed that she should travel to Providence as soon as possible to discuss the establishment of a convent of the sisters in the United States. It was not until May 23, 1923 that Mother Gerard and a companion finally were able to set sail for New York. Fr. Ward met the sisters in New York and, after spending three days in the New York area visiting the convents and schools of other orders, Fr. Ward accompanied the sisters to Providence to meet with Bishop Hickey.[191]

Bishop Hickey was not the first bishop to invite the sisters to his diocese, but his invitation came at a time the sisters were ready to come to the United States. When the prospect of the sisters opening a new mission field in Rhode Island first came up, it was suggested that the sisters might open a hostel for young women like the ones they maintained in several of the larger cities in England. However, during Bishop Hickey's meeting with Mother Girard, the two discussed not only what Hickey had referred to as "welfare work," but also the possibility that the sisters might take up the work of teaching in the schools of the diocese. During their stay in Providence, Mother Gerard and her companion, as they had done in the New York area, visited several of the Catholic schools in Providence. The sisters were also shown the house the bishop was considering purchasing as their residence and the site of a future hostel.[192]

The announcement that the Sisters of the Cross and Passion were to come to the diocese appeared in the *Providence Visitor* in July 1923. The following month, the *Visitor* announced that the bishop had purchased the estate of former Providence mayor Rosewell B. Smith, at 315 Elmwood Avenue, as the residence for the sisters. As with other religious orders when they came to the diocese, Bishop Hickey helped organize a group of Catholic women to prepare the sisters' new home prior to their arrival. In the case of the Sisters of the Cross and Passion, it was the newly formed St. Camillus Guild of Catholic nurses that undertook to raise money to furnish the new hostel. The guild's first event was a whist and entertainment which the members held in the sisters' new residence on February 20, 1924.[193]

[191] Ward to Hickey, January 5, 1922; Gerard to Hickey, August 1, 1922, PChA; "The Passionist Sisters in America," *The Sign*, August 1923, p. 3.
[192] Ibid.; Hickey to Gerard, January 23, 1923, PChA.
[193] *Providence Visitor*, July 26; August 9, 1923; February 14, 1924.

As events unfolded, the coming of the sisters became entangled in the complexities of the Immigration Act passed in May 1924. The sisters, who originally planned to leave England for Providence in January 1924, had to delay their departure until such time as a federal judge in New York ruled on the question as to whether or not religious teachers were exempt from the national quotas imposed by the 1924 act. Bishop Hickey worked with Fr. Ward, with the National Catholic Welfare Conference, and with Senator LeBaron B. Colt of Rhode Island to secure the admittance of the sisters. It would not be until February that the legal matters were cleared up and the original group of four sisters, headed by Mother Gonzaga McCunnin, arrived in Providence on March 8, 1924 in the midst of a snowstorm. The sisters spent their first few nights in Providence at the convent of the Franciscan Sisters, who staffed St. Joseph's Hospital, while the arrangements for their residence on Elmwood Avenue were completed. The sisters moved into their new home on March 14, 1924.[194]

The sisters named their first foundation St. Gabriel's Hostel. It was intended to be a home for young working women. In England, the hostels run by the Sisters of the Cross and Passion served girls who left their homes to come to find work in the industrial cities. The hostels offered them decent and safe places to live at a cost on a level with the small wages they earned. As the rents paid by the girls did not cover the cost of running the hostels, the difference between what the girls could pay and what the actual costs of running the hostels was made up by the monies other sisters of the Cross and Passions earned by teaching in Catholic schools where the English government paid their salaries. Part of the sisters' apostolate in running the hostels was to provide the girls who lived in them with guidance. Within a few months of the sisters arrival in Providence, the pastor of the Assumption Parish, Fr. Patrick J. Sullivan, arranged to have the sisters give catechetical instruction to the children in his parish and, particularly, to take charge of the preparation of the children of the parish for Confirmation. The sisters began their work on May 11 and the Confirmation was on May 27. At the ceremony itself, Bishop Hickey praised the sisters for the wonderful work they had done in a short period of time. In addition to the sisters' commitment to take over the catechetical program, Fr. Sullivan also secured a commitment from the sisters that they would staff the new parish school he was planning to build.[195]

The sisters received their first boarders at St. Gabriel's on June 14, 1924. In August, Bishop Hickey discussed plans for enlarging the facilities of the hostel with Mother Gonzanga and the architect, Ambrose Murphy. Later that year, the bishop formed the St. Gabriel Aid Association and appointed Fr. Hanley its director. Among the fund-raising endeavors un-

[194] Ibid., February 21, 1924; Mary Ann Strain, C.P., *The Women We Come From: The Sisters of the Cross and Passion in North America, 1924–1968* (Privately printed, 1998), 2–12.
[195] Ibid., 14–16.

dertaken by the association to support the sisters' new work was a concert offered by St. Mary's Industrial School Band of Baltimore, Maryland. The band, known as Babe Ruth's own because he traveled with the band on one of its tours, gave their concert on November 17 at Infantry Hall in Providence.[196]

On June 14, 1924, two additional sisters arrived in Boston to increase the size of the Providence community and to enable them to meet their new commitment at the Assumption. While the sisters looked forward to the opening of the new school and taking up residence in the new convent that Fr. Sullivan was also building, their work in running St. Gabriel's was faltering. Because the sisters teaching in Providence were not paid by the state as they were in England, but by Assumption parish, their income was not sufficient to offset the cost of running St. Gabriel's. In order to cover the cost of running the hostel, the sisters had to take in business and professional women, who were able to pay the full cost of their stay. The women who boarded there had little need to look to the sisters for guidance as did the residents of the sisters' hostels in England and Ireland. Rather, they tended to regard the sisters as "little more than housekeepers or maids and treated them as such." On November 2, 1925, sixteen months after the sisters welcomed their first boarders, Mother Gonzaga met with Bishop Hickey to discuss the future of the hostel. The bishop was well aware at the time of the increasing financial strain on the people of the diocese, who were supporting the existing institutions of charity. He was not about to commit the diocese to the support of another institution that could not pay its own way. At his meeting with Mother Gonzaga, the bishop informed Mother Gonzaga that he did not intend to build a house to put the hostel on a paying basis until he could be assured that it would be filled with "girls" able to pay. In reporting the contents of her meeting with Bishop Hickey to Mother Gerard, Mother Gonzaga wrote "I wouldn't be one bit sorry if [Bishop Hickey's] advisors said close it up as it will be a drag for many years." After the Assumption School opened on February 1, 1926, all the Sisters of the Cross and Passion eventually took up residence in the convent there and Mother Gonzaga became the superior of the house.[197]

In his initial enthusiasm for the establishment of the Sisters of the Cross and Passion in the United States, Fr. Ward had anticipated that the sisters would open a novitiate in the diocese soon after they came. The sisters in England were short of personnel to meet their many commitments. Mother Gerard and her council were convinced that it was important to the success of the order that Sisters of the Cross and Passion begin to attract and train American candidates in order to staff the foundations they anticipated would grow up in the American dioceses. The sisters' first choice was to

---

[196] Ibid., *12; Providence Visitor*, February 21; October 17, 1924; *Providence Journal*, November 15, 1924.
[197] Strain, *The Women We Come From*, 17–18.

seek to establish a novitiate close to a Passionist monastery. When she met with Bishop Hickey on November 2, Mother Gonzaga raised the question of a novitiate outside the Diocese of Providence, to which Bishop Hickey had no objection. When a few days later, the Passionist provincial in New York offered the sisters a position teaching Sunday school in a new Passionist parish in Jamaica, New York, Mother Gonzaga seriously explored the possibility of establishing a new foundation and a novitiate in the Diocese of Brooklyn. Negotiations with the Diocese of Brooklyn eventually failed to secure the desired permission for a novitiate and, in July 1930, Mother General, Rev. Mother Gerard raised the question of a novitiate in the Diocese of Providence. Bishop Hickey quickly gave his consent to its establishment. In April 1932, Mother Gonzaga considered three possible locations, one in Connecticut and two in Rhode Island, one in Warren and the other in Bristol. She eventually chose to purchase an estate in Bristol, the "Rockridge" home of the B. Thomas Potter family, which overlooked the waterfront at the entrance of Mount Hope Bay. On July 23, 1932, Bishop Hickey blessed the new novitiate, which would also serve as a vacation home for the sisters.[198]

Expansion of the Work of the Franciscan Missionaries of Mary

The novitiate of the Sisters of the Cross and Passion was not the first established by a religious order in the state. In 1929, the Franciscan Sisters of Mary opened a novitiate for their order's American candidates in their new convent on Olney Avenue in the Fruit Hill section of North Providence, which they dedicated to the Holy Family. In 1917, the Franciscan Missionaries of Mary had initially acquired the Fred W. Whipple estate at 100 Olney Avenue (later Fruit Hill Avenue) to use as a Procure or Motherhouse for their American Province. Besides their work among the poor in the United States, the Franciscan Missionaries of Mary staffed missions in many places in the world. Those sisters who were going to the missions came to the Procure to prepare for their assignments and to rest after them. Later the sisters acquired the Byron Angell estate, at 399 Olney Avenue, which lay at a considerable distance from their first purchase but offered them more room. The estate had a large and substantial house that the sisters initially used as a convent. In 1924, they began construction of a large, three-and-a-half story brick building which could better serve their needs. The new building was completed, dedicated and occupied in the spring of 1925. It was in their new convent on Fruit Hill that the sisters welcomed their first group of novices in 1929.[199]

---

[198] Ibid., 20–31; *Providence Visitor*, July 22, 29, 1932.
[199] *Providence Sunday Journal*, September 5, 1925; *Providence Visitor*, April 9, 1936.

The Introduction of the Discalced Carmelites

The closing of St. Gabriel's Hostel opened up possibilities for other ministries in the diocese. About a year previous to the closing of St. Gabriel's in May 1925, Bishop Hickey received a letter from a Discalced Carmelite nun of Our Lady of Guadalupe Monastery in Grand Rapids, Michigan, whose monastery was reaching its limit of twenty-one nuns, asking permission to open a new Carmel in the Diocese of Providence. Not wanting to refuse the nun's offer absolutely, Hickey put off sending a response. When on July 13, 1926 the bishop did send a reply, he offered to sell the nuns the Elmwood Street property as the site for a new Carmel.[200]

Although nothing came of the bishop's offer, the memory of his willingness to welcome a foundation of Carmelite Nuns to the diocese remained. On February 18, 1927, Bishop Hickey met with Emily Thorne Post, a convert to the Catholic faith and the widow of Edward C. Post of Newport, who wished to offer her Newport residence at 61 Narragansett Avenue as a site for a new Discalced Carmelite monastery. Mrs. Post's visit began a three-year long effort on Mrs. Post's part, an effort in which she was assisted by the Prior General of the Order of Carmelites, Fr. William of St. Albert, O.C.D., to see a Carmel established in Newport. Because Mrs. Post was determined to place her Carmel under the jurisdiction of the Carmelite Friars, her dream would prove difficult to accomplish. With Bishop Hickey's ready and patient co-operation, she sought to arrange a foundation with a number of different groups — a group from the Carmel, in Philadelphia; a group of exiled Mexican sisters from Guadalajara; a group from the Monastery of Piazza Farnese, Rome; and finally a group from the Carmel at Lisieux, France — all of which declined her offer of a foundation. In 1929, Fr. William of St. Albert, the Prior General, made a paternal visit to all the Carmels in the United States between June and October. At the close of his visit to New Orleans Carmel in August, he asked the community if they would like to go on a foundation. The response was unanimous. The Father General later wrote to the community from Washington, D.C. to officially request a foundation in Newport. On October 3, 1929, he visited Mrs. Post at Stoneleigh, her home in Newport, which she proposed to give to the new foundation. He blessed the house and named its titular patrons, Our Lady of Mt. Carmel and St. Theresa of the Child Jesus. The formal rescript for the foundation of the new Carmel was granted on March 20, 1930. The foundation was delayed until the Discalced Carmelite Fathers could name a chaplain and confessor for the new monastery. On May 14, Fr. Paschasius Heriz, O.C.D., of the Carmelite community in Washington, D.C., came to Newport to take up the duties of chaplain, and on May 16, 1930, the first group of foundresses of

---

[200] Rev. M. Teresa of the Immaculate Conception to Hickey, May 22, 1925; Hickey to Rev. M. Teresa, July 13, 1926, PChA.

the new Carmel arrived from New Orleans. Mrs. Post, a member of the Third Order of the Carmelites, herself became a member of the community. Mrs. Post did not endow the new community to which she turned over her home. However, she did support the foundation as best she could from her own income. On August 10, 1930, Bishop Hickey visited the monastery for the first time and officially established the enclosure.[201]

Word of the monastery's founding first appeared in the *Providence Visitor* and *Newport Daily News* on May 16, 1930. "Stoneleigh," Mrs. Post's estate, lay in the middle of the summer estates in Newport. When she first conceived of the idea of founding a Carmel in Newport, Mrs. Post had the stone wall surrounding her estate raised by several feet in order to provide the seclusion a monastery required. Part of the initial plan for the monastery was that it was also to be the site of a preparatory school or "college" where young men interested in joining the Carmelites might come for their training. Fr. Paschasius opened the preparatory school for the First Order of Carmelites in the former stables of the estate, which were renovated for that purpose, and he was shortly joined by a young student, Brother James, who attended classes at the nearby De La Salle Academy. Fr. Paschasius returned to his duties as Superior and Master of Novices in January 1931 and his place was taken by Father Innocent Delloroto, O.C.D., who came to help at the college in December 1930. Within a short time, the project of the preparatory school in Newport would be abandoned.[202]

The Order of Friars Minor, Capuchins

In July 1926, Fr. Nicholas Higgins, Provincial of the Order of Friars Minor, Capuchin of the Province of Great Britain, called on Bishop Hickey to raise the question of the order's establishing a house in the Diocese of Providence. The meeting went well and on July 30, Fr. Higgins wrote to Bishop Hickey to formally ask permission for the establishment of a Capuchin monastery in the diocese. Representatives of the order had approached Bishop Harkins in 1897 with the same request, but the diocesan consultors, in a meeting on January 10, 1898, recommended that a reply of "inexpedient" be given. As the popularity of retreats and parish missions increased during the early twentieth century, the sisters who ran retreat houses, such as the Cenacle in Newport, and pastors of the various parishes sought to engage members of religious orders to preach the re-

[201] Bishop Hickey's Diary, February 18; March 19, 1927; This paragraph is based on a manuscript history of the monastery prepared by Sister Vilma Seelaus, O.C.D, Prioress of the monastery, a copy of which is found in the Providence Chancery Archives. During Fr. William of St. Albert's second visit to Newport in 1935, Mrs. Post informed him that she could no longer financially support the monastery. She herself left the monastery in September 1935.

[202] Ibid.; *Providence Visitor*, May 16, 1930; *Newport Daily News*, May 16, 17, 1930; *Providence Journal*, May 17, 1930.

treats and missions they wished to offer. When Bishop Hickey brought this second proposal to his board of consultors on July 1, 1926, the consultors, this time, recommended the establishment of the monastery.[203]

On August 24, 1926, Fr. Higgins returned to Providence along with Fr. Brendan Casey, O.F.M., Cap., to work out further details of the establishment. The two had just completed a mission in Immaculate Conception Parish, Providence, and previously had preached a retreat at the Cenacle, Newport. They also had been engaged to preach a mission during the whole of Lent at the cathedral. The negotiations went well and, in November 1926, Fr. Casey and Fr. Daniel Hughes, O.F.M., Cap. took up temporary residence at the former St. Gabriel's Hostel, on Elmwood Avenue in Providence, while they awaited the arrival of three other members of their order from England. Within a few weeks they were joined by three other Capuchins, who, as did the first two Capuchins, had impressive academic credentials.[204]

Fr. Higgins was initially well pleased with the Elmwood Avenue property and agreed to take on the debt still on it but he later changed his mind in May, just before five laymen obtained a state charter of incorporation to enable the community to hold property tax free. Instead of the Elmwood Avenue property, the Capuchins purchased a substantial residence at 334 Norwood Avenue in Cranston. With the acquisition of the new house, a lay brother, Brother Alphonsus Reddy, joined the community in order to keep the house, while the others were away on their various missions. In 1938, the Capuchins acquired the former surgery of Dr. John W. Keefe at 262 Blackstone Boulevard, on Providence's east side, along with two adjoining lots. The former Keefe property consisted of a large, three story brick structure and grounds, which, along with the additional lots, provided ample space for the kind of monastery cloister prescribed by the rule of the Capuchins. After the house was remodeled, Bishop Keough blessed the new St. Francis Friary on November 4, 1938.[205]

The Society of St. Columban

On February 24, 1933, Fr. E. J. McCarthy, Superior of the Chinese Mission Society of St. Columban in St. Columbanus, Nebraska, and one of the founders of the Mission Society, wrote to Bishop Hickey to ask permission to locate a house of the society in the Diocese of Providence to serve as a novitiate, if he could find a suitable location. He explained that their existing houses left little room for expansion and that the number

[203] Higgins to Hickey, July 30, 1926; Minutes of Board of Consultors, January 10, 1898; July 31, 1926, PChA.
[204] Bishop Hickey's Diary, August 24, 1926; *Providence Visitor*, November 5, 26, 1926; *Providence Journal*, November 7, 1926.
[205] *Providence Visitor*, June 3, 11, 1927; May 19; November 3, 1938.

of vocations entering the society continued to increase. Rather than give Fr. McCarthy an immediate answer, the bishop invited him to come to Providence to discuss the idea, since requests for tax exemptions were unwelcome by many towns. Fr. McCarthy took the bishop up on his invitation and the two spent considerable time talking over the possibility of a Columban house in the diocese on April 7. Fr. McCarthy assured Hickey that the society had adequate funds and would not become a financial burden on the diocese. Rather, the house would be an asset for the diocese, since the priests of the society, who staffed the house, would be available to help out the pastors of the diocese when called on. While most of the other mission societies had houses in New England, one of the main sources of vocations in the country, the Columbans did not. Bishop Hickey was sufficiently satisfied with Fr. McCarthy's response to his questions that he brought up the possibility of a Columban foundation with his consultors at their meeting on April 8.[206]

Fr. McCarthy looked at several sites while in Rhode Island, one in Harrisville and another in Bristol, where Bishop Hickey encouraged him to settle, so that one of the priests in house might serve as chaplain to the Sisters of the Cross and Passion at their novitiate. Of the various places in Bristol that he looked at, Fr. McCarthy found the Lyons estate on the west side of Ferry Road near the Mt. Hope Bridge to be particularly well suited to their needs.

While in Bristol, Fr. McCarthy spoke with Luke Callan, a good Catholic and a prosperous contractor and businessman. Mr. Callan warned Fr. McCarthy about the strong anti-Catholic sentiments that existed in the town. Rather than negotiate for the sale of the Lyons property in his own name, Fr. McCarthy employed the services of a Chicago businessman, Charles C. Potter, who in turn employed the services of a non-Catholic lawyer. The negotiations were slowed also because there was not a clear title on the property. By August 2, 1933, Fr. McCarthy was able to give Bishop Hickey a date on which the purchase would be final and to ask his permission for a priest of the society to live there to get it ready for their use.[207]

In August, Bishop Hickey gave his formal written permission for the Columban foundation and Fr. William Kelly, formerly Vice-Rector of the Columban Preparatory Seminary at Silver Creek, New York, was appointed its first rector and master of novices. The *Providence Visitor* broke the news of the Columbans' plans in an article that appeared on August 25, 1933. Although the *Visitor* article presented the establishment as a temporary one, the experience of the Columbans in Bristol would prove to be a positive one for both the Columbans and the diocese because, as Fr.

---

[206] McCarthy to Hickey, February 24, 1933; Hickey to McCarthy's, March 7, 1933; McCarthy to Hickey, March 10; April 8, 1933; Minutes of Board of Consultors Meeting, April 8, 1933, PChA.
[207] McCarthy to Hickey, June 30; August 2, 1933, PChA.

McCarthy had said, the Columbans in Bristol did make themselves available to assist the pastor of St. Mary's, Bristol, as well as others. Bishop Hickey blessed the new novitiate on October 2, shortly after the first group of seven seminarians took up residence there.[208]

Good Works and Spiritual Devotions

The Society for the Propagation of the Faith

During the 1840s and 50s, when the bishop of Hartford lived in Providence, the diocese was financially assisted by the Society for the Propagation of the Faith of Paris and Lyon. While a local society was eventually established in the diocese, it languished in obscurity until January 1924, when Bishop Hickey appointed his fellow student from St. Sulpice, Paris, Fr. William P. Tally, then an assistant at St. Mary's, Providence, as the local society's director. In appointing Fr. Tally and encouraging his work, Bishop Hickey was being faithful to the underlying principles that lay beneath the High School Drive he had launched in 1923. As he believed that all the Catholics of his diocese should be concerned with supporting the work of Catholic education of all the young people of the diocese, he also believed that the Church of Providence should be concerned with supporting the missionaries, who were endeavoring to spread the Catholic Faith throughout the world. On receiving his new assignment, Fr. Tally established his office in the new Visitor Building on Fenner Street. He saw his responsibilities as being twofold: to recruit numerous and active members of the society, who would pay a one dollar regular or a six dollar special membership fee per year or a forty dollar perpetual membership fee, and to spread information regarding missionaries and the importance of their work. This last task was carried out mainly through articles submitted to the *Providence Visitor*.[209]

Fr. Tally represented the diocese at the first formal national convention that Msgr. William Quinn, the national director of the society, organized in New York City in January 1925. The idea for the convention came from a national meeting of the American bishops in Washington the previous September. In organizing a national meeting, the bishops were responding to the call of Pope Pius XI for the established churches to aid the work of missionaries throughout the world. The pope had urged the bishops of the world to unify their efforts in behalf of the missions. Under the papal plan, the Society was to be the official instruments through which collec-

---

[208] *Providence Visitor*, August 25; September 22, 1933.
[209] *Providence Visitor*, December 12, 1824.

tions and missionary gifts for both home and foreign missions were to be made in the future. Accordingly, at the 1925 convention of the Society, the delegates set as a goal for the coming year, the raising of $2,500,000 for the missions. When the American bishops assembled in Washington again in September 1925, they further streamlined mission assistance by creating the American Board of Catholic Missions to receive and distribute all funds for home missions.[210]

In September 1927, Bishop Hickey welcomed to Providence Msgr. Quinn and Archbishop Marchetti-Salvaggiani, director of the Sacred Congregation for the Propagation of the Faith, who in 1925 had organized the Vatican Missionary Exposition in Rome as part of the Holy Year observance. On Tuesday, September 27, Archbishop Francesco Machetti-Salvaggiani addressed the clergy of the diocese in Cathedral Hall. The archbishop urged the Providence clergy to support the fund-raising efforts of the Society for the Propagation of the Faith, which had as its new focus a national collection that was to be taken up annually in all parishes on Mission Sunday, the fourth Sunday of October. According to the plan worked out by Fr. Tally, each parish was to have a parochial director, who was usually the pastor or one of his assistants, who was to act also as spiritual director, and a lay secretary. They would collect the annual dues from the members of the society in their parish. There were also to be promoters of the work in each parish. An important part of the Society's program was the spiritual contributions asked of its members. They were to pray for the success of the missions and offer personal sacrifices for that success.[211]

Holy Years, Novenas and Retreats

Novenas and special devotions to the saints and the Virgin Mary continued to be popular during Bishop Hickey's years. The year 1925 witnessed the celebration of a Jubilee or Holy Year traditionally observed once every twenty-five years. During a Holy Year, a Plenary Indulgence could be gained by visiting Rome, where one confessed one's sins, received communion and visited twelve churches designated for the purpose during that year. To make this opportunity available to the people of the diocese, Bishop Hickey approved the itinerary of a diocesan-sponsored pilgrimage, which left for Rome from New York on July 29. Since the majority of Catholics could not make the pilgrimage to Rome, a plenary indulgence could gained by visiting twelve churches in the diocese designated for that purpose, or by visiting four of the designated churches three times. During the visits, the pilgrims were to say the special prayers provided for the occasion. Ordinarily a Catholic made the Holy Year devotions on one's own.

---

[210] Ibid., January 16; September 25, 1925.
[211] *Providence Journal*, September 27, 28; October 1, 1927; *Providence Visitor*, October 21, 1927.

But as the Holy Year came to an end, the priests of the cathedral parish obtained Bishop Hickey's permission to organize a pilgrimage on November 28, the last Sunday in November, to three other churches in the city for the benefit of their parishioners. More than a thousand people made the traditional visits on the designated day. Over the next three Sundays, the priests of the cathedral organized other processions both on Sundays and during the week, as did priests in other parishes in Providence and Pawtucket. On Sunday, December 12, nearly ten thousand people participated in the pilgrimages, which congested the Providence streets, and thousands more did so on the following Sunday in spite of the bitter cold that gripped the city on that day. In March 1929, Pope Pius XI proclaimed a Jubilee Year following the papacy's successful negotiations with the Italian government on the legal status of the Vatican State and to mark the pope's fiftieth anniversary of ordination. Yet another Jubilee Year was proclaimed in 1933 to mark the nineteenth century of the death of Christ. At the pope's request, virtually every church and chapel in the diocese began the holy year by holding a Holy Hour service on Holy Thursday. Bishop Hickey himself led the Holy Hour at the cathedral, and large crowds attended the various observances throughout the diocese. In 1933, the diocese again sponsored a pilgrimage to Rome.[212]

Eucharistic devotion also continued to be an important part of Catholic devotional life. Since most people went to communion only after having confessed the day before, Benediction was frequently held in all parishes as another form of Eucharistic devotion. In October 1927, an Apostolic Brief from the Holy See granted a plenary indulgence for the recitation of a third of the Rosary (five decades) in the Presence of the Blessed Sacrament, a favor which served to increase visits to the Blessed Sacrament. In 1930, five priests and a number of lay people took part in the official diocesan pilgrimage to Carthage, the site of that year's International Eucharistic Congress. In 1931, the diocese also sponsored an official pilgrimage to the International Eucharistic Congress in Dublin, Ireland. Unofficial reports noted that nearly seven hundred people from the diocese planned to attend the Dublin Congress.[213]

In June 1925, Bishop Hickey took advantage of the construction of the new Mt. St. Charles Academy, Woonsocket, to make a change in the location at which the annual retreats for the clergy of the diocese were held. Since Bishop Hendricken's time, the annual clergy retreat had been held at the College of the Holy Cross, Worcester, where one of the Jesuit priests served as retreat master. In 1925, half of the clergy made their retreat at

---

[212] *Providence Visitor*, July 10, 1925; December 27, 1926; March 3, 1929; April 7, 21, 1933; *Providence Journal*, November 29; December 13, 20, 1926.
When one visited only four churches, one made four distinct visits, even if made on the same day, by stepping out of the church three times. For a perspective on the spirituality this time cf. Jay P. Dolan, *The American Catholic Experience*, 221–40.

[213] *Providence Visitor*, October 27, 1927; April 4, 1930; September 12, 1931; January 15; June 3, 1932.

CHAPTER IV

The Church and Social Justice

Public Morality

The 1920 Federal census counted 604,397 residents in the state. In the same year, Kenedy's *Catholic Directory* listed the Catholic population of the state as being about 276,211. The upsurge in immigration that followed the First World War along with the natural increase of the state's population and internal migration caused the state's general population to rise to 679,260 in the 1925 census and the Catholic population to 284,267 in the Kenedy *Directory*. After the federal immigration acts of 1921 and 1924 introduced immigration quotas, the rate of immigration from Europe declined so that in 1930, the state saw only a moderate increase to 687,497 in the 1930 federal census, while the census of the diocese gave 319,903 as the number of Catholics. The impact of the Depression was seen in the last State Census, whose statistics were released in 1936. According to the census report, the state's population had declined slightly to 680,712. The Catholic population of the state in the 1936 according to diocesan figures was 339,672. These figures show that in 1925, Catholics made up about 42% of the population in the state. In 1936, Catholics made up approximately 50% of the state's population.[1]

The above figures reveal that by the 1920s the Catholic population of the state, if mobilized behind or against issues that bridged the gap between church and state, was a force to be reckoned with. Although Bishop Hickey's years coincided with the years of the greatest success and ultimate decline of the Ku Klux Klan, the American Catholic Church in general and the Church of Providence in particular, felt no anxiety about the joining the public debate on moral issues confronting the nation. Far more than his predecessor, Bishop Hickey was temperamentally inclined to involve himself and the Church in civic issues. The substantial expansion of

---

[1]   The state population figures are those given in the *Rhode Island Manual* and the Catholic population figures are those given in *The Official Catholic Directory* published yearly by P. J. Kenedy & Sons, New York, New York. The figures for the Diocese of Providence were supplied by the diocese itself.

338

the Catholic school system, which he made the focus of his administration, and Bishop Hickey's support of his clergy's efforts to create vacation schools in the diocese arose in part from his belief that the public schools presented a danger to the faith of the Catholic students who attended them. During an eleven day period in June 1932, Bishop Hickey, as was his custom, traveled throughout the diocese to preside at the various high school graduations and to confer the students' diplomas. The bishop used the forum of the addresses he gave to the graduates and their parents at each graduation to urge the parents to continue their Christian consistency by having their children attend Catholic colleges. He decried the atheism that he contended had crept into the public schools because of the schools' emphasis on temporal things. In an address he gave to the students and parents at St. Raphael's in Pawtucket in 1932, the bishop used the junior high school experiment of the Providence school system as an example of the dangers children were exposed to in the public schools. He accused the Providence schools, which offered a wide variety of subjects "from 'bed making' to 'cooking,'" of being "apparently lacking in disciplinary control" and "of weaning children away from respect for their parents and home" because the children became ashamed of their parents when they did not "measure up to the standard of living" set by the junior high schools. He also deplored what he saw as students' freedom "to choose any course of study and drop others because of inconvenience or hardship."[2]

While most Rhode Island Catholics probably did not share Bishop Hickey's alarm in regard to the Providence school department's experiment with junior high schools, many Rhode Islanders, both Catholics and non-Catholics, did share his concern about the godlessness of the public schools. In October 1934, the State Congress of Parents and Teachers held a seminar in the Pawtucket senior high school auditorium. The organizers of the meeting invited three members of the clergy, Fr. Lorenzo C. McCarthy, O.P., President of Providence College; Rev. Russell Hubbard, D.D., rector of St. Martin's Episcopal Church, Providence; and Rabbi Morris Shussheim of Temple Beth-Israel, Providence, to address them on the seminar's theme, "The Child and His Religion." In his remarks, Fr. McCarthy stated that he had "no grievance against the [public] school." However, he did express his serious concern that,

> Whether through ignorance or ambition, whether consciously or unconsciously, the school has so extended its functions or so over-emphasized its role in the educational process as to fail to take cognizance of the home and church as two other institutions of equal if not greater importance than itself.[3]

During the course of his remarks to the annual meeting of the Union of Holy Name Societies in March 1922, Bishop Hickey began by speak-

---

2   *Providence Visitor*, June 17, 1932.
3   *Providence Journal*, October 9, 1934.

ing generally of the need for Catholics to exert their influence to preserve virtue in the world and stressed particularly the duties of parents in the rearing of future men and women of character and solid virtue. He then addressed what he regarded as extremes in the fashions of the day, which he saw as a reversion to the habit of personal exposure and as "evidence of decadence." In the midst of the heat of the summer in 1925, Bishop Hickey returned to the subject again. In his sermons at the cathedral, he referred to some contemporary women's fashions as a "public scandal and an insult to God." Again citing a recent talk by the pope and the action taken by Roman authorities barring women who were not properly dressed from entering a church, the bishop declared that the same policy would be followed in the diocese unless "more respect was shown for the house of God."[4]

From the pulpit of the cathedral, Bishop Hickey warned his listeners of the dangers inherent in similar kinds of behavior when he believed that proper respect was not being shown. On one occasion after he observed a number of people leave the cathedral immediately after receiving Holy Communion, he announced that in the future acolytes with lighted candles would be posted at the doors of the cathedral to accompany those who left immediately after receiving for two blocks while ringing a bell. As in dealing with his clergy, Bishop Hickey generally never went beyond issuing a warning.[5]

In regard to the question of indecent literature and movies which the Union of Holy Name Societies, the Knights of Columbus and other Catholic organizations, addressed, Bishop Hickey supported their resolutions deploring the sale of such literature and the screening of such movies, but he did not make them the subject of a personal crusade of his own. However, when in February 1932, the management of the RKO-Albee theater in Providence proposed holding a wedding ceremony on the theater's stage, Bishop Hickey issued a strong statement condemning the idea as "a commercial stunt" which was offensive "both to Christian sentiments and good taste." He observed in his statement that the producers of live stage shows and theater managers were at particular pains during Lent to provide additional attractions in the hope of counterbalancing the patronage they traditionally lost during the season. The bishop took the occasion of his statement to renew the counsel contained in his annual Lenten letter to avoid frequenting theaters, dance halls and movies during the Lenten season.[6]

The issue of the sanctity of marriage arose in 1933 in another context, that of marathon dances. In January 1933, Representative James S. Lynch of Providence sponsored a bill in the General Assembly to prohibit

4   *Providence Visitor*, March 31, 1922; August 14, 1925; *Providence Journal*, March 27, 1922; August 10, 1925.
5   Interview with Rev. Joseph A. Besse, July 20, 1994.
6   Ibid., February 12, 1932.

marathon dance contests. What provoked Lynch to submit his bill was the spectacle of a marathon dance contest being held in Pawtucket at the beginning of January. Lynch found the building in which the contest was being held to be poorly ventilated and generally unhealthy given the fact that smoking was allowed in the low-ceilinged hall. According to his observations, the dance was a gathering place for children and the scene of drinking parties late at night. In the state that had laws against the staging of rooster and dog fights, he found the dance contest to be a "most disgusting pagan spectacle." What particularly raised his ire was the fact that the promoters of the contest had scheduled a wedding ceremony involving two of the professional dancers in an effort to lure paying spectators to the contest. Rather than being an unusual event, press clippings and photos supplied by the managers of the event revealed that marriage ceremonies were a regular part of these events. Lynch denounced the proposed marriage as a "commercial stunt" and quoted Bishop Hickey's statement on the RKO-Albee wedding as support for his position.[7]

Representative Lynch's statements promoted two women's groups in Pawtucket, the St. Raphael's Academy Ladies Auxiliary and the Diocesan Council of the National Council of Catholic Women, to protest the proposed marriage. The protests, together with that of Rep. Lynch, were enough to prompt the promoters to drop plans for the wedding. Furthermore, the new Pawtucket police committee, which was responsible for ruling on what public entertainments could be opened on Sundays, refused to renew the permission granted by the old board. Aroused by the publicity given the contest, the Pawtucket police stopped the contest on Monday, January 23, but the company sponsoring the event got a Superior Court judge to grant a temporary injunction preventing the police, the Board of Aldermen and the Common Council from "interfering with lawful business of the complainant." However, the Pawtucket Board of Aldermen, on January 25, voted unanimously to revoke the marathon company's license. Soon after the aldermen's action, the Pawtucket police closed the contest.[8]

In May 1933, another promoter applied for a license to hold a marathon dance contest in Newport for 102 days. In light of the experience in Pawtucket, the Newport Board of Aldermen refused to grant the license. The next year the promoter applied for a license in Tiverton, which the town council granted, but was forced by public opinion to rescind. He tried again to obtain a license to hold the event in Newport, but was again rebuffed. Finally, he turned to the town of Portsmouth, where he had previously run a dance hall at the Island Park amusement grounds. Here, in spite of the experience of Pawtucket and other places, he was granted a license to hold a "walkathon for the season of 1934," and a wooden building was hastily erected to house the event. A walkathon was essentially the

---

7   *Providence Visitor,* January 13, 1933.
8   Ibid., January 20, 27, 1933.

same thing as a marathon. The name change was simply an effort to avoid the notoriety attached to the former title. Although Mr. Lynch's bill to ban dance marathons passed the Rhode Island House in 1933 and 1934, in both years it was killed by a Senate committee.[9]

Birth Control and Abortion

Of all the moral issues of the early twentieth century, the two that perhaps most concerned Bishop Hickey were those of birth control and abortion. In 1923, the Voluntary Parenthood League of New York requested that Congress repeal the portion of federal law that prohibited the circulation of birth control literature through the mails. The League's initiative brought what had been a private, moral question into the public forum. The prohibition against the circulation of the literature by the advocates of birth control was part of a statue passed in the early 1870s that aimed to suppress the commerce in "salacious" literature. In April 1924, the subcommittees of the House and Senate Judiciary committees held hearings on the Cummins-Vaile bill, which would have opened the mails to both birth control literature and devices. Catholic opposition, in which a representative of the Evangelical Lutheran Synod joined, was led by Fr. (later Msgr.) John A. Ryan, as representative of the National Catholic Welfare Conference, and Miss Agnes G. Regan, as representative of the National Council of Catholic Women. The proposed bill was defeated but the proponents of contraception would make ongoing efforts to repeal the ban. In Rhode Island there were no state laws against the distribution of pro-birth control literature and the sale of contraceptive devices, because at the time it was thought none was needed.[10]

In August 1930, the issue of birth control took on a somewhat local dimension when Dr. Clarence A. Barbour, president of Brown University, speaking from the pulpit of the Lafayette Avenue Presbyterian Church of Brooklyn, urged the passage of a law that would prevent "propagation of 'inferior' children, born of sub-normal parents." A report of Dr. Barbour's sermon was picked up by the Associated Press and appeared in the *Providence Journal* on August 4. On the following Friday, the *Providence Visitor* printed a response by Bishop Hickey to the remarks attributed to Dr. Barbour. Bishop Hickey was careful not to attack Dr. Barbour personally, but rather directed his remarks to the "an unsocial and immoral measure" that Dr. Barbour advocated in his sermon. In place of an artificial method to achieve the eugenic end advocated by Dr. Barbour, Bishop Hickey urged

9   Ibid., May 12, 1933; January 5, 12, 26; June 22, 1934.
10 *Providence Visitor*, February 2, 1923; April 17, 1924; January 1, 1934; David M. Kennedy, *Birth Control in America: The Career of Margaret Sanger* (New Haven and London: Yale University Press, 1970), 224–71. For the context of this issues Cf. John T. McGreevy, *Catholicism and American Freedom: A History* (New York: W. W. Norton & Company, 2003, 221–227.

self-control and the acceptance of personal and corporate responsibility for sin. When interviewed by a *Journal* reporter, Dr. Barbour insisted that the matter of propagation of sub-normal people was merely incidental to his chief point. While he rejected the idea that self-control would cure the problems that he sought to address, he decried any intention of provoking a controversy between churches in Providence.[11]

As Leslie Woodcock Tentler has pointed out in her 2004 work, *Catholics and Contraception*, a more troubling development for Catholics was the fact that, by June 1930, four liberal denominational bodies in the United States—the Universalist General Convention, the American Unitarian Association, the New York East Conference of the Methodist Episcopal Church, and the Central Conference of American Rabbis—had publicly endorsed marital contraception. The action of these groups was followed in August by the Anglicans' Lambeth Conference, which reversed its previous stance against artificial birth control, and adopted a guarded blessing of its use in difficult marital circumstances. In was partly in response to these developments that Pope Pius XI issued *Casti connubii*, in which he set out the Catholic position of marriage and birth control on December 31, 1930. As Dr. Tentler noted in her 2004 work on *Catholics and Contraception*,

> The pope clearly and vigorously reaffirmed what he held to be the constant teaching of the Church against contraception. . . . The pope especially warned confessors against 'conniving in the false opinion of the faithful' by failing to question married penitents or giving evasive answers to their queries about birth control.
>
> The encyclical brought new pressure to bear on bishops and their priests with regard to reforming pastoral practice. And it made it much more difficult for lay Catholics to make a credible claim of good faith ignorance when it came to Church teaching on contraception.[12]

In February 1931, Sen. Gillett of Massachusetts introduced a bill in Congress that, if passed, would allow the importation, distribution, and sale of contraceptive literature, and instruments. Rather than speak out publically himself, Bishop Hickey encouraged the diocesan councils of Catholic men and women to urge their members to sign a petition against the passage of the Gillett bill. The Gillett measure died in the Senate, but the activities of the proponents of artificial birth control continued on both national and local levels.[13]

In March 1931, Dr. Clarence C. Little of Bar Harbour, Maine, who was associated with the Roscoe B. Jackson Foundation for Cancer Research and a former president of Michigan University, delivered a lecture to a meeting sponsored by the American Birth Control League in the Plantations Auditorium in Providence. The aim of meeting was to stir interest

11 *Providence Journal*, August 4, 9, 1930; *Providence Visitor*, August 8, 1930.
12 Leslie Woodcock Tentler, *Catholics and Contraception: An American History* (Ithaca and London: Cornel University Press, 2004), 72–73.
13 *Providence Visitor*, February 6, 13, 1931.

in forming a Rhode Island branch of the Birth Control League. In his lecture, Dr. Little contended that there was no longer any great opposition to birth control and that the problem was one of how best to promote the idea and eliminate misunderstanding of it. In the course of his remarks, Dr. Little held that liberal Catholics were not in agreement with the Catholic hierarchy on the question and that the "official" Catholic Church constituted the chief opposition to the spread of the idea of birth control.[14]

Bishop Hickey could not let Dr. Little's remarks, as reported by the *Providence Journal*, go without rebuttal, especially as the doctor had dismissed Pope Pius's recent encyclical on Christian marriage, *Casti connubii*, as neither accurate nor dignified. Although Dr. Little was right in saying that the Roman Catholic Church presented the chief opposition to the spread of the idea of birth control, Hickey properly noted that there were "great numbers of people outside the body of the Church that are staunchly opposed to contraception." In regard to Dr. Little's statements that the "ordinary, intelligent communicant of the Rhode Catholic Church is at odds with his hierarchy on the question," and that the average Catholic was "either quite upset at or quite ignorant" of the stand of the hierarchy on the question, Hickey stated that opposition or ignorance did not invalidate the doctrine as it was derived, not from the will of man, but of God as manifested in nature. That Catholics were ignorant of the Church's teaching was upsetting, Hickey remarked, especially to the Catholic clergy who deplored such ignorance.[15]

There is no scientific evidence as to the extent and nature of Catholic contraceptive practice during the depression years of the thirties. Basing their conclusions largely on demographic data, Catholic authorities widely assumed that a good many Catholics made at least intermittent use of forbidden means of family limitation. As Dr. Tentler has pointed out, various non-Catholic birth control advocates during this time claimed that from one quarter to one half of the patients in urban birth control clinics routinely identified themselves as Catholics, and sometimes as Catholics who had previously turned to abortion as a desperate means of family limitation. Drawing from the evidence offered by counselors and confessors who lived during this time period, and joining it with falling birth rates and a growing public acceptance of contraception, Dr. Tentler concluded, "that a significant minority of Catholics — some of them devout — had made a kind of personal peace with contraceptive practice." The evidence suggests that contraceptive use was strongly correlated with income and education. For the most part, during this period, the Catholics who took part in the studies on family planning that were done at this time, were the least educated group in the sample population.[16]

---

[14]   *Providence Journal*, March 5, 1931; *Providence Visitor*, March 6, 1931.
[15]   *Providence Journal*, March 5, 8, 1931.
[16]   Tentler, *Catholics and Contraception*, 76–77.

Particularly in the Depression, the reasons some penitents offered for their use of artificial birth control elicited sympathy from many of their counselors and confessors. *Casti connubii* cautioned confessors against failing in their duty by "permitting the faithful to err about this most serious law." Priests, in general, were reluctant to preach on the subject of birth control. Those who did were most often the religious who were engaged to preach the yearly parish mission. They spoke to men and women separately so that they had more time to discuss the subject. In 1932, new information on a woman's ovulatory cycle presented the compassionate confessors and troubled couples who had a legitimate reason for restricting or spacing out the size of their families another alternative. The use of the rhythm method, however, was unreliable. At best it was said that the method offered some hope for spacing out births in the case of some couples.[17]

Opposition on the part of the majority of Catholics and others to artificial birth control was not enough to prevent the establishment of a birth control clinic in Providence on July 30, 1931. The clinic, at 103 North Main Street, was sponsored by the Rhode Island Birth Control League and was intended to provide information on birth control only to married women, who were referred to the clinic by a private physician, hospital, clinic or social agency. The clinic was organized in May and subsequently incorporated. With its opening, it became the first such clinic in New England.[18]

In making the announcement of the clinic's opening, the *Providence Journal* gave the names of the committee of physicians who would attend each of the clinics and of the officers and members of the Rhode Island Birth Control League, which was sponsoring it. The article also provided the names of the members of the honorary committee that would sponsor the New England conference of the American Birth Control League that was planned for October in the Biltmore Hotel to show the support the purposes of the League had. The league's members and supporters were upper middle class professionals. Among the league's leaders were several Protestant ministers, and physicians. Six doctors ran the clinic with the aid of a social worker and a trained nurse. The "honorary committee of supporters" included the President, a dean, and several professors from Brown University, thirty-one doctors, the owner of the *Providence Journal*, a rabbi,

---

[17] Ibid., 79–122.
[18] Christine E. Nicoll and Robert G. Weisbord, "The Early Years of the Rhode Island Birth Control League," *Rhode Island History,* November 1986, 112; 114–15. Unlike other states, Rhode Island did not have a law forbidding the distribution of Birth Control information.

and three Protestant ministers. It also included a number of upper middle class women who lived predominately on Providence's East Side.[19]

As was the case with the attempts to repeal the Comstock Law against sending birth control information through the mails, Bishop Hickey was content to let lay people to speak out against the opening of the Providence Birth Control Clinic. Its opening particularly provoked the anger of a majority of the Providence Board of Aldermen who, on August 6, 1931, passed a resolution condemning the operation of the clinic and directing the City Solicitor and ordinance committee to consider and report on the legality of its operation. As directed by the Board, John C. Maloney, the City Solicitor, reported at the Board's September 3 meeting, that any action against the clinic had to be initiated by the Board of Public Safety. In spite of Mr. Maloney's report, Alderman Antonio C. Ventrone, who was a doctor, proposed a resolution instructing Mr. Maloney to prosecute the operators of the clinic and delivered a fiery attack on the whole birth control movement. Ventrone's motion, however, was tabled after Alderman Rush Sturges, the alderman for the East Side, defended those behind the movement and suggested that, before the Board took any action, it should hear from both sides of the questions. The motion remained tabled until after the clinic opened. Following the opening, Dr. Ventrone submitted a resolution to condemn the operation of birth control clinics in the city. After the clinic opened, Dr. Ventrone submitted another resolution in which the City Solicitor was directed to prosecute the operator of the clinic. After Dr. Ventrone made a fiery speech in support of the resolution and Alderman Sturgis made a lengthy one in the defense of those behind the clinic, the aldermen voted unanimously to table the resolution. Both resolutions were formally dropped the next year.[20]

When the clinic first opened, it offered its services only on Thursday and Friday mornings beginning at 10:30. However, the demand for the services the clinic provided was such that, within the clinic's first year, the committee in charge of the clinic extended its schedule to a full five days and its hours from 9:30 to 4:30. In spite of its extended hours, its consultation hours remained the same, Thursday and Friday from 10:30 to 12:30. Most of the clinics clients, as ascertained by a non-Catholic woman reporter hired in November 1933 by the *Providence Visitor* to investigate the clinic, were referred to it by the Family Welfare Society and other private

---

[19]   Ibid. Nicoll and Weisbord point out that the support of the upper class for birth control arose from "a curious combination of motives — mainly, humanitarian, but sometimes elitist . . . Eugenic, class, and nativist considerations undoubtedly informed the thinking of some birth control advocates in Providence and elsewhere. Birth rates among white Anglo-Saxon Protestants were lower than among the "hordes" of impoverished recent immigrants from southern and eastern Europe. If the fecund 'unwashed' alien population embraced birth control, a multiplicity of problems that afflicted urban slums could be mitigated and the traditional character of America preserved. Birth control was part of the process of Americanization." p. 115.

[20]   *Providence Journal*, July 29; August 7; September 4, 1931; Nicoll and Weisbord, "The Early Years of the Rhode Island Birth Control League," 121–22.

social agencies. It was suspected, but not proven, that public welfare agencies also referred clients, Catholics among them, to the clinic. By 1937, the RIBCL also maintained clinics in Newport and the village of Shannock in Washington County.[21]

When in October 1933, the Rhode Island League launched a well-organized campaign to expand its membership, Catholic women's groups in the state mobilized to counteract the League's efforts. On Monday, December 4, 1933, over five hundred women braved adverse winter weather to attend a meeting in the Biltmore Hotel organized by National Council of Catholic Women for a public demonstration on behalf of Christian marriage. At the dinner meeting, the women were addressed by Miss Regan, the executive secretary of the National Council of Catholic Women, Dr. William R. McGuirk, and Msgr. Peter E. Blessing. In addition to his talk at the Biltmore, Dr. McGuirk also contributed a series of articles that were printed in the *Providence Visitor* in which he questioned the particular methods employed by doctors to prevent births and the larger question of the impact of the use of artificial birth control methods on the life of the individual and on society. Debate on medical and moral aspects of artificial birth control would continue in the public form throughout the 1930s. Catholic women's groups and the *Providence Visitor* were among the loudest voices raised in defense of the Catholic position.[22]

In April 1931, three months after Pope Pius XI issued *Casti cannubii*, the three Catholic pastors in Cranston, led by Fr. Thomas Tiernan, pastor of St. Ann's, unanimously voiced their opposition to the very suggestion that the Cranston School Committee investigate the possibility of introducing a course on sex hygiene into the high school curricula. The clergy raised their voices in support of a resolution objecting to the proposition that the committee undertake a study of the question adopted by the Catholic Men's Club of Auburn. In taking its stand, the Catholic Men's Club and the clergy pointed to Pius XI's recent encyclical to show that their stand had the backing of Catholic teaching.[23]

The Ku Klux Klan

Of even more immediate concern to Bishop Hickey and the Rhode Island Catholics in the 1920s and 30s was the rise of the modern Ku Klux Klan. The modern Klan had its origins in Atlanta, Georgia, in 1915, but did not become a national concern until its founder, William J. Simmons, engaged the services in 1920 of the Southern Publicity Association found-

---

21 *Providence* Journal, November 4, 1932; *Providence Visitor*, November 3, 10, 17, 1933.
22 *Providence Visitor*, October 20, 27; November 10, 17, 24; December 8, 1933. For other articles that appeared in the *Visitor* during the 1930s, see the Birth Control file in the Providence Diocesan Chancery Archives.
23 *Providence Visitor*, January 9; April 2, 1931.

ed by Edward Young Clarke and Elizabeth Tyler. Clarke and Tyler perceived that there was in 1920 a considerable market for a mystical organization that focused not only on the danger to Southern "order" presented in Simmons' view by Africans Americans, but also on the danger to Democracy and Protestantism created by the flood of Catholic and Jewish immigrants that had come into the country in the three decades before the World War and whose numbers were increasing once again in postwar America. The growth in their numbers presented a real threat to the continued political dominance of what the Klan leaders regarded as the authentic American way of life.[24]

Bishop Hickey acknowledged the challenge the modern Klan posed to the Catholic Church as early as October 9, 1921, when in a Church Day address on the occasion of Pawtucket's 250th Anniversary, he asserted that the Catholic Church only became involved in politics to protect its God-given rights. Klan activities and support for it did not become an immediate concern until the beginning of 1923. On January 14, 1923, the *Providence Journal* carried a report that a Catholic priest, a state senator, and three businessmen in Woonsocket had all recently received threats signed "K.K.K." In February 1933, the Catholics of Westerly were aroused when Westerly school officials allowed high school students to debate the issue of whether or not the Klan posed a menace to American society. The team defending the Klan, moved by passion for their side, made derogatory statements in regard to the Catholic Church, which prompted the debate judges to call a halt to the exercise. In rendering their decision, the judges declared the pro-Klan team the winner of the debate. At a meeting of the Westerly School Committee subsequent to the debate, a representative of Westerly Catholics demanded that the School Committee issue a public apology for allowing such a volatile subject as the Klan to be debated by the students and for the religious slurs that resulted from it. Although the Catholics in the town were numerous, racist sentiments were also strong. In the town's Weekapaug section, landowners regularly wrote a prohibition against the purchasers selling, leasing, or conveying the land to Italians or persons of Italian heritage into their property deeds. The Westerly School Committee did express its regret that the debate incident had happened, but refused to make any apology. Edward Clarke, the Klan organizer, helped to stir up emotions a bit more when he wrote to the students on the winning team to congratulate them.[25]

It was not until October 1923 that the state's politicians began to take notice of the Klan's organizing activity. On Friday, October 19, at a meet-

---

[24] For background on the Klan, cf. David H. Bennett, *The Party of Fear: From Nativist Movements to the New Right in American History* (Chapel Hill: The University of North Carolina Press, 1988); Mark Paul Richard, *Not a Catholic Nation: The Ku Klux Klan Confronts New England in the 1920's* (Amherst & Boston: University of Massachusetts Press, 2015, 131–149); Kenneth T. Jackson, *The Ku Klux Klan in the City, 1915–1930* (New York: Oxford University Press, 1967).

[25] *Providence Post*, February 1, 6, 7, 1923; September 12, 1927; *Providence Journal*, September 9, 1927.

ing of the Democratic State central committee, the members expressed
their concern over reports that Klan organizers were meeting with some
success in their efforts "in South County and elsewhere in the State." The
committee passed a resolution calling on the people of the state to join the
fight against the Klan. It was at this same time that the night-riding activities of the Klan began. Edna Lovett (later Sr. Rita Lovett, F.C.J.), a resident of the Mt. Pleasant section of Providence, recalled a time in the fall
of 1923 that twenty white-clad riders carrying crosses went up Chalkstone
Avenue to what was known then as Violet Hill (the hill was across from
the Obadiah Brown estate on which the Triggs Memorial Golf Course is
now located) on three successive nights and set their crosses alight. On the
fourth night, the Klansmen burnt their cross on Mt. Pleasant Avenue between the Mt. Pleasant Primary School and George J. West School. When
firemen came to put out the fire, the horsemen went down the hill and
threw small red crosses on the steps of Blessed Sacrament church. When
they returned the next night, a Sunday night, they were met by a group
of men from Blessed Sacrament's Holy Name Society near the car barn
at the corner of Canton and Chalkstone avenues. The Holy Name men
blocked the road and three policemen, who were with them, ordered the
Klansmen to go back where they came from and leave the neighborhood
alone.[26]

In the rural town of East Greenwich, beginning in the second week of
April and extending into August 1924, a different sort of confrontation
between the Klan and Catholics took place. On April 10, the editor of the
Rhode Island Pendulum, Mrs. Fay R. Hunt, began printing a series of letters
between Morris S. Westervelt, who had been recently identified as a Klan
organizer from New Jersey, and George W. Gill, a local Catholic. Like the
high school students in Westerly, the debaters, especially Mr. Gill, found it
difficult to remain rational and dispassionate. On his part, Mr. Westervelt
had little in the way of original insight to contribute, but relied on material
from Klan publications to support his position. In the words of one historian who has reread the exchange of letters, the two "may have generated
more heat than light for avid readers."[27]

Reports of Klan activity in the various newspapers of the state increased
in 1924. While there were many who publicly denounced the Klan, there
were some, like Rev. Charles A. Meader, the general missionary of the
Episcopal Church in Rhode Island, who openly defended it. In June 1924,
the *Providence Journal* gave a report on the first public Klan initiation ceremony held in the state on the Old Home Day grounds in Foster. According to the report, some 8,000 Klansmen from five New England states,

---

[26] *Providence Journal*, October 20, 1923; Recollections of St. Rita Lovett, F.C.J., May 3, 1987. Cf. also Norman W. Smith, "The Ku Klux Klan in Rhode Island," in *Rhode Island History*, Vol. 37 (May 1978), 35–46. This section on the Klan owes much to Dr. Smith's article.

[27] *Rhode Island Pendulum*, April 10, 1924; Norman W. Smith, "The Ku Klux Klan in Rhode Island," p. 37.

among them many sailors from Newport and New London, gathered in
Foster for a rally and to welcome new members of their order. After a series of lectures, the candidates were divided into groups according to the
county in which they lived for their initiation ceremonies. The two largest
groups were residents of Providence and Kent counties, while a good number came from Newport County and a much smaller group from Bristol
County. Three days later, the *Journal* reported that the Klan held a smaller
ceremony near the Austin Farm in Exeter at which a hundred residents of
Washington County were initiated before three fiery crosses. The reports
prompted an editorial in the *Journal* advising the citizens of Rhode Island
not to join the Klan.[28]

In 1924, the Klan was not only concerned with recruiting new members but also with encouraging those who shared its views to register to
vote. In 1922, the Democrats in the state had taken advantage of the
widespread discontent with Republican Gov. Emery J. San Souci, who had
called out the state militia in the textile strike in 1922, and who failed to
veto the Peck Act, which put private schools until control of the State Department of Education, to win all the state's general offices except that
of Secretary of State. However, the Democratic Party lost the support of
many when they used the filibuster in an attempt to force the Republican-controlled General Assembly to consider political reform legislation, a
move that led deadlock and to the "stink bomb" incident of June 19, 1924
as noted above. In the fall election of 1924, Gov. William Flynn stood for
the office of senator and Lt. Gov. Felix Toupin for governor. The Republicans were particularly anxious to defeat both Democratic candidates and
regain control of the state house.[29]

In June 1924, the *Providence News*, an avowed enemy of the Klan, reported on the Klan's effort to register voters for the fall election. July 16,
1924 saw the first appearance of the *Rhode Island Klansman* through which
the Klan sought to advance its cause. The *Post* chose to see the paper as
a Republican organ. The Klan also distributed copies of *The Fellowship
Forum*, a national publication of the Klan, which in its June 28, 1924 issue
printed as a headline above the paper's masthead, "Poison Gas Used in
Rhode Island Senate as Rome Seeks to Control Legislature." On October
26, the Klan held an outdoor rally and initiation near Chepachet Road in
Greenville attended by some 3,000 Klansmen at which 200 men were initiated. The assembled Klansmen endorsed the Republican candidate, Senator Jesse H. Metcalf, who was running against Gov. William Flynn in the
then popular election for senator. As the day of the election drew near, the
Klan distributed thousands of copies of a broadside attacking the Roman
Catholic Church. The appearance of the broadsides prompted Fr. James

28 *Providence Journal*, June 22, 25, 27, 1924.
29 For a political overview, cf. Charles C. Carroll, "Six Decades in These Plantations," in *Rhode Island
History*, Vol. 59 (May 2001), 37–64.

P. O'Brien, editor of the *Visitor*, to castigate the publisher of the broadsides in uncommonly strong language.[30]

The hopes of the state's Democratic leaders that the Klan issue might sway voters and balance off their anger at the Democrats' tactics in the senate did not materialize. When the Republicans scored landslide victories in most races in the November elections, the Klan celebrated by burning crosses placed on hilltops throughout the state. One of the crosses was set afire at the corner of Eaton and River avenues on the campus of Providence College. On that evening the Apostolic Delegate, Archbishop Fumasoni-Biondi, who was in Providence for the dedication of the new LaSalle Academy building, presided at the ceremony in St. Pius Church, which was then located in Harkins Hall. The burning cross, the second set up on the campus in ten days, was discovered by the parishioners of St. Pius as they left the ceremony with the delegate.[31]

Following the election, the major newspapers' coverage of Klan events declined significantly. East Greenwich's *Pendulum*, however, continued to report on the Klan's efforts to recruit new members. It was between 1924 and 1928, that the Klan in Rhode Island enjoyed its greatest success in recruiting and retaining members. Since the Klan was a secret organization, membership numbers are at best estimates. Drawing from the bits and pieces of information published about the Klan in local newspapers, a reasonable estimate would place Klan membership at about six thousand men and women. As was true of the Klan in other states, the Rhode Island Klan saw changes in its leadership. Sometime during 1924, Mr. Westervelt left the state for Maine. It is unclear who exactly exercised leadership roles in the Klan between when Westervelt left and when John A. Domin, a United Electric Company motorman, in 1926 became Exalted Cyclops of Roger Williams Klanton No. 16, perhaps the largest Klan organization in the state, and John W. Perry became grand dragon or grand titan for the realm of Connecticut and Rhode Island in the same year. Nationally, scandals among Klan organizations in several states rocked the order as early as 1925. Although the Klan would claim credit for Republican victories in 1924, the political strength and influence of the Rhode Island Klan was not tested until 1927, when four different bills, similar to Klan-sponsored bills in other states, were submitted to the General Assembly. Two of them were offered by Senator Charles Weaver of Richmond in late January. The first of Weaver's bills would have made it illegal for parties to a marriage in Rhode Island to enter into a contract relative to the religious training of children of that marriage, as the Catholic Church required Catholic and non-Catholic couples who wished to be married in the Catholic Church to do. The second bill introduced by Senator Weav-

---

30 *Providence Post,* July 16, 17; October 27, 1924. The *Post* printed facsimiles of the Klan's newspapers. If there was more than one issue of the *Rhode Island Klansman*, there are no extant copies. *Providence Visitor,* October 21, 1924.

31 *Evening Tribune,* November 7, 1924; *Providence Post,* November 7, 1924.

er would have prohibited the marriage of white Americans with African
Americans. A third bill was similar to Weaver's second bill, and the fourth
was intended to prevent membership in societies with foreign leadership.
Although the General Assembly leadership could have killed the bills in
committee, they allowed them to come before the two houses for a vote in
February. Each of the four bills was soundly defeated.[32]

The public-spirited image of the Rhode Island Klan was besmirched on
March 17, 1928, when the *Providence Journal* ran an exclusive story revealing that three recently recruited companies of the First Light Infantry, a
chartered military organization headquartered in Providence's Cranston
Street Armory, had been recruited jointly as members of the Klan and of
the three suspect companies involved. The *Journal*'s revelation led to an
investigation of the recruiting practices of the First Light Infantry by the
State Adjutant General and the organization's commander, who convoked
a military board of inquiry. The Adjutant General's report eventually led
to an official inquiry by the House Committee on Military Affairs into the
Klan's infiltration of the Rhode Island militia units that had remained
outside of the National Guard. During the inquiry, various witnesses di-
vulged that the Klan had also sought to gain control of a Westerly-based
unit of the Guard. Among those who testified before the House committee
was John W. Perry, the Grand Titan of the Rhode Island and Connecticut
Klan. Mr. Perry presented himself, as did all Klansmen, as a one-hun-
dred-percent American and defender of Protestantism, Democracy and
American womanhood. Among other things, Perry stated that, as far as
he knew, his parents were born in the United States and that he had been
wounded while serving in France during World War I. Three days after
Mr. Perry appeared before the House committee, *The Rhode Islander* printed
a front page article disclosing that Mr. Perry's father was a native of the
Cape Verdean island of Madeira and that his mother was a native of St.
Michael's, the Azores; that he was baptized in a Catholic Church in New
London; and, while a police officer in New London, Connecticut, he had
been suspended after being charged with misconduct by a women whom
he had been sent to arrest. A subsequent article revealed that the wound
he claimed to have received in France was self-afflicted during a period of
despondency following his suspension from the police force.[33]

The political wrangling between those who favored the continuance of
private, state-chartered, military commands like the First Light Infantry,
and those who favored the bringing of all state-sponsored military units
under the control of the National Guard, prevented any legislative action
to remedy the dangerous situation revealed by the House inquiry. The incident resulted in a loss of prestige on the part of the Rhode Island Klan

---

[32] *Providence Visitor,* January 28, 1927; *Providence Journal,* February 3, 1927.
[33] *Providence Journal,* March 17, 1928; *The Rhode Islander,* March 23; April 6, 13, 1928; *Providence Visitor,*
      March 23, 30; April 20, 1928.

and had an impact on its membership. To revive interest in the Klan and its stated mission and to raise monies, the Roger Williams Klan arranged to bring U.S. Senator J. Thomas Heflin of Alabama to Rhode Island in order to deliver a lecture to a Klan gathering at the Klan's meeting place at Grant's Field, Stillwater Road, Georgiaville, in Smithfield, on June 8. Anyone who wanted admittance to the Klan compound to hear the senator was charged fifty cents.[34]

Sen. Heflin regularly traveled the country making speeches at Klan meetings. What made him a particular draw in the mind of the Rhode Island Klan was his recent attack on Bishop Hickey on the floor of the United States Senate on April 13, 1928. On that occasion, Heflin defended Elphege Daignault's right, as an American citizen, to sue Bishop Hickey in the civil courts. When J. A. Domin, Exalted Cyclops of Providence's Roger Williams Klan, and its secretary, Frederick T. Remington, along with Grand Titan John W. Perry gathered on Sunday afternoon, July 1, at Union Station to welcome him, they were taken by surprise when the senator did not get off the train. A newspaperman informed the Klan delegation that the Sen. Heflin had arrived during the morning at 12:45 and had gone to the Biltmore to get some rest. After the delegation collected the senator at the hotel, a Providence police motorcycle detail escorted the party out of the city along Smith Street to the North Providence line, where the State Police took over. The motorcade attracted little attention within the city and only a scattering of the curious along the route to Georgiaville.[35]

Some 8,000 people gathered at Grant Field to hear Sen. Heflin. Of those who gathered, 6,000 of them paid to enter the grounds. Another 2,000 chose to stand outside along the roads. According to the newspaper reports, Heflin reiterated his espousal of Elphege Daignault's cause; condemned the "foreign potentate" and American hierarchy that "sent their souls to hell as far as they had any authority"; and praised the insurgent Franco-American Catholics for resorting to "an American court" for justice. He portrayed himself as a man who had been "vilified, misrepresented and slandered" by the press, which he charged was under Catholic domination. He did not, however, make any direct attack on his party's recent nominee for president, Alfred E. Smith, although he did warn his hearers of the menace of New York's Tammany Hall's opposition to the dry law, which Congress had adopted after the passage of the Eighteenth Amendment. When on July 1, 1929, Sen. Heflin returned to Rhode Island to give another address in Georgiaville, only about 900 showed to hear his harangue.[36]

While Heflin did not attack Al Smith, who would run for president in the fall of 1928, the Rhode Island Klan's leaders did subsequently call

---

[34]   *Providence Journal*, April 21; June 24, 25, 1928; *The Rhode Islander*, June 29, 1928.
[35]   *Providence Journal*, July 2, 1928; *Providence Post*, July 2, 1928; *Woonsocket Call*, July 2, 1928.
[36]   Ibid.; *Providence Journal*, July 1, 1929. For a rebuttal of Heflin's 1928 address, cf. *The Rhode Islander*, July 6, 1928.

on the Klansmen to work for Smith's defeat. However, as Rev. E. Dean Ellenworth, pastor of the First Universalist Church, Woonsocket, and a frequent critic of the Catholic Church, pointed out two years earlier, the Klan's efforts tended to incite more Catholics to united action than they did Protestants. Al Smith would be the first Democratic presidential candidate since 1852 to win a majority of the state's popular vote.[37]

Although the vast majority of Klan-sponsored legislative acts were defeated on both state and national levels, the racist mentality of the age created an environment wherein Congress passed immigration acts in 1917, 1921 and 1924, based on the report of the Dillingham Commission, which sought to favor immigration by the races thought to be the easiest to assimilate into the existing American population. The 1921 and 1924 acts created quotas, which were distributed on a national basis. Neither act placed restrictions on immigrations from the nations of the western hemisphere, such as Canada or Mexico. The impact of the nationality-based quotas acts was to significantly reduce immigration from those nations, which, since 1890, had been sending the majority of the immigrants entering the United States. The changes in immigration policy had dramatic impact on American cities as the flow of new immigrants diminished and changed to focus on pastoral concerns in subsequent years. The amount of energy and resources that once were directed towards meeting the needs of the immigrants and helping them to assimilate into the American Church and culture, declined as ethnic parishes and institutions ceased to grow at the same rates as before. The changes in immigration law created minor problems in regard to the immigration of religious sisters as noted above and individual personal crises as the laws — one part of which was intended to make it easier to unite families — in fact created new dilemmas for families seeking admission to the United States.[38]

The Rhode Island Seminar on Human Relationships and the National Conference of Christians and Jews

The indignation felt by many Americans at the prejudice that surfaced during the years that saw the rise of the new Klan and its impact on Al Smith's campaign for the presidency in 1928, prompted many new members to join the newly formed Rhode Island Seminar on Human Relationships. After the Holy See reacted negatively to Catholic participation

---

[37]   For Ellenworth's comment, Cf. *Providence Journal*, October 11, 1926.
[38]   For an overview of the question of ecumenism in America, Cf. George H. Tavard, "Ecumenism in America," in Glazier and Shelly, *The Encyclopedia of American Catholic History, 476–78;* Winthrop Hudson, *Religion in America,* (New York: Charles Scibner's Sons, Third edition, 1981), 392–93; "What is the National Conference?" (National Conference of Christians and Jews, no date); Robert A. Slayton, *Empire Statesman: The Rise and Redemption of Al Smith* (New York: The Free Press, 2001), 326–27; *New York Times,* December 11, 1927.

in the World's Parliament of Religions during the Columbian Exposition in Chicago in 1893, Catholic participation in interdenominational efforts had almost entirely ended. The liberal bishops who organized Catholic participation in the parliament accepted the religious pluralism in American society as a logical consequence of America's freedom of religion. From Rome's point of view, Catholic participation in the parliament supported the claim that all religions were legitimate and equal. The position espoused by the papacy since the Protestant Reformation was that the Catholic Church was the only true Church and that the other churches were in error. In keeping with this understanding, Benedict XV in 1917 and Pius XI in his encyclical letter, *Mortalium animos*, rejected Catholic participation in the Faith and Order and Life and Work movements that had been inspired by the International Missionary Council at the Edinburgh Conference of 1910 and grew out of the common dangers faced by missionaries in non-Christian lands.

Among those who became affiliated with the Rhode Island Seminar on Human Relations was Joseph H. Gainer. Mr. Gainer was born in Providence in 1878 and was a graduate of La Salle Academy, Holy Cross College and the law school of the Catholic University of America. He took an active interest in politics and was elected as a Democrat to the School Committee, to the two-tier Providence City Council as a Councilman and also as an Alderman. He was elected mayor of Providence in 1913 and served until 1927, when he retired. In 1926, he ran on the Democratic ticket for governor, but was defeated by Aram Pothier, who was re-elected. At a dinner given him on his retirement from office, Bishop Hickey was the main speaker. After praising his faithfulness to his Christian principles, the bishop said:

> I must not forget to mention with particular pleasure the influence to be attributed to Mayor Gainer's personality in allying many forms of intolerance which threatened from time to time to upset the peace and harmony of our community. His broad mind and affectionate heart impelled him to grasp every chance that offered him a hearing before assemblies and organizations of all classes. Race, creed, or color by themselves meant nothing to him as lines of demarcation in social or political or civic life.

Given Gainer's background, it was not surprising that he was one of about ninety to one hundred Rhode Islanders, who came together about 1929 or 1930 to form The Rhode Island Seminar on Human Relationships. The entire membership of the Seminar met together initially. As would be typical of the organization, the membership chose an executive committee and three co-chairs to lead the Seminar. Mr. Gainer, along with Herbert W. Sheerwood, a Protestant, and Max Grant, a Jew, were elected the initial co-chairmen.[39]

---

[39] *Providence Visitor*, January 7, 1927; Gainer to Bishop Francis P. Keough, November 29, 1939, PChA.

In 1931 the Rhode Island Seminar became affiliated with the National Conference of Christians and Jews. The Conference was formed in 1927 by Charles Evans Hughes, Newton D. Baker, Rev. S. Parkes Cadman, and other distinguished Americans, who decided to take a common approach towards ensuring the right of freedom of religion by creating an association of individuals to promote justice, amity, understanding and co-operation among Catholics, Protestants and Jews to which they gave the name the National Conference of Christians and Jews. Unlike other ecumenical organizations, some American bishops, Bishop Hickey among them, were willing to allow Catholic participation in the work of the National Conference of Christians and Jews because the goal of the Conference was not to unite believers in one religious body but to bring about respect for the right of all to believe and live according to their beliefs. According to the Conference's bylaws, the Conference was founded "to analyze, moderate and finally eliminate intergroup prejudices which disfigure and distort religious, business, social and political relations, with a view to the establishment of a social order in which the religious ideals of brotherhood and justice shall become the standards of human relationships."[40]

In 1931 and '32, the Conference's executive director, Rev. Everett R. Clinchy, helped some forty local affiliates of the Conference to organize seminars on religion in a mutual effort to dispel some of the common misunderstandings of their respective beliefs. By the end of February 1932, the executive committee of the Rhode Island Seminar had held two local meetings for the purpose of organization and for mutual understanding of the objectives sought. The membership of the committee included Dr. Albert D. Mead, acting president of Brown University; Msgr. Peter A. Foley, who represented Bishop Hickey; Rabbi Samuel M. Gup of Temple Beth-El; Fr. Lorenzo C. McCarthy, O.P., president of Providence College; Rev. Arthur H. Bradford, president of the Rhode Island Ministers' Association; and Rev. W. Appleton Lawrence, rector of Grace Episcopal Church. With the approval of Bishop Hickey, Episcopal Bishop, James De Wolf Perry, Episcopal Bishop of Rhode Island, and Rabbi Gup, the seminar was planned for Tuesday and Wednesday, May 3 and 4. The seminar consisted of eight sessions held over the course of the two days. Tuesday's sessions met on the Brown University campus and Wednesday's at Providence College. According to a *Visitor* observer, the various sessions were characterized by a "frank and good-tempered discussion of the many differences, religious, social and racial, which create friction and hostility" between Catholics, Protestants and Jews. The meetings aroused widespread interest and were largely attended. The *Visitor* writer noted that nearly three-fourths of those attending were women. Among those who addressed the various sessions were Fr. Michael J. Ahern, S.J., of the Jesuit Theological

40 "What is the National Conference?", brochure found in National Conference of Christian and Jews folder, PChA.

School at Weston, Massachusetts; President Robbins W. Barstow of Hartford Theological Seminary; Judge Joseph M. Proskauer of New York City; George N. Shuster, editor of *Commonweal*; Prof. Mark Mohler of Skidmore College; and several local Catholic, Protestant and Jewish clergymen and lay leaders.[41]

In 1933, after the Nazi regime under Adolf Hitler stirred a persecution of the German Jews, the Rhode Island Seminar in conjunction with the Rhode Island Council of the American Jewish Council arranged for a protest meeting in Elks Auditorium in Providence on Sunday, May 30. More than 1,500 people crowded into the auditorium and several hundred who attempted to enter were kept out by the police after the space was filled. Speakers at the meeting included Providence Mayor James E. Dunne; Fr. Lorenzo McCarthy, O.P.; Clarence A. Barbour, president of Brown University; Rabbi William Braude of Temple Beth-el, and several other Jewish rabbis, clergymen and laymen. Former mayor Gainer presided. Those present at the meeting voted a resolution of protest against the discrimination against the Jews initiated by the German government.[42]

On Sunday, November 19, 1933, another "pilgrimage team" that consisted of Providence College's Fr. McCarthy, Rabbi Rudolph I. Coffee, of Temple Sinai, Oakland, California, and Benson Y. Landis, research secretary of the National Conference, helped initiate one of a series of nationwide campaigns for religious liberty with a mass meeting in Sayles Hall at Brown University, which was addressed by all three members of the team. The meeting was followed by a supper conference at Providence College at which nearly a hundred leaders of the various faiths discussed ways in which Rhode Islanders could express in practical terms the growing spirit of co-operation among religious groups. The participants made two definite recommendations to the Rhode Island Seminar: first, that a speakers' bureau be established, and, second, that the executive committee seek more publicity for its work. The following afternoon, the representatives of the three faiths went to Rhode Island State College in Kingston for an afternoon presentation, which was followed by an informal discussion in the Jewish fraternity house, Alpha Epsilon Pi. At the general meeting, the acting president of the State College, Dr. John Barlow, observed that the meeting was unique in that it was the first time the three faiths had gathered together on the same platform for a common purpose.[43]

---

[41] Ibid., April 29; May 6, 1932; *Providence Journal*, February 28; May 4,5, 1932.
[42] *Providence Journal*, May 1, 1933.
[43] *Providence Journal*, November 18, 20, 1933; *Providence Visitor*, November 24, 1933.

Social Justice and the Depression

From his early years in Providence, Bishop Hickey took a sincere interest in public affairs. During the early 1920s, he took an active part in the effort to secure enactment of a Mother's Aid law and, with the cooperation of the diocesan clergy, gave practical assistance to the legislative committee charged with investigating the problems mothers faced in the state. The clergy helped supply the facts and figures on which the law was based.[44]

Following the stock market crash in October and November 1929, confidence in the American economy declined and widespread unemployment followed as companies, unable to sell their products, had to cut back production or close entirely. The domino effect of the slowdown in manufacturing led to layoffs in the service industries. Towards the end of September 1931, Secretary of Labor W. N. Doak wrote to Bishop Hickey as he did to the other bishops, asking that the bishop might encourage his clergy to discuss the employment situation from their pulpits and the methods adopted to relieve it. Bishop Hickey replied that the clergy had already done much to help those unemployed and promised to convey the secretary's request to his pastors.[45]

The number of unemployed soon exhausted the traditional sources of help usually available in moments of economic crisis. Without income to make mortgage payments, the number of homeless increased dramatically in many parts of the country. Since Rhode Island's economy had been buffeted all during the twenties by weaknesses in the textile industry and the movement of jobs to other states, the impact of the Depression on the state was somewhat mitigated. Rhode Island private relief agencies as well as public assistance agents had a great deal of experience in dealing with the needs of the unemployed or underemployed, but resources in both the private and public sectors were limited and, in the case of the cities and towns, soon were exhausted, as several cities faced bankruptcy as a result of the sharp decline in municipal revenues.

Even in face of the record numbers of those unemployed, Bishop Hickey, as did many other Americans, shared the view that the American industrial and business structure was fundamentally sound. Nevertheless, he saw the need to get people back to work as quickly as possible. As the diocese began preparations for holding the 1930 Charity Fund Appeal, Bishop Hickey committed the diocese to an increase in the pace of construction work as far as that was possible and called his pastors and the general Rhode Island population to do the same. The construction industry in 1930 was still labor intensive and any increase promised a substan-

---

[44] *Providence Visitor*, October 6, 1933.
[45] Ibid., October 2, 1931. For another view of the response to the Great Depression in Rhode Island, Cf. Norma Lasa Daoust, *The Perils of Providence: Rhode Island's Capital City During the Depression and New Deal* (Ph.D. dissertation, University of Connecticut, 1982).

tial number of additional jobs. At the time he made his appeal to his pastors and the community at large, there was over a million dollars of diocesan and parish construction work in progress with another million dollars worth of work planned for the near future. In addition to large projects, Bishop Hickey urged his pastors to undertake repairs on their churches, rectories, schools, convents and other buildings as well as improvements of the grounds surrounding church buildings — anything that might provide work for the unemployed. In making his appeal to the Catholics of the diocese and to the citizens of the state to support the 1930 Catholic Charity Appeal, Bishop Hickey presented contributions to the appeal as a way to provide the resources to fund new projects and to continue to offer employment. In expressing his thanks to all who contributed to the Catholic Charity Appeal, Bishop Hickey referred to the $302,133 collected as an "amazing revelation of the kindness and charitable dispositions of the people [of the state]."[46]

Until the onset of the crisis created by the steadily increasing number of unemployed persons in the state, the focus of the Catholic Charity Appeals had been primarily on raising funds to allow the replacement or expansion of buildings. Beginning in 1933, Bishop Hickey began placing more emphasis on raising sufficient funds to pay the operating costs of the various institutions. As more and more parents exhausted all means of support for their families, increasing numbers began to turn to the Catholic Charities Bureau and to the various diocesan institutions that cared for children for help. The main thrust of the Catholic Charities Bureau was to keep families together whenever possible and to only place children in a diocesan institution when there were no viable alternatives. However, while the Bureau tried to ensure that institutional care was a last resort, the number of men, women, and children cared for by the various institutions of the diocese increased significantly during 1931 because of the impact of the Depression. Many of those who did seek the help of Catholic charitable institutions were no longer able to contribute anything towards the care they or their loved ones received.[47]

During the Great Depression, the various diocesan institutions not only provided for those in their care, but fed all those who came to their doors seeking food. Beginning in 1930, the St. Vincent de Paul Infant Asylum on Regent Avenue, Providence, began providing food for seventy-five people each morning. The Franciscan Missionaries of Mary in the Bell Street Industrial Home at the southerly end of Broadway in Providence began providing sandwiches twice daily to between two hundred and three hundred men who came to them looking for help. While two of the sisters spent most of their day making the sandwiches, two others spent their day soliciting the community for food and clothing to help those in need. Small-

46   *Providence Visitor*, April 4, 18; May 2, 29, 1930; *Providence Journal*, December 10, 1932.
47   *Providence Visitor*, February 6, 1931;

er numbers were helped by the St. Aloysius Orphan Asylum on Prairie Avenue, St. Joseph's Hospital on Broad Street in Providence and the Home for the Aged in Pawtucket, as well as by other diocesan institutions.[48]

In every other social crisis from 1853 on that confronted the state, local conferences of the St. Vincent the Paul Society had played a major part in alleviating the immediate physical needs and in addressing the spiritual needs of those affected. In 1930, the well-organized and efficient work of the conferences was particularly important. Prior to the onset of the Depression in the 1930s, there were approximately thirty-eight existing conferences, which had been established mostly in the larger urban parishes. In the earliest weeks of the Great Depression, individuals had some resources to fall back on and the cities and towns were able to meet the requests for help that the few, who normally did not ask for help, resorted to making. During the first five months in 1929, the conferences disbursed $9,482.56 to aid 247 families composed of 773 individuals. In the same period in 1930, the various conferences of the St. Vincent de Paul Society distributed $11,227.67, to aid 426 families composed of 1586 individuals. The monies distributed came from contributions placed in poor boxes or through tithing the members of the society.[49]

By 1930, the continuing wave of plant closings and work slowdowns gave warning that the current wave of unemployment would necessitate greater efforts on the part of the society, not only in the large city parishes, but throughout the diocese. Although Bishop Hickey, in an address at the dedication of the St. Teresa's Church in Pawtucket on September 28, urged his people to be optimistic about the future, he knew he had to make concrete plans to help those suffering in the present. On September 26, 1930, with winter coming on, Bishop Hickey sent a letter to all the pastors of the diocese urging those who did not have conferences of the St. Vincent de Paul Society in their parishes, to work with the Central Council of the society in the diocese to establish one so that they might handle the appeals for assistance that came to them from their parishioners in an organized manner. By February 1931, almost all the parishes of the diocese, with the exception of a few of the smaller ones, who lacked the resources, had established parish conferences. According to the extant summary reports of the Central Council, the conferences distributed $127,092 in direct monetary aid in 1931 and $147,996 in 1932. In 1933, after the state took some of the pressure off private relief agencies by borrowing money from the Federal government to distribute aid through the towns and cities, the total dropped to $71,497 and, in 1934, it was $80,753. In the first years of the Depression, when there was a great demand on the society's funds, Bishop Hickey, on November 20, 1930, informed his pastors that the annual collection taken up on the First Sunday of Advent for

[48] *Providence Journal*, March 15, 1931; *Providence Visitor*, February 10, 1933.
[49] *Providence Visitor*, July 25, 1930; "St. Vincent de Paul Society in the Diocese of Providence," PChA.

the Catholic University of America would, in that year, be taken up for the needs of the poor and the destitute in the face of the oncoming winter.[50]

In Woonsocket, where the city's working class population was hard hit by factory shutdowns and layoffs, Bishop Keough entrusted the task of revitalizing the existing parish St. Vincent de Paul Society and the establishing of new ones to Fr. Ernest Morin, the pastor of St. Ann's. During the spring of 1930, Fr. Morin met with the laymen and clergy of the city to fulfill his mandate. In St. Ann's itself, Fr. Morin's senior assistant, Fr. Adelard Laliberte, had charge of assisting the men of St. Vincent de Paul in their work. Collectively, Fr. Laliberte and newspaper publisher Philippe Boucher organized a committee of parishioners to raise funds to support the Cumberland Street Canteen, which the parish St. Vincent de Paul society opened to provide those in need with food, clothing, shoes, as well as money to help with rent and wood to heat their homes. Fr. Laliberte had charge of the society's funds that were donated by the citizens of Woonsocket who still had the means to do so, and oversaw the canteen. Businessmen also donated food, particularly bread and doughnuts. In addition to the soup kitchen, which provided food, the canteen made work space available where city-paid workers made clothing for distribution through the canteen. There was also a cobbler shop, where belting contributed by the various mills was used to repair old shoes, a room for reading and recreation, and a home visiting department.[51]

In order to provide fuel for the needy, Fr. Laliberte, who was also known as Father Liberty, obtained the permission of a gentleman who owned land in Glocester near the village of Chepachet to cut wood on his land. Woonsocket relief workers did the cutting. At times when a man asked for wood, he was sent to the Chepachet farm to cut two cords of wood. One would be delivered to his home, the other to some widow who had no one to cut it for her. Once one of the men employed to cut the wood remarked to Fr. Laliberte that he wished he had some place to spend the night rather than return to the city. The man's remark prompted Fr. Laliberte to propose to the men of the St. Vincent de Paul Society and to the owner of the land that the old farmhouse on the property be made habitable. After the plan was agreed on, the first floor partitions in the house were taken down to create one large room. The part of the house that was unserviceable was torn down and a large stone chimney was built to heat the remaining room. The upper part of the house was made into small bedrooms. In the spring of 1933, the first homeless men took up residence at the camp.

---

50 *Providence Visitor*, July 25; November 21, 1930; Hickey to Pastors, September 26, 1930, PChA; *Providence Journal*, September 29, 1930; Annual Reports, 1931, 1932, 1933, 1934, Diocesan Council Headquarters.

51 Marcel P. Fortin, ed., *Woonsocket, Rhode Island: A Centennial History, 1888–2000*, (State College, PA: Jostens Publishing and Printing Division), Millennium Edition, 96–97; Paul A. Bouget, ed., *St. Ann's Church, Woonsocket, R.I.: Towers of Faith and Family*, (State College, PA: Jostens Publishing and Printing Division), 1990, p. 74; *Providence Sunday Journal*, January 21, 1934.

They cleared land for a garden, built a dam to create a pond and enclosed a spring in a cement casement. Fr. Laliberte established the rules for living at the camp, which the men, who were mostly young and without other resources, were happy to live by. They did their own cooking with foodstuffs from the canteen and "policed" their own quarters. For each cord of wood they chopped, they were paid a dollar and a half. When a *Providence Journal* reporter did a story on the camp in January 1934, there were eleven men and boys there.[52]

In 1932, the state St. Vincent de Paul Society was given a check for $2,650 by the acting president of Brown University, Albert D. Mead. The money represented a part of Brown University's share from a charity "round robin" football tournament which pitted Brown against Yale and Holy Cross against Dartmouth in the Yale Bowl. In October 1931, Owen D. Young, the chairman of President Hoover's Committee on Mobilization of Relief Resources, had suggested that every college and school football team in the country play at least one game as a benefit fund-raiser for local employment relief agencies. In response, Providence's Mayor Donne and Edward P. Reidy, Director of Public Aid in the city, proposed that Providence College play Brown. Fr. McCarthy, Providence College's president, on the college's behalf, readily agreed to participate, but Brown was already committed to the tournament at Yale. Mayor Dunne then asked the President of the State College at Kingston, Raymond Bressler, if his team would play. Although Providence College teams had played the State College before in basketball in 1920 and baseball in 1922, Frank Keaney, the basketball coach at the college and its Physical Education Director, had refused to agree to any further games with Providence College after two athletes, who had agreed to enroll at the State College in the fall of 1922, changed their minds and enrolled instead at Providence College. Coach Keaney took offense at the loss of the two athletes and would not arrange any further contests between the two schools until Providence College adopted a policy of not playing freshmen and transfer students until they had been enrolled a year. In 1926, Coach Keaney wrote to John E. Farrell, the manager of Providence College's baseball team, who had previously suggested that the two colleges arrange meetings between the two schools in all sports, that, in view of the bad memories of the two students changing schools, "We had better wait a few years until that spirit of fatal rivalry ceases." However, Coach Keaney made an exception in view of the public need and agreed to have his football team play on November 28, after they and Providence College had finished their regular seasons. Brown University made its football stadium available for the game at no cost, so all the proceeds of the event could go to the fund established by Mayor Dunne to provide milk and fuel for the needy. The game was attended by Gov. Nor-

---

[52]   *Providence Sunday Journal*, January 21, 1934.

man Cass, Mayor Dunne and Bishop Hickey along with the presidents, faculties and students of the two colleges.[53]

Two other Catholic organizations volunteered to help the St. Vincent de Paul Society in providing for the needy in the crisis. The Knights of Columbus opened a drive to collect used clothing with Cathedral Hall as the drive's headquarters. Beginning on Friday, November 28, the Knights arranged that the members of the Queen's Daughters would staff the hall to receive and sort the clothing donated from ten to five daily and to do mending where that was necessary. Those who wished to take advantage of the services of the clothing depot were asked to bring a note from a clergyman or a St. Vincent de Paul conference. Where it was impossible for donors or those in need of clothing to get to Cathedral Hall, the Knights arranged with the donors to pick up the clothes and to deliver clothes where needed. Warm underclothing and men's and boy's shoes were in particular demand. By the end of December, the number of calls for assistance had increased from three hundred a day to five hundred. To cope with the continuing demand, the Knights and Queen's Daughters had to repeat their initial requests for donations. Donations came from both individuals as well as from companies. One of the larger donations received came from the Outlet Company. In all, during the ten weeks the clothing deport was open, from November 28, 1930 to January 31, 1931, approximately 25,000 articles of clothing were distributed to the needy of all creeds or none. At least 20 percent of those who came to the depot were referred to it by non-Catholic clergy. As many as five hundred articles were given out in one day.[54]

Share Your Clothes Drive

At the end of 1931, the Providence Central Relief Committee, which included among its members Mr. Joseph M. Tally, President of the Central St. Vincent de Paul Council, and Msgr. Peter E. Blessing, the society's Spiritual Director, announced a city-wide, "Share Your Clothes" appeal for Sunday, January 3, 1931, which Bishop Hickey endorsed in a letter to the committee's chairman. Various truck owners and drivers volunteered their vehicles and their services for the day. Boy Scouts rode with the drivers to do the actual collection. The drive's headquarters was on the street floor of the Infantry Hall building, 150 South Main Street. Bishop Hickey asked his priests to announce the drive at Sunday masses on December 27. The drive collected clothing, bedclothes and other items. When the various items were delivered to the clothing bureau, women from various

---

53   *Providence Visitor*, November 27, 1931; January 8, 1932; Memo explaining the circumstances of the game, no date; Keaney to John E. Farrell, Manager of Baseball, Providence College, January 14, 1926, Providence College Archives.
54   *Providence Visitor*, November 28; December 26, 1930; January 30, 1931.

organizations in the state, among them Catholic organizations, sorted and distributed the donated items. In addition to the clothes, various organizations and individuals contributed monies to purchase clothing. Three laundries in the city contributed by laundering soiled garments. During the time the program ran, over 51,708 articles were distributed to 5807 families.[55]

In January 1932, the Providence Central Relief Committee organized another "Share Your Clothes" campaign, this time in conjunction with the twenty-one Catholic churches in the city. On Sunday, January 1, the Providence police distributed more than 40,000 envelopes containing an appeal and brief instructions to assist the collectors who went around the following Sunday, January 8. In January 1933, the effort to provide clothing for the needy took a new tack. The U.S. Government made a large amount of cloth available through the American Red Cross. The cloth was precut but needed to be sewed into usable garments. In response to the government's offer of the cloth, Bishop Hickey, during the second week in January, sent letters to twenty-one Providence convents and five Catholic institutions in the city asking the superiors of the convents and institutions to organize sewing guilds among the sisters and lay people in order to turn the government cloth into wearing apparel for the needy. Twenty-four convents and institutions agreed to undertake the work, which was done by the nuns and laywomen who volunteered to help with the sewing. The finished clothing was turned back to the Red Cross for distribution. It was Bishop Hickey's and the St. Vincent de Paul's understanding, that the Red Cross would give the society a share in the distribution of the garments by honoring recommendations of worthy cases by the society's conferences. For a short time, the Red Cross abided by that understanding, but at a certain moment, Mrs. Edward S. Moulton, the local Red Cross Director, intervened and directed her workers to cease fulfilling orders from the St. Vincent de Paul Society. Bishop Hickey became incensed by Mrs. Moulton's action and, together with Mr. Tally, appealed her directive to the executive committee of the Red Cross's local organization. After an exchange of correspondence and telephone calls, the executive committee met in Mayor Joseph A. Gainer's office in Providence with Mr. Tally. By a unanimous vote, the committee decided "to recognize the St. Vincent de Paul Society as a trustworthy organization for relief, whose recommendations should be honored."[56]

[55] *Providence Visitor*, December 18, 1931; January 15; December 30, 1932; *Providence Journal*, February 18, 1932.
[56] *Providence Visitor*, January 13, 20, 1932; April 14, 1933; *Providence Journal*, April 10, 1933.

The Share Your Food Campaign

With Rhode Islanders' continuing loss of employment, the Providence Community Chest campaign in November 1931, like the Catholic Charity Appeal the previous spring, brought in less money than the year before. As a result, the Community Fund was unable to increase the monies allocated to the various member agencies whose client bases were increasing. At the same time, the city of Providence's tax revenues were reduced as many home and property owners were unable to pay their taxes. In March 1932, concerned citizens approached the Providence Central Relief Committee with the proposal that the Committee sponsor a Share Your Food campaign. The object of the campaign was to collect food that could be distributed to the clients of the Family Welfare Society and the Providence Department of Public Aid, which lacked the funds to purchase all the food needed to meet the requests for aid made by their clients, who were themselves unable to purchase sufficient food to satisfy their needs. The Relief Committee agreed to the plan on condition that a responsible administration committee be set up. In a short time, the Share Your Food Committee was created from among the socially conscious women of the city and Mrs. Virginia Gammell Cross was induced to serve as its chair. Under the committee's auspices over a hundred stores co-operated with the campaign by placing baskets and barrels into which donors could place cereals, potatoes, prunes, sugar, canned peas, salmon, string beans, tomatoes and other foodstuffs, which they bought for the purpose of donating to the needy. The stores, in their turn, pledged to contribute a certain percentage of goods in proportion to what the customers contributed. The Share Your Food Committee established the campaign's headquarters at 49 Dyer Street, Providence, where the donated foods were brought. Since several agencies were interested in having a role in the distribution of the collected foods, the Share Your Food Committee referred the question of distribution to the Providence Central Relief Committee. At its March 9, 1932 meeting, the Central Relief Committee decided:

> It would simplify the work of the volunteers workers of the Share Your Food Committee, decrease confusion and use to the greatest advantage the small amount of food available, if requisitions were limited to the [Providence Department of Public Aid and the Family Welfare Society] which at that time were carrying with extremely limited funds over 6,000 families.

The operating expenses of the Share Your Food Committee, approximately forty dollars per week, were underwritten by the Department of Public Aid and the Family Welfare Society. According to the procedure authorized, when food orders endorsed by the Family Welfare Society and the Providence Department of Public Aid were received and made up, they were then delivered to the needy families by an unemployed man who owned a truck. In order to increase the amount of food available for distribution, Mrs. Cross, on March 30, 1932, wrote to Bishop Hickey, as she did to other church leaders, to solicit the bishop's endorsement of the campaign, an endorsement the bishop quickly gave.[57]

The effort of the Share Your Food Committee was successful enough for the committee to undertake, in January 1933, a more ambitious campaign, in conjunction with the various service clubs in Providence and with the sponsorship of the Providence Journal Company, to collect both food and monies to purchase food. In anticipation of the campaign, Mrs. Gammell Cross, in a letter written on December 27, 1932, again asked Bishop Hickey to endorse the effort and to urge the pastors of Providence to support the effort from their pulpits. In her note, Mrs. Cross did not mention the involvement of the service clubs in the second campaign or the fact that this time monies would be collected. In thanking the bishop for his endorsement, Cross wrote, "It will be our endeavor to serve as many people as possible who are recommended to us by the Department of Public Aid and the Family Welfare Society." The bishop, however, was disturbed by what he read in the letter. His agreement to support this second effort of Mrs. Cross's committee was based on his understanding that the St. Vincent de Paul Society, in light of the support given to the campaign by the Catholic churches, would also be able to write food orders for distribution to those it served. When he read Mrs. Gammell Cross' letter, he asked Joseph Tally, along with Msgr. Peter E. Blessing, of the Providence Central Relief Committee, to seek a change in the stated policy. Mr. Tally raised the question of the St. Vincent de Paul Society's participation in the distribution of the food collected with Philip Simonds, the committee chairman. Mr. Simonds explained to him that:

> All the publicity appealing for funds had stated that the food would be distributed by the Director of Public Aid and the Family Welfare Society, and it was so represented to the Service Clubs that very generously ran the campaign.

Since the exclusion of the St. Vincent de Paul Society from the writing of food orders on the Share Your Food store came within a few weeks of the Providence director of the Red Cross having excluded the society from the distribution of Red Cross clothing supplies, the St. Vincent de Paul's second exclusion was not to go unchallenged.[58]

In its March 31, 1933 issue, the *Providence Visitor* printed a front page article stating that Mrs. Gammell Cross had refused to recognize the right of the St. Vincent de Paul Society to participate in the food fund after the society was "given every assurance that they would share in the results of

[57] *Providence Journal*, November 24, 25, 1931; March 30; April 1, 1932; Philip B. Simonds, Chairman, "Memorandum for Central Relief Committee;" "Statement Relative to the Distribution of Share Your Food," April 15, 1933, PChA.
[58] Cross to Hickey, December 27, 1932; Hickey to Cross, December 31, 1932; Cross to Hickey, January 21, 1933; Memorandum, Share Your Food Campaign, 1933, Simonds to Hickey, April 15, 1933, PChA; *Providence Visitor*, January 6, 1933.

the drive together with the Public Aid Department and the Family Welfare Society."

Four days after the *Visitor* article appeared, Mrs. Cross wrote to Bishop Hickey asking him to inform the editor of the *Visitor* of the letter she had sent to Hickey on January 31 in which she thanked the bishop for his endorsement of her committee's appeal and mentioned how the food collected was to be distributed. Bishop Hickey sent a reply to her the next day pointing out that she had not informed him of her intention to continue to limit the distribution of the food collected to the two agencies previously agreed on by the Providence Central Relief Committee in distributing the food collected in the previous campaign. Hickey stated that, after she had asked him to a urge the people of his diocese to support the second food collection, he had "quite naturally" concluded that the St. Vincent de Paul Society would "share in the recommendation of families needing relief." Furthermore, he informed her that he was unaware of the role of the Providence service clubs in the campaign until after his letter endorsing the campaign appeared in the newspapers. When Mr. Simonds informed Mr. Tally that the Providence Emergency Relief Committee was not able to alter its directive to Mrs. Gammell Cross's committee because of the manner in which the publicity announcing the campaign was written, the bishop decided, as he told Mrs. Cross, in his letter, "that the time had come for me to inform our people of the conditions surrounding the activities of Share-Your-Food-Committee to which presumably they had contributed." He could not understand, he told her, how her committee could "ask the help of the Catholic Church as such, and then, having accepted what has come in response to such an appeal, make known rules and regulations which exclude our Church Society from all share in the administration of such." He concluded by saying, "Whether this protest succeeds in bringing your Committee and its parent Committee to a change of view or not, it seems to me to have been necessary for me to stand for a principle and to express myself on what appears to our people very much like a reflection on the honor and efficiency of the St. Vincent de Paul Society."[59]

Bishop Hickey chose not to limit his protest against the way the St. Vincent de Paul Society had been excluded by the Providence Chapter of the American Red Cross and the Share Your Food Committee to a *Visitor* article. On Sunday, April 9, 1933, he used his scheduled address before the annual convention of the Holy Name Societies held in Cathedral Hall to review the manner in which he believed the society had been treated by both groups. While he did not directly accuse the leaders of the groups of being motivated by prejudice, in his extemporaneous address that he shared with the Holy Name men he said, "There is an attitude in

---

[59] *Providence Visitor*, March 31, 1933; Gammell Cross to Hickey, April 4, 1933; Hickey to Gammell Cross, April 5, 1933, PChA.

our city and State today that is not exactly hostile to the church and her organizations, though it may be at the bottom, but there is an attitude of high disdain and conscious superiority." In the course of his address, the bishop urged his audience to bring a knowledge of how the St. Vincent de Paul Society had been treated with "haughtiness" by the two organizations to all parts of the state and to demand from them "not a grudging recognition that our St. Vincent de Paul Society is efficient and honorable, but an unhesitating placing of the name of that society on the same line with Family Welfare and the Department of Public Aid." The Rhode Island newspapers headlined the bishop's address in their Monday editions. On the evening following his address, Bishop Hickey repeated his charges before the organizational meeting of pastors and lay trustees for the year's Catholic Charity Fund. He particularly noted that the morning newspapers, in reporting his remarks of the previous evening, had chosen to abridge his report of discrimination against the St. Vincent de Paul Society.[60]

On April 10, the day in which Bishop Hickey's charges appeared in the papers, Mrs. Gammell Cross wrote a short note to Hickey to inform him that she had turned over the copies of her correspondence with the bishop to the Central Relief Committee, which controlled the policies of her organization. The Central Relief Committee met on April 12 to consider the question of increasing the number of organizations which could make requisitions on the food supplies gathered by the committee. After the chairman, Mr. Simonds, read a statement explaining the method of distribution that the committee had adopted in 1932, some of the members presents expressed their belief that requisitions should be honored from other welfare organizations provided each bore their proportionate share of the expense of the cost of administering the program and that a practical method of operation satisfactory to the women operating the Share Your Food headquarters, the Providence Journal company, which had funded the campaign, and the service clubs, which had promoted it, could be worked out. No vote was taken at the meeting, but Mr. Simonds was asked to consult with the people interested and report the results at the committee's next meeting. When the committee met again on Saturday, April 15, the history of the Share Your Food Committee was reviewed. The majority of the committee members agreed with the opinion of the lawyers on the committee and with the Share Your Food Committee itself that, when in January the committee had appealed to prospective donors for funds and foodstuffs that would be dispensed by the Director of Public Aid and the Family Welfare Society, the Share Your Food Committee had created a legal and moral obligation to abide by the method of distribution specified in the appeal that it had to respect. In view of this situation, the Emergency Relief Committee chose

60 *News-Tribune*, April 10, 11, 1933; *Providence Journal*, April 10, 11, 1933, *Providence Visitor*, April 14, 1933.

to support the decision of the Share Your Food Committee that "it should keep its agreement with the campaign organization and the contributing public." The Emergency Relief Committee expressed its regrets for any misunderstanding which had arisen.[61]

In other parts of the state, the local Red Cross chapters worked with local public and social agencies and the St. Vincent de Paul conferences to distribute flour to needy families. In Woonsocket, the St. Vincent de Paul conferences worked with the Red Cross and the Woonsocket Public Aid Department to distribute not only flour, but a ton and a half of fish. In addition to the food donated by individuals and stores, Prof. G. E. Adams of the State College (later the University of Rhode Island) and Stanley E. Ainsworth of the State Unemployment Relief Commission worked together to organize the tilling of 236 acres of land throughout the state with seeds and tools provided by the state or local relief agencies. The gardens were of four types: home gardens worked by the individual landowner; community gardens worked by individuals on relatively large plots donated by various companies for the purpose; municipal gardens, where unemployed men raised crops for fifteen dollars a week; and industrial gardens, similar to the second type, but worked by individuals for the benefit of employees who needed aid. In all, some 3,000 jobless men cultivated some 1,037 subsistence gardens.[62]

At Bishop Hickey's suggestion, the Catholic Woman's Club joined in a non-sectarian, charitable effort of Providence women, to maintain a soup kitchen and recreation room for the unemployed. The kitchen was established by Mrs. Frank L. Hinckley shortly after Christmas in 1931, when she learned that there was no place for unemployed men to go during the day. It was intended to carry on the effort until warmer weather arrived in May. Mrs. Hinckley recruited a committee to assist in the effort and they were given the use of a vacant building at 262 North Main Street, where they served mid-day meals to about two hundred men each day. Various religious or church groups took charge of a different day. The Catholic Woman's Club was given Saturday and it was their responsibility to finance the project on that day and furnish members to assist in the serving.[63]

Other Forms of Diocesan Cooperation

In addition to supporting the diocese's own fundraising appeals and those of the Share Your Clothes and Share Your Food campaigns, Bishop Hickey lent his prestige and voice to support the fund raising efforts of the Providence Emergency Employment Plan. During the depression that fol-

61 "Memorandum for Central Relief Committee;" Statement Relative to the Distribution of Share Your Food, April 15, 1933, PChA.
62 *Providence Journal*, October 6, 1932; *Providence Visitor*, July 25, 1932.
63 *Providence Visitor*, February 26, 1932.

lowed the First World War, public-spirited citizens in Providence had organized the Providence Committee on Unemployment, which found temporary employment for hundreds of workers, many of them ex-servicemen, until such time as they could find regular work at their own trades. In response to the unemployment crisis that developed following the stock market crash in 1929, prominent men in Providence created a similar committee, the Providence Emergency Employment Committee, which in February 1931 began a campaign to raise $22,000 a week from the employed and their employers in order to provide temporary jobs paying fifteen dollars a week for a thousand people.[64]

Providence had a long history of paying unemployed men to work on public works projects in times of crisis and in a smaller way in the woodyard maintained by the city, which offered tramps and others a chance to earn money by splitting wood for distribution to the poor. The first time men were paid for working on various projects was during the economic crisis in the years before the Civil War when they leveled the grade of the bluff on north side of the cove. During the depression that followed the Panic of 1873, unemployed men, who were paid by the city, dug up Corky Hill in Fox Point and carted the sand away to fill in a cove in the Seekonk River. During the Great Depression in the 1930's, Rhode Island would place heavy emphasis on work relief, something that was not typical of other states.[65]

The organizers of the campaign to raise money to offer work to unemployed men asked those who were employed to contribute 1 percent of their wages each week for sixteen weeks to the Employment and Relief Fund. On Thursday evening, February 12, 1931, Bishop Hickey delivered addresses from stations WJAR and WEAN backing the committee's appeal for funds. In addition to lending his personal support to the effort, the bishop asked his priests to announce the program at all their masses on Sunday, February 22. According to the plan, the relief fund committee was to work with the St. Vincent de Paul Society and the Family Welfare Society to ensure that the neediest men and women were given preference. Persons out of work were to register with the State Employment Bureau on Weybosset Street, which was to act as a clearing house to assist the committee. After the first sixteen weeks, the committee launched a second campaign in June, which was also endorsed by Bishop Hickey. In his letter to Thomas H. West, Jr., the chairman of the committee, that committee's program would only reach 1,300 of the then 10,000 workers without jobs. In addition to funding jobs, the monies raised in the campaign were distributed among the various relief agencies in the city. From January 1931 to May 1931, the apportionment committee of the general commit-

64   *Providence News*, May 27, 1922; *Providence Visitor*, February 13; June 5; July 17; December 18, 1931; *Providence Journal*, February 13, 21; July 20, 1931.
65   James T. Patterson, ed., "Life on Relief in Rhode Island, 1934: A Contemporary View From the Field (*Rhode Island History*, Vol 39, August 1980), 79–91.

tee allocated nearly $18,000 to the St. Vincent de Paul Society. The sum represented the difference between what the society collected from various sources and the monies it expended on relief. By the time the Providence Employment Committee concluded its activities at the end of 1931, the St. Vincent de Paul Society received more than $40,000.[66]

In the midst of all the major efforts to relieve the many needs of people of the diocese, small gestures often passed unnoticed. Among the innovations of Edward L. Reed, who became manager of Strand Theater in 1921, was the showing of special Saturday matinee shows for children. It is said that under Reed the Strand were the first in the country to offer such shows. In order to attract the children of the city, Reed originated the idea of giving toys to those who attended the matinees. When the Depression hit, he substituted canned goods for the toys so that the children might have something to bring home to their needy families. In 1920, the town of Warren was hard it by the closures of mills there. Albert G. Jamiel, a Warren merchant who had immigrated from Lebanon, did something that many small grocery store owners in other depressions and Jamiel and others would later do in the Great Depression: gave away food to needy townspeople.[67]

Important as these various relief measures were, few, if any, direct attempts were made to deal with what became a defining image of the Great Depression — homelessness — in its early years. The large manufacturing companies, who housed their workers in company-owned houses, frequently did not press their laid-off workers to vacate the houses when they could no longer pay the rent. Others, who owned their own homes, were less fortunate, as they were forced out when they could no longer meet their mortgage payments. Relief monies could be only stretched so far. Many dispossessed families felt themselves fortunate to be able to find substandard housing that they could rent. They and many others had to do without electricity or gas. Even those who could make their rent or mortgage payments often had to sell their best furniture for whatever it would bring to make ends meet.[68]

---

[66] *Providence News*, May 27, 1922; *Providence Visitor*, February 13; June 5; July 17; December 18, 1931; *Providence Journal*, February 13, 21; July 20, 1931.

[67] Obituary of Edward L. Reed, *Providence Journal*, June 27, 1949; Obituary of Albert G. Jamiel, *Providence Journal*, October 31, 1961.

[68] *Providence Journal*, February 25, 1931; *Providence Visitor*, July 17, 1931. This article reflects a reporter's experience gained from visiting the homes of the unemployed.

The Consequences of the Involvement
on the Part of the Federal Government

During the early years of the Great Depression, the burden of relief for
the unemployed was carried entirely by the local governments and private
charitable organizations. The governor at the time of the onset of the
depression, Norman S. Case, a Republican, who shared a conservative
view of government with President Hoover, believed that "It was the duty
of the local communities, chiefly, to care for their own unemployed and
needy." If, however, the cities and towns exhausted their funds in helping
the needy with their existing monies, they might borrow money from the
state at 3 percent interest in order to meet the needs of their inhabitants.
Democrats such as Theodore Francis Green argued that the state should
provide emergency monies as outright grants with no restrictions on them.
The local governments could then use the monies as payment for work
done by its recipients. The General Assembly, where the Republicans controlled the Senate, voted for Case's plan as the Democrats in the House
chose not to stand in the way of state relief of some kind. However, in the
elections of 1932, Green defeated Case in the race for governor and, in
the organization of the new House of Representatives in January 1933,
the Democratic majority elected a Democratic speaker. Since the Republicans had retained control of the Senate, Gov. Green had to negotiate
the passage of relief acts that he advocated as the state's first priority. At a
four-hour conference on February 12, the respective party leaders agreed
that Green was to attempt to secure a three million dollar loan from the
Federal Reconstruction Finance Corporation, while the state would pass a
three million dollar bond issue to repay it out of the state gasoline tax over
a five year period. A few rural Republicans balked at the deal. But in the
face of Green's threat of a filibuster if the recalcitrants did not cooperate,
the legislature passed the relief measure without a single dissenting vote
and Green immediately signed it.[69]

Gov. Green successfully negotiated a $896,000 loan from the RFC to
cover state payments for the months of March and April to the local cities
and towns, who were providing relief for the unemployed. Following the
successful negotiation, "He announced," in the words of a biographer,
"that he and he alone would superintend the parceling out of the money
to the various towns and cities." In effect, Green promised that he would
not release RFC funds to localities for use in creating jobs for the unemployed that did not meet the standards he set for them. He also warned
that he would not tolerate mismanagement of funds or any kind of "politics" in handing out relief. Under his plan, local government could engage
only trained social workers hired by the state to administer aid. As the state
agency charged with carrying out his plan, Green created the State Unem-

---

[69]   Levine, *Theodore Francis Green*, 129–30; 145–53.

ployment Relief Commission and made Henry T. Samson, who had previously been employed by the Providence Community Chest, its secretary.[70]

Keeping politics out of state business was not in the Rhode Island tradition. The Republicans in the state senate criticized Green's plan since,
in their view, it would dramatically and unjustifiably increase the cost of
administering aid because of his insistence that trained social workers be
employed. To further their cause, on March 23 the Republican-controlled
Senate created a special five-man investigating committee to examine the
relief operation created by Secretary Samson. Gov. Green saw in the committee's creation a move by the Republican senatorial majority to regain
control of patronage. At one point during the first day of hearings, which
began on Saturday, March 25, Senator Luke H. Callan, an Independent
from Bristol, asked Mr. Samson if he considered St. Vincent de Paul men
and Red Cross officials qualified to serve as home visitors. The question
was a sensitive one, because under Gov. Green's plan the St. Vincent de
Paul men, who worked without pay, would be replaced by state visitors
hired by the state, who were to be paid between twenty and twenty-five
dollars a week. After trying to evade a direct reply, Mr. Samson said that
he believed a "trained worker" should assist them. At another point in his
testimony, Mr. Samson declared that, under Gov. Green's plan, the local
departments of public aid were prohibited from using volunteer assistance
to administer Reconstruction Finance Corporation or state funds.[71]

An account of the Senate committee's hearing appeared in the same
March 31 issue of the *Providence Visitor* that the article on the Share Your
Food Committee's decision not to include the St. Vincent de Paul Society
in the agencies authorized to write food orders appeared. In an editorial
he wrote for the same issue in which the senate committee's scrutiny of
Gov. Green's plan was reported, Fr. James P. O'Brien, the *Visitor*'s editor,
characterized the governor's relief plan as one that would de-humanize or
de-Christianize relief activities. Gov. Green was quick to take issue with
Fr. O'Brien's statement and challenged the critics of his plan to suggest
a substitute as practical and non-partisan as that he had proposed. In his
addresses to the Holy Name convention on April 9 and to the priests and
laymen at the Catholic Charity Fund meeting on April 10, Bishop Hickey
added his voice to Fr. O'Brien's in defending the honor of the St. Vincent
de Paul Society, which he believed was being besmirched by Gov. Green's
insistence on the use of "trained" social workers. Hickey did not believe
that such workers would bring to the work the same respect for the dignity
of man as did the men of the St. Vincent de Paul Society. He particularly
attacked Mr. Samson for proposing a relief system, which would invade
the privacy of aid recipients and employ social workers who lacked "the

---

[70]   Ibid., 153–55.
[71]   Ibid., 155; *Providence Visitor*, March 31, 1933. The *Visitor* printed an account of the Mr. Samson's
testimony.

sympathy, the elasticity and the wide power of making allowances that [was] required" in the current crisis. Specifically, Bishop Hickey pointed to the proposal that the "trained social workers," who would be hired by the state to administer state aid to the needy, would require that aid recipients provide their names and those of their families and children, the debts that they owed, the amount of clothing and furniture that they owned, all of which information would be kept in a card system. Hickey saw this whole idea as degrading of people, "never on the charity list anywhere before, to have their names and their families down on a card system" along with their personal data. He particularly disliked the idea that the aid recipients would be asked, "what church they belonged to," in view of the fact that both Gov. Green and Mr. Samson had promised "politics" would be kept out of relief work. At the conclusion of their meeting, the Holy Name men appointed a committee to draft a resolution supporting the bishop's stand in regard to both the Share Your Food committee and Gov. Green's proposed methods for delivering state aid.[72]

Bishop Hickey's criticism of the proposed methods of administering state aid prompted considerable comment in many quarters of the state. On Wednesday, April 12, the Republican floor leader in the state Senate, Cranston Sen. Harry T. Bodwell, who was also a member of the select senate committee charged with looking into Gov. Green's proposed re- lief methods, supported Bishop Hickey's remarks and quoted extensively from their reports in the press. In supporting the bishop, Sen. Bodwell, who would during his years in the Senate enjoy friendly relations with both Republican and Democratic politicians, asserted that he was speak- ing "neither as a Republican nor as the floor leader of his party," but that he "was voicing the sentiments of 90 per cent, of both Democrats and Republicans, who have any knowledge at all of relief methods employed in Rhode Island today."[73]

When the special senate committee resumed its hearings into the pro- jected cost of Gov. Green's aid plan on April 1, Sen. Alfred D. Chaffee of Scituate directed Mr. Samson's attention to the fact that the application form that was to be filled out by applicants for the state position of case work supervisor asked the applicant's religion. He asked why the question was there. Mr. Samson replied that the State Unemployment Commission had copied the forms used by New York State officials and neither himself nor his staff noticed it. The question of religion also came up when Sen. Chaffee questioned Mr. Samson's chief assistant, Miss Ruth G. Lindall, on April 13. When Sen. Chaffee asked Miss Lindall whether she believed the application for employment should include a question regarding the religion of the applicant, Lindall replied that the question, although used

72 *Providence Visitor*, March 31; April 7, 14, 1933; *News-Tribune*, April 10, 11, 12, 1933; *Providence Journal*, April 10, 11, 13, 1933. For an explanation of the need for trained social workers, Cf. *Providence Journal*, April 16, 1933.
73 *News-Tribune*, April 12, 1933; *Providence Journal*, April 13, 1933.

by "92 percent of the social agencies," had been removed because of the "misunderstanding" it had caused. Since Bishop Hickey and others had publicly objected to a person's being asked their religion on the state application for aid, Sen. Chaffee also sought an explanation from Miss. Lindall as to the reason for its inclusion on the form the Commission had sent out for use in the new system. Miss Lindall replied, as had Mr. Samson, that the question was on the New York State forms, which the Rhode Island commission had simply copied. She informed the senator that, within the last few days, she and Mr. Samson had called several of the city and town aid administrators to inform them that they might eliminate the question at their discretion, as some were already doing in spite of its inclusion on the state form. When Sen. Chaffee, in conversational tones, continued to press her as to whether or not the Commission had adopted any official rules prohibiting discrimination in granting of aid on the basis of religion or how comprehensive an effort had been made to inform the various public aid directors that it was better to leave off the question of religion, Miss Lindall managed to partially answer the senator's question. At this point, Lindall broke down sobbing and Sen. Chaffee asked if she wanted the committee to take a recess of a "few minutes." She was escorted from the room by a spectator at the hearing, Mrs. George H. Crooker, a prominent East Side welfare worker. Mrs. Crooker returned to the committee room within a few minutes to express her displeasure at how the committee had treated Miss Lindall.[74]

One outcome of the special Senate commission hearings was the introduction and subsequent unanimous passage of a bill in the Senate to limit the cost of administration of relief over the next eleven months to $135,000 or 2 percent of the funds to be distributed. The measure died in the House Finance Committee and Gov. Green did not have to carry out his threat to veto it. A second outcome was a surprise visit by Gov. Green to a meeting of state public aid directors and welfare workers on April 24. Because some of the aid directors had testified at the Senate hearings that some state case superiors had usurped their authority, the governor made a point of affirming that the aid directors' authority superceded that of the state case workers employed in their departments and that the directors could insist that workers with whom they were dissatisfied be replaced.[75]

Before any relief program could be inaugurated, the voters of the state had to approve the state's taking out the Unemployment Relief Loan. State officials paired the question of approving the loan with that of repeal of the Eighteenth Amendment. On May 1, 1933, when the voting was held, Rhode Island voted 7 to 1 to approve the loan and to repeal the Eighteenth Amendment. A majority in every district in the state voted to ap-

74 *Providence Visitor*, April 14, 1933; *Providence Journal*, April 14, 1933.
75 *Providence Visitor*, April 21, 28, 1933.

prove the loan, and in only two districts did the repeal proposal fail to get a majority.[76]

The Conference on Industrial Problems

Even though Bishop Hickey was politically and socially a conservative, who had publicly "pledged to the fight against atheism, paganism, Godless Socialism, Communism and Bolshevism," as he had announced to the crowd gathered for the dedication of the new La Salle Academy in 1925, he was not blind to the flaws in American society and its economy, which led to the depression. Like President Hoover, he too believed that the America's industrial and business structure was fundamentally sound, but he also believed that the country's move toward centralization of wealth and the means of production in the interest of efficiency had led to a disregard for the individual. In a *Visitor* editorial, which he wrote under the direction of the bishop for the paper's September 26, 1930 issue, Fr. O'Brien said that the root cause of the failure of America's industrial leaders to avert the current financial crisis and to provide guarantees for future betterment lay in the idea that an efficiently organized:

> Society can be made to harmonize . . . with man, as a social being." It seemed clear, the editorial went on, "that we have arrived at a stage in our national development where conflict has arisen between our traditional individualistic system and a society which by reason of its rapid increase in number and growing complexity requires an ever greater degree of social organization. . . . Justice, and indeed, ordinary common-sense requires than an earnest and sustained effort be made to bring the legitimate aspirations of the individual into harmony with the general social needs of the day.

The path to the solution of America's social and economic problems that the editorial proposed lay in the modification of the cult of individual success and in providing opportunity for "the development of social thinking along just and reasonable lines."[77]

Bishop Hickey addressed the growing social and economic crisis confronting the United States in a talk given to the Holy Name men on the occasion of the eighth triennial Holy Name parade in Providence on September 20, 1931. He observed that it was clear to all thinking persons that fundamental and far-reaching changes in America's economic structure were inevitable. He proposed that the criteria by which the various changes to the economic order were to be judged was "the extent that they hold the promise of better achievement of distributive justice." Such criteria were "in accordance with the mind of the Church as reaffirmed recently

---

[76]   *Providence Journal*, May 2, 1933.
[77]   *Providence Journal*, September 28, 1925; *Providence Visitor*, April 4, 1930; September 26, 1930. Hickey's call for social leadership was applauded by Frederick P. Kenkel, director of the Central Bureau of the Catholic Central Verein of America, Cf. *Providence Visitor*, December 26, 1930.

by Pope Pius in his encyclical on Reconstructing the Social Order." In that encyclical, the bishop reminded the men, Pope Pius XI had repeatedly called on both clergy and laity to carefully study Christian social principles in their efforts to restructure both society and the economy. It was through the Catholic Action urged by the pope that Catholics could hope to achieve "that harmony [between the interests of individual and society] which should exist as between the spheres of the visible and invisible."[78]

To spur discussion of social and economic questions in the light of the Gospels and Catholic social teaching, particularly the social encyclicals of the popes, Fr. John A. Ryan, following his appointment as chairman of the Social Action Department of the National Conference of Catholic Bishops, along with other priests and laymen interested in the issue of social justice, organized the Catholic Conference on Industrial Problems at Chicago, Illinois on December 29, 1922. The object of the organization was to "promote the study and understanding of industrial problems by the calling of conferences." In the fall of 1929, Bishop Hickey agreed to host a regional meeting of the Conference in Providence the following December. However, when the Conference's Field Secretary, Linna E. Bresette, who did much of the work of planning and running the various conferences, was seriously hurt in a automobile accident, Fr. Raymond A. McGowan, the Secretary-Treasurer of the Conference and Fr. Ryan's assistant in the Social Action Department, wrote to Bishop Hickey on November 14, 1929 conveying the information that the conference in Providence would have to be delayed until Miss Bresette had sufficiently recovered to resume her duties. The delay proved to be longer that either Fr. McGowan or Bishop Hickey suspected. Fr. McGowan did not formally bring up the question of a conference in Providence again until June 1, 1932, when he was in the process of making plans for the fall and winter months. Once again, Bishop Hickey agreed to host a conference in Providence. The two men initially agreed on October 14 for the holding of the event, but, when it developed that the Providence Community Fund was planning to host its opening dinner for its 1932 campaign on that date, Bishop Hickey and Fr. McGowan agreed on Tuesday and Wednesday, November 15 and 16.[79]

On Friday, October 21, Bishop Hickey sent invitations to eighty-five prominent laymen and women and forty-five priests inviting them to serve on a general committee, which together with Miss Bresette, would organize the conference. The committee met at Providence's Biltmore Hotel, the site of the forthcoming conference, on Tuesday, October 25, where the volunteers were appointed to sub-committees charged with arranging the various aspects of the meeting. Personal invitations went out from

---

[78] *Providence Visitor*, September 25, 1931.
[79] Brochure, "The Catholic Conference on Industrial Problems;" Bresette to Hickey, October 14, 1929; McGowan to Hickey, November 14, 1929; June 1, 1932, PChA.

the committee on attendance and from Msgr. Peter E. Blessing, the general chairman of the conference, to all Catholics and non-Catholics who were thought to be interested in such a conference. In order to make sure that every parish in the diocese was represented at the conference, Bishop Hickey sent a letter to his pastors asking them to appoint a committee of five men and five women to attend the conference's sessions.[80]

Bishop Hickey personally opened the conference at the Biltmore on October 15. During the course of its six sessions, those attending heard addresses on a variety of topics from Fr. Francis J. Haas, Director of the National Catholic School of Social Service in Washington; Dr. Edmund Bigge, Professor of Economics at Brown University; Edward Reidy, Providence Director of Public Aid; Fr. C. H. McKenna, O.P., Professor of Political Science at Providence College; Francis J. Gorman, International First Vice-President of the United Textile Workers of America; Harold A. Fasick, Division Manager of New England Telephone and Telegraph Company, in Providence; Percival De St. Aubin, Treasurer of Vest Underwear Company, Providence; and from Frs. John A. Ryan and Raymond McGowan among others. At the dinner meeting on Wednesday evening, which was to be the capstone of the conference, Fr. James I. Corrigan, S.J., Professor of Sociology at Boston College and Michael Williams, editor of *The Commonweal*, were the featured speakers. As many as a thousand people attended the six sessions. At the closing dinner, Providence City Treasurer Walter F. Fitzpatrick attributed the large response to the conference to Bishop Hickey's intense interest in its proceedings and viewed the number who attended as a tribute to the bishop. The *Providence Visitor* gave the conference extensive publicity and its November 18 issue printed the text of the majority of the talks given.[81]

Additional Issues

In April 1933, some members of the State Employment Commission raised the question whether people receiving state relief continued to qualify to vote under the terms of the state's constitution, Bishop Hickey issued a statement, which the *Visitor* included in an article on the issue in its May 11 issue, in which the bishop held that there was no need to "add anything of the suffering of the people" by raising such a question. The provision in the constitution, [he asserted], contemplated a condition of pauperism due

---

80   *Providence Visitor*, October 21, 28; November 4, 11, 1932.
81   Ibid., November 18, 1932. The text of Fr. Ryan's and Fr. McGowan's talks appeared in subsequent issues on November 25 and December 2. On Monday, May 1, 1933, Protestants and Jews in the state held a similar conference at Providence's Central Congregational Church under the sponsorship of the Interdenominational Commission on Social Action which was attended by several Catholics. The two conferences differed in that at the conclusion of the interdenominational Conference the participants took formal votes on various resolutions aimed at economic reform. Cf. *Providence Journal*, May 2, 1933; *Providence Visitor*, May 5, 1933.

to criminal neglect or habit" and did not apply to the present circumstances "when even the best of men are reduced to the necessity of accepting aid." In the same issue, the *Visitor* printed the opinion of Attorney General, Benjamin M. McLyman, given in response to the State Employment Relief Commission that the state constitutional provision did not apply to persons receiving aid from the Commission.[82]

A month earlier, on March 4, 1933, when the loss of confidence in banks in other parts of the country began to have its impact on Rhode Island's banks, acting governor, Robert E. Quinn, in the absence of Gov. Green, closed all the banks in Rhode Island to avert a run on them. On March 6, the new President, Franklin D. Roosevelt, declared a four-day banking holiday. After receiving reassurances that every bank in Rhode Island was sound, Bishop Hickey joined other civic and religious leaders in a call for patience and calmness by having a letter of his read at all the masses on Sunday, March 6, in which he passed along the assurances he had received that there was no need for concern about the safety of the monies deposited in Rhode Island banks. Later in the week, he amplified his remarks by expressing the hope that "the results of this banking holiday will be beneficial to all and more particularly to the small businessman." In order to deal with the problem of protecting the Sunday collections taken up at the various churches in the state, city and town officials arranged for the local police forces to guard them. In Providence, the police took the collections from each of the rectories and placed them in a vault at police headquarters until such time as the banks reopened.[83]

When Congress, at President Roosevelt's urging, adopted the compromise National Industrial Recovery Act in an effort to put the unemployed back to work, Bishop Hickey agreed to lend his voice to the state campaign organized to enlist the voluntary co-operation of employers and consumers in the planned economy envisioned by the measure. When asked by the local organizers of the effort to speak at an organizational meeting of the local campaign committee at the Turks Head Club, Bishop Hickey expressed himself as "proud, glad and enthusiastic" to be associated in the work, which he said was motivated by "the principle of justice for all." In response to a request by Arthur Henius, secretary of the Providence Campaign Committee, the bishop wrote a letter to the pastors of the diocese in which he called on all of them to support the efforts the National Recovery Administration, particularly the effort on August 27, which the NRA dubbed "NRA Sunday," to secure the signatures of as many people over eighteen as possible to a pledge to patronize stores whose owners had themselves signed an NRA pledge. Going further in support of the campaign to convince people to sign the NRA consumer pledge, Hickey agreed to make an address over radio station WEAN in which he praised

---

[82]   *Providence Visitor*, May 11, 1932.
[83]   Ibid., March 10, 1933; *Providence Journal*, March 5, 11, 1933.

President Roosevelt's program as the "best preliminary step that could be taken in the approaching new era." He called on the people of the state to sign the consumer pledge as a "patriotic duty."[84]

A snapshot of the conditions prevailing in Providence in 1934 was offered by the U.S. Commerce Department as part of a series of studies that the department did based on data collected in 1934 and released in October 1937 in a document entitled "Consumer Use of Selected Goods and Services by Income Classes." Among the department's finding was the fact that 63 percent of Providence families had incomes of less than $1,500 annually. In addition, 41 percent received less than $1,000 annually to operate their homes, and 5.2 percent had no income at all. Among other points: Providence residents owned three times as many automobiles as mechanical refrigerators; forty-four percent of the city's residents still used stoves, rather than central heating plants, for heat; one sixth of the families surveyed— 16.9 percent—had neither bath tubs nor showers in their homes; sixty-one-and-a-half percent had no cars—only 13 percent of the 7,741 families had more than one car; the average family consisted of four persons, living in five-and-a-half rooms for which the annual rental was $285 a year; six out of ten families lived in one or two-family houses—only 5.2 percent lived in apartment buildings; ninety-seven percent of all families surveyed lived in wooden construction; families reporting incomes between $1,000 and $3,000 owned about 57 percent of all automobiles used in Providence and almost 56 percent of all mechanical refrigerators in the city; coal still was used by 67 percent of all Providence families for heating: kerosene by 18.1 percent, and oil burners by only 6.2 percent; Electricity was used for lighting by all families with incomes of $3,000 or more and by 98 percent of the other reporting families.[85]

Epilogue: The Death of Bishop Hickey

On Wednesday, October 5, 1933, the feast of St. Francis of Assisi, Bishop Hickey had one of his usual, active days. He had risen early in order to be at the new St. Francis Home for the Aged on Blackstone Street in Woonsocket before eight. The bishop said mass in the home's small chapel for the nuns who staffed the new home and a few lay persons who had heard of the bishop's coming by word of mouth. The bishop said a few words at the conclusion of the mass about the saint whose feast day it was and af-

---

[84] *Providence Visitor*, August 18, 25; September 1, 1933. Another article printed in the August 18 *Visitor* listed the names of prominent Catholics who had been appointed over the last weeks to federal positions in the state, where they would direct established agencies and carry out the new projects instituted under the National Recovery Act.

[85] Excerpts of the Commerce Department report were reprinted in the *Providence Journal*, October 11, 1937.

terwards blessed the chapel and the rooms of the new home. After spending a brief time at the reception that followed, he returned to Providence
before noon and went right to his office. He took care of routine matters
which he generally got to after lunch because he wanted to listen to a few
innings of the world series. He lunched, as usual, with the priests of the
cathedral and the chancery staff. After lunch he went back to his office to
finish what work remained and to pray part of the Divine Office before
the game came on. Late that afternoon, he went to his dentist for a regular
check-up. At five, he stopped at the office of Curran, Hart, Gainer and
Carr to visit with his nephew, David B. Lovell, as he frequently did when
time allowed. After dinner with Fr. Thomas J. McKitchen, the rector of
the cathedral, and other the priests of the cathedral, he went to the chapel in the rectory for evening prayer. However, almost immediately after
he retired to his room, he called Fr. McKitchen and asked him to come
to his room. When McKitchen arrived, the bishop told him that he was
not feeling well. Since the bishop's appearance confirmed his words, Fr.
McKitchen hurried to a phone to call Dr. John A. Bolster, the bishop's
doctor. At the bishop's request, Fr. McKitchen administered the Sacrament of the Sick and, with the bishop, he began to pray for the grace of a
happy death. When Dr. Bolster arrived the bishop had already lapsed into
unconsciousness. The doctor's stimulants failed to revive him, and three
minutes after the doctor's arrived, Bishop William A. Hickey was dead at
age sixty-four.[86]

Bishop Hickey's death came as a shock to many. He had shown no signs
of frailty as had Bishops Hendricken and Harkins before him. He seldom
took a vacation or a day off. The exception was an occasional round of
golf. He did not particularly enjoy travel. The only times he was away
from the diocese for any length of time was when he made his two visits
to Rome. Only in the later stages of his life did he form friendships among
the clergy of the diocese.

He enjoyed working. The day he died was typical of how he filled each
day. He was a skilled and talented administrator who closely oversaw both
diocesan and parochial affairs. Having been a pastor before becoming
bishop, he continued to identify himself with the lives of the people he
served, in both a private and public manner. He believed that the Church
ought to be involved in public life as advocate and defender of public morals. "For this reason," as a *Visitor* editorial said, "he was not only willing but
eager to make use of the press and the radio, through which, with courage
and eloquence, he bore witness to the Faith and condemned those things
in public life which he judged to be evil.[87]

His solicitude for the spiritual progress of his diocese prompted him
to write numerous letters and to have them read from the pulpit since he

---

[86]   *Providence Journal*, October 5, 1933; *Providence Visitor*, October 6, 1933.

[87]   *Providence Visitor*, October 6, 1933. The next few paragraphs lean heavily on the editorial written
       as part of the special edition the *Visitor* published following Bishop Hickey's death.

conceived it as one of his chief responsibilities to be pastor of every soul in his diocese. His concern for the spiritual welfare of his priests prompted him to be an active participant in their annual retreats and the semiannual diocesan clergy conferences. As bishop, he was keenly aware of the importance of the liturgy. As chief celebrant, he sought to carry out his role in church services faithfully and exactly. His love for the Eucharist and for the Lord caused him to urge the development of the liturgy in the diocese as fully as possible.

In order to promote the spiritual well-being of the people of the diocese, he encouraged the work of the religious orders which were present in the diocese when he arrived and welcomed new orders, both active and contemplative orders. His concern for the preaching of the gospel went beyond the confines of the diocese. Although he realized that the needs of the parishes and institutions of the diocese were pressing, he encouraged and actively promoted the work of the Propagation of the Faith. Among the last of the ceremonies he performed was the blessing of the Columban Fathers' novitiate in Bristol.

The obituary articles in both the *Visitor* and the *Providence Journal* spent a good deal of space on Bishop Hickey's efforts in behalf of Catholic education in the diocese and the role he played as a leader in encouraging the co-operation of the people of his diocese with their fellow citizens in every good work consistent with Catholic principles. In the midst of the economic crisis which beset the country in the fall of 1929, he joined with his fellow Catholic bishops and with the Social Action Department of the N.C.W.C. in calling for a reevaluation of the basis of American society and sought to bring the light of Catholic social teaching to bear as a guide to social reconstruction.

The notices also made reference to Bishop Hickey's generosity. His name consistently led the published lists of donors to the Catholic Charity Appeal. When approached to support various civic causes such as the Providence Community Fund, the Red Cross fund-raising drives, or the "Forget-Me-Not-Day" appeal of the Disabled American Veterans of the World War, he not only agreed to write letters in support of such fund raising efforts but also sent a personal check as his own contribution. To illustrate Hickey's constant concern in regard to the needy, the *Visitor*'s obituary notice recalled the time when a despairing mother sent the bishop a letter detailing her plight and that of her children. Moved by the letter, the bishop sent a St. Vincent de Paul man in a cab to bring the woman money that the bishop took from his own pocket. As a result of this incident, Bishop Hickey had constant private surveys made during the winters of 1931 and 1932 so as to keep himself informed on unemployment conditions in the state.[88]

In speaking to the LaSalle Academy alumni in December 1931, Bish-

---

[88]   Ibid., October 6, 1933.

op Hickey referred to what he called his "rashness" in urging the LaSalle alumni not only to buy a few acres as a site for a new academy building but the whole parcel. He could also have been speaking of launching the campaign to build not only a new LaSalle Academy building but to raise a million dollars to build other new high schools.

In making this remark, Bishop Hickey recognized that he did not always foresee the entire consequences of his actions. For the most part, his talent as an administrator ensured that his undertakings were successful. However, that same rashness that prompted him to undertake actions which were not fully thought out from the beginning also prompted him to say things to people which they took in ways he did not anticipate. A person who knew the bishop and was of strong character might well have challenged the validity of one of the bishop's critical remarks. When the reply was spoken with even handedness, Bishop Hickey would reconsider his position. Those who knew him were aware that "he was solicitous of souls to such an extent as to be deeply disturbed at any act of his which he thought might in any way cause spiritual harm." While he had his regrets, his zeal for his ministry never deterred him from speaking out whenever he thought it was necessary.

Pope Pius XI was among those who expressed their sorrow at the death of Bishop Hickey. Pope Pius and Bishop Hickey had come to know one another during Bishop Hickey's visits to Rome in 1922 and 1929. Hickey's efforts in behalf of Catholic education and the success of the Catholic Charity Drives set him apart from among the American bishops. Pope Pius and the Roman officials also had another reason to remember Bishop Hickey as Bishop Hickey and Pope Pius XI bore a striking physical likeness to each other.

Bishop Hickey's death was a cause of general sadness in Rhode Island. His funeral was attended not only by his fellow bishops but by a wide spectrum of the religious, educational and civil leaders of the state, who knew him personally because of his involvement in community affairs. All of the bishops of New England were there except Cardinal O'Connell and Fall River bishop, Daniel Feehan. One of his closest friends in the episcopacy, Most Rev. James E. Cassidy, the apostolic administrator of the Diocese of Fall River, was the celebrant of the mass. Most Rev. John B. Peterson, the Bishop of Manchester, a former auxiliary bishop in Boston and another friend in the New England episcopacy, preached the eulogy. The Archdiocese of Boston was represented by its new auxiliary bishop, Francis J. Spellman.[89]

Bishop Peterson praised Bishop Hickey as being "pre-eminently a man of duty" who "made his life the life of his people, their needs his needs and their troubles and difficulties his very own." In a reference to the Sentinel-list crisis, Bishop Peterson said of him that, "He was a man of much tried

89   Ibid., October 13, 1933.

Most Rev. Francis P. Keough, D.D.

CHAPTER V

The New Bishop of Providence

The Interim

On October 6, 1933, three days after Bishop Hickey died, the Diocesan Consultors met to choose a diocesan administrator, who would serve until such time the Holy Father announced his choice of a successor to Bishop Hickey. To no one's surprise, the man the consultors chose to take charge of the affairs of the diocese was the man both Bishop Harkins and Bishop Hickey had chosen to serve as Vicar General, Msgr. Peter E. Blessing.[1]

At the time of Bishop Hickey's death, the American bishops met every two years with the archbishops of their provinces to discuss possible candidates for the episcopacy. After having selected two names from among those submitted, the list was arranged alphabetically and sent to Rome along with the archbishop's comments and all the available information as to the qualifications of the individuals whose names appeared on the list. The apostolic delegate, who would have forwarded the list to Rome, might also add his own comments on the potential candidates. The length of time required for the choice of the fourth Bishop of Providence was dependent in large measure on when the question of a successor to Bishop Hickey was placed on the agenda of the Consistorial Congregation in Rome. On February 12, 1934, Archbishop Amleto Cicognani, the new apostolic delegate, who had been appointed to replace Archbishop Fumasoni-Biondi in March 1933, sent a telegram to Fr. Francis P. Keough, the assistant chancellor of the Diocese of Hartford, notifying him that he had been appointed Bishop of Providence. Because Bishop John Nilan of Hartford was seriously ill, the bishop-elect delayed his coming to Providence for more time than a new bishop might ordinarily have. In the interval, the diocese continued to be administered by Msgr. Blessing.[2]

Although as administrator, Msgr. Blessing was to maintain the status quo rather than to launch any new initiatives, he was expected to use his best judgment when new issues arose. The successful passage of the vari-

---

[1]   *Providence Journal*, October 13, 1933.
[2]   Ibid., February 13, 1934; *Providence Visitor*, February 16, 1934.

ous New Deal initiatives sparked a revival of the effort to secure passage of a proposed amendment giving Congress the "power to limit, regulate and prohibit the labor of persons under 18 years of age," which was popularly referred to as the Child Labor Amendment. Congress had submitted the proposed amendment to the states on June 21, 1924. Within three years, five states ratified it while twenty-six rejected it. During the 1920s the percentage of underage children working had dropped substantially as rising wages enabled a single wage earner to support a family. Nevertheless, proponents of the amendment, which included among them the president's wife, Eleanor Roosevelt, and Secretary of Labor, Frances Perkins, renewed their efforts to secure its adoption. In Rhode Island, Gov. Green had appointed a committee headed by Prof. George E. Bigge of Brown University to advise him on social problems. The committee recommended passage of the amendment and the governor had included such a recommendation in his address to the legislature at the beginning of January 1934. Aware that the amendment's national proponents were going to push for its passage in Rhode Island, Archbishop John T. McNicholas, Archbishop of Cincinnati and episcopal chairman of the N.C.W.C.'s Department of Education, wrote to Msgr. Blessing alerting him to the situation. As he wrote to Msgr. Blessing, Archbishop McNicholas' concern and that of the American hierarchy was "that if the Child Labor Amendment be adopted in its present form Congress will be able to control the educational system of the country."[3]

Msgr. Blessing, who shared the archbishop's concern about the potential for federal control of education, engaged the legal firm of Curran, Hart, Gainer & Carr to prepare a brief that argued against passage of the amendment and which set forth the objections of Archbishop McNicholas and others who opposed it as being overly broad and susceptible to misuse in ways beyond what was intended by its proponents. He also asked several attorneys, who were members of the legislature, to look over the wording and to gather data that could be used in opposing it. In addition to preparing a brief arguing against passage of the amendment, one of the attorneys of the firm hired by the diocese, David B. Lovell, who was Bishop Hickey's nephew, arranged to meet with Gov. Green on January 11 to set out the diocese's argument against passage. The governor explained why he had urged passage and asked Mr. Lovell to share his objections with Prof. Bigge. He agreed to halt all action on the amendment's behalf until he had secured from Rhode Island's congressmen information on Msgr. Blessing's concern that its adoption would mean federal control of education.[4]

In addition to seeing the governor, Mr. Lovell also met with Democratic state senator, Francis J. Kiernan, who had been designated as the senator

---

3   McNicholas to Blessing, December 28, 1933, PChA.
4   David B. Lovell, "Memorandum re Amendment to the Constitution Related to Child Labor," January 12, 1934; Blessing to McNicholas, January 11, 1934, PChA.

to introduce a resolution of approval into the Senate. Sen. Kiernan agreed not to introduce the resolution and added that he would see to it that no other member of his party offered such a resolution. As the House Committee on Special Legislation had already voted to recommend passage of the amendment, Mr. Lovell next turned to the leadership of the House. Time was important because the House was scheduled to vote on a resolution approving the amendment on the day that Mr. Lovell went to the State House. Lovell spoke with both Democratic and Republican members of the House. His most important conversations were with Democratic Representative William Reddy, the Speaker of the House; James Kiernan, the Deputy Speaker; and Edmund Flynn, the Democratic floor leader. Mr. Flynn assured him that after the resolution was referred back to the Committee on Special Legislation, it would die there unless its supporters asked for a hearing. Lovell's last conference of the day was with Lt. Gov. Robert E. Quinn. Quinn assured him that the act would never pass the Senate so long as he was president of it. In his lobbying efforts, Mr. Lovell was helped by Fr. Martin Reddy, pastor of St. Patrick's, Providence, who was the brother of the House Speaker. When the House met later in the afternoon, the only business the representatives took up was a resolution to recommit the proposed amendment to the House Committee on Special Legislation. Before he left the State House that day, Mr. Lovell received assurances from politicians in both House and Senate the amendment would not pass the legislature.[5]

Like Msgr. Blessing's opposition, Mr. Lovell's lobbying effort caught those who favored the Child Labor Amendment off guard as they were not expecting any opposition. After the amendment was recommitted to the Committee on Special Legislation, the proponents of the amendment, among whom were Alice Hunt, a veteran worker for child welfare legislation in her own name and that of the Consumers' League of Rhode Island of which she was president, and labor leaders, Frank Gorman and Thomas McMahon, asked for a hearing on the amendment. The House Committee on Special Legislation scheduled the hearing for Wednesday, January 31.

On January 29, 1934, Msgr. Blessing met with the Diocesan Board of Consultors. He reviewed with the board his concept of the powers contained in the proposed amendment and the arguments of its opponents. He explained that he had had a pamphlet prepared explaining the provisions of the amendment and had had a complete account of the proposed legislation printed in the previous week's *Visitor*. Since it was in the Board of Consultors that Canon Law placed episcopal authority during a vacancy in the diocese, Msgr. Blessing asked for a vote from the board in regard to the actions he had taken and in view of the scheduled hearing on the amendment before the House Committee on Special Legislation. The consultors were unanimous in their opinion that Msgr. Blessing should

---

[5]   Ibid.

continue his opposition to the proposed amendment and that he should authorize his legal advisors, who were to testify before the House committee, to oppose the proposed Child Labor Amendment in its present form.[6]

In addition to the lobbying efforts that the diocese financed, Msgr. Blessing had the strong support of the *Providence Visitor* and its editor, Msgr. Michael O'Brien, in publicizing the concerns many of the nation's Catholic bishops had in reference to the Child Labor Amendment. Msgr. O'Brien had built up the circulation of the *Visitor* to the point where it could claim the largest circulation of any diocesan newspaper. Beginning on the Friday before the House hearing, the *Visitor* began running a series of front page, bold print articles. The first article consisted of the brief that Curran, Hart, Gainer & Carr had prepared at Msgr. Blessing's request. Another article in the same issue reported the substance of a talk Msgr. Blessing gave to the Daughters of Isabella on Sunday, January 21, in which the monsignor voiced his criticism of the amendment. In an interview with a *Visitor* staffer reported in the same article, Msgr. Blessing responded to the argument of Msgr. John Ryan and others, who personally supported the amendment, that Congress would never use the broad powers granted to it, if the amendment was passed, to invade the personal rights of parents and the prerogatives of the individual states in the manner its critics foresaw as possibilities. He pointed to the recently voided Volstead Act as an instance where Congress, under the control of a minority of the citizens, passed a law, which led to the gross violations of individual rights. He also described two of the four women who drafted the amendment passed by Congress as associates of communists or socialists.[7]

On February 2, the *Visitor* printed a lengthy report of the hearing before the House committee, again in large and bold print. During the hearings, Patrick Curran appeared as counsel for the Diocesan Council of Catholic Men and Women. His main argument was that "the control of persons under eighteen years of age with respect to their labor ought to be kept at home, first with their parents, their natural guardians, and secondly with . . . their lawfully elected state representatives." Miss Hunt; Bishop Granville Gaylord Bennett of the Episcopal Diocese of Rhode Island; Rabbi William Breude of Temple Beth-El, Providence; Mrs. Royal C. Taft, president of the Rhode Island League of Women Voters; and Mrs. Albert Kenyon of the Rhode Island Parent-Teacher Association were among those who spoke for passage of the resolution approving the amendment. The amendment's supporters were joined by a Newport Catholic lawyer, Cornelius Moore. In his testimony before the committee, Francis Gorman, vice-president of the United Textile Workers of America, one of several labor officials who supported the amendment, urged ratification and re-

---

6   Minutes of the Board of Consultors, January 29, 1934.
7   *Providence Visitor*, January 26, 1934.

ferred to the opposition of leading Catholics in the diocese as "unfair and unfortunate."[8]

The task of rebutting the witness given by the proponents of the amendment was taken on by Joseph H. Gaynor, a former mayor of Providence and, with Mr. Curran and Mr. Lovell, counsel for the Diocesan Council of Catholic Men and Women. A telling part of his testimony, and one highlighted by the *Visitor* in a separate article, was his review of the attempts made in the U.S. Congress to limit the scope of the proposed amendments by qualifying its wording, all of which were defeated through the efforts of the lobby which supported the proposed amendment as it was introduced. Mr. Gaynor also made a point of demonstrating that Msgr. Ryan, whom Cornelius Moore had cited as favoring the amendment, quite readily admitted that, on the issue of the amendment, he was speaking in his own name as a citizen, not as a representative of the Catholic Church. Besides Curran, Gaynor and Lovell, an impressive list of other witnesses, both Catholics and non-Catholics, spoke against the amendment. Among the proposals that came up at the hearing was one offered by Albert A. Baker, a Providence attorney, who supported the businessmen opposed to the amendment. Mr. Baker suggested that the amendment be placed before the voters of the state in a referendum, something the supporters of the measure were against because they believed that the opposition Msgr. Blessing had organized to the amendment would ensure its defeat. The *Visitor* continued printing front page articles, which were exclusively against the amendment, until fifty days had passed, the required time within which the committee had to act on a piece of legislation.[9]

In January 1937, again as a result of pressure from the Democratic administration in Washington, a renewed attempt was made to convince the state legislatures that had not acted on the amendment or had rejected it, to consider or reconsider its passage. Once again the *Providence Visitor* took a strong editorial stand in opposition to the adoption of the amendment. Many of the same arguments advanced for and against the amendment in 1934 were repeated in 1937 by the priests of the diocese in their addresses to diocesan and parish groups. Once again, the diocesan and parish lay organizations passed numerous resolutions, which they forwarded to their state senators and representatives, opposing passage of the amendment. The labor organizations in the state though the local labor paper, *The Labor News*, the official newspaper of the Rhode Island State Federation of Labor, sought to offset the opposition of the clergy by reprinting a statement of Msgr. Ryan in support of the amendment. The *Visitor* was quick to contradict Msgr. Ryan's statement that the Church in the United States had not taken a stand on the issue. For evidence to the contrary, the editor, Fr. Francis Deery, pointed to an article the paper had run in its February

---

8   *Providence Visitor*, February 2, 1934.
9   Ibid., February 2, 9, 16, 23, 30; March 2, 9, 16, 23, 30, 1934; *Providence Journal*, February 1, 1934; *Pawtucket Times*, February 1, 1934.

25 issue reporting the opposition of the bishops of New York and Massachusetts as "a striking indication of the unanimity that exists among the members of the hierarchy with regard to the proposed amendment." When Bishop Keough himself addressed the question in a talk to the annual convention of the Holy Name Society in the cathedral, he echoed the stand taken by many other bishops that they would eagerly welcome a child labor proposal that he could support but feared the loss of parental and church authority that potentially would result from the wording of the proposed amendment. Once again, the Rhode Island legislature took no action on the proposed amendment other than to ignore it.[10]

Bishop Keough's Early Life

Francis Patrick Keough was born in St. Mary's parish, New Britain, Connecticut, on December 30, 1891. He was the second son of Patrick Keough and Margaret (Ryan) Keough, who had named their first son, Michael, in honor of their pastor, Fr. Michael Tierney. When the question of a name for the new baby came up, an aunt, who was an admirer of the third Bishop of Hartford, Francis Patrick McFarland, announced, according to tradition, "Francis is his name." Apparently, everyone agreed, and it was the name given him at his baptism. When it came time for confirmation, the young man himself chose Patrick as his middle name.[11]

His father, Patrick, a gasworker, died when Francis was three years old. (There were also two girls in the family, who died when they were children). Rather than stay home when his older brother began the first grade at St. Mary's Parochial School, young "Frank" begged his mother to be allowed to go to school with him. His mother consulted the nun in charge of the school, who agreed to allow Frank to come along with his brother in anticipation that "perhaps one day will cure him." Frank was not cured and, earlier than most, began what was to be a distinguished academic career.[12]

The Keoughs were a devout family, who held the clergy in high esteem. From the age of six, young Francis talked of becoming a priest. As a widow, Mrs. Keough faced a difficult task in raising her two surviving children. It was important, if not necessary, for the two boys to find jobs, even while they were in school, to help out financially. Francis worked as a grocery boy, newsboy, and clerk while he was in school. In his free time, he played baseball with other boys and, if forced to, could hold his own in a fight. Among those who befriended the boy when he was about twelve

10   Ibid., January 21; February 4, 18, 25; March 18, 25, 1937; *Evening Bulletin*, April 26, 1937.
11   Ibid.; *Providence Visitor*, May 18, 1934; Thomas F. Cullen, *The Catholic Church in Rhode Island* (North Providence, Rhode Island: The Franciscan Missionaries of Mary, 1936), p. 200. In St. Mary's baptismal register, the new bishop's name is spelled Kehoe.
12   *Providence Visitor*, May 18, 1934.

was an immigrant Jewish cobbler from Kiev, Samuel Greenburg, who had come to live across the street from the Keoughs. Greenberg, who at the time had no children, came to love his young neighbor as a son. It was Sam Greenburg who urged Francis' mother to open a grocery store in the first story of her home so that she might have the money to send her sons to high school when it was time. Mrs. Keough took his advice and the store prospered. Francis and Mr. Greenburg had many long talks together in Sam's shop while he worked. They talked about their respective religions and Sam spoke of how he once thought of becoming a rabbi. He encouraged Francis to get a good education and, when the time was right, to enter the seminary.[13]

After Fr. Michael Tierney was made Bishop of Hartford in 1894, he made it a priority to establish a minor seminary in his see city. During the time he was rector of the Providence cathedral, Fr. Tierney had opened the Boys Academy on Fountain Street that Bishop McFarland had founded. St. Thomas's Preparatory Seminary opened in the fall of 1897. It offered four years of high school and two years of college training in the classics to boys who could either reside at the seminary or attend classes during the day. When young Francis Keough graduated from St. Mary's, New Britain, in 1906, he was accepted at St. Thomas in the following fall.[14]

Francis Keough's academic career at St. Thomas was such that Bishop John J. Nilan, Bishop Tierney's successor, chose Francis and two of his classmates to do their philosophical and theological studies at the renowned Sulpician seminary of St. Sulpice, at Issy, just outside of Paris. The three young men from the Hartford diocese began their studies in October 1911. While they would have taken French as part of their studies in Hartford and thus have some knowledge of the ordinary language of the seminary in which they were to live, the constant use of French reinforced their formal knowledge and helped the students to become fluent and comfortable in the language. According to the reports of the seminary authorities, Francis Keough's intellectual abilities, combined with habits of diligence and exactness, made him one of the outstanding students in the house. They also discovered in him "a love of cultural pursuits, soundness and depth of judgment, an amiable and sympathetic disposition, and a profound sense of reverence and piety." When the Germans invaded Belgium in August 1914, Bishop Nilan recalled his students and sent Francis Keough to Street Bernard's Seminary, Rochester, New York, to continue his studies. For the last months before ordination, he served as a prefect at St. Thomas Seminary. Bishop Nilan ordained Francis P. Keough a priest at St. Joseph's Cathedral, Hartford, on June 10, 1916.[15]

13 Jack Harrison Pollack, "The Cobbler and the Archbishop," *Catholic Digest*, 22, June 1958, 15–18.
14 For St. Thomas Seminary, cf. James H. O'Donnell, "The Diocese of Hartford," in William Byrne et al., *History of the Catholic Church in the New England States* (Boston: Hurd & Everts, Co., 1899), Vol. II, 452–59.
15 *Providence Visitor*, February 16, 1934; *Catholic Transcript* (Hartford), February 15, 1934.

For his first assignment, Bishop Nilan appointed him an assistant at St. Rose's parish, Meriden, Connecticut. Years later Msgr. John Neale, pastor of St. Rose's, would write of his young assistant, "To us, he was always the cultured gentleman and the ideal priest. He was an eloquent preacher, the friend and advisor of youth, a man of great executive ability, a keen sense of justice and fair play, tactful, prudent and withal simple and most approachable." Fr. Keough was in Meriden when the Spanish Influenza pandemic struck in 1918–19. The young priest worked tirelessly to help where he could, even digging graves so as to relieve the sexton of some of his labor.[16]

In December 1919, Bishop Nilan chose Fr. Keough to be the Diocesan Director of the Society for the Propagation of the Faith, as well as chaplain at St. Agnes' Infant Home, which was staffed by the Sisters of Mercy, and the House of the Good Shepherd, which was staffed by the Sisters of the Good Shepherd. Both homes were in the Hartford area. Fr. Keough would also take an interest in St. Mary's Home for the Aged, also run by the Sisters of Mercy. Keough lived at St. Agnes' in West Hartford and traveled throughout the diocese on Sundays preaching on behalf of the mission society. When he did not have a speaking engagement, he helped local pastors. Over the years, the Sisters of the Good Shepherd frequently turned to him for advice and assistance in remodeling and reconstructing their home. He designed their new chapel and, more importantly, assisted the sisters in establishing courses in typewriting, housekeeping, hairdressing and cosmetics to prepare the women in the home for the time when they would be released.[17]

In 1925, Bishop Nilan appointed Fr. Keough assistant chancellor and secretary to the bishop with his residence at the cathedral. Bishop Nilan soon developed a warm friendship with his new secretary, who became one of the bishop's closest advisors. His position as chancellor and secretary gave the young priest a broad understanding of diocesan administration. Although the focus of his work shifted at this time to the Chancery Office, Fr. Keough now said mass at St. Mary's Home for the Aged. It happened on occasion that he brought the Eucharist to up to one hundred elderly and infirm residents of the home before beginning his day in the chancery office.[18]

At the time of his ordination as bishop, Bishop Keough would be one of the youngest men in the American episcopacy. The new bishop was, for his day, of medium height, perhaps five feet seven inches tall, and solidly built. He was mild-mannered and amiable and, as a result, was popular among the priests of Hartford, where he had many friends, as well as

---

16 Ibid.
17 Ibid., February 17, 1934; May 18, 1934. In appreciation for his services to the House of the Good Shepherd and the women who lived there, the girls at the home made the rochet, a close-fitting linen vestment with sleeves extending to the hands, that Bishop Keough would wear on the day he was ordained bishop.
18 *Providence Journal*, February 13, 1934; Cullen, *The Catholic Church in Rhode Island*, 203–204.

among the laity. He had no interest in sports or hobbies. His chief exercise
for the years before he came to Providence was a methodically undertaken
two-mile walk, frequently with his bishop. According to his friends and
associates, who were interviewed when Fr. Keough's appointment was announced, he had a "pronounced talent for getting things done easily and
pleasantly." Those who knew him spoke of the steadfastness with which
the new bishop pursued an appointed task and of how he was never satisfied until the work at hand had been throughly accomplished. One of his
intimate friends was quoted as saying, "He is wonderfully consistent with
himself. He has a genius for maintaining his personal integrity."[19]

It fell to the new bishop to decide when and where he was to be ordained
to the episcopacy. His decision as to where came quickly. On the day after
he was named bishop, the local newspapers announced that the new bishop would be ordained in the cathedral of SS. Peter and Paul's, Providence,
"sometime after Easter." In order to set a date for his ordination, Bishop-
elect Keough traveled to Washington to see Archbishop Cicognani in order
to ask him to preside at the liturgy and to be the ordaining prelate. They
agreed on May 22 as the date for the ordination. Although the bishop-elect
might have chosen any agreeable date after Easter Sunday, which fell on
April 1, the bishop-elect chose the twenty-second in part because he was
aware the Bishop Nilan was seriously ill and his death was near. At their
meeting, the delegate suggested to the bishop-elect that he call on Boston's
Archbishop, Cardinal O'Connell, to ask him if he would do Keough the
honor of installing him as Bishop of Providence. Cardinal O'Connell gra-
ciously agreed to do so and, with that gesture, ended the long estrangement
between the cardinal and the Diocese of Providence.[20]

On the day after Bishop-elect Keough's appointment was announced,
Msgr. Blessing, Fr. Thomas McKitchen, the rector of the cathedral, Fr.
William Tally, who had been a student with Keough at Issy, and Fr. Charles
C. Curran, director of the Diocesan Charities Bureau, went over to Hartford to offer their congratulations and to begin to prepare to receive their
new bishop in Providence. Keough did not make his first trip to Providence until March 28, when he made a brief visit to the Chancery Office
and spent some time with Msgr. Blessing and the Chancery staff. At Msgr.
Blessings' urging, the bishop-elect made his first official visit to his diocese
on April 9, to address the meeting of pastors and trustees that annually
launched the Catholic Charity Drive. The bishop-elect purposely waited
outside Cathedral Hall until after the meeting began as he intended to
leave the leadership of the drive in Msgr. Blessings' hands. At the agreed
upon time, Fr. Thomas J. McKitchen, the rector of the cathedral, escorted
him into the meeting. Keough spoke only a few words and then closed the

19 *Providence Visitor*, February 16, 1934; *Providence Journal*, February 16, 1934.
20 Keough to Cicognani, March 14; April 12, 1934, PChA.

meeting with a prayer. Afterwards, he joined Msgr. Blessing, the clergy and the laymen for the traditional picture in front of the cathedral.[21]

While he was anxious to take up his new work in Providence, Bishop Nilan's illness prompted him to stay in Hartford so that he might be with his friend and mentor. Bishop Nilan died on April 13 and was buried on the seventeenth. A week later, Hartford received word from Rome that Auxiliary Bishop Maurice F. McAuliffe had been appointed to succeed Bishop Nilan. The same issue of the *Visitor* that carried the news of Bishop Nilan's death and funeral also carried the official announcement that Bishop-elect Keough had set May 22 as the date on which he would be ordained and of the prelates who would ordain him. It would not be until Sunday afternoon, May 20 that the bishop-elect moved from Hartford to the Cathedral rectory on Fenner Street.[22]

Bishop Keough's First Years

SPIRITUAL CARE OF THE MEMBERS
OF THE CIVILIAN CONSERVATION CORPS

Among the first pastoral challenges Bishop Keough took up was the spiritual care of the young men, who had enlisted in the Civilian Conservation Corps, of which there were three camps established within the diocese during 1933. The Civilian Conservation Corps was one of the more popular of the New Deal programs. Congress passed the legislation creating the corps on March 31, 1933. The legislation was intended to address two unique segments of the nation's unemployed population. The first was young men between 18 and 25. In ordinary times, men of this age would have entered business or industry as apprentices or helpers. As they gained experience and knowledge, the young men would have gradually worked themselves up into the better paying job categories. With the onset of the depression, married men of much greater experience filled the jobs once given to the young. With no work to fill their time and exhaust their energies, the young were in danger of drifting into delinquency of one kind or another. The second segment the creation of the CCC was intended to help were the unemployed veterans of the First World War.

The federal government moved quickly to organize, train and deploy the forest army created by Congress. The U.S. Army was put in charge of the program and men from the regular army and the reserves were placed in command of the companies of 215 men, who were to be assigned to each Reforestation Camp. Rhode Island officials began to invite qualified

---

21 *Providence Visitor*, February 16; March 30; May 18, 1934; *News-Tribune*, April 9, 1934; *Providence Journal*, April 10, 1934.

22 *Providence Visitor*, April 20, 27, 1934; *News-Tribune*, April 18, 1934; *Evening Bulletin*, April 18, 19, 1934; *Providence Journal*, 19, 20; May 18, 1934.

young men to fill out application forms to fill the quotas allotted to each city and town in the state during the third week of April 1933. Those selected then went to the Army recruiting station at 100 Union Street in Providence, where they were given a physical examination. After passing the physical, the young men were bused to Fort Adams, Newport, for ten days to two weeks of physical conditioning before being assigned to camps. The first group of Rhode Islanders enlisted in the program were sent to Rangeley Lake, Maine, on Monday, June 5, 1933; others were later sent to camps in Vermont and New Hampshire. Both of Rhode Island's Congressmen, Francis Condon and John O'Connell, as well as Gov. Green, worked to secure federal approval for opening CCC camps in Rhode Island. Initially three camps were designated for the state. They were located on state forest lands in the towns of Charlestown, West Greenwich and Coventry. The 141st company was assigned to Burlingame State Forest near Watchaug Pond, Charlestown, which the state had acquired in 1930, and the 142nd at the George Washington Memorial Forest, which had been donated to the State in August 1933 by the Edgewood Woman's Club. The camp was on the Putnam Pike in Glocester, near the village of Chepachet. Later, the 1161st was stationed at Primrose, in the town of North Smithfield; the 1186th company was posted to Beach Pond, Escoheag, West Greenwich; the 1187th was sent to Mount Vernon, at Greene, in the town of Coventry; and the 1188th was assigned to Arcadia Management Area, Hope Valley, in the town of Exeter. In 1938, the 1188th Company was transferred to East Jeffrey, New Hampshire and replaced at Hope Valley by the 1116th Company, which was made up of war veterans. Also in 1938, the 1161st Company was transferred from Primrose to Chepachet.[23]

In the weeks after the establishment of the first camps, many bishops and others conveyed to Archbishop Cicognani, the apostolic delegate, their concerns about the spiritual welfare of the young men in the CCC camps. Several bishops suggested that the delegate establish a central clearinghouse for information about the religious situation in the camps that could be forwarded to the bishops concerned about the welfare of the young men of their dioceses. Accordingly, the delegate asked Fr. John Burke, C.S.P., General Secretary of the N.C.W.C., to gather the desired statistics and make them available. On August 14, 1933, the delegate wrote to Bishop Hickey to inform him of the arrangement he had made with Fr. Burke. In his reply to the delegate, Bishop Hickey reported that, Fr. John T. Fahey, the chaplain at Newport's Mercy Home and School, had heard the confessions and said mass for the men while they were at Fort Adams. Subsequently, the Marists at Immaculate Conception, Westerly, began saying

---

[23] *Providence Journal*, April 7, 8, 16; June 6, 1933; The designations of the companies and their
    locations are found in a report submitted to Bishop Keough by Fr. Arthur A. Sullivan, "Summary
    of the Religious Census of the Six Civilian Conservation Corps Camps in the State of Rhode
    Island," September 21, 1937.

mass for the men at Burlingame after the camp opened in July 1933, and continued to do to do so for a year until the spiritual responsibility for the camp passed to Fr. John O'Rourke, the pastor of St. Francis, Wakefield. The camp at Escoheag was cared for by the pastor of Our Lady of Mercy in East Greenwich and his assistants, who took turns driving the twelve miles to the camp on Sundays. The camp near Chepachet was served by Fr. Valmore Lambert, chaplain at St. Francis Home, Woonsocket, who said mass there on Sundays and Holy Days. Otherwise, the boys there might go to Fr. Laliberte's camp for homeless men and boys, which was nearby. While the priests who offered mass in the camps had not taken a census as the delegate suggested, the bishop assured him that they would.[24]

The problem of ministering to the young men at the camps was primarily one of personnel. The priests in Wakefield, East Greenwich, and other parishes, which had camps within their boundaries, were hard pressed to keep up with their ordinary responsibilities. Fr. William Delaney, to whom Bishop Keough would entrust youth work in the diocese in September 1935, visited the first three camps on occasion to hear confessions, say mass and to give a short talk to the whole camp. But his duties made it impossible for him to visit the camps every Sunday. On June 9, 1937, Arthur J. Spring, the Educational Advisor at the Beach Pond Camp at Escoheag, West Greenwich, wrote to Bishop Keough praising Fr. Delaney's work, but suggesting that a Catholic chaplain whose sole responsibility was ministry to the young men in the camps was needed. He pointed out that 85 percent of the men in his camp were Catholics and there was a real danger of their slipping away from the faith as contract or reserve Army Protestant chaplains regularly visited the camps.[25]

The ordination of a large number of new priests for the diocese in May and June 1937 gave Bishop Keough the opportunity to assign one of them, Fr. Arthur A. Sullivan, as full time chaplain to the CCC. camps. During the summer of 1937, Fr. Sullivan spent his time traveling from one of the five camps then in Rhode Island to another, saying mass in each camp, hearing confessions and otherwise making himself available to the young men. On weekends, he said an early mass in one camp and a later mass in another. During his visits to the camps, Fr. Sullivan took a census. He reported that out of the 898 men enrolled in the camps, 801 or 91 percent were Catholics.[26]

At the end of the summer of 1937, Bishop Keough sent Fr. Sullivan back to the Catholic University in Washington where he had pursued his theological studies for graduate work and appointed Fr. William Beane, who at the time of his appointment was an assistant at the cathedral, to

---

[24] Cicognani to Hickey, August 14, 1933; Hickey to Cicognani, August 19, 1933, PChA; *Providence Visitor*, August 3, 1934.

[25] "Report of CCC. Duty: November 1, 1936 – June 1, 1937; Arthur J. Spring to Keough, June 9, 1937, PChA.

[26] Fr. Sullivan's reports are found in the Civilians Conservation Corps file, PChA.

take over the work, which Fr. Sullivan had clearly shown there was a need for. Although the federal government had begun paying clergy who acted as "contract" chaplains $30 a month and five cents a mile in 1934, Bishop Keough had not sought to secure compensation for the services of the parish priests who attended the camps, or for those of Fr. Delaney. When he assigned Fr. Beane as chaplain of the CCC. camps, Fr. Beane inquired about securing an appointment as a reserve Army chaplain. After a long exchange of letters between Bishop Keough and various church and army officials, Fr. Beane received a reserve chaplain's commission in February 1938. He continued in the camp ministry even after he was called to active duty with the army in February 1941. Because of the wartime demands for labor, all the Civil Conservation Camps were closed by 1942.[27]

The Catholic Youth Organization

While the Civilian Conservation Corps was the U.S. governments' response to the problem of unemployed youth, the Catholic Church developed its own. In 1931, Auxiliary Bishop Bernard J. Sheil, who had recently been appointed pastor of St. Andrew's parish on the near north side of Chicago, created the Catholic Youth Organization out of existing parish programs and some fund raising and social welfare operations run by the archdiocese. The CYO welcomed young people of all races and creeds, not just Catholics, and sought to teach moral and spiritual values through athletics. The CYO in Chicago had programs for young girls and boys from 10 to 18 and for young men from 18 to 25 years old.[28]

On December 14, 1934, Bishop Keough discussed his desire to see the Catholic Youth Organization established in the Diocese of Providence with the Board of Consultors. His desire was motivated by his concern that too many young people were growing away from the Church and contributing their share to the delinquency in the community. He stressed with the consultors the spiritual side of the CYO's programs. At the meeting, Keough outlined his plans to enlist the support of the pastors of the diocese. Although he had been planning to organize the CYO in his diocese for a while, the first practical steps towards that organization took place hurriedly. While on a visit to Chicago in early July 1935, he apparently inquired about the CYO organization in that city. As a result of his inquiries, he learned of a program in Boy Guidance offered by the Knights of Columbus at the University of Notre Dame. On July 4, he sent a telegram to his secretary, Fr. Charles Maloney, asking him to notify Frs. William M.

27 Burke to Keough, June 15; July 9, 14, 1934; December 18, 1937; Keough to Burke, June 22, 1934; Keough to Captain J. J. Donovan, Acting Assistant Adjutant General, First Corps Area, Boston, September 22, 1937, PChA; *Providence Visitor*, February 24, 1938.

28 Steven M. Avella, "Bernard James Shiels (1886–1969), in *The Encyclopedia of American Catholic History* (Collegeville, Minnesota, The Liturgical Press: 1997), 1290–92.

Delaney and Frederick M. Moreau that he wished them to take the course. Fr. Delaney was ordained in 1929, and since the fall of that year, he had been an assistant at the Immaculate Conception parish, Providence. Fr. Frederick M. Moreau, who was ordained in June 1933, had served first in Holy Family parish, Woonsocket, and had recently been transferred to St. Ann's, Woonsocket. Since he was still relatively new to the diocese, the bishop had asked for advice as to which two priests he might ask to direct the CYO programs he envisioned. Fr. Delaney came to his attention because of his involvement with the youth activities of his parish, particularly playing ball with the boys at Hopkins Park. In addition, in December 1933, Delaney had initiated a Parochial Basketball League for the Providence city parishes, which the principal of LaSalle Academy agreed to sponsor and to allow the new league the use of LaSalle's gym. The following spring, Fr. Delaney also created a parochial basketball league. Fr. Moreau was recommended to the bishop because of his interest in scouting. At the request of his pastor, Fr. Morin, Moreau had organized Troop 2, Woonsocket, in St. Ann's, which was the first Catholic Scout Troop organized in the diocese since the 1920's. He then went on to organize two others in Holy Family and Precious Blood.[29]

Catholic Scouting

After each received a call from Fr. Mahoney informing them of Bishop Keough's wishes, the two priests, who had not met before, arranged to meet that day in Immaculate Conception rectory. They agreed to start for Notre Dame the next day in Fr. Moreau's new Plymouth. The trip took three days. After their return from Notre Dame towards the end of July 1935, Bishop Keough appointed the older of the two, Fr. Delaney, director of youth activities in the diocese and Fr. Moreau, associate director. When Fr. Delaney met later with Bishop Keough, he sounded the bishop out as to which of the two programs that were discussed at Notre Dame, the Boys Brigade or the Boy Scouts, the bishop favored. There were then three scout troops in Woonsocket and one in St. Brendan's, Riverside, and a Boys Brigade at Blessed Sacrament in Providence. Bishop Keough made it clear to Fr. Delaney, as he would later to all his priests when he met with them, that he wanted a Boy Scout and a Girls Scout troop in every parish.[30]

Backed by Bishop Keough's dictum and with the enthusiastic cooperation of the Narragansett Council of Boy Scouts and its executive, J. Harold

---

[29] "Board of Consultors Minutes," December 14, 1934; Telegram from Keough to Mahoney, July 4, 1935, PChA; *Providence Visitor*, December 15, 1933; July 11, 1935; September 19, 1935; Interview with Msgr. William M. Delaney, August 7, 1990. For the earlier history of the scouting movement in the diocese, Cf. Hayman, *Catholicism in Rhode Island and the Diocese of Providence*, II, 612–14.

[30] *Providence Visitor*, August 22; September 12, 1935; Interview with Msgr. Delaney.

Williams, Fr. Delaney and Fr. Moreau began setting up meetings between pastors who were willing to have troops in their parishes and the scouting professionals who worked for the Narragansett Council. One of the basic principles enunciated during the course Frs. Delaney and Moreau took at Notre Dame, and one supported by the National Scout Office, was that whenever a Catholic troop was formed, Catholics who had previously joined other troops had to join the new unit or resign from the Boy Scout organization. Pastors who were willing to host troops in their parishes were asked to commit the same space each week to the scouts for their troop meetings. In order to provide training for the new Scoutmasters, Assistant Scoutmasters, and the five men who would serve as the troop committee, Fr. Delaney arranged with Chief Williams for the holding of training courses for the new leaders. The course met one night a week over a period of eight weeks. On his part, Fr. Delaney established the first troops in the English-speaking parishes. Although Fr. Delaney had to overcome the opposition of certain pastors who were suspicious that he was checking up on them or who were reluctant to have their facilities used by the scouts who might damage them, the movement spread rapidly through the diocese.[31]

Even before the new scout troops were set up in the Catholic parishes, Catholic scouts, who belonged to already established troops, looked forward to spending a week at Camp Yawgoog, the Narragansett Council's camp in the town of Hopkington. Until Fr. Delaney began going down to Yawgoog on Sundays to say mass for the scouts during the summer of 1936, Catholic scouts, who wished to go to mass on Sunday, were obliged to go the five miles to St. Joseph's, in Hope Valley, a mission of Immaculate Conception, Westerly, where they were often unable to enter the chapel because of the lack of room. Fr. Delaney would also say mass for the scouts during the Winter Camping Season of 1936–37. In May 1937, Bishop Keough assigned him as full-time chaplain at Camp Yawgoog for the next summer season. As had the Marists who served St. Joseph's and who had visited the camp on Sundays to say mass during the summers previous to 1936, Fr. Delaney offered mass on the porch of one of the camp's buildings. During his sermon to the scouts, who were camping during the opening week of the 1936 season, Delaney asked them to make a weekly donation to cover the cost of purchasing an altar and mass equipment. Because of the many distractions that took place while saying mass outdoors, Fr. Delaney soon began thinking about building a Catholic chapel at the camp. It would not be until 1949 that the hope became a reality.[32]

31 *Providence Visitor*, August 22; September 12, 19, 26, 1935; Interview with Fr. Delaney, August 7, 1990. Sr. Mary Winifrid Motherway, R.S.M., "Catholic Youth Organization of the Diocese of Providence," M.A. dissertation, Catholic Teachers College, May 1944, p. 40.
Fr. Delaney wrote a weekly column for the *Providence Visitor* in which he detailed the growth of the scouting movement in Catholic parishes during 1935–36.
32 Ibid., July 16, 1936; May 20, 1937.

In large part because of Bishop Keough's endorsement of scouting and the energy and enthusiasm Fr. Delaney brought to his new assignment, in the years between 1935 and 1939, the Narragansett Council experienced one of its greatest periods of growth. Frs. Delaney and Moreau collectively would assist in the organization of sixty-two troops by May of 1937. The Council reached a peak of 10,022 men and boys during 1939. By 1941, the number dropped back to 9398. During the Second World War, 60 percent of the Council's troops lost their leaders. There would be resurgence beginning in 1944 with much of the gain coming from the organization of Cub Scout Packs. Once again, Bishop Keough lent his support. At the kickoff meeting of the Narragansett Council's effort to organize sixty-one new troops, the leaders read a letter from Bishop Keough in which he expressed the hope that "there will be a troop in every Catholic Church in the diocese." In 1947, when Fr. Delaney made his yearly report on the activities sponsored by the CYO in the diocese, he noted that there were 102 Catholic Boy Scout and Cub Scout troops with some 2800 scouts.[33]

Several months before he sent Frs. Delaney and Moreau to Notre Dame, Bishop Keough met with Mrs. Nicholas F. Brady, chair of the Girl Scout board of directors, to discuss the organizing of troops under Catholic leaders. To assist in the effort, the bishop asked Mrs. Marion de St. Aubin, the wife of Percival de St. Aubin, who in 1934 had been honored by Pope Pius XI with the "Pro Ecclesia et Pontifice" cross for her private works of charity, to serve on the Providence Girl Scout Council as his representative. Mrs. de St. Aubin agreed and later chaired the finance committee of the Providence Council. During 1935, Mrs. de St. Aubin helped organize thirty-five troops in various parishes in the diocese. In February 1936, Girl Scout leaders in Woonsocket helped organize a Girl Scout troop among the girls in St. Francis Orphan Home in Woonsocket, the first such troop of girls in any charitable institution in the diocese.[34]

As was true of the Boy Scouts, many of those who joined the Girl Scouts also looked forward to attending Camp Hoffman, in West Kingston, the Girl Scouts' summer camp. Until 1941, the director at Camp Hoffman had arranged for the transportation of the Catholic campers to St. Francis, Wakefield, for Sunday mass. In April 1941, the camp director, Yolande Delys, wrote to Bishop Keough asking if he might assign a priest to say mass at Camp Hoffman on the Sundays the girls would be there. Although he would never have enough priests to fulfill all the requests he received for masses, Bishop Keough made the scouts a priority and arranged for Fr. Francis Deery, then the editor of the *Providence Visitor*, to say mass for

---

33   Ibid., May 20, 1937; *Providence Journal*, February 11, 1944; "Activities Sponsored by the CYO of the Providence Diocese," [1947]; J. Harold Williams, *Scout Trail, 1910–1962: History of the Boy Scout Movement in Rhode Island, An Eyewitness Report* (Rhode Island Boy Scouts and Narragansett Council, Boy Scouts of America, 1964), p. 41.
34   *Providence Visitor*, December 14, 1934; January 30; February 6, 1936.

the girls. Even when the Second World War stretched the supply of priests even further, the bishop was able to arrange for mass at the camp.[35]

Catholic Youth Activities

Bishop Keough and Fr. Delaney saw scout troops as one dimension of a program of Catholic youth activities. In September 1935, Fr. Delaney turned his attention to also organizing athletic competitions. He began with the parochial schools in Providence whose boys' basketball and base-ball teams he had previously organized into a Parochial School League under the sponsorship of LaSalle Academy. Under Fr. Delaney, the Dioc-esan Catholic Youth Organization took over the sponsorship of the Paro-chial School League. According to the plan he formulated, each pastor in the Providence area was asked to appoint an assistant to take charge of CYO activities in the parish. While Fr. Delaney planned to begin CYO competition by organizing a Parochial League of Softball Teams in Sep-tember 1935, the delay in opening schools that September caused by an infantile paralysis epidemic forced him to start with a league of basketball teams, who began play during the week before Christmas. Besides teams from the Providence city parishes, the league included one from Sacred Heart, East Providence, and one from the St. Aloysius Orphan Home.[36]

While the CYO would be associated in the minds of many with its cul-tural, social and athletic programs, the spiritual dimension of the program was emphasized from the beginning by its early leaders. Ideally, religion was the motivating force and final objective of all the activities embraced by the program. As Sr. Mary Winifrid, R.S.M., who wrote an early history of the CYO program in the diocese, noted, the stress on spirituality and morality was present from the beginning:

> Participants in athletic events are governed by the C.Y.O. Pledge of Sportsmanship. The C.Y.O. player must ever keep in mind that he represents an organization which is under the direction of the Catholic Church; that the public recognizes him as a Catholic and consequently expects his conduct and his ideals to be influenced by his religious beliefs and training. Therefore, he takes the following pledge whereby is regu-lated his participation in C.Y.O. athletics: 'I promise upon my honor to be loyal to my God, to my Country, and to my Church; to be faithful and true to all my obligations as a Christian, a Man, and a Citizen. I pledge myself to live a clean, honest and upright life; to avoid profane, obscene and vulgar language, and to induce others to avoid it. I bind myself to promote, by word and example, clean, wholesome and manly sport. I will strive earnestly to be a youth of whom my Church and my Country may be justly proud.'

---

35 Delys to Keough, April 9; July 7, 1941; Keough to Delys, April 10; July 11, 1941, PChA.
36 *Providence Visitor*, November 21; December 5, 1935.

To promote spirituality, many parish CYO units had a monthly corporate Communion Sunday followed by a Communion breakfast.[37]

A particularly important part of the CYO program in Chicago, which was a model for programs elsewhere, was boxing. This was true for the older boys and young men, particularly those between seventeen and twenty-five who were unemployed because of the depression. Church sponsorship of boxing competitions was criticized by some as morally dubious, but Bishop Shiel defended his program as the best way to rehabilitate impoverished young men, whose other alternatives were gangs and a life of urban crime.[38]

While some saw boxing as an antithesis of moral sport, Fr. Delaney did not share the scruples of those opposed to it. He saw instruction in boxing as a way to teach boys "the art of self-defense and to provide them with sport under excellent leadership." CYO boxing tournaments would become popular features of the program in its early years. In order to participate in the sport, boys needed to write to Fr. Delaney about their interest and to present a letter of recommendation from their pastors. In addition to boxing for the older boys and young men, Fr. Delaney also organized a Senior Parish Baseball League in the summer of 1936 and in January 1937, a basketball league, which had two divisions, heavyweight and lightweight. The initial season of the basketball league saw teams entered from parishes in Providence, North Providence, West Warwick, East Greenwich and East Providence. The highlight of each season would eventually be the state championships contested in the various sports.[39]

In order to begin the program of boxing instruction in January 1936, Fr. Delaney secured the use of the Knights of Columbus gymnasium in the Knights Building on Greene Street, Providence. The Catholic Working Boys Home was also used for some CYO activities. A year later, Bishop Keough arranged for the use of the gymnasium on the third floor of Infantry Hall on South Main Street as a site for the boxing program as well as basketball, handball and gymnastics. According to the schedule arranged by Fr. Delaney, when the CYO gym opened on March 30, 1937, the gym was open from 2:00 to 4:00 each afternoon, except Sundays, for the boys 17 and older, many of whom were unemployed. From 4:00 to 6:00, the grammar school boys used the gym, and, from 7:00 to 10:00, the older school boys, 17 and older, had use of it. On the opening day for the gym, both Bishop Keough and Providence Mayor Dunne were present and spoke briefly. Fr. Delaney used the occasion to pass out trophies to the winners in the CYO basketball leagues and to stage several boxing bouts to demonstrate what the young men had learned. In his brief remarks at the opening of the gym, Bishop Keough reiterated for the audience what he had said when he first discussed CYO activities with his consultors, that

---

37 Sr. Winifrid, "Catholic Youth Organization," p. 18.
38 Avella, "Bernard James Shiel," p. 1290.
39 Ibid., January 16, 1936.

"the athletic program was not an end in itself but is to serve as a means to bring youth nearer to God and to the teachings of His Church."[40]

The gym, along with the whole CYO program, was supported by the funds raised by the Catholic Charity Fund. Besides the renovation of the space used by the CYO and its rental, the fund paid the salary of the full-time gymnasium director, initially Robert Dwyer, a Providence College graduate and a graduate of the Boy Guidance course at Notre Dame. In the first days that the gym was open, Mr. Dwyer was assisted by volunteers Edmund Martineau, who taught wrestling; Billy Lynch, a one-time professional boxer, who along with Leo J. Hunt, the Athletic Director at St. Raphael's, taught boxing; and Jack Keating, a former La Salle Academy coach, who taught track. To help him at the CYO office, which was first located in Infantry Hall, Fr. Delaney had the services of Archie Cardillo, who came to him in 1938 as a National Youth Administration Worker. When Bobby Dwyer later moved out of state, Mr. Cardillo took his place as athletic director. Cardillo was devoted to the CYO and he and Fr. Delaney worked well together.[41]

Although not immediately related to CYO activities, the *Providence Visitor*, in March 1933, began publishing articles on sports written by Thomas J. Connery. The *Visitor* had printed occasional articles on Providence College sports as well as those of the Catholic high schools and the Columbian Squires, before Mr. Connery began writing for the paper. By the end of June 1933, the *Visitor* began devoting an entire page to sports. When the CYO began its athletics activities, the results of the CYO competitions were also included. In addition to the attention CYO activities received from the *Visitor*, WEAN, the Providence radio station, in 1941, began offering the CYO Radio Program, with Archie Cardillo as the CYO reporter. The program featured news about CYO activities and, during the war, interviews with the various priest sectional directors as well as with former CYOers serving with the armed forces, who were home on leave.

The first sports program offered for girls was bowling. In September 1944, the CYO ran an announcement in the *Visitor* that, in response to many requests, it would begin sponsoring a bowling league for girls composed of parish teams from Providence and its vicinity. Also in 1944, the CYO sponsored its first "mixed" activity, a stage show at the Loew's State Theater, which according to the *Visitor*, was a hit with the large audience in attendance.[42]

In its early days, cultural activities were an important part of the CYO. In cooperation with the National Youth Administration, Fr. Delaney launched a variety of cultural programs. Msgr. O'Brien at Immaculate Conception placed the second and third floors of the parish institute at

40 Ibid.; February 11; March 18, 25; April 1; May 13, 1937; *Providence Journal*, April 1; April 20, 1937.
41 *Providence Visitor*, January 31, 1985.
42 Ibid., September 28; November 21, 1944.

Fr. Delaney's disposal. The CYO scheduled classes in knitting, crocheting, cooking, home nursing and arts and crafts for girls. For boys, there were classes in art, metal and woodworking as well as sign painting and photography. Cameras and dark room materials were supplied by the NYA. With the cooperation of the Bishop Hendricken Council, Fourth Degree Knights of Columbus, the CYO organized a Public Speaking Class for boys, which was taught by Dr. Harry Nugent. Dr. Nugent had taught at La Salle Academy for seventeen years before he joined the state Department of Education in 1937 as head of its division of Americanization and Adult Education.[43]

The renting of Infantry Hall for the CYO gym provided Fr. Delaney with office space. He kept his door open for young men, who wished to stop in and talk. As CYO activities multiplied, so did the responsibilities involved in their oversight. Because Fr. Moreau was interested in scouting rather than in the athletic part of the CYO program, Fr. Delaney recruited Fr. Theodore Peloquin, who had been transferred to Precious Blood, Woonsocket, from Central Falls in 1935, to serve as the first sectional or regional director of CYO activities. In December 1937, Fr. Delaney appointed five other young priests as regional directors. Fr. Delaney also appointed Fr. J. Leo Lyons as his associate diocesan CYO director. At Delaney's request, in September 1937, Bishop Keough removed Fr. Delaney from Immaculate Conception parish and appointed him chaplain to the Mercy Sisters at Villa St. Rose in Greenville so that he might have more time for the CYO.[44]

In October 1938, on the Feast of Christ the King, the feast chosen by CYO directors at a national conference in May 1937 in Chicago as the patronal feast day of the CYO, Fr. Delaney organized the first CYO parade Sunday. Pastors, who chose to cooperate with the program on that day, set aside the Sunday as a communion Sunday for the youth of their parishes. In the afternoon, there was a parade from Market Square in Providence to the cathedral, which consisted of twenty-nine divisions and a dozen bands. At the cathedral, Fr. Delaney preached at the service and Bishop Keough addressed the CYOers. The Boy Scout pledge was led by J. Russell Gray, a district commissioner for the Boy Scouts. The Girl Scout pledge was led by Miss Marie Lamond, captain of Girl Scout Troop 33 at Blessed Sacrament, and the CYO pledge of sportsmanship by Robert Dwyer, the CYO athletic director. The entire assembly then pledged allegiance to Christ the King. The service ended with Benediction celebrated by Fr. Lyons. The CYO parades on the feast of Christ the King became a regular event until 1942, when wartime rationing made it difficult to transport the CYO members to Providence. During and after the war years, the feast of Christ the King was the occasion of parish recognition of the youth groups.[45]

[43] Sr. Mary Winifrid, "Catholic Youth Organization," 22–24; *Providence Visitor*, September 21, 1944; March 8, 1945.
[44] Interview with Msgr. Delaney; *Providence Visitor*, December 16, 30, 1937.
[45] *Providence Visitor*, October 27, 1938; October 29, 1942 *Providence Journal*, October 31, 1938;

The CYO suffered its first tragedy in 1941 during a CYO-sponsored hockey league game at the Rhode Island Auditorium on North Main Street, Providence. On February 13, one of the young men, aged 21, playing at the Auditorium fell during a game and was injured. The young man was taken to a hospital, but later died of complications resulting from his injuries.[46]

On Sunday, October 4, 1942, Fr. Delaney and the organization suffered another kind of tragedy when a mentally disturbed young man, who had escaped fifteen times from what was then called the Exeter School, set fire to the Infantry Hall building. The building suffered damage estimated at $160,000, while the top two floors, including the fourth floor, where the CYO gym was located, were destroyed. In the wake of the fire, Fr. Delaney salvaged what he could from his office and set up a new office in the Visitor Building on Fenner Street. A few days after the fire, Providence Mayor Dennis J. Roberts, through Charles F. McElroy, Director of Public Works, offered Bishop Keough the use of the facilities in the Point Street fire station as a temporary gymnasium that would serve the needs of the boxing program and offer space for ping pong, checkers and other games. The Fire Department had used the third floor of the building as a training and conditioning center.[47]

Following the Second World War, Bishop Keough and Fr. Delaney explored various possibilities for opening a new gym. At the beginning of 1946, the bishop had an inspection made of the Federal Street School on Federal Hill, which the city was willing to sell. However, engineers reported that the city's building code would not allow the auditorium in the school, which was being considered for use as a gym, to be used for that purpose. As an alternative, Bishop Keough considered having the existing building torn down and a new building erected to house CYO central headquarters and a gymnasium as a memorial to the CYO boys who died during the war. This alternative was presented as a possibility at the April 1946 opening meeting of the Catholic Charity Fund.[48]

Another alternative developed when Fr. Martin Reddy, pastor of St. Patrick's, Providence, agreed to allow the CYO to use the gymnasium, which the parish had built as part of its new parochial school on Smith Street. Fr. Delaney officially opened the new Smith Hill CYO center on Tuesday, November 12, 1946. It was open to youth of the city and vicinity regardless of race, color or creed. To direct the new center and the volunteers who would help out there, Fr. Delaney hired Edward J. Roth, a former Providence College football player and a physical training instructor while in the Army Air Force. A second gym suitable for basketball was made available to the CYO in Our Lady of Loreto Hall, East Providence. During the summer of 1947, the interior of the hall was repainted. The

October 24, 1942.

[46]   Delaney to Keough, February 15, 1941, PChA.

[47]   *Providence Journal*, October 5, 8, 1942; *Providence Visitor*, October 8, 1942.

[48]   *Providence Visitor*, April 23, 1946.

center was under the charge of Fr. Donald King and lay director, Cecil J. Ryan.[49]

A good deal of Fr. Delaney's time and that of other staff members in the period after the war was given to listening to and counseling returned veterans, a goodly number of whom he noticed were "nervous, worried and unstable." Fr. Delaney well realized that the CYO organization was wholly unprepared to offer the kind of help these young men needed. He described the situation in a report to Bishop Keough in September 1945.

> We have listened to their problems, advised them, directed them to the Veterans' Guidance Bureau and obtained employment for them. Those who need help are not isolated cases. At times we have had ten servicemen in the office at one time and four of them would be waiting to get my advice. Directed to Government agencies set up to help them, they hesitate, claiming they would rather not go to these Bureaus. This is a good sign because it seems to indicate that these ex-servicemen remember what the Church did for them in wartime through their chaplains. They want guidance from the Church now that the war is over.[50]

Care for the Deaf and Hard of Hearing

While Bishop Keough took the initiative in responding to the needs of the young people in his diocese, one of his priests, Fr. Everett W. McPhillips, was the initiator of several initiatives aimed at meeting the spiritual needs of the deaf and hard of hearing in the diocese. While still a seminarian at St. Mary's, Baltimore, Fr. McPhillips became interested in the spiritual care of the deaf. In addition to his regular course work, he studied the various sign-language systems and the history of the aid of the deaf throughout the nation under the tutelage of Fr. Michael A. Purtell, S.J., whom Cardinal Gibbons had asked years before to interest himself in the care of the deaf and the mute. After he was ordained in June 1929, McPhillips served for several weeks at St. Patrick's, Providence, and then, in September, was appointed an assistant at St. Mary's, Pawtucket. During McPhillips' first year as a priest, Msgr. Peter A. Foley, who, since 1914, had been moderator of the Society of St. Francis Xavier for the Deaf, passed on that responsibility to him. Under McPhillips, the society continued to meet every third Sunday of the month in the cathedral. In 1931, Fr. McPhillips persuaded Fr. Purtell to come to Providence to preach a mission during the first week of June to those under his care. It was the first mission preached to the deaf in several years. Subsequent missions were preached in the chapel of Holy Name church on Camp Street in Provi-

---

49 *Providence Visitor*, November 7, 1946; Fr. William Delaney, Twelfth Annual Report, p. 3, October 1, 1946–September 30, 1947, PChA.

50 Delaney, Tenth Annual Report, October 1, 1944–September 30, 1945, PChA.

dence, which was convenient to the State School for the Deaf on Hope Street.[51]

In 1936, Fr. McPhillips asked Bishop Keough for permission to form a guild whose members would work to raise money to support his work among the deaf and hard of hearing. Bishop Keough gave the necessary permission and McPhillips proceeded to form the St. Francis de Sales Guild to Assist the Deaf and Hard of Hearing. The membership of the Guild was made up of men and women from throughout the state. Guild members paid dues and met four times a year. They organized an annual bridge tournament as their chief fundraiser. With the funds they raised, the Guild financially supported the yearly missions the ministry offered.[52]

Fr. McPhillips recognized that those who were profoundly deaf and those who were hard of hearing had different needs and different experiences. In October 1941, Fr. McPhillips organized a mission at the cathedral specifically for the hard of hearing. To assist those who attended the mission, Bishop Keough provided special lighting so those who could lip read might see the lips of the preacher. For those who had no personal hearing aids and for those whom the loud speakers installed in the pews were not sufficient, the bishop supplied individual earphones connected to amplifiers. After the mission, those who attended were urged to go to their own parishes for confession. At that time, seven parishes had hearing aids in certain confessionals to assist the hard of hearing. In the December following the mission, Fr. McPhillips organized the Bishop's Auricular Group, a society for the spiritual cultivation of the hard of hearing, which held its first meeting on December 11 in the Columbus Club on Greene Street, Providence. Many at the meeting used the hearing aids supplied by the bishop for the mission in October. For the next few years, Fr. McPhillips organized separate missions for the profoundly deaf and the hard of hearing. Important as the work of the St. Frances de Sales Guild was, the need for the financial assistance they offered was greater than what they could raise by their dues and annual bridge. Although by the late 1940 the Guild was one of the largest in the state, funds from the Catholic Charity Appeal were needed to supplement the monies the Guild was able to provide.[53]

---

[51] Ibid., June 5, 1936; September 26, 1946.
[52] Ibid.
[53] Ibid., September 11, 25; October 23; December 18, 1941; October 8, 24, 1942; October 13, 1949.

CHAPTER VI

New Parishes and Schools

New Parishes and Missions

New Italian Parishes

SACRED HEART, *Natick, West Warwick*

Sacred Heart had been built in 1928–29 as a chapel for the use of the Italians, who had previously attended mass at St. Joseph's. Even though the Italians now had their own chapel and worshiped apart from the French Canadians, they, like other immigrant groups, continued to meet with prejudice in their daily lives. Some of the older immigrants and their children blamed the slowness of the newer immigrants to abandon the old ways for the prejudice experienced by all Italians.

On his part, Fr. Tirocchi, the Missionary of the Sacred Heart, who had charge of the chapel, paid particular attention to the newcomers and helped them feel at home. Rather than be cowered by prejudice, the Italian community in Rhode Island [and presumably in Natick] found ways to express their pride in their heritage. In 1934–35, Ulbaldo U. M. Pesaturo, at the request of the *Providence Evening Bulletin*, wrote a series of articles on various towns of Italy and the contributions of the immigrants who came from them. On Sunday, May 28, 1934, the Federation of Italian War Veterans organized a ceremony to commemorate Italy's entrance into the First World War at which the acting Italian Vice Consul in Providence, Dr. Vincenzo Verderosa, along with Lieut. Vittorio Orlandini, an Italian war veteran and a Boston lawyer, were the main speakers. The president of the Veterans Federations, Lieut. Antonio Pace, began the meeting by calling on all those present to pledge themselves to keep up the fight for the betterment of "not only our people, but for all those racial elements that are held back by the barriers of hate and prejudice." In his speech, Dr.

Verderosa declared that the meeting was called not to solemnize the spirit of war, but "to exalt the national awakening of Italy."[1]

In the 1920s and 30s, Benito Mussolini, who rose in 1922 to head a Fascist government, deliberately set out to reignite the Italians' sense of pride in themselves. This resurgence of patriotism also touched the Italians who had settled overseas. Supported by the Army and business interests which feared communism, Mussolini was able to quickly consolidate his power. His suppression of the Popular (Catholic) Party in the process created tension with the Papacy and the Italian Church, but in February 1929 Mussolini and the Papacy signed a series of agreements known as the Lateran Treaties, which restored papal temporal power although only over the Vatican State, and defined the place of the Church in the Fascist state. In the spring of 1931, Mussolini's suspicions about the role of the Catholic Action movement in Italy led him to dissolve the thousands of male and female groups. In response, Pius XI issued the encyclical *Non abbiamo bisogno* on June 29, 1931, which branded fascism as a pagan idolatry of the state. However, on September 2, 1931, the papacy reached an agreement with the Fascist state; this allowed the Catholic Action groups to exist but limited their field of activity to the purely religious sphere. Prior to Mussolini's Fascist government's first break with the Church in Italy, Bishop Hickey, before leaving for Rome for his *Ad limina* visit in 1929, sought to obtain a meeting with the Prime Minister. However, the brevity of Bishop Hickey's stay made it impossible to arrange a meeting.[2]

Mussolini fanned the flames of Italian nationalism both in Italy and in the United States when in October 1935 he invaded Ethiopia and thereby provoked League of Nations sanctions because of his aggression. Limited by America's neutrality laws, Italians in the United States supported the war effort by contributing to a fund established by the Italian Red Cross to aid the widows and orphans of war casualties. Even though many families' resources were reduced by the Depression, Italian women were encouraged to donate their gold wedding rings to the cause and several hundred Rhode Islanders did.[3]

In Rhode Island, Dr. Pasquale Conca, who involved himself in many organizations that promoted Italian culture, was one of the organizers of the Fascio Vittorio Veneto, a local organization that was part of the

[1]   In addition to the series of articles that appeared in the *Evening Bulletin*, Mr. Pesaturo also published a work detailing the events and accomplishments of Italian immigrants and their descendants: *Italo-Americans of Rhode Island: An Historical and Biographical Survey of the Origin, Rise and Progress of Rhode Islanders of Italian Birth or Descent* (Privately published, 1940), Second edition; *Providence Journal*, May 28, 1934.
[2]   For a brief overview of the Catholicism in Italy during the twentieth century, cf. Hubert Jedin, editor, *History of the Church: Volume IX. The Church in the Modern Age* (New York: The Crossroads Publishing Co., 1981), 569–583; R. Montecchi, Vice Consul, to Msgr. Peter E. Blessing, May 27, 1929, PChA.
[3]   *Providence Journal*, May 4, 11, 25, 1936.

Fascisti League of North America. In March 1927, he was the featured
speaker at a meeting held in the Providence Plantations Club to celebrate
the birth of "Fascismo" in Italy. The secretary of the local Fascisti unit at
that time was Fr. Carlo Sasso, an assistant at Our Lady of Mt. Carmel in
Providence. In addition to the pro-Facist organizations, there was also a
Providence Branch of the Amalgamated Anti-Fascist League of the World.
In 1930, this organization was headed by Gennaro Onorato, a one-time
candidate for Lt. Governor on the Socialist ticket.[4]

After Fr. Tirocchi's sudden death in March 1935, one of the assistants
at St. Joseph's, Fr. Michael Caron, M.S.C., took charge of the chapel along
with Fr. Adrien McShane, M.S.C., who served as his assistant. Having agi-
tated for many years to have their own church and a priest of their own
nationality, the Italians in the Pawtuxet Valley accepted Fr. Caron's services
only as a matter of necessity. During the few months he had charge of
Sacred Heart, Fr. Caron managed to say and do things that angered the
Italians. The pastor of St. Joseph's was Fr. Pierre L'Esperance, M.S.C., an
American, born of Canadian parents, who became pastor in 1904. When
in 1912 the Missionaries of the Sacred Heart formed a quasi-province
that included Rhode Island, Fr. L'Esperance was elected quasi-provincial.
Over the years, there had been various times when he and the Italians in
the parish had disagreed. In addition to his occasional differences with
his Italian parishioners, Fr. L'Esperance had his disagreements with the
two Italian priests attached to St. Joseph's who were assigned to care for
the Italians in the parish. As noted above, one of the them, Fr. Santolini,
was transferred in 1917 and eventually left the Missionaries of the Sacred
Heart after his hopes for erecting a separate chapel for the Italians were
frustrated by America's entrance into the First World War. Fr. L'Esperance
and Fr. Tirocchi also disagreed at times, primarily over the wisdom of
building a separate chapel for the Italians.[5]

On his part, Bishop Keough insisted on Fr. L'Esperance's securing
the services of another Italian priest to serve Sacred Heart. The priest
selected, Fr. Francesco Russo, M.S.C., was, like Fr. Tirocchi, a priest of
the order's Italian province, and, like Fr. Tirocchi when he first arrived in
Natick, was ordained only a short time. Fr. Russo arrived in New York on
November 14, 1935, and went first to Waterbury, Connecticut, where he
stayed the night as the guest of the pastor of Our Lady of Lourdes, Fr.
Joseph Valdembrini. The two were joined by Fr. Alvaro Santolini, who
had formerly served in Natick and had recently been an assistant at Our
Lady of Lourdes under Valdembrini. At the time of Fr. Russo's arrival,
Fr. Santolini was pastor of St. Anne, Highwood, near New Haven. The
three priests traveled to Natick on Friday, arriving at St. Joseph's in the
evening. At St. Joseph's rectory, Fr. Russo was welcomed by the priests of

---

4   *Providence News*, March 24, 1927; *Providence Journal*, January 26, 1930.
5   Committee for the Italian Community of Natick to Cicognani, September 10, 1936; Fr. Pierre A.
     Pillarella to Keough, October 22, 1936, PChA.

St. Joseph's and by delegations from all the Italo-American religious and fraternal organizations in the parish, who invited him to a banquet in his honor planned for Sunday afternoon. Over five hundred Sacred Heart parishioners turned out for the banquet held in the hall in the basement of Sacred Heart. Fr. L'Esperance headed the list of speakers, which included several of the Italian priests of the diocese, local Italian political figures, and representatives of the various parish and Italian societies. When it came time for Dr. Verderosa to speak, he suggested that the assembly rise when the clock struck six and shout "Viva Italia" to mark the beginning of the League of Nations sanctions against Italy for its invasion of Ethiopia.[6]

While Bishop Hickey had appointed Fr. Tirocchi as pastor of the chapel of the Sacred Heart, Bishop Keough appointed Fr. Russo, administrator, a common enough practice when a priest is without experience and is unknown to the bishop. Fr. Russo proved to be a very zealous, self-sacrificing priest in the carrying out of his parochial duties. He would become particularly popular among the women of the parish, in part because he took special care to provide for the religious instruction of the children who attended Sacred Heart. As devoted as he was to his religious duties, he was equally passionate in his love for Italy. Because he had grown up in Italy during Mussolini's early years, he had imbibed a good deal of Mussolini's nationalist propaganda. As did many priests at the time, he saw Italy's Fascists as a bulwark against the threat posed by the Communists. At the start of the campaign among the Italians in Rhode Island to collect gold on behalf of Italy, he was the first Italian priest in the state to embrace the cause. On Sunday, May 3, 1936, the Italian vice-consul, Dr. Verderosa and Fr. Russo arranged a special blessing of the steel rings provided by Mussolini's government in compensation to the 130 Italo-American women in the Valley who had donated their gold wedding rings to the collection. The rings were blessed at a special 10:00 o'clock solemn high mass celebrated by Fr. Russo, who was assisted by Frs. Caron and Bourke, who served as deacon and sub-deacon. Fr. Cesare Schettini of St. Mary's, Cranston, who had served during the First World War as a chaplain in Italy's army, and a number of Italian war veterans attended the dinner in the afternoon at which the rings were given to the women at the end of a round of patriotic speeches.[7]

While Fr. Russo's priestly zeal and his fervent patriotism endeared him to his new parishioners, his relationships with his fellow priests at St. Joseph's and particularly with his immediate superior, Fr. L'Esperance, deteriorated rapidly. Within a short time of Fr. Russo's arrival in Natick, representatives of a lay committee of Sacred Heart parishioners organized a group to build a rectory for Fr. Russo as a way of further separating him

6   *News-Tribune*, November 15, 18, 1935; *Pawtuxet Valley Daily Times*, November 16, 18, 1935.
7   Letter of the Committee for the Rectory to Bishop Keough, no date; *Providence Journal*, May 4, 1936; *Italian Echo*, September 25, 1936; *Sacred Heart Church, West Warwick, Rhode Island: Its People, Its History, and Its Faith* (So. Hackensack, NJ: Custombook, Inc., 1979), 7–8.

and themselves from the French-Canadian clergy and people in St. Joseph's from whom they had encountered abuse in the past. Although the
building of another rectory in the parish could easily be seen as redun-
dant, Bishop Keough, after talking the matter over with Fr. L'Esperance,
who was initially against the idea, agreed to grant permission in hopes that
the separation would finally bring about an end to the lingering hostilities
between the Italians and the French Canadians. The bishop did, however,
place a condition on his permission. Before he would give his approval for
the project to begin, the Italians would have to raise $5,000 of the esti-
mated $15,000 that a new rectory would cost. In spite of the fact that the
economic situation of many in the parish had suffered as a result of the
Depression, the committee for the rectory succeeded in raising the money
the bishop asked.[8]

After he was pastor of Sacred Heart for a short time, Fr. Russo began
making social visits to the leaders of the Italian community in the Valley.
The conversations often turned to Italy's war in Ethiopia and the sanctions it had provoked as well as international politics and internal politics
in Italy. In these conversations, the anti-French sentiments Mussolini had
aroused in Italy merged with the hostility and resentments the Italians in
Natick had developed towards the French Canadians. Furthermore, Fr.
Russo portrayed his own difficulties with Fr. L'Esperance and the other
French-Canadian priests at St. Joseph's as another aspect of the conflict
between the Italians and the French.[9]

By the spring of 1936, the tensions in St. Joseph's rectory had increased
appreciably. Not only did Fr. Russo have difficulties with Fr. L'Esperance,
he also created problems with Bishop Keough over the manner in which
he managed the project of building the new rectory for Sacred Heart. Fr.
Russo deposited the money collected by the committee for the new rectory
in the Centreville Bank in Arctic in the name of the Bishop of Providence
but allowed it to remain under the control of the committee who raised it.
Without Bishop Keough's permission, he awarded the contract for the new
rectory to Fr. Tirocchi's brother in spite of the fact that his bid was four
thousand dollars higher than the next. Since this was a case of poor administration, Bishop Keough, who had signed the bank note guaranteeing
a $10,000 bank loan to the parish for the rest of the money needed for the
rectory, felt he had to intervene and give the project to the lower bidder.[10]

All involved in Natick acknowledged that Fr. Russo lacked prudence.
Being made a pastor at a young age inflated his ego. In the latter part of
1936, he happened to meet a diocesan priest, Fr. Eugenio Cormuto, who,
like himself, was Italian-born. Fr. Cormuto had been ordained in 1920, but
did not come to the United States until 1925. Rather than being named
a pastor as Russo had, Fr. Cormuto was an assistant at Our Lady of Mt.

[8] Archbishop Cicognani to Fr. Pillarella, October 1, 1936, PChA.
[9] Ibid.
[10] Ibid.

Carmel parish, Providence at the time the two met. During the course of their conversation, Fr. Russo suggested that Fr. Cormuto must be stupid because he was still an assistant after ten years in the diocese, while he was a "pastor with a curate [Fr. Caron] who was of little value."[11]

By the summer of 1936, Fr. Russo's fanning of the nationalism of his parishioners had created a situation where antagonism had turned to hatred of the French Canadians. In order to work out some kind of an arrangement between himself and Fr. L'Esperance that would give Russo the independence he sought, Fr. Russo set up a meeting between the two of them and Bishop Keough for September 4. Upset that Fr. Russo had gone over his head to the bishop and wishing to have him removed in hopes that his leaving would leave to a calming of the popular furor Russo had created, Fr. L'Esperance had met with Bishop Keough two days before and arranged that Fr. Russo's provincial would send him a cablegram recalling him to Italy. Fr. L'Esperance informed Fr. Russo of the outcome of his meeting with the bishop on the day the two of them were to meet with Bishop Keough.[12]

When news of Fr. Russo's recall spread through Natick, the Italian community "immediately went aflame with hate, with wild rumors, and with a belligerent spirit," as a Sacred Heart parishioners later recalled. A delegation was quickly appointed and deputized to call on Bishop Keough to have him reverse the decision. However, when the delegation did meet with the bishop on September 12, Keough told them there was nothing he could do since personnel matters concerning the Missionaries of the Sacred Heart were internal matters of the order to decide and were outside his jurisdiction. The bishop did promise those who called on him that he would send another Italian priest to Sacred Heart. The committee offered a compromise by suggesting that Bishop Keough allow Fr. Santolini to take over the parish. Since Fr. Santolini was a priest of the Diocese of Hartford, such a proposal was more complicated that the committee knew and the bishop rejected it. On September 9, the *Pawtuxet Valley Daily Times* ran a short article noting that Fr. Russo had been recalled by his provincial and that Bishop Keough would name his successor in a few days.[13]

When Fr. Tirocchi died, Bishop Keough, out of respect for the Missionaries of the Sacred Heart, had asked them to supply another Italian priest acceptable to the congregation at Sacred Heart. Since the experience with Fr. Russo had been so negative, Bishop Keough decided, after talking the matter over with Fr. L'Esperance, that the best course of action would be to separate Sacred Heart from St. Joseph's and establish Sacred Heart as an Italian national parish with a diocesan priest as its pastor. Since the

---

11 Report by Fr. Cormuto to Bishop Keough by way of Fr. Charles Mahoney, October 15, 1936, PChA. Two priests were needed at Sacred Heart because there were four masses on Sundays.

12 Pillarella to Keough, October 22, 1936, PChA.

13 *Sacred Heart Church, West Warwick*, p. 8; *Pawtuxet Valley Daily* Times, September 9, 1936; *Italian Echo*, September 25, 1936; Memo of meeting, PChA.

1917 Code of Canon Law required the permission of the Congregation of
the Council for the establishment of any national parish, Bishop Keough,
on September 8, 1936, formally requested the faculties for doing so in
a letter to Cardinal Raphael Rossi, the congregation's secretary, and forwarded his letter to Archbishop Cicognani at the Apostolic Delegation in
Washington. The congregation had then to consult Archbishop Cicognani,
who supported the petition after Bishop Keough cleared up a few details.
Contrary to popular belief among many Italians, the diocese, rather than
the Missionaries of the Sacred Heart, held the title to the Sacred Heart
Church property and the revenues from the collections in the church
were kept in the church's own bank account. To ensure equity in the diocese's dealings with St. Joseph's, Bishop Keough would pay St. Joseph's
one thousand dollars to compensate the parish for any monies it spent on
Sacred Heart's behalf.[14]

In addition to sending a delegation to call on Bishop Keough, representatives of the parish's societies were also sent to call on the apostolic delegate, Archbishop Cicognani, in Washington. They presented to the delegate a short summary of their past and present grievances. The document
stated that until their grievances were addressed they would prevent the
Canadian priests from using the church; cease going to church themselves
(or, if they did go, not contribute anything); cease sending their children
to St. Joseph's school; and finally, in the event that the delegate did not
do them justice, they intended to take their case to Rome. After hearing
them out, the delegate told them that it was their duty to submit humbly
to the decisions of their ecclesiastical superiors. He pointed out that, in
the present instance, they had no grounds for complaints because Bishop
Keough had promised to send an Italian priest to replace Fr. Russo. In his
letter to Bishop Keough notifying him of the delegation's call, Archbishop
Cicognani volunteered to repeat his counsel in a letter to some member
of "the so-called 'Committee,' if such a note would serve a good purpose.
The delegate also sent the document the representatives had left with him
and asked Keough for a brief statement of the situation in Natick.[15]

On Monday, September 7, the committee for the Italian community in
Natick, as they signed themselves in their letter to the delegate, held a mass
meeting of the Italians of the Pawtuxet Valley. As Pasquale Parente, the
spokesman for the committee, reported to Bishop Keough in a brief note,
"the community unanimously voted to oppose with any means the departure of Father Russo." Convinced that Fr. Russo's actual leaving Natick
would help to calm the situation, Fr. L'Esperance arranged for his departure in the early darkness of September 9 to avoid arousing the commu-

---

14   Keough to Rossi, September 8, 1936; Cicognani to Keough, October 12, 1936; Keough to
     Cicognani, October 17, 1936, PChA. According to the *Italian Echo*, many Italians believed that
     since the Missionaries of the Sacred Heart administered the parish, they collected the "profits" of
     the church. Cf. *Italian Echo*, September 25, 1936.
15   Cicognani to Keough, September 10, 1936, PChA.

nity. However, news of Fr. Russo's impending departure leaked out, and the Italians increased the number of people they had keeping watch on the rectory to the point where Fr. L'Esperance called the West Warwick police. At four o'clock, when Fr. Russo left the rectory, the bells in Sacred Heart began ringing and hundreds of people gathered at the rectory. As Fr. Russo was leaving under obedience to his superiors, he realized he was the only one who could calm the crowd, who were imploring him not to leave and promising that they would aid and protect him. He asked for quiet and calm, because, he said, "I will return very shortly—be assured of that—to live among you and you alone." It was his intent, on his return to Rome, to place his case before his superiors. Mollified enough by Fr. Russo's promise to return, the crowd allowed him to drive away from the rectory on his journey to the train station. Two days after Fr. Russo left Natick, the *Pawtuxet Valley Daily Times*, on Friday, September 11, ran the story that Bishop Keough had appointed Fr. Eugene Cormuto, pastor of Sacred Heart, and Fr. Anthony De Angelis, a young Italian-American priest, as assistant pastor.[16]

Aware of the divisions and resentments among the parishioners of Sacred Heart, Bishop Keough, asked his secretary and vice chancellor, Fr. Charles J. Mahoney, to accompany Frs. Cormuto and De Angelis to Natick in order to support the two priests. When on Saturday, September 12, the two priests went to Sacred Heart to take up their new duties, the platform in front of the main doors of the church and the neighboring sidewalks were filled with an angry crowd. One contemporary witness described it as "a mob scene with yelling, cursing and menaces." The leaders of the crowd absolutely refused to turn over the keys of the church to Fr. Cormuto. They did agree, however, to allow Fr. Mahoney to remove the Blessed Sacrament from the church as the bishop would not allow it to remain as long as the church was in the hands of the crowd. As the sacrament passed them, the people genuflected and asked God to bless Fr. Russo. During the course of the following week, Bishop Keough held talks with the various factions in order to try to resolve the impasse. Since many of the parishioners were persistent in their demand that Fr. Russo be allowed to return and were scornful of any other resolution of the problem, Bishop Keough arranged for Frs. Cormuto and De Angelis to take up temporary residence in St. James, Arctic, and to offer one mass each Sunday in Italian for the parishioners of Sacred Heart, who wished to attend. Initially, few did.[17]

Fr. Russo did not go directly to New York, where he planned to take ship for Italy. As he had nine months earlier on coming out from Italy, he stopped in Connecticut, this time at St. Anthony's, Bristol, where Fr. Santolini, was then pastor. On the following Sunday, September 13, several

---

16   The scene is described in the *Italian Echo*, September 25, 1936; *Pawtuxet Valley Daily Times*, September 11, 1936.
17   *Sacred Heart Church, West Warwick*, 9–10; *Italian Echo*, September 25, 1936.

of his former parishioners went over to Bristol to say goodbye to him. According to the apostolic delegate's report to his Italian provincial, Fr. Russo "urged them to reject any other pastor, promising them that he would continue the battle in Rome, even taking the matter to the tribunals of the Holy See." In addition to his admonition to his visitors, Fr. Russo also gave them a letter to the parish as a whole in which he expressed "similar thoughts."[18]

When Bishop Keough heard of Fr. Russo's stay at Fr. Santolini's, he feared that Fr. Russo was not going to return to Italy, but rather that he was going to ignore his provincial's order. The bishop's fears increased after Joseph Tally, in his capacity as a steamship agent, telegraphed the agent of the Italian Line to inquire if Fr. Russo was listed among the passengers, who sailed on the *Comte Savoia* or on the *Vulcania*, both of which sailed on September 19. The agent for the Italian Line responded that Fr. Russo's name was not on the passenger lists of either ship. Bishop Keough also was informed that Fr. Russo had sent letters to other of his former parishioners similar to the one he gave to those who called on him at Bristol. After Bishop Keough reported this news to Archbishop Cicognani, the delegate telegraphed an official in the Vatican Secretariat of State asking him to pass on a request to Fr. Russo's provincial that he prevent Russo from communicating with his former parishioners. Keough would later learn from Fr. Russo's provincial that Russo had in fact left on the *Comte Savoia* on September 19, and that he had written only the one letter.[19]

On Monday, September 21, six hundred people, of whom the greater part were women and girls, gathered in the basement of Sacred Heart. The meeting was presided over by Pasquale Parente, the chairman of the Italian Committee of Natick, who opened the meeting by extending Fr. Russo's greetings to the his former parishioners. The main speaker at this meeting was Vincenzo De Orchis, the editor of the Italian-language section of the *Italian Echo*, who briefly reviewed the community's past struggles with the French-Canadian clergy in St. Joseph's and with Fr. L'Esperance in particular. Mr. De Orchis then went on to praise Fr. Russo as being a true patriot and a model priest. After this, he urged the crowd to be calm and respectful toward Bishop Keough, who he believed would "provide for Father Russo's return to Natick." He ended by again urging calm and having faith in a complete victory.[20]

Although the events surrounding Fr. Russo's leaving and the two mass meetings held to protest his recall by his religious superior were newsworthy, nothing appeared about them in either the *Pawtuxet Valley Daily Times,* *Providence Journal, Evening Bulletin* or any of the English-language newspa-

---

[18]   Cicognani to Pillarella, October 1, 1936, PChA.
[19]   Italian Line to Tally, September 25, 26, 1936; Keough to Cicognani, September 19, 1936;
       Cicognani to Monsignor Tardini, September 30, 1936; Pillarella to Keough, October 22, 1936,
       PChA.
[20]   *Italian Echo,* September 25, 1936.

pers in the state. The only newspaper which carried a report of the events, which occurred after Fr. Russo was recalled, was the weekly *Italian Echo*, which printed its articles in either English or Italian at this time. The first of the *Echo*'s articles did not appear until September 25, where they were written in Italian. In the retelling of the events of this time that is found in a parish history published during Fr. De Angelis' years as pastor of Sacred Heart, the writer of the narrative attributes the lack of news coverage to Bishop Keough's influence. At the time of the protest, Fr. Russo's partisans frequently remarked on the lack of coverage and attributed the lack in part to the *Pawtuxet Valley Daily Times*' deference to Fr. L'Esperance and in part to the fact that the paper's editor was also of French-Canadian heritage. Without coverage in the English-language papers, Fr. Russo's partisans realized that they were deprived of an important means of pressuring Bishop Keough to secure Fr. Russo's return. In protest, many canceled their subscriptions to the *Times*.[21]

On Saturday, October 10, 1936, Frs. Cormuto and De Angelis tried again to gain possession of Sacred Heart church. However, as soon as they arrived at the church, word of their arrival quickly spread and a crowd of several hundred quickly gathered. In a short time the West Warwick police arrived and the captain in charge sought unsuccessfully to convince the crowd to reopen the church since the property belonged to the bishop, not to them. After the captain's initial attempt failed, he ordered his officers to withdraw and granted the leaders two hours to reconsider before he took action. When he returned at the stated time, the crowd had swollen to several thousand. While a good number were merely there to see what would happen, the captain realized that any use of force would be ill advised. In his report on the confrontation for the *Italian Echo*, Mr. De Orchis, who was apparently a resident of the Valley, argued that the unrest, which motivated the crowd:

> Did not result from Father Russo's departure. At issue is the dignity of a race of people; at issue is the desire for revenge for the more than 40 years of harassment caused by the Provincial of the Sacred Heart.

De Orchis made his comments on the root of the problem at Sacred Heart in response to a letter he printed in the body of his article from Maria Calabro, who had asserted that leaders of the resistance to Fr. Cormuto did not constitute "the entire population but are a few proud insatiable men and women who had gotten the upper hand during Fr. Russo's time." She labeled the resistance to the opening of the church, "capricious and arbitrary" and "an insult to religion" since it "deprived good people and youngsters of a great many spiritual benefits."[22]

Among those who came to the church that afternoon was Dr. Verderosa,

---

21   *Sacred Heart Church, West Warwick*, p. 10; *Italian Echo*, September 25, 1936. The owner and editor of *Pawtuxet Valley Daily Times*, Irving P. Hudson, was not French, at least on his father's side.

22   *Italian Echo*, October 16, 1936.

the acting Italian vice-consul. Dr. Verderosa tried to convince the leaders and their supporters in the crowd in front of the church that, while their complaints against past injustices and insults might be well-founded, Bishop Keough had already responded to their complaints by removing Sacred Heart from the jurisdiction of the Missionaries of the Sacred Heart and placing it under his own direct control. In refusing to open the church, they were depriving the bishop of the use of his property and were clearly in the wrong. While Dr. Verderosa's arguments made sense, the crowd was in no mood to listen to reason and booed him intermittently. Rather than listen to logic, the crowd responded more readily and more enthusiastically to other speakers, who urged them to continue their resistance. To many in the crowd, Dr. Verderosa was not entirely unbiased. During the First World War, he and Fr. Cormuto had first met in a German prisoner of war camp after they had been captured while serving in the Italian army and had remained friends. Since neither Fr. Cormuto nor Dr. Verderosa wished to see force used, Dr. Verderosa was able to use the prestige of his office to persuade the police captain to withdraw his men once more. Dr. Verderosa himself left the church deeply offended that the crowd did not pay him the respect he believed his office as vice-consul of the Italian government demanded, but instead had booed him as he sought to convince them to respect the law. Later in the week, the leaders of the committee called on Dr. Verderosa to "make excuses for not having received the Consul well and to thank him for his good offices in having the police withdraw." In a conversation with Fr. Mahoney, Bishop Keough's secretary, Dr. Verderosa stated that he "would not go to Natick again unless assured of respect for his office."[23]

On Saturday, October 17, the day after Dr. Verderosa called at the Chancery Office, four Natick Italians came to Providence to see Bishop Keough. As the bishop was not available, they spoke with Fr. Mahoney. The youngest of them, Mrs. Petrarca, made an earnest plea for the return of Fr. Russo. She said that she knew of two or three hundred women, who would enter the sanctuary and remove any priest from the altar other than Fr. Russo. Almost two weeks before Mrs. Petrarca made her request, Bishop Keough had received a telegram from the General of the Missionaries of the Sacred Heart, which stated briefly and simply, "Russo will never return." When Fr. Mahoney gave her no encouragement at all that the bishop was in any position to grant her request, she offered an alternative proposal. Although two different versions of the background of the request circulated later, Mrs. Petrarca claimed that she had been in contact with Fr. L'Esperance through a go-between and that she believed that Fr. L'Esperance would be agreeable to having the bishop cede jurisdiction over Sacred Heart to the Italian province of the Missionaries of the Sacred Heart, who would then send two priests from Italy to staff

---

[23]   Ibid.; Report of the incident given by Verderosa to Fr. Charles Mahoney, October 16, 1936, PChA.

the parish. She professed to have knowledge of a document signed by Fr. L'Esperance affirming that Sacred Heart would be transferred to the Missionaries of the Sacred Heart's Roman province when Fr. Tirocchi died. According to one report, Mrs. Petrarca and her fellow spokespersons went to the bishop's office, confident that he would accept their proposal to end the impasse. Bishop Keough entered the meeting at this point. He refused to hear any proposal that the committee had to make. Rather, he frankly told them that if the church was not opened soon, he would place it under interdict.[24]

Bishop Keough had already suggested to Fr. Cormuto that he and Fr. De Angelis find lodging in Natick so as to be as close to the church as possible. Accordingly, Fr. Cormuto rented rooms in the home of a Protestant lady, Mrs. Alice Bryer, widow of Dr. Barton H. Bryer, who lived at 790 Providence Street, and the two priests moved in a the end of the month.[25]

After having met with the four representatives from Natick, Bishop Keough advised Fr. Cormuto to be prepared to alter his living situation once again because he had decided that the time had come to take control of Sacred Heart church. The bishop consulted with State Attorney General John Hartigan, who in turn alerted the State Police to be ready to assist the bishop's delegates. On Saturday, October 24, the day Bishop Keough set for the third attempt to take control of the church, about thirty State Policemen took up position in the vicinity of the church. Again, news of the state police appearance spread quickly through the Italian community in Natick. Dr. Verderosa also came down to Natick that day to make a second attempt at mediating a peaceful end to the standoff. At his suggestion, the Superintendent of State Police, Frs. Mahoney, Cormuto and De Angelis, the consul—whoever wished to—went into the church hall beneath the church to talk the matter over. Dr. Verderosa's chief argument that the primary question before them was no longer one of the Italians receiving the respect they deserved from other nationalities, but of law and order. Sacred Heart church was clearly Bishop Keough's property. In preventing his delegates from using the church, the Italians were violating the bishop's rights. Furthermore, by defying the law, the Italians were harming the good name of Italians in general. Verderosa's appeal to their patriotism provided the leaders of the protest movement an honorable way of ending the impasse. They handed the keys of the church over to him as the official representative of the Italian government. He in turn handed them to Fr. Cormuto.[26]

The protest of a large part of the Italian community in Natick did not end with the handing over of the keys. While many of the parishioners came to mass on Sunday, November 1, others continued to boycott the

---

24   Telegram, Janssen to Keough, October 4, 1936; Notes of meeting with committee kept by Fr. Mahoney, October 17, 1936, PChA; *Italian Echo*, October 23; November 13, 1936.
25   *Sacred Heart Church, West Warwick*, p. 10.
26   *Italian Echo*, November 13, 1936; *Sacred Heart Church, West Warwick*, p. 10.

masses offered by Frs. Cormuto and De Angelis. Those Italians who did
defy the boycott received threatening letters from the protesters, which
were duly turned over to the West Warwick police. The dispute divided the
community and even split families. Merchants who supported Fr. Cormuto
were boycotted by the partisans of Fr. Russo and vice versa. Fr. Cormuto
moved quietly to undermine the position of the protesters. As would be
required of any new parish, Fr. Cormuto, in cooperation with Bishop
Keough, secured the incorporation of the parish. He chose as the parish's
first two trustees, Luigi Senerchia and Alberic DiMasi.[27]

Together with others in the parish, Fr. Cormuto and the trustees drew
up plans for a rectory. As part of the settlement with the protesters, Bishop
Hickey had agreed to the return of the $5,000 collected under Fr. Russo
for the construction of a rectory. According to the agreement, individual
contributors who wished their money back were paid immediately, while
organizations that had contributed to the rectory fund had first to consult their members on whether or not they wished to have the money returned. Dr. Verderosa acted as a facilitator between the bishop and the
committee that had collected the funds. On November 25, 1936, the
bishop authorized Verderosa to make withdrawals from an account set up
in the Centreville National Bank under the name of the "Roman Catholic Bishop of Providence, Sacred Heart, Natick, Rhode Island, New Rectory Fund." On their part, the committee agreed to deposit the money
it collected, in order to repay the contributors, into that particular account. Since a rectory had a symbolic as well as practical purpose, Bishop
Keough did not insist on the raising of another $5,000, but gave permis-
sion for the project to begin as soon as possible. Ground on a site adjacent
to the church was soon broken for the Spanish-style, two-and-a-half story
rectory, which was designed to blend with the architecture of the church,
in the spring of 1937.[28]

During the time when the Italian Committee of Natick dominated the
parish, those parishioners who disagreed with the committee's leaders and
their course of action were themselves divided. After Fr. Cormuto took
over at Sacred Heart and established the corporation and parish organizations, those who disagreed with the Italian Committee had a focus around
which they could unite. As a result, the number of parishioners who attended mass began to rise. On April 25, 1937, Fr. Cormuto made use of
the Congregation of the Council's approval of the establishment of Sacred
Heart as a national parish devoted to the service of the Italians to provide
an outlet for the expression of the faith and patriotism of those who had
returned to the church by arranging a banquet in the parish hall to formally receive the document by Cardinal Rossi. Frs. Cormuto and De Angelis

[27]   Keough to Cicognani, November 7, 1936; A good church member to Keough, November 27,
1936, PChA; *Sacred Heart Church, West Warwick*, p. 10.
[28]   Agreement concerning rectory fund, no date; Keough to Verderosa, November 25, 1936; Keough
to Centreville National Bank, November 25, 1936, PChA; *Providence Visitor*, April 8, 1937.

were the guests of honor at the dinner. The scroll establishing the parish was presented to Fr. Cormuto by Dr. Verderosa. Fr. Mahoney represented the bishop and Gov. Robert E. Quinn, himself a resident of the Valley, extended the greetings of the state. Supreme Court Justice Antonio A. Capotasto was among the guests. When called on to speak, Judge Capotasto, with an eye to recent events, urged the Italo-Americans to be ready to fulfill their obligations as well as to demand their rights as American citizens. He praised Fr. Cormuto as one "who knows how to lead and to forgive." Another speaker, Fr. Paul Perrotta, O.P., a professor at Providence College, counseled patience and forbearance in order that peace and harmony may reign in the parish. Similarly, Fr. Cormuto made the dedication of the new rectory on Sunday, September 12, an occasion for another dinner with another round of talks. A month earlier, Bishop Keough enhanced Fr. Cormuto's prestige when he chose him to deliver the eulogy at the solemn requiem the diocese held on August 21 in the cathedral to honor Guglielmo Marconi, the famous Italian scientist.[29]

Perhaps the most important advantage Fr. Cormuto had in gaining the support of the Italians in Natick was the fact that he was the celebrant of the masses held on the various saints days that were important to the people of his parish. In the celebration of the various feasts, Italian faith and patriotism came together in a unique way. The feasts that were important to the Italians in Natick were those of Our Lady of Mt. Carmel, which was celebrated in the middle of July; the feasts of St. Peter Martyr and St. Dominic Abbot, the patronal feasts of the immigrants from Fornelli, which were celebrated at the end of August or in early September; and the feast of St. John the Baptist, the patronal feast of the immigrants from Grazzanise, which was observed in the middle of September.

To offer an alternative to the feasts in which the church played a prominent role, Fr. Russo's partisans, in January 1937, formed the Benito Mussolini Society for the men. In addition to this society, there was also the Donna Rachele Society for the women and the Il Duce Athletic Club for the young men. On April 25, 1937, the day on which Sacred Heart parish celebrated its formal establishment with a dinner, the Benito Mussolini and Donne Rachele Mussolini societies also held a dinner in Palazzo Hall at which the presidents of the two societies, Pasquale Parente and Elisa Coletta, were honored. In 1937, on the same Sunday, Fr. Cormuto led the celebration of the feast of Our Lady of Mt. Carmel in Sacred Heart Church, the Donna Rachele Society held their annual picnic at Goddard Park. In August 1938, on the same Sunday, the immigrants from Grazzanise were celebrating the feast of St. John the Baptist with a mass,

---

29 *Providence Visitor*, April 29, 1937; *Pawtuxet Valley Daily Times*, August 13; September 10; October 25, 1937.

parade, and carnival in Natick, the Mussolini Society hosted its annual outing at Brush Neck, Oakland Beach.[30]

In 1937, in addition to their annual outing, the Benito Mussolini and Donna Rachele Mussolini societies along with the Grazzanise society and the Il Duce Athletic Club organized a celebration of Columbus Day in Natick on Sunday, October 10. The starting point of the parade was Palazzo's Hall, 770, Providence Street, Natick, where the various organizations held their meetings. The parade passed through the principal streets of the village and returned to the hall. The organizers of the parade hired three bands for the occasion: the Natick Columbus Band; the Warwick Aerie of Eagles Band; and Sockannosset School Band. On the Saturday before the parade, the *Pawtuxet Valley Daily Times* printed an article that included the information that the Mussolini Society would parade in the black shirts and hats of the Italian Fascisti, while the women of the Donna Rachele Society would wear black skirts and white blouses. On the day of the parade, the Sockannosset School Band did not appear. The day was rainy, but the parade went on with over six hundred participants, exclusive of the two bands, when those who marched and those who rode in the motorcade in the rear of the parade were counted. On Monday, the *Pawtuxet Valley Daily Times* gave a verbal description of the parade but the *Evening Bulletin* printed both a description of the parade and a picture under the caption, "In West Warwick: Black Shirts On the March." The *Bulletin* articles detailed the difficulties the parade organizers experienced in obtaining the seventy-five black shirts worn by the marchers.[31]

The Mussolini societies' wearing of black shirts and hats and their giving the Fascist salute during the Columbus Day parade while marching behind the stars and stripes aroused the ire of the West Warwick Post of the American Legion. On the Friday following the parade, sixty-five members of the Post meeting in the Legion Home in Arctic, adopted resolutions affirming its opposition to "Communism, Fascism and Nazism and other forces and organizations that seek to destroy the free institutions of the United States" and condemning the Italian societies' actions as "audacious effrontery." They also voted to ask the West Warwick Town Council to deny the privilege of parading through the streets of the town to any group or organization whose ideals and creeds were disloyal to the government of the United States. A few days later, all the American Legion posts in the third district upheld the action of the West Warwick Post at a meeting in Greenwood. In addition to the Legion posts, Camp McGregor, Sons of Union Veterans of the Civil War, meeting in Odd Fellows' Hall in Riverpoint, on October 19, passed similar resolutions.[32]

---

30 *Pawtuxet Valley Daily Times*, April 26, 1937; July 16, 1937; August 29, 1938; *Sacred Heart Church, West Warwick*, 10–11. According to an article in the *Daily Times* on January 18, 1937, 135 Italo-American men of the Valley formed a society, initially unnamed, to "better work for the interests of the Italians of the Valley."

31 *Pawtuxet Valley Daily Times*, October 11, 1937; *Evening Bulletin*, October 11, 1937.

32 Ibid, October 16, 18, 20, 27, 1937; July 16, 28, 1938.

The presidents of the Grazzanise, Benito Mussolini and Donna Rachele Mussolini societies quickly challenged the West Warwick Post's accusations that they were Communistic, Fascist or Nazis or that the wearing of black shirts and hats and the using of the Fascist salute "were disloyal or un-American." However, the indignation of the community at large towards the actions of the three Italian organizations was such that the West Warwick Town Council quickly acted on the requests of the West Warwick Post and Camp McGregor and on October 26 passed a resolution that it would in the future "withhold its permission for parades or demonstrations to any group or organization whose purpose is to demonstrate or display their allegiance to any foreign country or government."[33]

Almost a year later, Pope Pius XI began issuing a series of statements, in which he first criticized ultra-nationalism in general for creating barriers between peoples and then criticized Mussolini's government more specifically when it began to imitate the Nazis in persecuting the Jews. Pope Pius's criticism of Mussolini culminated in a Christmas Eve statement in 1938 in which he complained about the Italian government's treatment of Catholic Action groups and its violation of its concordat with the Vatican, especially by its mandating the racial laws, which violated the marriage regulations of the concordat.[34]

Although the hold of the group that came to dominate the parish during Fr. Russo's time weakened after Frs. Cormuto and DeAngelis took control of the church, they did not easily give up their struggle. On April 16, 1938, the apostolic delegate received a letter signed by Anselmo Coletta, the son of Elisa Coletta, who had been elected the first president of the Donna Rachele Mussolini society and who was one of Fr. Russo's strongest partisans. In the letter, Mr. Colleta again asked that Sacred Heart be given to the Roman province of the Missionaries of the Sacred Heart as, he claimed, was promised in the agreement concerning the building of the rectory during Fr. Russo's time. To support his request, he offered an overview of the spiritual conditions, which he claimed were prevailing in Sacred Heart. He informed the delegate that 400 out of the 525 families in the parish remained away from the church since Fr. Russo's removal in September 1936; that hundreds of children were kept from going to catechism by their parents; that weddings, baptisms, first communions and confirmations were few; and that the faith of the children in the parish was endangered by the fact that many of the girls and boys were attending sewing, cooking, manual training and gymnastic classes held by the Christian Center of Natick. He further claimed that the minority, who did go to church, caused inflated numbers of those attending parish events to appear in the local papers. As usual, the delegate sent Mr. Coletta's letter

---

[33] Ibid.

[34] Jedin, *History of the Church*, X, p. 579. After Pearl Harbor, the FBI sent agents to West Warwick to investigate the leaders of the Mussolini societies, an action which speeded their demise. Cf. *Sacred Heart Church, West Warwick*, p. 11.

to Bishop Keough with a request for comment. In his reply to the delegate, Bishop Keough identified Mr. Coletta's mother as one of the five members of Sacred Heart who formed "the bulk of the opposition" to Fr. Cormuto, and suggested that, given the extent of Mr. Coletta's education, he was not likely the true author of the letter which bore his name. In contrast to Mr. Coletta's dismal picture of the spiritual condition of the parish, the bishop offered a much more positive one, especially in regards to the attention the priests of the parish paid to its children. A year later, Bishop Keough sent another report on the spiritual condition of the parish to the delegate, this one containing specific statistics to support his contention that the parish was flourishing under its current pastors. He stated the parish population as consisting of 425, of whom all but 80 regularly attended mass at Sacred Heart. Of the 80 who did not, 50 had never attended mass even in Fr. Tirocchi's time, and 30 attended mass in other parishes. In regard to the reception of the sacraments, he reported that the number of children receiving the sacraments was higher than under the Sacred Heart fathers. It was his general observation that Sacred Heart was in charge of two of the ablest priests of the diocese and that the parish was recovering well "from the severe shock it received by the indiscretions committed against its peaceful members."[35]

ST. ANTHONY, *North Providence*

After the Second World War, many places in Rhode Island experienced substantial growth as the state sought to cope with an usually high demand for new housing. The Woodville section of North Providence was one of those places. Both St. Edward's on Branch Avenue and St. Anthony's on Woodward Avenue saw their parish populations increase sharply. At the time, St. Anthony's was a mission of St. Ann's, Providence. Some of the Italians — particularly the Italo-Americans who moved into the area — joined St. Edward's. Many more joined St. Anthony's. In January 1946, early in the post-war building boom, Bishop Keough elected to separate St. Anthony's from St. Ann's and appointed Fr. Anthony L. Dimeo, the first pastor of the new parish.[36]

Like most of his Irish contemporaries, who were now American born, Fr. Dimeo was born in Providence in 1906 in St. Ann's Parish, Providence. He attended St. Ann's School, before entering the public schools for his high school courses. Following high school, he enrolled at Providence College. After Bishop Hickey accepted him as a candidate for the diocese, the bishop sent him to the Collegio Leoniani, at Anagni, near Rome. Fr. Dimeo was ordained in 1933. On his return from Italy, he was assigned to

[35] Anselo Coletta to Cicognani, April 16, 1938; Cicognani to Keough, April 18, 1938; Keough to Cicognani, April 23, 1938; Keough to Cicognani, May 22, 1939, PChA.
[36] *Providence Visitor*, January 17, 1946; Richard A. Walsh, *The Centennial History of Saint Edward Church, Providence, Rhode Island, 1874–1974* (Privately printed, 1974), p. 165.

St. Rocco's as an assistant to Fr. Bartolomeo Marenchino, C.S. In August 1941, Bishop Keough named him to the original faculty at Our Lady of Providence Seminary. Since the priests assigned to the seminary also assisted in parishes on Sunday, in 1942, he was appointed administrator of St. Anthony's, North Providence. When the mission's population rapidly increased after the Second World War, he was named pastor.[37]

New French-Canadian Parishes

ST. VINCENT DE PAUL, *Anthony, Coventry*

Although the 1920s and 30s saw a steady decline in the textile industry in Rhode Island, many mills continued in operation. Among those that managed to continue making a profit for its owners was the Anthony Mill on Washington Street, in Coventry, owned by the Berkshire Fine Spinning Associates. Cotton spinning had begun on the Flat River at Anthony in 1806. In 1873, the then owners of the mills at Anthony built a new five-story mill building, which came to employ a number of French Canadians. The French Canadians, who settled in Anthony, had to travel about two miles to Jericho, as the Canadians called Arctic Center, to attend mass at St. John the Baptist.

Following the death of the long time pastor of St. John's, Fr. Joseph R. Bourgeois, in March 1928, Bishop Hickey appointed a younger, more energetic priest, Fr. Henri Vincent, to replace him after an interim of several months in July 1929. At the time of Fr. Vincent's appointment, the population of the parish numbered over 7,500 people. As St. John's church was too small to accommodate those who wished to attend the Sunday masses, Fr. Vincent had already urged Bishop Hickey to split off the Centreville section of West Warwick in 1931. As St. John's continued to be crowded, even after the establishment of Christ the King in July 1935, Fr. Vincent arranged with the David Papineau American Legion Post at the corner of Washington and Anthony streets, in Anthony, for the use of their building as a place in which to offer two Sunday masses for the French Canadians in Coventry. Previously, in 1933, Fr. Vincent had arranged with the Post for the use of two rooms on the first floor of their building as a schoolhouse. Beginning in September 1935, two additional classes were added in Anthony as St. John's School, like the church, was overcrowded. Initially, three Sisters of the Presentation of Mary came out from their convent in Arctic every day to staff the school.[38]

---

[37] *Providence Visitor*, April 28, 1972; August 21, 1986.
[38] Joseph A. Cichon, Jr., *St. John the Baptist Church: Faith and Sacrifice Build a Parish* (Hackensack, New Jersey: Custombook, 1974), 22–26; Richard Siembab, "St. Vincent de Paul, Anthony, Rhode Island: Golden Jubilee Celebration, 1937–1987" (Privately printed); *Pawtucket Valley Daily Times*, July 9; 15, 1935.

In September 1937, at Fr. Vincent's urging, Bishop Keough appointed Fr. Oliva H. Brouillette, a close friend of Fr. Vincent, as first pastor of Anthony. The bishop named the new parish St. Vincent de Paul to honor Fr. Vincent, who was the chief instrument in its establishment. The new parish, which began with 217 families, extended from Bates Avenue in Quidneck to the Connecticut state line. Fr. Brouillette was no stranger to the Pawtuxet Valley as he had previously served as an assistant in St. James and St. Mary's, Arctic, for more than eight years. Since leaving the Valley in 1926, he had served in five French-Canadian and mixed parishes before his appointment as pastor.[39]

At Fr. Vincent's invitation, Fr. Brouillette resided initially at St. John's Rectory in Arctic, while he took a census of his new parish and introduced himself to his parishioners. At the same time, he undertook the task of securing funds to build a church. Later, in 1938, he would rent a house at 43 Station (now Laurel Avenue). Before he left Arctic, Fr. Brouillette earned a reputation as one who possessed "unusual ability in the conducting of bazaars and other social events for the raising of funds for the church." He now employed his talents in the service of his new parish. The Berkshire Fine Spinning Associates, for whom many in the parish worked, made a major gift to the new parish in the form of four acres of land on which the company had earlier grazed its horses and more recently had been used as a baseball field. Fr. Brouillette announced the company's gift on June 6, 1938. Although money was scarce, the new parishioners of St. Vincent's were anxious to have a church of their own. In Arctic, meanwhile, Fr. Vincent had proposed to his parishioners the building of a new church to replace the old wooden one, which had been dedicated in 1880. The men of St. Vincent's helped in the tearing down of the old church, which, in June 1938, was in the last stages of its demolition. Wood and brick salvaged from St. John's was stored temporally behind John Pierson's home on Mapledale Avenue. St. John's made these materials available to the parishioners of St. Vincent's for their new church.[40]

Plans for the new St. Vincent de Paul church, with a seating capacity of 300, were drawn by Lodias J. Allard of Woonsocket. It was to be a brick building in the colonial style with two wings on the west end. There was to be a parish hall in the basement. Bishop Keough approved the plans in September 1938, but ground breaking for the new building did not take place until June 15, 1939. As in Bishop Hickey's years, church construction was viewed as one way the diocese could address the problem of unemployment. To help those without resources, Fr. Brouillette established a branch of the St. Vincent de Paul Society in his parish in August 1938. Many out of work men found jobs in Arctic with the building of the new St. John's and, in Anthony, with the building of St. Vincent's. When the carpenters went home, the men and boys of St. Vincent's, who had al-

---

[39]   *Providence Visitor*, September 30, 1937.
[40]   Siembab, "Golden Jubilee Celebration"; *Pawtuxet Valley Daily Times*, October 1, 1926.

ready spent many hours sorting the timber and cleaning the brick salvaged from the old St. John's, came to the church to paint and varnish. The last part of the construction was to move the old oak pews from St. John's into the new church and move the altar from the chapel in the legion hall. Fr. Brouillette celebrated the first mass in the new church on December 25, 1939. Bishop Keough blessed the new building on Sunday, June 16, 1940 when he came to Coventry to confirm the children of the parish.[41]

Since a parochial school was already in existence in Anthony when St. Vincent's was established, Fr. Brouillette directed his efforts at enlarging it to a full eight grades. As Fr. Vincent at St. John's had built a new convent for the Sisters of the Presentation, there was room there for the additional sisters who came to teach in St. Vincent's. In order to provide sufficient classroom space, Fr. Brouillette, in the summer of 1938, arranged with the Coventry School Committee to lease the Quidnick primary school, which the town had closed in 1937 and the Town Council wished to sell, for two hundred dollars a year.[42]

New English-language Parishes

ST. RITA, *Oakland Beach, Warwick*

The establishment of St. Peter's in the Pawtuxet section of Warwick in 1933 was but one sign of Warwick's growth in the period between the wars. By the 1930s, many of Warwick's residents had become convinced that the increasing population of the town had rendered its town meeting obsolete, especially in the financially difficult times of the Depression. On April 21, 1931, after the town's residents had twice refused a city charter, backers of the proposal succeeded in convincing a majority to accept it. With the onset of the Depression in 1929, many families in the state, faced with the loss of employment, had to cut expenses and liquidate what assets they had. In the Oakland Beach and many other of Warwick's summer resorts, so many cottages were offered for sale that their price dropped, making them affordable to people with some resources, who were in need of housing. Oakland Beach in particular became a place where various welfare agencies in the state sent their clients, who could not afford to live anywhere else.[43]

In view of the growth of Oakland Beach in the early 1930s, Bishop Keough, after consulting with Fr. Patrick Canning, the pastor of St. Catherine's, Apponaug, who was in charge of the mission, and with the Board of Consultors, chose to set off St. Rita's, with its 231 families and a total of

---

[41] Siembab, "Golden Jubilee Celebration"; *Pawtuxet Valley Daily Times,* May 16, June 14, 15, 17, 1940; *Providence Visitor,* June 13, 1940; *Providence Journal,* August 8, 1942.

[42] *Providence Journal,* August 30, 1938; Siembab, "Golden Jubilee Celebration."

[43] Donald D'Amato, *Warwick's 350-Year Heritage: A Pictorial History* (The Downing Company, 1992), 132–37.

969 individuals, from St. Catherine's and give it its own pastor. On October 10, 1935, Bishop Keough formally appointed Fr. John W. Marren pastor of the new the parish. At the time of his appointment, Fr. Marren was the pastor of St. Andrew's, Block Island. Earlier in his priesthood, he had served as a summer assistant at St. Rita's when it was a mission of Our Lady of Mercy in East Greenwich.[44]

During his first year in Oakland Beach, Fr. Marren rented a house on Ottawa Avenue. A rectory was an obvious need, and on March 20, 1936, he started work on a brick, two-and-a-half-story house on the south side of the new church that Fr. Peter J. Malone has built in 1913–14, and which Fr. Peter Keeley, at St. Catherine's, had doubled in size in 1921. In addition to the rectory, Fr. Marren was also concerned about the physical needs of the people of his parish. The various federal work programs offered some relief, but those unable to secure work of any kind or who needed help for a short time looked to the city's Director of Public Aid, who had some monies for the "Outside Poor"; to the Family Aid Society, which distributed milk to needy families; and to the Red Cross, which distributed seventy-five hundred bags of flour between November 1932 and April 1933. In addition to these sources of help, the parish organized fund raising events for the benefit of the St. Vincent de Paul Unemployment Fund. The sensitive task of seeking out the needy and distributing the society's funds most often fell to John Bannon, one of the parish's first two trustees.[45]

The Hurricane of 1938

The development of new parishes and the building of new churches during the 1930s was a testament to the faith and sacrifice of Rhode Island's Catholics. All parishes found it difficult to meet expenses and to provide for the many who were in need. In September 1938, those who struggled to meet the day to day challenges of securing food and housing were forced to meet a new challenge: the challenge of staying alive in the midst of the most devastating storm to hit Rhode Island in over a century. On September 21, a storm that had its origins near the Cape Verde Islands on September 4, ended its journey across the Atlantic by crashing into Long Island and Connecticut during the morning hours and later that day it crossed into Rhode Island. Weather instruments in Providence recorded sustained winds of 100 mph and gusts of 125 mph. The storm surge produced by the storm created 18 to 25 foot tides along the Rhode Island coast and a twelve to fifteen foot surge up Narragansett Bay. Down-

44 *Providence Visitor*, December 29, 1933.
45 D'Amato, *Warwick's 350-Year Heritage*, p. 134; Leo and Donald Thuotte, "St. Rita's, Warwick, Rhode Island, 1935–1984: 50th Jubilee (Privately printed, 1985).

town Providence was submerged under a foot more water than had inundated the west side in the Great Gale of 1815.[46]

During the course of the storm, 312 men, women and children lost their lives. Included among the dead were two priests, Fr. Timothy A. Fitzgerald, a priest of the Diocese of Worcester, who was vacationing at the shore in Charlestown, and Fr. Patrick Crowley, a seventy-year old priest of the Diocese of Helena, Montana who was visiting with family in Pawtucket. Fr. Crowley was riding in a car near the reservoir in Newport with Fr. John T. McConnell, an assistant at St. Mary's, Pawtucket, when the full force of the hurricane struck. Fr. McConnell's car was hurled into the reservoir. Fr. Crowley drowned, but McConnell was rescued after three hours in the water, and, although initially in critical condition, he survived. At Conimicut Point, which was devastated by the storm as were other Rhode Island coastal communities, several fishermen and boys aided Fr. Thomas F. McKitchen, then rector of the cathedral, and his mother, who attempted to leave his summer home on the point in a skiff after the road to the point was flooded, and safely brought them to a nearby home.[47]

At Oaklawn Beach, on the morning of the storm, Fr. Valmore Savignac, Fr. Marren's young assistant, a powerfully built man who had played football at LaSalle Academy and Providence College, after hearing the news of rising waters, went to warn his aged and infirm parishioners of the danger. Joined by a young man, Edward Thompson, the two waded and swam through the rising waters to every house where Fr. Savignac believed that people might be trapped. The two, together with others who joined in their efforts, carried more than fifty people to safety. When the priest got back to St. Rita's rectory, he found seventy people being cared for there and another forty in the church.

In the aftermath of the storm, Fr. Charles Curran, head of Catholic Charities in the diocese, offered to Gov. Robert Quinn and to the state, the services of the various charitable facilities of the diocese. Bishop Keough followed this offer of help with a letter, sent by special messenger, in which he offered the services of the priests and nuns of the diocese for any kind of relief work needed. Also, at the direction of the bishop, the men of St. Vincent de Paul Society, visited all the pastors in the areas most seriously affected by the hurricane in order to make thousands of food orders available to those in need.[48]

In addition to the loss of life, many of the parishes and diocesan institutions suffered heavy property damage from the storm's high winds and heavy rains. In the weeks following the storm, many pastors were forced to undertake extensive repairs of church properties. Some buildings, like St. Cecilia's School in Pawtucket, were total losses. To pay for the repairs, par-

---

46   "The Great Hurricane and Tidal Wave, Rhode Island, September 21, 1938," Providence Journal Company, 1938.

47   *Providence Visitor*, September 23, 29, 1938; *Woonsocket Call*, September 24, 1938.

48   *Providence Visitor*, September 23, 29, 1938; *Providence Journal*, September 25, 28, 1938.

ishes like St. James in Arctic had to undertake special fund raising drives to
meet the unexpected expense entailed in the repair of its church. For the
unemployed men of the state, the storm was a boon, as much work had to
be done on an emergency basis.[49]

ST. JOSEPH, *Hope Valley, Hopkinton*

Among the buildings that were severely damaged by the 1938 hurricane
was the former Episcopal Methodist Church on the northwesterly side of
Main Street in the village of Hope Valley. Hope Valley is one of several
small villages in the town of Hopkinton. Bishop Hickey had purchased
the property in behalf of the diocese in May 1922 for a thousand dollars.
The church, which held a hundred people, had been built originally in
Rockville about 1846. However, in 1851, it had been taken down board-
by-board and re-erected on a site facing the Providence-New London
turnpike (now Main Street) near the Wyoming bridge. After the bishop acquired the property, the Marist Fathers at Immaculate Conception, Westerly, had the building remodeled and Fr. Jules P. Cassagne, S.M., an assistant at Westerly, began saying mass in the church after Bishop Hickey
dedicated the new mission to St. Joseph on May 10, 1922.[50]

At the time of its dedication, the mission served mostly Polish immigrants and their families. The Poles had come to the town to work in two
of the town's woolen mills, the Hopwood Mill and Bailey's Woolen Mill.
In addition to the Polish and a few Irish families in Hopkinton, the mission
also served other families scattered through the towns of West Greenwich,
Exeter, and Richmond. With the establishment of the Yawgoog Scout
Camp in neighboring Rockville in 1916 and later the CCC Camp of Veterans in the Acadia State forest, the boys and Catholics among the veterans also came to mass in Hope Valley.[51]

The hurricane caused St. Joseph's church steeple to fall into the building. The church was so badly damaged that Hopkinton's inspector of
buildings condemned the structure. In the aftermath of the hurricane, Fr.
Daniel Sullivan, S.M., at Immaculate Conception, arranged to use the
Grange Hall, the former Advent Church, before it was purchased by the
Grange, as a convenient place to offer mass. The renting of the hall was
a practical arrangement for the moment. Fr. Arthur Sullivan's report on
the religious conditions of the young men, who were enrolled at the CCC
camps, suggested that the religious education of the boys from the rural
areas of the state was being neglected. As a practical step towards remedy-
ing that situation, Bishop Keough undertook to have the remains of the

49 Ibid.; *Pawtuxet Valley Daily Times*, October 6, 1938.
50 Hopkinton Land Evidence, Book 32, p. 688; *Providence Visitor*, June 22, 1923; "History of St.
    Joseph's Parish," in "St. Joseph's Church, Hope Valley, Rhode Island: Silver Anniversary, 1940–
    1965 (Privately printed, 1965).
51 Ibid.

old St. Joseph's church removed and a new, much larger church, one capable of seating 310, built on the same site that would be the center of a new parish in Hopkinton. On October 11, 1939, while the new church was still under construction, Bishop Keough transferred Fr. Jeremiah P. Murphy from St. Andrew's, Block Island, to be the first pastor of the newly established parish of St. Joseph's. The Immaculate Conception's Fr. Sullivan introduced Fr. Murphy to the people of St. Joseph's on Sunday, October 15, 1939. At the time of its founding, there were ninety-five families in the parish. For almost two years, Fr. Murphy lived in rented quarters, until the parish was able to purchase a rectory on August 12, 1941. On Sunday, June 9, 1940, Bishop Keough dedicated the new church. An important part of the new structure was the parish hall in the basement beneath the church. Fr. Murphy began utilizing the hall as early as the previous March, when the first parish societies were organized.[52]

The first pastor of St. Joseph's, Fr. Murphy, was, like the great majority of the priests appointed pastor at this time, a first generation American. He was born in Newport on October 27, 1888. After graduating from his parish school, St. Joseph's, he went to the local public high school before studying at Holy Cross College and St. Mary's Seminary, Baltimore, where he was ordained in on May 27, 1914. In the summer and fall of 1914, he served as an assistant in Our Lady of Mercy, East Greenwich, and divided his time between Oakland Beach and Conimicut. In January 1915, he was appointed assistant at St. Edward's, Pawtucket. After two years in Pawtucket, he was transferred to St. Patrick's, Valley Falls, where he served for twenty years before being appointed pastor of St. Andrew's, Block Island.[53]

ST. JOSEPH, *Scituate*

At the same time and for the same reasons he set off St. Joseph's, Hope Valley as a new parish, Bishop Keough also appointed a full time pastor for St. Joseph's, Scituate. Scituate lay at the head of the Pawtuxet River Valley. Priests from Providence had begun saying mass in the town in 1905 and, since 1915, clergy from the cathedral had been going out Sundays on the trolley that ran through the villages of Scituate on its way to Danielson, Connecticut. By 1916 at least, a priest said mass first in Rockland, in the southern part of the town, at 9:30, and then would take the 10:30 trolley to North Scituate, where he said mass at 11:15. If the priest missed the trolley, the people waited until he came. Between 1921 and 1926, the city of Providence radically altered the landscape of Scituate in the course

---

[52] *Hope Valley Advertiser*, October 20, 1938; October 19, 1939; *Providence Visitor*, March 7; June 6, 13, 1940. In 1938, the Marist Fathers took a census of the mission. According to the report, there were 407 individuals within the mission territory, 190 adults and 110 children. Of these 217 were of Polish origin; 141 were Irish (English-speaking); 17 French Canadian; 14, Italian; with a scattering of others.

[53] *Providence Visitor*, December 29, 1961.

of developing its reservoir. With the development, the priests ceased saying mass in Rockland, which was inundated, but continued to come out to
North Scituate. Fr. J. H. Champagne had begun saying mass in North Scituate about 1913 on an altar made of boxes and old boards in a little building on the shores of Lake Mowswansicut. At this time, Mrs. Ida Phillips
played a leading role in organizing the small Catholic community scattered
through the towns of Scituate, Johnston, Greenville and Foster. Later, larger quarters were secured in the basement of a house on the Danielson Pike
near the reservoir. When during the 1920s the number of Catholics who
attended mass in North Scituate swelled further, they purchased the Mack
house on the Danielson Pike and used its first floor tenement as a place
for the visiting priest to say mass. After four years, the Mack house was no
longer able to accommodate the number of people who wished to attend
mass, and in the mid-1930s, the Catholics arranged with Harry J. Hall to
rent the old hall he owned on Silk Lane as their meeting place.[54]

When in 1925 Bishop Hickey appointed Fr. Thomas Cassidy Diocesan
Visitor of Parochial Schools and moved him from St. Charles, Woonsocket, to the chaplaincy at St. Vincent de Paul Infant Asylum, Fr. Cassidy took
over the responsibility of saying mass on Sundays in Scituate. It was Fr.
Cassidy who first recognized that the growth of the Catholic population of
the mission was such that there would soon be need to build a church for
their use. The site he envisioned as a proper building site lay near the corner of the Danielson Pike and Hope Road, one of the parcels condemned
on Providence's behalf for the reservoir. In order to secure the site, permission needed to be obtained from the State, the city of Providence and the
town of Scituate. The state and town readily agreed but the city held out
for a larger sum than was originally offered. Finally a deal was struck for
$700. One of the principal money-raising efforts the people of the mission
undertook to build a church during the Depression times was the holding
of a raffle at the Chopmist Hill Inn, where large articles were offered for
sale.[55]

After Fr. William Delaney was transferred from Immaculate Conception, Providence, and appointed as chaplain at the Sisters of Providence's Villa St. Rose, Greenville, in September 1937, he replaced Fr. Cassidy as the priest in charge of North Scituate. Construction of a small,
Barrington-brick church of modified English Gothic design began during 1939. Although the church was not finished, as the windows had not
yet arrived and neither the permanent altar nor the pews had been installed, the people insisted that Fr. Delaney offer the first mass in the new
church on Christmas Eve. The new church was dedicated to St. Joseph,

54   *Providence Visitor*, August 18, 1916; December 21, 1938; *Providence Journal*, December 18, 1938; "St.
     Joseph Church, North Scituate, Rhode Island, 50th Anniversary" (Privately printed, 1990).
55   "St. Joseph's Church, North Scituate, Rhode Island." The site on which St. Joseph's was built had
     formerly been the site of John Whipple's tavern and a hundred years later of the Congregational
     Church of Scituate.

on his feast day, March 19. Fr. Cassidy said the mass and Fr. Thomas J. McKitchen, the rector of the cathedral, preached. In October 1939, at the same time Bishop Keough named Fr. Murphy to St. Joseph's, Hope Valley, he also appointed Fr. William P. Tally first pastor of St. Joseph's, North Scituate [56]

Like his fellow pastor, Fr. Tally was a first generation Irish-American. His father, Philip Tally, was born in Drumish, County Longford, and came to Providence with his parents when he was eleven. He began as a journeyman tailor and later formed a partnership with John Slattery. The two opened their shop in the Hoppin Homestead Building in Providence. Philip Tally became a trustee of the cathedral parish and a member of the corporation of the St. Aloysius Orphan Asylum. William P. Tally was born in Providence on October 12, 1869. He attended the Federal Street School before enrolling in La Salle Academy, from which he graduated in 1908. After four years at the College of the Holy Cross, Worcester, he was adopted by Bishop Harkins for the diocese in 1913. Harkins sent him to study theology in France at St. Sulpice, outside of Paris at Issy, where he was a classmate of the future Bishop Keough. With the outbreak of the First World War, Tally transferred to the Grand Seminary at Montreal and was ordained in the cathedral in Providence on June 19, 1916. His first diocesan was as an assistant at St. Ignatius Church, Sanford, Maine. In November 1916, he was appointed an assistant at St. Matthew's, Cranston, where he served four years before he was transferred to St. Mary's, Providence. It was while he was at St. Mary's that Bishop Hickey appointed him Diocesan Director of the Propagation of the Faith.[57]

The Impact of the Automobile

Three more years passed before Bishop Keough moved to establish other parishes. While the Depression had slowed the development of the rural towns around Providence, the populations of Barrington, Smithfield and West Warwick, had continued to slowly increase. With the continued development of the Rhode Island road system and the increasing popularity of automobile as the preferred mode of travel, more and more people were moving from the urban centers to these towns. The increase in population caused the small churches in these towns, which had originally been mission churches, to be increasingly crowded. In September 1942, Bishop Keough chose to alter the status of three of the mission chapels and create three new parishes.

---

[56] *Providence Journal*, December 18, 1938; February 11; March 20, 1939; *Providence Visitor*, December 21, 1938; February 9; March 16, 1939.

[57] *Providence Visitor*, August 24, 1944.

ST. LUKE, *Barrington*

In 1934, the Catholics living in the West Barrington and Bay Spring areas of Barrington, with the support of their pastor, Fr. John Toohey, pastor of St. Brendan's, Riverside, petitioned Bishop Keough for a church closer to their homes. Barrington, famous for its brick works, also saw the development of a number of summer colonies along its bay shore. The growth of these summer colonies was originally encouraged by the rail and trolley lines, which ran through the town and provided easy access to Providence. The 1938 hurricane would later severely damage the road-beds of both kinds of rail and both would be discontinued. However, by the time this happened, many preferred commuting by car. In 1934, the number of the people who lived in Barrington year round as well as the number of summer residents, whose presence annually continued to cause overcrowding at St. Brendan's, even though it had been expanded in 1931, more than justified Bishop Keough's granting the petition. The new mission church would also serve the Catholics who lived or summered at Nayatt and Hampden Meadows, who usually attended mass at St. Mary's, Warren. Although not encouraged at the time, some of the English-speaking Catholics in Barrington also attended mass at Holy Angels, on Maple Avenue, when, after 1914–15, this Italian-speaking parish was dedicated and given a full-time pastor.[58]

As early as 1923, Fr. Joseph E. Hughes, then pastor of St. Brendan's, anticipating the need for a church in Barrington, had purchased an acre of land on Washington Road. With a site for a church already in hand, Fr. Toohey began discussing the building of a church dedicated to St. Luke during the summer of 1935. Work on a church designed by Joseph M. Mosher of West Barrington began a week after Fr. Toohey blessed the site on October 7, 1936. Bishop Keough came down to Barrington to bless the completed church on the feast of the Assumption in August 1937. The church was of Gothic design, measuring 38 by 90 feet, with two wings for a priest's sacristy and an altar boys' sacristy on each side. It had a full basement for social activities. Following the church's dedication, Fr. Toohey arranged for the offering of two masses there on Sundays, at least during the summer months, at 8:00 and 10:00.[59]

By September 1942, the growth of the Catholic population in Barrington prompted Bishop Keough to appoint Fr. John A. Kelly, the senior assistant at St. Patrick's, Providence, the first pastor of St. Luke's. Fr. Kelly was born in Providence on June 3, 1893 and educated at St. Joseph's, Cleary School, and at La Salle Academy, from which he graduated in 1911. After studies at Mt. St. Mary's College, Emmitsburg, Maryland, Bishop Harkins sent him to the American College in Louvain, Belgium in

---

58   "St. Luke's Parish, Silver Jubilee, 1942–1967" (Privately printed, 1967).
59   *Providence Visitor*, October 15, 1936; August 12, 19, 1937; *Star-Tribune*, June 21, 1937.

1913. The outbreak of the Great War interrupted his studies after a year
and a half and he completed his studies at the Grand Seminary, Montreal,
prior to his ordination on December 22, 1917. He served as an assistant in
Cranston, Providence and Ashton, prior to going to St. Patrick's. Fr. Kelly
spent his first few weeks as pastor living in St. Brendan's rectory until the
house he had secured in Barrington was ready for occupancy.[60]

ST. PHILIP, *Greenville, Smithfield*

At the same time St. Luke's was given its own pastor, Bishop Keough
also appointed Fr. Charles J. O'Neill, pastor of St. Philip's, Greenville, in
the town of Smithfield. A priest was first assigned to care for the Irish mill
workers in Greenville in 1855 and, in September 1858, Bishop Francis P.
McFarland had dedicated a small church on what is now Smith Street in
the southern part of the village in honor of St. Philip and appointed a
pastor. An Irish immigrant from Kilkenny, Patrick Magner, who was the
superintendent of the Pooke and Steere mill on the Putnam Pike to the
west of Greenville, was perhaps the leading force in the establishment of
the church. In 1873, a fire destroyed the Stillwater Woolen Company mill.
Also in the 1870s, the Pooke and Steere mill was one of many mills to
cease operations because of financial problems. The mill was eventually
sold to new owners. As a result of the mill's closing, many of the Irish, who
worked there had to move in search of employment elsewhere. In 1875, Fr.
William Wiseman, who was at that time the newly appointed pastor of St.
Philip's, established his residence in Georgiaville, a village five miles away,
which then had a much larger Irish and French-Canadian population. In
Georgiaville, Fr. Wiseman built another church, this one dedicated to St.
Michael, which in time became the center of the mission. The pastors of
St. Michael's continued to say mass in St. Philip's on a regular basis. From
at least the 1870s, the priests who served both St. Michael's and its mission, read the gospel in both English and French and frequently preached
in both languages. In 1911, the Catholics of Greenville undertook to make
extensive repairs and alterations to the church there. The congregation celebrated their work with a special service on Sunday afternoon, November
19. At the time of service, an observer wrote that the Catholics in Greenville composed "perhaps the smallest Catholic congregation in the state."[61]

In spite of the Pooke and Steere's mill closings, the village of Greenville
continued to be the largest village in the town, especially after 1871, when
parts of Smithfield were split off and given to Woonsocket and the newly
created towns of Lincoln and North Smithfield. In the twentieth century,

---

[60]   *Providence Visitor*, September 17, 1942; January 8, 1959; *Providence Journal*, September 28, 1942.
[61]   Hayman, *Catholicism in Rhode Island and the Diocese of Providence*, I, 112, 119, 169–70, 211; Kulik and
       Bonham, *Rhode Island: An Inventory of Historic Engineering and Industrial Sites*, 227; *Providence Visitor*,
       November 24, 1911.

the present day town of Smithfield saw an increase in its population as new mills were built in the eastern part of the town and new housing plats were developed in the western. The Providence Street Railway, which ran to Chepachet, opened in 1914 and continued to provide passenger service until 1924. At this time, the state improved both the Powder Mill and Putnam turnpikes, making it an easier commute into Providence for those who preferred country living. According to the 1940 census, there was an estimated 4,611 people in Smithfield. Four years earlier, a parish census noted that only 270 people regularly attended mass at St. Philip's and more than a third were children. However, by 1942, there were about 250 families who attended mass at the mission. While increasing numbers partially explains the stationing of a priest in Greenville, the providing of good pastoral care for those who lived in Greenville was perhaps the strongest motive. Accordingly, in September 1942, when Bishop Keough raised the mission church in West Barrington to the status of parish, he did the same for St. Philip's, Greenville.[62]

Fr. O'Neill, the first pastor of the restored St. Philip's parish, was a native of Providence. Born on November 25, 1890, he attended the Messer Street School, La Salle Academy, and St. Charles College, Catonsville, Maryland. After two years at St. Charles, he went to the American College in Louvain, Belgium, for two years, 1912–1914, and finished his studies at the Grand Seminary, Montreal. He was ordained in St. James Cathedral, Montreal, on June 2, 1917. Beginning in June 1917, he began a twenty-year assignment as an assistant at St. Joseph's, Pawtucket. In July 1937, he was appointed an assistant at Blessed Sacrament, Providence. It was while he was at Blessed Sacrament that he was named pastor of St. Philip's. During his first years in St. Philip's, Fr. O'Neill lived at the newly built St. Aloysius Orphanage on Austin Avenue.[63]

ST. MARY, *Crompton, West Warwick*

The third parish established in September 1942, St. Mary's, Crompton, was, like St. Philip's, one of the older parishes in the diocese. In 1891, Bishop Harkins had reversed the relationship of St. Mary's with its mission, St. James, in the Arctic section of West Warwick, at the urging of the pastor at that time. The change was dictated by the fact that the majority of the people of the parish then lived closer to the new church of St. James in Arctic than to the older church of St. Mary's in Crompton. By 1942, the southern part of West Warwick had seen the building of a number of new homes with a consequent increase in population. Although some distance from West Warwick, the construction of a naval air station at Quonset Point, which began in July 1940, impacted West Warwick in

---

62 Rhode Island Historical Preservation Commission, "Historic and Architectural Resources of Smithfield, Rhode Island," 1992.
63 *Providence Visitor*, May 15, 1964.

that the base came to employ many civilians, many of who lived at some distance from the base.[64]

As pastor of St. Mary's, Bishop Keough chose Fr. Barton J. Daggert. Fr. Daggert was born in Seekonk, Massachusetts on February 16, 1892. A convert to the Catholic faith, he received his early education at St. Joseph's School, Pawtucket, and later enrolled at La Salle Academy. He began his college education at St. Charles College, Catonsville, Maryland, and studied philosophy and theology at St. Mary's Seminary, Baltimore. After his ordination in Baltimore on May 29, 1919, he served as an assistant at Sacred Heart, Woonsocket, and later at Sacred Heart, East Providence. He was subsequently chaplain at St. Maria's Home, Providence, and the East Providence sectional director of the Catholic Youth Organization.[65]

ST. FRANCIS, *Hillsgrove, Warwick*

As was true of the Oakland Beach section of Warwick where St. Rita's was set off as a separate parish in 1935, the Pontiac and Hillsgrove sections of the newly chartered city had also seen their share of growth. During its heyday in 1912, the Elizabeth Mill on Jefferson Boulevard in the Hillsgrove section employed 346 workers, many of whom lived in the mill houses to the west of the mill. To meet the religious needs of the mill workers, Fr. Daniel Lehane, M.S.C., then pastor of St. Joseph's, Natick, had built a chapel on land donated by a trustee of the Elizabeth Mill, where mass was said for the first time on Christmas Day 1900. Two years later, Bishop Harkins dedicated the new chapel to St. Francis on June 1, 1902. Earlier, the extension of the Elmwood Avenue trolley line down Post Road to East Greenwich and Wickford in 1892 had helped to end the isolation of Hillsgrove, as it opened up large parts of Warwick for housing development and connected the villages of Warwick to a wider world. In 1928, the Warwick Town Council passed a resolution urging Gov. Pothier to use his influence and authority to build a proposed state airport on the scrub lands in the Hillsgrove section of the town. In July 1929, the selection board charged with choosing a site selected Hillsgrove over Gaspee Point and the other proposed sites. When the airport officially opened in 1931, its facilities consisted only of a leveled grass landing field. During the Second World War, the much-expanded airport was used as a training field for fighter pilots.[66]

In April 1942, Fr. Laurent Bourke, M.S.C., who a few months earlier had come to St. Joseph's, Natick, as an assistant, was appointed administrator of St. Joseph's and then pastor of St. Joseph's and St. Francis in

---

64 Robert W. Hayman, "Old St. Mary's Church, Crompton, Rhode Island, 1844–1944" (Manuscript in Providence Diocesan Archives).

65 *Providence Visitor*, December 4, 1947.

66 Rhode Island Historical Preservation Commission, "Warwick, Rhode Island," 35–43; Donald D'Amato, "Pontiac changes during the Depression Years, *Warwick Beacon*, June 6, 1991.

October 1942. In the months following his appointment, Fr. Bourke approached Bishop Keough to request that St. Francis be set off as separate parish. In August 1943, with very little fanfare, Bishop Keough, after consultation with the Missionaries of the Sacred Heart, appointed Fr. Xavier Caron, M.S.C., the first pastor of St. Francis. It was not until the administration of St. Francis' second pastor, Fr. Fernand A. Roberge, M.S.C., tenure, which began in 1946, that the parish purchased a rectory for its pastor.[67]

South County[68]

ST. CLARE, *Misquamicut, Westerly*

In September 1946, Bishop Keough, in face of the increasing number of Catholic families who were electing to live in the southern part of the state, created four parishes out of the four mission stations that the Marist Fathers in Westerly continued to serve. The 1938 hurricane destroyed some four hundred cottages as well as the Catholic chapel at Misquamicut, which was swept from its foundation on Crandall Avenue. St. Clare Chapel at Misquamicut had been opened in 1916. In 1931 it was enlarged by Fr. J. F. Vincent, S.M., then the pastor of Immaculate Conception, Westerly, because an average of five hundred people attended mass there on Sundays during the summer. During the summer of 1939, Fr. Jules Cassagne, S.M., who had succeeded Fr. Vincent as pastor of Immaculate Conception, and whose assistants now served the mission, arranged for mass to be said in the Atlantic Beach Casino and the Pleasant View House. At the end of July 1939, Fr. Cassagne announced the formation of a Fund Drive Committee of mainly summer residents of Watch Hill and Misquamicut, headed by Percival de St. Aubin, who had agreed to assist in the raising of funds to rebuild the chapel. One of the main fund raising efforts was a series of weekly parties, sponsored by the church, which were held each Wednesday night at the casino. Prior to his announcement of the formation of the committee, Fr. Cassagne had purchased land on Crandall Avenue, further away from the shore, as the new site for the church. Providence architect, John F. Hogan, designed the new Gothic style church, which was built for approximately $30,000. The new church was a relatively large building for a mission church. It was ready for use before the summer season in 1940. Bishop Keough dedicated the new St. Clare's Chapel on Sunday, August 11, 1940. Only two objects from the

67   "St. Francis Church, Warwick, Rhode Island," (South Hackensack, N.J.: Custombook, 1969); *Providence Visitor*, April 26, 1969; "History of Missionaries of Sacred Heart in RI, 1899 to 1989," three type-written sheets, PChA.

68   South County refers to a geographic area. In many ways it is co-terminus with Washington County, the southernmost of the five Rhode Island counties.

first St. Clare's had been salvaged after the hurricane, a granite holy water font and a ciborium. Both of these were part of the furnishings of the new church.[69]

As the first pastor of St. Clare's, Bishop Keough named Fr. Philip S. McKenna, who at the time of his appointment, was an assistant at St. Charles, Woonsocket. Fr. McKenna was a native of East Providence, where he was born on October 1, 1896. He graduated from La Salle Academy, and studied at St. Charles College, Catonsville, Maryland, before moving St. Mary's Seminary, Baltimore, and then to the Sulpician Seminary at Washington, D.C. He was ordained a priest on May 20, 1922. His first assignment was as an assistant at the cathedral in Portland, Maine. Later he served at St. Michael's, Providence, and St. Matthew's, Cranston, before going to Woonsocket.[70]

With Fr. McKenna's appointment, St. Clare's, which previously had only been opened during the summer months, now was open year round. Fr. McKenna quickly acquired a rectory on Maplewood Avenue, both as a place for him to live and as a place to offer mass during the winter, since St. Clare's, having been built as a summer chapel, was not insulated. Within the first year of the parish's establishment, Fr. McKenna oversaw the insulating of the church.[71]

ST. MARY, *Carolina, Charlestown*

At the same time St. Clare's was set off as a separate parish, Bishop Keough also appointed a full time pastor at St. Mary's, Carolina, which was the oldest of the missions served by the Marist Fathers. St. Mary's was already a mission station of Immaculate Conception parish, Westerly, when the Marists took charge there in 1906. Beginning in 1920, when he was first assigned to Westerly as an assistant, Fr. Cassagne visited the homes of each one of his parishioners, who were scattered through the four towns served by the Marists, at least once each year. To accomplish this, he used whatever means of transportation available to him. At times he walked, rode horseback, rode a handcar or the occasional freight train. Sometimes he traveled by boat; other times by passenger train. He ate at whatever house or farmhouse he happened to be and many times embarked on his rounds without knowing where he was going to spend the night. Eventually, he was provided with an automobile, which made his life easier. On the evening of May 15, 1932, Fr. Cassagne spent Sunday night in Carolina, in the home of a parishioner, because he planned to offer mass in St. Mary's the next day. At 6:45 on Monday morning, two men spotted a fire in the rear part of the church. Although the first firemen were on the scene in only five minutes, the entire rear part of the church

---

[69] *Providence Journal,* July 25, 1939; *Providence Visitor,* August 8, 1940; *Evening Bulletin,* August 12, 1940.
[70] *Providence Visitor,* December 17, 1971.
[71] Ibid., April 26, 1968.

was already enveloped when they arrived. Eventually over a hundred firemen and volunteers from Richmond and Charlestown fought the blaze. Unfortunately, their efforts were hindered by the fact that hose had to be laid almost a quarter of a mile to the Pawcatuck River. In the end, their efforts were to no avail and the church was a total loss, which in dollar value was estimated at between $12,000 and $15,000.[72]

Although the Depression was very much in people's minds, within days of St. Mary's destruction, Fr. Cassagne, as the priest in charge of the mission, began laying plans for a new church. Through the pages of the *Providence Visitor*, Fr. Cassagne appealed to the pastors of the diocese for donations of church furnishings, which they no longer had use for. While Catholics were still very much in the minority in South County and prejudice against them continued, in the aftermath of the fire, Rev. Leon F. Kenny, pastor of the Carolina Free Baptist Church, offered the use of his church to his Catholic neighbors and Miss Ann Hoxie offered the use of the Episcopalian chapel in Shannock. A number of Catholic neighbors also volunteered their support to any lawn parties or other social events that Fr. Cassagne might hold to raise funds to build anew. Grateful as he was to Rev. Kenny and Miss Hoxie, Fr. Cassagne accepted the offer of the use of Memorial Hall in Shannock, which was tendered by Ernest Champion, chairman of the Memorial Hall Committee, and George P. Clark, president of the Columbia Narrow Fabric Company, over the time needed to rebuild St. Mary's.[73]

During the week of September 11, 1932, work began on a new church on a site on the opposite side of the street from the razed church. As the old chapel, which could accommodate about 200, had been filled to overcrowding by the number of people who regularly attended mass, the new church, designed by John P. Hogan in colonial style, was almost double in size and provided seating for 350. By the time the church was opened on Christmas Eve, 1932, the parishioners had raised about $4,000 of the approximately $13,000 the church cost. Nearly all its furnishings were donated, not by pastors who had surplus goods, but by parishioners and others outside the parish, Catholics and Protestants both, who had read Fr. Cassagne's appeal in the *Visitor*. Bishop Hickey dedicated the new church on Sunday, June 25, 1933. Later in 1933, Fr. Francis Vincent, S.M., who was pastor of Immaculate Conception, at the time of the fire and the dedication of the new church, left Westerly and Fr. Cassagne replaced him.[74]

As the first pastor of St. Mary's after it was established as a parish, Bishop Keough chose Fr. Anthony S. Cotter. Fr. Cotter was born in Susquehanna, Pennsylvania, on November 3, 1898 of parents, who had recently moved from Providence. He was educated at St. John's School, Susquehanna, and at Laurel Hill Academy prior to enrolling at Mount St.

72 *Providence Journal*, May 17; June 5, 1932; *Providence Visitor*, May 20, 1932; "St. Mary's, Carolina: A Heritage of Holiness (South Hackensack, N.J.: Custombook, Inc., 1972), 12–13.
73 *Providence Journal*, June 5, 1932.
74 *Providence Visitor*, September 16; December 22, 1932; June 23, 30, 1933.

Mary's College, Emmitsburg, Maryland, from which he graduated in June 1919. He continued his education at Mt. St. Mary's Seminary and was ordained in Emmitsburg on June 24, 1923 for the Diocese of Providence. His family had strong ties to Rhode Island and two of his uncles, Frs. James and Michael O'Brien, were priests of the diocese. As a young priest, he served at the cathedral for a short time and was then was appointed assistant at St. Lawrence, Centredale, while at the same time serving as a teacher of Latin and Greek at La Salle Academy. In 1927, he was assigned to St. Mary's, Newport, where he remained until 1941, when he was transferred to Holy Trinity, Central Falls. During his years in Newport and in Central Falls, he served as the area director of CYO activities.[75]

Since there was no rectory when St. Mary's was set off as a parish and the income from collections was meager, Fr. Cotter first stayed with a Mrs. Molloy of Tockwotten until such time as he moved into a house in Quonochotaug loaned to him by Capt. and Mrs. Thomas Higgins. Since both places were quite a distance from the church, Fr. Cotter decided to set up living quarters in the sacristy of the church. Here the lack of kitchen facilities and his tendency to neglect his own health in his zeal for the service of others led to illness. In June 1947, he secured the use of a house in Shannock, which still was at some distance from the church itself. Finally, in June 1949, Fr. Cotter received permission to build a rectory next to the church. Much of the labor and materials that went into the small cape were donated by the parishioners.[76]

Shortly after Fr. Cotter took up his new assignment, Fr. James McKenna, S.M., who had replaced Fr. Cassagne as pastor of Immaculate Conception, told the new pastor that he was having the Chrysler automobile which the Marists had used to serve the parish repaired before turning it over to him. Anxious that the children in his widespread parish be able to have religious instruction, Fr. Cotter wrote to Bishop Keough to ask if he might turn the Chrysler in towards a Beach Wagon in order to furnish better transportation for the children to their scattered homes after their weekday religious education classes. The bishop readily agreed to the idea. Later a twenty-two-seat parish bus was used. Initially, various parishioners opened their homes as places where the religious education classes were taught. Although the parish lacked a rectory, it did have a parish hall, an old house on Columbia Heights in Shannock Village. In October 1947, a Teenage Canteen was opened in the house by the women of the parish and a juke box was installed. The parish bus provided free transportation to and from the Canteen for the teens, who had no other transportation.[77]

When he arrived in Charlestown, Fr. Cotter began saying two masses in Carolina, at eight and ten on Sunday mornings. During his first summer in the parish, he obtained Bishop Keough's permission for a third mass.

75 *Providence Visitor*, March 10, 1955.
76 "St. Mary's, Carolina," 15–16; Rev. Charles J. Mahoney to Fr. Cotter, June 7, 1949, PChA.
77 Cotter to Keough, November 7, 1948; Keough to Cotter, November 9, 1946, PChA; "St. Mary's, Carolina," p. 16.

Beginning on the second Sunday in July, Fr. Cotter arranged for a mass to be said at Legiontown to accommodate the large number of Catholic boys there. In the summer of 1948, he began offering mass in the Fire Station at Cross Mills, a practice that continued until 1958, when the site of the mass was changed to the Stables, a barn on Matunuck School House Road. The Stables proved so suitable that the parish soon purchased the property. In order to provide the extra masses during the summer, Bishop Keough began sending Fr. Cotter one of the newly ordained priests as a summer assistant.[78]

ST. VINCENT DE PAUL, *Bradford, Westerly*

The third of the parishes established in 1946 was St. Vincent de Paul, Bradford, on the Westerly-Hopkinton town line, which had been founded as a mission of the Immaculate Conception, Westerly. In 1910, the Marists had built a church in the village to serve a mainly Italian-immigrant congregation. By 1946, an average of 150 persons attended mass in the chapel on Sunday, but, as with the other new parishes established at this time, the number was rising. Bishop Keough chose Fr. William D. McKitchen to be St. Vincent's first pastor. Fr. McKitchen's older brother, Thomas, was, at the time of his appointment, rector of the cathedral. Fr. William McKitchen was born in St. Mary's Parish, Pawtucket on July 27, 1896. He attended St. Mary's School and La Salle Academy before spending six years at Mt. St. Mary's College and Mt. St. Mary's Seminary, from 1914 to 1920. In September 1920, he was sent to the American College at the University of Louvain, Belgium, and was ordained in Belgium on June 18, 1922. After a short time at the cathedral parish, he was appointed assistant at St. Catherine's, Apponaug, in Warwick, while serving at the same time as an instructor in Greek at La Salle Academy. In September 1930, he was transferred to St. Michael's, Providence, as a full time assistant prior to his being named pastor.[79]

One of Fr. McKitchen's first concerns as pastor was to obtain the services of a priest who could hear the confessions for a group of Italian women in the new parish known as The Christian Mothers. A Marist at Immaculate Conception was willing to help him but, when he wrote to Bishop Keough, the bishop advised him that it "was far more satisfactory" to secure the help of a diocesan priest. An able administrator, Fr. McKitchen almost immediately began to plan for the repair of St. Vincent's and for the building of a rectory. While the parish had the money

78   Cotter to Keough, September 8, 1947; "St. Mary's, Carolina," 18–19.
79   Hayman, *Catholicism in Rhode Island and the Diocese of Providence, II,* 198–99; *Providence Visitor,* April 5, 1984.

for the repairs, there were not sufficient monies at that time for a rectory also.[80]

After six months of effort failed to realize the necessary funds for a rectory, Bishop Keough, in August or September 1947, directed Fr. McKitchen to live in a house on Sunset Avenue, just off Main Street in Ashaway, which had previously been occupied by Fr. Vincent Crawford, who was appointed pastor of a new parish in Ashaway, at the same time as Fr. McKitchen. Fr. Crawford had succeeded in building a new rectory in Ashaway and was preparing to move into it. After living with his family at their summer house in the Conimicut section of Warwick while Fr. Crawford completed his move, Fr. McKitchen tried to move into the Sunset Avenue house at the beginning of October. To do so, he found he had to move some of Fr. Crawford's things, which were still in the house, into the garage. On discovering what had happened, Fr. Crawford complained to Bishop Keough. The result was that Fr. McKitchen went to live with his mother in Pawtucket and drove down to his parish for the day until Fr. Crawford completed the moving of his belongings to the new rectory in Ashaway. Fortunately for Fr. McKitchen, a family in his parish, unable to sell a house on the Ashaway Road as they had planned, offered to rent the property to Fr. McKitchen. Upset by what had happened over the Sunset St. house, Fr. McKitchen asked the bishop's permission to take up the offer, if only because renting the property would enable him to live within his own parish. Fr. McKitchen never did build a rectory before he was appointed pastor of Sacred Heart, Woonsocket, in March 1949. His successor, Fr. Joseph A. Devaney, finally succeeded in solving the problems that had frustrated Fr. McKitchen's plans.[81]

OUR LADY OF VICTORY, *Ashaway, Hopkinton*

Of the three missions of Immaculate Conception raised to the status of parishes, the only one that did not have a church was the youngest of them, the Catholics who gathered in Circle Hall, at Potter Hill, a small village in the southwestern part of Hopkinton, near the Rhode Island-Connecticut state line. In 1943, in the midst of World War II, the rationing of gasoline made it difficult for the Catholic families who lived in the villages of Potter Hill and neighboring Ashaway to secure enough gas for the trip to Westerly for mass. Under the leadership of Joseph E. Murray, the Catholics in the two villages signed a petition asking their pastor, Fr. James T. McKenna, S.M., to say mass for them closer to their homes. Towards the end of the year, Fr. McKenna secured a lease on Circle Hall at Potter

80 McKitchen to Keough, October 10, 1946; Keough to McKitchen, October 11, 1946; McKitchen to Keough, March 3, 1947; Keough to McKitchen, March 4, 1947; McKitchen to Keough, May 12, 1947; Keough to McKitchen, May 20, 1947, PChA.
81 McKitchen to Keough, October 14, 1947; October 21, 1947, PChA; *Providence Visitor*, April 26, 1968.

Hill for $250 a year and, on the feast of the Immaculate Conception, December 8, 1943, Fr. Joseph V. Demers, S.M., one of Fr. McKenna's assistants, said the first mass there, at which sixteen people were present. When at the beginning of 1944, Fr. Demers was assigned to cover St. Mary's, Carolina, Fr. John W. Lynch, S.M., another Marist at Immaculate Conception took over the duty of saying mass in Potter Hill at 7:00 a.m. each Sunday before going on to Bradford for a mass at 9:00 a.m.[82]

While there was no church in Potter Hill or Ashaway, the local postmaster, a convert to the faith, had donated to Immaculate Conception a piece of property on Sunset Avenue, off Nooseneck Hill Road, or Main Street, as it was known, in the village of Ashaway, as a site for a church. The pastor of Immaculate Conception passed on the property to the diocese for the use of the new parish when Bishop Keough decided to set it off. Bishop Keough chose to dedicate the new parish to Mary under the title of Our Lady of Victory in thanksgiving for the allies' victory in the Second World War. Shortly after receiving his appointment as first pastor of Our Lady of Victory, Fr. Raymond J. Crawford took up residence in a house on Sunset Avenue.[83]

The new parish embraced the area from the Westerly-Hopkinton town line at the Meeting House Bridge to a point one and half miles north of Hopkinton City and from the Connecticut line to the Hopkinton-Westerly line in Bradford. There were about fifty families in the parish when it was created. The new pastor, Fr. Crawford, was born in Woonsocket on February 9, 1897. He attended St. Charles School for nine years, before spending four years at La Salle Academy. After graduation from the College of the Holy Cross, Worcester, he was sent by Bishop Harkins to St. Mary's, Baltimore for three years, and then by Bishop Hickey to the Suplician Seminary at the Catholic University in Washington for one year. After his ordination in Baltimore on May 26, 1923, he began his career as a priest as an assistant at St. Benedict's, in the Conimicut section of Warwick, while also teaching at La Salle Academy from the time of his first appointment until 1931. In 1935, Bishop Keough appointed him an assistant at Blessed Sacrament, Providence. It was while he was at Blessed Sacrament, that he received his appointment to Our Lady of Victories.[84]

The land, which had originally been donated for a church in Ashaway, failed to pass a perk test. Fr. Crawford was forced to seek another and found a suitable site, the Arthur Main property, on Broad Street (now Main Street), which also included a house suitable for use as a rectory. The transaction was completed on July 19, 1947 and, by the end of October, Fr. Crawford finished moving his belongings from the Sunset Avenue

---

[82]   "Our Lady of Victory Parish, Ashaway, Rhode Island: Twenty-Fifth Anniversary, October 24, 1971."

[83]   Ibid.; *Westerly Sun*, September 27, 1946; Conservation with Rev. John F. Farrell, former pastor of Our Lady of Victory, June 16, 2004.

[84]   Rev. Raymond J. Crawford, personnel record, PChA.

house into the Broad Street house. On October 23, 1947, the day after he wrote to Bishop Keough informing him of his move to the Broad Street house, Fr. Crawford sent another letter to Keough to inform him that the owners of Circle Hall were selling the building and that the new owners planned to turn it into a two-tenement house. Since the parish's lease on the hall was paid up until December 1, Fr. Crawford had time to look for another hall. To his mind, the hall in the Ashaway Volunteer Fire Station would suit the parish well. However, not all in Hopkinton were as yet comfortable having Catholics as neighbors. As a first step toward securing the use of the Firemen's Hall, Fr. Crawford hired it for a Thanksgiving Social and Raffle on November 22. His calculated approach to hiring the hall was successful and the parish was able to rent the hall on Sundays and Holydays for $240 a year. Daily mass was celebrated in the rectory, where religious instructions were also held for the children of the parish.[85]

Fund-raising for building of a church began as early as January 1947, when the Gordon Greene Post of the American Legion put on a two-hour show for the benefit of the parish in Immaculate Conception School Hall in Westerly. Weekly bridge and whist parties were held in the Lantern Glow Restaurant every Tuesday from March 1947, for the next two years. The chief fundraiser for the new church, however, would be the Annual Summer Festival, which was held on the newly acquired church property on Main Street. In addition to what the parish raised for its church, several of Fr. Crawford's former parishioners in Blessed Sacrament, particularly the ladies of the Rosary and Altar Society, contributed money to help the new parish. The Rosary and Altar Society alone contributed $630.[86]

Fr. Crawford would consider several possibilities before settling on a final plan for the building of a church. One idea was to obtain one of the military chapels the government had built on various military bases before and during the war, which the government had declared as surplus, take it down, and transport it in sections to Ashaway. Bishop Russell McVinney, who was named to succeed Bishop Keough in June 1948, considered the idea but thought the difficulties made the effort not worth the trouble. Rather, he urged Fr. Crawford to pursue the first idea the two had discussed, building a chapel similar to the ones Bishop Cassidy in Fall River had recently built on Cape Cod. In December 1948, Fr. Crawford sent the bishop a letter containing the conclusions he reached after examining the churches at Bass River and Orleans and after consulting a Providence contractor. What he proposed was a wood-frame church with a seating capacity of two hundred, which would have a full basement, and could be built at estimated cost of $65,000. Bishop McVinney quickly approved the plan and authorized him to go ahead. In the same letter, the bishop informed him that the chancery office would be sending him a monthly check of

85 Crawford to Keough, October 22, 23, 1947; "Our Lady of Victory: Twenty-Fifth Anniversary."
86 Crawford to Keough, October 22, 1947; *Providence Visitor,* January 23, 1947; "Our Lady of Victory: Twenty-Fifth Anniversary."

one hundred dollars with which he could hire a housekeeper, who might prepare his meals in order to ensure that he got the proper nourishment. Like Fr. Cotter in Carolina, Fr. Crawford's financial situation had forced him to do without certain comforts and his spartan living had had an impact on his health.[87]

Fr. Crawford broke ground for the new church on April 29, 1949. The blessing of the cornerstone occurred on May 30. Progress on the church was sufficient to allow the basement hall to be used for mass for the first time on August 7, 1949. Bishop McVinney dedicated the completed church on October 9, 1949. Although Bishop McVinney made Fr. Crawford pastor of St. Catherine's, Apponaug, on September 13, 1949, Fr. Crawford returned to Ashaway to be the celebrant of the first mass celebrated in the new church following its blessing.[88]

ST. JUDE, *Lincoln*

Besides the four South County parishes created in September 1946, Bishop Keough also merged territory taken from St. Patrick's, Valley Falls, and Holy Trinity, Central Falls, into a new parish centered on the Prospect Hill section of Lincoln. The various mills on the western side of the Blackstone River in Lincoln had prompted a good number of workers to settle in their vicinity over the years. In addition, the building boom of the post-war World War I period spurred the rapid development of new homes in the area and caused the population of the Prospect Hill section to rise accordingly. The creation of a parish in the area might have come sooner, but for the respect generally accorded the pastor of St. Patrick's, Fr. Thomas J. Fitzpatrick. Fr. Fitzpatrick took charge of St. Patrick's in March 1908 and, when he died on December 15, 1945, he was the oldest priest in the diocese.[89]

As pastor of the new parish, which was to be placed under the patronage of St. Jude, Bishop Keough named Fr. James J. Loughran, who had recently returned from military service in the U.S. Army as a World War II chaplain. Fr. Loughlan was born in Warren on October 2, 1895. He spent seven years in the Warren public schools. When his family moved to Providence, he attended St. Mary's School on Broadway before entering La Salle Academy. After La Salle, he attended St. John's Preparatory School, in Danvers, Massachusetts, prior to admittance to the College of the Holy Cross. He spent two years at Holy Cross, before beginning his preparation for the priesthood at St. Bernard's Seminary, Rochester, New York, where he did both his philosophical and theological studies. Following ordination on June 9, 1922, he served for twelve years as an assistant at Blessed Sacra-

[87] McVinney to Crawford, November 2; December 3, 1948; Crawford to McVinney, December 2, 1948, PChA.
[88] "Our Lady of Victory: Twenty-Fifth Anniversary;" *Providence Visitor*, May 26; September 29, 1949.
[89] *Providence Visitor*, September 19, 1946.

ment, Providence, before going to St. Patrick's, Valley Falls, for four years. In November 1938, he was appointed an assistant at St. Augustin's, Newport. It was while he was at St. Augustin's that he volunteered for military service.[90]

Following his appointment, Fr. Loughran arranged for the use of the meeting hall of McKeown Post, Veterans of World War I, on Front Street. The American Legion Hall would serve as the site for mass for several years. In November 1948, Fr. Loughran announced the purchase of five acres of land bordered by Front, West and Charles streets from the Lonsdale Company as a site for a new church and rectory. Taking a prudent approach to the construction of a church, the parish soon broke ground for a basement church over which it hoped to build a superstructure. The new church was used for the first time on May 11, 1950. That same evening, Bishop McVinney came to the parish to celebrate the Sacrament of Confirmation in the recently completed building. It would not be until August 24, 1952, that Fr. Loughran undertook the task of building a rectory next to the church. Bishop McVinney blessed the new rectory on December 18, 1952.[91]

NEW MISSION CHURCHES

In addition to the new parishes he created, Bishop Keough also authorized the building of a mission church in St. Philomena's Parish, Narragansett [now St. Thomas More Parish], to principally serve the summer vacationers in the Point Judith area. In March 1940, Bishop Keough gave Fr. Matthew F. Clarke, the pastor of St. Philomena's, permission to sign contracts for the construction of a brick church of colonial design, with a seating capacity of four hundred, on the eastern side of Point Judith Road. Ground was broken for the new chapel, which was dedicated to Mary under the title, St. Mary's, Star of the Sea, on the feast of the Annunciation, March 25. The building was ready for use a year later and mass was celebrated in the chapel for the first time on June 22, 1941. Bishop Keough blessed the new chapel on July 6.[92]

New Educational Efforts

NEW PARISH SCHOOLS

Under Bishop Keough the number of parochial schools continued to grow in spite of the financial restraints imposed by the Depression. In Coventry, hopes for a parish school for the Polish children of the Paw-

---

[90]   *Providence Visitor*, June 4, 1959.
[91]   *Providence Visitor*, September 29, 1967.
[92]   *Providence Visitor*, March 21, 1940; July 2, 10, 1941.

tuxet Valley had begun to take concrete form in 1926, when Fr. Bronislaus Rosiak, the administrator of Our Lady of Czestochowa, which lay in the Quidnick section of the town, gathered his people for a meeting on Sunday, February 28. The meeting was prompted by the growing desire of the Poles in the Valley to have a school where their children would have a thorough religious education while at the same time being exposed to American ideals. At the meeting Fr. Rosiak expressed the hope that the children of his parish might not only learn American history, but also come to know the part Poles had taken in it. Those present at the meeting agreed to undertake a fund raising campaign to purchase a school site. Over four hundred Poles gathered six weeks later on another Sunday to complete arrangements for a fund-raising drive in the parish. In the fall of 1927, the parish purchased two, four tenement houses with four acres of ground in the vicinity of the church. The larger of the two buildings was once a Quaker Meeting House. Fr. Rosiak oversaw the conversion of the two-and-a-half-story building into a combination school and convent. Four classrooms were created on the first floor and the second was renovated as a convent for the five Felician Sisters of the Third Order to St. Francis, who came to open the school in August 1934. The sisters opened in September with seven grades, as three of the classrooms accommodated two grades apiece. Prior to the school's opening, Bishop Keough came down to the Valley on August 12, 1934, to dedicate the new school.[93]

In September 1935, almost two weeks before Bishop Keough was to dedicate the new St. Casimir's Church in Providence, the pastor of St. Casimir's, Fr. John Vaitekunas, announced plans to convert the old church into a parish school. Like the Poles, the Lithuanians, who worshiped at St. Casimir's, wished to see their children come to a knowledge of their faith and their Lithuanian heritage. Fr. Vaitekunas' plan was to substantially rebuild the old St. Casimir's in two stages. The first involved enlarging the footprint of the building and adding a second story to accommodate four classrooms and an assembly hall. Because of a lack of space around the building, he initially planned to construct a flat roof over the new second story that would serve as a playground for the children. He had bowling alleys installed in the basement of the building, which would be used during the evenings as a parish club. On two evenings during the week, Fr. Vaitekunas offered classes in religion, language and philosophy to his older parishioners. When Bishop Keough dedicated the combination school and recreation building on Sunday, April 11, 1937, the second story of the building had still not been added. Although Fr. Vaitekunas expressed the hope at the time of the building's dedication that the large room on the first floor would be divided into three classrooms and a school would be opened in September, it was not until a year later, September 1938, that the school actually opened. To staff the school, Fr. Vaitekunas arranged

---

[93] *Providence Visitor*, March 5; April 23, 1926; August 10, 17, 1934; January 14, 1937.

for three Sisters of St. Casimir from Chicago to come to Providence. The school opened in 1938 with twenty-three children. Within a year there were forty. Since there were only three classrooms and three sisters, two and later three grades were accommodated in one room.[94]

Also in 1938, Fr. Brouillette, the pastor of St. Vincent de Paul's in Coventry, arranged with the Coventry School Committee to lease the Quidnick primary school, which the town had closed the year before. The leased building allowed him to expand St. Vincent's school, which had begun as an annex of St. John's in Arctic in 1932, to eight grades, which were taught by the Sisters of the Presentation of Mary.[95]

In 1940, Fr. Thomas McGrath, pastor of St. Leo's, Pawtucket, took a slightly different approach to building a parish school. Fr. McGrath became pastor of St. Leo's in September 1936. At the end of May 1939, he announced that he was having plans drawn by John Hogan, who had designed the church almost twenty-five years earlier, for a twelve-room convent to house the Sisters of Mercy, who taught in the parish's religious education program. Work on the convent began in July and finished about the first of the new year. Bishop Keough privately blessed the new convent on Monday, September 6, 1940, after five Sisters of Mercy had moved into the new building. During the parish's celebration of its twenty-fifth anniversary in May 1940 at St. Raphael's Academy, Fr. McGrath announced plans for a parish school, also designed by Mr. Hogan, to be built on the site of the former Central Avenue Grammar School next to the church. Work on the new, two-story, Barrington brick school, designed to accommodate 350 children, began towards the end of May. As with other building projects at the time, there was initially some concern about being able to obtain the necessary steel, but the project was able to go forward on schedule. While the building was under construction, the Sisters of Mercy began the school by holding two classes in the old Parish Hall. With the opening of schools in September 1942, 264 children registered for the school's nine grades before the doors were opened on September 14. The Saturday before the opening, Bishop Keough formally blessed the building.[96]

In August 1943, Fr. John X. Murphy, who was appointed pastor of St. Brendan's in the Riverside section of East Providence in February 1942, bought a large two-story house as well as three lots on Turner Avenue across the street from the church for use as a parish convent. Previously, Fr. Murphy had arranged with the town of East Providence for the lease of the Turner Avenue School. Up to this time, the children of the parish who wished to go to a Catholic school had enrolled in St. Mary's Academy,

94 Ibid., September 12, 1935; April 8, 1937; November 7, 1959.
95 *Providence Journal*, August 30, 1938; Siembab, "Golden Jubilee Celebration."
96 *Pawtucket Times*, May 29, 1939; *Providence Journal*, July 14, 1939; August 30, 1940; July 28, 1941; *Providence Visitor*, October 1, 1939, September 5, 1940; September 17, 1942; "Solemn Observance of the Golden Jubilee of St. Leo's Parish, Pawtucket, Rhode Island, 1916–1966, (Privately printed, 1966).

a grammar school and high school run by the Sisters of Mercy at Bay-view. However, because St. Mary's was a considerable distance from the homes of many of the children, who lived in the south end of Riverside, Fr. Murphy's predecessor, before the outbreak of the war, had intended to build a parish school on several lots adjoining the church. The war caused a postponing of his plans, but the combination of distance and traffic con-ditions, forced Murphy to adopt the alternative plan of leasing a school building.[97]

In October 1934, Bishop Keough acknowledged the work Fr. Bronislaus Rosiak had done in Coventry by appointing him pastor of St. Adalbert's, Providence. From the parish's beginnings in 1902, its pastors and people had sought to have not only a church but a school as well. Financial dif-ficulties frustrated the desire for a school until after Fr. Rosiak became pas-tor. The country was still immersed in the Depression when Fr. Rosiak came to Providence and a heavy debt limited what he could do. However, the same desire to strengthen both his parishioners' Catholic faith and Polish heritage that had prompted him to open a school in Coventry also motivated him to invite the Felician Sisters to come to St. Adalbert's. To provide for the sisters, the parish purchased and renovated a house at 138 Florence St. Three Felician Sisters from Enfield, Connecticut, took up resi-dence in the house on November 26, 1937, and Fr. Rosiak blessed it two days later. The sisters held classes on the ground floor of their convent. During their first year, 130 students registered for religion and Polish lan-guage classes. It was not until 1946 that Fr. Rosiak could move forward. During the summer of 1946, Fr. Rosiak had the convent and the parish hall renovated for parochial school use. The first floor of the convent was divided into two classrooms, which would accommodate two grades each. The annex was partitioned for the use of the fifth and sixth grades and the kindergarten. St. Adalbert's School opened on September 9, 1946 with an enrollment of fifty-two students, whose numbers increased to sixty-nine in kindergarten through sixth grade by the end of the school year. When numbers increased further in subsequent years, the parish obtained the use of space first in the Academy Avenue public school in 1948 and then in the Putnam Street School in 1949. In September 1954, the school was con-solidated in the former Sixth Precinct Police Station at 36 Chaffee Street. Before the opening of school, the interior of the building was complete-ly renovated into five classrooms, a two-room kindergarten and a nurse's room. By that year there were 105 pupils and five Felician Sisters.[98]

The opening of a parish school was also a dream of Fr. Anthony Bainotti, C.S., who became pastor of Our Lady of Loreto, East Provi-dence in October 1939. In October 1946, he welcomed the Maestre Pie Venerini Sisters to the parish where he had purchased a cottage across

---

[97] *Evening Bulletin*, August 23, 1943.
[98] "St. Adalbert's Church, Providence, Rhode Island, 75th Annviersary, 1902–1977 (Privately print-ed, 1977), p. 18.

the street from the church and had converted it into a convent for their use. After their arrival, the sisters opened a kindergarten in their convent. The kindergarten enrolled more than thirty boys and girls of all nationalities in a program that ran all year. Disaster struck the parish in February 1947 when a blaze destroyed the interior of the church. Fr. Bainotti had the damage repaired by the following June. In spite of the setback caused by the fire, Fr. Bainotti had the pleasure of seeing the sisters add a first grade program to the classes they offered in their convent during September 1947. To accommodate, the first grade, the sisters moved their kindergarten to the second floor of the CYO building in the back of the rectory. The sisters continued to add a grade each year until there were nine grades in the school. Ground for a new school building was broken in September 1954, and new school was blessed in November 1955.[99]

With the five new schools opened during Bishop Keough's years, the total number of parish schools in the diocese rose to sixty-four. Since during these years, fourteen parishes were added to the 110 parishes already established, the percentage of parishes with schools rose slightly to approximately fifty-four percent from approximately fifty-two percent at the end of Bishop Hickey's administration.

Catholic Teachers' Institute

The increase in the number of schools was due mainly to the initiative of the pastors in the diocese. One area in which the bishop himself lent support for Catholic education was in the area of continuing education for all Catholic schoolteachers. In April 1939, after several meetings with representatives of the various teaching communities in the diocese, a plan was agreed on for a two-day Teachers' Institute that was to be held in October 1939 on the same days the public school teachers held their institute at the Rhode Island Institute of Instruction. In addition to achieving agreement on the necessity of a teachers' institute for the some eight hundred lay and religious Catholic school teachers in the diocese, the representatives who met in the preliminary sessions chose committees to plan the sessions and chose officers for the planned institute. Bishop Keough was named the institute's honorary president and Msgr. Blessing the honorary vice president. Fr. Gerald F. Dillon, Dean of Men at Catholic University, was named president, a religious brother vice-president and two religious sisters, secretary and treasurer. Fr. Cassidy, the Diocesan Visitor of Parochial Schools, was named chairmen of the executive committee whose membership was drawn from the ranks of both the men and women religious. As a sign of his interest and concern, Bishop Keough presided at the eight institutes that were held while he was bishop.[100]

---

[99] *Providence Visitor,* June 19, 1947; September 16, 1954; November 9, 1955.

[100] *Providence Visitor,* April 27; October 19, 1939.

ST. CATHERINE'S ACADEMY, *Newport*

The combination of increased income taxes, local property taxes, continuing maintenance costs, and limited use of essentially summertime property created opportunities for the diocese to acquire valuable property in many places in the state. In October 1939, Herbert Claiborne Pell, then the American Minister to Portugal, offered his spacious Bellevue Avenue home in Newport, formerly known as the Osgood Villa, to the city of Newport for use as a high school, with the proviso that it be named the Pell School. Mr. Pell wished to honor his family, who had been connected with Newport for more than a hundred years. The city, however, declined the offer because the school department felt that, from the standpoint of location and size, the villa was unsuitable for use as a high school. In January 1940, Mr. Pell offered the villa to Bishop Keough for a similar use. In 1925, Bishop Hickey, through Fr. Baggott of St. Mary's and Dr. Philip E. Clark, had bought the Gray estate, at the corner of Kay Street and Cranston Avenue, in Newport, for use as a girls' high school. However, with the opening of De LaSalle in 1924 and the departure of the boys from St. Joseph's High for the new school, St. Joseph's had enough space to accommodate all the girls who wished to attend and the idea of utilizing the Grey property for a girls school was dropped. However, when Mr. Pell offered his estate to the diocese, the idea was revived. Mr. Pell suggested that the new academy be named St. Catherine's in honor of St. Catherine of Siena and in his memory of his mother and grandmother, both of whom were named Catherine. Bishop Keough was happy to comply with the request when forming a new corporation to hold the property. Mr. Pell's interest in advancing education in Newport was one of long standing. Earlier he had fostered a movement to establish a college in Newport "to help develop the seasons as well making for longer stays of families." A month or so after the diocese acquired the Pell estate, an anonymous benefactor purchased the Eustic Corcoran villa at the corner of Bellevue Avenue and Webster Street from the Savings Bank of Newport and donated the property to the diocese for use as a convent by the Sisters of St. Joseph, who had previously staffed St. Joseph's High School, which would close before St. Catherine's Academy opened in September 1941.[101]

School Busing, Textbooks, and Religion
and the Public Schools

SCHOOL BUSING

In the course of the "bloodless or Green revolution" of 1935, which

---

[101] *Providence Visitor*, May 22, 1925; March 28, 1940; April 3, 1941; *Providence Journal*, May 17, 1925; October 13, 1939; March 25, 1940 *Newport Herald*, March 25, 1940.

saw the Democrats in Rhode Island break the political hold of the Republican Party and its bosses on the state, the Democratic controlled legislature passed an omnibus bill, which brought about a reorganization of state government. The reorganization led to the removal of many Republicans from administrative positions and their replacement by Democrats. Among the new appointees was Dr. James F. Rockett, who was Superintendent of Schools in Woonsocket at the time of his appointment as State Director of Education. During the waning hours o f the January 1937 session of the Rhode Island legislature, the assembly passed a bill submitted by Dr. Rocket without a hearing or debate, which empowered the local school committees in Rhode Island to provide for "the same rights and privileges as to transportation to and from school . . . [for] pupils attending private schools of elementary and high school grades [except such schools as are operated for profit] as are provided for pupils attending public schools." Under this legislation, it was left to the local school committees to determine, after "giving consideration to age of children, local conditions and hazards involved," the distance from school at which children would be bussed. The school committees could arrange for special school buses to transport the children or provide them with bus passes so that the children might take the public buses.[102]

Rhode Island was not the first state to pass a law enabling the local school committees to provide for the busing of private school children. The issue had arisen in several other states along with the advent of motor transportation and centralized schools. Illinois passed a law providing for free transportation of both public and private school children in 1933, and in 1936, Ohio, New York and Massachusetts passed similar laws. The New York law was challenged in the state courts as a violation of New York's constitution, but on March 1, 1937, a justice of the New York Supreme Court upheld the validity of the law.[103]

Regardless of the legal precedents in other states, when the Rhode Island State Baptist Convention met in Providence in May 1937 the delegates adopted a resolution in which they vigorously protested what they saw as an attack on Rhode Island's "time-honored principle of separation of Church and State." The following month, the New England Southern Conference of the Methodist Episcopal Church joined in the protest. In an unusual front page editorial, the *Providence Visitor* offered a rebuttal to the Baptist State Convention's resolution in its May 13 issue. The editorial rejected the Baptists' view that the legislation violated the principle of separation of Church and State. Basing itself on the recent opinion of U.S. Supreme Court Chief Justice Charles Evans Hughes in the Louisiana school text book case, the *Visitor* argued, as did Justice Hughes, that, "In extending transportation facilities to the children of Catholic schools the

---

[102] Edward M. McEntee, *Laws of Rhode Island Relating to Education* (Providence: State Department of Education, 1948), 22–23.

[103] *Providence Visitor*, May 18, 1928; July 28, 1933; March 4, 1937.

state is not aiding or supporting sectarian institutions. It is the child and
not the school that is aided." As a practical example to show the need for
the law, the *Visitor* editorial cited the case of the village of Nasonville, in
the town of Burrillville, where there were two schools:

> One, the Catholic school, is a modern brick building with four teachers and eighty
> pupils. The other, the public school, is a wooden structure with three teachers and
> seventy-one pupils. Before the transportation act was passed the public school children
> were given transportation while the Catholic school children were deprived of this
> convenience, although some of them were forced to walk four miles to school, in rain
> or shine and sometimes at the expense of ridicule from their companions.

The new law impacted high school students more than others, as Rhode
Island towns, in particular, had but one high school, if they had any at all,
and many students in these schools lived at a distance from their schools.
The new law placed an added burden on the towns. Since Rhode Island
towns still retained the tradition of a financial town meeting, getting transportation money for public school students in previous years had proved
difficult.[104]

TEXT BOOKS AND HIGH SCHOOL TUITION

In 1929, Louisiana Gov. Huey P. Long had legislation passed that
enabled the state to supply free textbooks to both public and parochial
schools. The enabling legislation was challenged and in 1930 reached the
U.S. Supreme Court, which upheld the law. Rhode Island's political parties
began to consider having Rhode Island do the same during the 1938 legislative session. During the darkest days of the Depression in October 1933,
the *Providence Visitor* had printed the results of a survey of Catholic schools
and estimated that the diocesan school system saved Rhode Island's cities
and towns in those cash-strapped years $2,562,526 a year in education
costs. This savings was exclusive of the cost of erecting and maintaining
school buildings. The *Visitor* offered a similar estimate in November 1935
in response to a reader's letter.[105]

Since many Rhode Island cities and towns in 1935 were struggling to
meet the costs of maintaining public services, the relief offered by Catholic
schools was considerable. Nevertheless, some towns had to choose which
bills to pay. In the case of the of Johnston, the town treasurer in 1935
chose not to pay the bills submitted by St. Xavier's and LaSalle academies
for the tuition of Johnston students during the 1934–1935 academic year.
As part of a move to improve high school education, the General Assembly had passed a law in 1909 providing that any town that did not maintain its own high school, as was the case in Johnston, was required to make
provision at the expense of the town for free attendance of its children at

---

[104] *Providence Journal*, May 13; June 11, 1937; *Providence Visitor*, May 13; June 10, 1937; *Woonsocket Call*, June 8, 1937.

[105] *Woonsocket Call*, May 15, 1937; *Providence Visitor*, October 27, 1933.

some high school or academy approved by the State Board of Education. Although the Johnston Town Treasurer had made an agreement regarding the overdue tuition bill it had received from Providence, the private schools had not been included in the agreement. The money owed to St. Xavier's alone amounted to $1,775. In addition to what Johnston owed the two academies, the town was also in arrears when it came to its grammar school teachers. Prior to the financial crisis in 1934–35, Johnston had also paid the cost of the books that high school students were required to buy. When the Johnston students at St. Xavier's asked the town to supply them with books, their requested was refused on the grounds that the cost of books was included in tuition, which it was not. The publicity given to the dispute caused some Johnston residents to grumble about "money grabbing" on the part of the town's Catholics. The matter was left for the next financial town meeting.[106]

Because of the "bloodless revolution," there were members of the Rhode Island legislature, who believed that the state should financially aid the parochial schools because of their public utility and who believed they were in a position to offer the diocese such aid. In his later years, Msgr. Thomas V. Cassidy, who continued as Diocesan Visitor of Catholic Schools and secretary of the Catholic School Board under Bishop Keough, recalled that at this time Bishop Keough was approached by a member of the General Assembly, who claimed he would see to it that the Catholic schools of the diocese would get all the money they needed from the state. According to Msgr. Cassidy, Bishop Keough's first impression was that the diocese would be "taking an awful chance," if it accepted the offer, but he did not immediately say no. Before giving his decision, Bishop Keough met for two hours with various diocesan and school officials, Msgr. Cassidy among them, to discuss the offer. Msgr. Cassidy recalled that Msgr. Peter Blessing, whom he credited with knowing the mind of the community better than Bishop Keough, was very strong in saying, "No, keep away from it." Bishop Keough chose to follow his advice.[107]

RELIGION AND THE PUBLIC SCHOOLS

Before Dr. Rockett's tenure as Director of the Department of Education, Rev. J. M. Hunter, an East Greenwich resident, beginning in October 1921, had promoted a campaign to have the public grammar schools

[106] Charles Carroll, *Public Education in Rhode Island* (State Board of Education, the Commissioner of Public Schools, and the Trustees of the Rhode Island Normal School, 1918), p. 236; James A. Feeley to Fr. Charles Mahoney, October 21, 1935; October 1935.

[107] *Providence Visitor*, November 27, 1935; Interview of Joseph Cicione with Msgr. Thomas V. Cassidy, no date, PChA. The issue of accepting state support of Catholic education was similar to that of federal support of public education. While Bishop Keough was not as strident as was Bishop Hickey in regard to the issue, he essentially agreed with the views offered by Msgr. Edward B. Jordan, vice president of the Catholic University of America, in a talk to the Catholic Woman's Club on Thursday, February 10, 1944, namely that federal aid to education would mean an increased tax burden to support schools to which the consciences of Catholics parents prevent them from sending their children. Cf. *Providence Journal*, February 11, 1944.

in the various towns and cities of the state release their students for hour during the course of the week so that the children might go to churches or synagogues of their choice for religious instruction. Within a period of twenty weeks, Hunter and others were able to persuade twenty-six school boards to adopt the program of religious training. One of the first towns to adopt the idea was West Warwick. School officials there dismissed the children of the grammar schools on Thursday afternoons. In September 1922, the school committees in Cumberland and Lincoln also authorized the release of public school children so that they might take religious instruction. Cumberland schools released the children for the last hour on Wednesdays, while Lincoln released the children for the last hour on Fridays. Then State Commissioner of Education, Walter E. Ranger, in an address to a union meeting of clergymen held under the auspices of the Rhode Island Baptist Ministers' Association in the First Baptist Church, Providence, in December 1924, supported the idea of "Release time," especially in the light of decrease in the practice of Bible reading in the public schools that had occurred over the last fifty years. Citing Dr. Thomas E. Young, one of the seven national directors of week-day religious education as his source, Dr. Ranger said that there were 27,000,000 children of school age in America, who had received no religious instruction whatever. Although he believed that it was within "the province of the various school committees throughout the state to grant release time for religious instruction, if they so desired, Dr. Ranger added, "A little legislation of the right sort on the matter would clear the atmosphere and prevent the unthinking crank from serving an injunction to stop the week-day religious instruction."[108]

While few parents were concerned about the legality of release time, many were concerned about the dangers students encountered while passing through the streets on their way to religious instruction. In January 1930, following an incident when a child on release time darted onto Main Street and caused an accident, six clergymen in East Greenwich asked the East Greenwich School Committee to consider what alternatives there might be. The School Committee responded by extending the use of fifteen classrooms in the James G. Eldridge Grammar School on First Avenue to the pastors of all the churches in the town for one hour during which they and the teachers that assisted them might give religious instruction to the children of their parishes. Those who did not wish to attend the class offered were given a study period. This practice continued for four

108 *Pawtuxet Valley Daily Times*, April 4; May 5, 1922; *Providence Journal*, September 19, 1922; *Evening Bulletin*, December 15, 1924. In April 1926, after Dr. Edgar F. Hamlin, senator from North Smithfield submitted a proposed bill to the state senate that would have made it compulsory to read the Bible daily in the public schools, William A. Newell, Superintendent of Schools in Pawtucket, in an article in the *Pawtucket Times*, on April 2, 1926, opposed the idea on the grounds of the lack of consensus that existed among the various religious as what text of the Bible was acceptable. He noted that in Pawtucket schools, parts of the psalms were read daily, but without comment, and that the day began in most classes with the saying of the Lord's Prayer.

years, but in August 1935, the School Committee decided to go back to the previous arrangement whereby children were allowed to leave school one hour early to attend instructions in their own churches.[109]

Another of Dr. Rockett's initiatives was to extend an invitation to Catholic, Protestant and Jewish leaders in April 1937 to meet with him at the Rhode Island College of Education to discuss a possible plan for religious instruction in the public schools of the state. Dr. Rockett first discussed the question in a radio address delivered on November 24, 1936 in regard to the program of the Rhode Island Congress of Parents and Teachers. In that address he raised the possibility of introducing religious instruction into the public schools as part of the schools program.[110]

Dr. Rockett issued his invitation to the clergy of the state to meet to discuss a possible plan of religious instruction in the schools of the state the day after Rev. Charles H. Temple, chairman of the Department of Religious Education of the Rhode Island Council of Churches, and Fr. Thomas V. Cassidy held an informal meeting on the subject on Thursday, April 29, 1937. Dr. Rockett described himself as "a firm believer in religious education as furnishing the fundamental principles upon which all moral education and good citizenship may be placed." Fr. John J. Dillon, O.P., president of Providence College, in an address to the graduating seniors of the Rhode Island College of Education on May 13, 1937, applauded Dr. Rockett's initiative in seeking to include instruction in dogmatic religion within the public school curriculum. In the course of his address, Fr. Dillon criticized the "Godless education" offered in the public schools, which sought to teach goodness and discipline without any grounding in religion. He offered thanks to God that "Rhode Island [was] waking up to the need of introducing religious instruction in public schools."[111]

Dr. Rockett's advocacy of religious instruction in the public schools did not go unchallenged. In his Memorial Day sermon, Rev. A. Mason Brown, pastor of the First Presbyterian Church, Woonsocket, challenged the wisdom of Dr. Rockett's proposal. In words that revealed both his bias and his patriotism, Rev. Mason held that the problem of religious education "will not be solved by introducing dogmatic religious instruction, founded often on tradition and superstition, into State-supported and against the constitution. Rather, he endorsed the suggestion previously advanced by other

---

[109] *Providence Journal,* January 8, 16, 1930; *Providence Visitor,* August 15, 1935.
[110] *Providence* Journal, May 1, 1937; Woonsocket *Call,* May 15, 1937.
[111] *Providence Journal,* May 1, 14, 31; June 5, 1937. In an address to the Westerly High School graduates at their baccalaureate exercises, Rev. G. Edgar Tobin, rector of Christ Episcopal Church, Westerly, also praised the idea of religious instruction in the public schools. Cf. *Providence Journal,* June 21, 1937.

Woonsocket pastors, that Woonsocket students be released from school in order to study religion at their respective churches.[112]

Because some of the Protestant clergy, like Rev. Brown, were opposed to the idea of religion classes in the public school, Dr. Rockett sought to have the various denominations first work out a consensus among themselves as to the time, the place, the method and the teacher of religion courses that he proposed to add to the state's public school curriculum. However, Fr. Cassidy and Fr. Cornelius Holland, the erudite pastor of St. Charles, Woonsocket, pressed on before such a consensus was in place. In June 1937, they sought to convince the Woonsocket School Committee to introduce a program wherein the students in the Woonsocket school system could elect to take courses offered by Protestant, Catholic and Jewish teachers within the structure of their regular school day and, more importantly, in the public school classrooms. In a speech delivered before a gathering of alumnae and seniors at St. Xavier's Academy on Sunday, June 6, Fr. Cassidy argued for holding the religion classes in the public school building on the grounds that such an arrangement would respect the rights of parents "who pay for the building" and the practicality of "associating religion with other school subjects and in making it a part of life.[113]

Frs. Cassidy and Holland's Woonsocket proposal was immediately attacked by Rev. E. Dean Ellenwood, pastor of the First Universalist Church in Woonsocket on June 20, 1937, who assailed the teaching of "sectarian religion" to school children as a menace to American democracy. In the second of his sermons on the subject, Rev. Ellenwood held that the "segregation of the representatives of the various sects into separate rooms of the public school buildings for such instruction," as envisioned in the plan offered by the Woonsocket clergy, "condemns itself as utterly out of harmony with our American system of public education, if not positively inimical to the very spirit of democracy itself." On the following Sunday, Fr. Cornelius J. Holland responded to Rev. Ellenwood's criticism from his pulpit. In his sermon, Fr. Holland, as reported by the *Providence Journal*, asserted that the suggestion that the Woonsocket plan would menace the ideal of the separation of Church and State was "nothing more than a nightmare" and that there was "no possible likelihood of such an outcome, nor is there any desire on the part of any proponent of the plan for such a consummation." Fr. Holland readily admitted that the proposal was an

---

112 *Woonsocket Call,* June 1, 1937. While greatly diminished, anti-Catholic prejudice in society and in the public school system continued to exist. What was different in the 1930's was that the number of Catholics and their political influence was such that even a causal remark delivered in a public forum by an educator that was deemed prejudicial towards Catholics could lead, as it did in the case of Harry A. Jager, principal of Hope High School in Providence, in the fall of 1936, to disciplinary action being taken against that educator. While Catholics applauded Mr. Jager's demotion from principal to teacher, various Protestant congregations protested. Mr. Jager sent a letter of apology to Bishop Keough and had a similar letter published in the *Providence Visitor*. Cf. *Providence Visitor*, October 22, 29; November 5, 12, 1936; January 7, 1937; *Providence Journal*, November 10, 16; December 14; January 8, 1937.
113 *Woonsocket Call,* Providence *Journal*, June 7, 1937.

innovation and its results unpredictable, but asked that it be given a trial in order that representatives of all religion may be able to unite "against the things that all commonly condemn and dread, namely the devastating effects of a refined but deadly paganism and the threatened dangers of an atheistic communism."[114]

In the face of the publicly expressed opposition of some of the Woonsocket clergy to the idea and the unresolved question of the constitutionality of the idea of dogmatic religious instruction as part of the public school curriculum, Woonsocket Superintendent of Schools Leon M. Farrin and the Woonsocket School Committee did not pursue the idea. Fr. Cassidy did not let go of the idea readily. In an address at Cumberland's Alhambra Isabella Silver Anniversary banquet, Fr. Cassidy criticized those, principally the clergy, who had turned down the proposal to institute a program of religious training in the public schools of Rhode Island and dismissed the charge that the church ultimately would dominate the state if religion was taught in the public schools as a "smokescreen." He charged that the plan was stalemated "simply because of the narrowness, the short vision, the intolerance of those—principally clergymen—who talk much about the need of religion in education and then throw a smoke-screen of keeping the church and state apart."[115]

Superintendent Farrin was not unsympathetic to the idea of introducing religion into the curriculum of the Woonsocket Schools. After considering various ideas, he wrote to Dr. Rockett on February 14, 1940 in order to get his reaction to a plan he had formulated but not yet fine-tuned. After reading an article in the *Journal* of the National Education Association regarding a recently adopted religious education plan in Pittsburgh, and taking into consideration the release time plan in operation in East Greenwich and the objections raised in Woonsocket to Fr. Cassidy's plan for religious instruction within the public school building, Mr. Farrin proposed releasing the Woonsocket grammar and high school students for a period of time within the school day so that those who wished to, could go to places designated by their respective parishes or synagogues for religious education classes. The novel part of Mr. Farrin's plan was that the students in the elementary and junior high classes would receive a mark, furnished by the church or synagogue, on their report cards, and the high school students would be given credit for the course they took.[116]

Mr. Farrin sent Bishop Keough a copy of his letter to Dr. Rockett. On February 16, two days later, Farrin wrote to Fr. Cassidy to ask if he and Fr. Holland would wish to get together a group of the Catholic priests in

[114] Ibid., June 21, 28, 1937; January 15, 1940; *Providence Visitor*, July 1, 1937. In March 1948, in the Champaign, Illinois case, brought by Mrs. Vashti McCollum, the rationalist or atheist mother of a student in Champaign schools against the Champaign School Board, ruled 8 to 1 that the holding of religions education classes in the public school during school hours was unconstitutional. Cf. *Providence Visitor*, September 20, 1945; March 11, 1948.
[115] *Providence Visitor*, January 15, 1940.
[116] Farrin to Rockett, February 14, 1940, PChA.

Woonsocket to give him an opportunity to explain his plan and to give them an opportunity for offering suggestions. He extended a similar invitation to French-speaking Catholic clergy in the city. Several weeks later, Mr. Farrin presented his idea before a community gathering at the annual meeting of the Woonsocket Y.M.C.A. In his talk, he stressed the fact that his proposed plan would work only if it received the co-operation of the various religious groups of the city.[117]

On Friday, March 29, Mr. Ferrin discussed his idea with the members of the congregation of B'nai Israel Synagogue and on Tuesday, April 2, he met with the Protestant ministers of Woonsocket in the First Universalist church to do the same. Many Protestants ministers and Jewish rabbis shared the concerns of the Catholic clergy that the lack of religion in the country's public schools was creating a moral vacuum and contributing to the increase of crime. On Thursday, April 11, Farrin held the last of his series of meetings with Woonsocket's Catholic clergy at the School Administration Building on North Main Street. The priests who attended agreed to support the plan as had the Jewish and Protestants leaders. A representative from each of the religious groups then met with Mr. Ferrin to work out the final plans for introduction of the religious training system at the beginning of school in September 1941. The Woonsocket School Committee formally adopted the plan at its meeting on May 8, 1940. Under the plan, students in the grammar and junior high grades were released on Mondays to attend classes in the various Catholic and Protestant churches of the city. Not all the Protestant churches elected to offer classes, but those that did welcomed all children, regardless of whether their parents were members of the congregation of that church or not. High school students were released on Tuesday afternoons. The Protestant junior and high schools students went to the Y.M.C.A. building on Federal Street for their classes. The implementation of the program was not without some problems, but in the main most were satisfied with it.[118]

The Confraternity of Christian Doctrine

From the earliest days of Catholicism in Rhode Island, the pastors of the diocese recognized that the teaching of religion to the young was one of their most important responsibilities. In the larger of the parishes, such as the cathedral parish, the rectors of the cathedral, as did pastors elsewhere, organized a branch of the Confraternity of Christian Doctrine to run the cathedral's Sunday School. When he came to the diocese, Bishop

---

[117] Ferrin to Cassidy, February 16, 1940; Ferrin to Rev. J. M. L. Giroux, February 21, 1940; *Providence Journal*, March 31, 1940.

[118] *Providence Journal*, March 31; April 12; May 9, 1940; September 22, 1941; June 8, 1942. For insight into mindset of the community in general over the question of religion and the schools, see the report of the seminar held at the State Congress of Parents and Teachers in Pawtucket's senior high schools given in the *Providence Journal*, October 9, 1934.

Keough brought with him a personal concern for the religious welfare of youth. He was well aware that many young people lacked religious and moral training, especially if they were public school students. While he continued to stress the importance of parochial schools as a vital element in the Church's efforts aimed at sharing the faith with the next generation, he also recognized that the expansion of the parochial school system in the diocese required greater resources than were immediately available. His initiative in 1935 in appointing Fr. William Delaney diocesan head of the Catholic Youth Organization was one aspect of his concern for the welfare of the youth of his diocese. A second aspect was the strengthening of the religious education programs aimed at young people who were not enrolled in a Catholic school. With the ultimate aim of establishing a unit of the Confraternity of Christian Doctrine in every parish, in late 1936, Bishop Keough appointed Fr. Cornelius B. Collins the diocese's first Diocesan Director of Catechetics.[119]

Fr. Collins would prove an excellent choice. After he finished his college course at St. Francis Xavier University, Antigonish, Nova Scotia, he enrolled at the Provincial Normal College at Truro, Nova Scotia, where he received a Superior First Class License. He then made the decision to study for the priesthood, and, after being accepted as a student for the diocese, he went to Montreal for an additional year of philosophy and then to St. Paul's Seminary, St. Paul, Minnesota for theology. In 1920, Bishop Hickey sent him to the newly re-opened American College in Louvain for his last two years of theology. Fr. Collins was ordained in Louvain in June 1922. On his return to the United States, he was appointed Dean of Religion and Latin at LaSalle Academy while also serving as an assistant at St. John's, Providence. In 1931, Bishop Hickey consented to the request of the Archbishop of Winnipeg that he allow Fr. Collins to take charge as president of the archbishop's newly founded diocesan college. Financial difficulties forced the archbishop to offer his college to the Jesuits and Fr. Collins returned to the diocese in 1933 and was appointed an assistant at St. Joseph's, Providence. In September 1935, he became Spiritual Director at LaSalle Academy and assistant at St. Thomas Parish, Providence.[120]

Just as he was aware of the work of Bishop Shiel in organizing a CYO program in Chicago, Bishop Keough was also aware of the work of Bishop Edwin V. O'Hara of Great Falls, Montana, who in 1933 was a leading figure in the movement to establish a national headquarters for the catechetical movement in the United States at the Catholic University of America. In 1934, Bishop O'Hara was named chairman of the newly formed Episcopal Committee of the Confraternity of Christian Doctrine. In that same year, at Bishop O'Hara's invitation, fifteen diocesan directors of CCD met for the first time. In the following year, a National CCD

---

[119] Other than a mention that Fr. Collins was appointed Diocesan Director in 1936 in later articles regarding the program, there was no publicity given to Fr. Collins' appointment when it was made.

[120] Diocesan Personal Records.

Center was set up as part of the National Catholic Welfare Conference. In January 1936, Bishop Keough was named assistant episcopal chairman of the NCWC Education Department and in that same month he appointed his own diocesan CCD director.[121]

Fr. Collins' first initiative was to offer a training course for approximately two hundred public school teachers, which was designed to provide the teachers with certification for catechetical work in the diocese. He himself taught a course in apologetics while Fr. Thomas Cassidy, the Diocesan Visitor of Catholic Schools, taught a course in catechetical methods. The first half of the program ended on December 16. The second half, which included a course on liturgy, was scheduled for March of the following year.[122]

After this modest beginning, Fr. Collins began organizing a series of four regional meetings in Providence, Pawtucket, Woonsocket and Newport beginning on Tuesday, February 23, 1936, in order to outline his plans for extending the work of the Confraternity of Christian Doctrine in the diocese. The meetings were intended for the priests of the area and the representatives of the religious teachings orders and of various Catholic lay groups. The main speaker at the each of the meetings was Miss Miriam Marks, the national secretary of the Confraternity. As presented by Miss Marks, the CCD program aimed first at the recruiting and training of Catholic public school teachers and graduates of Catholic high schools, who would assist the pastors in teaching catechism to the children of grammar and junior high age who attended public school in the parishes. This was something that was already being done in Providence. In the parishes that did have parochial schools, religious sisters would often volunteer to help with this work. In addition to the catechism classes, the second phase of the program introduced by Fr. Collins and Miss Marks aimed at forming study clubs for Catholic students attending public high schools and for adults. The program's third phase was the conducting of religious vacation schools where they were deemed necessary, again something that was already being done. The teachers in this last program were public school teachers, seminarians and other members of the laity, who were paid by the diocese for their services. Together, they constituted the majority of those who belonged to the Confraternity of Christian Doctrine prior to Fr. Collins' expansion of the program. The fourth phase of the program was the lay home visitors. The visitors were to be recruited by the pastors of the various parishes. The work of the home visitors was to visit the parents who neglected to send their children to religious instructions or who had fallen away from the Church completely and to attempt to persuade them to resume the practice of their faith and of their responsibilities. As the work envisioned by Fr. Collins was too great for one man to oversee and assist, Bishop Keough appointed a group of young

[121] "The Confraternity of Christian Doctrine," in *Encyclopedia of American Catholic History*, 366–67; *Providence Visitor*, January 30, 1936.
[122] *Providence Visitor*, December 23, 1936.

"priest visitors" whose function was to assist the pastors in their designated regions in the forming of parish units of the Confraternity. In several of the regions, French-speaking or Italian-speaking priests were specifically appointed to assist pastors of the French and Italian parishes. In several of the regions, parts of the meetings would be conducted in both English and French. On the Monday prior to the regional meetings, Fr. Collins met with the priest visitors at the St. Vincent de Paul Infant Home to discuss details of the work. In addition to the assistance provided by the priests, Fr. Collins also recruited the help of a number of lay women. Fr. Collins named Miss Julia M. Sheridan as executive secretary. In addition to Miss Sheridan, Miss Margaret Mahoney was the lay assistant in charge of study clubs; Miss Mary Gormley assisted with the teachers; Miss Mary Farrell with teacher helpers; and Miss Ethelyn Henry with home visitors.[123]

During the first years of Fr. Collins' tenure as CCD director, he placed particular emphasis on the organization of the study clubs for high school students and adults as did Third National Catechetical Congress of the Confraternity of Christian Doctrine that was held in St. Louis in October 1937. In that same month, in the Diocese of Providence, forty-eight parishes, which had organized clubs, began meeting. Initially, Fr. Collins organized an eight-week program that focused on a study of "The Ceremonies of the Mass," a booklet specially prepared for club use by the national CCD organization. The booklet was supplemented with material published in the *Providence Visitor*. Private homes, parish halls and club rooms were all used for the weekly gatherings. Each club was to have a spiritual director in addition to a leader and a secretary chosen from the group. Meetings began and ended with prayer and lasted for about a hour and a half. While most parishes offered only the eight week program, the cathedral parish, where Fr. John F. O'Neil was spiritual director of the clubs, was the first to plan to continue the weekly meetings of the clubs throughout the school year. In order to promote the work, the national office developed additional pamphlets to serve as the focus of the clubs' discussion. In 1938, a new dimension was added to the program when a number of Mothers' Clubs were formed to discuss Pope Pius XI's 1930 encyclical on Christian Marriage, *Casti connubii*. As in all the programs introduced in the diocese, not all the pastors of the diocese shared Bishop Keough's perception of the pressing necessity of improving the religious education programs they offered. However, a substantial majority did.[124]

Bishop Keough gave evidence of his own interest in the catechetical movement by personally leading delegations of priests and laity to the National Congresses of the Confraternity held in Hartford in October 1938, in Cincinnati in November 1939 and in Los Angeles in October 1940. At the Los Angeles congress, Bishop Keough addressed the General Session for Teaching Sisters and the Laity on "The Growth of the Confraternity

---

[123] *Providence Visitor*, February 11, 18, 25, 1937; *News-Tribune*, February 19, 1937.
[124] *Providence Visitor*, October 14, 21, 28; November 23; December 16, 1937; December 13, 1938.

Catholicism in Rhode Island

of Christian Doctrine in the Diocese of Providence." Fr. Collins and other Providence priests also were among the speakers at various sessions of the three congresses. Fr. Collins' work as diocesan director brought him to the attention of Bishop O'Hara and the other bishops on the Episcopal Committee on the Confraternity. In October, Bishop Keough announced that he had given Fr. Collins leave to serve as Director of the National Center in Washington. To replace him as diocesan director, Bishop Keough, in March 1941, named Fr. John H. Flanagan, an assistant pastor at St. Edward's, Pawtucket, who previous to his appointment, had been a member of the faculty of St. Raphael's Academy.[125]

Diocesan Seminary

While there had been a shortage of priests to serve the parishes of the Providence diocese after the Diocese of Fall River was created in 1904, that shortage had been quickly made up. Even in the face of the shortage of priests caused by the division, Bishop Harkins continued to maintain high standards for adoption of those who wished to study for the priesthood. These standards remained in place under Bishops Hickey and Keough, in part, because the number of men ordained each year was sufficient to meet the needs of the diocese, and in part, because lowering them created problems that the bishops wanted to avoid. Over the years, many young priests ordained for Providence of Providence, were loaned for a time to other dioceses, such as the Diocese of Portland, Maine, until places opened up for them in their own diocese. However times were changing, and, in order to insure an adequate number of priests, Bishop Keough began making plans early in his administration for the establishment of a minor seminary in the diocese for young men in their high school and early college years, who aspired to the priesthood.

In the sixteenth century, the reform-minded bishops who met in the Council of Trent had made the renewal of priestly formation one of the centerpieces of the council's reforms. All bishops were urged to establish seminaries in their dioceses to foster and direct vocations to the priesthood. As seminarians studying for Bishop Keough's native diocese of Hartford profited from their exposure to the wider world outside of New England or, at least, outside of Connecticut, so too did seminarians for the Diocese of Providence. While Bishop Keough realized that a major seminary in the diocese would mean a further duplication of Church resources, a minor seminary, such as he envisioned, would serve to nurture priestly vocations and provide the rigorous and intense classical training that would prepare candidates for further studies in philosophy and theology in a major seminary. In addition, Bishop Keough was aware that over the last few years

---

[125] Ibid., September 23, 1938; November 9, 1939; October 3, 1940; March 27, 1941.

there had been a general decline in vocations in the country as a whole, in part because of economic and social disruptions caused by the Depression. He believed that a minor seminary would serve to prevent Providence from experiencing a decline in the number of priests who served the diocese.[126]

Bishop Keough himself apparently left no record of his thinking on the subject of a seminary. The process for creating a seminary might well have begun when Edward B. Aldrich offered to sell his estate, Indian Oaks, in the Warwick Neck section of Warwick, to the bishop in the fall of 1934. After the death of his father, Senator Nelson W. Aldrich, in 1915, Indian Oaks had been placed in trust for the lifetime of the senator's wife. When Mrs. Aldrich died in 1917, the trust ended and the nearly 200 acre estate was divided among Aldrich's seven living children. In 1927–28, six of the seven conveyed their interests in the estate to the seventh, Edward Aldrich. Edward became the sole owner of some ninety-six acres, which included a manor house, a casino or boat house and several other service buildings. Before the division of the estate, the Aldrich heirs had removed most of the costly furnishings, an action which reduced the value of the estate's intangible property from the $1,000,000, at which it had originally been valued, to $200,000. In 1938, the town of Warwick assessed the land and buildings of Edward Aldrich's part of the estate at $272,040, with a resultant tax of $5984.84, a sum which, according to local lore, Aldrich felt to be excessive. In addition, the passage of the Revenue Act of 1935 meant that wealthy families were faced with significantly higher personal income taxes. This new tax, together with the taxes on the property, which Mr. Aldrich's family used only occasionally, when added to the expense involved in maintaining the property were probably factors in his entertaining an offer by Roger Williams University to buy the estate. Roger Williams, which recently had been granted a state charter, made an offer to purchase the estate for educational purposes in 1932. When the principals in the newly chartered university failed to raise their offer to what Mr. Aldrich considered a sufficient one, a Providence real estate man, Richard Hurley, contacted Bishop Keough to inform him of Mr. Aldrich's interest in selling his property.[127]

When he was first approached by Mr. Hurley in November 1934, Bishop Keough did not express any immediate interest for he did not see how the property met any of the diocese's needs. Nevertheless, he promised to look over the main house, a promise he fulfilled when he met with Mr. Hurley at Indian Oaks on March 18, 1935. Keough's first thought was that the estate might be used as the site of a new diocesan orphanage

---

[126] John F. Cox, Draft copy of a "History of the Seminary of Our Lady of Providence," PChA; Interview with Msgr. Cox, July 12, 2004.

[127] *Providence Journal,* June 13, 14, 1939; *Providence Visitor,* June 15, 1939; *Warwick Beacon,* January 31, 1984. Local folklore in Warwick held that part of Mr. Aldrich's motivation in selling the property to a tax-exempt entity such as the Diocesan Seminary was that he was angry with the town for the high evaluations it had placed on the property.

that he planned to build to replace both the St. Aloysius Home in Providence and the Mercy Home and School in Newport. On October 8, 1935, the bishop raised the prospect of purchasing the property at a meeting of the diocesan consultors and outlined the results of a recent survey of the condition and needs of the charitable institutions in the diocese. The consultors accepted the bishop's invitation to visit the estate in a body the following week.[128]

Aldrich and the bishop discussed the possible sale of the estate again at the beginning of 1936, but Bishop Keough was not particularly anxious to conclude a deal. When the diocesan consultors again met with the bishop on March 24, 1936, he solicited their views on acquiring the property as the site for a new orphanage. There was not a great deal of enthusiasm for the idea and, in the end, they unanimously approved the bishop's suggestion that "in view of the special circumstances" it would be better to look around for some other available property. The bishop was not the only possible buyer of the property. At about this time, Mr. Aldrich also held discussions with officers of the U.S. Navy who were looking for a place to base navy seaplanes that could not be accommodated at Newport.[129]

When the consultors met again on April 13, 1937, Bishop Keough informed them that he had decided to build the new orphanage that he was considering at Villa St. Rose in Greenville, but that he had obtained from Mr. Aldrich the promise of a five-year option on his Warwick estate. Although the bishop had as yet made no definitive decision as to where he would open a minor seminary, in September 1937, he sent four young priests, Frs. Edmund J. Brock, John J. Cox, Henry J. Crepeau, and Arthur A. Sullivan, who were to become the core group of a prospective seminary faculty, to the Catholic University of America to pursue doctoral degrees in philosophy, education and social science. In doing so, Bishop Keough was continuing a tradition of sending priests to Washington for graduate degrees that had begun with Bishop Harkins. In giving these priests their assignments, he said nothing publicly about his future plans.[130]

As a first step toward the formal organization of a diocesan seminary, Bishop Keough engaged Bishop Hickey's nephew, David B. Lovell, Jr., to draw up a charter of incorporation for submission to the Rhode Island General Assembly during its January 1938 term. The measure passed both houses of the legislature by unanimous votes and was quickly signed by the governor in April. Later that year, on September 21, 1938, an extraordinarily fast moving hurricane hit Rhode Island. The wind and storm surge did considerable damage to the Aldrich estate. The boat house and

---

[128] Hurley to Keough, November 27, 1934; March 12, 15, 1935; Minutes of the Board of Consultors, October 8, 1935, PChA.

[129] Hurley to Keough, February 27, 1936; Keough to Hurley, February 28, 1936; Minutes of the Consultors Meeting, March 24, 1936; May 5, 1941. There is no mention in the meeting's minutes as to what the special circumstances were.

[130] John F. Cox, Draft copy of a "History of the Seminary of Our Lady of Providence," PChA; Interview with Msgr. Cox, July 12, 2004.

sea wall were heavily damaged by the storm surge and the strong winds knocked down many of the trees for which the estate was famous and ripped branches from countless others. The winds also tore many of the slates from the roof of the manor house. Since the estate was still in Mr. Aldrich's hands, repairs were his responsibility. He gave his efforts primarily to repairing the boat house and the sea wall. In addition to the property damage done by the hurricane, Mr. Aldrich also had to deal with various episodes of vandalism which occurred, in part because his family was not in continuous residence on the property.[131]

Mr. Aldrich and Bishop Keough finally came to an agreement in regard to the estate in June 1939. With the time for tax assessment approaching on June 15, Mr. Aldrich was anxious to dispose of his property without having to pay another year's real estate taxes. Although Mr. Aldrich was asking $75,000 for the property, Bishop Keough, through Mr. Hurley, the real estate agent, suggested that $50,000 would simplify the "financing" of the property, but Mr. Aldrich held firm to his price of $75,000 for seventy-five acres with all the buildings on them. Under the terms of the agreement worked out with Bishop Keough, Mr. Aldrich was granted the right to the continued use of the boat house during the summer months for as long as he wished. In return, he agreed to compensate the diocese for any taxes incurred by the diocese as a result of the agreement. In addition, the sale was subject to the lease Mr. Aldrich had given to B. Thomas Potter of the "Caretakers Cottage," which was to run until May 31, 1940. Two days after news of the sale of the property appeared in the *Providence Journal*, a front page article in the *Providence Visitor* disclosed that Bishop Keough had purchased the estate as the site for his diocesan seminary. Shortly thereafter, Bishop Keough met with the mayor of Warwick, the Warwick town solicitor and the Board of Assessors during which the Warwick officials agreed to recognize the tax exemption of the Roman Catholic Bishop and Bishop Keough agreed to pay a tax on the lease of the boathouse.[132]

While the ninety-nine rooms in the Indian Oaks manor house offered adequate space for use as a seminary, the damage done by the hurricane had to be repaired and certain modifications had to be made before the seminary could open. Bishop Keough engaged John F. Hogan to prepare the plans and specifications for the conversion of the house to its new use and entrusted oversight of the renovations to Fr. Thomas McKitchen, the rector of the cathedral. Among the changes thought necessary was the paving of some of the roads on the estate. The contractor engaged to do the paving was Luigi Vallone. As a personal gift to the seminary, Mr. Vallone, who, with his wife, had previously donated the main altar of St. Mary's, Cranston, had a statue of Our Lady carved out of Westerly granite, which he set up on a pedestal in the circle in front of the manor house

---

[131] *Providence Journal*, April 20, 1938; *Warwick Beacon*, January 31, 1984.

[132] Hurley to Keough, June 2, 1939; Edward V. Doyle to Roman Catholic Bishop of Providence, June 21, 1939, PChA; *Providence Journal*, June 13, 15, 16, 1939.

in September 1940. He also planted a ring of flowers and flowering plants around the statue, which he continued to care for over many years.[133]

The conversion of the manor house was well underway, when, at the beginning of 1941, rumors reached Bishop Keough that the Navy was interested in the Warwick Neck property as part of its coastal fortifications. As a result, on March 24, 1941, Bishop Keough wrote to Senator Theodore Francis Green, asking him to inquire as to whether or not the Navy was indeed looking into acquiring the property. Senator Green had previously suggested to the government that the property would make a wonderful site for a naval hospital. While the bishop was not unwilling to have the Navy take over the property, he did not wish to put any more money into Indian Oaks if the diocese would not be able to occupy it. On receiving the bishop's letter, the senator forwarded it to Frank Knox, the Secretary of the Navy. On April 3, 1941, one of Knox's aides wrote to Senator Green that the Navy Department had no interest in the property and noted that he was forwarding the senator's letter to the Commandant of the First Naval District in Boston to inquire if he had any plans concerning the property. On May 5, 1941, Bishop Keough reported to the consultors on the progress of preparing Indian Oaks for its new use. He made mention of his correspondence with the Navy, but noted he was prepared to open the seminary in September. The bishop added he was determined to go ahead with opening the seminary, which involved the loss to parish ministry of the priests assigned to the faculty, even though eight priests had already left the diocese for military service. The new seminary was to be call Our Lady of Providence.[134]

As it was customary in most seminaries of the time to entrust the running of the domestic department of a seminary to a religious order, Bishop Keough invited the Carmelite Sisters for the Aged and Infirm to take on the care of the faculty and seminarians of his new seminary. This particular branch of Carmelites had only been founded in 1929 in New York by Cardinal Patrick J. Hayes and Sr. M. Angelina Teresa. The six women who joined with Mother M. Angelina to establish the new order had wished to create a new type of home for the aged where both those with means and those without were welcomed as guests in a family-like atmosphere. In the Carmelite tradition, the Carmelite Sisters for the Aged and Infirm regarded prayer for priests and those preparing for the priesthood as part of their vocation. While care for the aged was the particular charism of their order, to the sisters' mind, serving priests in rectories and seminaries was but an extension of this apostolate of prayer.[135]

The cofounder and head to the order, Mother M. Angelina, came up

[133] John F. Hogan, Billing statement, September 20, 1940, PChA; *Providence Visitor*, September 19, 1940; John F. Cox, "History of the Seminary of Our Lady of Providence."
[134] Keough to Green, March 24, 1941; Green to Keough, March 27; April 7, 1941; Keough to Green, April 9, 1941; Board of Consultors Minutes, May 5, 1941, PChA.
[135] *Providence Visitor*, January 15, 1948.

to Providence at the end of March 1941 to meet with Bishop Keough and to see the new seminary. The order had been blessed with numerous vocations and was anxious to have places for the sisters. At the beginning of August, Mother M. Angelina met with Bishop Keough again to finalize arrangements and returned to Rhode Island a few weeks later with a group of sisters to make preparations for the reception of the community that would live at the seminary.[136]

As a way of introducing the priests of the diocese to the new seminary, Bishop Keough, on June 10, the day on which he was to celebrate his twenty-fifth anniversary of his ordination to the priesthood, invited the priests of the diocese to dinner at Warwick Neck following a mass held in the cathedral. Several weeks later, on August 7, 1941, the *Providence Visitor* carried an announcement that Bishop Keough had set Monday, September 15, as opening day for the new minor seminary. As initially conceived, Our Lady of Providence Seminary would offer four years of high school training and the first two years of college. According to the announcement, those interested in applying for admission needed to send their application to the Chancery Office before September 1.[137]

Since Bishop Keough had earlier accepted an invitation to be present at the ordination of Bishop James J. Sweeney in Honolulu, Hawaii, at the time of the seminary's planned opening, he arranged to offer the first mass on Wednesday, August 13, in the manor house's former ballroom, which had been converted into the seminary's chapel. Present for the mass were the new community of Carmelite Sisters and several lay persons, among them, Mrs. Percival de St. Aubin, who had donated the main altar in the chapel in honor of her late husband, and Mr. and Mrs. Luigi Vallone, who had donated the statue of Our Lady of Providence. Following the mass, the bishop blessed both the main house and the statue of Our Lady of Providence in the front of the building. August 14 also saw the beginning of the first of the priests' retreats that were held at the new seminary for the first time.[138]

Following the blessing of the seminary, the *Visitor* printed the list of the priests Bishop Keough had chosen for the seminary faculty. As rector, Bishop Keough appointed Fr. Russell J. McVinney. Following his ordination in Louvain, Belgium, on July 13, 1924, Fr. McVinney filled in for the priests assigned to the cathedral while they took vacation. When the assistant at St. Patrick's, Harrisville, became ill, Bishop Keough sent Fr. McVinney there as his replacement. In 1929, the bishop transferred him to St. Edward's, Pawtucket, where he was a part-time assistant and teacher at the new St. Raphael's Academy. In 1935, McVinney went to the

---

[136] Mother M. Angelina to Keough, April 2, 1941; Keough to Mother M. Colette, May 9, 1941; Mother M. Angelina to Keough, August 6, 1941; Keough to Cardinal Francis J. Spellman, August 12, 1941, PChA.
[137] *Providence Visitor*, June 12; August 7, 1941.
[138] Cox, "History of the Seminary of Our Lady of Providence."

University of Notre Dame for a master's degree in journalism, and on his return to Providence, in July 1936, Bishop Keough appointed him an assistant editor at the *Providence Visitor* and a part-time assistant at the cathedral. During his time at the cathedral, Bishop Keough came to appreciate Fr. McVinney's talent for leadership and administration. As a priest who was well known in the diocese, many thought that Fr. McVinney was the natural choice to be rector.[139]

Since Bishop Keough had already sent Frs. Brock, Cox, Crepeau and Sullivan for graduate studies, they were available to serve on the faculty of the seminary. Fr. McVinney's first responsibility as rector was to interview various priests to fill out the faculty. In addition to the four already chosen, Frs. Anthony Dimeo, Norman Leboeuf, Joseph Lamb, and Christian Guilbault were appointed to the faculty prior to its opening. Fr. McVinney called his new faculty together for a meeting for the first time in the cathedral rectory on September 14, 1941. At that time the new professors received their class assignments and were given their special duties in the seminary. Fr. Sullivan was appointed Dean of Studies; Fr. Brock was made Spiritual Director; Fr. Guilbault was given charge of Discipline; and Fr. Lebeouf of the seminary liturgy.[140] Our Lady of Providence Seminary officially opened on September 15, 1941. The main ceremony of the day was a mass in the new chapel attended by the faculty, the seminary's first students, their families, and visiting clergy. Msgr. Peter E. Blessing, the diocese's vicar general, presided at the mass and read a telegram from Bishop Keough expressing his congratulations, good wishes and giving his blessing. Msgr. Blessing also addressed the faculty, students and guests. After the mass the students were free to tour the manor and the grounds. The seminary began with thirty-two students spread over four years of high school and the first year of college. During this first year, several of the students were day students. Many of them took a bus from Providence as far as the bus turn-around on Warwick Neck Avenue. They then walked up the hill to the seminary. At night, they reversed their route. At the close of the seminary's first year, the practice of allowing some students to commute to class was discontinued.[141]

While, in general, the seminary's first few months went well for both the students and faculty, experience showed that some adjustments had to be made to the schedule and living situation. On October 17, Augustus Menders arrived from six years of study in the Azores to become the seminary's first prefect. His ordination to the diaconate on March 30, 1942, was the occasion for Bishop Keough's first official visit to the seminary.[142]

---

[139] "As We Remember Him: The Life and Work of Bishop McVinney," (State Council of the Knights of Columbus, 1971).

[140] Cox, "History of the Seminary of Our Lady of Providence."

[141] *Providence Visitor*, September 18, 1941. Various sources record different numbers as to the number of students in the first year. The number given here is that found in Msgr. Cox's history of the seminary.

[142] Cox, "History of the Seminary of Our Lady of Providence."

Although relatively isolated from the larger world by the seminary schedule and discipline, world events managed to intrude into the life of study and prayer. At first, the threat of war that promoted an expansion of the American military touched only the faculty. Since only two priests at most were needed for Sunday mass at the seminary itself, those faculty members who were not scheduled to say mass helped out in various parishes. On November 30, priests from the faculty began taking turns saying mass at the new naval air station at Quonset Point until such time as the Navy assigned a Catholic chaplain to the base. In September 1942, the faculty took on a similar commitment when they began saying mass at the Hillsgrove Air Base where the Army was training fighter pilots. America's entrance into the Second World War after the attack on Pearl Harbor would make the challenge of operating the seminary even more challenging for its rector and faculty.[143]

The influence of the war on the seminary was felt only gradually. The timing of the legislature's grant of a charter for the seminary meant that the new seminary fell within the guidelines established by the National Military Service Commission, which ran the draft, as a legitimate ecclesiastical school whose students were exempt from the draft. On April 26, 1942, Rhode Island was declared a military area and its citizens were ordered to dim all lights. Although the seminary lay a considerable distance from the ocean, the fear of aiding submarines by showing any lights forced the seminary staff to place black out curtains on all the windows facing the bay. After the government instituted the rationing of strategic materials and food at the beginning of the war, Fr. McVinney's task of feeding the community became more complicated. The bishop collected ration cards from the seminarians and took them to the Weboysset Food Market in Providence, where the owner, a devout Catholic, helped where he could. Throughout the war the seminarians and faculty did not experience any severe privations.[144]

Because of the food shortage, the faculty and students began a victory garden on the land that Sen. Aldrich had farmed and they had cleared of brush to use as athletic fields. Beginning May 7, 1943, Fr. McVinney declared a week's "farm holiday" so that the faculty and students could prepare the field for the planting of potatoes, corn and other vegetables. In order to do the actual plowing, Fr. McVinney asked Bob Chilton, the man he had hired to do maintenance work, to purchase a horse because gas was difficult to obtain for tractors. The first day the horse was there, the students took the horse down near the bay where they allowed the horse to eat some green apples. The next day was warm and, after working in the hot sun, the horse collapsed and died. The exact cause of death was

---

[143] Ibid.
[144] Ibid.; Interview with Msgr. Arthur A. Sullivan, July 26, 1994.

never determined. During the summer of 1943, four students stayed at the seminary in order to work the farm.[145]

It was during these early years that Fr. Laboeuf persuaded Fr. McVinney to purchase a lamb. Laboeuf was very much interested in the efforts of the modern liturgical movement to reform and revive the Roman liturgy. The movement had its roots in Europe and in St. Meinrad's Abbey, Collegeville, Minnesota, in the United States. On December 4, 1941, at Laboeuf's urging, Fr. McVinney introduced the "Dialogue Mass," wherein the entire student body, rather than just the altar servers, responded to the celebrant, a practice that initially was to be followed every Tuesday. The dialogue mass was the first of many innovations that Fr. Leboeuf would suggest. In purchasing the lamb, Laboeuf anticipated that the seminarians would raise it until the following spring when it would be slaughtered and served at the main meal following the liturgy of Holy Thursday when lamb was traditionally eaten. While Fr. McVinney agreed to the purchase of the lamb, he and the entire community had second thoughts about the rest of Fr. Laboeuf's proposal and the lamb was given to a local farmer after being at the seminary only a few days.[146]

The seminary began its second year in September 1942 with forty-one students, two deacon prefects, and a new faculty member, Fr. Arthur T. Geoghegan. During the previous December, Fr. Lamb, who had continued as Assistant Director of Catholic Social Services, had left the faculty to take up the position of assistant at St. John's, Providence. Fr. Geoghegan was his replacement. With the progress of the first year college students to second year, the seminary began offering a full, six-year program for the first time. In order to accommodate the larger student body, some rooms on the second floor of the manor house that had originally been used as classrooms became dormitories and new classrooms were created in the basement. June 19, 1943 saw the first six students graduate from the seminary with the completion of their second year of college. The problem of finding space for the increasing number of students continued into the seminary's third year. In September 1943, the number of students increased to fifty, a twenty-five percent increase over the year before. To accommodate the additional students, Fr. McVinney had the former superintendent's house near the farm prepared for use as a dormitory by the first and second year high school students. The farm and superintendent's house were enclosed with a stone wall similar to that which bordered the main part of the estate. Consequently, the new dormitory was called St. Paul's after the basilica near Rome, which was "outside the walls" of ancient Christian Rome.[147]

The biggest change that occurred during the first years of Our Lady

[145] Ibid.
[146] Ibid. Cf. Keith F. Pecklers, *The Unread Vision: The Liturgical Movement in the United States of America: 1926–1955* (Collegeville, Minnesota: The Liturgical Press, 1998).
[147] Ibid.; *Providence Visitor*, September 10, 1942.

of Providence was introduced in July 1944. As a war emergency measure, the bishops who served on the executive committee of the Department of Education of the National Catholic Welfare Conference organized a twelve month "speed-up" of seminary education on both the major and minor levels. In order to replace the increasing number of priests, who had and were volunteering for military service as chaplains, the bishops directed an acceleration of seminary programs. For the faculty and students of Our Lady of Providence, the school year in 1944–45 was divided into four terms. The first began on July 5 and ran to September 20; the second from October 1 to December 20; the third from January 4 to March 20; and the fourth from April 1 to June 10. The work of an entire scholastic year was to be covered in three of the terms. In addition to the need for more priests, the program was initiated because of the difficulties the seminarians, especially the major seminarians, were encountering when they were home on vacation. While the vast majority of the seminarians were as anxious to do what they could to serve their country, the importance of priests as chaplains and as parish priests had prompted the government to exempt seminarians from the draft in both the First and Second World Wars. Frequently enough when the seminarians were at home, they were subject to ridicule and affronts because they were not in the service. The accelerated courses decreased the time the seminarians were exposed to criticism for their choice of vocation. While the acceleration was well intentioned, it took its toll on faculty and seminarians alike. After the war ended in August 1945, the American seminaries, including Our Lady of Providence, returned to their traditional calendars. It was in 1944 also that Fr. McVinney and the faculty decided that the seminary would no longer accept students in the first year of high school. Finding space to accommodate the increasing number of students was one consideration, but the main reason was that the faculty had come to realize that ninth graders were too immature and were better served by finishing the ninth grade in their parish schools.[148]

Providence College

By September 1933, Providence College, which Bishop Harkins had founded, the Dominican Provincial Fr. Raymond Meagher, O.P., had carefully nurtured, and Bishop Hickey had loyally supported, had seen its enrollment increase from 75 freshman in 1919 to 750 students. The onset of the Depression had cut into the number of freshman admitted from 1930 to 1933, but by 1933 the number of incoming freshmen was again rising. Although there would be another dip as a result of the so called "Roosevelt depression" of 1936, the number of freshmen would

---

[148] *Providence Visitor*, May 11, 1944; Interview with Msgr. John Cox, July 12, 2004.

quickly rebound. As early as June 1930, Bishop Hickey spoke of the need
for the college to expand while addressing the college's commencement
exercises. Key to that expansion was the construction of new buildings to
provide the necessary space needed to accommodate the increased number of students and programs. During Bishop Hickey's years, he and Fr.
Lorenzo C. McCarthy, O.P., who served three terms as president of the
college from 1927 to 1936, had a sometimes tense relationship because of
Bishop Hickey's insistence that the college was essentially diocesan in character. After the choice of Fr. Francis Keough as the next Bishop of Providence was announced, Fr. McDermott, O.P., the recently elected Dominican Provincial, was determined to gain recognition that the college was a
Dominican institution, something that could have been done unilaterally
by the Dominican majority on the corporation board if they elected Fr.
McDermott president of the corporation rather than the bishop. On his
part, Fr. McCarthy counseled approaching the matter carefully, for if he
chose, the new bishop, who was reputed to be extremely friendly with the
Jesuits, could invite them to establish a college in the diocese that would be
a competitor to Providence College.[149]

When Fr. McCarthy met with Bishop-elect Keough in Hartford shortly
after his appointment was announced, the two had an amicable conversation. In his report to Fr. McDermott on the meeting, Fr. McCarthy wrote
that the bishop-elect:

> [c]onsented to be present at the Commencement exercises and to be elected president
> of the corporation. In proposing the latter, I told him of the constitution of the Cor-
> poration as being predominantly Dominican from the legal point of view and entirely
> so from the ecclesiastical one.

After Fr. McCarthy urged the advantage of presenting a united front,
Keough responded, "It takes two to make a fight; and I won't be one of
them." By 1936, after three terms as president of the college, Fr. McCarthy
was ready to retire. Although Fr. McDermott chose several times during Fr.
McCarthy's third term as president not to accept his offer of resignation,
he finally agreed to allow McCarthy to resign following the college's graduation in June 1936.[150]

In August 1936, Fr. McDermott announced his choice of the next president of the college, Fr. John J. Dillon, O.P., who was duly confirmed as
president at a corporation meeting in September. Following Fr. Dillon's
confirmation as president, Bishop Keough made a major gesture of his
good will towards the Dominicans when he agreed to turn over to the
college the remaining funds from the 1920 Providence College Drive. Although the money had been invested in securities, which had decreased by

[149] McCaffrey, "The Origins and Early Development of Providence College through 1947," pp. 298–
304; McCarthy to McDermott, April 15, 1934, PCA.
[150] McCarthy to McDermott, May 11, 1934; October 27, 1936, PCA.

more that $20,000 in value, Bishop Keough made up the difference from diocesan funds and presented Fr. Dillon with a check for $127,342.30, which Fr. Dillon then applied to the college's outstanding mortgage obligations.[151]

In the same letter in which he reported to Fr. McDermott that Bishop Keough had turned over to him the remaining monies from the 1920 Providence College Fund Drive, Fr. Dillon also noted that, "Bishop Keough is very favorable towards us. He realizes this is a Dominican institution; he just wants to help us grow not control." Given Bishop Keough's attitude towards the Dominicans and the college, the bishop readily acquiesced in May 1938 to the election of McDermott as president of the corporation. After Fr. McDermott's election, Bishop Keough continued as a member of the college corporation.[152]

The main impact of the change was that any fundraising to finance the physical expansion of the college would primarily be the responsibility of the Dominicans rather than of the diocese. In November 1937, Fr. Dillon announced the beginning of a program of building expansion at the college which looked to the adding of a dormitory, science building, library, chapel and athletic field house. Although the Dominicans took over the task of fund raising, they, like Bishop Harkins and Hickey, turned primarily to the civic and business leaders in Rhode Island for support of their contemplated drive. They began, in November 1937, by recruiting a number of prominent Catholic laymen to serve with four Dominicans as members of a building fund committee. Unlike the diocesan drives, this third fund raising effort on the college's behalf looked forward to enlisting the help of the college's alumni, who had been urging expansion of the college. The drive, with a goal of $350,000, began on Wednesday, February 10 and ran through February 23, when final reports were to be made. Fr. Dillon's hope was that the drive would raise enough money in the two weeks to insure a start of the work on a dormitory. When the final results were totaled in June 1938, the drive had realized approximately $55,000.[153]

Of the five possible choices for a first project funded by the campaign, Fr. Dillon chose to build a dormitory for the increasing number of out of state students who were electing to enroll at the college. Although founded to serve the young men in Rhode Island, by 1938 Providence College's reputation had attracted over a hundred and fifty out of state students who boarded in houses in the neighborhood of the college. These out of state students, concentrated as they were in the vicinity of the college,

[151] Dillon to McDermott, October 27, 1936; McDermott to Keough, November 1936, PChA. There is no record of when Fr. McDermott was elected president of the corporation. He was certainly president by February 1939 as evidenced by his name appearing as such in the *Providence College Bulletin.* Most likely the change was made at the annual corporation meeting in May 1938.
[152] Ibid.
[153] Dillon to McDermott, October 27; McDermott to Keough, November 2, 1936; Dillon to McDermott, June 1938, PCA; *Providence Journal,* November 19, 1937; January 9; February 3, 1938; *Providence Visitor,* December 16, 1937; February 3, 1938.

were seen as important to the development of the spirit of the college. Fr. Dillon broke ground for the new building on Friday, December 14, 1938. The four-story, u-shaped, brick building was designed by Oresto Di Sala, a prominent Rhode Island architect who had designed many important buildings in the state. Besides accommodations for 200 students, it was intended to also house twenty-four members of the faculty. Besides a kitchen, dining room, recreation room and lounge, the building included a chapel to replace the smaller chapel in Hawkins Hall. Work on the building was pushed forward as rapidly as possible and it was ready to receive its first occupants in September 1939. By the time of its completion, its estimated $350,000 cost had risen to $500,000. Bishop Keough dedicated the building in honor of St. Thomas Aquinas on March 7, 1940.[154]

In addition to providing out of state students with housing, Fr. Dillon, in his first years as president of Providence College, also successfully confronted two other continuing problems that the college faced. He further strengthened and expanded the college's curriculum and engaged additional professors and instructors to teach the new courses. Besides the changes in the college's regular undergraduate program, a much broader Extension School program was developed and, in October 1936, the college announced that in addition to holding Saturday morning classes for its Extension School, it would also begin offering evening courses. All of these changes resulted in a continued rise in the college's enrollment.[155]

At the beginning of his tenure, Fr. Dillon found that he also had to give his attention to the college's athletic program. Over the last few years, the college's three major varsity sports teams, its baseball, football and basketball teams, had suffered so many losses that the college's alumni were complaining. To deal with the situation, Fr. Dillon set up a new Athletic Board and with it, for the first time, an alumni advisory board. He also appointed a new faculty director of athletics from among the Dominicans, who brought in three new coaches for the three main varsity sports to provide the student athletes with more uniform coaching and training. In addition to this, Fr. Dillon decreed that all students should engage in some form of physical education. Practically this meant, that students were to participate in at least one year of intramural sports or physical education.[156]

In June 1940, Providence College graduated 151 seniors and nineteen students who took their classes in the Extension School. The following September the college opened for its twenty-second academic year with

---

[154] *Providence Visitor*, September 8; December 13, 1938; March 7, 1940; *Providence Journal*, December 9, 1938; October 1, 1939; March 8, 1940.

[155] *Providence Visitor*, October 1, 1936; *Providence Journal*, August 20, 1939.

[156] Ibid. Two years prior to Fr. Dillon's election as president of Providence College, John E. Farrell, the college's first graduate manager of athletics, successfully arranged for Providence College and Rhode Island State College to renew athletic competition between the two colleges that Rhode Island State's Athletic Director, Frank W. Keaney had broken off over the question of Providence College's use of freshman on its varsity teams, particularly over two freshmen who had initially indicated that they would enroll at Rhode Island State. Cf. *Evening Bulletin*, March 31, 1934; *Providence Visitor*, November 16, 1934.

over 800 undergraduates. However, in that same September, Congress passed the Selective Training and Service Act in the aftermath of the breakout of war in Europe in September 1939. Drafting of those who registered began in October. The act provided for deferments for college students until they graduated. However, the patriotism of many young men caused them to consider dropping out of school to work in a defense industry or to enlist in the armed forces. Fr. Dillon felt compelled to try to convince young men and the wider public of the value of a college education, even in wartime. In a talk given to the Kent County Club of Providence College at Club 400 in West Warwick, Fr. Dillon told the college's alumni, "Our American way of life cannot afford to discontinue, interrupt and impede the education of our youth. If it does to any extent, I fear the America of the future may not be worth defending." Twenty-eight of Providence College's 155 seniors received draft notices before they graduated, but all were deferred until July 1 so that they might finish their college courses.[157]

In May 1942, the number of graduating seniors dropped to 116 while degrees were also given to eight members of the extension school. Within a few weeks thirty of the graduates had enlisted in the armed forces. In response to wartime demands, Providence College offered courses during the summer of 1942, so that the 129 members of the class of 1943, rather than graduating in June, finished their classwork and received their degrees in December 1942. This change came out of the conference in Baltimore in January 1942 that created the National Educational War Time Effort. By instituting a trimester system, a student was able to graduate from college before he was twenty and thus before he was drafted. Wartime demands cut deeply into the college's enrollment. In August 1943, when the college held its twenty-second commencement, only 88 students received diplomas, and, of these, 44 had already been drafted and assigned to the reserves until they finished college, while six were already on active duty. During the academic year of 1943–44, Providence College's enrollment plummeted to its lowest levels since its earliest years. Only 182 were enrolled in the fall; 160 in the spring; and 143 in the summer semester that year. When PC held its twenty-third commencement in April 1944 after adopting a six day a week schedule in September 1943, only 32 seniors and 10 members of the Extension School received diplomas.[158]

In addition to seeing students leave the college for the war, Dominican members of the faculty—Frs. Joseph D. Donovan; Edward P. Doyle; Francis J. Fanning; Dennis B. McCarthy; George C. Reilly; John F. Ryan; and Philip C. Skehan—left the college for service as military chaplains. The

---

[157] *Evening Bulletin*, June 13, 1940; *Providence Visitor*, September 26, 1940; *Providence Journal*, April 2; May 11, 1941.

[158] *Providence Visitor*, May 14; July 30, 1942; August 5, 1943; *Providence Journal*, December 21, 1942; *Evening Bulletin*, August 2, 1942; April 17, 1944; Registrar's Office, *Student Register*, 1910–1 911, PCA. The information on the National Education War Effort is found in McCaffrey, "The Origins and Early Development of Providence College through 1947," 411–412.

bravery of a former Providence College Dominican faculty member, Fr. Paul J. Redmond, was cited several times in the local papers.[159]

The sharp drop in Providence College's enrollment due to the war created a financial crisis for the college. Without an endowment of any appreciable size, the college was almost totally dependent on tuition to cover the expenses involved in its operation. Prior to the war, the tuition revenues were sufficient to pay off the bank debt it incurred in building Aquinas Hall and to meet current expenses. However, after the War Department and President Roosevelt approved the Army Specialized Training Program in December 1942, which provided that talented soldiers under the age of twenty-two would be given the opportunity to receive college-level training so as to ensure an supply of doctors, lawyers, and engineers after the war, Providence College was among the 122 colleges in the country chosen to participate in the program. Fr. Dillon enlisted the help of the state's congressional delegation as well as that of Gov. J. Howard McGrath to secure a group of military students for the College. Their combined efforts paid off. An Army representative toured the college on March 8 and made a favorable report. Fr. Dillon was informed that he needed to be ready to accept an Army detachment by April 5. Although the college was ready by the specified date, the commander of the Providence College unit, Major Howard Smith, did not arrive on campus until July 1943. The first of the more than five hundred soldiers assigned to Providence for studies in basic engineering came in August. They were billeted in Aquinas Hall (five to a room) and in Guzman Hall. The student-soldiers attended class in Harkins Hall, drilled on the Hendricken baseball/football field, and exercised in the multi-purpose gym in Harkins or on the training field, which is now Slavin Center and Alumni Hall. The first twenty of the soldiers completed the basic phase of their training and were given certificates indicating the satisfactory completion of their courses on Friday, January 28, 1944. The program was suddenly shut down the following month, when the military, in view of the impending invasion of Europe, decided that there was greater need for the men on active duty. On March 19, 1944, after the college had given them a going away party, the soldiers marched down to Union Station to join new units. The college ran the military program conjointly with its normal program. When the college held its twenty-third commencement in April 1944, thirty-two seniors and ten students of the Extension School received degrees, the smallest number since the college's first graduating class.[160]

The infusion of government money from the Army Specialized Training Program stabilized the financial situation of the college. However, not

---

[159] *Veritas*, 1945.
[160] *Providence Visitor*, July 15, 1943; *Providence Journal*, January 29; April 17, 1944; McCaffrey, "The Origins and Early Development of Providence College through 1947," 416–23; Robert L. Deasy, "History of the Army Specialized Training Program at Providence College," Commemorative Ceremony, October 17, 1998, PCA.

all the attention the government paid to the college during the war was appreciated. In early April 1944, the District Medical Officer for the First Naval District toured the college to ascertain whether its facilities could serve the needs of a naval hospital. The prospect of the Navy's taking over the college prompted Fr. Dillon to argue strenuously against the idea and to seek the help of Massachusetts Senator David Walsh to forestall the Navy's plans. He would be much relieved to hear in late June that the project had been definitely abandoned.[161]

With the continued existence of Providence College resolved, Gov. McGrath (PC, Class of 1927 and, in August 1943, the first graduate of the college to be invited to be the main speaker at a college graduation) hosted a "big gifts" thousand dollar dinner at the Biltmore Hotel on Wednesday, November 29. On the following day, McGrath also hosted a giant rally of 1,200 alumni and solicitors to greet Lt. Com. James H. Crowley, U.S.N.R., one of the immortal four horsemen of Notre Dame at Harkins Hall. Both events marked the beginning of a fund drive, directed by local business man and alumnus Thomas A. Monahan and chaired by Fr. Bernard A. McLaughlin, O.P. The drive's goal of $350,000 was targeted at building a gymnasium at the college. Fr. McLaughlin had earlier reorganized the dramatics program at the college and had founded the Pyramid Players. It would be nine years before the alumni raised a sufficient sum for the college to begin work on a gym.[162]

On December 1, 1944, the college and the state suffered a great loss when Fr. Dillon, whose health had been declining for several years, died at St. Raphael's Hospital in New Haven. In his eulogy for Fr. Dillon, Fr. Arthur H. Chandler, O.P., the dean of the college, recalling the excessive strain that the administrative and enrollment problems of the college during the war years had put on Fr. Dillon, said of him, "He was a veteran of the first war and a casualty of the second." In addition to having gained the respect of the college's faculty and students, Fr. Dillon had been highly esteemed by his fellow educators in the state. In the early 1940s, Gov. McGrath had appointed Fr. Dillon to a committee of educators charged with reorganizing the laws relating to the management of the state's public-supported colleges. Dr. Henry M. Wriston, president of Brown University, was also a member of the committee. At its June 1941 commencement, Brown University conveyed an honorary degree of Doctor of Laws on Fr. Dillon in which he was cited for his service on the committee. Fr. Dillon's death prompted many prominent figures in the state, including many educators, to issue statements praising him. Hundreds of clergy and lay people crowded the Cathedral of SS. Peter and Paul for Fr. Dillon's funeral on December 5, 1944. Because of his navy service during

[161] McCaffrey, "The Origins and Early Development of Providence College through 1947," 423–25.
[162] *Providence Visitor*, November 21, 30, 1944.

World War I, he was buried with military honors in St. Francis Cemetery, Pawtucket.[163]

When Fr. Dillon's successor as president, Fr. Frederick C. Foley, O.P., took office in December 1944, the nation had reason to hope that the end of the war was near. Unlike World War I when Congress did not make any provisions for the reentry of the millions of demobilized servicemen into the civilian economy, Congress in June 1946 passed the Servicemen's Readjustment Act, or GI Bill. Among its provisions was the government's commitment to pay the tuition of servicemen, who wished to pursue an education. While most chose to attend vocational and technical schools, more than two million ex-servicemen elected to apply to colleges and universities. In September 1945, the college's enrollment totaled 322. By January 1946, the number of students had swollen to 754. The summer trimester in 1946 saw 517 students, and in September 1946, 1,245 students were accepted. For the spring semester, the last class enrolled under the trimester system, there were 1,203.[164]

In order to accommodate the swelling numbers and to plan for the future, Fr. Foley, in January 1947, announced a $1,500,000 expansion drive. Since the need for more space was immediate, Fr. Foley could not wait for funds to accumulate. By November 1, 1946, he applied for federal financing of three facilities under Public Law 697, which authorized the Federal Works Agency to provide additional educational facilities for colleges educating veterans under the GI bill. Fr. Foley immediately began negotiations with the Bureau of Community Facilities for the acquisition of surplus Navy property, specifically a one-story, frame dispensary building on the Naval Air Station at Charlestown. Fr. Foley had the building dismantled and trucked to Providence where it was re-erected near St. Thomas Hall, the two-story, white house the college acquired when Fr. McCarthy bought the land along Wardlaw Avenue. When the reconstructed building opened in September 1947, it housed classrooms, laboratories, offices and other facilities. The new structure was named Donnelly Hall in tribute to John J. Donnelly, who served the college for twenty-five years as Superintendent of Grounds and Maintenance.[165]

While Donnelly Hall helped to relieve the demand for space, much more was needed as enrollments continued to climb. In September 1946, Fr. Foley broke ground for a one-story brick building situated between Aquinas Hall and Donnelly Hall which was intended to serve as a home for the college's Business Administration programs. The new building, dedicated in honor of St. Antoninus, was ready for use in the fall of 1947. During his tenure as president, Fr. Foley also set in motion the long desired, but long delayed, science building project. He laid the ground-

[163] *Evening Bulletin*, December 2, 5, 1944; *Providence Journal*, December 2, 3, 3, 6, 1944; *Providence Visitor*, December 7, 1944.

[164] McCaffrey, "The Origins and Early Development of Providence College through 1947," p. 441.

[165] Ibid., 443–45.

work when he negotiated a loan on favorable terms from the Rhode Island Hospital Trust Company, which would be the main source of the building's financing. After securing Fr. McDermott's permission to proceed, Fr. Foley had plans for the building drawn, which was to be located on the south side to the main drive approaching Harkins Hall. Although ill health would force him to resign as president in May 1947, Fr. Foley had the pleasure, in June 1947, of seeing Fr. McDermott bless the ground on which the new building, Albertus Magnus Hall, would rise.[166]

Salve Regina College, Newport

While Bishop Hickey had been able to implement the greater part of the education plan that he made the main work of his episcopate, he died without seeing a women's college established in the diocese. He first vocalized his hopes to see a women's college in Rhode Island in an address at a reception tendered him by the Catholic Club and the Catholic Woman's Club in La Salle Auditorium on April 21, 1926. The main topic of his address was his concern about the spread of atheism in the country. He declared that the "great bulwark against the destructive tendencies of the times" was Catholic education. In addition to his hope to see Catholic schools for girls equal to those established in the diocese for boys, he expressed the desire "to see a girls' College in Rhode Island." The bishop vocalized the same hope a week later in an address to the Rhode Island Chapter of the International Federation of Catholic Alumnae that was also held at La Salle.[167]

Apparently, Bishop Hickey's original idea was to build a women's college in Providence that would be affiliated with Providence College. During Providence College's commencement exercise in June 1930, Bishop Hickey expressed great pleasure in informing the gathering that "we are coming nearer and nearer, day by day, to the realization of the project [of a woman's college]." The Dominicans, he said, had assured him that they would soon have a sufficient number of professors to make a "university of Providence College." What remained was for the people of the diocese "to provide the necessary funds." A year later, however, during a meeting with the Diocesan Consultors on October 31, 1931, Bishop Hickey raised the question of "the advisability of establishing a Woman's College," not in connection with Providence College, but with St. Francis Xavier Academy. The consultors recommended the project as a step toward completing the education plan that the bishop had initiated.[168]

The first concrete step toward realizing the desire for a women's col-

---

[166] Ibid., 443–55.

[167] *Providence Visitor*, April 26, 1926; *Providence Journal*, May 2, 1926.

[168] *Providence Visitor*, June 13, 1930; *Providence Journal*, June 13, 1930; Minutes of Board of Consultors, October 31, 1931.

lege was the submission and passage of a bill incorporating Salve Regina College of Rhode Island in the legislature's January 1934 session. The diocesan administrator, Msgr. Peter E. Blessing, had Rep. Edmund Flynn introduced a bill chartering the proposed college. While the name of a Dominican, Fr. Daniel M. Galliher, O.P., Providence College's registrar, along with those of Msgr. Blessing and Dr. Charles Carroll, then the supervisor of Public Education, were included among the incorporators, Msgr. Blessing acted primarily at the request of the Sisters of Mercy for whom the idea of establishing a college had been an ambition of long standing. In 1929, the Sisters of Mercy had restructured their American foundations and divided the various Mercy communities into nine provinces. The Province of Providence included the Providence community as well as the Mercy communities in Fall River, New York city, Gabriels, N.Y., and the sisters' missions in British Honduras. In the aftermath of the restructuring, the sisters purchased an additional 130 acres adjoining their property in Cumberland, which they had acquired at Grant's Mills in Cumberland 1913 and used as a vacation house and retreat house. The sisters named the property Mt. St. Rita's. Mother Mary Matthew Doyle, R.S.M., had a large bungalow on the former Clovis Bowen estate remodeled for use as a provincial house. The sisters first occupied the house in September 1932, a move necessitated by overcrowded conditions at St. Xavier's Convent in Providence. The new Province of Providence retained two novitiates, one on their property in Cumberland, where the sisters had moved from St. Xavier's, and a second at Tarrytown, N.Y. When the Cumberland novitiate quickly became overcrowded since it served as a novitiate for both the Providence and Fall River communities, work began in November 1933 in Cumberland on an addition for the novitiate. The work was aided in large measure by a ten thousand dollar gift offered by a generous benefactor. The addition was complete by May 1, 1934. It was in light of the completion of these projects that Mother Mary Matthew began to make preparations for the sisters next venture, the establishment of a women's college.[169]

Following the granting of a college charter, the Sisters of Mercy began making the necessary preparations for opening a college. While the diocese had bought or built many of the high schools in the diocese, and had bought the land and raised the money with which to build Providence College, Bishop Keough was content to allow the Sisters of Mercy as well as the Dominicans of Providence College the freedom to advance the interests of their colleges. From the very beginning, the Sisters of Mercy envi-

[169] *Providence Visitor*, February 9, 1934; *Acts and Resolves*, January Session, 1934; *Providence Visitor*, August 27, 1927; March 25; September 16; October 21, 1932; November 24, 1933; May 4; September 14, 1934; Sr. Mary Loretto O'Connor, *Mercy Marks the Century* (Providence: Sisters of Mercy, 1951), 36–37; 138–41. The Province of Providence would prove to be too large an entity and was divided April 1935 when Providence and Fall River were united as one province and New York and Gabriels combined to form another.

sioned a college under their own control. While Msgr. Blessing would be a member of the board of Salve Regina, Bishop Keough would not.

After Mother Matthew had secured a charter, both she and Mother Mary Hilda Miley, R.S.M., who was elected Provincial in 1936, sent sisters to secure doctorates in various subjects. The sisters also began accumulating the necessary books to create a college library. Both of these steps were well within the sisters' control. They had, however, to depend on the goodness of God and the continued generosity of friends, in addition to their own prudential management of their revenues, for the funds necessary to open the college. Before the sisters could undertake the new venture, they had first to pay down the debt that they were already carrying.[170]

At Salve Regina's annual corporation meeting on May 19, 1944, with the end of the Second World War in sight and with much of the Mercys' debt paid, Mother Mary Matthew, who had been reelected Provincial in 1942, and Mother Mary Hilda, who was now assistant provincial, along with a third sister, were appointed a special committee to call on Bishop Keough in order to discuss the opening of Salve Regina in a new building to be built at Mt. St. Rita's. It was apparently not until September 1945, that the three sisters actually met with Bishop Keough. The bishop encouraged the sisters to go ahead and open their college, but he did not give his approval for the Cumberland site. Bishop Keough thought that there would be transportation problems because of the rural nature of the proposed location. Mother Matthew accepted the bishop's decision, but, shortly after their meeting, wrote a very polite note in which she informed the bishop that, in the year it would take for the sisters "to arrange their plans and to settle on what is required for the erection of the [college] building," the sisters would pray to Mary under the title of Our Lady of Fatima, that the bishop would change his mind.[171]

The sisters believed that Mary answered their prayers in a manner neither they nor Bishop Keough had foreseen. In 1947, Mr. and Mrs. Robert Goelet, who owned a large estate on Ochre Point Avenue in Newport, offered to donate it to the diocese. The estate had been created in the 1880s by Mr. Goelet's father, Ogden Goelet. The Goelets were no longer able to make the estate their home. Rather than simply sell the estate, the Goelets wished to see the premises devoted to a use that would be beneficial to the state and particularly to the city of Newport. When informed of the Goelets' hopes for their estate, Bishop Keough suggested to Mother Matthew that the estate would make an excellent site for the Mercys' college. After the bishop and Mother Matthew toured the property together, Mother Matthew agreed that Ochre Court and its surrounding grounds

---

[170] "Salve Regina College, 1934–1984," (Privately printed, 1984); Sr. Mary Eloise Tobin, RSM and Sr. Mary Jean Tobin, RSM, *With Courage and Compassion: A Reflection on the History of Salve Regina in the Light of the Spirit Which Engendered and Sustains It (1993)*, Faculty and Staff - Ebooks, Book 1. https://digitalcommons.salve.edu/fac_staff_ebooks/1, 3–31.

[171] Minutes of the Annual Corporation Meeting of Salve Regina College, May 19, 1944; Sr. Mary Matthew to Keough, September 24, 1945, PChA.

met her requirements in every respect. The *Visitor* carried the news of Mr. and Mrs. Goelet's gift in a front page story on March 20, 1947, the same day on which the Salve Regina college corporation voted to accept the property.[172]

Simultaneously with the announcement of the Goelet's gift, Mother Mary Matthew, who was the college's president in addition to being provincial, announced that Salve Regina College would open on September 24. Four days after the announcement of the college's opening appeared, the Sisters of Mercy began accepting applications from freshman, who would form the entire student body during the first year of the college's operation. The application period ran through April 12. That the sisters could announce an opening so quickly testifies to the extent of the planning Mother Mary Matthew and Mother Mary Hilda had already done. Opening the college in September 1947 would mean that the first class would graduate from Salve Regina in 1951, the year in which the Sisters of Mercy would celebrate the One Hundredth Anniversary of their arrival in Providence.[173]

While Mother Mary Matthew played a leading role in the college's creation, so did Mother Mary Hilda Miley, first vice president in 1935 and Mother Mary's successor as provincial in 1950, when Mother Mary resigned because of ill health. Mother Mary Hilda was one of the first Sisters of Mercy in the Providence Province to earn a doctorate degree. Hers was a doctorate in Education. She has been described by the sisters who were aware of her contributions to Salve Regina College "as the masterful force behind the college plan." Another important member of the college's first administrative team was Sister Mary James O'Hare, R.S.M. In 1947, Sr. Mary James, Ph.D., was completing her eleventh year as principal of St. Xavier's Academy. Mother Mary Matthew appointed her the college's first dean. In addition to Sr. Mary James, who as dean would direct the day to day operations of the college, Mother Mary Matthew appointed six other Sisters of Mercy to the college's faculty; of these seven, four had earned doctorates. In addition to Mother Matthew's appointments, Bishop Keough appointed Fr. Gerald F. Dillon, who had recently returned from service as a Navy chaplain during the Second World War and who had previously served as Dean of Men at Catholic University prior to the war, as the college's chaplain. Fr. Dillon would also serve as professor of religion and philosophy. To round out the faculty, two lay women were hired, one to serve as an instructor in speech and the other to direct the physical education classes and the college's sports program. Dr. Harry Nugent, State Director of Adult Education, was also hired to be the debate coach.[174]

In order to prepare Ochre Court for its new role as a college complex, the Sisters of Mercy took out a $650,000 bank loan to finance the altera-

---

[172] *Providence Visitor*, March 20, 1947.
[173] Ibid.; March 27, 1947.
[174] *Providence Visitor*, July 31; September 18, 1947; "Salve Regina College, 1934–1984."

tion and furnishing of the estate to serve its new role. Bishop Keough formally opened the college on the announced date, September 24, the feast of Our Lady of Mercy, with a mass in the estate's former ballroom that had been converted for use as the college's chapel. At the mass, he greeted the college's faculty and administrators, a large number of diocesan priests, the college's benefactors, Mr. and Mrs. Goelet and the fifty-eight young women who comprised the student body. Most of the women chose to board in the college's dormitories on the third floor of Ochre Court, while a few others commuted to classes. All that was necessary for the first year students was in place when the college opened. However, during the college's first year, construction continued on the facilities that would be needed in succeeding years.[175]

The Development of Catholic Teachers College

In June 1941, when classes began at the Catholic Teachers College, 572 sisters, belonging to twenty different religious orders, were enrolled for classes during the summer session. About 250 enrolled for Saturday classes during the school year. Although the Catholic Teachers College had proven to be an important instrument in the in-service training of the religious sisters who taught in the Catholic schools in the diocese, many of whom began teaching before they had completed work on a college degree, the program it offered did have its drawbacks. Since the sisters were able to attend classes on a full time basis only during the summer and on Saturdays during the school year, it took four years for most to earn a teaching certificate and six years to earn a bachelor of education degree. Taking courses on Saturdays meant that the sisters had only Sunday as a day free of classes and, with classes and class preparations, little time for themselves. A second problem was that by taking courses on an extension basis, the sisters lacked the thorough, well-planned program that a full-time program could afford them. In the spring of 1941, the college's Board of Incorporators, of which Bishop Keough was president, voted to ask the religious communities whose members were teaching in the diocese to send their sisters to the Catholic Teachers College on a full-time basis year round. The response of the religious communities was positive. To accommodate the expanded mission of the college, Bishop Keough began renovating the buildings of the St. Aloysius Orphans Home on Prairie Avenue in Providence, which had been vacated when the orphan asylum moved to Greenville in the summer of 1941, to provide classrooms, laboratories and a library. The formal opening of the Catholic Teachers College with full-time and extension courses was held in the chapel of the old orphanage

---

[175] *Providence Visitor*, September 25, 1947; *Evening Bulletin*, January 14, 1948.

CHAPTER VII

Charitable Institutions and Institutional Support

The Catholic Charity Appeal

Like Bishop Hickey, the originator of the annual Catholic Charity Appeal, Bishop Keough devoted a great deal of time and effort to its success. Bishop Hickey had essentially utilized the services of his lay chairman and other volunteers to help him run the appeal. He also did much of the work himself. However, Bishop Keough was more comfortable about sharing responsibility than Bishop Hickey and was more inclined to assign tasks related to the drive to his clergy. After Bishop Hickey appointed Fr. Thomas J. McKitchen, rector of the cathedral, in February 1933, Fr. McKitchen had taken charge of the appeal's headquarters in Cathedral Hall. Under Bishop Keough, McKitchen became the appeal's executive director. At Cathedral Hall, McKitchen directed a staff that ranged from five to seven people. During the 1930s, Charles Beirne of Providence served as the appeal's secretary and George Houlker of Providence as shipping clerk responsible for seeing that the appeal's posters, prayer cards and other appeal printed matter were sent out to the various parishes. During the 1937 appeal, a typical appeal about which there is some information, an estimated one million pieces of printed matter was sent out. In addition to the two laymen, Misses Marie Foley, Kathleen Breen and Helen Arsenault served as stenographers from the period when appeal headquarters opened at the beginning of April until it closed at the beginning of June. During the time when parishes were making their reports to appeal headquarters, two other stenographers were added to the staff. Because of the time commitment involved, the headquarters staff were paid for their efforts. All other appeal workers were volunteers. The parishes made their reports to headquarters every three days during the appeal period and reports were compiled for Bishop Keough at regular intervals. The headquarters staff compiled the parish reports not only for the bishop, but for distribution to the local newspapers, which printed the names and amounts contributed by the larger donors. In addition to the headquarters staff, each parish had its own staff to assist the pastors, who directed the appeal at the parish level. In addition to the volunteers who made personal calls on parishioners, Fr. McKitchen helped Bishop Keough organize and encourage the efforts of the diocesan Special Gifts Committee and its regional branches, which called on local businesses to ask their support of the appeal. Because of the extensive use of clergy and volunteers, the administrative costs of the appeal during the 1930s, which were primarily invested in printing, amounted to but two cents out of every dollar raised, one of the lowest administrative costs of any charitable appeal in the country.[1]

In addition to the assistance provided by Fr. McKitchen, Bishop Keough gave Fr. Charles C. Curran, the director of the Diocesan Bureau of Social Services, and his associate, Fr. Joseph Lamb, charge of directing the radio campaign in support of the appeal. The main component of the radio campaign were the speeches Bishop Keough and the appeal's lay chairman delivered at the beginning of each year's appeal. The air time was provided free of charge by the various Rhode Island radio stations. In addition to the bishop's and lay chairman's appeal, other prominent priests and laymen also were invited to speak in order to publicize the appeal. The bishop gave his secretary, Fr. Charles J. Mahoney, charge of outdoor advertising and the special gifts committee in the Newport area. Finally, the bishop entrusted Fr. Francis J. Deery, editor of the *Providence Visitor*, and his assistant editor, Fr. Joseph F. Bracq, with the responsibility of directing publicity for the campaign. For several years the *Providence Journal* and *Evening Bulletin*, the *Tribune*, which appeared under various names during the 1930s, as well as the *Providence Visitor*, printed by-lined articles, prepared by their reporters, on the various institutions and programs supported by the Charity Appeal. Other Rhode Island papers also supported the appeal by printing similar stories.[2]

Bishop Keough's appointment as Bishop of Providence coincided in 1934 with the beginnings of President Roosevelt's New Deal. The boost that the injection of federal funds into the American economy on a large scale gave to employment and the continuing sufferings of the poor was reflected in increased giving to the Charity Appeal. The 4 percent increase in the 1934 total was the first increase since the less than 2 percent gain in 1931. The 1935 appeal, which brought in $309,644 saw an almost 18 percent increase over the previous year. Smaller gains of almost 3 percent and 8 percent in the succeeding years were followed by only a 1 percent increase in 1938 as the federal government sought to cut back its investment in the economy. Better than 3 percent and almost 7 percent gains followed in 1939 and 1940. In 1941, with increased employment due in part

1   *Star-Tribune*, April 15, 1937; *Evening Bulletin*, May 16, 1938; *Providence Visitor*, June 27, 1957.
2   *Star-Tribune*, April 10, 1937.

to government military and military related spending, the appeal realized $446,777, an almost 14 percent gain. The 1942 campaign raised only approximately four thousand dollars more than that of the year before. However, in 1943 the appeal collected $588,695, a better than 30 percent gain; in 1944, the total rose to $709,523, a better than 20 percent increase; and in 1945, $810,721 was contributed, a better than 14 percent increase. The postwar campaigns did not fare as well. Between 1946 and 1948, a period of rising inflation and sporadic unemployment, the appeal brought in $859,635 in 1946, $899.018 in 1947 and $909,018 in 1948.[3]

The Continued Development of Diocesan Charitable and Social Institutions

Within only a few months of Bishop Keough's taking up his new responsibilities as Bishop of Providence, the diocese arranged with Dr. John O'Grady, the dean of Catholic University's new School of Social Work, for the loan of the services of Anna Schneider, an instructor in child welfare. Beginning at end of August 1934, Miss Schneider undertook a six-month survey of the diocese's charitable institutions with the aim of improving the services they rendered. One area Miss Schneider was asked to address in particular was the Diocesan Charities Bureau's legal inability to make provision for foster home care. At the end of her survey, Miss Schneider presented her findings and recommendations to a board of pastors and laymen named by Bishop Keough, who then presented the results of the survey to the bishop.[4]

Even before the survey was completed, the Charities Bureau applied for and received a license from the State Public Welfare Commission to function as a child-placing agency. The license, similar to that already held by the institutions for children in the diocese, directly enabled the Bureau "to receive, secure homes for, or otherwise care for children." When the license was granted in December 1934, Fr. Charles C. Curran, the director of the Charities Bureau, explained for the benefit of a *Visitor* reporter that it was "a recognized belief among those engaged in social work that a child should be placed in a foster home whenever feasible." While all the child caring institutions in the diocese had placed children in private homes on occasion, none had done it extensively. Fr. Curran did not envision the wholesale placing of children in foster homes, but a greater effort to place children in them when the opportunity presented itself. For the most part, the Bureau believed that it was easier to place older children in foster care rather than younger. In essence, Fr. Curran and the Charities Bureau believed that the diocese's child care institutions should only accept

---

3   The figures are based on the figures provided in the published reports provided each year by the Catholic Charity Fund Appeal.

4   *Providence Visitor*, August 17, 1934.

children for whom there was some hope that they could be returned to their homes or to the care of a family member. These were children whose parents or parent had not surrendered their parental rights. Because the diocese did not possess unlimited resources, the staff of the Charities Bureau agreed with the director of the State's Children's Bureau, Miss Ann I. Griffth, that only children, who were truly orphaned, should be placed in the care of the state. Given the concern many Catholics had had in the past about the dangers to a child's faith presented by the lack of opportunity available to the Catholic children at the State Home and School to practice their faith, this represented a considerable change in the diocese's policies. The Bureau's reluctance to place children in the State Home and School was not limited to religious concerns. The State Home in the 1930s had many limitations in regard to its physical equipment, services and its ability to place children in foster homes. Furthermore, the state was slow in providing casework with the families of the children under its care. The Diocesan Bureau did not begin committing children to the State Home until around 1940. When it did, the cases involved several children from the same family. However, when after some time Bishop Keough raised questions about the State Home and School, the practice was suspended. It was not resumed until 1947, when the Bureau again committed children to the care of the State Child Welfare Services although problems continued where placements in the State Home and School were involved.[5]

Laudable as the Charities Bureau's efforts were to return children to their families and to place children in foster care whenever possible, the economic realities of the 1930s made the challenge daunting. During the 1930s, the Bureau made several appeals to Catholic groups asking their members to consider welcoming a child into their homes either as foster children or, in the case of older children, as boarders. In the Charities Bureau's 1934 and 1935 reports, there is no distinction made between the terms foster care and adoption. In 1933, there were 48 requests to adopt children, or put them into foster care, of which 13 were approved. In 1934, the requests dropped to 29, of which only 6 were approved and 5 were withdrawn. While the impact of the Depression continued to limit the families who were financially able to provide homes for foster children for some time, the out placing of children would continue to be the focus of Fr. Curran's efforts.[6]

Shortly after the creation of the Catholic Charities Bureau, Fr. Curran and his staff decided that the Rhode Island Working Boys' Home on Park Street in Providence had outlived its usefulness. The home had been established in 1898 to provide a safe residence for boys thirteen and fourteen, who had formerly lived at the Rhode Island Catholic Orphan Asylum on Prairie Avenue. As teenagers, the boys were judged able to go out to work.

---

5   *Providence Visitor*, August 17; December 3, 7, 1936; Lamb and McGovern, "The Diocesan Bureau of Social Service: Historical Sketch."

6   *Providence Visitor*, February 7, 14, 1935.

Originally, the home had been placed in charge of a male superintendent, William J. Wallace, who was assisted by a matron, Miss Mary Callahan. Miss Callahan had previously been employed as a teacher in a Providence evening school. When Mr. Wallace left after ten years, Miss Callahan was put in charge. Over the years, new state laws regarding child labor meant that the many of the younger boys in the home, now unable to work, had to continue in school for several years after they came to the home. When the Diocesan Charities Bureau was founded in 1927, Fr. Curran, given his belief that young people should be brought up in families if at all possible, sought to reduce the number of boys at the home. Over the years, the number of residents, which at one time had been as high as fifty, dropped to fifteen. The Charities Bureau only admitted boys to the home for whom no other plan was feasible. For those for whom there were placements in a family environment, the Bureau began providing subsidies to the parents or relatives of the boys so that families could stay intact. About the same time in 1932 that Miss Callahan retired, the Providence Board of Health condemned the home's plumbing. In 1934, in view of the home's many other physical deficiencies, the Charities Bureau decided that the home should be closed. It took almost two years for the staff of the Charities Bureau to find satisfactory placements for the boys, who were residents of the home at the time when the decision to close was made. The Bureau did eventually find homes for them and paid for their board, schooling, clothing and medical care until each became self-sufficient. The home ceased to exist in September 1936.[7]

Coincidental with the closing of the Working Boys' Home, the change in the Charities Bureau focus from institutional care to foster care and the increased number of requests for aid generated by the Depression demanded an increase in the Bureau's staff. In June 1935, Bishop Keough appointed Fr. Joseph J. Lamb, who had recently finished a year's training in social work at the Catholic University in Washington, assistant director of the Bureau. When Miss Schneider's contract with the diocese expired on June 1, 1935, Fr. Curran hired Miss Julia Rager as the Bureau's executive secretary and chief social worker. Miss Rager, a native of Ohio, was a recent convert to Catholicism when she came to Providence in 1935. She was a graduate of the master's program in the School of Applied Social Science at Western Reserve University and had worked in the Cleveland Children's Bureau prior to accepting a position in Providence. In addition to Miss Rager, who took Miss Schneider's place, the Bureau also employed two other lay social workers, Miss Gertrude Olsen, who was a graduate of Fordham University, and Miss Mabel Cooney, who had a B. A. degree from Trinity College, and an M.A. from Brown University. Since the Bureau's original space at 25 Fenner Street could not be expanded, Fr. Cur-

---

7   Hayman, *Catholicism in Rhode Island and the Diocese of Providence*, II, 512–16; *Providence Sunday Journal Magazine*, August 21, 1932; Lamb and McGovern, "The Diocesan Bureau of Social Service: Historical Sketch."

ran had to look elsewhere for the space he needed for his staff. The closing of the Working Boys' Home in 1936 made that space available for other uses. The three-story building that had housed the Boys' Home was extensively repaired and renovated to provide separate offices for the two priests, Miss Rager, Miss Olsen, Miss Cooney, and Miss Alice Beaudet, who was hired after the Bureau moved from Fenner Street, as well as two stenographers. Later a fourth case worker would be added to the staff. The move to Park Street enabled the staff to have private offices in which to interview those who applied for aid. In addition, there was space for a conference room. The renovations were funded by the Catholic Charity Appeal. In addition to the physical changes in the Bureau, Bishop Keough moved to secure an act of incorporation for the Bureau under a name that better reflected its mission, the Diocesan Bureau of Social Service. The act was approved by the legislature on April 2, 1935.[8]

In order to supply the staff of the Bureau with a cross-section of community thinking on various religious, social and economic problems, and, secondarily, to acquaint the community with the work of the Bureau of Social Services, Bishop Keough, in 1935, suggested that the Bureau hold monthly case conferences. The members of the conferences, which began in Providence in 1935, were drawn from the clergy, the judiciary, the bar, the medical profession, business, teaching, civic organizations, the St. Vincent de Paul Society and other organizations. At each of the conferences, a staff member of the Bureau presented a problem that had come to the Bureau's attention and invited comments and suggestions from the conference participants. In order to have the widest possible influence, conferences were also organized in Pawtucket, Newport, West Warwick, and Woonsocket. In Newport, the conference met in the music room of St. Joseph's Church. In Pawtucket, the conference there met in the Chamber of Commerce on Main Street. The Woonsocket Case Conference did much to bring the English and French-speaking elements of Woonsocket's population together and paved the way for the opening of a Woonsocket branch of the Bureau of Social Services in June 1948.[9]

The Bureau's Woonsocket office was opened by Fr. Henry J. Crepeau. Fr. Crepeau did graduate work at the Catholic University at Washington in 1937. From September 1941 to June 1944, he served on the faculty at Our Lady of Providence Seminary. In June 1944, Bishop Keough appointed him an assistant at Precious Blood in Woonsocket and Associate Director of the Diocesan Bureau of Social Service. It was Fr. Crepeau who opened the Woonsocket office of the Bureau in June 1948 at 48 Hamlet Street.

8 *Providence Visitor*, March 4, April 8, 1937; September 1, 1967; *News-Tribune*, April 22, 1935; *Providence Journal*, April 18, 1937; Acts and Resolves, January Session, 1935.
9 *Providence Visitor*, December 17, 1936; November 4, 1938; November 17, 1938; Lamb and McGovern, "The Diocesan Bureau of Social Service: Historical Sketch."

During the Woonsocket office's first year, Fr. Crepeau and his first secretary, Miss Bernadette Boudreau, handled twenty-four cases.[10]

In October 1936, the Diocesan Bureau of Social Service organized the first of what would be a regular series of meetings of the sisters who ran and served in the various child care institutions in the diocese: the orphanages, the day nurseries and the protective home of the Good Shepherd. Because the Sisters of the Good Shepherd were the only semi-cloistered order in the group, to accommodate them, the Conference of Religious meetings were held at the Catholic Training School on Eaton Street. The motivation behind holding the monthly conferences, which ran from October to May, was to provide the sisters from the various child care institutions with the information they needed to improve the level of care each institution offered. The first part of the conference was given over to one or more talks by experts in a particular field. Topics included nutrition, medical care, emotional problems, general health, discipline, school programs, and religious training and practices. After the talk or talks, the sisters broke up into three groups. Fr. Curran led the group that discussed administration; Fr. Lamb took charge of the health and recreation group; and Miss Rager worked with the behavior section. In May 1938, the Conference of Religious organized a special health conference for the last of their monthly meetings in order to disseminate and discuss the latest developments in the field of health care as it related to children. This health conference became an annual event.[11]

In addition to working to inform the community about the social and economic challenges faced by those in need and to assist the religious who ran the various charitable institutions in the state, at Bishop Keough's suggestion, Fr. Curran also sought to support and inform Catholics, who were working in the various areas of social service. In November 1937, the Bureau for Social Services inaugurated a series of Sunday evening talks on various topics of concern to the laymen and women engaged in social work in the state, a group whose numbers had expanded greatly because of the various New Deal initiatives. The lectures were held in Cathedral Hall in Providence. Following the talk, the 150 social workers who attended the meeting began to discuss the forming of a permanent organization of Catholic social workers. A committee of organization was nominated from the floor. Those nominated agreed to meet the following Friday at the Diocesan Bureau of Social Work offices. The organization committee reported on its efforts at the next scheduled lecture on December 12. The result was the formation of the St. Thomas More Guild for Social Work-

---

10   Lamb and McGovern, "The Diocesan Bureau of Social Service: Historical Sketch," *Providence Visitor*, June 5, 1958.
11   *Providence Visitor*, December 3, 1936; January 21, 1937; May 8, 1938; Lamb and McGovern, "The Diocesan Bureau of Social Service: Historical Sketch."

ers, which elected Edward P. Reidy, director of the State Department of Public Welfare, its first president.[12]

All three groups discussed above met regularly in the years after their founding. However, after the United States entered the Second World War, the activities of all three groups were curtailed because of transportation difficulties and lack of staff time caused by the new demands generated by America's involvement in the war and the pressures on families it created. After the war, the St. Thomas More Guild became one of the Thomistic Guilds at Providence College. Fr. William Clark, O.P., the head of the Sociology Department at the college gave a great deal of time to the Guild. After his sudden death in June 1957, the Guild ceased to exist.[13]

In addition to the Diocesan Bureau of Social Services' work with groups within the diocese, the Bureau also provided leadership through its director, Fr. Curran, and its executive secretary, Miss Rager, in helping the Rhode Island Conference of Social Work establish an accredited branch of the Boston College School of Social Work in Providence. Bishop Keough provided $5,000 to help sustain the school through its early years of operation. Miss Rager was a casework consultant and an official member of the Boston College faculty.[14]

St. Vincent de Paul Infant Asylum

While the local conferences provided the information and encouragement for the various administrators to raise the standards of their respective institutions so as to stay abreast of the best practices in the field of child care, the Diocesan Bureau played a more active role in regard to some institutions. The institution that caused Fr. Curran and his associates the most concern was the St. Vincent de Paul Infant Asylum. While the name of the institution suggested that only infants lived at the home, the reality was that certain older girls and boys were allowed to stay at the home after the time their peers were sent, at the age of six, across the city to the Rhode Island Catholic Orphanage on Prairie Avenue. These older boys and girls lived in cottages on the grounds. In addition to the older girls, the rule of the Sisters of Divine Providence required that, if unmarried mothers wished to place their child in the home, the mother herself had to agree to stay with the child at the home for one year. Part of the idea behind the rule was that the sisters believed that a child needed the

12 *Providence Journal*, November 13, 15, 1937; *Providence Visitor*, November 18; December 16, 1937; October 16, 1941.
13 Lamb and McGovern, "The Diocesan Bureau of Social Service: Historical Sketch;" *Providence Visitor*, June 6, 1957.
14 Lamb and McGovern, "The Diocesan Bureau of Social Service: Historical Sketch." In 1962, the Conference chose to recognize Miss Rager's leadership in and service to the social work community in Rhode Island by giving her a special award of appreciation from her peers, Cf. *Providence Visitor*, October 11, 1962.

care of its mothers during the child's early years. The mother worked with the sisters to pay for the board of her child and for herself. She was given clothes for herself and fifty cents a week. Unfortunately, the sisters tended to treat these young mothers differently than the older girls, who they allowed to remain at the home and who assisted the sisters in the care of the children. The sisters referred to the mothers as "the women" to set them apart from the other girls.[15]

Beginning in 1936, the staff of the Bureau of Social Services began to introduce changes in the program at St. Vincent's. Prior to this time, it was the accepted practice that the children brought to the home as infants stayed there until they were six and then were transferred to the Rhode Island Catholic Orphan Asylum. The staff found the program for children over three at St. Vincent's to be limited, restricted and repressive. In contrast, St. Francis Orphanage in Woonsocket, which was run by the Franciscan Missionaries of Mary, had an excellent pre-school program, which utilized the programs for children worked out by Dr. Maria Montessori, an Italian physician and educator. Dr. Montessori developed her program for children three to five in a Franciscan Missionaries of Mary school in Rome. The sisters also utilized programs that had been developed by Friedrich Froebel, a German educator, who, in the first half of the nineteenth century, had organized the first *kindergartens*. The Bureau began sending children from St. Vincent's to St. Francis Orphanage as a stopgap measure. Ideally, in keeping with its operative philosophy, the Bureau believed that as many children as possible should be placed in foster or adoptive homes. The option of sending the children to Woonsocket was employed until such time as the Bureau could develop a more extensive foster home program or make better use of foster care under public auspices.[16]

Because of the Bureau's efforts, the cottages for the older children were closed by 1943. By 1946, the mothers' stay was eventually reduced to six months by which time a salary scale for each mother was inaugurated. By 1958, the practice of having unmarried mothers stay at the home was completely abandoned and salaried employees were hired to help the sisters care for the children. The changes in regard to the mothers of children born out of wedlock introduced by the Bureau for Social Services at St. Vincent's flowed out of a shift of emphasis from shielding the parents of such children to one of recognizing their rights in regard to their children. Rhode Island orphanages, like orphanages elsewhere in the country prior to the 1930s, had deliberately not kept careful records of the parents of a child placed in their care. However, by the 1930s, the sisters who ran Catholic orphanages had begun to realize that their attempts to shield and protect the mothers of children born out of wedlock caused more heartache than they prevented, especially when such mothers tried

15 Lamb and McGovern, "The Diocesan Bureau of Social Service: Historical Sketch."
16 *The Rhode Islander*, Ma6 6, 1927; *Evening Bulletin*, April 28, 1936; Lamb and McGovern, "The Diocesan Bureau of Social Service: Historical Sketch."

unsuccessfully to reestablish contact with their children. With the establishment of the Diocesan Bureau in 1927, the staff of the Bureau utilized the modern casework approach when unmarried women turned to the Bureau for help. The idea behind such an approach was expressed in a *Providence Journal* article in 1939:

> The sisters and workers who have been intimately identified with this problem for 70 years know from experience that the complete and accurate records are apt to indicate complete and thorough treatment which, in the long run, is more charitable and more likely to result in a happier future for the mother and her baby.[17]

Changes to Various Diocesan Institutions

While the Diocesan Bureau for Social Service played an important role in assisting the various child care facilities in the diocese to improve the services they offered to the community, only the increases in the amounts collected by the annual Catholic Charity Appeal could provide the monies necessary to improve the physical facilities operated by the sisters. From the beginning of the annual appeal in 1927, the amounts realized from the campaigns were barely able to cover the deficits the various agencies funded by the appeal ran and limited the amounts that could be allotted to those agencies that totally depended on the appeal to cover for their annual budgets. Since the 1935 Charity Drive Appeal raised $309,644.99, an approximately eighteen percent increase over the previous year, Bishop Keough and his advisors were able to allocate funds to cover the costs of pressing repairs and long overdue improvements at several institutions. In speaking to the pastors and parish trustees who gathered for the opening meeting of the 1937 Fund Appeal, Bishop Keough informed those present that among the improvements made during 1936 was a new laundry and renewed heating plant at the St. Vincent de Paul Infant Asylum; the purchase of a new home for the Little Sisters of the Assumption in Woonsocket, who visited the homes of the poor and the sick in that city as did the White Sisters elsewhere in the state; and the establishment of the Bureau for Social Services in its new home. In addition, an extensive project of repair and improvement was begun at the Home for the Aged in Pawtucket. Between 1937 and 1938, the interior of the home was repainted, an elevator was installed, a modern heating plant, laundry and kitchen were built, and two fireproof staircases and three new entrances as well as a four-story addition were added. Throughout the thirties, many of the stories written about the institutions supported by the Charity Fund that appeared in the local papers focused on the need for repairs and the expansion of programs at the various Catholic orphanages in the state. Some repairs and renovations were of such a nature they they had to done immediately.

---

17 Lamb and McGovern, "The Diocesan Bureau of Social Service: Historical Sketch;" *Providence Journal*, May 5, 1939.

In 1937, prudence demanded that the diocese address the dangers of fire at St. Francis Orphanage in Woonsocket. Although the newest of all the orphanage buildings in the diocese, its needs were the most pressing. The orphanage was completely renovated. The old, creaky fire escapes were replaced by modern firewells, fire resistant doors were built in, and a new elevator was installed for normal and emergency use. At the same time, a new building was built to house a new boiler and modern laundry equipment. It was connected with the main building by an enclosed bridge.[18]

When both the 1936 and 1937 campaigns yielded even slightly higher returns than the 1935 campaign, Bishop Keough used the increase to begin to address the need for new construction on the part of several of the diocesan charitable institutions. The two most urgent needs were new buildings for the Rhode Island Catholic Orphan Asylum in Providence and for L'Hospice St. Antoine in Woonsocket. In early January 1937, a fire in the chapel of L'Hospice St. Antoine caused considerable damage, but was quickly repaired. In the aftermath of the fire, the state fire marshal condemned the hospice's buildings as being unsafe. Besides the fact that the men's and women's quarters, which dated back to 1907, were constructed of wood and thus vulnerable to fire, the home was overcrowded. To relieve the overcrowding of the home, the Grey Nuns, who ran the home, had bought several neighboring apartment buildings in 1926 and used some of the apartments to house their guests. In view of the state's condemnation of the hospice's buildings, Bishop Keough, in May 1937, purchased the Montgomery Farm on the Woonsocket-Smithfield line as the site for a building. The land had previously been designed as a potential site for an airport.[19]

The bishop engaged a local Woonsocket architect, Walter F. Fontaine, to design the new home. After researching the subject, Mr. Fontaine drew up plans for a five-story, fireproof, brick building with the capacity for housing 225 guests, which he presented to the bishop in June 1939. The scale of the proposed new building looked not only to meeting current needs, but to enable the sisters to plan for future demands. The initial estimated cost of the proposed building was $428,857. Among the provisions included in the plans for the new building were living quarters for elderly priests. In early November 1939, the diocese awarded the general contract to the E. Turgeon Company of Providence and the company began work on the building immediately, pouring the foundations of the new building before the cold weather set in. Although the sisters initially hoped to move into the new building during the summer of 1940, difficulties in obtaining materials and furnishings, which were subject to government priorities, conspired to delay construction. It was not until August 1941 that the sisters were able to move the 145 residents in their Hamlet Avenue home to

---

18 *Providence Visitor,* June 13, 1935; April 21, 1938; *Evening Bulletin,* May 3, 1938.

19 *News-Tribune,* May 12, 1937; *Woonsocket Call,* July 23, 1926; April 20; December 20, 1927; *Evening Bulletin,* April 28, 1936; April 23, 1937; *Providence Visitor,* May 13, 1927.

the new facility. Bishop Keough blessed the cornerstone of the new building on Friday, July 18, 1941, and returned to Woonsocket on the feast of the Assumption, Friday, August 15, 1941, to solemnly bless the building and its new residents. By the time the building was opened, its cost had risen to $650,000.[20]

The success of the Charity Fund Appeals from 1935 through 1938 allowed Bishop Keough to announce at the opening of the 1939 appeal that the Little Sisters of the Poor and the Sisters of the Good Shepherd had ceased their traditional practice of begging throughout the year. The bishop told the assembled pastors and trustees that he wished to spare the sisters any embarrassment that they occasionally experienced and, more importantly, the ending of the practice would allow them to give more of their time to running their respective institutions.[21]

The Consolidation of Orphanages and the Building of a New St. Aloyius in Greenville, Smithfield

With the St. Antoine project underway, Bishop Keough began considering the building of an entirely new facility that could accommodate the children living at the Rhode Island Catholic Orphanage in Providence as well as those at the Mercy Home and School in Newport and the St. Vincent de Paul Home in Woonsocket. The St. Vincent de Paul Home in Woonsocket was an old wooden structure in serious need of repair. The Providence orphanage, which since its opening in 1862 had housed nearly 18,000 children, was badly overcrowded and outmoded. The Mercy Home and School in Newport that was housed in the former Bruguiere mansion on Miantonomi Hill, also had been overcrowded at times. In May 1936, there were sixty-nine children at the home, a number which strained its capacity. Interest first focused on a place along the shores of Narragansett Bay as the site for a new orphans' home. However, when the decision was finally made to build, the location chosen was just outside the country village of Greenville, on Austin Avenue, in the town of Smithfield, where the diocese owned a large farm, the Villa St. Rose. The villa, which was run by the Sisters of Divine Providence who staffed the St. Vincent de Paul Infant Asylum, supplied the asylum with milk and vegetables.[22]

Bishop Keough engaged John F. Hogan, who had already done a number of diocesan churches, to draw the plans for the new orphanage, which would be known as St. Aloysius Orphan Asylum, the name by which the Rhode Island Catholic Orphan Asylum on Prairie Avenue was also

---

20   *Providence Journal*, June 20; November 19, 1939; April 6; August 16, 1941; *Providence Visitor*, November 2, 9, 1939; August 7, 14, 1941.

21   Ibid., April 11, 1939.

22   *News Tribune, April 28, 1936; Providence Journal*, May 9, 1936; April 14; May 2, 1937; April 16, 1939; *Providence Visitor*, April 20, 1939.

known. Mr. Hogan presented his design in April 1939. The new red-brick building was intended to accommodate two hundred children with complete convent facilities for thirty-six sisters, who would have charge of the home and school. A chapel that could accommodate 250 persons was a main feature of the building. On the second floor there was a complete infirmary with receiving room, an observation parlor and special quarters for the convalescents as well as offices for physicians and dentists and quarters for the chaplain. The large dormitories were planned to accommodate twenty-four beds, with study rooms and lavatories adjoining each sleeping room. Bishop Keough broke ground for the main building on Monday, October 23, 1939. The following February, work began on a separate, eight classroom, school building, also designed by Mr. Hogan, on the grounds of the new home. Bishop Keough returned to Greenville on Monday, November 17, 1941, to dedicate the new buildings to their patrons, the home to St. Aloysius and the school to St. Peter. The two buildings, together with their furnishings, cost well over a half million dollars. At their dedication, Bishop Keough gave credit for the erection of the new home and school to the "great charity of our citizens," both Catholics and non-Catholics.[23]

On April 1, 1941, the *Visitor* printed a short article stating that the federal government had purchased some fifty-one acres of the property adjoining Newport's Mercy Home and School as the site for a defense housing project for civilian workers at the Newport Naval Torpedo Station. Although the diocese cooperated with the government in the matter, the government gave the diocese little choice. While the Mercy Home and School had been overcrowded in 1936, by April 1939, because of the Social Service Bureau's policy of placing children in foster or adoptive homes and doing whatever was possible to reunite families, the number had dropped to less than twenty in spite of the fact that the home had temporally taken in thirty-three children left homeless when the hurricane of 1938 destroyed their parents' homes in the Island Park section of Portsmouth. While Bishop Keough announced as early as May 1938 that the children in the Mercy Home and School would be moved to the new orphanage in Greenville, he did not reject the idea of securing a site for a new orphanage to serve the children on Aquidneck Island who needed help. On March 11, 1941, Herbert E. Macauley, the mayor of Newport, wrote to Bishop Keough in support of the idea that a new location for the home might be found in Newport. In spite of an extensive search for a suitable piece of property, the heightened demand for housing in the Newport area caused by the increases in the military establishments in and around the city made it impossible for the diocese to purchase another site until after Bishop Keough left the diocese. In April 1940, there were only six boys and nine girls at the home, down from ninety plus only a few

---

23   *Providence Visitor*, April 20; October 19, 26, 1939; February 1, 1940; April 3; November 13, 18, 1941; *Providence Journal*, April 28, 1940; November 18, 1941.

years before. These would be moved to Greenville when St. Aloysius was opened. When no new site could immediately be found in the Newport area for an orphanage to serve the Newport area, the decision was made to place the Mercy Home's furnishing in storage against the time when a location could be found.[24]

The Impact of the Hurricane of 1938 and the Second World War on Diocesan Institutions

As was the case with the fire at Hospice St. Antoine, accidents occasionally forced Bishop Keough's hand and prompted the spending of monies on immediate needs rather than on planned projects. Such was the case after the 1938 hurricane. The hurricane caused considerable damage to diocesan institutions, among them, St. Francis Orphanage in Woonsocket, St. Aloysius Home and School in Providence, and St. Joseph's Hospital in Providence. The most seriously damaged of all the agencies supported by the Catholic Charity Fund was Tower Hill House near Wakefield. The hurricane so destroyed the old summer hotel used to provide summer vacations for children in the cities that the building had to be torn down. Bishop Keough had been considering replacing the building since he had ordered that the upper two floors of the four-story hotel not to be used because of the real danger of fire. After the old hotel was torn down, Bishop Keough had two smaller buildings built to replace it. One was single-story dormitory building capable of accommodating one hundred beds, which was built on the foundation of the old hotel. To the left of the dormitory he had a two-story administration building built, which contained an office, kitchen, and accommodations for the priest in charge and the staff. Another one-story building was built for a dining room and playroom, which served to connect the two. All was in readiness in July 1939 when the first busload of children arrived.[25]

American military preparations before the Second World War and particularly the war itself would have a great impact on the Diocesan Bureau for Social Services and the various charitable institutions of the diocese. The difficulties contractors experienced in securing the materials necessary to build Hospice St. Antoine and St. Aloysius Home and School increased to the point where any private construction had to be suspended until after the war's end. The Bureau's efforts towards reducing the population of the diocese's child care institutions were thwarted in large measure by an in-

---

24 *Providence Visitor*, April 3, 1941; *Providence Journal*, April 14, 1940; *The News*, Newport, May 14, 1938; Macauley to Keough, March 11, 1941; Keough to Macauley, March 13, 1941, PChA. Under Bishop Keough's successor, Bishop Russell J. McVinney, the diocese did acquire the James Estate in Newport in November 1951 with the intention of using the property for a children's home. However, changes in the diocese's approach to child care would mean that the planned use of the property was never carried out. Cf. *Providence Visitor*, December 6, 1951.

25 *Providence Journal*, April 11, 20, 1939.

creased demand for temporary care of children. While the Charity Appeal brought in more money during these years, the gains were partially offset by the increase in prices charged for goods before the government imposed limits. The expansion of personnel at the Newport Navy base and the Torpedo Station, the building of a naval air station at Quonset Point, North Kingston and the establishment of the Kaiser Shipyard at Field's Point in Providence all brought thousands of young men and women into contact with each other, resulting in a substantial increase in the number of pregnancies among unmarried women. In the years before the war, the Bureau for Social Services had persuaded the sisters who ran St. Joseph's Hospital to accept unmarried girls. In addition, the Bureau and the hospital cooperated in setting up a special prenatal clinic, which operated at a time different than other hospital clinics in order to provide quicker and more confidential service. Furthermore, the sister in charge of social services at the hospital worked with the private physicians in the area to encourage referrals so that unmarried mothers might receive counseling and guidance. To protect the privacy of the women, Bishop Keough authorized the payment of one hundred dollars by the Bureau to the hospital for maternity care. During the war, the House of the Good Shepherd also accepted unmarried mothers referred to it by the Bureau. The influx was so heavy that the diocese's resources proved inadequate. The Bureau referred some women to private homes, which the Bureau financed, and others to out-of-state maternity homes. Many women had to turn to their own dioceses for care.[26]

---

26   Lamb and McGovern, "The Diocesan Bureau of Social Service: Historical Sketch."

CHAPTER VIII

Catholic Action, World War II and the Promotion of Bishop Keough

Since the time of Pope Pius X, the popes of the twentieth century had been urging the priests, religious and laity to make their religion relevant to their lives as Catholics and to bring the light of the Gospels and Catholic social teaching to bear on the economic problems of modern society and their social consequences. According to the *Manual of Catholic Action*, published in New York in 1936, Catholic Action, defined as "the participation of the laity in the apostolate of the hierarchy," was designed to return society, threatened by "pagan forces," to its Christian foundations. Lay men and women were to be mobilized and trained under episcopal direction to bring the Church's teachings into practice. The most notable effort on the part of the bishops of the American Catholic Church during Bishop Keough's years was to bring Catholic teachings on morality and human values to bear on the debate as to the kind of films produced in Hollywood by the film industry.[1]

Morality in Theater and Motion Pictures

In the early history of Providence, many different Protestant groups denounced the theater as a nursery of vice. Individuals and congregations sought to either close the one theater that existed in Providence in early national times or limit the hours and patronage of it and its successor. The popularity of amateur theatricals in the late 1850s and of the professional German and Italian opera troupes that played in the city during the Civil War spurred the demand for a first-class theater and led to the opening of the Providence Opera House in 1871, which was quickly followed by a second, Harrington's Opera House. Burlesque and vaudeville houses followed between 1874 and 1887. They were soon joined by peep shows and nickelodeons in the 1890s. During the first decade of the twentieth century, small motion picture theaters began to appear, which were often merely

---

[1]   The *Manual* is quoted and placed in context in David O'Brien, *American Catholics and Social Reform: The New Deal Years* (New York: Oxford University Press, 1968), 181–184.

reconfigured storefronts. Short motion pictures were also shown in the existing theaters as part of their entertainment. Seeking to attract yet larger, more diverse audiences than the early storefront theaters attracted, the first motion theaters began to give way to larger, purpose built theaters where their patrons could enjoy feature films like *The Birth of a Nation*, which first played in Providence in 1917.[2]

The showing of some of the early films was not without controversy. When in May 1907, the Lyric Theater in Providence screened a series of short pieces entitled *Murphy's Wake*, the presentation provoked the ire of a group of Irishmen from Pawtucket, which was then a hotbed of Irish nationalism. After viewing the film, one of the Pawtucket Irishmen telephoned Mayor Patrick McCarthy, who was himself Irish-born, at his home to complain that the depiction of the Irish in the film was insulting. The caller promised that if the theater did not discontinue showing the film that "a party of loyal sons of the Emerald Isle from Pawtucket would create a small-sized riot." On the following day, Mr. McCarthy purchased a ticket to see the film himself. After viewing the film, McCarthy went immediately to see the theater's manager and, although without authority, insisted that manager cease showing the film, which he also believed was insulting to the respectable Irish citizens of Providence. The manager confessed that he had not previewed the film before screening it and, in view of the mayor's protest, agreed to discontinue showing it.[3]

While many recognized the recreational value of the new motion pictures, parents, educators and clergy became concerned about the possibility that the new medium could also work to degrade the minds and artistic taste of children. The concern of the various groups moved the state legislature to pass the Cinematography Act of 1909, which became law on July 1, 1909. The act provided each city and town with the authority to license and regulate motion picture machines and forbid the use of dangerous films. In 1913, the Rhode Island Congress of Parents and Teachers, a federation of thirty-seven mothers' clubs whose children attended both private and public schools, suggested to the Providence City Council that Providence follow the lead of such cities as Chicago and New York and establish a civilian censorship board staffed by volunteers from the congress' fifteen hundred members. Volunteers pledged to work "constructively" with theater managers to make "the movies wholesome and entertaining." The expenses of the effort were to be paid by a tax on each movie reel. The congress' petition added another dimension to the frequent complaints made to the Watch and Ward Society in regard to certain movies and stage productions. The end result was that Board of Police Commissioners created the Office of Amusement in the Providence Police

---

2   Cf. John S. Gilkeson, Jr., *Middle-Class Providence, 1820–1940* (Princeton, New Jersey: Princeton University Press, 1986), 67–68; 219–20; 257–258.
3   *Providence Journal*, May 3, 1907. This was not the first protest by the Irish of the manner in which the Irish race was presented in the theaters and now on film.

Department and appointed one of the city's best detectives, Inspector John T. Maguire, to inspect each of the city's theaters. Inspector Maguire filled his new position on a part-time basis while carrying on with his other duties. The position proved to be unpopular as well as controversial as people were always complaining about his decisions. After a number of other officers, who really did not want the job, held the position briefly, the position was given in the fall of 1913 to Sergeant Richard N. Gamble. Gamble, who would hold the position of Amusement Inspector (his official title beginning in 1917) as a full-time one, was promoted to lieutenant following his appointment. The Board of Police Commissioners retained final authority over whether or not a theatrical piece or movie could play in Providence in its entirety or in censored form.[4]

Initially, the bulk of the Amusement Inspector's work lay with supervision of the entertainment presented in the city's legitimate theaters and the burlesque and vaudeville venues. In order to promote clean and wholesome entertainment, the Catholic Theater Movement, which was organized in 1912, published a "White List" of plays, which every member of a Catholic family could safely attend. Omission from the list did not mean that reviewers for the Theater Movement found the omitted plays without merit. Rather, omission meant that theatergoers had to use their own discretion in choosing to attend plays that were not on the list. In 1910, the American Federation of Catholic Societies launched an appeal to theatrical managers and playwrights for a clean stage, a campaign which the Diocesan Holy Name Union was happy to support. In 1911, the play that caused the greatest uproar in Providence was not one to which citizens took exception because of bad or suggestive language or immoral content, but one which many Irish Americans found to be offensive. The play was an Irish Players production of J. M. Synge's *The Playboy of the Western World*, which had been booked at the Opera House. The delegation of Irish Americans, who asked the Providence Board of Police Commissioners to prohibit the production, did so on the grounds that it would "offend the Irish people" and hinted that there might be trouble in the theater if production of the play was allowed. The Board rejected the delegation's request and saw to it that there were a sufficient number of officers in the theater to prevent any demonstrations.[5]

In order to deal with the increasing number of motion pictures that came to be offered in Providence, Lieut. Gamble relieved heavily on the

---

4   For a fuller discussion of this matter Cf. Richard L. Testa, Jr., *Movie Exhibition and Procedures During the Hollywood Studio Era in Providence, Rhode Island* (Ph.D. dissertation, University of Maryland, 1992), pp. 101 & Fl. (Hereafter, *Movie Exhibition and Procedures*); Carl B. Hunt, "What Effect Have the Movies on 45,000 Catholic Children in R.I.," *Providence Visitor*, September 1, 1922; June 23, 1933. The women who wished to see an improvement in the quality of the movies shown in Providence continued their efforts by organizing the Better Film Committee during the winter of 1922–23, which met periodically with local theater managers. The Providence committee was part of a nationwide Better Film Movement. Cf. Gilkeson, *Middle-Class Providence*, 259–60.

5   *Providence Visitor*, November 3, 1911; November 15, 1912; April 10, 1914; *Providence Journal*, October 31, 1911.

movie rankings of the National Board of Censorship, which sent a list of all movies they had passed and approved for general patronage to city censors. The National Board was created in 1909 by the People's Institute of New York, which had been asked by the Motion Picture Patents Company "to exercise unofficial control over the motion pictures." In 1916, the board changed its name to the National Board of Review of Motion Pictures.[6]

In Providence, as elsewhere in the country, private groups were not content to leave the question of what films were acceptable for viewing by the general public to a public official. In 1913, the Rhode Island Branch of the Congress of Mothers and Parent Teacher Association (CMPTA) called for a civilian state censorship board. The plan was well received by the *Providence Journal* and by Superintendent of Police John A. Murray, but the local theater owners and managers opposed the plan. They had developed a close working relationship with Lieut. Gamble and were fearful that women's groups would attempt to exhibit too much control. The theater owners were able to convince the City Council that a board was not needed.[7]

Public protest to the showing of a particular motion picture surfaced again in 1917. Its focus was D. W. Griffith's *The Birth of a Nation*, which first appeared in theaters in March 1915. In the case of this film, Lieut. Gamble had initially refused to allow the exhibition of the film. Opponents of the film claimed that it encouraged racial prejudice and lacked historical accuracy. Although Gamble was initially backed up by the chairman of the Board of Police Commissioners, after a few scenes were cut from the film, the board later voted to allow the showing of the film both in 1915 and 1921. On another occasion, a portion of the film was presented as a stage play. The Board's decision to allow the showing of the film provoked protest from the local chapter of National Association for the Advancement of Colored People. The Board's handling of the case was also criticized by the Rhode Island branch of the CMPTA, who, as a result of this incident, renewed its call for a local censorship board. A bill calling for a statewide board of censors was introduced into the General Assembly in early 1921. The bill was sent to House judiciary committee where it died.[8]

Griffith's film was re-released in 1921. It again fell to the Providence Board of Police Commissioners to decide whether a censored version of the film could be shown again in Providence. In making its decision in 1921, the Board held that the state statute, which authorized it to censure certain material under specified circumstances, did not apply to the film and its suppression would violate the producer's right of free speech.[9]

The commercial success of Griffith's *The Birth of a Nation* spurred the

6   Testa, *Movie Exhibition and Procedures*, p. 102.
7   Ibid., 103–107.
8   Ibid., 107–118.
9   *Providence Journal,* June 18, 1921.

production of feature films and the building of larger theaters. Between 1912 and 1919, motion picture entrepreneurs opened eight theaters in downtown Providence. Of these, both the Strand and the Shubert Majestic, which were built exclusively for the showing of motion pictures, had more than two thousands seats. As the popularity of motion pictures increased, their subject matter and the manner of its presentation evoked complaints from various individuals and groups as well as a demand for censorship of the offending films. Beginning in 1919, the National Association of the Motion Picture Industry, in the face of a growing demand for national censorship of movies, committed itself to a campaign to clean up the movies of its members. The same year also saw the formation of a Motion Picture Committee under the auspices of the newly formed National Catholic Welfare Council (in 1922, renamed the National Catholic Welfare Conference) whose chairman was charged with working quietly with producers to eliminate indecent pictures. After the committee reviewed what films it could, it published a white list in the pages of the *NCWC Bulletin*. If the producers refused to cooperate in cleaning up a film, the chairman of the committee could resort to calling the Church's attention to the offending producer through the pages of the *NCWC Bulletin*. The role of the NCWC was only to inform and advise the bishops. Each bishop could choose to do as he pleased in regard to the movies shown in his diocese. Independent of the NCWC, the International Federation of Catholic Alumnae (IFCA) created a Motion Picture Committee in 1922, which began advising Catholic schools about what was suitable entertainment for children. Like the NCWC, the IFCA issued a whitelist. The IFCA's list divided its recommended films into two categories, one suitable for church entertainment or Catholic schools, and one appropriate for mature audiences. Each film was also given an aesthetic rating of "good," "very good," or "excellent." With a large staff of volunteers, the IFCA reviewed far more films that the NCWC committee. The story of the interaction of the various secular private and public agencies, of the NCWC and the IFCA and of individual Catholics, such as Martin Quigley, publisher of *Exhibitor's Herald*, with the NAMPI and its successor, the Motion Picture Producers and Distributors of America, in promoting the self-regulation of the movie industry has been told in several recent publications.[10]

Until May 2, 1926, state law kept theaters closed on Sundays. After the law was amended, theater managers, both those who showed only movies and those who presented both movies and vaudeville, reported they did a brisk business on the first Sunday they were allowed to open. The *Providence Journal* noted that "In order to 'break the ice' and bridge the difference

---

10 Gregory D. Black, *Hollywood Censured: Morality Codes, Catholics and the Movies* (New York: Cambridge University Press, 1994); _____, *The Catholic Crusade Against the Movies, 1940–1975* (New York: Cambridge University Press, 1997); Frank Walsh, *Sin and Censorship: The Catholic Church and the Motion Picture Industry* (New Haven and London: Yale University Press, 1996).

Catholicism in Rhode Island

between the weekday and Sabbath feeling, one theater added to its program a soloist who sang 'The Rosary' and semi-sacred songs."[11]

While other bishops were very vocal in condemning immorality and indecency in movies, Bishop Keough's predecessor, Bishop Hickey was apparently content to leave the enforcement of public morality in the hands of Captain George W. Cowan, who had replaced Lieut. Richard Gamble as Providence's Amusement Inspector in 1922. When Capt. Cowan first took over the assignment in 1922, he had little technical knowledge of the theater. But, by study, observation and practical experience, he endeavored to keep pace with the rapidly changing stage and the new motion picture industry. In the course of his duties, Capt. Cowan acquired a considerable archive of information on all forms of entertainment in his third floor office in police headquarters on Fountain Street.[12]

Across the country, the presence of a Catholic newspaper in a diocese proved to be the key element in mobilizing Catholic opposition to indecency and immorality in public entertainment. In its May 19, 1933, issue, the *Visitor* printed an editorial calling attention to the increasing tendency of motion picture producers to present sordid love dramas in a manner "crafty enough" to retain "scenes and suspense tending to the immoral." The particular object of the editorial's ire was the recent showing in Providence of a Paramount picture, *The Story of Temple Drake*, based on William Faulkner's novel, *Sanctuary*. In an article printed in the *Visitor* in the same issue as the editorial lamenting the showing of the film, the *Visitor* writer detailed the research Capt. Cowan did on the film and reprinted the various reviews of it secured from the National Board of Review in New York, a private effort funded by the motion picture industry, the IFCA, and the *Boston Post*, as well as the comments of two representatives of the *Visitor*, one a priest, who also attended the special showing of the film. Although Capt. Cowan, as did many, found the movie's theme extremely sordid, he believed that there was nothing actually shown that he could use under the law to ban the film or to demand cuts.[13]

Following the showing of *The Story of Temple Drake*, the *Visitor* ran a five-part series on the challenge of securing "clean" films. The series began with a description of the work of Capt. Cowan in policing the seventeen Providence theaters. According to his annual report for 1932, Cowan made 850 visits to the various theaters. While Capt. Cowan commended the theater owners for their cooperation in his reports, he also pointed out that they were often caught in the middle between the companies that owned the theaters or supplied the live entertainment and the people who attended the theaters and occasionally objected to what they saw or heard.

Providence Journal, May 3, 1926.
[12] *Providence Visitor*, February 24; June 23, 1933; Various women's organizations as well as individual women continued the censorship debate into the 1930's. Cf. Testa, *Movie Exhibition and Procedures*, 118–163.
[13] Ibid., May 19, 1933.

Both Cowan and the author of the *Visitor* series concluded that an informed public was the best hope of securing clean films and stage shows. After the movie theaters reopened following their traditional closing for the summer period in the fall of 1933, the next chorus of complaint came from Pawtucket, where a movie theater there showed a film that had not been approved by the National Board of Review. The city clerk there, who was charged with granting the weekly licenses to the theaters, responded to the complaints by insisting that the theater managers indicated in writing whether a film had been approved by the National Board or not.[14]

When in November 1933, the majority of the American bishops gathered in Washington for the annual meeting of the National Catholic Welfare Conference, it was in the wake of Bishop Hickey's death on October 4, 1933. No Bishop of Providence was present then when the bishops made the question of the "growing moral menace of the lurid American movie" the main topic of one of their sessions. After listening to a report by Bishop John J. Cantwell of Los Angeles, which jolted many bishops who were uninformed about the problem, the body of the bishops decided to appoint an episcopal committee of five bishops, chaired by Archbishop John T. McNicholas, to study the problem further and make recommendations to the whole body of bishops at their meeting in 1934. The bishops were inspired to act in part by a speech given to the Catholic Charities Convention in New York city by the newly appointed apostolic delegate to the United States, Archbishop Amleto Cicognani on October 1, 1933, in which the delegate was persuaded by two Catholic laymen involved in efforts to clean up the movies to include in his remarks a section charging the film industry with a massacre of youth and a call for a united effort on the part of American Catholics to purify the cinema.[15]

The Episcopal Committee on Motion Pictures began its work before Bishop Keough was ordained on May 22, 1934. The committee considered many options before deciding in April 1934 to put pressure on the industry to produce clean movies by promoting the organization of a Legion of Decency in each diocese whose members would swear "to remain away from all motion pictures except those which do not offend decency and Christian morality." In a letter dated May 16, 1934 sent to Msgr. Peter Blessing, then Administrator of the diocese, Archbishop McNicholas, in the name of the Episcopal Committee, urged that "some form of pledge will be approved by each Bishop for his diocese, and some form of organization set up." What the committee envisioned was that individual Catholics, including the children in Catholic schools, would sign the pledge composed by the committee to support a boycott of unsuitable films. The *Providence Visitor* printed a copy of the "Pledge of the Legion of Decency" in its April 13, 1934 edition. Bishop Keough did not make the Legion a priority following his May ordination. However, the *Visitor* continued to allot space

14   Ibid., June 23, 30; July 7, 14, 21; November 3, 1933.
15   Walsh, *Sin and Censorship*, 85–88; *Providence Visitor*, November 24, 1933.

on its front page to the Legion of Decency's crusade as it developed in other dioceses. Even though Bishop Keough did not issue a pastoral letter on the subject in 1933 as did other bishops, the *Visitor*, by printing the weekly box office receipts reported by the Providence theaters in the trade paper, *Variety*, suggested that the national campaign was having an effect in Rhode Island as well.[16]

Bishop Keough attended his first meeting of the National Catholic Welfare Conference during the week of November 11, 1934. At that meeting the bishops listened to a report of Archbishop McNicholas' committee. While they readily lent their common support to the Legion of Decency campaign, divisions surfaced at the meeting and in McNicholas' committee as to what kind of guide the Church should offer to Catholic movie goers, especially those who had taken the Legion Pledge. One group of bishops and laymen interested in the question favored continuing the practice of recommending good films and ignoring those found to be offensive since they saw the blacklisting of films as counterproductive. A second group favored publishing both whitelists of acceptable films and blacklists of objectionable ones. At the November meeting the majority of the bishops agreed, for the sake of unity and to avoid the confusion of competing lists, to urge Cardinal Mundelein of Chicago to continue to publish a classified list of films, which the bishops were ask to instruct the editors of their diocesan newspapers to print in preference to all others. The *Visitor* published the Chicago list the week following the bishops' conference in the same issue in which it printed the bishops' statement on the Legion of Decency that summarized the decisions of the meeting.[17]

When Bishop Keough did follow the example of other American bishops in writing a pastoral on the question of immoral or indecent entertainment, his concerns were wider than the movies. After praising the efforts of his fellow bishops in beginning and supporting the Legion of Decency, in a pastoral dated December 5, 1935 to be read on the feast of the Immaculate Conception, Bishop Keough wrote as his conclusion:

> Reverend and dear Father, we urge you on this Feast of the Immaculate Conception, commemorating the spotless purity of the Mother of God, to exhort your people to lead a holy life, to respect the ideal of Catholic womanhood, to cherish Christian modesty not only in dress but especially in sports and athletic recreations; to pledge your parishioners to patronize only those motion pictures that are clean and wholesome and finally to refuse to frequent theatres where nudism is exploited out of a fixed policy.[18]

---

[16]   McNicholas to Blessing, May 16, 1934, PChA. From June 1 on, most issues of the *Providence Visitor* contained an article on the Legion campaign nationally and oftentimes on its local impact.

[17]   Walsh, Sin and Censorship, 95–130; *Providence Visitor*, November 23, 1934. The Chicago list was eventually replaced by one prepared by the Archdiocese of New York's Legion of Decency which utilized the expertise of the International Confederation of Catholic Alumnae.

[18]   *Providence Visitor*, December 5, 1935.

Following the reading of the bishop's letter, it soon became the practice to ask the people to stand and publicly take the Legion of Decency pledge.

Within a month of the reading of Bishop Keough's pastoral, the Loew's Colonial Theater in Newport began advertising the film *High School Girl* as one of its coming attractions. Since the film had been listed by the Legion of Decency as a Class C film, one unfit for public entertainment, the Catholic clergy of the city informed the manager of the theater that the showing of the film would be seen by Catholics as an offense. The manager, however, refused to withdraw the film. On Sunday, December 29, 1935, Fr. Edward A. Higney, the pastor of St. Joseph's in Newport and his two assistants, spoke against the showing of pictures in Newport discountenanced by the Legion and made particular reference to *High School Girl*, which was scheduled to open that afternoon. They also reminded their congregations of Bishop Keough's letter and urged their parishioners to stay away from Class C films. The priests' protests were soon followed by protests directed to the manager of the Colonial Theater by the Newport Council of the Knights of Columbus, St. Joseph's Holy Name Society, the Newport Father Matthew Total Abstinence Society, and the County Board of the Ancient Order of Hibernians. Reportedly, according to an article in the *Providence Visitor*, the manager of the Colonial "thanked the Catholics of Newport for boosting its business." In their sermons, the priests praised the three Newport theaters that were co-operating with the campaign for clean pictures.[19]

When the Community Theater in the North Providence village of Centredale screened the same picture beginning on Sunday, September 27, Lieut. William F. McTernan, Capt. Cowan's assistant in the office of Amusement Inspector, went out to see the film and survey the audience, even though the theater was outside his jurisdiction. In a letter written the next day to Fr. Thomas J. McKitchen, then the rector of the cathedral, Lieut. McTernan observed that the film played to a standing room audience made up "mostly of girls and boys of very young age." Fr. Francis Deery, the editor of the *Visitor*, cited McTernan's comment in an editorial he wrote on the following Wednesday which appeared in the *Visitor* the next day. The editorial, entitled "Centredale's Shame," protested the showing of the film and called attention to the advertisement for the film, which invited the public to "see why this picture cannot be shown in Providence." The editor challenged the members of the North Providence community to take action to protect the morals of the youth of Centredale.[20]

Five days after the editorial appeared in the *Visitor*, the manager of the Community Theater wrote the *Visitor* a letter of apology. In his defense,

19 *News-Tribune*, December 30, 1935; *Newport Herald*, December 30, 1935; *Providence Journal*, January 2, 1936.
20 McTernan to McKitchen, September 28; October 4, 1936; *Providence Visitor*, October 1, 1938. In his report to the Providence Superintendent of Police at the end of 1936, Capt. Cowan made it clear that films rated as Class C by the Legion were never approved by either he or Lieut. McTernan for public exhibition in Providence, Quoted in the *Providence Visitor*, February 4, 1937.

the manager pointed out that the same picture had been shown in Woonsocket and Pawtucket without any discrimination as to age and had not provoked any public protest. Furthermore, he had shown the film to seven "official and public spirited agencies" of the town whose general reaction was favorable. He also noted that the picture had been endorsed by a number of educators. Nevertheless, the manager promised that, in the future, the theater would not show any films which did not meet with the approval of the Legion of Decency.[21]

Although newly ordained at the start of the Legion of Decency Drive, Bishop Keough's ability as an administrator soon attracted the attention of his fellow bishops. In November 1936, he was elected to the Administrative Board of the NCWC as an Assistant Bishop. At the bishops' meeting in November 1941, Bishop Keough was chosen to be a member of the Motion Picture Committee and, in November 1943, he replaced Archbishop McNicholas as chairman. He served as chair until November 1946. While serving on the committee and afterwards, Bishop Keough screened movies in a room in the basement of the cathedral rectory. After his term as chairman, when a controversy arose in October 1947 between the Legion and the president of Twentieth Century-Fox over the Legion's condemnation of the studios' most expensive project to date, *Forever Amber*, Bishop Keough personally did not agree with the Legion's classification of the film. Nevertheless, he saw to it that the film was not shown in Providence and successfully pressured other theater owners not to book the film. In November 1947, the *Visitor* lamented the fact that the studios had recently released two Class C movies and that 1946 had seen a rise in the number of Class B movies. By the early 1950s, a combination of increasing independence on the part of Catholic theatergoers and a growing sensitivity on the part of the courts for First Amendment rights of writers, producers and directors began to sap the influence of the Legion of Decency.[22]

In contrast to the co-operation Capt. Cowan received from the managers of the motion picture theaters in Providence, the owners of the city's burlesque theaters were willing at times to challenge the Amusement Inspector's orders to cut lines or acts from their shows. When in September 1934, Capt. Cowan refused to grant a license to the owners of the Modern Theater to present a new burlesque show that had played in Boston the week before, the owners appealed the Amusement Inspector's decision to the Providence Board of Safety. When the Safety Board upheld Capt. Cowan, the owners went to court to overturn the order. In the course of the proceedings, Fr. McKitchen, Rev. W. Appleton Lawrence, rector of Grace Church, and Rev. Allen E. Claxton, rector of Trinity Union Methodist Episcopal Church, who had each sent a letter of complaint to the board against the type of shows presented at the Modern, were called to

---

21   Ibid., October 8, 1936.
22   Walsh, *Sin and Censorship*, 211, 262–81; Black, *The Catholic Crusade Against the Movies*, 143–75; *Providence Visitor*, November 20, 1947.

testify and were subjected to an attack by the counsel for the petitioners for their trouble. Only one of the three had actually attended a burlesque show at the Modern. Their complaints were based on statements made by their parishioners. The defense's chief argument was that Safety Board was influenced in making the decision it did by a member of the Board, who was engaged in a dispute with the theater's owner. The judge in the case ruled in favor of the Safety Board. When the following week, Capt. Cowan ordered eighteen specific deletions of what he regarded as indecent material in the current show, the president of the theater acquiesced in making the cuts so as not to provoke the Safety Board to ban all burlesque shows.[23]

Fr. McKitchen was the sole focus of another protest against another show scheduled to open in Providence. In October 1935, the RKO-Albee advertised a performance by Sally Rand, a well-known fan and bubble dancer, a show that Capt. Cowan had approved after Miss Rand agreed to make two changes. However, Fr. McKitchen, pastor of the cathedral parish that included the theater, protested Rand's proposed appearance to the Police Board of Public Safety. The board held a hearing on the theater's request for a license. After Fr. McKitchen stated his objections, the theater's manager withdrew his request. Miss Rand did not take the cancellation of her show meekly. She went to the cathedral rectory on the day the request was withdrawn and made a personal appeal to Fr. McKitchen. Fr. McKitchen was unmoved by her appeal, and was quoted by Rand as saying, that "he had no objection to the show or to me personally, but because I am Sally Rand who was arrested in Chicago, I couldn't appear on a stage in his parish if I came on wrapped in the back drop." Although Miss Rand showed him a certified copy of the Chicago court decision exonerating her of what she called "trumped up political charges," Fr. McKitchen remained unmoved.[24]

Providence was not the only venue for theatrical performances in the state where stage productions might stir up adverse public sentiment. In August 1937, the Theatre-by-the-Sea at Matunuck, in South Kingstown, presented *Devil's Moon* in which the clergy and the Sisters of Mercy were presented in an unkind light. During the course of the season theatergoers had mentioned aspects of other plays presented by the Theatre-by-the-Sea that they found objectionable, but particular complaints mentioned about the portrayal of the clergy and sisters in *Devil's Moon* provoked the pastor of St. Francis, Wakefield, Fr. James E. Greenan, and his assistants, to read a message from the pulpit vigorously criticizing the play.[25]

23 *Providence Visitor*, September 21, 28, 1934.
24 *News-Tribune*, October 15, 1935.
25 *Providence Journal*, August 9, 1937; *Providence Visitor*, August 12, 1937.

RADIO PROGRAMS

Radio was a form of entertainment as well as of news and public service that the Catholic Church and other groups monitored for decent and
moral programming. The local radio stations, WJAR, WPRO and WEAN,
were originally set up and run as separate corporations by the three large,
family-owned, Providence Department stores, The Outlet Company, The
Shepard Company and Cherry and Webb. Beginning in 1928, each of the
stations at various times offered Bishop Hickey and later Bishop Keough
free air time to promote the Catholic Charity Drive. As was true of many
of the early radio stations, the local Rhode Island stations needed pro-
graming to fill up the time they were on the air and were ready to sell air
time at reasonable rates to religious organizations. In September 1929, the
various Knights of Columbus councils in Rhode Island financed a series
of talks on Sunday evenings over WJAR on Catholic doctrine and teaching and their relation to social questions. A committee chosen by Bishop
Hickey planned the talks and arranged for the speakers. Bishop Hickey
gave the first talk in the series on Sunday, September 29, as well as the last,
on March 22, 1930. The speakers on the other evenings included both diocesan and religious priests. Bishop Keough also saw the radio as a potent
asset for the communication of Catholic doctrine and tradition. In October 1941, he sponsored a series of talks directed by Fr. Joseph F. Bracq, assistant editor of the *Visitor* over WPRO on Thursday mornings at 8:30. By
1947, nine different Catholic programs, of both national and local origin,
were carried over various Rhode Island stations.[26]

Just as the *Providence Visitor* was a catalyst in rousing the Catholics of the
state to make their views known where stage shows and movies crossed
the line of what was perceived as decent, the *Visitor* also played a crucial
role in calling its readers attention to offensive material broadcast over the
radio. When a regularly scheduled program on NBC radio sponsored by
the Chase & Sanborn Coffee Company broadcast a skit based on the Garden of Eden story featuring Mae West and Don Ameche, many Catholics took offense at the manner in which the skit was presented. Various
Catholic groups wrote the sponsors in protest and Fr. Maurice S. Sheehy,
head of the Department of Religion at Catholic University in Washington,
urged the Catholic editors of the country to join in the protest, a request
that Fr. Deery at the *Visitor* was happy to comply with. The resulting outcry
prompted the Chase & Sanborn Company to broadcast a public apology
during a later program and to send individual letters to those who wrote
the company.[27]

---

26   *Providence Visitor*, September 27; October 4, 1929; March 28, 1930; October 16, 1941; April 17,
     1947. The radio programs in 1947 were *The Catholic Hour, Catholic Round Table* (Rev. David J.
     Coffey), *Catholic Truth Period, CYO Program, From the Pilot's Seat* (Fr. Cyprian Trust, OFM, Cap., *Part-
     ners in Industry*, (Fr. Henry Crepeau); *Sacred Heart Program, Safeguards for America*, and *Sursum Corda* (Fr.
     Joseph F. Bracq).
27   Ibid., December 16, 22, 1937.

The *Visitor* also played a pivotal role in calling the Catholic population of Rhode Island to action in response to the attacks on Catholic beliefs and practices contained in the radio sermons of Joseph F. Rutherford.
Rutherford was the successor of Charles Taze Russell, the founder of the
Jehovah's Witnesses movement. Like Russell before him, Rutherford questioned the central doctrines of the mainline Christian churches and attacked their "pretensions." In June 1933, Rutherford began a new series
of radio broadcasts in New England over the Yankee network stations,
which included WEAN in Providence. Sponsored by the Watchtower Bible
and Tract Society, Rutherford, during the first of his new series on Sunday, June 25, attacked Pope Pius XI's recent declaration of a Holy Year
as well as the pope himself. Alerted to the broadcast by an advertisement
in the local papers, Fr. Deery had a stenographic record made of the sermon during which Rutherford used language derogatory of the Catholic
Church as well as Protestants and Jews. Two Knights of Columbus councils adopted resolutions of protest at the station's continued broadcasting
of the program and many individuals sent their own letters of protest. The
Visitor itself carried several articles on Rutherford in which it highlighted
the fact that Rutherford's sermons had provoked protests in many parts of
the country, particularly in the Midwest where they had been heard earlier.
The manger of WEAN defended his station's carrying of the Rutherford
broadcast when first approached by the *Visitor*. He claimed that, until he
heard from the *Visitor*, no one had complained about the sermon. In a
statement issued by the Yankee Network explaining the policy of WEAN
and other stations, the acting network manager informed the protesters
that it was the network's policy to make airtime available to all denominations for the expression of their beliefs. However, he also said that it was
never the network's to allow obnoxious broadcasts. "In the final analysis," the statement continued, "the radio audience is our judge and jury."
The station went ahead with a second broadcast of a Rutherford sermon
on the following Sunday, but by that time the members of the Catholic
Press Association, the *Visitor* among them, had stirred their readers to action. On Thursday, July 6, the Shepherd Broadcasting service, which was
headquartered in Boston, announced that it was reconsidering its position. Shortly thereafter, John Shepherd III, the president of the Yankee
Network, announced that his station, WEAN, was joining in the action of
other stations and canceling the remainder of their contract with Rutherford's sponsor in keeping with the station's policy of pleasing "the majority
of its radio audience."[28]

Rutherford did not immediately disappear. The Cherry & Webb station, WPRO, included the Rutherford program in its Sunday schedule on
July 23, two weeks after WEAN had dropped it. In his defense, the station
director, Mr. Oury, informed the *Visitor* that he was unaware of any controversy surrounding Rutherford's sermons. Aroused by previous exposure

---

[28]   Ibid., June 30; July 7, 14, 1933.

to Rutherford and by the crusading of the *Visitor*, listeners quickly flooded WPRO with telephone calls and letters protesting the station's decision to carry the program. On reading of the controversy surrounding the program in Rhode Island and elsewhere in the country in the pages of the *Visitor* when the paper was brought to his attention, Oury made the decision to immediately drop Rutherford. Aware that reaction to the program might turn people against the station as well as against the Cherry & Webb department store, Oury personally accepted the responsibility for the program's being on the schedule and stated that the Cherry family had no previous knowledge of the station's agreement to carry the broadcast.[29]

Since stations in both the East and Midwest had taken Rutherford's program off the air or refused to sell his sponsor air time, Watchtower agents, in December, began circulating a petition addressed to Congress asserting that in refusing to allow Mr. Rutherford's program the various stations were infringing his freedom of speech. The agents seeking signatures passed out pamphlets that sought to explain the Watchtower Bible and Tract Society's position. According to the *Visitor*, some of the agents went so far as "to suggest to the gullible that unless 'freedom of the air' is maintained, even Father Coughlin may no longer be able to broadcast." Agents also sought funds to finance a radio hour in opposition to Fr. Coughlin.[30]

While the *Visitor* under Msgr. O'Brien and Fr. Deery neither embraced nor opposed Fr. Charles E. Coughlin's socio-economic message, they recognized the newsworthiness of the radio priest from Royal Oak, Michigan. According to a local survey done in 1933, Coughlin had the largest radio audience in New England. In his radio addresses, which touched on social and economic issues, Coughlin made it clear that his messages were "delivered not as a spokesman of the Catholic Church, but as an American citizen speaking to other Americans."[31]

Prior to the national convention of the Union Party, which Coughlin helped organize, on August 14, 1936, Fr. Coughlin undertook a campaign tour in behalf of the party's announced presidential candidate, William Lemke. On Sunday, August 2, Fr. Coughlin addressed a gathering of about 15,000 in Clara Andrews Stadium on Massassoit Avenue, East Providence, as part of a tour of New England. He returned to the state again in October to address a rally at the Rhode Island Auditorium in support of the local congressional candidates of the Union Party. The rally drew a crowd of eight thousand. The day after the rally, Fr. Coughlin visited the St. Vincent de Paul Infant Asylum where he sliced the cake given him the evening before and offered each child a piece. While the *Visitor* reported on the events as did the *Providence Journal*, Fr. Deery never endorsed Coughlin's efforts. When in the aftermath of the Union Party's poor showing in the 1936 election, Fr. Coughlin sought to regain the national spotlight, in part

---

29   Ibid., August 4, 1933.
30   Ibid., December 29, 1933; February 9, 23; March 2, 9, 1934.
31   Ibid., March 3; April 7; October 27, 1933; March 14, 1935.

by calling attention to what he regarded as Jewish complicity in the nation's economic and political troubles, the *Visitor* continued to treat Coughlin as a news story in the same manner as did the secular papers.[32]

CENSORSHIP OF MAGAZINES AND BOOKS

While stage shows, the movies and radio programs were important sources of entertainment and information, the print media continued to touch more people than any other. In order to strengthen the influence of the *Providence Visitor*, which the Notre Dame School of Journalism referred to in the 1930s as "the best Catholic paper in the country," Bishop Hickey had authorized the expansion of the paper's offices in the last months of 1932. In what would be his last Catholic Press Message, which appeared in the *Providence Visitor* on February 3, 1933, Bishop Hickey cited the School of Journalism's praise. During his administration, Bishop Keough, in an effort to increase the circulation of the *Visitor*, authorized a new method of seeking subscriptions. Prior to the introduction of the method in February 1938, the editor and assistant editor of the *Visitor* made the rounds of the various parishes each year and preached a sermon on the importance of the *Visitor* as a source of reliable information about the Church and the Church's concerns. The new method adopted under Bishop Keough employed the good offices of the sisters teaching in the Catholic schools who, after training by a committee of priests, were to supervise the work. The sisters were to encourage the students in the Catholic schools to seek out subscriptions among their families, friends and neighbors. The schools and students who brought in the most subscriptions were recognized by being awarded prizes. The Student Press Crusade was begun each February with a pontifical mass in the cathedral celebrated by Bishop Keough at which a special sermon was preached by one of the priests of the diocese. On the Sunday following the opening of the Crusade, the parish priests were to devote their sermons to the promotion of the *Visitor* and to Catholic literature in general and to stir up the resolve of their people to avoid indecent and immoral publications.[33]

On the Sunday following the appearance of Bishop Hickey's message in 1933, two priests in West Warwick, Fr. Stephan Grenier, pastor of Our Lady of Good Counsel, Phenix, and Fr. John J. McLaughlin, assistant pastor at St. James, Arctic, devoted their sermons to amplifying the bishop's statement and applying it to the local situation in West Warwick as they

---

[32]   Ibid., September 26; October 29, 1936; July 20; November 16, 1939; *Providence Journal*, July 22; August 2, 3, 5, 1936. While Fr. Deery elected not to take Fr. Coughlin to task for his remarks, Rabbi Israel M. Goldman of Temple Emanuel, Providence, in a sermon given from the pulpit of the First Baptist Church, Providence, on Sunday, March 10, 1935, pleaded for Godly leaders to deal with the "narrow nationalism of a William Randolph Heart and a Father Coughlin," *Providence Journal*, March 11, 1935. Cf. Donald Warren, *Radio Priest: Charles Coughlin, the Father of Hate Radio* (New York: The Free Press, 1996).

[33]   *Providence Visitor*, February 3, 1933; September 23, 1938; January 19; February 9, 16, 1939.

saw it. In addition to urging the reading of Catholic literature in order to counteract the evils of the day and make Catholics better informed, both priests attacked the presence of pornographic magazines in West Warwick stores. Since about nine-tenths of West Warwick's population was Catholic, the priests' remarks stirred the community. Prompted by the sermons and by a letter from a mother, who complained that she found her high school student purchasing a pornographic paper in an Arctic store, the chief of the West Warwick police personally undertook a canvas of the local newsstands and ordered any and all magazines that did not bear the second class postage rating of the government to be removed. The chief's actions were supported by a petition from the St. Vincent de Paul societies in the town asking that the town authorities enforce the state laws regarding the sale and distribution of obscene literature.[34]

On his part, Fr. Deery and the *Visitor* chose to focus on the books available through the various commercial lending libraries operating in Providence. In an article published in the *Visitor* of February 17, the paper called attention to the fact that the Rhode Island law relating to "obscene, indecent or impure" literature was being widely violated in the city by the private lending libraries. Calls for action on the part of Catholics to halt the lending and sale of obscene or indecent literature had been made in the past and were being made with increasing frequency in many parts of the country and on a national level. Among the resolutions the American bishops agreed on during the meeting of the National Catholic Welfare Conference in November 1933 was one of concern in regard to the "increasing flood of immoral and unmoral books, periodicals and pamphlets" then coming off the American presses. The bishops declared that such literature presented "one of the greatest menaces to our national well-being." The bishops asked the Catholic people of the nation "to make it part of that crusade of Catholic Action" which Pius XI had urged Catholics to undertake. With proportionally the largest Catholic population of any state in the union, Bishop Hickey's attack on immoral literature, when taken up by the *Providence Visitor*, was to rouse the conscience of the state in a way that even surpassed the Legion of Decency's crusade against objectionable motion pictures.[35]

In his February 1933 Lenten message, Bishop Hickey called upon his people:

> [t]o avoid the degenerate reading matter of the age, and give our minds and hearts to books, papers and meditation on the Life, Passion, Death and Resurrection of the Son of God Made Man, in Whose honor our Holy Father had declared a Jubilee to mark the Nineteenth Centenary of the Redemption of Mankind.

In support of his admonition and of the drive the *Visitor* had begun against

---

[34] *Providence Visitor*, February 10, 17, 1933.
[35] Ibid., May 1, 1926; January 15; November 25, 1932; January 20; February 10, 1933.

indecent literature, the bishop amplified his message by making a special statement in which he commended:

> [t]he call of the American hierarchy to protest the almost unrestricted trafficking in obscene literature whose prevalence on newsstands and in circulating libraries constitutes a real menace to the morals of youth and even to those who have reached their maturity.[36]

Bishop Hickey made it a point in his sermon in the cathedral on Sunday, February 26, to express his support of the *Visitor* and the clergy, who had preached against "dirty" books. The *Visitor*'s call for enforcement of the law and the ensuing complaints made to State Attorney General John P. Hartigan by various Catholic organizations brought quick results. On March 3, Attorney General Hartigan issued a statement aimed at warning the circulating libraries and drugstores that were distributing books containing "obscene, indecent and impure language" that they would be prosecuted unless such distribution stopped immediately. The books referred to in the complaints were of rather recent origin and were not allowed in the public libraries.[37]

As in West Warwick, the police in Warren and Providence quickly joined in the campaign. Providence Superintendent of Police Edward J. Kelly, on March 11, ordered all his precinct commanders to see to it that all the proprietors of establishments where obscene books were available were served notice that distribution of such books violated the law. As a follow up to this general notification, the chief appointed a special detail to conduct an investigation of all the known dealers of the books the *Visitor* complained about. Many managers of the chain and private circulating libraries immediately heeded the Attorney General's warning. To deal with those who chose not to heed the warning, Superintendent Kelly prepared a "blacklist" of books whose possession would lead to the immediate arrest of the seller. On their part, the women of the Diocesan Council of Catholic Women created a vigilance committee to follow the police as they made their checks on the circulating libraries. The women agreed that they would offer to place a small placard of endorsement on any bookstand that consistently displayed only such books as the police and they approved. When several Providence dealers asked the Attorney General for a list of books that violated the state law, Mr. Hartigan agreed to provide one. While no local dealers were arrested during the campaign, two New York salesmen were. One salesman, who was arrested in March, pleaded not guilty after being stopped by a traffic officer who found obscene literature in his car. He was bound over to a grand jury, which found cause for him to be held for trial. Attorney General Hartigan personally prosecuted the case against the accused salesman. At his trial the salesman did not contest the charge against him and was sentenced to a month's confinement in the

---

[36]   Ibid., February 24, 1933.
[37]   Ibid., March 3, 1933.

state prison. A second salesman was arrested a little better than a year later, in July 1934. He too pleaded no contest and likewise was sent to the state prison for a month.[38]

The *Visitor*'s campaign effectively dealt with the particular problem posed by the private, circulating libraries. The wider problem of indecent, obscene and immoral magazines being available to children remained. In March 1937, the Pawtucket police vice squad began a campaign to rid the city's newsstands of twenty-one different magazines the city's Public Safety Director, Harry F. Curvin, had determined violated the state law. The activity of the Pawtucket Police prompted the *Visitor* to undertake a survey of newsstands in other Rhode Island cities and towns and found that the twenty-one magazines banned in Pawtucket were on sale throughout the state.[39]

In late May or early June a Woonsocket priest informed Lucien San Souci, the Woonsocket agent for the Rhode Island Society for the Prevention of Cruelty to Children, that a Woonsocket newsdealer was selling indecent pamphlets and magazines to children in the city. The agent began an investigation, which soon focused on the store of Barnat Ephraim at 301 Social Street. On Saturday, August 28, 1937, San Souci and Inspector Wilfred Messier of the Woonsocket Police raided the store and confiscated 350 immoral booklets and magazines. Many of the pamphlets and magazines carried England or France as the place of publication, but Ephraim told the investigators that they were printed in Brooklyn, Manhattan, Detroit and Philadelphia. Shortly before the raid, the chief of police in Woonsocket, Alfred O. Perron, had established a system for censoring the publications sold in the stores of the city, but Ephraim had bypassed the system of censoring because the agent who supplied him with the materials had failed to submit the publications to the police as required. When his case came up for trial, Ephraim was found guilty and sentenced to twenty months at the state prison.[40]

The success that the Legion of Decency experienced in the diocese and in the country inspired Fr. Deery to launch a similar campaign against the "tidal wave of filth" at the beginning of January 1938 aimed at the Rhode Island News Company, the primary distributor of immoral and indecent magazines and "the rotten crew with whom they deal." With Bishop Keough's support and blessing, the *Visitor* called on the priests of the diocese to "preach this campaign in season and out of season." Secondly, the paper called on the teachers in the Catholic schools to get their pupils to pledge total abstinence from magazine filth. Thirdly, it called upon Catholic parents to "lock the doors of their homes against this agency of the devil and to boycott every place — drug store, variety store, or whatever it may be — where these rotten magazines were sold." Finally, it called on the

[38]   Ibid., March 17, 24, 31, 1933; October 13, 20, 1933; July 14, 1934.
[39]   Ibid., March 25, 1937.
[40]   Ibid., September 2; November 4, 1937.

active Catholic organizations of the state to join in the fight. The paper printed the titles of the magazines that violated the standards of morality or decency and promised to add to its initial list. One key component of the campaign was Fr. William Delaney's making available the services of the Catholic Youth Organization. Under the direction of the priests, who were the CYO sectional directors, members of the organization were to interview the magazine dealers to ascertain their attitude in regard to the sale of objectionable magazines. The *Visitor* committed itself to publish the names of the dealers co-operating with the crusade in a weekly Honor List. Those who agreed not to carry the products of the "Devil's Press" were given placards to place in their windows notifying the public of their support for the campaign. A second major component was the signing of a pledge by individuals, a copy of which was printed in the paper, that they would "refrain from the purchase and reading of any magazine listed as objectionable by the *Visitor*. The *Visitor* was quite frank about its tactics:

> We struck at rotten movies through the boxoffice. We now propose to strike at rotten magazines through the cash register.[41]

The campaign quickly won support from the various mayors of the state; state officials; numerous educators; J. Harold Williams, State Boy Scout Executive; and a few clergymen of other denominations as well as from the Master Barber's Association of Rhode Island and the Ladies' Hairdressers Association of Rhode Island, both associations urging their members to aid the campaign. The members of the Diocesan Council of Catholic Women and of the various Holy Name societies followed the initial approach to the newsdealers by the members of the CYO and lent their own weight and that of their organizations to the campaign to secure the dealers co-operation with the campaign. The students in the Catholic High Schools in the state pledged to refrain from purchasing the magazines listed in the *Visitor*. By March 10, 330 dealers were on the Honor List and by April 28, the *Visitor* had received 210,061 signed pledge cards.[42]

As the American bishops did in regard to their concerns about immoral scenes in motion pictures, the NCWC created a committee of bishops to study the traffic in printed and pictured obscenity. Following a meeting in Chicago at the end of January 1939, the five bishops on the Bishops' Committee on Obscene Literature announced a plan to create the National Organization of Decent Literature (NODL) as a parallel organization to the Legion of Decency in order to encourage all the dioceses of the country to unite in the effort to eradicate immoral and indecent periodicals. The committee was chaired by Bishop John F. Noll of Fort Wayne, Indiana. Bishop Keough was also a member of the committee. As was the case with motion pictures, the aim of this parallel national effort was to

---

[41]   Ibid., January 13, 20, 1938.
[42]   Ibid., January 27; February 3, 10, 17, 24; March 10; April 28, 1938.

convince the producers or publishers of the magazines judged to be immoral or indecent, that such magazines were not profitable. In an editorial commenting on the announcement of the formation of the NODL the *Visitor* observed:

> It is noteworthy that while the Bishop's campaign for decency in print waged through the *Providence Visitor* was at its height, the smut publishers were scared off. But when of necessity it relaxed, the rats came out of their sewers surreptitiously and warily to feed on the delectable pabulum of innocent souls. Gradually the dirty magazines are becoming more bold. It proves that constant vigilance must be the watchword. We cannot relax. There must be no respite. Eternal vigilance and unrelenting warfare alone can keep the periodicals clean.

In promoting the first Student Press Crusade at the beginning of 1939, Bishop Keough referred to the formation of the NODL and reminded the people of the diocese of the pledges they had signed in the previous year.[43]

Spiritual Awakening and Social Action
Among Franco Americans:
Fr. Arthur Bienvenue and the Jocist Movement

Many of those who promoted social action on the part of the laity recognized the importance of the link between prayer in which one comes to a knowledge of and relationship with Christ and the work one undertakes to bring about God's kingdom on earth. In the 1930s, the retreat movement continued to gain in strength. Rather than wait for lay people to come to retreat houses, some of those, who believed in the importance of retreats, sought to reach out to the laity and create opportunities to make retreats in places and at times that more readily facilitated the making of a retreat. The Jesuits in the United States were particularly active in this field as were their confreres in Canada. During the early 1930s, if not before, individuals from the several French-speaking parishes in the diocese made retreats with the Jesuits at Quebec and Montreal. In 1936, the Jesuits in Montreal secured Bishop Keough's permission and his support for the holding of a series of closed retreats at Mt. St. Charles Academy during July and August. The retreats were conducted by Frs. Joseph Belanger, S.J., and Jean d'Auteil Richard, S.J. Several of the retreats were open to any man who wished to attend. Others were specifically directed towards young men and professional men. By the end of the five retreats, 146 men had taken part. During the second year, Fr. Richard returned along with another Jesuit, Fr. G. D. Desjardins, S.J., who was a native of

---

[43]   Ibid., February 2, 9, 1939.

Pawtucket, to offer seven retreats. One was a general retreat and one was for workingmen, the others were given specially for businessmen and merchants, professional men, and priests. A total of 229 men attended the retreats that year.[44]

At the end of the final retreat in 1937, the one given for priests from August 30 to September 8, Fr. Desjardins, who was the director of the retreats that year, helped the laymen interested in the movement to form the Franco-American Closed Retreat Association. More than four hundred men attended the organizational meeting. In testimony to at least a partial healing of the divisions that had arisen among the French-speaking Catholics during the Sentinellist controversy, Antonio Prince of Woonsocket was elected president of the group. Fr. J. M. L. Giroux, pastor of Our Lady of Victories, Woonsocket, was elected chaplain. Eugene Dursin, Eugene L. Jalbert, and Wilfred Laferriere of Woonsocket; Guillaume Myette of Central Falls, and Albert Coutu of West Warwick were elected vice presidents; Elie Boucher of Woonsocket, Secretary; Roderique Hemond, of Woonsocket, Assistant Secretary; and Mathias Thibault of Woonsocket, Treasurer. The meeting was addressed by Fr. Joseph-Pepin Archambault, S.J., an internationally known sociologist, on the topic of "Catholic Action or the Laymen's Apostleship." Fr. Archambault told his audience that every Catholic man should carry out the principles of his faith wherever he went, and by his own example he should promote justice, charity, and Catholic action.[45]

In the summer of 1939, the Closed Retreat Association faced a crisis when, for various reasons, the Brothers of the Sacred Heart withdrew from hosting the retreats at Mt. St. Charles. Rather than see this valued movement end, Fr. Stephen Grenier, pastor of Holy Family Parish, Woonsocket, offered the Jesuits and the retreatants the use of Holy Family church and school. From 1939 to 1949, the closed retreats for men continued at Holy Family. In early 1942, with many men then serving in the military and others engaged in vital defense work, the Jesuits expanded their retreat apostolate by offering to hold retreats for women. These retreats were held in the Sisters of Jesu-Marie convent in Precious Blood parish. The women, who took advantage of the opportunity to make a closed retreat, imitated the men in forming their own retreat association, the Franco-American Women's Closed Retreat Association. On January 16, 1942, Bishop Keough appointed Fr. Arthur L. Bienvenue, then an assistant at Precious Blood, Woonsocket, chaplain of the group.[46]

Since the Jesuits were concerned both with encouraging retreats and active involvement of laymen in the social action movements, some of the

---

[44]   Ibid., July 11, 1936; July 15; August 5; September 7, 1937.
[45]   Ibid., September 7, 1937. The French name for the group was Association des Retraitants Franco-Americain.
[46]   "Holy Family Parish, 1902–1977," privately printed, 1977; Fr. Bienvenue's biographical record, PChA.

workingmen who made closed retreats with the Jesuits at Quebec, Montreal or in Woonsocket formed a local branch of the Ligue Ouvrière Catholique sometime during 1939. Fr. Bienvenue, who was involved in the formation of the Ligue, secured the permission of his pastor, Fr. Georges Bedard, to serve as the Ligue's chaplain. The Ligue was an organization found in many places in French Canada, which strove to inject, in the words of labor historian, Gary Gerstle, "Christian values into the labor movement and reestablish the importance of the parish as the institution best equipped to offer Catholic guidance in the problems of daily life." By September 1942, when the Ligue held its third annual Labor Day Picnic at Lincoln Woods, there were eight Franco-American cells from the Blackstone Valley parishes represented and two cells from West Warwick. In all, the picnic attracted approximately seven thousand men, women and children.[47]

When the Woonsocket branches of the Ligue Ouvrière Catholique were formed in 1939, the French-Canadian clergy in Woonsocket were becoming increasingly concerned about the direction of the labor movement in their city. The Independent Textile Union (ITU) had replaced the United Textile Union as Woonsocket's largest union. The president of the ITU, Joseph Schmetz, a Belgian-born mulespinner, had left war-ravaged Belgium with his family in 1919 for Canada. After having worked for a short time in various places, Schmetz came to the United State and worked for a while in Lawrence, Massachusetts. In 1924, after being blacklisted for his union activities during the famous textile strike in Lawrence, he moved to Woonsocket where he settled among the Franco-Belgians on Woonsocket's Social District's northern rim. Although Schmetz initially joined the local United Textile Workers Union in Woonsocket when he first found employment there, he and a small group of mulespinners, who shared the militant, socialist views of his native land, seceded from the UTW in 1931 and formed the Independent Textile Union. In writing the new union's constitution, Schmetz and his associates avoided socialist rhetoric in order to attract workers to the new union. However, after 1936 when the new union was firmly established, Schmetz began to express his radical views in his union's publications. In order to move the ITU more surely toward the socialist vision that Schmetz and other Franco-Belgians shared, Schmetz in 1936 used his influence as president of the union to secure the hiring of Lawrence Spitz, a twenty-five year old, Providence-born, UTW organizer as the union's General Secretary. Spitz's radicalism grew out of different circumstances than did Schmetz's. Although occasionally accused of being a Communist, Spitz never openly espoused the Communist cause.[48]

The majority of the French-Canadian textile workers in Woonsocket, who came to join the ITU, never shared the radical, class warfare views of Schmetz and the core leadership group allied to him. However, Schmetz

[47] Gary Gerstle, *Working Class Americanism: The Politics of Labor in a Textile City, 1914–1960* (Cambridge: Cambridge University Press, 1989), p. 252; *Providence Journal*, September 8, 1942.
[48] Gerstle, 78–89; 158–66.

recognized that the cultural forces that had shaped the French-Canadian community in Woonsocket—namely, the struggle for *survivance*, which had animated many during the Sentinellist controversy—could be exploited to help build the new union. In his writings Schmetz would represent the French-Canadians cultural struggle in class terms. Just as the Sentinellist leaders had depicted Bishop Hickey as an oppressor of the French community, Schmetz depicted the wealthy French mill owners in Woonsocket as aristocrats, who despised their French-Canadian workers and sought to exploit them. A riot in front of the Woonsocket Rayon mill on September 12, 1936, during the course of a nationwide strike of textile workers, was the occasion during which a young Woonsocket worker was killed. The riot and death focused Woonsocket's attention on the Manville Jenckes Corporation, which owned the mill. Formed in a merger in 1923, the Providence based company had a history of labor troubles and shaky finances. Rather than bargain with their unionized workers and potentially raise manufacturing costs, the company had chosen to close its cotton mills in Manville and Woonsocket. In October 1933, the company violated the labor provisions of the National Industrial Recovery Act by firing Woonsocket Rayon Company workers, who had joined a newly organized UTW local. Resentment toward the company fueled the violence on September 11 and 12, which focused on Woonsocket Rayon. The ITU's leadership during the September strikes demonstrated, in Gerstle's words, "that it could provide the leadership and organization necessary to alter significantly the conditions of working-class life." As a result, the union became the chief beneficiary of the class resentment demonstrated in September 1934. Membership in the ITU swelled by 50 percent from late 1934 through 1936.[49]

The shift of workers' allegiance to the foreign-born, radical leadership of the ITU disturbed the Catholic clergy of Woonsocket. When in 1939, Fr. Ernest Morin, pastor of St. Ann's, Woonsocket, preached an anti-radical sermon in which he denounced the ITU's leaders, the union members in the congregation walked out en masse. The Ligue Ouvrière Catholique offered an alternative to a direct and public contest between the traditional and conservative Catholic leaders of Woonsocket and the radical unionists for leadership in the French-Canadian community.[50]

In his sermon on Sunday, February 4, 1940, Fr. Grenier at Holy Family charged that:

> A communistic organization masquerading as an agency for the promotion of the industrial worker's welfare has established itself in Woonsocket and is working to sow the seeds of discord among employers and their employees.

He assured his parishioners of his support for unions, but declared his opposition to "workers' organizations that looked to communists for leadership." Grenier's expression of support for unions broke with a fifty-

---

[49]   Ibid., 128–140.
[50]   Ibid., 247–51, 252.

year tradition of opposition on the part of the French-Canadian clergy
in Woonsocket to local unionism. Given the support of the papacy and
of many of the American bishops for the concept of corporatism, which
Pius XI advocated as a middle way between the laissez-faire of the right
and the collectivism of the left, the clergy in Woonsocket began to support
the rights of labor and to argue for the positive role of trade unions. In
Gerstle's words, Pius XI's vision of corporatism:

> [m]eant a humane and regulated capitalism made possible by the organization of
> society's main occupational groups — capitalists, workers, farmers, professionals and
> small businessmen — into guild-like bodies that would simultaneously promote the
>
> interests of their members and enlarge each group's consciousness of its dependence,
> for its own well being, on the welfare of other groups.[51]

Fr. Arthur Bienvenue, who, along with other Woonsocket priests, served
as an advisor to the Ligue, had been ordained a priest in June 1933 after
completing his studies for the priesthood in Montreal. After two temporary
assignment following his ordination, Bishop Keough sent him to Precious
Blood as an assistant. It is probable that Fr. Bienvenue acquired a knowledge of the specialized Catholic action movement founded in Belgium in
1924–25 by then Canon (in 1965, Cardinal) Joseph Cardign while he was
a student in Montreal. In 1925, Pope Pius XI had given his approval to
an outgrowth of Cardign's Jeunesse syndicaliste, the Jeunesse Ouvrière
Chretienne (JOC) or Young Catholic Worker movement. It is from the
acronym, JOC, that the common name for the movement, Jocist, is taken.
As envisioned by Fr. Cardign, a small group, which formed a cell or section, would systematically observe their environment and meet weekly to
discuss it, judge the situation in light of the gospel, and end their gathering
with a decision for action. In contrast to the study club method adopted by
the Confraternity of Christian Doctrine, the thrust of the Jocist movement
was clearly on action. By defining itself as specialized, the Jocist movement, of which Jeunesse Etudiante Catholique or JEC groups were a part,
indicated that its cells or sections were oriented towards specific ages, sexes,
groups or professions such as young workers, students or married couples.
Fr. Bienvenue, with the assistance of the Sisters of Jesu-Marie, founded
in 1935 the first Jeunesse Etudiante Catholique groups at the Jesu-Marie

---

[51] *Woonsocket Call*, February 5, 1940. Union leaders were particularly sensitive to the charge of their
being communists as such an accusation readily caught the attention of the community at large.
Union leaders in Woonsocket and in Saylesville, a mill village in Lincoln where two men were
killed in a confrontation with the National Guard, Deputy Sheriffs, and private security men,
similar to that which occurred in Woonsocket, blamed outside agitators for the violence. Cf. *Woonsocket Call*, September 14, 1934, for a list of alleged communists arrested in Providence. Cf. also,
Providence Journal, September 14, 27, 1934.

Academy and St. Claire's High School, which were in Precious Blood parish, after he had been in Woonsocket for about three years.[52]

When Fr. Bienvenue became involved with the Ligue, he kept the focus of the members on labor issues. The initial inspiration and direction of the Ligue came from the Jesuits who had begun the Closed Retreat movement in Woonsocket. According to the information obtained during interviews done in 1983 by Gerstle with three former members of the Ligue and presented in his study of the labor movement in Woonsocket, the Jesuits selected certain men and women for membership in the Ligue and gave them "brief but intense bursts of instruction on subjects ranging from theology and papal encyclicals to organization skills to family economics." Not all the members of the Ligue were workers. The instruction provided during the courses of the various retreats and on special study days was intended to "enrich their religious lives, improve their effectiveness as lay leaders in parish affairs, and prepare them for the task of infiltrating Woonsocket's labor movement, propagating religious values and ousting the radicals."[53]

After its founding, the Ligue grew to about fifty members, who were spread out among the city's six French-Canadian parishes. Two men active in the league, Arthur Fortin and Phileas Valois, held strategic positions in the community. Fortin was the owner of a service station and Valois operated a grocery store. The two, in Gerstle's words, "orchestrated plans by Ligue members to make themselves available to Catholic workers in need, to inject their religious values into the currents of daily discourse, and to stimulate opposition in the ranks of the [ITU] to its radical leadership." Membership in the Ligue in its early days could easily have been much larger as a number of ITU French-Canadian officials wanted to join, but, as Gerstle noted, the Ligue refused to accept them. "the Ligue wanted as member unobtrusive infiltrators who seemed to spring naturally from the rank and file."[54]

The Ligue's first challenge to the radicals' leadership of the union occurred when the radicals scheduled union meeting on Easter Sunday. The Ligue cadre did not challenge the radicals openly, but rather prevailed on a brother of a Ligue member, who was an overseer, to pass the word to ITU members in his department and to overseers in other departments. The overseer quickly marshaled sufficient opposition to force the radicals to cancel the meeting. Early efforts on the part of Ligue members to oust the ITU's radical leadership were readily blunted, but in August 1943, Joseph Schmetz was forced out as president of the union for reasons unconnected with the Ligue efforts and replaced in September by another, less talented,

---

[52] *Providence Visitor*, February 27, 1941. For a short overview on how the movement inspired by Fr. Cardign entered the United States apart from Fr. Bienvenue's initiative, Cf. Jay P. Dolan, *The American Catholic Experience: A History from Colonial Times to the Present* (New York: Doubleday & Company, 1985), 415–16.

[53] Gerstle, p, 252.

[54] Ibid., 253–55.

radical. In that same month, Lawrence Spitz was drafted and was forced to leave the city and his position as General Secretary.[55]

On June 10, 1943, Fr. Bienvenue undertook to transform the Ligue along the lines developed by the Jocist movement, by forming parish sections, each with its own section leader and chaplain. With the changed focus there came, in 1947, a different name, the Christian Family Movement. In 1944, after he began organizing the sections, Fr. Bienvenue invited Fr. Edmund Brock, the director of the newly formed Diocesan Social Action Institute, to give a talk to a study day for perspective chaplains "so that the priests would have a clear conception of the relation between the Ligue and Social Action." Fr. Bienvenue followed this study day for priest-chaplains with one in November 1944 for workers. As a result of this second study day a method for the formation of parish sections was agreed on. The method consisted of individual training until the leaders were ready for the formal meeting of their sections or sections. As later described in an article in the *Providence Visitor*:

> The leaders would be convinced that they were not being called upon for their own spiritual benefit but to do Apostolic work among others. In one case, a chaplain spent sixteen months in individual contacts with his leaders before starting a formal meeting. After the leaders had been sufficiently prepared the establishment of a section begins in earnest. One of the Federation Committee leaders conducts a series of fourteen meetings which are held weekly.
>
> The members of the Federation Committee are the section leaders and the workers. The workers are mostly mill workers and Union members. Besides Father Bienvenue, there are five other members of the committee: Arthur Fortin, Philias Valois, Adelard Durand, Rene Masse, and Mederic Ethier. Rev. Adrien Menard, Rev. Lucien Roussell are assistant Federal chaplains.[56]

On November 25, 1944, Fr. Bienvenue wrote to Bishop Keough to inform him of what happened on Sunday, November 19, when the Ligue held its first general reunion. The reunion was attended by eleven chaplains and fifty leaders from fifteen parishes. The day itself was prepared and conducted by the five laymen who, along with Fr. Bienvenue, made up the Ligue's Federation. Fr. Bienvenue reported that the working men, who attended, were actually in the stage of formation. They represented twenty-nine different trades in thirty-two mills, shops, or public agencies located in eight cities or towns in Rhode Island. Several of them were of special interest to Fr. Bienvenue and his leadership team because of their responsibilities in the ITU, which they hoped to influence through the movement. He reported that the Ligue's program for the year dealt with the professional and vocational responsibilities of the laboring class.

---

[55] Ibid., 251, 270–73.
[56] Members of the Federal Committee to Keough, September 11, 1944, PChA; *Providence Visitor*, February 27, 1947. The date for the founding of the Christian Family Movement is taken from a biographical sheet Fr. Bienvenue prepared for the *Providence Visitor* on July 7, 1956, PChA.

The leaders of the meeting stressed the necessity of taking an active part in parochial activities and of gaining influence in workers' organizations.[57]

The efforts of the members of the Ligue to gain influence in the ITU were not without their setbacks. However, by the end of 1944, the ethnic corporatists, as Gerstle refers to members of the Ligue, had managed to capture four crucial staff posts—the two organizing positions, the editorship of *ITU News*, and a newly created business agent job. In a report to Bishop Keough submitted several months before the September contest for president of the union that saw Gagnon elected, Fr. Bienvenue wrote to Bishop Keough that:

> The L.O.C. had also been progressing in a very encouraging manner during the past few months. The leaders are following a program of study of their social milieu whereby they are becoming more and more aware of unchristian conditions. Our action is penetrating more deeply into workers' unions where many members are beginning to better understand the need of more authentic Christian leaders in the unions.
>
> Other activities of the L.O.C. consist in monthly meetings of the presidents and bi-monthly meetings of section leaders at which the problems and program of the movement are discussed. The men are also helping to promote the work and assure the success of closed retreats. At present, we are preparing an intensive campaign among workers which we hope will bring about a deeper penetration of the Christian spirit.

By September 1945 the ethnic corporatists had gained control of three of the top elective positions in the union. The election in that same September of Ligue member Herve Gagnon as president of the ITU completed the ethnic corporatist ascension to union power. Subsequently, the new leaders of the ITU "moved quickly to remake the ITU in their religious and ethnic image."[58]

The Ligue's concerns were not just limited to the working conditions of laborers and mill hands, but embraced the whole environment in which they lived. Late in 1945, the Ligue members began visiting stores and other establishments in Woonsocket, which displayed advertising posters for Nipmuc Park in Mendon, Massachusetts, where there was a strip club. Members of the Ligue found the advertisements themselves offensive and the entertainment at the club degrading. In his December 1945 report to Bishop Keough, Fr. Bienvenue noted that by speaking to the owners of the establishments where the posters for the park were, the Ligue members were able to persuade the owners to remove all but five of the fifty-seven advertisements found in Woonsocket.[59]

While the members of the Ligue had initially chosen not to draw attention to themselves, Fr. Bienvenue believed it important to demonstrate the strength of the Ligue and the size of its following in order for the Ligue

---

57 Bienvenue to Keough, November 25, 1944, PChA.
58 Gerstle, 273–74; Bienvenue to Keough, June 20; December 21, 1945, PChA.
59 Bienvenue to Keough, December 21, 1945, PChA.

"to impose itself all the more on other organizations or institutions detrimental to a Christian spirit in the working class." To that end, in 1945 he organized a Ligue-sponsored picnic in Lincoln Woods State Park. The second of the Ligue's picnics, the one held on August 25, 1946, was attended by almost five thousand people. Members of the Ligue spread their message through personal contacts, a few speeches and Benediction of the Blessed Sacrament with which the day ended.[60]

The success of the Ligue's members, who were formed by the corporatist vision of industrial relations, in driving the radicals from control of the ITU and placing its members in important positions did not mean the triumph of corporatism. While manufactures had made substantial profits on the government's World War II cost-plus contracts, the wages of labor were controlled by the federal government as was labor's right to strike. In the post-war period, which saw a significant rise in inflation, labor throughout the country sought to negotiate raises in wages. The ITU was among the unions that sought wage increases for its members. The aggressiveness of the ITU was fueled in part by the social and religious perception that the owners were being immoral in refusing to accord their workers a just share in the wealth that they had helped to produce. In the changing world of post-war Woonsocket, many of the young people had been exposed during the war to the wider world beyond the French-Canadian enclave dominated by French-Canadian culture. Consequently, the new corporatist leaders of the ITU began to look for inspiration and support from the Social Labor School, an initiative of Fr. Brock's Social Action Institute. Brock was more enthusiastic about the labor movement than any French-Canadian clergyman in the city, with the exception of Fr. Henry Crepeau, who, like Fr. Brock, had studied at the Catholic University of America under Msgr. John A. Ryan. Brock's influence in the labor movement would eventually replace that of the Jesuits and Fr. Bienvenue. Subsequent to the ouster of the radicals from the leadership of the ITU, Fr. Bienvenue began taking the men of the Ligue Ouvrière Catholique in a different direction.[61]

While the Ligue had initially focused on labor issues, the Jocist movement, which Fr. Bienvenue introduced to Woonsocket in 1936 and whose methods also informed the Ligue, was concerned with the Christianization of the whole of society. Fr. Bienvenue, along with a group of young French-Canadian priests with whom he shared his interests, and a core of lay leaders, spent six years of experimentation in which they sought the best way to apply the Jocist techniques to the American situation. In 1942, Bienvenue asked and received Bishop Keough's permission to spread the Jeunesse Etudiants Catholique (Young Christian Students) Movement, which he had established in Precious Blood parish, to other schools in the city and beyond. Later that year, in July, Bishop Keough approved the organization of

---

[60] Bienvenue to Keough, September 6, 1946, PChA.
[61] Gerstle, 278–330; *Providence Visitor*, February 27, 1947.

a Diocesan Committee, whose responsibility was the foundation of cells in various schools. In his first report to Bishop Keough on work of the Jocist movement in the diocese at the end of 1943, Fr. Bienvenue noted that there were JEC sections in sixteen Catholic grammar schools in Woonsocket, Manville, Central Falls, Pawtucket and Providence, four in French-speaking Catholic high schools — St. Claire's and Mt. St. Charles in Woonsocket, Sacred Heart in Central Falls, and St. Jean Baptiste in Pawtucket — as well as sections in Marlborough, Lawrence, Lowell and Worcester, Massachusetts that kept in touch with the Federation in Rhode Island.[62]

As to specific actions undertaken by the sections, Fr. Bienvenue informed Bishop Keough in his December 1943 report that leaders of the movement in the various schools worked in co-operation with the Confraternity of Christian Doctrine to make personal contacts with public school students in order to bring them to the July catechism classes, taught classes themselves, and organized recreation periods between classes. The three young women who, along with Fr. Bienvenue, made up the Federal Committee of the JEC, attended the annual Catholic Action Students Study Week at the University of Notre Dame in May and the Study Week of the JEC in Montreal during the summer. The whole of August was taken up in preparing for the second annual Diocesan Study Day, which was held by the Federation at the end of August, and was attended by twenty-five priests, sixty nuns and eighty lay leaders from both within and outside the diocese in contrast to the twenty-five priests, forty nuns and fifteen lay leaders who attended the first one the year before. The study days during the summer focused on the program that the sections would stress in the coming year. The growth of the movement in Rhode Island was such that by May 1943, Fr. Bienvenue felt the need to open an office in the St. John Baptiste building at 1 Social St., Woonsocket, which was staffed by Miss Madeleine Bordes, Field Secretary for the JEC, and serviced section leaders who wished to stop in and talk.[63]

In October 1943, Fr. Bienvenue attended the Priests' Study Days held by the Catholic School of Social Action in Chicago. In the summer of 1938, another priest, Fr. Donald Kanaly, from Ponca City, Oklahoma, who had studied in Louvain, Belgium, where he came to know Fr. Cardign's work, had first spoken on the Jocist movement. In the 1943 Chicago meeting, Fr. Bienvenue spoke on "The Role of the Priest in the Formation of Lay Apostles."[64]

In his December 1943 report, Fr. Bienvenue also informed the bishop that he was beginning the formation of Jeunesse Oeuvriere Chretienne sections. To that end, he was meeting with leaders from five parishes every

---

62   *Providence Visitor*, February 27, 1947; Keough to Bienvenue, July 17, 1942; Report of Activities from May to December 1943, PChA.

63   Report of Activities from May to December 1943; *Providence Visitor*, February 27, 1947.

64   Jeffrey M. Burns, *Disturbing the Peace: A History of the Christian Family Movement, 1949–1974* (Notre Dame, Indiana: University of Notre Dame Press, 1999), 14–15. While Burns mentions the talk of Fr. Kanaly, he does not mention that of Fr. Bienvenue nor does he mention the work that Fr. Bienvenue had been doing among the French-speaking in Rhode Island.

Thursday evening and was expecting leaders from three additional parishes to join them. The report listed as the immediate aim of the group the "reestablishment of the Holy Name Society on a Catholic Action plane, i.e.: inside the Society, the Catholic Action leaders are to render the Holy Name Society a militant organization."[65]

In another report, dated June 12, 1944, Fr. Bienvenue informed Keough of additional developments. One was that he had begun meeting with a Catholic Action Discussion Club for married men on Thursday evenings. After the training in Christian principles, the work of the men would be to endeavor, under the direction of their parish priests, to instill a Christian attitude of mind in their co-parishioners. In order to facilitate the work of this and the other Catholic Action initiatives, Fr. Bienvenue asked Bishop Keough's permission to publish a newspaper, which would "favor their apostolic endeavors." The proposed paper would be "limited to the development of a Christian attitude of mind in our Catholic population on the problems discovered by the leaders of the various sections in their investigations." Fr. Bienvenue saw the paper as a way of uniting all the Catholic Actions cells under his control "in the same program in order that strength be not divided." Bishop Keough does not seem to have agreed to the idea. However, in his December 21, 1945 report, Fr. Bienvenue mentioned that the JEC Federation had recently begun publishing its own bulletins, which were an adaptation of the Jocist program in Montreal.[66]

One of the prouder moments of Fr. Bienvenue's life came during and after a Jocists priests' meeting in Chicago in August 1946. Canon Cardign came from Belgium and presided over the meeting during which the Diocese of Providence was recognized as "the best organized and richest in realization in the field of Catholic Action." Following the meeting, Canon Cardign came to Providence on Sunday, September 1. That afternoon, the canon met with the members of the JEC and the JOC Federation Committees. In the evening, Canon Cardign gave a conference to some forty priests, sixty religious and two hundred lay leaders in the Jesu-Marie convent. Before he left on the following morning, he shared with Fr. Bienvenue that in his report to Pius XII:

> There will be a special chapter concerning the diocese of Providence. I shall tell the Holy Father that I saw here an organization of specialized Catholic Action the like of which I desire to see in the whole of the United States.

Success brought its own problems. On October 30, 1946, after having previously asked for help and having Bishop Keough assigned Fr. Lucien Rousell, the junior assistant at St. Ann's, Woonsocket, to assist him, Fr. Bienvenue wrote to the bishop again to ask for the assistance of yet another young priest in Woonsocket, Fr. Adrian Menard. After a short delay,

65   Report of Activities from May to December 1943.
66   Bienvenue to Keough, June 12, 1944 (There is no record of a response to this letter); Bienvenue to Keough, December 21, 1945, PChA.

Bishop Keough agreed to this second request as well and Fr. Bienvenue gave over the direction of the Jeunesse Oeuvriere Chretienne sections to Fr. Menard.[67]

Spiritual Awakening and Social Action Among Catholics in General: Fr. Edmond Brock and the Labor School Movement

While the Ligue was an outgrowth of the Closed Retreat Movement in Woonsocket and drew its support in part from it, Fr. Edmund Brock's social action ministry would eventually turn to retreat work in order to advance the aims of his ministry to labor and management. After his ordination to the priesthood at St. Sulpice International Seminary, in Issy, France, on June 29, 1936, Fr. Brock spent his first summer back in the United States helping out in various summer parishes. In the fall of 1936, Bishop Keough sent him to the Catholic University at Washington to pursue a master's degree in the School of Social Work. He wrote his master's thesis, "A Study of Some Aspects of the Economic, Social and Religious Life of a Selected Group of Young Catholic Workers," on the sources of juvenile delinquency among young men in the Olneyville section of Providence, then an Irish and Italian working-class section of the city. He stayed on at the university's School of Social Work and earned a Ph.D. in sociology in the spring of 1941. During the course of his studies, he also did work in the field of sociology at Columbia University in New York. His doctoral dissertation, *The Background and Recent Status of Collective Bargaining in the Cotton Industry in Rhode Island*, was done under the direction of Msgr. John A. Ryan, and reflected the main lines of Ryan's thought. When he returned to the diocese, Bishop Keough appointed him spiritual director at the new seminary at Warwick Neck where he was also to teach Latin, Greek and Geometry.[68]

With his background in labor studies, Fr. Brock was anxious to become involved in the labor movement in Rhode Island. As a seminary student in France, Brock had encountered students and workers, who were members of cells or sections that were part of Canon Cardign's Jocist movement. Like Fr. Bienvenue before him, Brock knew that there were major differences between the European and American economies. With Bishop Keough, he shared a concern about Communists' influence in American unions. Shortly after he took up his new duties, Fr. Brock approached Bish-

---

67 Bienvenue to Keough, September 6; October 30, 1946, PChA; *Providence Visitor*, September 12, 1946. Canon Cardign visited the diocese a second time on Sunday, July 13, 1947.

68 *Providence Visitor*, October 1, 1981; October 22, 1998; Edmund J. Brock, *The Background and Recent Status of Collective Bargaining in the Cotton Industry in Rhode Island* (Catholic University of America Press, 1942).

op Keough to ask if he might pursue, in his spare time, his interest in labor and management relations. The bishop agreed to the creation of a Diocesan Social Action Institute which, under Fr. Brock, would seek to bring the insights and vision of Leo XIII and Pius XI, who had written encyclicals on the relationship of labor and capital, as these were interpreted and applied to the American situation by Msgr. Ryan and the Social Action Department of the NCWC. Brock's first effort was to renew his contacts with the heads of the various labor unions in the state, some of whom he had met while doing the research for his dissertation, and with the State Director of Labor and other professionals in the field. He also organized a study group composed of other young priests in the diocese, who were interested in the labor question.[69]

In 1944, with Bishop Keough's support, Fr. Brock gathered 125 priests of the diocese at Our Lady of Providence Seminary on Tuesday, June 20, to listen to himself and other speakers outline a plan for a Labor School for priests of the diocese, which was aimed at enabling them to become better acquainted with the current and post-war problems growing out of labor-management relations. The rector of the seminary, Fr. McVinney, welcomed the priests and the day's main speaker, Fr. Raymond McGowan. Fr. McGowan was the associate director of the Social Action Department of the NCWC and the author of the column "The Yardstick," which was carried in the *Visitor.* For many years, McGowan traveled across the country organizing and speaking at Catholic social action conferences. Fr. Brock also spoke to the priests. He focused on the papal origins of the movement for social justice in the workplace and suggested, as a first step toward implementing the pope's economic and moral vision, the formation of study clubs among the priests.[70]

Having instructed the priests who were interested in the work, Fr. Brock's Social Action Institute then opened labor schools in Providence, Pawtucket and Woonsocket in October 1944, which were intended for the laity. The schools, which were supervised by a priest, were to run for eight weeks. The announced purpose of the schools, which were open to all interested parties, Catholics and non-Catholics, was to "provide general knowledge of the principles and techniques essential to solution of labor problems." Each of the three schools was to offer a co-ordinated three-period program, divided into three sections. The first was to run from 7:30 until 8:10, the second from 8:15 until 9:05 and the third from 9:15 until 10 o'clock. The ten minute break between the second and third periods was to allow for smoking and informal conversation. Those attending were allowed a choice during the first period between a course on parliamentary procedure and public speaking in order to develop the ability to conduct

---

[69]   Interview of the author with Msgr. Brock, August 10, 1971; Gerstle, 282–83, recounts an interview he did with Msgr. Brock on July 7, 1983; Obituary of Msgr. Brock, *Providence Visitor,* October 22, 1998.

[70]   *Providence Visitor,* June 22, 1944.

a meeting and to speak well in public; the other choice was one on the history of the labor movement. The second period was to be devoted to the main focus on the schools, labor ethics, and dealt with the rights and duties of workers, employers and government. The third period offered a choice of courses between Labor Economics, which dealt with such topics as wages, profits, rents, interest and other phases of the modern economic system, and a course on Current Labor Problems. The Labor Problems course was held in a forum setting. Whenever possible the speakers at the forums included a priest, who gave the Church's position, a labor leader and a representative of management. One of the principal objectives of the labor school, according to Fr. Brock, was to teach the workingman his fundamental rights as a member of a labor union, to cultivate in him an ability to discuss union matters at meetings, and to help make more democratic the functioning of trade unionism. With such skills, it was hoped that workers would keep their union out of the hands of crooked or Communist leaders. Besides the classes themselves, the Institute for Social Action sought to disseminate sound social and economic principles pertaining to the problems of capital and labor at the schools through the sale of pamphlets and newspapers which were made available each week at the rear of the halls.[71]

The Woonsocket school, which was directed by Fr. Henry Crepeau, associate director of the Diocesan Bureau of Social Service, was the first to open in the McFee School on Tuesday, Oct. 2. The Providence school, which was directed by Fr. Brock and held in the Knights of Columbus Building on Green Street, opened the next night. The Pawtucket school, directed by Fr. Daniel Ryan, an assistant at St. Mary's, Pawtucket, opened on Friday, Oct. 4. Eight priests of the diocese, Frs. John Cox, Arthur Geoghegan and Henry Robitaille, all of whom taught with Fr. Brock at Our Lady of Providence Seminary, and Frs. David Coffey, John Duffy, Anthony DeAngellis, Edward Flannery, and Joseph Charon, assisted the three directors in this initial effort as did Joseph Breen, James J. McAleer, and Eugene L. Jalbert, attorneys-at-law; M. B. Horan, personnel director of Owens Corning Fiber Glass Company of Ashton, and Charles Shea, principal of Samuel Slater Junior High School, Pawtucket. The initial announcement of the labor schools also carried a long list of names of labor, business and state officials, who had agreed to address the labor school attendees from time to time. The initial response to the opening of the labor schools was encouraging. Two hundred showed up for the Woonsocket school and 250 for the Pawtucket one. The responses in Woonsocket and Pawtucket were such that the meeting places of the Woonsocket school had to be moved to the Jesu-Marie Convent and the Pawtucket school to the Pawtucket Public Library. Experience would show that attendance at the schools fell off slightly after the first week. Sixty percent of all those

---

[71] Ibid., September 6: October 4, 25; November 8, 1945.

who registered for the first sessions were members of trade unions and the percentage went up in succeeding weeks. In Providence, the American Federation of Labor had the largest representation. In Pawtucket, the newly formed Congress of Industrial Organizations predominated, and, in Woonsocket, it was the Independent Textile Union. A large sprinkling of personnel men attended as did some employers. In reviewing the first semester of the schools, Fr. Brock noted that over a thousand men and women attended the sessions in the three schools at least once. Approximately three hundred came back every single week. At the end of each semester, the schools awarded certificates of merit to those who attended six of the eight sessions.[72]

Given the success of the first semester, Fr. Brock organized three additional schools for the second semester, which began during the third week of February and ended during the second week of April. The "new" schools met in the Knights of Columbus Hall in Arctic, to serve the Pawtuxet Valley and South County; in the Columbus Club in Centredale, in North Providence; and in the Junior High School, East Providence. In the fall of 1946, two other schools were opened for a time in Providence's Federal Hill and North End. In September 1947, a school was held in Apponaug. Those who attended the first session took up where they left off at the end of the first semester. In organizing the schools, Fr. Brock envisioned a three-year program in order to adequately cover the content which he believed needed to be conveyed.[73]

With the start of the labor schools, Fr. Brock began writing a column for the *Visitor*, "Labor School Notes," which first appeared on October 25, 1944 while the schools were in session. The idea behind the column was to publicize the work of the schools. In his column, Brock reviewed the happenings in the schools and discussed the Church's social teachings. In his January 17, 1945 column and in a radio address on September 27, 1947, Brock began a defense of the Church's involvement in labor and management issues by setting forth the fundamental principle that economic relationships were moral relationships. As summarized by Gary Gerstle:

> [Brock] rejected the old fiction that the market was a self-regulating mechanism that would tolerate no human intervention and the notion that scientific considerations of efficiency or technological considerations of productivity were paramount in determining the economic health of an industrial system. What mattered was how well labor and management could co-operate, which depended on how able they were to respect each other's God-given rights. Capital's rights consisted chiefly of the right to own property and the right to 'receive a reasonable return for the productive use of one's property.' Labor's rights, according to Brock, consisted of the right to a just wage which would allow a worker's family to live 'decently, with a reasonable amount of security and freedom,' the right to associate freely with workers and bargain collectively

---

[72]   Ibid., September 6: October 25; November 29, 1945.
[73]   Ibid., November 29, 1945; October 17, 1946; September 25, 1947.

with one's employer, and the right of a worker to 'share in a responsible, effective way in control over his economic and political destiny.'[74]

This last right was perhaps the most ambiguous and most controversial. In another radio address on March 5, 1949, Fr. Brock held that private property was:

[t]he material basis for . . . [man's] independence, and freedom. Psychologically, it is the most effective way of engaging his interest, and initiative, and of developing his sense of responsibility. Therefore the more widely it is distributed, the more whole-some, healthy and genuinely prosperous society will be. But when property became concentrated, as it had, in the hands of a few, the right of property was no longer absolute. Rather, he argued, "it must be controlled and used so as to promote the in-dependence and well-being of all members of the community.

Though Brock preferred that workers and employers decide, independent-ly of the government, how to control private property in the interests of the community, he believed that "the government has a positive obligation to protest the personal rights of workers and employers, especially those most in need, and to promote those institutions and policies which will bring about public well-being."[75]

Many of the business people of the state challenged Fr. Brock's asser-tion that the right to private property was not absolute since the Church had stoutly defended the right to private property against the socialists. In his retirement during a 1971 interview, Fr. (then Msgr.) Brock recalled that the businessmen of the diocese were "antagonistic" when they first heard him express his views on private property and regarded them as "commu-nistic doctrine." In order to educate anyone willing to listen, Fr. Brock, in the fall of 1947, with help of a few businessmen, initiated a monthly series of meetings for business and professional men at the Metacomet Country Club in East Providence. For $1.50 a plate, the men had supper at 6:00 o'clock after which they listened to a speaker.[76]

As the labor school forums, which treated current labor problems, were among the more popular aspects of the labor schools, Fr. Brock, in order to educate a wider spectrum of the people of the diocese, began to offer forums apart from the labor schools. One of the first was held at the Elks Auditorium in Providence on December 17, 1947. The topic was the re-cently adopted Taft-Hartley Act, to which labor had objected strenuous-ly. Brock engaged Isadore Katz, General Counsel of the Textile Workers Union, CIO, to represent labor; Theodore Iserman, Corporation Counsel from New York, to represent management; and George Brenner, a New York Attorney, to represent the public. The admission charge was thirty-

74 *Providence Visitor*, January 17, 1946. Gerstle had access to a draft of the radio address, Cf. Gerstle, *Working-Class Americanism*, p. 283.
75 This summary of Brock's March 5, 1949 address is also taken from Gerstle, *Working-Class American-ism*, 283–84.
76 *Providence Visitor*, November 25, 1947.

five cents. In retrospect, Brock believed that the forums "developed a sort of spirit in the community that the Church was involved in labor-management relations and had something to say about them.[77]

At the beginning of 1946, the Knights of Columbus turned over a major portion of their radio time on WFCI to Fr. Brock as a means of explaining the activities of the Social Action Institute and the reasons for the Church's interest in labor problems. Brock gave the first talk and other priests, who were working with him in the labor schools, gave the others. In subsequent years, other radio stations provided air time for a program, which Brock called, "Partners in Industry." Brock welcomed guests to his program and even had a talk-back program. He saw the program as a way of sharing the Church's social message with an wider audience than the other programs offered by the Social Action Institute.[78]

Other Forms of Catholic Action

PRE-CANA CONFERENCES

Lay retreats were also the starting point for a movement aimed at deepening the spirituality of married couples and later for couples preparing to marry and for separated persons. In 1943–44, Fr. John P. Delaney, S.J., began giving retreats for married couples in New York City as well as in St. Louis during which he sought to explore the challenges of married life in a less formal way than other retreat masters did. His conferences focused on the everyday problems married couples encountered. His retreats, which he called Cana Conferences, proved popular and spurred a demand for similar retreats, particularly for Pre-Cana Conferences for those preparing to marry. In October 1946, Fr. James J. Lamb, moderator of Our Lady's Sodality at Sacred Heart Church in East Providence, under the patronage of the Sodality, organized a series of meetings for young people over the age of sixteen, which were held that first year, every first Friday following the Holy Hour devotions at Sacred Heart. The forum was opened to all and was intended to instruct young people on the meaning of a true Christian home. Fr. Lamb gave the first talk and he recruited a secular lawyer, a canon lawyer, a doctor, a nurse, a financial expert, a housewife and mother, and a judge to give the others in the series. At the end of each talk, Fr. Lamb moderated a question and answer period. When Fr. Lamb organized another series the following year, the program began at 2:00 o'clock at Bayview Academy and ran until 8:00, with supper provided by the Sisters of Mercy in the convent. Those who attended the conference were asked to receive communion in their own parishes in the morning.[79]

---

[77] Ibid., November 25, 1947.
[78] *Providence Visitor*, January 17, 1946; Brock interview, August 10, 1971.
[79] *Providence Visitor*, November 11, 1947; September 16, 1948.

INITIATIVES OF THE SISTERS OF MERCY

Clergy were not the only ones moved by the popes' calls for Catholics to involve themselves in apostolic work. In 1933, Sister Mary Matthew, the Provincial of the Sisters of Mercy, conceived the idea of establishing a special school to promote Catholic Action, which was to be based at St. Francis Xavier Academy, Providence. Mother Matthew's initiative was inspired by Pope Pius XI's call for social action during the Holy Year that was to mark the nineteen-hundredth anniversary of the Death and Resurrection of Christ. With Bishop Hickey's support, Mother Matthew organized the St. Xavier's School of Catholic Action, which offered study clubs in religion, art, music, English and foreign languages. Mother Matthew, who was the honorary president of the St. Francis Xavier Academy Alumni Association, sent an announcement of invitation to join the clubs to the academy's alumnae, but membership was not limited to alumnae. The study groups got underway in October 1933. Msgr. James P. O'Brien directed the Liturgy study club, which met on Monday evenings. Fr. George G. Harold, O.P., conducted the course on Shakespeare, which met on Tuesdays. On Wednesday night, Mrs. Henry Donovan began a course in voice culture; Henri Faucher worked with those interested in orchestra; and sisters of the academy's faculty supervised the activities of those interested in a glee club or an art club. On Thursday nights, the sisters conducted clubs in Latin, French and Spanish.[80]

In addition to the study clubs, Mother Matthew also organized three other units to be formed from among Catholic mothers, Catholic teachers, and patronesses of Catholic Action. In order to initiate a Mother's Club, better known as the Marian Motherhood Assembly, Mother Matthew sent out letters to the mothers of Catholic high school students in the Providence area. In the letter, Mother Matthew invited them to an initial meeting at the Academy on the fourth Friday of October 1933. After the initial meeting, about 150 women gathered the next month to form the organization and elect officers. At the November meeting, it was decided that the Assembly would undertake fund-raising activities in order to give material aid to St. Xavier's. The Columban Fathers, who were newly established in the diocese, were invited to supply a spiritual director for the Assembly and Fr. Ambrose Gallagher, S.S.C., attended all the meetings during the Assembly's first year. The stated mission of the Assembly, beyond that of aiding St. Xavier's and co-operating with its teachers, was the fighting of juvenile delinquency by using the members' influence to combat legislation that corrupted morals and family life; defending the sanctity of the home; and objecting to indecent literature and moving pictures.[81]

In addition to the Marian Motherhood Assembly, Sr. Matthew also organized the Catholic Teachers' Conclave, which met on the second Fri-

---

[80] *Providence Visitor*, August 18; October 13, 1933.
[81] *Providence Visitor*, October 13, November 3; December 1, 1933; January 24, 1957.

day of each month at the Academy beginning in December 1933. The evenings often began with a short business meeting. The main feature was an address by a knowledgeable figure in a field related to education, which sometimes was followed by a discussion. The evening concluded with a musical program and Benediction. In addition to the monthly meeting, there was an annual Communion Breakfast on the Feast of Christ the King following mass in the convent chapel. Through the 1930s and into the 40s, the monthly sessions of the conclave were attended by several hundred members and presided over by an elected president assisted by an executive board. The Patronesses were a group that supported Catholic Action initiatives through prayer and financial support.[82]

<h2 style="text-align:center">FIRST FRIDAY CLUBS</h2>

The laity also took initiative in seeking to bring Gospel values into the world in which they lived. In June 1941, John E. Smith, a Pawtucket real estate man, who lived in East Greenwich, and five other Catholic gentlemen, got together to organize a First Friday Club. Previous to the meeting, Mr. Smith had written to Bishop Keough asking his permission to organize a Catholic Layman's First Friday Club. The movement began in New York city in 1936 at the urging of Fr. Herman I. Storck, a Jesuit retreat master, who was anxious to find a way to sustain the fervor of the men, who made retreats at the Loyola Retreat House in Morristown, New Jersey. Fr. Storck urged retreatants to seek year-long interior perfection by carrying on Catholic action in the form of study clubs, forums, public speaking, parish activities and frequent meetings of men, who had made a retreat together. Two men who had made retreats with him decided to have luncheon meetings on the First Friday of every month as it would be an easy date to remember, and could be combined with reception of Holy Communion. As the idea developed, it was decided that each man who attended the luncheon was to invite a guest. The group was to have a chaplain, who would give a short talk at each meeting and who could invite a fellow priest to give a longer one. There were to be no dues, no officers and no bylaws. Each year the group was to make a retreat together.[83]

A friend of Mr. Smith had told him about his First Friday Club when Smith had visited him in New York City. A year after Smith's New York visit, the friend wrote Smith suggesting that Smith organize a First Friday Club in Providence. In his letter to Bishop Keough on June 5, 1941, Smith informed the bishop that he had already asked the second assistant at St. Joseph's, Pawtucket, Fr. Edward H. Flannery, if he would be willing to serve as the group's chaplain. As he was anxious to have Bishop Ke-

---

[82]   Ibid., October 13, 1933; *Providence Journal,* January 12; November 9; December 14, 1935; January 11; February 13, 1936.

[83]   Joseph W. Burns, "Catholic Layman's First Friday Clubs, a history and directory" (Privately printed, 1961), 12–13.

ough's permission to organize the club and have Fr. Flannery as chaplain before the prospective club members had their first meeting, Smith followed up his letter with a phone call to the bishop's office. The bishop gave the requested permission and wished Smith success in the undertaking. The Catholic Layman's First Friday Group of Providence County or the Rhode Island First Friday Club, as it was also called, first met at noon at Butler's Diner on the Providence and Pawtucket line on June 6, 1941. After the initial meetings, the meeting time was changed to 6:45. Butler's Diner would be their regular meeting place until the diner closed down in March 1951 after which meetings were held at the Lindsey Tavern on Smithfield Avenue in Pawtucket.[84]

In his talks, Fr. Flannery sought to strengthen the devotion of the group's members by speaking on the Mass and the Sacraments. The group was encouraged to receive communion daily if possible. The speakers at the meetings were either suggested by the members of the group and or by Fr. Flannery himself and were most often priests, although there was the occasional layman. Those who addressed the group frequently shared Flannery's own conviction that one should keep oneself informed on social affairs to which Catholics were to bring their Catholic point of view. One of the initial efforts of the club was to appeal to its members and friends to send none but religious Christmas cards during the Christmas season. An important yearly activity on the part of the club was the organizing of a weekend retreat for its members, which in the club's early years, was held at the Benedictine Priory in Portsmouth. About the middle of 1946, a Laywoman's First Friday Group, which met at the Howard Johnson's on North Main Street, was also organized. The men's and women's groups occasionally held joint meetings to hear a prominent speaker from out of state. In April 1946, a group of men and women in Newport asked Bishop Keough for permission to form a joint group there. Like the earlier groups, the Newport group wished to follow the example of the Providence group by emphasizing the spiritual development of its members as a preparation for social action as part of other groups. Specifically, the organizers of the Newport club saw its aims as furthering "Catholicism through its works of Liturgical education, revolving around the Mass and Sacraments."[85]

BOOKSTORES AND READING GROUPS

The witness and apostolate of St. Margaret Mary Alacoque, which inspired the practice of attending mass and receiving communion on First Fridays, also played a role in Mrs. Percival de St. Aubin's establishing a bookshop and lending library in Froebel Hall on Brown Street, on the

---

[84] Ibid., 19–20; Smith to Keough, June 5, 1941; Keough to Smith, June 6, 1941, PChA; *Providence Visitor*, March 22, 1951.

[85] *Providence Visitor*, February 7; November 24, 1942; November 7, 1946; Albert J. McAloon, et al. to Bishop Keough, April 7, 1947, PChA.

East Side of Providence, which she named in honor of St. Margaret, in October 1940. When Mrs. de St. Aubin opened her bookstore, she already had over five hundred persons as subscribers. The shop was stacked with over a thousand books drawn from all fields of scholarship and popular writing. The bookshop's incorporators were five priests, headed by Bishop Keough. After a year's operation, Mrs. de St. Aubin initiated a series of book reviews, the first of which was presented by Fr. Russell J. McVinney, the rector of Our Lady of Providence Seminary. Bishop Keough was present on the occasion and urged the wide reading of good books. He particularly urged the mothers present to scrutinize the reading done by their children. When Mrs. de St. Aubin died in February 1942, Agnes C. Burke, according to Mrs. de St. Aubin's wishes, took over the bookshop. However, patronage of the shop began to fall off and, in October 1942, Bishop Keough and the other directors decided to discontinue operation of the bookstore until after the Second World War ended. Against that day, the bookshop's lending library was stored in the Visitor Building Library.[86]

In 1946, a group of ladies from Sacred Heart Church in East Providence attended the Catholic Book Fair and Author's Luncheon organized and sponsored by Agnes Burke's Marion Book Shop and Lending Library at the Narragansett Hotel in Providence on November 16, the first such Catholic book fair held in Rhode Island. The ladies returned to East Providence determined to organize a similar book club in their own community. They chose the name St. Catherine's Book Club and secured the services of Fr. James J. Lamb, an assistant at Sacred Heart, as their moderator. The club met on the last Friday of each month to discuss a current book and to listen to a guest speaker. While the core of the group that founded the club were parishioners of Sacred Heart, the club was open to all and members who were particularly encouraged to join. One of the club's first projects was the founding of a parish library.[87]

In 1945, a group of Catholics in the Westerly-Pawcatuck area felt the need for a religious lending library. They founded the Catholic Library of Westerly, Inc. and initially established the library in a classroom in St. Michael's School, Pawcatuck. After about a year, they secured an upstairs room in a building on West Broad Street, about ten yards across the state line in Pawcatuck. Beginning in 1948, Mrs. James Smith, the wife of one of the founders of the library, with the help of her husband took over the library, which served the parishes in South County and southeastern Connecticut for twenty-five years. In 1953, the library corporation secured another building on the bridge that spanned the Pawcatuck River as the site for the library. In addition to lending books, the library also operated a religious gift shop as a way of financially supporting the library. At the

---

86 *Providence Visitor*, October 31, 1940; October 30, 1941; Agnes Burke to Keough, March 23, 1942; Keough to Richard A. Hurley, October 31, 1942, PChA.
87 Agnes C. Burke to Bishop Francis P. Keough, November 6, 1946, PChA; *Providence Visitor*, March 6, 1947.

time of the move, there was still a problem with vandalism motivated by intolerance and misunderstanding in a town with deep Protestant roots. In 1955, in the same storefront, the Postal Service opened its first post office in Pawcatuck. Mrs. Smith served as the community's first postmaster. After Mrs. Smith died in March 1971 and Mr. Smith later became seriously ill around Christmas time, it was thought that the library would have to close for good. However, Mr. Smith recovered and with the help of Fr. William Loftus, the pastor of St. Mary's, Stonington, and with financial assistance from the pastors in the Westerly area, the library reopened on April 1, 1972, after a three months hiatus.[88]

OTHER ORGANIZATIONS

Any issue of the *Providence Visitor* printed in the 1930s or '40s contained notices of the meetings of Holy Name and Altar societies, Ladies' guilds, sodalities, and other organizations whose moderators and lay leaders sought to deepen the spirituality of the organizations' members and direct their spiritual zeal in useful and important directions for their own welfare and that of the Church. Some of these were organized into state organizations that held yearly general meetings at which speakers were invited to address the representatives of the members' groups in order to renew their energies and zeal. During the Second World War the ranks of the men's organizations were depleted by the younger men's entering the armed forces and many of the older men having to work longer hours in defense work. Furthermore, energies that might have gone into supporting the works of the Church went into supporting the American war effort with a resulting lapse in vitality of many Catholic organizations, particularly the men's groups.

EUCHARISTIC CONGRESSES

All forms of Catholic Action were rooted in an awareness of the God's love for his people and in the apostolic mission of the Church, which was the Mystical Body of Christ. A tradition of holding an annual Eucharistic Congress in the United States began in 1928. While clergy and laity of the diocese made trips to the annual observances, there was no organized, diocesan pilgrimage to a national Eucharistic Congress until 1935. In September 1935, Bishop Keough publicly announced that he had accepted the invitation of Bishop Joseph Schrembs, the Bishop of Cleveland, who was the Promoter of Eucharistic Congresses in the United States and Protector of the Priests' Eucharistic League, to attend the congress planned for Cleveland, between September 23 and 26. The bishop named Msgr. Peter A. Foley, then pastor of St. Joseph's, Pawtucket, to direct the pil-

---

[88] *Providence Journal*, April 2, 1972; *Providence Visitor*, 1975.

grimage. Msgr. Foley was to be the contact person for the clergy and laity aiming to attend the congress who wanted information as to transportation and housing in Cleveland. The Rhode Island pilgrimage committee, which Msgr. Foley headed, arranged for a special railroad car to carry the pilgrims. Bishop Keough accompanied the Rhode Island party. Among those who made the trip was Frederick A. Wilmot, a Protestant minister and the religion writer for the *Journal* and *Bulletin* newspapers. In giving his impressions of the congress, Mr. Wilmot noted particularly "the spiritual alertness, disarming humility, unfailing courtesy and personal charm" of Bishop Keough. Bishop Keough also encouraged wide participation on the part of the clergy and laity of the diocese at the Eucharistic Congress held in New Orleans, October 17 to 20, 1938.[89]

World War II

Like the vast majority of the clergy, religious and laity in Rhode Island, Bishop Keough was a sincere American patriot. His patriotism flowed out of both his personal background and his convictions. Most of the time his patriotism was expressed in formal statements addressed to the diocese as a whole when he sought to rouse the support of his diocese for some civic cause. There were, however, occasions when the bishop spoke from his heart without the benefit of a carefully prepared script. One such was the address he gave on June 29, 1938 during a Confirmation ceremony at the camp of the 141st Civil Conservation Company in Charlestown. This was the first time the bishop had confirmed at any of the CCC camps in the state. The seventy-six young men confirmed that evening came not just from the 141st but also from three other CCC companies in Rhode Island and one in Voluntown, Connecticut.[90]

In his address to the young men of the five companies, Bishop Keough urged them to build their citizenship standards through strict adherence to their Roman Catholic faith. He told the young men that, "Through being good Catholics, you will be good Christians. And through being good Christians, you will become better citizens." He pointed out that a requirement of the faith was obedience to civil law and this involved respect for the American government regardless who was president. Furthermore, he urged the young men to not let their "ideas wander away from the American form of government. No matter what 'isms' others may try to teach you, never sell the flag short! Love your country and defend it with your life if necessary."[91]

---

89 *Providence Visitor*, August 22, 29; September 5, 12, 19, 1935; September 23; October 20, 1938; June 26, 1941; *News-Tribune*, September 6, 12, 17, 27, 28, 1935; *Providence Journal*, September 28, 1935; June 26, 1941.
90 *Providence Journal*, June 30, 1938.
91 Ibid.

Early Efforts to Aid the Victims of Oppression

When in March 1934, Adolph Hitler and the National Socialist or Nazi Party, with the help of the Nationalist Party and deputies from the Catholic Center Party, secured the passage of an Enabling Act, which firmly established a Nazi dictatorship in Germany, the new government enacted a series of racial laws, which initiated a ruthless persecution of the Jews in Germany. The harshness of the laws prompted a significant number of German Jews, Catholics and Protestants to leave Germany and take refuge in other countries. The economic plight of the refugees, who frequently had to leave most of their material possessions behind, prompted Jewish organizations in America, who were working in conjunction with the League of Nations High Commissioners for German Refugees to help the refugees, to undertake fund-raising campaigns to provide them with relief. On August 2, 1934, Ilie Berger, a Providence dentist, wrote to Bishop Keough in behalf of the fund-raising effort in Rhode Island to ask if Bishop Keough would allow Fr. Edward A. Higney, pastor of St. Joseph's, Newport, to lend his name in support of the committee in Newport. According to Dr. Berger, 40 percent of the refugees were Catholics and Protestants and the funds raised by Jewish agencies were being distributed to the refugees without distinction of religion.[92]

Tragic as the situation in Germany was for both Jews and Christians, in 1934, the attention of American bishops was focused more on Mexico than on Germany. When the government of President Lazaro Cardenas renewed the persecution of the Church in Mexico, the American bishops, at the annual meeting of the National Catholic Welfare Conference, agreed to organize a crusade of prayer in their respective dioceses. The crusade began on first Sunday of 1935, the Feast of the Epiphany.[93]

The Conflict of Loyalties among the Italian Americans

The Italian army's invasion of Ethiopia in October 1939 focused the attention of at least the Italian Catholics in the diocese on Italy and stirred the nationalism of many of the Italians, which were further inflamed when the League of Nations sanctioned Italy in November. Several hundred women in the state donated their gold wedding rings in support of the Italian cause. At the war's end, the Italian government presented women, who had contributed their wedding bands, with steel rings in ceremonies in May 1936 in Providence and Natick. On May 11, 1936, over five thousand

---

92 Dr. Ilie Berger to Keough, August 2, 1934, PChA. For background material on the American Catholic Church and World War II, cf. "World War II and American Catholics," *The Encyclopedia of American Catholic History*, 1519–22, and the bibliography at the end of the article.
93 *Providence Visitor*, November 23, 1934; Keough to pastors, January 4, 1935, PChA.

Italo-Americans and their guests gathered at Rhodes-on-the-Pawtuxet to celebrate the Italian government's victory in Ethiopia.[94]

American goodwill towards the Italian Fascists in general began to ebb, however, after Mussolini's Italy concluded a political and military alliance with Hitler's Germany in May 1937, but it remained strong in the Italian community. During the Columbus Day parade held on October 10, 1937 in West Warwick, as discussed above, the men's and women's Mussolini societies paraded in black shirts for the men and black skirts for the women and gave the Fascist or Roman salute. On hearing of the Fascist parade, the veterans' groups in the town protested what they regarded as the Italians' betrayal of the loyalty due their adopted country. The West Warwick Town Council responded by passing an ordinance that would withhold permission for parades or demonstrations whose purpose was to express allegiance to a foreign country or government. A year later, on election day, November 8, 1938, Rhode Islanders voted 101,023 to 79,501 to make Columbus Day a full state holiday.[95]

Because of the passage of the referendum making Columbus Day a full holiday, the celebration of the day in October 1939 took on a heightened importance for the Italians. The passing of the referendum marked a victory for the Columbian Central Committee, an organization of more than one hundred independent religious, civic, fraternal and social organizations of Italian background that had organized to push for having Columbus Day made a full holiday and to celebrate the day with a parade and public speaking. After the day became a full legal holiday, the Providence City Council created a committee headed by Alderman Frank Rao to organize a municipal celebration and Rao's committee invited the Columbian Central Committee to participate. Friction developed between the two when the City Committee on Columbus Day passed a resolution requiring that all military salutes given in the Columbus Day parade be "American salutes." The Columbian Central Committee immediately protested the ban on the Roman salute. Capt. Angelo Martella, chief marshal of the parade and head of the Italian World War Veterans organization, protested what he saw as the implication of the city committee's order, "[The Roman salute] doesn't mean allegiance to Italy or to Fascism. It's just the salute of a military organization and a gesture of respect to authorities."[96]

---

94 *Providence Journal*, May 4, 25, 1936; *Evening Bulletin*, May 11, 12, 1936.
95 *Providence Journal*, October 11, 1937; November 9, 1938; *Pawtuxet Valley Daily Times*, October 16, 18, 20, 27, 1937.
96 *Providence Journal*, October 7, 1939.

The Challenges Created by the Spanish Civil War and German Refugees

While many Catholics were concerned by the rise of Nazism in Germany and Fascism in Italy, the attention of the bishops shifted to Spain in July 1936 when a civil war broke out in the aftermath of elections that brought a leftist government to power, which renewed the anti-clerical policies of previous governments. Many of those Americans who took an interest in foreign affairs divided over supporting the popular front government that had won power in the 1936 elections or the rebel nationalist forces under Gen. Francisco Franco. Since Spain's leftist government persecuted the Catholic Church, the majority of American Catholics supported Franco's cause, while American liberals supported the elected Spanish government. The war was a bloody one in which both sides committed atrocities. In March 1938, Secretary of State Cordell Hull issued a statement on behalf of the American government deploring aircraft attacks on the city of Barcelona. In response to Hull's statement, Fr. Francis Deery, editor of the *Providence Visitor*, took issue with Hull's seeming sympathy for the Spanish government's cause in a front page editorial. Political passions and prejudices clouded the judgment of many on either side of the issue and Fr. Deery was not exempt. Fr. Deery made little of the fact that Franco's cause was supported by military forces from Hitler's Germany and Mussolini's Italy; rather, he based his criticism of the Spanish government on the fact that he believed the leftist government was operating on the orders of the Communist government in Moscow, which, like the government of Spain, was notoriously hostile to the Church. His main criticism of Hull's protest was that Hull's statement was unbalanced and based on inaccurate information. The following week the *Visitor* printed an editorial from the Jesuit magazine *America*, wondering why the State Department protested the bombing of civilians in Barcelona and had said nothing about those killed by the Spanish government for holding political opinions hostile to the government's.[97]

A few months after Secretary Hull's statement, the Providence chapter of the Medical Bureau to Aid Spanish Democracy held a fund-raising dinner in Providence at the Narragansett Hotel in May 1938 at which one of the speakers was a Spanish Franciscan, Luis de Sarasola. About 125 people attended the dinner. Sarasola's presence was intended to blunt Catholic criticism that the Spanish government was hostile to the Church. At the end of the dinner and speeches, Dr. Alexander Burgess, the chairman of the dinner, invited questions from the audience. A Providence lawyer, William A. Needham, who asked Dr. Burgess if he had any concerns about misleading people in the statements he had made that evening. Needham went on to read an article from the *New York Times* of October 27, 1936, in which the acting Provincial of the New York Province of the

---

[97] *Providence Visitor*, March 24, 31, 1938.

Order of Friars Minor had stated that Sarasola, who had been presented as a priest in good standing, was in fact an apostate from the Order and the Church. Dr. Burgess defended Sarasola and, when Needham sought to press the issue, announced that there would be no further discussion of Sarasola's status. When Needham persisted, Dr. Burgess announced that the meeting was adjourned.[98]

If the audience that gathered in the Narragansett hotel to support the Medical Bureau's effort was biased towards the Spanish government's cause, another talk entitled "The Truth about Spain," by Dr. A. Hamilton Rice, a geographer and explorer, which took place in May 1940, expressed support for the other side of the issue. Dr. Rice gave his talk at the annual open forum of the Catholic Woman's Club in Providence. Rice declared the reports that General Franco was opening the doors of Spain to the Italian and German armies "nothing but lies." In his remarks before Dr. Rice's talk, Bishop Keough criticized the secular press for its unfair and unbalanced reporting on the war and he expressed his concern that the Spanish government's Loyalist sympathizers in the United States were about to increase their efforts to lift the embargo the American government had imposed on shipping military equipment to Spain. In the weeks that followed, the *Visitor* lent its weight to efforts to defeat attempts to have the embargo lifted.[99]

At the same time that the issue of the embargo on arms shipments to Spain came to the fore, the American bishops at their annual meeting in Washington, concerned about the rise of extremism of all kinds, adopted a Pastoral Letter, which initiated a campaign to educate Catholic children on the nature of true Christian democracy. The bishops designated Sunday, November 20, as a day of prayer for all refugees from political tyranny and for all victims of racial or religious persecution. Many bishops, Bishop Keough among them, informed the National Conference of Christians and Jews of their intentions for observing the day. In his letter to his pastors, Bishop Keough urged that the Catholics of the diocese direct special attention to the plight of those in Europe of Jewish blood whether Jewish or Christian in faith whose plight had been detailed in the secular press. The same news reports about the plight of the oppressed minorities in Germany prompted representatives of several Protestant churches, synagogues and civil organizations to launch a $150,000 fund-raising drive during the second week of December 1938 with the aim of distributing the funds collected by the Jewish, Catholic and Protestant committees to help the refugees.[100]

In face of the plight of Catholics in Germany who suffered under the Nazis, the American bishops created the Committee for Catholic Refugees from Germany, which was headed by Archbishop Joseph Rummel of New Orleans and employed Fr. Joseph D. Ostermann as its executive director.

---

[98] *Providence Journal*, May 17, 1938; *Providence Visitor*, May 19, 1938.

[99] *Providence Visitor*, January 5, 12, 19, 1939.

[100] Ibid., November 17, 22, 1938; *Providence Journal*, December 16, 1938.

On December 30, 1938, Archbishop Rummel wrote to Bishop Keough, as he did to other bishops, bringing to his attention the plight of the various German religious communities that had lost the income they depended on to support themselves when the Nazis expelled them from the schools and institutions they had been conducting. Secondly, at the request of Cardinal Pacelli, the Vatican Secretary of State, Rummel asked Keough to consider helping to place German professors who were converts to the Catholic faith from Judaism and had been driven from their academic positions, in suitable positions in a university or hospital. Thirdly, he asked that the diocese be ready to participate in national fund-raising efforts aimed at assisting all political refugees. When a collection was taken in the diocese on March 19, 1939, following an appeal from Bishop Keough in which he strongly criticized the actions of the Nazis in relation to the Church, $3,800 was donated and sent to aid the Catholic Committee.[101]

On May 2, 1939, Fr. Ostermann wrote to ask assistance in the writing of affidavits of good conduct necessary to the bringing of individual German refugees to the United States under the prevailing immigration laws and, on May 11, he wrote again asking if Keough could find a place in his diocese for one or more of the German refugees. When protests arose within the United States that the country was being flooded with refugees, the Catholic, Protestant and Jewish committees, concerned with the problem, published a pamphlet in 1939 with facts and figures that showed that, when return German immigration was taken into consideration, there were actually fewer German nationals in the country than there had been before the refugee problem had developed.[102]

When England came under air attack in 1939, many English parents began to worry about the safety of their children. Many English children were sent from the cities to the comparative safety of the English countryside. Others were sent to live with relatives or acquaintances in Canada and the United States. Besides the English children, in 1940, there were also more than 40,000 French, Belgian and Polish children who had taken refuge in England. Fr. Charles Curran, director the Diocesan Bureau of Social Service, advised the Rhode Island Committee for the Care of European Children of the bureau's willingness to receive 200 to 300 children. Under the plan Fr. Curran submitted, the children would be temporarily placed in the diocese's institutions until arrangements could be made to place them with foster families. In addition to the United States Committee for the Care of European Children, of which the Rhode Island unit was a part, the American bishops set up a Bishops' Committee for Refugee Children to specifically care for Catholic children. There is no known record of how many children were actually provided for in Rhode Island by these various organizations.[103]

---
[101] Rummel to Keough, December 30, 1938, PChA; *Providence Visitor*, March 9, 1939; *Evening Bulletin*, March 13, 1939.
[102] Osterman to Keough, May 2, 11; July 7, 1939; "Refugee Immigration: Facts and Figures, PChA.
[103] *Providence Visitor*, July 11, 18, 1940.

The Church experienced a crisis of its own when on February 10, 1939, Pope Pius XI, who had given much of his pontificate to the cause of maintaining peace among the nations of the world, died. Pius XI's death and the election of his succession, Cardinal Eugenio Pacelli, who took the name Pius XII, came in the midst of a worsening political situation in Europe. While much of Europe's attention was focused on Germany's occupation of what remained of Czechoslovakia, Mussolini's Italy, on Good Friday, April 7, 1939, began an invasion of Albania. The fighting in Albania was but the prelude for a wider war which engulfed Europe when, on September 1, 1939, German forces invaded Poland. Among Pius XII's first messages as pope was a request made to the bishops and faithful to offer special prayers during the month of May to invoke the assistance of the Blessed Virgin in the cause of peace. When Germany invaded Poland on September 1, Bishop Keough ordered that the prayer for peace be said in place of the prayer for the pope at every mass until further notice.[104]

The Outbreak of World War II
and the Plight of the Diocese's Seminarians

Coming as it did in September, the outbreak of the war caught the seminarians of the diocese who were studying at the American College in Louvain on vacation in various places in Europe. The rector of the American College, Msgr. Percival DeStrycker, immediately ordered all the students of the college to return to Belgium immediately. Five of the diocese's seminarians at the college were in Italy, one was in Poland and another was in Polish-occupied Lithuania. Their return trips to Louvain would be complicated by the fact that their pre-war visas were no longer valid. The one who was at Lake Como made his way back to Louvain by way of Munich. The two who were at Assisi traveled to Turin and then to Paris on their way back. The two who were at Rimini on Italy's Adriatic coast went first to Milan and then to Geneva, before making their way through Germany to then neutral Belgium.[105]

John Dzienkowski, the student who was vacationing in Vilna, the Polish-held capital of Lithuania, had a more difficult time making his way back to Louvain when Germany invaded Poland. Since in his August 1939 pact with the Russians, Hitler had agreed to Russian control of Lithuania, Dzienkowski sought to flee the city, along with many of its inhabitants, after the city was bombed by the Russians. He suffered a broken rib when the vehicle he was riding in was struck by a careening ambulance. He sought medical attention at a Lithuanian hospital, but, being suspected of being a German spy, he had difficulty getting the help he needed. He eventually made his way to Kaunas, where the American consul gave him

---

[104] *Providence Visitor*, April 27; May 4; September 7, 1940.
[105] *Providence Visitor*, January 18, 1940.

papers that enabled him to get to Berlin by way of East Prussia and the Baltic. Although he was detained again at the Dutch-German border, he made it safely to Louvain.[106]

When Dzienkowski arrived back in Louvain, he was carrying a letter from the other Providence seminarian, who had been vacationing in Poland, Michael Dziob. Dziob was visiting relatives in Dobrzechow, a village near Rzeszow in southeastern Poland. Msgr. DeStrycker tried to contact Dziob through the American ambassadors in Warsaw, Berlin and Brussels and through church channels in Poland, but was unsuccessful. He had no word of Dziob until John Dzienkowski returned to Louvain. Dziob was not able to leave Dobrzechow until conditions in Poland settled down after the German occupation of the country. In December, he used the money he had to buy a first class ticket to Louvain through Berlin and made the journey through Germany in a compartment with seven German generals who eyed him with suspicion and said little. In Berlin, he stopped at the American embassy to send word to Louvain that he was alive and well. The embassy staff hurried him back to the train station as his ticket did not provide for any stops. Nevertheless, he made a stop at Cologne to make contact with a fellow student at Louvain, who lived in that city. The student, who had been drafted into the army, also pointed out the danger of stopping, but helped Dziob avoid a problem by explaining Dziob's situation to the officer in charge at the Cologne station.[107]

With the beginning of the German invasion, Msgr. DeStrycker had cabled Bishop Keough to ascertain whether he wanted his seminarians to return to the United States. Since Belgium was a neutral country, Keough had decided to let them stay at Louvain. However, on September 12, he wrote to Msgr. DeStrycker to ask that he might use his own good judgment as to when his students should return. After most of the seminarians had arrived back at the American College, the University of Louvain opened at its usual time and the American students returned to class. On October 20, Msgr. DeStrycker received his first letter from Bishop Keough, a letter sent September 12, in which Keough added a word of direction to his permission to let his students stay. The bishop left it to the rector's better judgment that if the situation in Europe began to cause him anxiety that "he should "remove our students to a place of safety when they may eventually make their way home." Msgr. DeStrycker replied that same day giving the bishop what news he had of the Providence seminarians and sharing his concerns about Michael Dziob.[108]

Dzienkowski and Dziob were not the only ones caught in the path of war in 1939. Anthony Kacevicius was studying at the Vilkaviskis Seminary in Lithuania, when the Germans attacked Poland. He was immediately ordered home by Bishop Keough. He was not allowed to cross the Polish

---

[106] Ibid.
[107] Ibid., December 28, 1939; February 10, 1940; Interview with Msgr. Dziob, July 8, 2005.
[108] Keough to DeStrycker, September 12, 1939; DeStrycker to Keough, October 20, 1939, PChA.

corridor but had to go by way of Pillau to Berlin. He made his way to Rotterdam where he boarded the *New Amsterdam* for the trip home.[109]

On December 7, 1939, Msgr. DeStrycker cabled Bishop Keough asking him whether he wanted his students to remain in Europe after the university closed for the Christmas break. With uncertainly continuing to surround the question of whether Germany would respect Belgium's neutrality, Bishop Keough elected to call his students home from Belgium rather than have them remain there over Christmas. He cabled Msgr. DeStrycker to send his six seminarians, by way of France, to Genoa, where he arranged passage for them on the *Rex* of the Italian line. The six young men, John Dzienkowski, John Corrigan, Timothy Gillen, Leo McKenna, Bernard McKenna and William Pyne left Genoa on January 2 and arrived in the United States without incident. After Michael Dziob made his way back to Louvain, he found the other students at the American College gone and only Msgr. Destrycker in the college. The rector quickly sent him on his way again and Dziob followed the same route taken by his fellow seminarians to Genoa and arrived in New York on February 8. When the Germans invaded Belgium in May 1940, Msgr. DeStrycker left Louvain and made his way to Bordeaux, France. From there he cabled Bishop Keough to ask him to sponsor his admission to the United States. Keough readily did as Msgr. DeStrycker requested.[110]

The American College in Louvain was not the only European seminary to close down. After the Germans attacked Holland, Belgium and France in May, Italy declared war on England and France on June 10. The prospect that Mussolini would soon join Hitler in his war on France and Great Britain prompted many American bishops and religious superiors to recall their priests and seminarians, who were studying or working in Europe. At the beginning of June, the United States liner *Manhattan* carried more than 450 priests, seminarians and nuns among its 1,907 passengers on its voyage New York. Among those who left Rome at the end of class in June were three Providence seminarians — Alfred Santagata, who had been a student at the North American College, and Anthony Robinson and Bernard Kelly, who had been studying at the Lateran Seminary, both of which seminaries were in Rome. Four other seminarians, who had been studying at St. Brieuc, in the Normandy region of France — John Condon, Joseph Gallagher, Ernest Ferland and Raymond Beaulieu — and one who had been a student at Limoges in the Loire Valley, returned home by way of Lisbon and Galway on the American ship *George Washington*. Two other Providence seminarians, Paul Daley and James Cassidy, had been studying at Orleans, France. They had transferred to Orleans from the Sulpician Seminary at Issy, an industrial suburb of Paris, when the war broke out.

---

[109] *Providence Visitor*, October 5, 1939.
[110] DeStrycker to Keough, December 7, 1939; Keough to DeStrycker, no date; Destrycker to Keough, May 26, 1940; *Providence Visitor*, January 18; February 2, 1940; *Providence Journal*, February 10, 1940.

They arrived home in the middle of July on the *S.S. Examiner,* which sailed from Lisbon.[111]

Military Chaplains in World War II

On September 16, 1940, the same day on which Congress enacted the Selective Service and Training Act, the Federal government inducted the 243rd Coast Artillery Regiment of the Rhode Island National Guard into federal service. The regiment was mustered to augment the regular army troops assigned to the coastal defenses around Narragansett Bay. The headquarters of the regular troops, who manned the bay defenses, was Fort Adams. The fort's pre-war garrison of 250 men was not large enough to have a regular army chaplain assigned to take care of their religious needs. Therefore, the army contracted with Fr. John T. Fahey, the chaplain at Mercy Home and School in Newport, to supply religious services for the Catholics stationed at the forts. Fr. Fahey said mass in the service club for which Bishop Keough donated a new altar in February 1939. When the diocese closed Mercy Home and School in late 1940 and later sold the property to the government for a housing project, Fr. Fahey's service at the fort ended. With Fr. Fahey's departure and the increase of troops at the fort, the army assigned a regular army chaplain to succeed him. With the activation of the 243rd, Fr. Joseph McNamara, the regiment's Catholic chaplain, took over the responsibility of offering mass for the troops manning Forts Getty and Wetherill on Jamestown. As the regiment's chaplain, McNamara was responsible for providing religious services for the men of all faiths in the regiments. At the same time, he was also the regiment's recreation officer. With the continued buildup of forces around the bay, Fr. McNamara, who was a captain with seven years' service in the Guard, was appointed Harbor Defense Chaplain in January 1941 with responsibility for providing for all the army units in the area and command responsibilities for other chaplains assigned there.[112]

Among Fr. McNamara's first concerns was to secure for his command area several of the $21,000 chapels authorized by Congress as a part of the defense build-up. His work resulted in a groundbreaking ceremony on June 10 for a chapel at the top of a rocky hill at Ft. Wetherill. The new chapel, which was to be available for use by all religious denominations, was used for the first time on Sunday, September 28, 1941. A second chapel was opened for services at Fort Adams on Sunday, October 26, 1941. Besides the chapels, the government also funded the conversion of a former hardware store and warehouse on Commercial Wharf in Newport into a Federal Recreation Building, to be run by the USO, to which

---

[111] Ibid, June 13, 20; July 11, 1940; *Evening Bulletin,* June 22, 1940.
[112] *Providence Journal,* November 16, 1940; January 27; April 20, 1941; *Providence Visitor,* March 5, 1942.

Catholics as well as other citizens contributed. The building was dedicated in March 1942. Bishop Keough was represented at the dedication by Fr. Edward Higney, the pastor of St. Joseph's and treasurer of the federal community building.[113]

Since the planned expansion of American armed forces necessitated the recruiting of more chaplains, in February 1941, Fr. William J. Beane, who had been serving as a CCC chaplain, transferred to the regular army. By March, five other priests of the diocese, Frs. Lawrence Deery, John P. McGuire, Leonerd J. McAteer, Lionel Beaudet and Stephen K. Callahan had volunteered for military service and were assigned to various army posts.[114]

Clergy were not the only specialists needed by the military, who needed to volunteer for duty if the government was to have their services. The new conscription law did not provide for the conscription of women nurses. Accordingly, on March 19, 1941, the Rhode Island Red Cross Nursing Service Committee arranged for the medical officer at Fort Adams, Capt. G. Edward Crane, to address the annual Jane Delano Memorial meeting, in the auditorium of St. Joseph's Hospital nurses' home. Capt. Crane informed his audience that seventy-five nurses would be needed to meet the medical needs of the men, who would man the defenses of Narragansett Bay. Other speakers described the work of navy nurses and of the nurses of the Army Nursing Corps Reserve, who had been called to duty at Camp Edwards in Massachusetts. Although the government considered drafting nurses if war came, that course of action would not prove to be necessary.[115]

Bishop Keough recognized the necessity for the United States to ready its defenses in case the war in Europe was carried to American shores or if the United States' dispute with Japan over Japanese aggression in China escalated. More particularly, he was concerned that the United States would be drawn into the European war by the propaganda of one side or another. In an address to the annual Knights of Columbus dinner on February 2, 1941, at which the main speaker was the Minister from Ireland to the United States, Keough warned the Knights that bigotry must never enter their words or deeds. He saw the strength of the United States "in the unity of all races and all creeds."[116]

While wishing to see the United States stay out of the European war, Bishop Keough was not unaware or unmoved by the suffering the peoples of Europe were enduring. Rather than see a plethora of fund-raising campaigns aimed at providing relief to Europe, the American bishops in November 1940 set up a Bishops' Relief Committee, which decided to con-

---

[113] *Providence Journal*, March 29; June 11, 14; September 27; October 25, 27; December 7, 1941; *Providence Visitor*, August 14; September 25, 1941.

[114] *Providence Visitor*, March 20, 1941.

[115] *Providence Journal*, March 20, 1941.

[116] Ibid., February 3, 1941.

duct a single fund-raising campaign in March 1941 to finance the numerous relief problems committed to its care. Bishop Keough supported the committee's efforts and arranged for a collection to be taken in the diocese on Sunday, March 23. This would be the first of many such collections in the years ahead. In July, the bishop endorsed another kind of collection. With the great increase in defense work, aluminum was in short supply. Accordingly, the Office of Civilian Defense conducted an Aluminum Collection Campaign from July 21 to 26, which Bishop Keough supported and urged the clergy, religious and laity of the diocese to do likewise. During the war, there were drives held to collect other metals, rubber and paper. Because rubber items tended to be small, the schoolchildren of the diocese were organized to undertake the collection. The rationing of fuel oil as a result of the war meant that many parishes had to curtail some of their activities in order to save heat, but driving to church was allowed while pleasure driving was discouraged as a fuel saving measure. Although not directly related to the war, in February 1942, Bishop Keough gave permission for a noonday mass to be celebrated in the cathedral during Lent. The mass proved very popular and drew large crowds. With the onset of food rationing dictated by the war, Bishop Keough, did not alter the Lenten regulations covering fast and abstinence, but, in his 1943 Lenten message, he stated that the regulations needed "to be applied with prudence." A chancery office official explained that, since meat was scarce and difficult to obtain, if meat could be had on a Friday, a family could considered itself excused from fasting on that day.[117]

When the Japanese government chose to go to war rather than agree to reverse Japan's course in China, Bishop Keough returned to the themes of unity and loyalty as vital needs in facing the crisis of war. He recognized that the struggle would be a long and hard one. He urged the people of his diocese not to take the duties of patriotism lightly and to pray to God and his Blessed Mother for the strength and courage to do their duty as citizens. As to practical measures, the bishop said there should be a large response to the requests for the purchase of defense bonds and stamps and a willingness on the part of all workers to maintain production for defense on the highest possible level. Four days after Pearl Harbor, Bishop Keough pledged to the governor, J. Howard McGrath, and to the mayor Providence, Dennis J. Roberts, the resources of the diocese for the defense of the nation. The bishop's words and deeds were echoed by many of his pastors on Sunday, December 14. After the federal government asked him to serve as chairman of the Clergy Division of the Defense Savings Staff for the Catholic Church in Rhode Island, Bishop Keough, within a week of the start of the war, sent a letter to all his pastors for them to read at mass urging the people of the diocese to purchase Defense Savings Bonds. He also appointed various priests to canvass the diocese in support of the

---

[117] *Providence Visitor*, March 6, 13; July 17, 1941; February 26; June 4; October 1, 1942; March 4, 1943.

government's fund-raising efforts. At the same time he sent out his letters to the parishes in support of fund raising, Bishop Keough also sent out prayer leaflets to each parish which contained a prayer for the welfare of the nation to be read after all masses and distributed to parishioners for their private use.[118]

In pledging the resources of the diocese, Bishop Keough continued to release priests who volunteered for war service. On the home front, Mayor Dennis J. Roberts appointed Fr. Charles J. Mahoney, who was a licensed and experienced shortwave radio operator, a member of the Communications Division of the Providence Civilian Defense Organization. Mahoney's appointment was made specifically so that he could organize a mobile radio patrol as part of the city's civil defense program. In addition to Fr. Mahoney, Mayor Roberts also appointed Fr. John J. Dillon, O.P., the president of Providence College, to be a member of the Civilian Defense Council and Director of the Welfare Division. When Fr. Dillon resigned in June 1942 because of ill health, the mayor appointed Fr. Joseph J. Lamb to succeed him.[119]

After the attack on Pearl Harbor, many more of the diocesan and religious priests serving in the diocese volunteered for military service. In February 1942, Fr. Rene Malboeuf entered the Army and Frs. Gerald F. Dillon and Paul J. Redmond, O.P., a member of the faculty of Providence College, the Navy. In March 1943, Frs. John J. Callanan and George Brennan became Army chaplains and Raymond F. McManus and Timothy Shea, O.P., who was serving in St Pius Parish, the Navy. In June 1942, Frs. Valmore Savignac and George Labonte also entered the Army. In addition to these men, Fr. T. Edward McGrath, M.S.C., an assistant at St. Joseph's, Natick, and a native Australian, returned home to serve in the missions there. Fr. Francis L. McGann, O.S.B., a Benedictine at Portsmouth Priory, left for service in the Navy as did Joseph T. Keown, C.S.Sp., an assistant at St. Anthony's, Portsmouth.

During 1943, yet more priests, both of the diocese and from religious orders working in the diocese, left for military service. Frs. Joseph Lamb, James Sullivan, William Spinney, and Paul Llyod joined the Navy along with Dominican Fathers Patrick Skehan, O.P. and George Reilly, O.P. Also in 1943, Frs. Anthony E. Czubak, James Loughran, Timothy Gillen, Francis Boudreau, and John Condon became Army chaplains as did Fr. George Favier, O.F.M., Cap., John Ryan, O.P., Edward Doyle, O.P. and Dennis McCarthy, O.P., the last three priests were on the faculty at Providence College. As the military continued to recruit and train new units, the need for chaplains for these units and as replacements for men serving existing units prompted continued calls for clergy enlistments. During 1944, Frs. Lionel Dorais, Thomas Scott, and Edmund Mullen joined the Army

---

[118] Ibid., December 11, 18, 1941; *Evening Bulletin*, December 11, 12, 1941; *Providence Journal*, December 15, 1941.

[119] *Providence Visitor*, December 18, 1941; June 11, 1942; *Evening Bulletin*, June 10, 1942.

chaplains and Joseph Gallagher, James Connolly, and August Mendonsa the Navy.

When American troops went into combat, their chaplains went with them and shared the danger. During the invasion of North Africa, Fr. Lawrence Deery, then a captain, risked his life to rescue two wounded soldiers at St. Cloud, Algeria, during the Oran offensive. In recognition of his gallantry, Fr. Deery was awarded the Silver Star. Later in the North African campaign, Fr. Deery was slightly wounded in another engagement and was awarded the Purple Heart. Towards the end of the war, Fr. George Brennan, who served with the Third Cavalry Group, which was part of Gen. Patton's Army, was awarded the Bronze Star for meritorious service between August 1944 and February 1945 during operations in France and Germany. Likewise, Fr. Edward P. Doyle, O.P., also was awarded a Bronze Star for meritorious service in connection with operations in Belgium, Holland and Germany. Like many of the men they served, the devotion to duty of the chaplains who served on the front lines and under fire went officially unrecognized because all shared the common danger. In October 1944, the Secretary of the Navy, James Forrestal, instituted a program of recognition of the diocese and parishes that sent priests to serve as Navy chaplains. On Sunday, October 8, Fr. James J. Casey, the senior Catholic chaplain at the Naval Construction Center at Davisville, represented the Navy in presenting Bishop Keough with certificates recognizing the nine parishes, Portsmouth Priory, and Providence College from which priests entered the Navy.[120]

Out of the forty-three priests who were serving in the diocese when they volunteered for duty with the armed forces, thirteen were religious priests from four different orders. The remaining thirty were diocesan priests. Of this thirty, two died while serving their country and their God. Fr. Valmore Savignac, who had already shown his love for his people and his personal courage during the 1938 hurricane when he swam through the rising waters at Oakland Beach to rescue people trapped in their homes, could have in good conscience stayed at home. But such was his desire to serve, he underwent a major operation at St. Joseph's Hospital in February 1942 to eliminate a physical problem that would have kept him out of the military. Following his recovery from the surgery, he went on active duty on June 22, 1942. He was assigned to Fort Eustis, Virginia. For a brief time, he was transferred to Fort Miles Standish, while awaiting orders to disembark for Europe, which he did on January 16, 1943. He was on the troopship *Henry Mallory* bound for Iceland when it was torpedoed on February 7 during a severe storm and sank in the North Atlantic. Fr. Savignac survived the explosion and made it to the deck of ship before it sank. When he got on deck, he gave his lifejacket to a man who did not have one since he himself was a good swimmer. However, he died in the icy waters before he could

---

[120] *Evening Bulletin*, January 14, 1943; *Providence Journal*, March 21, 1943; *Providence Visitor*, July 22, 1943; October 5, 11, 1944; May 3; December 13, 1945.

be rescued. On February 23, the Army notified his stepmother that her son was missing in action. Another man who was on the same ship and was rescued, George Dunningham, on May 3, sent a letter to Fr. Savignac's sister in which he confirmed her brother's death. On Monday, May 31, 1943, Bishop Keough offered a solemn requiem mass for his deceased priest at which Fr. Henry Shelly preached in honor of his friend. The mass in the cathedral was attended by Fr. Savignac's family, over a hundred priests, representatives of the Army and hundreds of parishioners from St. Rita's, Oakland Beach. On September 16, 1943, President Roosevelt posthumously awarded him the Purple Heart.[121]

On February 7, 1945, word arrived in Providence of the death of another priest. Fr. Anthony Czubak, then a captain, was serving with the 7th Armored Division in Belgium when he was killed in action on January 22. Prior to entering the service, he had been an assistant at St. Patrick's, Valley Falls. On February 13, Bishop Keough celebrated the funeral mass for Fr. Czubak and offered his prayers and consolation to the deceased priest's family, friends and fellow clergy. A classmate, Fr. Norman Leboeuf offered a moving and compassionate eulogy. One of Fr. Czubak's former parishioners, who was then serving as a representative from Cumberland in the General Assembly, submitted a resolution, which the Assembly adopted, that paid tribute to Fr. Czubak's sacrifice and offered its condolences to his parents.[122]

At the war's end, most of the chaplains from the diocese would return home to take up their former lives again as did the great majority of the men and women they served. As was true of other servicemen and women, some of the priests suffered psychological trauma as a result of their service with which they would struggle for the rest of their lives. To meet the physical and psychological needs of World War II veterans, the federal government substantially increased the number of hospitals that offered medical care to veterans. After the government built the Veterans' Memorial Hospital in Providence at Davis Park, on land given it by the city of Providence, federal and state officials gathered along with various veterans' organizations to dedicate a memorial chapel in the new hospital to Frs. Savignac and Czubak. Bishop Keough's successor, Bishop Russell J. McVinney, blessed the oratory and was one of the speakers on the occasion.[123]

---

[121] *Providence Visitor*, June 18, 1942; February 25; May 20; June 3; October 14, 1943; January 18, 1951; *Providence Journal*, June 1, 1943. It was not until July 31, that the War Department formally notified Fr. Savignac's stepmother of his death.

[122] *Evening Bulletin*, February 7, 13, 1945; *Providence Visitor*, February 8, 15, 1945. In April 1948, Fr. Czubak's body was disinterred and returned to the United States. On April 10, a funeral mass was celebrated in St. Anthony's, Providence prior to his body's reburial in St. Francis Cemetery, Pawtucket, *Providence Visitor*, April 8, 1948.

[123] *Providence Visitor*, May 24, 1951.

The Diocese during World War II

Among the most important physical assets that Bishop Keough could make available to the government was St. Joseph's Hospital. The hospital was designated as a "clearance hospital," which meant that, in any wartime emergency, its principal function would be to care for injured persons who arrived by ambulance, litter, or were carried or walked into the hospital or placed in relief or refugee centers. To fulfill its mission, the hospital stockpiled the necessary medical supplies and equipment. Although it ordered refrigeration equipment to store blood plasma in the spring of 1942, St. Joseph's Hospital did not receive the equipment until the first week of January 1943 because of government priorities. Once the equipment was received, the hospital issued a call for blood donors in order to secure a supply of plasma in case of emergencies. In addition, the various religious communities in the diocese committed themselves to provide the hospital with all possible assistance in the case of an emergency. Fortunately, the hospital's chief wartime contribution was to provide trained nurses for the military.[124]

The only diocesan-owned building that the military took over directly was the former St. Aloysius Home and School on Prairie Avenue. Prior to the start of classes in the fall of 1941, the Board of Incorporators of the Catholic Teachers' College voted to launch a four year, full-time program using the former orphanage building, which it committed itself to renovate, as the site for the school's classes. The Board asked the religious communities teaching in the diocesan schools to send their subjects to this four-year training program, which welcomed its first students in September 1941. With the outbreak of the war, the board's plans for the expanded program were dropped and the Catholic Teachers' College continued to hold its classes at St. Xavier's as before. Early in 1942, the Coast Guard began looking for barracks and drill ground space in the Providence area for men who manned fire boats in the Providence area. Housing in the Providence area in general was tight because of the need to accommodate workers engaged in war production. After examining the property, the Coast Guard agreed to rent the former orphanage for a thousand dollars a month. Initially, 150 were assigned to the building with the possibility that another 150 would be assigned later. Another structure that the military used on an occasional basis was the water tower on Senator Aldrich's former estate in Warwick, which had become the diocesan seminary. When the military organized a mock air raid on Rhode Island from January 20 to 23, 1941, the Army used the room, which the senator had built above the water tower, as an observation post from which to spot "enemy" aircraft.[125]

---

[124] Ibid., December 18, 1941.

[125] *Providence Visitor*, September 18, 25, 1941; August 6, 1941; Contract, April 11, 1942, PChA; *Providence Journal*, December 1, 1940.

Because civilian defense planners believed that they had to be concerned about possible air raids, John F. McFadden, Special Investigator of the Bureau of Fire Prevention in the city of Providence, addressed the January 1942 meeting of the Diocesan Conference of Religious in the auditorium of the Catholic Training School run by the Sisters of the Good Shepherd. He outlined procedures that should be followed in all the diocesan child-caring institutions during air raid alarms and also addressed the duties of air raid wardens, whose organization had been recommended by the Rhode Island State Council of Defense. In addition to instruction given to the heads of Catholic child-care institutions, the principals of all the Catholic schools in and near Providence were appointed air raid wardens and given classes by state instructors outlined by the United States Office of Civil Defense. Fortunately, the chief impact of the war on child care institutions of the diocese was the expansion of the size of the population they cared for as the draft and war work forced more parents to seek help caring for their children. Because of the proximity of Tower Hill Camp to various defense positions along the Rhode Island coast, the diocese kept the camp closed for much of the war.[126]

The war brought about many changes, some temporary, some permanent. After the United States declared war on Japan on December 8, Germany and Italy honored their treaty obligations to Japan and declared war on the United States on December 11. The Italian government's declaration of war meant that the Italian immigrants in the state who had not taken out citizenship papers and had not become citizens were liable to the restrictions of the Enemy Aliens Act. On Sunday, January 18, Judge Luigi De Pasquale, chairman of the State Defense Council's welfare committee arranged for a meeting of Italians in Providence at the Federal Hill House at 400 Atwells Avenue to provide information to the Italians who wished to become citizens. Judge De Pasquale expected a turnout of possibly four to five hundred from the Providence area. Instead, over 3,000 Italians from all over the state converged on the Federal Hill House, which could only accommodate 250 people in its auditorium. De Pasquale had to twice ask those who could not be accommodated and who were blocking the street, to go home, something the majority did reluctantly. Among those who addressed the meeting was Congressman John E. Fogarty, who, along with a Michigan colleague, had introduced several amendments to the existing naturalization laws, which would make it easier for those who had been living in the United States for many years to become citizens. Fogarty's amendments meant, in essence, that Italians who had been living in the United States before the passage of the immigration acts in the 1920s were be removed from the enemy aliens list. After the speaking program, volunteers from several Italian organizations assisted those who had questions or needed specific help in attaining citizenship. To accommodate those

---

[126] Ibid., January 22; February 19; March 19, 26; May 17; June 25, 1942.

who were not able to gain admittance to the meeting, Judge De Pasquale announced that another meeting would be held the following Saturday at the Bridgham Junior High School. Over 1,400 showed up for this second meeting to obtain information on naturalization.[127]

Although there were many thousands of "enemy aliens" in Rhode Island at the start of the war, there was no public roundup of Italians, who would have been the most numerous, or of German nationals. Neither was the only Japanese national living in the state, Matazo Ishakawa, incarcerated. Mr. Ishakawa has come to study in the Unites States before the turn of the century. He had lived in California and Wisconsin before coming to Rhode Island in 1902. Between 1902 and 1942, with the exception of two periods, he served as cook and houseboy to the Jonathan Comstock family in Cranston. During the first hiatus from his employment with the Comstocks he worked as a houseman in St. Francis Rectory, Wakefield from 1912 to 1913. During the second in 1924, he returned to Japan, but decided he preferred to live in the United States and returned to Rhode Island. The outbreak of the war caused him great anguish, and he died on June 20, 1943.[128]

Among other changes, Providence College, on Thursday, January 22, 1942, suspended intercollegiate football games, and later all varsity sports for the duration of the war, although the college played some games against other schools during the war. The annual CYO parade, which was begun in 1936 and held in the fall of each year on the Feast of Christ the King, was canceled in 1942 and never resumed. The Triennial Holy Name Parade, which was last held in 1937, was also canceled and not revived after the war. Membership in the various parish Holy Name societies slipped as a result of the young men of the parish going off to war. Because of blackout regulations, Bishop Keough withdrew permission for midnight masses at Christmas in 1942, but, with the relaxing of the restrictions in some areas such as Woonsocket, allowed the practice to resume in these areas in 1943.[129]

Prayers for peace, for a swift end to the war and for the safety of those who left home to serve their country became regular features of masses and weekly novenas during the course of the war. At the beginning of the war, many parishes set up honor roles with the names of those from the parish, who had gone off to war. Beginning on April 23, 1942, the *Visitor* began printing the names of those on the various parish honor rolls. Many parishes also held special services in which an American flag and a service flag with stars representing those in the military was blessed and dedicated to those in the armed services. As the casualty lists began to appear, funeral masses were said for those who died in the war. The blessing

---

[127] *Providence Journal*, January 15, 25, 1941.

[128] *Providence Journal*, June 21, 1943.

[129] *Providence Journal*, January 22; September 19, 1941; December 13, 1943; *Providence Visitor*, September 16, 23, 1937.

of American flags and the custom of placing them in prominent places in churches during the course of the war expanded what had been a limited admittance of the flag inside the churches.

In 1910, Bishop Harkins had halted the Italian custom of blessing flags in church ceremonies. The Italian priests had continued to bless both the American and the Italian flags, but in ceremonies held in the halls of the various societies. In 1911, Cardinal James Gibbons, on behalf of the a past commander of a Grand Army of the Republic post in Brooklyn had asked Rome whether the national flag could be permitted in church religious ceremonies, and, specifically, whether, the G.A.R. could bring a flag-draped coffin of one its members into church. In May 1911, the Congregation of the Holy Office considered the question and conveyed its reply to Cardinal Gibbons through the Apostolic Delegate, Archbishop Falconio. The Congregation said that, "In so far as there will be no disrespect resulting in regard to the Church or the Sacred Liturgy, there is no objection." Until World War II, the blessing of national flags had not been a common custom.[130]

The Second World War would have a dramatic impact on the economy of Rhode Island. In 1939, when the Rhode Island Unemployment Compensation Board made the first complete and comprehensive check on unemployment in the nation as a part of a national survey, the Board noted that there were 40,000 men and women registered for work in the various public employment offices. The Board's tally did not include WPA workers or the thousands of workers, who had not renewed their registration with the Board at the end of the three month period for which the registration was active. In the eighteen months before Pearl Harbor, the U.S. government awarded Rhode Island manufacturers more than $115 million in defense work, some of it on experimental contracts. Nearly seventy-five million went into textiles and most of the rest into the metal trades.[131]

Even before the United States became involved in the actual fighting of the Second World War, the government had begun expanding the defense installations in the state. When the Navy began looking for a site for a northeastern naval air station, Theodore Francis Green, who had won election as U.S. senator in 1936, used his influence with President Roosevelt to help bring the projected base to Narragansett Bay. On May 25, 1939, Roosevelt signed a bill appropriating one million dollars for the purchase of land at Quonset Point. Part of the land that was to become the naval air station was state property and had been the site of Camp Green, a National Guard training base. The land to the north was the site of a colony of summer cottages, which the government tried to buy out rather than take by condemnation. The last of the property owners had until September 6, 1940 to vacate their property. Work on the base for the seaplanes of the neutrality patrol, which had previously been based at the

---

[130] Hayman, *Catholicism in the Rhode Island and the Diocese of Providence, 1886–1921*, 214–15; *Providence Visitor*, May 5, 1911.
[131] *Providence Journal*, December 17, 1939; Keller and Lemons, *Rhode Island: The Independent State*, p. 136.

lower end of Gould Island, began in 1939. Work on the buildings, run-
ways and piers that would serve as the home base for navy carriers began
later in 1940. Work on the patrol plane base was sufficiently well along for
the base to go into commission at the beginning of October 1940. The
construction of the naval air station and later of the naval construction
base, Camp Endicott, at nearby Davisville, attracted hundreds of construction workers to the area and later the two bases would employ thousands
of workers during the war. The navy supplied a chaplain to meet the religious needs of the men and women at the bases, but the influx of civilian workers taxed the capacities of the neighboring parishes. In order to
provide for the recreational needs of the servicemen at the bases, the USO
opened a recreation center in East Greenwich.[132]

In early 1942, the United States Maritime Commission selected Field's
Point in Providence as the site for a shipyard and employed the Rheem
Manufacturing Company to construct six ways on which to build ships.
The Rheem Company had previously manufactured water heaters and
cartridge cases. Since one of the last, if not the last, ships built in Providence, the *Haidee*, was launched in 1853, the company would have to hire
and train thousands of workers in ship-making skills in order to fulfill its
contract. Apprentice schools for the new yard workers began in mid-May
and the keel of the Rheem Company's first liberty ship was laid at the end
of June 1942. The new ship, the *William Coddington*, was launched on November 28, 1942, after a blessing by Bishop Keough and the traditional
christening. The filling of the jobs in the Providence shipyard and those
of three smaller yards at Bristol, Wickford and Chipiwanoxet in Warwick,
where smaller vessels were built for the Navy, as well as those at Quonset
Point and the Torpedo Station in Newport, was done by men and women
drawn from the entire state and beyond. Where once the majority of the
young people who went out to work found employment in mills and fac-
tories dominated by one ethnic group or another and where their fathers
often had a say in their being hired, the new work environment meant a
loosening of the hold the ethnic family and community had on its young
people. Ethnic pride among the workers in the shipyard, however, was
not absent. When an article in the company newspaper, *The Yardarm*, appeared prior to St. Patrick's Day in 1944, insinuating that the Irish would
celebrate the day by carousing, there was a public outcry among the workers, which forced the management of the yard to repudiate the article and
issue an apology.[133]

Since increasing numbers of women were drawn out of their homes
and into war industries, the resulting challenge to what most of society

---

[132] *Providence Journal,* January 11; March 10; May 10; September 1; October 2, 1940; February 22,
1942; Patrick T. Conley, *An Album of Rhode Island History, 1636–1986* (Downing Company, 1986),
212–13.

[133] *Providence Journal,* June 28, 1942; April 8, 1943; *Providence Visitor,* December 3, 1942; March 16, 23,
1944; Conley, *An Album of Rhode Island History,* p. 213.

then regarded as a woman's place was cause for concern on the part of many observers. Not only was Bishop Keough concerned about the weakening of family structure and values that could come from women working outside the home, but he was also alarmed when the government began drafting fathers in later 1943, without providing adequate compensation for their families. Speaking at the fifth annual Catholic School Teachers' Institute at LaSalle Academy on October 28, Bishop Keough criticized Congress for squabbling over whether to allow ten dollars per child or twenty to provide for the maintenance of children when their fathers were drafted. At the same time, billions of dollars in materiel were being sent to America's allies and countless single men who could have been inducted were passed over or thought to be too valuable in the jobs they were doing. A few weeks later, the American bishops as a whole stressed the importance of protecting the rights and dignity of the family, not only in America, but in any post-war peace.[134]

After a fire destroyed the fabrication plant at the Field's Point shipyard, the Maritime Commission replaced the Rheem manufacturing company with the Walsh-Kaiser Company. Henry J. Kaiser's expertise was in assembly line production. He adopted his techniques to shipbuilding with outstanding results. Msgr. Peter E. Blessing was called on to bless the third of the ships, the *Samuel Gorton*, that came from the yard after the fabrication plant was rebuilt under Walsh-Kaiser, on April 6, 1943. Bishop Keough returned to the yard again in May 1944 to bless the *U.S.S. Artemis*, the first cargo-combat vessel ever built by the Maritime Commission. In December 1944, the bishop was invited to bless the new light cruiser, *Providence*, prior to its christening on December 28 by Mrs. Mary A. Roberts, mother of mayor of Providence, Dennis J. Roberts, at the Bethlehem Steel Plant yard at Quincy, Massachusetts.[135]

In that same month, the government launched its Second War Loan campaign. Rhode Island's goal in the campaign was $76,000,000. In order to give a focus to the campaign, the government listed the kinds of military equipment and numbers of each that could be purchased by the government with the monies invested in the hope that various groups in the state might chose the funding of one or several as their goal. The idea caught on and, in June 1943, the Franco-American fraternal and social organizations in New England committed themselves to raising $6,000,000 to pay for the construction of three Liberty Ships, of which Franco Americans in Rhode Island agreed to raise $1,150,000. Bishop Keough served as the honorary chairman of the Rhode Island committee organized to support the effort, which was broken up into parish quotas. By August 31, a total of $1,200,586 dollars in Liberty Bonds sales had been reached. In announcing the total to date on August 31, 1943, Laure B. Lussier, vice-

---

[134] *Evening Bulletin*, February 25, 1942; October 28, 29, 1943; *Providence Visitor*, December 3, 10, 1942; July 28; November 18, 1943.
[135] *Providence Visitor*, April 8, 1943; *Providence Journal*, May 21; December 29, 1944.

chairman of the New England Committee credited the leadership of the Franco-American clergy for the drive's success. When all the Rhode Island contributions were tallied, the Franco Americans in Rhode Island bought $1,680,000 worth of bonds. Although few in numbers when compared to their Roman Catholic brethren, the parishioners of St. John's Romanian Orthodox Church in Woonsocket joined with their Franco-American neighbors in contributing to the drive. While the drive had focused on raising sufficient funds to build three Liberty Ships, the funds actually raised by the Franco Americans in New England were sufficient to build seven ships. Of the three names submitted by the Rhode Island Committee, one, that of Msgr. Charles Dauray, was agreed upon by the entire New England Committee as the name of one of the seven.[136]

As the Treasury Department hoped, patriotism combined with ethnic pride among the Polish in Rhode Island. In July 1943, leaders of the Polish war relief effort in the Blackstone Valley proposed to the Poles of the state that they undertake to purchase $100,000 in bonds to buy a bomber to replace the one in which Gen. Wladyslaw Sikorski, the Premier of the Polish Government-in-exile, was killed in a crash off Gibraltar. Acting on this suggestion, the Poles in Rhode Island organized the General Sikorski Memorial War Bond Committee, under the patronage of Our Lady of Czestochowa, and elected Alexander Chmielewski, the state chairman of the Polish Group of the Foreign Origins Division of the Treasury Drive, chairman of the Polish Bond Committee. The drive was endorsed by the Polish-American fraternal and social organizations. As he did with the Franco-American drive, Bishop Keough agreed to chair the honorary committee of the Polish drive. The drive's working committee held a series of rallies throughout the state to encourage contributions to the effort at which socially and politically prominent Poles spoke. As with the Franco Americans, the parish priests in the various Polish parishes played important roles. In some parishes, they helped to organize a house-to-house canvass. When the drive officially ended on October 24, the total amount of sales and pledges committed to the Third War Loan Drive had reached $829,400. The final total was $869,534. New Army regulations against the use of individual or personal names on American plans frustrated the desire of the Poles to have bombers bear the names of the Polish heroes, General Sikorski or Ignace Paderewski, but the committee asked the Treasury Department to name one of the B-17s the "Spirit of the Polish People of Rhode Island." On Sunday afternoon, October 31, 1943, Mrs. J. Howard McGrath, the wife of the governor, christened a new B-24 Liberator, "Spirit of Polonia of Rhode Island.[137]

Patriotism and competition also played an important role in the Knights

---

[136] *Providence Visitor*, April 13; June 17, 24; July 1, 8, 15, 22, 29; August 19, 26; September 2, 9, 1943; January 13, 1944; *Providence Visitor*, July 26, 1943.

[137] *Providence Journal*, July 16, 1943; *Providence Visitor*, July 29; August 5, 12, 19, 26; September 2, 16, 23, 30; October 28; November 4; December 2, 1943.

of Columbus annual war bond campaign in 1944. The Rhode Island State Council set a goal of $3,000,000 for the drive, which it held during the month of January. Councils throughout the state were divided into six districts under the supervision of District Deputies. With six days to go, the councils had surpassed their goals. Before the drive was ended, the Knights had sold $4,253,675 in bonds. In recognition of the Knights' accomplishment, the Maritime Commission gave the Knights' the honor of naming a ship, which was built in the New England Ship Yard in South Portland, Maine. A party of twelve, headed by Msgr. Peter E. Blessing, State Champlain of the Knights, who went to bless the ship, and Mrs. John B. O'Rourke, wife of the past State Deputy, during whose term the bonds were sold, went to South Portland for the christening. The name chosen by the Knights for the new ship was that of the first bishop who lived in Providence, William Tyler.[138]

In each of the bond drives, bonds were sold not only in the various rectories of the diocese, but also through the schools. During the first two drives, the schoolchildren of the diocese purchased a significant number of bonds and stamps. During 1944 alone, $1,085,592 worth of bonds and stamps were sold through the Catholic Schools, which represented a per capita rate for the 31,330 students of $34.67 per pupil. This was in addition to the students' efforts in collecting salvage material and other patriotic services.[139]

The state and federal government along with civic and religious groups were not the only ones who contributed to the war effort. Private individuals often made largely unheralded but nevertheless important contributions. Such was the case with Mrs. Robert L. "Ma" Sheridan, who lived at the beginning of the war at 421 Cranston Street with her husband, four sons and four daughters. Her husband operated a grocery store at Cranston Street and Cutting Avenue in Cranston. Prior to the war, Mrs. Sheridan had made it part of her routine to visit poor and elderly persons. According to an obituary that appeared in the *Providence Journal* on April 19, 1963, after the war began, "Ma" Sheridan's "door was open to any man in uniform 24 hours a day" who wanted some home-cooking or motherly advice. . . . The gray-haired little woman wrote about a hundred letters a week during the war to servicemen she had cared for in her home. When not frying eggs, she was baking apple pie for them or listening to their troubles." She lost one of her sons in Sicily, who was later awarded a Purple Heart, Air Medal and Distinguished Flying Cross, a loss she never got over.[140]

After the allied armies liberated much of Italy, Catholic War Relief Services, which had been organized under the auspices of the National Catholic Welfare Conference, in May 1944, initiated a nationwide collection

---

[138] *Providence Visitor*, January 13, 27; February 10; August 10, 17, 1944; *Evening Bulletin*, August 14, 1944.
[139] *Providence Visitor*, January 20; June 20; September 21, 1944.
[140] *Providence Journal*, April 19, 1963.

of used clothing in behalf of the people of Italy. In this endeavor, Catholic Relief Services worked in co-operation with the national organization, American Relief for Italy, Inc., which was centered in the Italian-speaking parishes of the country. In Rhode Island, the diocesan campaign was organized by the Italian pastors, who urged the people of their parishes to contribute what they could. Parishioners were urged to bring useful clothing to the schools in parishes, which had them, or to the church basement. Volunteers in the individual parishes sorted the clothes, which were then sent to the Cathedral Hall in Providence. Here they were packed for shipment to New York, from which port they would be sent on to Italy. This initial drive in the diocese collected some thirty-eight tons. In September 1944, Catholic War Relief Services agreed to participate in a clothing drive to collect new and useful clothing and bedding for all of Europe as part of an effort organized by the United Nations Relief and Rehabilitation Administration. This second drive netted over eighty tons of clothing and bedding. Clothing drives in behalf of the peoples of Europe became a regular feature of the postwar years.[141]

In February 1945, the attention of the war relief agencies in the country turned to the collection of canned goods and soap. Again, Bishop Keough lent his good offices to the national effort and sent a letter to the pastors of the diocese asking them to undertake a collection of relief supplies during the week of March 4, 1945. The people of the diocese were again asked to bring their donations to their parish churches where the donations were packed and shipped to a central collection point at Cathedral Hall. All contributions received from Italian parishes went to American Relief for Italy, Inc. while those received from Polish parishes went to Polish War Relief. Both organizations maintained warehouses in New York. Donations from other parishes were divided equally between the two organizations. Well over 150,000 items were received during this collection. Again the children of the diocese played a significant role, going around their neighborhoods soliciting donations. A second National Food for the War Stricken drive was held from December 9 to 16, 1945.[142]

The Japanese government's acceptance of the allied peace terms on August 14 meant that the observance of the Feast of the Assumption on August 15 took on a particular joyfulness. As the Catholics of Rhode Island had so frequently gathered in great numbers to pray for peace and for the protection of those serving their country, they gathered in similar numbers to give thanks for the war's end. In his sermon in the cathedral, Bishop Keough paid special tribute to those who died in the war and those who had been wounded or taken prisoner. From the cathedral's pulpit, he particularly recognized the sacrifices of the 65 out of the 986 men of the cathedral parish who had lost their lives in the service of their country.[143]

---

[141] Ibid., May 25; June 1, 8, 15; August 17; September 21; October 11, 1944.
[142] *Providence Visitor*, February 22; March 8; November 29, 1945.
[143] Ibid., August 16, 1945.

Bishop Keough's Promotion

On December 3, 1947, the local news outlets carried the announcement that Pope Pius XII had appointed Bishop Keough to be the new
Archbishop of Baltimore. By 1947, Bishop Keough had created a strong
legacy not only in the Diocese of Providence, but on the national scene
as well. Early in his episcopal career, his fellow bishops recognized his administrative ability and, at the annual meeting of the National Conference
of Catholic Bishops on November 19, 1936, they elected him to be one
of the Assistant Bishops on the Administrative Board elected that year. In
1937, he was named to the Board that oversaw the work of the Educational Department of the NCWC. In 1941, he would be elected chairman and
served in that post until 1944. As noted above, in January 1939, he was
also appointed to the Bishops' Committee on Indecent Literature and as
also noted above, he became a member of the Motion Picture Committee
in November 1941 and two years later, 1943, was elected its chairman. In
addition to these NCWC positions, in 1943, he was elected as a member
of the Board of Trustees of the Catholic University of America. In 1939,
he was appointed to a committee headed by Patrick Cardinal Hayes of
New York, which had supervision of the work of the Propagation of the
Faith in the United States. In that same year, the Holy Father named him
a director of the Catholic Near East Welfare Association. The scrapbook
of newspaper clippings kept during his years in Providence contains numerous articles on the ordination of various bishops, which Keough attended. At many of these ordinations, he was asked to be the main preacher. In October 1938, he preached at the installation of Matthew F. Brady
as the fourth Bishop of Burlington. In January 1945, after having preached
at the installation of Archbishop Richard Cushing in Boston, he again
preached for Bishop Brady at his installation as the Bishop of Manchester, New Hampshire. In a different context, in June 1941, Bishop Keough
was the principal speaker before government officials and public service
groups at the ninth National Eucharistic Congress in St. Paul, Minnesota.
In the judgment of Thomas W. Spalding, who has written a history of the
Archdiocese of Baltimore, "Bishop Keough's executive ability, gracious-
ness, and contributions to the NCWC were doubtless factors in his choice
as Archbishop of Baltimore.[144]

Spalding has written of Bishop Keough that he "was not a man given
to publicizing his feats or to encouraging others to do it for him." Spalding
noted that "When news of his appointment to Baltimore was released the
Baltimore Sun described him as 'modest almost to the point of shyness' and
marveled that 'one so lacking in assertiveness' could have accomplished

---

[144] *Providence Visitor*, December 3, 1935; December 4, 30, 1947; February 19, 1948; Thomas W.
Spalding, *The Premier See: A History of the Archdiocese of Baltimore, 1789–1989* (Baltimore: The John
Hopkins University Press, 1989), p. 386. Archbishop Keough asked Bishop Brady to preach at his
installation mass in Baltimore on February 24, 1948, *Providence Journal*, February 25, 1948.

so much in Providence. In its February 19, 1948 issue describing Bishop
Keough's farewell to the Diocese of Providence, the *Providence Visitor* pondered the question of which of Keough's accomplishments it should highlight. The writer's first choice was the remarkable increase in the receipts
of the annual Catholic Charity Appeal, which rose during Keough's years
from $270,589 in 1934 to $902,000 in 1947. In his farewell to the diocese,
Bishop Keough made it a point to stress his appreciation not only to the
Catholics of the diocese, who had contributed so generously to the Charity
Appeal, but also "to those who do not worship in the same church as we
do." Another of the writer's choices was the diocese's service to the country under Bishop Keough in terms of the number of priests he allowed
to serve as chaplains during World War II and in the sale of stamps and
bonds which he encouraged. Although the *Visitor* writer did not mention it
in his short summary of Keough's major accomplishments, he could also
have included the establishment of Our Lady of Providence Seminary in
1939. When Bishop Keough departed the diocese in 1947, he left behind
74 more priests than when he arrived, 15 more parishes, 13 more chapels,
a new college, 1362 more Catholic college students, 1889 more Catholic
high school students, five more academies and high schools, and approximately 99,000 more Catholics.[145]

In an editorial that appeared on December 4, 1947, the *Providence Journal* expressed what was the image of Bishop Keough that would remain,
not only among Catholics, but in the minds of the larger Rhode Island
community:

> He will leave behind him as he departs for his new field, remembrance of a sweet na-
> ture, a gracious personality and a rare gift of friendliness. Quietly and without osten-
> tation, he had become an influential part of the life of the community. Pervasively he
> spread a fine feeling of understanding throughout the diocese, encouraged a generous
> spirit and was grateful beyond measure for the way in which the community respond-
> ed to his appeal for charity. His consideration of others is eloquent of a gentle nature,
> and his natural modesty bespoke of a courtly character.

When Archbishop Keough died on December 8, 1961, the paper's editors
again praised the man more than his accomplishments. An article in the
Evening Bulletin said of the late archbishop that he was "remembered . . . as
an extremely approachable man, possessed of heart-warming personality,
a priestly man, simple, humble and with a tremendous amount of common sense."[146]

One example of Bishop Keough's simplicity and humility was spoken
of by the clergy in Maryland. According to the story that circulated in the
archdiocese, Bishop Keough, on learning of his appointment to Baltimore,

---

[145] Spalding, *The Premier See*, 387–88; *Providence Visitor*, February 12, 19, 1948.

[146] *Providence Journal*, December 3, 1947; *Evening Bulletin*, December 8, 1931; Andrew
    J. Robinson, "Bishop Keough and the Development of Rhode Island Catholicism,
    1934–1948," Seminar paper prepared for Dr. Patrick T. Conley, May 13, 1975.

Index

Herald News, Fall River, 167
heresy, 205
Heriz, Fr. Paschasius, O.C.D., 331
Herman, Bishop J. S., 94
Herreshoff, Julia, 312
Hickey, Bishop William Augustine,
    48n119, 81n1, 83, 140–141, 146,
    221, 238, 240, 240n229, 242–244,
    243n235, 506–507, 522, 536
  abuse of authority, 222
  accusations against Fr. Beland, 122
  accused of misusing parish monies,
    150
  address on WDWF, 51
  address to Queen's Daughters, 39
  Administrator of the Diocese, 3
  admonition about reading material,
    516
  Advent pastoral urging those censured
    by church to repent, 200–201
  American Committee for Relief in
    Ireland and, 73
  on birth control and abortion, 342–
    344, 346
  calls for removal from diocese, 139
  Catholic Charity Appeal and, 249,
    486
  Catholic education and, 1–80
  Catholic Press Message of, 515
  censures, 234
  Chairman of the Charity Fund's
    Drive's Grand Committee and
    Treasurer, 42
  Christian Brothers' Superior General,
    56
  civil trials and, 147–148, 150–154,
    156, 159–163, 166–168, 170–171,
    173–174, 176, 180
  commissioned historical study of the
    agitation, 235
  commitment to expanding number
    and scope of Catholic Schools,
    325
  copy of "Fiat Lux," 203
  correspondence with Cardinal
    Donato Sbaretti, 196
  correspondence with Cardinal
    Rouleau, Archbishop of
    Quebec,195
  court decision in favor of, 180
  criticism of, 88
  Daignault and, 48, 154, 159–160, 235
  death of, 77, 380–383
  declares pastorate of St Louis Parish
    vacant, 146
  dedication of new schools, 64
  diaries of, 135
  "Documents au subjet de L'Agitation
    Sentinellist," 161
  Dominicans and, 25–26
  Drive's Rules and Regulations, 44
  early life, education, and career of,
    1–4
  ecumenical revolt and, 85–88
  education and, 53–60, 480–481
  education initiative, 67
  elementary schools and, 60–68
  end of the affair, 229, 231–234, 237
  excommunications and, 154, 175–
    176, 181–182, 184, 186–188,
    191–192, 194–195, 197–203, 205,
    207–210
  foreign language skills, 2
  Franco-Americans and, 101, 112,
    158, 164
  French-Canadian papers and, 127
  French language and, 2–3, 221
  Fr. Lavergne and, 88–89
  Gainer and, 355
  Great Depression and, 357–363,
    364–380, 381
  growing discord and, 102–105
  Holy See and, 38, 142, 154, 223–224
  Holy Years and, 335–336
  on industrial problems, 375–378
  instututional growth and, 244–337
  intervention of Boston priests in his
    diocese, 164
  Ku Klux Klan and, 348, 353
  La Salle Alumni dinner and, 91
  lawsuits and, 126, 128, 130–133,
    135–136, 140, 143–144
  letters of, 71, 121, 124, 127, 145, 150,
    154, 172, 179, 191, 232
  list of dogmatic errors printed in La
    Sentinelle, 157n168
  Million Dollar High School Drive
    and, 38–53, 85- 87, 106–111, 208
  Drive's Rules and Regulations, 42,
    44–45
  missionaries and, 335
  National and Local Context, 4–36